Communications
in Computer and Information Science   **580**

Commenced Publication in 2007
Founding and Former Series Editors:
Alfredo Cuzzocrea, Dominik Ślęzak, and Xiaokang Yang

More information about this series at http://www.springer.com/series/7899

Philippe Desfray · Joaquim Filipe
Slimane Hammoudi · Luís Ferreira Pires (Eds.)

Model-Driven Engineering and Software Development

Third International Conference, MODELSWARD 2015
Angers, France, February 9–11, 2015
Revised Selected Papers

 Springer

Editors
Philippe Desfray
SOFTEAM
Paris
France

Slimane Hammoudi
MODESTE/ESEO
Angers
France

Joaquim Filipe
INSTICC
Polytechnic Institute of Setubal
Setubal
Portugal

Luís Ferreira Pires
University of Twente
Enschede
The Netherlands

ISSN 1865-0929   ISSN 1865-0937   (electronic)
Communications in Computer and Information Science
ISBN 978-3-319-27868-1   ISBN 978-3-319-27869-8   (eBook)
DOI 10.1007/978-3-319-27869-8

Library of Congress Control Number: 2015950049

Printed on acid-free paper

This Springer imprint is published by SpringerNature
The registered company is Springer International Publishing AG Switzerland

Preface

The present book includes extended and revised versions of papers selected from the Third International Conference on Model-Driven Engineering and Software Development (MODELSWARD 2015), held in Angers, Loire Valley, France, during February 9–11, 2015.

The purpose of the International Conference on Model-Driven Engineering and Software Development is to provide a platform for researchers, engineers, academicians, as well as industrial professionals from all over the world to present their research results and development activities in using models and model-driven engineering techniques for software development.

MODELSWARD 2015 was sponsored by INSTICC (the Institute for Systems and Technologies of Information, Control and Communication) and co-organized by École Supérieure d'Électronique de l'Ouest (ESEO). MODELSWARD was held in cooperation with ACM SIGMIS – ACM Special Interest Group on Management Information Systems, ACM SIGSOFT – ACM Special Interest Group on Software Engineering, The Open Group – SOA Work Group, The Institute of Electronics, Information and Communication Engineers (IEICE), IEICE Special Interest Group on Software Enterprise Modeling (SWIM) and technically co-sponsored by the AIS Special Interest Group on Modeling and Simulation (AIS SIGMAS), IEEE Computer Society (IEEE CS), Technical Council on Software Engineering (IEEE CS – TCSE), and IEEE Technical Committee on Business Informatics and Systems (IEEE CS – TCBIS).

The conference received 94 paper submissions from 30 countries, covering all continents. To evaluate each submission, a double-blind review was performed by the Program Committee. After a stringent selection process, 15 papers were published and presented as full papers (30-min oral presentation), leading to a full-paper acceptance ratio of about 20 %, which shows our commitment of offering a high-quality forum to our community.

The MODELSWARD program included panels and five invited talks delivered by internationally distinguished speakers, namely: Bran Selic (University of Toronto, Canada), Sébastien Gérard (CEA, France), Marco Brambilla (Politecnico Di Milano, Italy), and Mark van den Brand (Eindhoven University of Technology, The Netherlands), and an invited lecture by Philippe Desfray and Etienne Brosse (SOFTEAM, France).

This book contains 24 papers from MODELSWARD 2015, which have been selected, extended, and thoroughly revised.

We would like to thank the authors, whose research and development efforts are recorded here for future generations.

September 2015

Philippe Desfray
Joaquim Filipe
Slimane Hammoudi
Luís Ferreira Pires

Organization

Conference Co-chairs

Philippe Desfray — SOFTEAM, France
Joaquim Filipe — Polytechnic Institute of Setúbal/INSTICC, Portugal

Program Co-chairs

Slimane Hammoudi — ESEO, MODESTE, France
Luis Ferreira Pires — University of Twente, The Netherlands

Program Committee

Silvia Abrahão — Universitat Politecnica de Valencia, Spain
Hamideh Afsarmanesh — University of Amsterdam, The Netherlands
Guglielmo de Angelis — CNR – IASI, Italy
Keijiro Araki — Kyushu University, Japan
Paris Avgeriou — University of Groningen, The Netherlands
Elarbi Badidi — United Arab Emirates University, UAE
Franck Barbier — University of Pau, France
Bernhard Bauer — University of Augsburg, Germany
Luca Berardinelli — University of L'Aquila, Italy
Lorenzo Bettini — Università di Torino, Italy
Paolo Bocciarelli — University of Rome Tor Vergata, Italy
Jan Bosch — Chalmers University of Technology, Sweden
Jean-Pierre Bourey — Ecole Centrale de Lille, France
Achim D. Brucker — SAP Research, Germany
Philipp Brune — University of Applied Sciences Neu-Ulm, Germany
Christian Bunse — University of Applied Sciences Stralsund, Germany
Dumitru Burdescu — University of Craiova, Romania
Fergal Mc Caffery — Dundalk Institute of Technology, Ireland
Sergio de Cesare — Brunel University, UK
W.K. Chan — City University of Hong Kong, Hong Kong, SAR China
David Chen — Laboratory IMS, France
Yuting Chen — Shanghai Jiaotong University, China
Chihung Chi — CSIRO, Australia
Antonio Cicchetti — Malardalen University, Sweden
Tony Clark — Middlesex University, UK
Bernard Coulette — University of Toulouse Jean Jaurès/IRIT Laboratory, France

Jacek Kesik	Lublin University of Technology, Poland
Jun Kong	North Dakota State University, USA
Grzegorz Koziel	Lublin University of Technology, Poland
Martin Kropp	University of Applied Sciences Northwestern Switzerland, Switzerland
Uirá Kulesza	Federal University of Rio Grande do Norte (UFRN), Brazil
Yvan Labiche	Carleton University, Canada
Anna-Lena Lamprecht	Potsdam University, Germany
Kevin Lano	King's College London, UK
Dongxi Liu	CSIRO, Australia
Francesca Lonetti	National Research Council (CNR) Pisa, Italy
Roberto Lopez-Herrejon	Johannes Kepler, University Linz, Austria
Der-Chyuan Lou	Chang Gung University, Taiwan
Eda Marchetti	ISTI-CNR, Italy
Tiziana Margaria	University of Limerick and Lero, Ireland
Beatriz Marin	Universidad Diego Portales, Chile
Steve McKeever	Uppsala University, Sweden
Dragan Milicev	University of Belgrade, Serbia
Marek Milosz	Lublin University of Technology, Poland
Dugki Min	Konkuk University, Republic of Korea
Valérie Monfort	LAMIH Valenciennes UMR CNRS 8201, France
Sascha Mueller-Feuerstein	Ansbach University of Applied Sciences, Germany
Debajyoti Mukhopadhyay	Maharashtra Institut of Technology, India
Halit Oguztüzün	Middle East Technical University, Turkey
Olaf Owe	University of Oslo, Norway
Gordon Pace	University of Malta, Malta
Patrizio Pelliccione	Chalmers University of Technology and University of Gothenburg, Sweden
Dana Petcu	West University of Timisoara, Romania
Alexander Petrenko	ISPRAS, Russian Federation
Rob Pettit	The Aerospace Corp., USA
Luis Ferreira Pires	University of Twente, The Netherlands
Malgorzata Plachawska-Wójcik	Lublin University of Technology, Poland
Elke Pulvermueller	University of Osnabrück, Germany
Wolfgang Reisig	Humboldt-Universität zu Berlin, Germany
Werner Retschitzegger	Johannes Kepler University, Austria
Laurent Rioux	THALES, France
Colette Rolland	Université Paris 1 Panthéon-Sorbonne, France
Jose Raul Romero	University of Cordoba, Spain
Gustavo Rossi	Lifia, Argentina
Francesca Saglietti	University of Erlangen-Nuremberg, Germany
Rick Salay	University of Toronto, Canada
Comai Sara	Politecnico di Milano, Italy
Giuseppe Scanniello	University of Basilicata, Italy

Jean-Guy Schneider	Swinburne University of Technology, Australia
Peter Sestoft	IT University of Copenhagen, Denmark
Marten van Sinderen	University of Twente, The Netherlands
John Slaby	Raytheon, USA
Arnor Solberg	Sintef, Norway
Richard Soley	Object Management Group, Inc., USA
Stéphane Somé	University of Ottawa, Canada
Jean-Sébastier Sottet	Public Research Center Henri Tudor, Luxembourg
Alin Stefanescu	University of Pitesti, Romania
Hiroki Suguri	Miyagi University, Japan
Massimo Tivoli	University of L'Aquila, Italy
Salvador Trujillo	Ikerlan, Spain
Naoyasu Ubayashi	Kyushu University, Japan
Sabrina Uhrig	Universität Bayreuth, Germany
Andreas Ulrich	Siemens AG, Germany
Cristina Vicente-Chicote	Universidad de Extremadura, Spain
Gianluigi Viscusi	EPFL-CDM, Switzerland
Christiane Gresse von Wangenheim	UFSC – Federal University of Santa Catarina, Brazil
Michael Whalen	University of Minnesota, USA
Franz Wotawa	Graz University of Technology, Austria
Amiram Yehudai	Tel Aviv University, Israel
Tao Yue	Simula Research Lab, Norway
Gefei Zhang	Celonis GmbH, Germany
Haiyan Zhao	Peking University, China
Olaf Zimmermann	HSR Hochschule für Technik Rapperswil, Switzerland
Elena Zucca	University of Genoa, Italy
Zyla	Lublin University of Technology, Poland

Additional Reviewers

Michele Amoretti	University of Parma, Italy
Xabier De Carlos	IK4-Ikerlan Research Center, Spain
Christian Colombo	University of Malta, Malta
Hamid Gholizadeh	McMaster University, Hamilton, Canada
Aitor Murguzur	IK4-IKERLAN, Spain
Chris Porter	University of Malta, Malta
Christelle Urtado	LGI2P/Ecole des Mines d'Alès, France
Kim Voellinger	Humboldt-Universität zu Berlin, Germany
Shuai Wang	Simula Research Lab, Norway
Johannes Wettinger	University of Stuttgart, Germany

Invited Speakers

Bran Selic	University of Toronto, Canada
Sébastien Gérard	CEA, France
Marco Brambilla	Politecnico Di Milano, Italy
Mark van den Brand	Eindhoven University of Technology, The Netherlands
Philippe Desfray	SOFTEAM, France

Contents

Methodologies, Processes and Platforms

Applications and Software Development

Invited Paper

Safety Case Development with SBVR-Based Controlled Language

Yaping Luo[1], Mark van den Brand[1(✉)], and Alexandre Kiburse[2]

[1] Eindhoven University of Technology,
P.O. Box 513, 5600 MB Eindhoven, The Netherlands
{y.luo2,m.g.j.v.d.brand}@tue.nl
[2] Klee Group, La Boursidière, 92350 Le Plessis-Robinson, France
alexandre.kiburse@kleegroup.com

Abstract. Safety case development is highly recommended by some safety standards to justify the safety of a system. The Goal Structuring Notation (GSN) is a popular approach to construct a safety case. However, the content of the safety case elements, such as safety claims, is in natural language. Therefore, a common understanding of the meaning of a safety claim may be difficult to reach. Consequently, the confidence of a safety claim can be misplaced. In this paper, we propose to use an SBVR-based controlled language to support safety case development. By using the controlled language, the ambiguities caused by natural language can be mitigated. Furthermore, an SBVR editor for building a vocabulary and a GSN editor with vocabulary support are developed. Finally, a case study has been carried out to show the benefits of using the controlled language for safety case construction.

Keywords: Safety case · SBVR · Controlled language · Conceptual model

1 Introduction

A safety case is a well-structured argument for justifying that systems are safe. A safety case is defined as: "a documented body of evidence that provides a convincing and valid argument that a system is adequately safe for a given application in a given environment" [6]. It is used to show that a system, service or organization will operate as intended for a defined application in a defined environment. In some international safety standards, explicit safety cases are required for safety-critical systems. For example, ISO 26262 [13] in the automotive domain and DO 178C [4] in the avionic domain, stimulate the use of safety cases to demonstrate the product safety [24]. Besides, MOD Def Stan 00-55 [21] for safety-critical software in defense equipment requires producing safety cases with explicit safety requirements. Due to these characteristics, a safety case must be represented in a correct and understandable structure. Thus, the safety case should be carefully developed and defined.

© Springer International Publishing Switzerland 2015
P. Desfray et al. (Eds.): MODELSWARD 2015, CCIS 580, pp. 3–17, 2015.
DOI: 10.1007/978-3-319-27869-8_1

There are mainly two ways to document a safety case: textual and graphical. For textual safety case documents, the logic and structure of a safety case are implicit [2]. This could bring inconsistencies and confusion, and thus the understandability of the safety case can be harmed. For graphical safety case documents, the Goal Structuring Notation (GSN) has been proposed for representing the argument structure [14]. It provides a number of graphical symbols to assist the development of safety cases. By using GSN, the structure of a safety case is explicit and clear. However, as more and more users (argument readers and writers, such as safety engineers, or safety assessors) are involved in safety case development, shared understanding of the meaning of safety case elements are important. If the shared understanding is missing, the confidence of a safety case can be misplaced.

To address this, some research has been done on the understandability of safety arguments. In [12], assured safety arguments are proposed as a clear argument structure to demonstrate how to create clear safety arguments. Besides, in [11], a precise definition of the context in GSN arguments is proposed to achieve a better understanding. However, the content of a safety case element is still documented in natural language. The ambiguities caused by natural language are still unsolved.

In our previous research, we proposed a methodology to use an Semantics of Business Vocabulary and Rules (SBVR) based controlled language [23] to support the development of clear safety arguments [18]. By using a controlled language, all the concepts (noun concepts and verb concepts) in a safety case are well-defined in an SBVR vocabulary. Argument readers can check the definitions or examples of those concepts to get a shared understanding of them. In this way, the understandability of safety arguments can be improved. However, the process of our previous methodology can only be done manually. To address this issue, in this paper we propose a model transformation to generate SBVR vocabularies from EMF conceptual models. This reduces the manual work involved in vocabulary development. Moreover, we built two editors to facilitate the safety case construction. An SBVR editor is implemented for modifying or creating a vocabulary, and a GSN editor is developed to enable argument writers to edit GSN elements in the controlled language. Finally, we carried out a case study to show the benefits of using the controlled language for construction safety cases.

The remaining paper is organized as follows: Sect. 2 introduces GSN and SBVR. Section 3 presents the three main phases in our vocabulary-based methodology for safety case development. Section 4 shows a case study on two existing safety cases. Section 5 discusses the related work of this paper. Finally, Sect. 6 summarizes our conclusions and future work.

2   Background

In this section the basic information used in the remainder of this paper is discussed. We give a brief description of Goal Structuring Notation (Sect. 2.1) and Semantics of Business Vocabulary and Rules (Sect. 2.2).

2.1 Goal Structuring Notation

Goal Structuring Notation (GSN) is a graphical notation which is widely recommended for presenting safety cases [15]. It provides a clear and well-structured argument in terms of basic graphical elements, such as goals, solutions and strategies. As mentioned before, safety standards such as ISO 26262 (automotive) and DO 178C (avionic), require documentation of safety cases for safety-critical systems, and GSN provides the standard format to document the safety cases graphically. The most stable and referenced documentation of GSN is called GSN Community Standard [3]. Some elements of the standard GSN are introduced in Fig. 1.

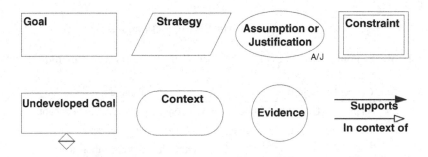

Fig. 1. Some elements of the Goal Structuring Notation.

2.2 Semantics of Business Vocabulary and Rules

Semantics of Business Vocabulary and Rules (SBVR) is a standard business-focused specification proposed by the Object Management Group (OMG) in 2008 [23]. It is designed for domain experts to capture business rules in a formal, structured and understandable language. It consists of a highly flexible structure that can capture and define most of the subtle intricacies of the natural language. The SBVR specification defines, among others, a metamodel to develop models of business vocabulary (comparable to conceptual models) and business rules (comparable to constraints that should be enforced). Figure 2 shows the relevant subset of the SBVR metamodel regarding the concepts presented in this paper. The definitions of some of the main concepts in SBVR specifications [25] are:

Vocabulary, a set of noun concepts, verb concepts, as well as various specialized concepts such as categorizations.
Concept, a unit of knowledge created by a unique combination of characteristics.
Rule, a proposition that is a claim of an obligation or necessity.
Business Rule, a rule with a business focus.

In this paper, all SBVR examples are given in SBVR Structured English (SSE), which is introduced in SBVR Annex C [23]. The font styles used in this paper are shown in Table 1. Note that, for the font style of *Name*, we use the same font style as *Term*.

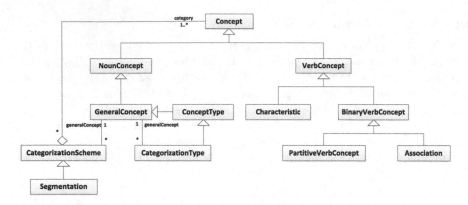

Fig. 2. Extract of the SBVR metamodel.

Table 1. Font styles and color with formal meaning used in this paper.

SSE Concepts	Font Style	Color	Denotes
Term	Underlined	Green	Noun concepts or Individual concepts
Verb	Italic	Blue	Verb concepts
Keyword	Normal	Orange	Other linguistic symbols used for definitions and statements

3   Methodology

Based upon our previous approach, we propose a vocabulary-based semi-automatic approach for constructing safety cases. An overview of our current approach is shown in Fig. 3. There are three phases: Conceptual Phase (P1), Vocabulary Phase (P2), and Modeling Phase (P3). In the conceptual phase (P1), a conceptual model of the target domain will be manually built from scratch [19] or semi-automatically refined from other conceptual models [17]. The conceptual model is used as an input for the vocabulary development. The metamodel that

Table 2. Mapping between EMF and SBVR concepts.

EMF concepts	SBVR concepts
Class	General concept
Enumeration literal	Individual concept
Attribute	Role
Association	Verb concept
Generalization/Enumeration	Categorization
Multiplicity	Necessity

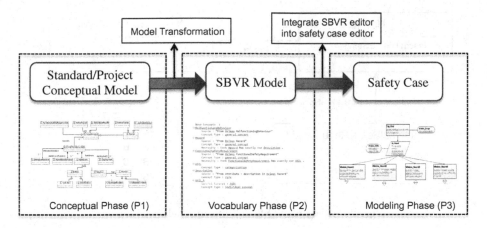

Fig. 3. An overview of our methodology.

we use for describing conceptual models is an Ecore metamodel. After the creation of the conceptual model, a model transformation is applied to transform the conceptual model from an EMF format to an SBVR specification. Then in the vocabulary phase (P2), users (argument writers) can build their own vocabulary based on the generated SBVR model. Note that, users can also skip the previous phase and start by creating a new SBVR vocabulary. Finally, in the modeling phase (P3), the vocabulary is used to facilitate safety case construction. The details of these three phases are described in the following subsections.

3.1 Conceptual Phase: From Conceptual Model to SBVR Model

As a preparation phase, the main goal of the conceptual phase is to make the domain knowledge explicit and develop a common understanding. As a result, the development of a conceptual model was proposed in [18]. A conceptual model represents the main terms and their relations that need to be considered for safety cases. As mentioned before, to facilitate the formulation of safety cases, a model transformation is introduced to transform a conceptual model in the EMF format to the SBVR format. The definition of this model transformation is created based on a mapping between the concepts of those two formats (Table 2), and implemented in the Epsilon Transformation Language (ETL) [16]. Finally the conceptual model in SBVR can be used as an input for an SBVR vocabulary in the vocabulary phase. Note that, in our previous research, an SBVR vocabulary can be only built during vocabulary phase.

To demonstrate our current approach and show the improvement on our previous approach, we selected the same example as in the previous study. Figure 4 illustrates a simple EMF schema, which is derived from the industrial ISO 26262 metamodel presented in [26]. It represents the relations between *Malfunctioning Behaviour*, *Hazard*, and *Functional Safety Requirement*. Besides it includes an

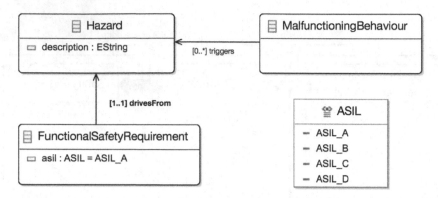

Fig. 4. A part of ISO 26262 metamodel in EMF.

enumeration type, *ASIL*. By applying the model transformation, an SBVR representation of the original conceptual model can be generated. All concepts are categorized into noun concepts and verb concepts. For our example, there are ten noun concepts (three instances of *General Concept*, one instance of *Categorization*, four instances of *Individual Concept*, and two instances of *Role*) and two verb concepts (instances of *Association*) derived from the EMF model. Some of the noun concepts and verb concepts are shown in Figs. 5 and 6 respectively. In these two figures, *Concept Type* represents the type of a noun concept or a verb concept, while *Source* shows the traceability information.

3.2   Vocabulary Phase: Creating Vocabulary with an SBVR Editor

To support safety case development, the generated vocabulary needs to be checked by domain experts or refined with additional safety-related concepts. In this phase, an SBVR editor is developed to support argument writers to build their own vocabulary. As mentioned before, the vocabulary can be a new construction or a modification of an existing one. The detailed information of our SBVR editor will be described in this section.

Main Functions of the SBVR Editor. The main functions of the SBVR editor include a vocabulary editor and a rule editor. The vocabulary editor enables users to define noun and verb concepts, while the rule editor enables users to define SBVR rules with the vocabulary. In our SBVR editor, the "noun" font represents general concepts, individual concepts, roles and categorizations whereas the "*verb*" font represents verb concepts. Besides, there are two types of keywords defined in our editor: default keywords and structural keywords. Note that, all keywords are predefined. The default keywords are keywords defined in the SBVR specification. They are displayed in "keyword" font style, for example, "each" and "exactly one". The structural keywords are implemented for the structure of a vocabulary or the characteristics of noun and verb concepts.

```
Noun Concepts :
⊖ MalfunctioningBehaviour
        Source : "From Eclass MalfunctioningBehaviour"
        Concept Type : general concept
⊖ Hazard
        Source : "From Eclass Hazard"
        Concept Type : general concept
        Necessity : Each Hazard has exactly one description .
⊖ FunctionalSafetyRequirement
        Source : "From Eclass FunctionalSafetyRequirement"
        Concept Type : general concept
        Necessity : Each FunctionalSafetyRequirement has exactly one ASIL .
⊖ ASIL
        Concept Type : categorization
⊖ description
        Source : "From Attribute : description in Eclass Hazard"
        Concept Type : role
⊖ ASIL_A
        General Concept : ASIL
        Concept Type : individual concept
```

Fig. 5. An example of SBVR Noun concepts generated from EMF concepts (screenshot of our editor).

```
Verb Concepts :
⊖ MalfunctioningBehaviour triggers Hazard
        Concept Type : association
⊖ FunctionalSafetyRequirement is_derived_from Hazard
        Concept Type : association
⊖     Necessity : Each FunctionalSafetyRequirement is_derived_from at least one
        Hazard .
    ;
```

Fig. 6. An example of SBVR Verb concepts generated from EMF concepts (screenshot of our editor).

They are shown in a gray font style. For instance, in Figs. 5 and 6, "Noun Concepts" and "Verb Concepts" are defined to categorize concepts into noun or verb. The field of "Concept Type" shows the concept type of a noun or verb concept. The field of "Source" keeps the traceability information from a EMF model to an SBVR model. Moreover, the field of "Necessity" describes the constraints of noun or verb concepts.

There are also predefined noun concepts and verb concepts. The concepts in the SBVR metamodel are predefined noun concepts, such as general concept. The predefined verb concepts are extracted from the SBVR specification to represent some basic association types. The verb concept "*has*" or its passive form "*is_property_of*" identifies the essential properties of a given noun concepts. The containment association is represented by "*includes*" (active form) or "*is_included_in*" (passive form). Besides, the categorization association is represented by "*specializes*", "*generalizes*", "*is_category_of*", or "*is_a*".

According to the SBVR specification, our rule editor supports four types of model operations: obligation formulation, necessity formulation, possibility formulation, and permissibility formulation. A number of keywords are predefined for those model operations. "it_is_obligatory_that" and "it_is_prohibited_that" are defined for obligation formulation. "it_is_necessary_that" and "it_is_impossible_that" are defined for necessity formulation. "it_is_possible_that" is for possibility formulation. "it_is_permitted_that" is for permissibility formulation.

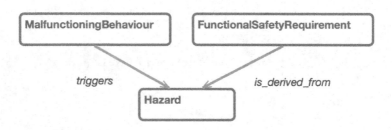

Fig. 7. An illustration of the graphic diagram of verb concepts shown in Fig. 6.

Graphical Editor for Vocabulary. Along with the textual editor, a graphical editor has been implemented to enable users to modify or build their vocabulary via a diagram. A diagram provides an overall picture of a given vocabulary.

All noun concepts and verb concepts defined in the vocabulary are represented in a corresponding diagram. Figure 7 shows a diagram of verb concepts defined in Fig. 6. We can see that, the noun concepts (MalfunctioningBehaviour, Hazard, and FuctionalSafetyRequirement) are shown as nodes, while the verb concepts (*triggers* and *is_derived_from*) are shown as links between those nodes. As the textual and graphic editor are synchronized, a noun concept or verb concept can also be added or modified via the diagram. In addition, the properties of concepts can be found in the property view of the graphical element. Labels of noun and verb concepts in the diagram are displayed in the same font color as in the textual editor.

Vocabulary Checking. When building a vocabulary, duplicated noun and verb concepts can be created. This causes a risk of ambiguities and inconsistencies in the vocabulary. Consequently, the confidence of the safety claims, which use those duplicated concepts, will be hampered. To address this, vocabulary checking is implemented in our editor. The goal of the vocabulary checking phase is to check the size of a vocabulary and find duplications in a vocabulary. The output of the vocabulary checking is a report, which shows the number of defined noun and verb concepts and duplicated concepts that need to be addressed. A checking report is automatically generated after a vocabulary created. An example of the checking report is shown in Listing 1.1.

Listing 1.1. An example of vocabulary checking report shows: There are 55 noun concepts defined (line 3–6), 16 verb concepts defined (line 7–10). Besides, there are two noun concpets with the same name "ASIL" (line 11–14).

```
1    <?xml version="1.0" encoding="UTF-8" standalone="no"?>
2    <reports>
3       <report>
4          <check> Definitions of Noun Concepts </check>
5             <reason> 55 noun concepts are defined </reason>
6       </report>
7       <report>
8          <check> Definitions of Verb Concepts </check>
9             <reason> 16 verb concepts are defined </reason>
10      </report>
11      <report>
12         <check> Duplicated Concepts </check>
13            <reason> 2 noun concepts with the same name: ASIL </reason>
14      </report>
15   </reports>
```

3.3   Modeling Phase: Construct Safety Cases with Vocabulary

In the modeling phase, the safety argument will be constructed in GSN with vocabulary support. We propose to use SBVR to express the content of each safety case element. By integrating our SBVR editor into the GSN editor, the noun and verb concepts defined in a vocabulary will be highlighted when safety engineers edit a GSN element. Figure 8 shows a screenshot of our GSN editor. When a GSN element is edited, a list of suggested concepts is given via content assistant. For example, after typing "p", a list of concepts in the vocabulary that start with "p" is provided. In this way, the number of errors, such as ambiguities of a safety case can be reduced. Users can always look into the vocabulary to check the definitions of nouns and verbs used in their safety cases to avoid misunderstanding.

4   Case Study

To demonstrate how the controlled language can facilitate safety case construction, we chose two published safety cases for our case study. One is a preliminary safety case for a Whole Airspace Air Traffic Management (ATM) System [1], the other is a safety case for a hypothetical Air Traffic Services Unit (ATSU) [10]. Finally, two main benefits of using controlled language for safety cases are found: the ambiguities in the safety case can be reduced, and the structure of the safety case can be simplified.

Reduce Ambiguities in Safety Case. Figure 9 shows a part of the Whole Airspace ATM system safety case. The concepts or terms which can introduce ambiguities into the safety case are circled. We can see that different terminology is used for expressing the same thing. For example, *Area* and *geographical areas*, *ATM rules* and *Basic ATM rules*, *Assumptions for Area safety* and *safety*

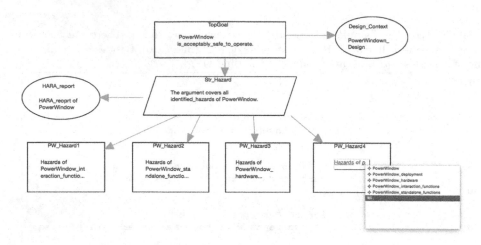

Fig. 8. Illustration of our graphical editor.

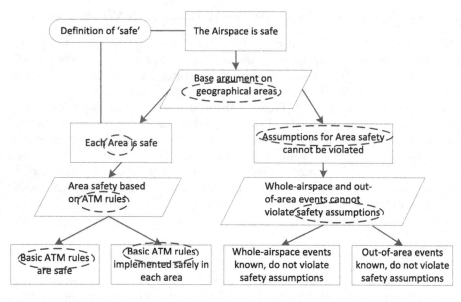

Fig. 9. Extract from 'Complete Structure Based On Geographical Areas Strategy' (Figs. 4, 5 and 6 from [1]).

assumptions. For those similar concepts, some questions can be raised. "Are *geographical areas* a part of or the same as the *Area*?" "Are *Basic ATM rules* a part of or the same as the *ATM rules*?" "Are *Assumptions for Area safety* a part of or the same as the *safety assumptions*?"

If these ambiguities exist in a safety case, the clearness and understandability of the safety case can be affected. Consequently the confidence of the safety case may get harmed. By introducing a controlled language, this issue can be

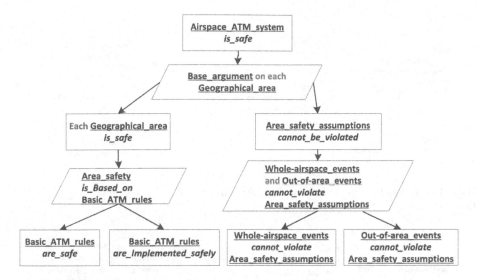

Fig. 10. The SBVR format of the safety case example shown in Fig. 9. The context element *Definition of 'safe'* is removed because the definition of 'safe' can be added in the SBVR vocabulary.

addressed. All the concepts used in the safety case have an explicit definition in the SBVR vocabulary. In this way, the ambiguities in the safety case can be reduced. Figure 10 shows the SBVR format of the previous safety case example (Fig. 9).

Simplify the Structure of Safety Case. Sometimes, in a GSN safety case, safety engineers might add detailed information to the safety case by introducing more GSN elements, for instance a context element. In Fig. 11, we can see that there are three context elements and one constraint element added to a safety claim. These context elements and constraint element can help safety case reviewers to understand the safety claim. However, if the safety case consists of a huge number of safety claims, then elements linked to these safety claims might make the structure of the safety case more complex. Besides, some of these elements are only used to explain the meaning of the terms in a safety claim. For example, in Fig. 11, the context element *C001* and the constraint element *Cr001* are used to provide the definition or guideline for the used terms in the safety claim *Arg0*. By using the controlled language, the information or meaning of terms are provided in the SBVR vocabulary. Therefore, the structure of the safety case can be simplified. Figure 12 shows the SBVR format of the safety case example in Fig. 11. We could see that by moving the definitions of the terms into the SBVR vocabulary, the structure of the safety case gets simplified.

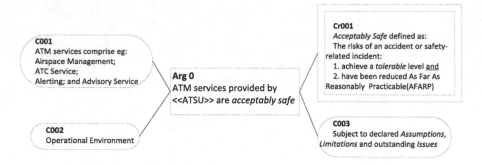

Fig. 11. Extract from 'Overall Safety Argument for a Unit Safety Case' (Fig. 12 from [10]).

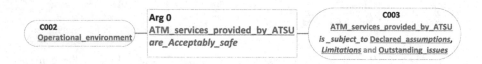

Fig. 12. The SBVR format of the safety case example shown in Fig. 11.

5   Related Work

Tool Support for SBVR. In 2006, an SBVR editor called SBeaVeR [8] was developed. SBeaVeR is an Eclipse based plug-in which implements the Structured English notation and provides a number of features: automatic syntax highlighting, automatic completion, dictionary, standard text editing. In 2010, another tool called VeTIS [22], based on the SBVR 1.0 metamodel, was created. Concerning the editing and the validation of SBVR business rules, VeTIS tool provides the same features as SBeaVeR. Both tools provide the main feature for editing SBVR vocabulary, however the vocabulary can only be created from scratch. Whereas in our approach the vocabulary can be derived from a conceptual model.

Tool Support for Safety Case Construction. There exist a number of open source and eclipse-based safety case editors, such as AdvoCATE [9], D-case [20], and CertWare [5]. Besides typical features, they also support safety case modules, patterns, and other advanced functions. In this paper, our focus is on the controlled-language support. Our GSN editor only supports basic features for creating safety cases. However, our vocabulary editor can be integrated into other existing eclipse-based safety case editors. In this way, our approach can be used for other applications.

SBVR and Other Techniques. A model transformation from SBVR to UML with OCL constraints is provided by using ATL (ATL Transformation Language) [22]. Moreover, a study of transforming UML models to SBVR models can also be found in [7]. In this paper, we discussed a model transformation from EMF models to SBVR models.

6   Conclusions and Future Work

In this paper, based on our previous research we presented a vocabulary-based semiautomatic approach for safety case development. By using an SBVR vocabulary, it enables the explicit connection between conceptual models and safety cases to ensure that certification data is built properly and can be reused efficiently. Moreover by utilizing SBVR, the content of safety case elements is well-structured and well-controlled. It can reduce mistakes and misunderstanding between the different roles involved in producing, assessing, and using the safety case. There are four main contributions of this paper:

1. A model transformation from an EMF model to an SBVR model is proposed. A vocabulary can be automatically generated from a conceptual model, which facilities the vocabulary creation.
2. An SBVR editor is implemented. This editor supports the development of SBVR vocabularies and rules, and provides graphical editing and checking of a vocabulary.
3. A GSN editor with SBVR vocabulary support is implemented. This editor enables users to construct safety cases with their own SBVR vocabulary.
4. A case study has been carried out to show the benefits of using controlled language for safety case construction. The results show that by using controlled language, the ambiguities in the safety case can be reduced and the structure of the safety case can be simplified.

Thus, our method supports improving the clarity and correctness of safety cases, and increasing the confidence in the claimed safety assurance. As future work, we plan to extend our approach on safety case pattern development for reuse of certification data. Finally, we aim to cooperate with industrial partners to use our approach in large scale applications.

Acknowledgements. The research leading to these results has received funding from the FP7 programme under grant agreement n° 289011 (OPENCOSS).

References

1. EUR Whole Airspace ATM System Safety Case (2001). http://dependability.cs. virginia.edu/research/safetycases/EUR_WholeAirspace.pdf
2. Tube Lines Contractual Safety Case (2004). http://dependability.cs.virginia.edu/ research/safetycases/Tube_Lines.pdf
3. GSN Community Standard Version 1 (2011). http://www.goalstructuringnotation. info/documents/GSN_Standard.pdf
4. Software Consideration in Airborne Systems and Equipment Certification: RTCA DO-178C, December 2011
5. Barry, M.R.: CertWare: a workbench for safety case production and analysis (2011)
6. Bishop, P., Bloomfield, R.: A methdology for safety case development. In: Redmill, F., Anderson, T. (eds.) Industrial Perspectives of Safety-Critical Systems, pp. 194–203. Springer, London (1998)

7. Cabot, J., Pau, R., Raventós, R.: From UML/OCL to SBVR specifications: a challenging transformation. Inf. Syst. **35**(4), 417–440 (2010)
8. De Tommasi, M., Corallo, A.: SBEAVER: a tool for modeling business vocabularies and business rules. In: Gabrys, B., Howlett, R.J., Jain, L.C. (eds.) KES 2006. LNCS (LNAI), vol. 4253, pp. 1083–1091. Springer, Heidelberg (2006)
9. Denney, E., Pai, G., Pohl, J.: AdvoCATE: an assurance case automation toolset. In: Ortmeier, F., Daniel, P. (eds.) SAFECOMP Workshops 2012. LNCS, vol. 7613, pp. 8–21. Springer, Heidelberg (2012)
10. EUROCONTROL: Safety Case Development Manual (2006). http://www.eurocontrol.int/sites/default/files/article/content/documents/nm/link2000/safety-case-development-manual-v2.2-ri-13nov06.pdf
11. Graydon, P.J.: Towards a clearer understanding of context and its role in assurance argument confidence. In: Bondavalli, A., Di Giandomenico, F. (eds.) SAFECOMP 2014. LNCS, vol. 8666, pp. 139–154. Springer, Heidelberg (2014)
12. Hawkins, R., Kelly, T., Knight, J., Graydon, P.: A new approach to creating clear safety arguments. In: Dale, A., Anderson, T. (eds.) Advances in Systems Safety, pp. 3–23. Springer, London (2011)
13. ISO: ISO 26262: "Road Vehicles - Functional Safety" (2011)
14. Kelly, T.: Arguing Safety - A Systematic Approach to Managing Safety Cases. Ph.D. thesis, University Of York (1998)
15. Kelly, T., Weaver, R.: The goal structuring notation - a safety argument notation. In: Proceedings of Dependable Systems and Networks 2004 Workshop on Assurance Cases (2004)
16. Kolovos, D.S., Paige, R.F., Polack, F.A.C.: The epsilon transformation language. In: Vallecillo, A., Gray, J., Pierantonio, A. (eds.) ICMT 2008. LNCS, vol. 5063, pp. 46–60. Springer, Heidelberg (2008)
17. Luo, Y., van den Brand, M., Engelen, L., Klabbers, M.: From conceptual models to safety assurance. In: Yu, E., Dobbie, G., Jarke, M., Purao, S. (eds.) ER 2014. LNCS, vol. 8824, pp. 195–208. Springer, Heidelberg (2014)
18. Luo, Y., van den Brand, M., Engelen, L., Klabbers, M.: A modeling approach to support safety assurance in the automotive domain. In: Selvaraj, H., Zydek, D., Chmaj, G. (eds.) Progress in Systems Engineering. Advances in Intelligent Systems and Computing, vol. 330, pp. 339–345. Springer International Publishing, Switzerland (2015)
19. Luo, Y., van den Brand, M., Engelen, L., Favaro, J., Klabbers, M., Sartori, G.: Extracting models from ISO 26262 for reusable safety assurance. In: Favaro, J., Morisio, M. (eds.) ICSR 2013. LNCS, vol. 7925, pp. 192–207. Springer, Heidelberg (2013)
20. Matsuno, Y.: D-Case Editor: A Typed Assurance Case Editor. University of Tokyo (2011)
21. Defence Standard 00-55 Part 1 (1997). http://www.software-supportability.org/Docs/00-55_Part_1.pdf
22. Nemuraite, L., Skersys, T., Sukys, A., Sinkevicius, E., Ablonskis, L.: VeTIS Tool for Editing and Transforming SBVR Business Vocabularies and Business Rules into UML & OCL Models (2010)
23. OMG: SBVR: Semantics Of Business Vocabulary And Rules (version 1.2), Sepetember 2013
24. Safety Case Repository (2013). http://dependability.cs.virginia.edu/info/Safety_Cases:Repository

25. Spreeuwenberg, S., Healy, K.A.: SBVR's approach to controlled natural language. In: Fuchs, N.E. (ed.) CNL 2009. LNCS, vol. 5972, pp. 155–169. Springer, Heidelberg (2010)
26. Taguchi, K.: Meta Modeling Approach to Safety Standard for Consumer Devices (2013)

Modeling Languages, Tools
and Architectures

Realizing a Conceptual Framework to Integrate Model-Driven Engineering, Software Product Line Engineering, and Software Configuration Management

Felix Schwägerl[(✉)], Thomas Buchmann, Sabrina Uhrig,
and Bernhard Westfechtel

Applied Computer Science I, University of Bayreuth, 95440 Bayreuth, Germany
{felix.schwaegerl,thomas.buchmann,sabrina.uhrig,
bernhard.westfechtel}@uni-bayreuth.de

Abstract. Software engineering is a highly integrative computer science discipline, combining a plethora of different techniques to increase the quality of software development as well as the resulting software. The three sub-disciplines Model-Driven Software Engineering (MDSE), Software Product Line Engineering (SPLE) and Software Configuration Management (SCM) are well-explored, but literature still lacks an integrated solution. In this paper, we present the realization of a conceptual framework that integrates those three sub-disciplines uniformly based on a filtered editing model. The framework combines the checkout/modify/commit workflow known from SCM with the formalism of feature models and feature configurations known from SPLE. The implementation is model-driven and extensible with respect to different product and version space models. Important design decisions are formalized by means of Ecore metamodels. Furthermore, we propose several optimizations that increase the scalability of the conceptual framework.

Keywords: Model-driven software engineering · Software product line engineering · Software configuration management

1 Introduction

The discipline *Model-Driven Software Engineering* (*MDSE*) [25] is focused on the development of *models* as first-class artifacts in order to describe software systems at a higher level of abstraction and to automatically derive platform-specific source code. In this way, MDSE promises to increase the productivity of software engineers, who may focus on creative and intellectually challenging modeling tasks rather than on repeated activities at source-code level. Models are typically expressed in well-defined languages such as the *Unified Modeling Language* (*UML*), which define the structure as well as the behavior of model elements. The *Eclipse Modeling Framework* (*EMF*) [21] provides the technological foundation for many model-driven applications.

© Springer International Publishing Switzerland 2015
P. Desfray et al. (Eds.): MODELSWARD 2015, CCIS 580, pp. 21–44, 2015.
DOI: 10.1007/978-3-319-27869-8_2

Software Product Line Engineering (SPLE) [13] enforces an organized reuse of software artifacts in order to support the systematic development of a set of similar software products. Commonalities and differences among different members of the product line are typically captured in *variability models*, e.g., *feature models* [8]. Different methods exist to connect the variability model to a *platform*, which provides a non-functional implementation of the product domain. The concept of *negative variability* considers the platform as a multi-variant product, which constitutes the *superimposition* of all product variants. To automatically derive a single-variant product, the variability within the feature model needs to be resolved by specifying, e.g., a *feature configuration*.

Software Configuration Management (SCM) is a well-established discipline to manage the *evolution* of software artifacts. A sequence of product *revisions* is shared among a *repository*. Besides storage, traditional SCM systems [2,3, 23] assist in the aspects of *collaboration* and *variability* to a limited extent, by providing operations like *diff*, *branch* and *merge*. Internally, the components of a versioned software artifact – most frequently, the lines of a text file – are represented as *deltas*. The most commonly used delta storage type are *directed* deltas, which consist of the differences between consecutive revisions in terms of change sequences, whereas *symmetric* deltas [15] constitute a *superimposition* of all revisions, annotated with *version identifiers*.

In literature, many approaches to pair-wise combinations of MDSE, SPLE, and SCM are described. *Model-Driven Product Line Engineering (MDPLE)* is motivated by a common goal of MDSE and SPLE — increased productivity. MDPLE may be realized using positive variability, e.g., by *composition techniques* [24], or using negative variability by creating a *multi-variant domain model* whose elements are mapped to corresponding feature model elements [6]. *Model Version Control* subsumes the combination of MDSE and version control [1], with the goal of lifting existing version control metaphors *check-out* and *commit* up to the model level. *Software Product Line Evolution* deals with common problems occurring during the management of the life-cycle of software product lines, for instance propagating changes from the variability model to the platform. A survey can be found in [11].

In [17], we have presented a conceptual framework to realize an integrated combination of the three disciplines. It is built around an editing model oriented towards version control systems, where the developer may use his/her preferred tool to perform changes to versioned software artifacts within a single-version workspace. The workspace is synchronized with a repository, which persists the entirety of product versions. In addition to revision graphs, feature models are provided to adequately define logical product variants. Version selection is performed in both the revision graph and the feature model. In the latter case, a feature configuration is selected, which allows for the combination of various logical properties in a consistent product variant. The adoption of a version control oriented editing model to SPL development implies advantages such as unconstrained variability: single-version constraints do not affect the multi-version repository. Furthermore, the distinction between variability in time and

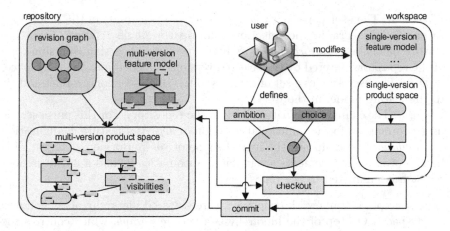

Fig. 1. The integrated editing model underlying our conceptual framework.

variability in space is blurred: our conceptual framework allows to postpone the decision, whether a change to a product constitutes a temporal evolution step or a new product variant or feature, until the commit.

The current paper deals with the model-driven realization of a conceptual framework [17], discussing important design decisions using the formalism of Ecore models. Furthermore, extensions to the generated source codes are presented, which implement behavioral parts of the framework. In addition, this paper proposes several optimizations that improve the scalability of the framework's implementation.

2   The Conceptual Framework

The conceptual framework presented in [17] provides an integrated solution to MDSE, SPLE, and SCM based on the *uniform version model* (UVM) presented in [27]. UVM defines a number of basic concepts (*options*, *visibilities*, *version rules*) for version control. A prototype of our conceptual framework, *SuperMod*, uses EMF both for its own implementation and as the primarily targeted product space. In [18], SuperMod is presented from the end user's perspective and the added value of the integration of MDSE, SPLE and SCM is discussed.

2.1   Overview

As illustrated in Fig. 1, the conceptual framework defines an *editing model* oriented towards version control metaphors. The basic assumption is that the user edits a single version selected by a *choice* (the *read filter*), but the changes affect *multiple* versions, which are defined by a so called *ambition* (the *write filter*). Editing a product version consists of three – partly automated – steps:

1. *Check-out:* The user performs a *version selection* (a *choice*) in the repository. In the revision graph, the selection comprises a single *revision*. From the feature model, a *feature configuation* has to be derived. A single-version copy of the repository, filtered by the selected version, is loaded into the workspace.
2. *Modify:* The user applies a set of changes to the single-version product and/or to the feature model in the workspace.
3. *Commit:* The changes are written back to the repository. For this purpose, the user is prompted for an additional selection of a *partial* feature configuration (an *ambition*) to delineate the logical scope of the performed changes. Visibilities of versioned elements are updated automatically, and a newly created revision is submitted to the repository.

The conceptual framework proposes a three-layered hierarchy of version and product spaces. On top of the hierarchy is a *revision graph*, which controls the evolution of both the *product space* and the *feature model*, which plays a dual role: From the revision graph's perspective, it is versioned the same way as the product space; for the product space, it incorporates an additional variability model.

The *product space* is represented as a *superimposition* of product versions. The connection between the product space and the version space is established by *visibilities*, which are assigned to elements of the product space and the feature model and in turn refer to the version space. The primary product space is a heterogeneous file system, consisting of EMF models and further contents such as plain text or XML files. The interaction between different spaces is described below.

Please note that the conceptual framework's implementation shown in the current paper is restricted to single-user operation. Therefore, the repository is persisted locally in the user's development environment. Collaborative versioning will be addressed by future research.

2.2 Version Space

The term *version space* subsumes the revision graph and the feature model. After introducing a set of general concepts, we show the mapping of those concepts to the feature model and to the revision graph, before an integration is described.

General Concepts. The version space is defined by a set of concepts described in [27] using set theory and propositional logic.

Options. An *option* represents a (logical or temporal) property of a software product that is either present or absent. The version space defines a global *option set:*

$$O = \{o_1, \ldots, o_n\}. \tag{1}$$

Choices and Ambitions. A *choice* is a conjunction over all options, each of which occurs in either positive or negated form:

$$c = b_1 \wedge \ldots \wedge b_n, \ b_i \in \{o_i, \neg o_i\} \ (i \in \{1, \ldots, n\}) \tag{2}$$

An *ambition* is an option binding that allows for unbound options ($b_i = true$, such that this component can be eliminated from the conjunction):

$$a = b_1 \wedge \ldots \wedge b_n, \ b_i \in \{o_i, \neg o_i, true\} \ (i \in \{1, \ldots, n\}) \tag{3}$$

Options occurring positively or negatively in the conjunction are *bound*. Thus, a choice is a *complete binding* and designates a specific version, whereas an ambition may have unbound options (*partial binding*) in order to describe a *set* of versions. The version specified by the choice is used for editing, whereas the change affects all versions specified by the ambition. The ambition must include the choice; otherwise, the change would be performed on a version located outside the scope of the change. Formally, this means that the choice must imply the ambition:

$$c \Rightarrow a. \tag{4}$$

Version Rules. The version space defines a set of *version rules* — boolean expressions over a subset of defined options. The *rule base* $\mathcal{R}$ is composed of a set of rules $\rho_1, \ldots, \rho_m$ all of which have to be satisfied by an option binding in order to be consistent. Thus, we may view the rule base as a *conjunction*:

$$\mathcal{R} = \rho_1 \wedge \ldots \wedge \rho_m \tag{5}$$

A choice c is *strongly consistent* if it implies the rule base $\mathcal{R}$:

$$c \Rightarrow \mathcal{R} \tag{6}$$

In the case of ambitions, only the *existence* of a consistent version is required. An ambition is *weakly consistent* if it overlaps with the constrained option space:

$$\mathcal{R} \wedge a \neq false. \tag{7}$$

Feature Model. Concepts such as options, rules and choices should not be exposed to the user directly because they are represented at a too low conceptual level. *Feature models* [8] meet the requirements of SPLE in a satisfactory way.

Feature Options. A *feature* is a discriminating logical property of a software product. It is adequate to map each feature to a *feature option* $f \in O_f$, where $O_f \subseteq O$.

Feature Dependencies and Constraints. Feature models offer several high-level abstractions: First of all, features are organized in a tree, which makes them existentially depend on each other. Non-leaf features may be grouped as AND- or OR-features. If an AND-feature is selected, its mandatory child features have to be selected as well. In the case of an OR-feature, exactly one child has to be selected (exclusive disjunction). Additionally, cross-tree relationships may be defined: *requires* and *excludes* constraints. It is straightforward to map feature models to propositional logic (see Table 1).

Table 1. Mapping feature models to version space rules.

Pattern	Transformation
root feature f_r	f_r
child feature f_c of parent feature f	$f_c \Rightarrow f$
AND feature f and mandatory child f_c	$f \Rightarrow f_c$
OR feature f and child features $f_1, \ldots f_n$	$f \Rightarrow (f_1 \otimes \ldots \otimes f_n)$
f_1 *excludes* f_2	$\neg(f_1 \wedge f_2)$
f_1 *requires* f_2	$f_1 \Rightarrow f_2$

Version Selection. As aforementioned, *feature configurations* describe the characteristics of a single product of the product line and thus may be considered as a *version selection* within the feature model. A feature configuration is derived from a feature model by assigning a *selection state* to each feature. A feature configuration can be mapped to a choice or ambition by setting the binding b_i for a *feature option* $f_i \in O_f$ as follows:

$$b_i = \begin{cases} f_i & \text{if feature } f_i \text{ is selected.} \\ \neg f_i & \text{if feature } f_i \text{ is deselected.} \\ true & \text{if no selection is provided for } f_i. \end{cases} \tag{8}$$

Please note that *partial* feature configurations allow for unbound options ($b_i = true$). These are allowed only for ambitions, not for choices.

Revision Graph. In SCM, the *evolution* of a software product is addressed. The history of a repository is typically represented by a *revision graph*. Revision control deviates from variability management in two aspects. First, revisions are organized *extensionally*, i.e., only product revisions that have been committed earlier may be checked-out [4]. Second, revisions are *immutable*: Once committed, they are expected to be permanently available.

Revision Options. Temporal versioning can be realized by *revision options* (transactions options in [27]) $r \in O_r$, where $O_r \subseteq O$. For each commit, a new revision option is introduced automatically. In order to achieve *immutability*, neither a revision option itself nor a visibility referring to it may ever be deleted.

Revision Rules. Automatically derived *revision rules* reduce the number of selectable versions within the revision graph considerably: it equals the number of available revision options. As summarized in Table 2, implications are introduced for consecutive revisions transparently.

Choice Specification. A version in the revision graph is selected as a single revision r_c by the user. Since each revision option requires the corresponding options of its predecessor revision ($r_i \Rightarrow r_{i-1}$), a choice in the revision graph is created

Table 2. Mapping revision graphs to version space rules.

Pattern	Transformation
initial revision r_0	r_0
new revision r_i as immediate successor of revision r_{i-1}	$r_i \Rightarrow r_{i-1}$

by conjunction of the selected revision with all of its predecessors. All other revisions appear in a negative binding. For each revision option $r_i \in O_r$ within a revision choice c_r, the option binding b_i is determined as:

$$b_i = \begin{cases} r_i & \text{if } r_i \text{ is the selected revision } r_c \text{ or a predecessor of it.} \\ \neg r_i & \text{else.} \end{cases} \qquad (9)$$

Choices referring to the revision graph are necessarily complete since the binding *true* may never appear.

Ambition Specification. In contrast to choices, ambitions in the revision graph only consist of one bound option, namely a transparently introduced revision option that is a successor of the previously selected revision choice. As a consequence, a *revision ambition* a_r consists of exactly one positive option r_n; positive bindings for predecessors are set implicitly.

$$a_r = r_n, \quad r_n \text{ is a successor of } r_c. \qquad (10)$$

Hybrid Versioning. The combination of the revision graph and the feature model causes interaction between elements of both spaces. Thus, we provide the following extensions to our framework.

Hybrid Version Space. Both the option set and the rule base are decomposed into two disjoint subsets for the feature model and for the revision graph, respectively:

$$O = O_f \,\dot\cup\, O_r \qquad (11)$$

$$\mathcal{R} = \mathcal{R}_f \,\dot\cup\, \mathcal{R}_r. \qquad (12)$$

Hybrid Choice Selection. A *version selection* has to be performed in both the revision graph and the feature model. Correspondingly, a *hybrid choice* is a complete option binding on $O_f \,\dot\cup\, O_r$. It must be ensured that each selected feature option is visible under c_r, the choice among the revision graph.

$$c = c_r \wedge c_f. \qquad (13)$$

Hybrid Ambition Specification. From the user's perspective, the specification of a *hybrid ambition* does not differ from a specification in the feature model. A hybrid ambition a is a conjunction of the selected feature configuration a_f and a transparently introduced revision option r_n.

$$a = r_n \wedge a_f \qquad (14)$$

Since a revision ambition is always weakly consistent, a hybrid ambition only needs to be *weakly consistent* with respect to the feature part of the rule base:

$$\mathcal{R}_f \wedge a_f \neq false \tag{15}$$

Similarly, it is sufficient to require that the feature part of the choice and the ambition imply each other:

$$c_f \Rightarrow a_f. \tag{16}$$

2.3 Product Space

Our conceptual framework makes only few assumptions with respect to the primary product space. These assumptions are discussed in this section, providing the basis for the realization of a multi-variant heterogeneous file system, consisting of EMF, XML, and plain text resources, in Sect. 3.

Set-Theoretic Definition. We assume that the product space consists of a base set of products. It depends on the implementation of the concrete product space, in which granularity elements are modeled, e.g., lines of code or model objects.

$$P = \{e_1, \ldots, e_n\}. \tag{17}$$

Hierarchical Organization. Elements are arranged in a tree, and the product space defines a unique *root element* e_r. Furthermore, each non-root element $e \in P \setminus \{e_r\}$ element has a unique *container* that is returned by the container function $cont(e)$. Basically, the hierarchy is invariant, i.e., the container of an element may not vary among multiple versions.

Visibilities. Each element e of the product space defines a *visibility* $v(e)$, a boolean expression over the variables defined in the option set. An element e is *visible* under a choice c if its visibility is implied by the choice, i.e., it evaluates to *true* given the option bindings of the choice:

$$c \Rightarrow v(e). \tag{18}$$

Filtering. The operation of *filtering* a product space P by a choice c can be realized as a conditional copy, where elements e that do not satisfy the choice are omitted.

$$filter(P, c) = P \setminus \{e \in P \,|\, c \not\Rightarrow v(e)\} \tag{19}$$

Unfortunately, we cannot assert any properties to the result of this function. In particular, it may be syntactically ill-formed, which raises new questions with respect to product consistency control. Those will be further discussed at the end of Sect. 3.2.

3   Model-Driven Realization

This section describes the underlying design decisions made in advance to the realization of the conceptual framework presented in Sect. 2. Unless specified differently, the presented implementation is included in our research prototype *SuperMod* [18]. First, we introduce a set of Ecore metamodels for the repository. Next, the local workspace and the synchronization between repository and workspace are addressed. Subsequently, the operations *check-out* and *commit* are specified. All behavioral components have been implemented in a modular and extensible way using the Google Guice [22] dependency injection framework.

3.1   Metamodels for the Repository

In the realization of the conceptual framework, the repository, where products are contained in their multi-variant representation, is represented as an EMF model instance. This section explains underlying design decisions by presenting the repository's core metamodel, which is divided into several Ecore models.

The Core Metamodel. The presented realization is highly configurable with respect to the concrete product and version space used in a specific versioning scenario. Figure 2 shows an Ecore Metamodel for the *core*, which is extended by specific product and version dimensions. Below, we assume a three-layer architecture consisting of a revision graph, a feature model, and a file system as primary product space (cf. Fig. 1).

A *repository* combines a version space and a product space, which are in turn divided up into several *product* and *version dimensions*. A product dimension contains a tree of *versioned elements*, to which a *visibility* may be assigned. Those visibilities are organized in an optimized data structure, the *visibility forest*, which is explained in Sect. 4.2. A version dimension contains *options* and *(version) rules*, which have been formalized in Sect. 2.2. Both visibilities and rules are represented as *option expressions*.

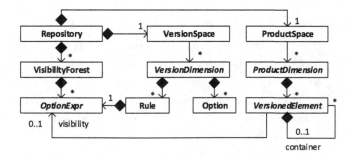

Fig. 2. The core metamodel implements the conceptual framework and is extensible with respect to specific product spaces and version spaces. [18]

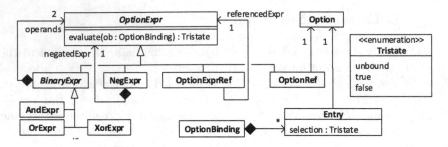

Fig. 3. Metamodel for option expressions and option bindings.

Option Expressions and Option Bindings. Option expressions are logical expressions on the option set. As shown in Fig. 3, there exist three categories of option expressions: *Option references* target an existing option. *Compound expressions* are used in order to combine option expressions (e.g., the negation ¬ is represented by NegExpr, the conjunction ∧ by AndExpr). *Option expression references* re-use existing expressions in order to avoid their repeated duplication (see Sect. 4).

Choices and ambitions appear as temporary data structures; they are internally represented as *option bindings*, sets of entries binding an option to a selection state. The enumeration Tristate defines the three states allowed in *three-valued logic*. The value *unbound* indicates that no selection has been performed for a specific option, which is only allowed within ambitions. Option expressions may be evaluated with respect to a given option binding. This has been realized by corresponding implementations of the operation evaluate in the subclasses of OptionExpr. During evaluation, options are virtually replaced by the bound tristate value. Table 3 shows how three-valued literals are combined.

Table 3. Value table for three-valued logic and basic logical operators. Symmetric cases have been omitted. Complex logical operators such as ⇒ are derived by laws of propositional logic.

a	b	$\neg a$	$a \wedge b$	$a \vee b$
true	*true*	*false*	*true*	*true*
true	*unknown*	*false*	*unknown*	*true*
true	*false*	*false*	*false*	*true*
unknown	*unknown*	*unknown*	*unknown*	*unknown*
unknown	*false*	*unknown*	*false*	*unknown*
false	*false*	*true*	*false*	*false*

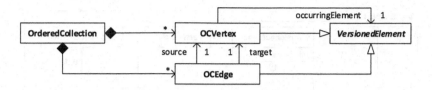

Fig. 4. Multi-version representation of ordered collections as directed graphs.

Ordered Collections. Ordered collections appear in several places in the product space. A text file is a sequence of lines; furthermore, in case a multi-valued structural feature is indicated as *ordered* in an Ecore metamodel, the order of its instances should be preserved whenever possible. The metamodel for multi-version ordered collections, shown in Fig. 4, is used in several concrete product space metamodels.

The underlying design decision is to represent a single version of a collection as a linear directed graph, where succeeding elements are connected by an edge. A corresponding multi-version representation in the repository may form an arbitrary directed graph, whose vertex set and edge set are variable. Furthermore, the vertices of a graph refer to *occurrences* of elements rather than to elements themselves. In order to convert a multi-version collection into a single-version representation (i.e., a *list*), this graph is linearized by a topological sort algorithm. This problem is discussed in detail in [20] in the context of three-way merging of ordered collections.

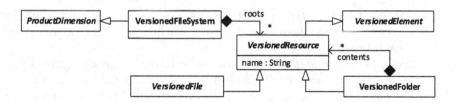

Fig. 5. Ecore class diagram for the metamodel of multi-version heterogeneous file systems.

Heterogeneous File Systems. The class diagram shown in Fig. 5 defines the primary product space, *heterogeneous file systems*, which organize files and folders in a tree. The presented realization supports different *file content types*. As one representative, EMF models are discussed below. In a similar way, support for plain text files and XML files has been realized.

EMF Models. EMF models are structured in a specific way: A (single-version) EMF resource contains a set of hierarchically organized objects. The state of each

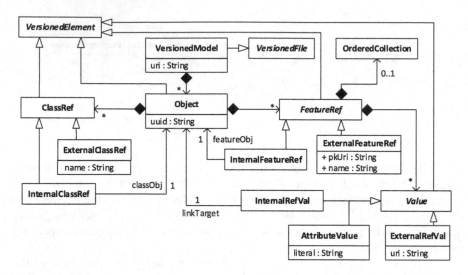

Fig. 6. Simplified Ecore class diagram for the metamodel of the multi-version EMF product space.

object is encoded in the specific values of its structural features, which are divided up into attributes and references. For attribute values, primitive data values are allowed. The values of references are links to existing objects. The metamodel in Fig. 6 realizes the following design decisions with respect to multi-variant EMF models:

(a) *Unconstrained Variability:* Each detail of an object may vary arbitrarily. For this purpose, the meta-classes for structural features and their values extend `VersionedElement`.

(b) *Optionally Versioned Meta-data:* The metamodel of the versioned model may or may not be versioned itself. Classes and structural features are divided up into the categories internal and external. Internal classes/features define a reference to a co-versioned meta-object, while external classes/features are identified by their package URI and class name, or their feature name, respectively.

(c) *Variable Object Classes:* An object may be instance of different classes in different versions. Therefore, the conformance relationship between objects and their corresponding classes is expressed by an ordinary object link that may vary among different versions. Technically, a multi-version EMF model represents two modeling layers (model and metamodel) at the same modeling level, which enables co-versioning of models and metamodels.

(d) *Variable Object Containers:* An object may have different containers in different versions. Thus, the containment hierarchy of objects inside a resource is flattened.

Furthermore, we assume a unique identifier (`uuid`) assigned to each object. Attribute values are represented by string literals; reference values may be internal, by defining a link to an existing object, or external, by specifying a workspace-global object URI. Variability among the order of multi-valued features is achieved by an `OrderedCollection` (see above) that refers to instances of `Value` that must be contained in the corresponding `FeatureRef`.

Revision Graphs. Revision graphs are realized as a *version dimension* comprising a directed graph of *revisions*, for which details such as the revision number, the commit date and message, as well as the username are recorded (see metamodel in Fig. 7). In order to conceptually prepare three-way merging, a revision may have multiple predecessors and successors. Furthermore, specific references to low-level version space elements ensure that the mapping shown in Table 2 may be realized. On instance level, the corresponding options and rules are introduced transparently during the *commit* operation.

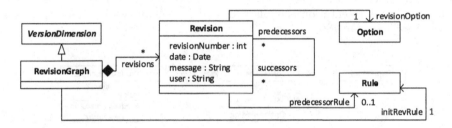

Fig. 7. Ecore metamodel for revision graphs in the repository.

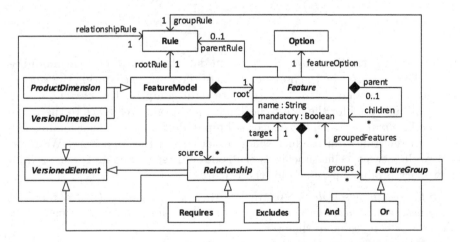

Fig. 8. Ecore class diagram for the metamodel of multi-version feature models.

Feature Models. As mentioned above, the feature model plays a dual role. Therefore, the corresponding class in the Ecore model in Fig. 8 extends both `ProductDimension` and `VersionDimension`. A feature model arranges features within a tree. Each feature is uniquely identified by its name. Multiple sibling features may be arranged in either an *AND* or *OR* group. Furthermore, cross-tree *requires* and *excludes* relationships are allowed. Since features, feature groups and cross-tree relationships are subject to evolution, the corresponding classes extend `VersionedElement`.

For each feature, a feature option is introduced transparently in advance to a *commit*. Furthermore, the semantics of feature groups and cross-tree relationships explained in Table 1 is enforced by links to corresponding *rules*, for which the metamodel provides corresponding references.

3.2   Workspace and Local Synchronization

After having explained the repository, whose internals are not directly exposed to the user, we now switch to workspace abstractions which allow the user to communicate with the repository. First, we describe the realization of the meta-data section of the workspace. Next, the synchronization between single- and multi-version representation is explained. Last, mechanisms for product consistency control are outlined.

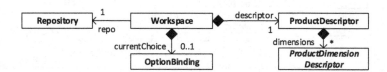

Fig. 9. Simplified metamodel for workspace meta-data in Ecore class diagram representation.

Workspace Meta-data. Workspace meta-data keep track of local modifications and allow to restore the previous state of the workspace during the *commit* operation (see metamodel in Fig. 9). Meta-data comprise the *current choice*, which has been used for the latest check-out operation, a reference to the *repository*, and a *product descriptor*, which is composed of specific dimension descriptors, each referring to a product space dimension of the repository. We informally outline two specific subclasses of `ProductDimensionDescriptor` used for the primary product space and for the feature model.

- The *file system descriptor* keeps track of the versioning state (*added, removed, modified, unmodified, non-versioned*) of files and folders in the workspace. This descriptor is invisible to the user.
- The *feature model descriptor* contains a copy the revision of the feature model that has been selected in the previously specified choice. For the purpose of its modification, an EMF-generated *feature model* editor is provided.

Import and Export Transformations. Within the repository, the product space is represented in a multi-variant representation. In order to make the selected product version available for modification, it needs to be converted into a specific single-version representation. The conversion between single-variant and multi-variant products, and vice versa, is realized by two transformations, namely *import* and *export*. For those, the core module provides an interface, which needs to be implemented by each specific product dimension, e.g., for the file system and for the feature model.

- The import/export transformation pair for the *file system* converts between a physical file system and an instance of the metamodel shown in Fig. 5. The operations are further divided up into specific resource types, i.e., plain text, EMF, and XML. For instance, the EMF-specific *export* transformation maps each multi-version object of the repository to a corresponding EObject in the workspace, setting attribute and reference values accordingly. The flattened containment links are converted back into a hierarchical object tree.
- The *feature model* in the workspace (see meta-data) is represented as an instance of the multi-variant feature metamodel shown in Fig. 8. Therefore, the import/export transformations correspond to the *identity function*.

Product Consistency Control. Multi-version models within the repository are not restricted by single-version constraints and may therefore vary arbitrarily. *Version rules* introduced in Sect. 2.2 cannot guarantee that the outcome of the *export* transformation, i.e., the conversion between multi- and single-variant representation, is syntactically correct. Thus, a mechanism for *product consistency control* is required in addition.

For the purpose of conflict detection, we introduce an additional operation, which has to be implemented by specific product dimensions. The *validation* operation takes as input a filtered multi-version representation and returns a set of *conflicts*, which forbid the transformation into a corresponding single-version representation. It has been implemented for the file system and for the feature model as follows:

- Once again, the validation of a multi-version *file system* is passed to resource-specific validation operations. For multi-variant EMF models, generic constraints such as referential integrity, spanning containment hierarchy, type correctness, and the cardinality of structural features are checked. In the case of an *ordered collection*, a conflict is raised whenever a topological sort of the corresponding collection graph (cf. Fig. 4) does not produce a unique result.
- For the feature model, the following constraints are enforced: unique root feature, unique parent feature, unique feature name, non-contradicting requires/excludes relationships, and unique group membership.

After having detected conflicts, they must be *resolved* by the user, which is not in focus of this paper. An approach to *interactive conflict resolution* is described in [19] in the context of three-way merging of EMF models.

3.3 Realization of Check-Out and Commit

Below, we finalize our editing model sketched in Sect. 2.1 by detailing the operations *check-out* and *commit*. In the description below, we refer to the conceptual framework presented in Sect. 2 as well as to local synchronization operations defined in Sect. 3.2.

Check-Out

1. The user is prompted for a revision r_c from the revision graph, by default the latest revision. The derived *revision choice* is $c_r = r_0 \wedge \cdots \wedge r_c \wedge \neg r_{c+1} \wedge \cdots \wedge \neg r_n$.
2. The multi-version feature model is *filtered* by elements e_f that satisfy the revision choice $(c_r \Rightarrow v(e_f))$. The filtered feature model is *exported* into the workspace and made available for modification.
3. The user performs a *feature choice* c_f on the filtered feature model by specifying a *completely bound* feature configuration. Options for invisible features f_i are automatically negatively bound: $b_i = \neg f_i$. The feature choice must be *strongly consistent* according to the rule base: $c_f \Rightarrow \mathcal{R}_f$.
4. The *effective choice* c is calculated as the conjunction $c = c_r \wedge c_f$ and recorded within the meta-data section of the workspace.
5. The primary product space is *filtered* by selecting elements e_p that satisfy the effective choice $(c \Rightarrow v(e_p))$. The filtered product space is *validated*; in the case of conflicts, the user is prompted for conflict resolution. Finally, the conflict-free filtered product space is *exported* into the workspace and provided for modification.

Modify

6. Between *check-out* and *commit*, the user may apply arbitrary modifications to the primary product space and/or to the filtered feature model provided in the local workspace. Model or non-model files within the workspace belonging to the primary product space may be modified with arbitrary editors, e.g., GMF-based graphical or Xtext-based textual editors. For the modification of the feature model, a generated EMF tree editor is provided, which ensures single-version constraints, although the feature model itself is represented in its multi-version metamodel.

Commit

7. The previous version of the product space is reproduced using the recorded choice. The current state of the product space is obtained by applying the *import* operation to the current workspace contents. Next, *differences* between the previous and the current state of the product space are detected. *Updates* are broken down to insertions and deletions of element versions.
8. A new revision option r_n is added to O_r transparently. The rule $r_n \Rightarrow r_c$ is added to $\mathcal{R}_r$.

9. Next, the user specifies an *incomplete feature configuration* a_f that delineates the logical scope of the change. The feature ambition must be *weakly consistent* according to the rule base: $\mathcal{R}_f \wedge a_f \neq false$. Furthermore, the feature ambition must be *implied* by the feature choice: $c_f \Rightarrow a_f$.

10. The applied modifications are written back under the *effective ambition a*. For changes to the feature model, $a = r_n$; for the primary product space, the *hybrid ambition* $a = r_n \wedge a_f$ is applied. Each modified element e is processed as follows:
    - Inserted elements e_{ins} are appended to the primary product space or to the feature model, respectively. Their visibility is set to the ambition: $v(e_{ins}) := a$.
    - For re-inserted elements e_{reins}, which have not been visible under c, the visibility is modified as follows: $v(e_{reins}) := v_{old}(e_{reins}) \vee a$.
    - Deleted elements e_{del} remain in the repository. Their visibility is modified accordingly: $v(e_{del}) := v_{old}(e_{del}) \wedge \neg a$.

4 Optimization

The representation of the product space as a superimposition will inevitably result in a growing memory consumption. Since revisions are immutable, product space elements will never be effectively deleted from the repository. Furthermore, the evaluation of the constantly growing visibilities will be noticeable in terms of higher runtimes for *check-out* and *commit*. In this section, we present three mutually independent optimizations for the implementation of the conceptual framework, which significantly improve the scalability of the framework's implementation. All three optimizations have been realized in the tool SuperMod [18].

4.1 Hierarchical Evaluation of Visibilities

As explained in Sect. 2.3, one of the few assumptions with respect to the product space is that its elements are organized *hierarchically*. This inherently implies two drawbacks:

- *Duplication of Visibilities:* The insertion of a tree of new elements under the same logical ambition will result in multiple copies of the same visibility during the application of Sect. 3.3, step 10.
- *Consistency of Parent/Child Relationships:* Many modeling frameworks including EMF assume that non-root elements e *existentially depend* on their respective container element $cont(e)$, if any. This constraint should be ensured in any version described by the superimposition; conflicts may be avoided by requiring that the child element's visibility must imply the parent element's visibility: $v(e) \Rightarrow v(cont(e))$.

In order to compensate these drawbacks, we introduce the concept of *effective visibility* v_{eff} of an element, which is defined by conjunction with the visibility of its container element as follows:

$$v_{eff}(e) = \begin{cases} v(e) & \text{if } e \text{ is a root element.} \\ v(e) \wedge v_{eff}(cont(e)) & \text{otherwise.} \end{cases} \tag{20}$$

Furthermore, the visibility of an element is made *optional*; in case an element e does not define a visibility, we implicitly assume $v(e) = true$. This improvement has been conceptually prepared in the core metamodel: In Fig. 2, the cardinality of the reference `visibility` is `0..1`.

The *editing model* shown in Sect. 3.3 is modified as follows: When a tree of elements is inserted/removed in the workspace, only the corresponding root element's visibility needs to be updated during step 10.

Replacing visibilities with effective visibilities improves scalability for the following reasons:

- *Reduced Commit Runtimes:* The above modification of the editing model significantly reduces the number of elements to be processed by visibility updates and therefore the entire runtime of a commit.
- *Reduced Check-out Runtimes:* Likewise, the number of visibilities to evaluate during the *filter* operation, which is applied during a check-out, is reduced. In case an element is filtered, all sub-elements must be filtered, too, removing the necessity to evaluate their visibilities.
- *Improved Consistency Control:* The constraint $v(e) \Rightarrow v(cont(e))$ is ensured automatically for each non-root element e.

4.2 Visibility Forests

Now, we discuss how the connection between product space elements and visibilities can be realized. One possibility would be to make an element directly contain its visibility, which has two obvious drawbacks:

- *Duplication of Visibilities*: The insertion of a large set of new elements (not necessarily connected by containment) under the same logical ambition will result in repeated copies of the same visibility during the application of Sect. 3.3, step 10.
- *Repeated Evaluation of Equivalent Visibilities*: During the *filter* operation, the visibility of all product space elements is evaluated with respect to the specified choice. However, many elements share an equivalent visibility. Without any optimization, the filter operation would repeatedly evaluate the same visibility with respect to the same choice, causing additional runtime.

These drawbacks are removed by *visibility forests*, a global data structure for the storage of visibilities, which has been conceptually prepared in the core metamodel (cf. Fig. 2). Rather than subordinating an element's visibility by containment, a cross-reference is established between `VersionedElement` and `OptionExpr`. This allows several elements to share the same visibility. Furthermore, *option expression references* (see Fig. 3) allow to re-use existing visibilities in the case of element re-insertions or removals. By the mechanisms described below, several hierarchies of interconnected visibilities are created, giving the *visibility forest* its name.

The following modifications are applied to the editing model from Sect. 3.3:

– *Commit, step 10*: The visibility of an element is modified by adding corresponding new entries to the visibility forest and re-using the old visibility by means of expression references. The graph patterns presented in Fig. 10 describes how visibilities of inserted and deleted elements are updated. For instance, in the case of an element deletion, the old visibility is re-used as the first operand of an **AndExpr**, and the second operand consists of the negated ambition. Both the old visibility and the ambition are connected by *option expression references*, which ensure that these expressions may be re-used within different visibilities. As a consequence, no duplicate visibility will ever be inserted into the visibility forest.

– *Check-out, steps 2 and 5*: The visibility forest ensures that equivalent visibilities are represented by the same runtime object. Therefore, the runtime object's identity is used to *cache* the evaluation result (i.e., the **Tristate** returned by **evaluate**, cf. Fig. 3) in a hash map. Before an element's visibility is actually evaluated, a lookup is performed. In the case of a match, the cached result is returned.

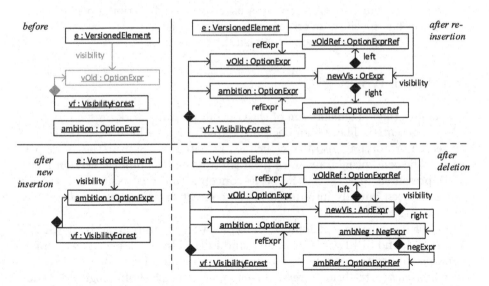

Fig. 10. Object diagrams describing optimized visibility updates of newly inserted, re-inserted and deleted elements in the visibility forest as graph patterns. It is assumed that the **ambition** is passed as a parameter. In the case of a new insertion, the elements shaded in grey are omitted.

4.3   Substitution of Ambition Expressions

The mechanism of writing back changes using an ambition results in corresponding option expressions appearing in the visibility of all affected elements. These expressions increase the size of the superimposition and/or the visibility forest, regardless of whether hierarchical visibilities are used.

In order to reduce the size of serialized feature expressions, we propose to introduce a third component to the option set and the rule base, namely *change options* $\Delta \in O_\Delta$ and *change rules* $\rho_\Delta \in \mathcal{R}_\Delta$ by redefining Eqs. 11 and 12 as follows:

$$O = O_f \,\dot{\cup}\, O_r \,\dot{\cup}\, O_\Delta \tag{11'}$$

$$\mathcal{R} = \mathcal{R}_f \,\dot{\cup}\, \mathcal{R}_r \,\dot{\cup}\, \mathcal{R}_\Delta \tag{12'}$$

The *change space* is completely invisible to the user and used transparently for optimization purposes. After a logical ambition a_f has been specified by the user (cf. Sect. 3.3, step 9), the editing model is modified as follows:

1. A new *change option* Δ is introduced to O_Δ.
2. The rule $\Delta \Rightarrow a_f$ is added to $\mathcal{R}_\Delta$.
3. The change is committed to the repository under the ambition $a_f' := \Delta$.

Besides improved commit runtimes, this optimization brings an additional advantage: It becomes easer to modify a user-specified ambition a posteriori. In case the user has specified an erroneous ambition, it is only necessary to correct a_f in the rule base rather than in the visibility forest.

5   Related Work

In this paper, the implementation of the conceptual framework presented in [17] has been presented. The design decisions explained here have been realized in the research prototype *SuperMod*, which is presented in [18] from the user's perspective. The conceptual framework itself is based on the *uniform version model* (UVM) presented in [27]. UVM's basic concepts (*options, visibilities, version rules*) have been initially introduced in the context of *change-oriented versioning* (*CoV*) [12].

A detailed comparison of approaches to pairwise integration of MDSE/SPLE, MDSE/SCM, and SPLE/SCM, can be found in [17]. In the following, we confine our comparison to tools that address both temporal and logical versioning.

With *branches*, traditional version control systems [2,3] offer logical variants to a limited extent. Albeit, it is only possible to restore variants that have been committed earlier (*extensional* versioning, see [4]). In contrast, our approach allows to create new variants based on a predicate on variant options, i.e., feature configurations (*intensional* versioning). This reduces the overhead of product derivation considerably.

The tool *EPOS-DB* [12] is an implementation of CoV concepts at a low level of abstraction when compared to our approach. Propositional formula are exposed to the user directly, e.g., to specify *choices* and *ambitions*. The product space is based on an *EER* (*Enhanced Entity-Relationship*) model, and is also capable of versioning plain text files. In [12], a global storage for visibilities is introduced, which shares many conceptual similarities with *visibility forests* discussed in this paper.

In [14], an approach for *orthogonal* version management is proposed. In the version control tool VOODOO, a version cube is formed by product, revision, and variant space. The user interface is capable of versioning a complete file hierarchy, which may itself vary along all three dimensions. Albeit, the approach does not consider that the variant space may be subject to temporal evolution.

The commercial SCM system Adele [5] has logical variants built into its object-oriented data model as symmetric deltas, which are exposed to the user. Temporal variability is realized by a versioning layer on top, which relies on directed deltas. Thus, logical and temporal versioning are not integrated at the same conceptual level.

In [28], an approach to *unified versioning* based on *feature logic* is presented. In the version control system *ICE*, versions of artifacts (i.e., text files) are stored with selective deltas; visibilities are controlled by feature-logical expressions. Constraints on feature combinations are expressed by version rules, which are enforced by means of *unification*. The editing model slightly differs from the approach presented in this paper: The user performs only a *partial* version selection. As a consequence, the workspace may still contain variability, which is exposed to the user in the form of C preprocessor directives [10]. Concurrent changes are orchestrated by means of a pessimistic versioning strategy, i.e., write locks.

In [26], an approach to filtered (*projectional*) editing of multi-variant programs is described. The motivation is a reduction of complexity gained by hiding variants not important for a specific change to a multi-variant model. As in our approach, visibilities are managed automatically. Conversely, the restriction of a *completely bound choice* does not exist since the user operates on a partially filtered product, which still contains variability. Temporal versioning is not addressed by the approach presented in [26].

In the field of SPLE, there exist several approaches to partially apply filtered editing to software product lines. These approaches can be considered as a conceptual extension to *multi-version editors* [16]. The source-code centric tool *CIDE (Colored IDE)* [9] generalizes preprocessors using a colored representation to distinguish features. The changes performed in a filtered view may only affect the selected feature or variant, i.e., *choice* and *ambition* must be equal. The MDPLE tool *Feature Mapper* [7] offers the possibility of *change recording* during domain engineering. However, only *insertions* are recognized while recording.

6 Conclusion

We have described the model-driven realization of a conceptual framework [17] that integrates MDSE, SPLE and SCM. The framework defines an editing model that is oriented towards version control metaphors and uses the operations *checkout* and *commit* in order to make a single-version workspace communicate with a multi-version repository. In addition to revision graphs, which manage temporal variability, feature models and feature configurations are used in order to define logical variability and the logical scope of a change. With respect to the repository's architecture, the presented implementation is highly configurable. In this paper, we have focused a three-layered approach, where a revision graph is used to control the evolution of a feature model and a primary product space, which may consist of arbitrary model- or non-model resources. The feature model plays a dual role since it is also used as an additional variability model.

The conceptual framework is based on a *uniform version model*, which builds upon the formalisms of set theory and propositional logic. The static structure of the framework's core is defined by a basic metamodel that abstracts from concrete product and version dimensions. On top of the core metamodel, the model-driven realization of the tool has been presented by means of several concrete extending metamodels, e.g., for the revision graph, for the feature model, and for the heterogeneous file system. The operations *check-out* and *commit* have been fully specified. Last, we have presented three optimizations that increase the scalability of our approach: hierarchical visibilities, visibility forests, and substitution of ambition expressions.

Future work will address the realization of a multi-user component, which requires a mechanism to synchronize multiple, remotely distributed copies of a repository. This extension will advance our prototype *SuperMod* [18] to a full-fledged distributed version control system. Furthermore, conflict resolution still needs to be improved, especially with regard to collaborative versioning. For evaluation purposes, we are planning a case study of industrial scale, which will allow for a quantitative comparison with related SPLE and SCM approaches.

References

1. Altmanninger, K., Seidl, M., Wimmer, M.: A survey on model versioning approaches. Int. J. Web Inf. Syst. (IJWIS) **5**(3), 271–304 (2009)
2. Chacon, S.: Pro Git, 1st edn. Apress, Berkely (2009)
3. Collins-Sussman, B., Fitzpatrick, B.W., Pilato, C.M.: Version Control with Subversion. O'Reilly, Sebastopol (2004)
4. Conradi, R., Westfechtel, B.: Version models for software configuration management. ACM Comput. Surv. **30**(2), 232–282 (1998)
5. Estublier, J., Casallas, R.: The Adele configuration manager. In: Tichy, W.F. (ed.) Configuration Management, Trends in Software, vol. 2, pp. 99–134. Wiley, Chichester (1994)
6. Gomaa, H.: Designing Software Product Lines with UML: From Use Cases to Pattern-Based Software Architectures. Addison-Wesley, Boston (2004)
7. Heidenreich, F., Kopcsek, J., Wende, C.: FeatureMapper: mapping features to models. In: Companion Proceedings of the 30th International Conference on Software Engineering (ICSE 2008), pp. 943–944. ACM, New York, May 2008
8. Kang, K.C., Cohen, S.G., Hess, J.A., Novak, W.E., Peterson, A.S.: Feature-oriented domain analysis (FODA) feasibility study. Technical report CMU/SEI-90-TR-21, Carnegie-Mellon University, Software Engineering Institute, November 1990

9. Kästner, C., Trujillo, S., Apel, S.: Visualizing software product line variabilities in source code. In: Proceedings of the 2nd International SPLC Workshop on Visualisation in Software Product Line Engineering (ViSPLE), pp. 303–313, September 2008

10. Kernighan, B.W.: The C Programming Language, 2nd edn. Prentice Hall Professional Technical Reference, Upper Saddle River (1988)

11. Laguna, M.A., Crespo, Y.: A systematic mapping study on software product line evolution: from legacy system reengineering to product line refactoring. Sci. Comput. Program. **78**(8), 1010–1034 (2013). http://dx.doi.org/10.1016/j.scico.2012.05.003

12. Munch, B.P.: Versioning in a Software Engineering Database – The Change Oriented Way. Ph.D. thesis, Tekniske Høgskole Trondheim Norges (1993)

13. Pohl, K., Böckle, G., van der Linden, F.: Software Product Line Engineering: Foundations Principles and Techniques. Springer, Berlin (2005)

14. Reichenberger, C.: VooDoo a tool for orthogonal version management. In: Estublier, J. (ed.) ICSE-WS/SCM 1993/1995. LNCS, vol. 1005, pp. 61–79. Springer, Heidelberg (1995)

15. Rochkind, M.J.: The source code control system. IEEE Trans. Software Eng. **1**(4), 364–370 (1975)

16. Sarnak, N., Bernstein, R.L., Kruskal, V.: Creation and maintenance of multiple versions. In: Winkler, J.F.H. (ed.) SCM. Berichte des German Chapter of the ACM, vol. 30, pp. 264–275. Teubner (1988)

17. Schwägerl, F., Buchmann, T., Uhrig, S., Westfechtel, B.: Towards the integration of model-driven engineering, software product line engineering, and software configuration management. In: Hammoudi, S., Pires, L.F., Desfray, P., Filipe, J. (eds.) Proceedings of the 3rd International Conference on Model-Driven Engineering and Software Development (MODELSWARD 2015), pp. 5–18. SCITEPRESS Science and Technology Publications, Portugal (2015)

18. Schwägerl, F., Buchmann, T., Westfechtel, B.: SuperMod – a model-driven tool that combines version control and software product line engineering. In: Proceedings of the 10th International Conference on Software Paradigm Trends (ICSOFT-PT). SCITEPRESS Science and Technology Publications, Portugal, Colmar, France (2015, to be published, accepted for publication)

19. Schwägerl, F., Uhrig, S., Westfechtel, B.: Model-based tool support for consistent three-way merging of EMF models. In: Proceedings of the workshop on ACadeMics Tooling with Eclipse, ACME 2013, pp. 2:1–2:10. ACM, New York (2013)

20. Schwägerl, F., Uhrig, S., Westfechtel, B.: A graph-based algorithm for three-way merging of ordered collections in EMF models. Science of Computer Programming (2015, in press, accepted manuscript). http://www.sciencedirect.com/science/article/pii/S0167642315000532

21. Steinberg, D., Budinsky, F., Paternostro, M., Merks, E.: EMF Eclipse Modeling Framework. The Eclipse Series, 2nd edn. Addison-Wesley, Upper Saddle River (2009)

22. Vanbrabant, R.: Google Guice: Agile Lightweight Dependency Injection Framework (Firstpress). APress, New York (2008)

23. Vesperman, J.: Essential CVS. O'Reilly, Sebastopol (2006)

24. Völter, M., Groher, I.: Product line implementation using aspect-oriented and model-driven software development. In: Proceedings of the 11th International Software Product Line Conference, SPLC 2007, pp. 233–242. IEEE Computer Society, Washington, DC (2007). http://dx.doi.org/10.1109/SPLC.2007.28

25. Völter, M., Stahl, T., Bettin, J., Haase, A., Helsen, S.: Model-Driven Software Development: Technology, Engineering, Management. Wiley, Chichester (2006)
26. Walkingshaw, E., Ostermann, K.: Projectional editing of variational software. In: Generative Programming: Concepts and Experiences, GPCE 2014, Vasteras, Sweden, 15–16 September 2014, pp. 29–38 (2014). http://doi.acm.org/10.1145/2658761.2658766
27. Westfechtel, B., Munch, B.P., Conradi, R.: A layered architecture for uniform version management. IEEE Trans. Softw. Eng. **27**(12), 1111–1133 (2001)
28. Zeller, A., Snelting, G.: Unified versioning through feature logic. ACM Trans. Softw. Eng. Methodol. **6**(4), 398–441 (1997)

Composition of Heterogeneous Modeling Languages

Arne Haber[1], Markus Look[1], Pedram Mir Seyed Nazari[1]([✉]),
Antonio Navarro Perez[1], Bernhard Rumpe[1], Steven Völkel[2],
and Andreas Wortmann[1]

[1] Software Engineering, RWTH Aachen University, Aachen, Germany
nazari@se-rwth.de
http://www.se-rwth.de
[2] Volkswagen Financial Services, Braunschweig, Germany

Abstract. Model-driven engineering aims at managing the complexity of large software systems by describing their various aspects through dedicated models. This approach requires to employ different modeling languages that are tailored to specific system aspects, yet can be interpreted together to form a coherent description of the total system. Traditionally, implementations of such integrated languages have been monolithic language projects with little modularization and reuse of language parts.

This paper presents a method for engineering reusable language components that can be efficiently combined on the syntax level. The method is based on the concepts of language aggregation, language embedding, and language inheritance. The result is the ability to efficiently develop project-specific combinations of modeling languages in an agile manner.

1 Introduction

Engineering of non-trivial software systems requires reducing the conceptual gap between problem domains and solution domains [1]. Model-driven engineering (MDE) aims at achieving this by raising the level of abstraction from programming of a complete system implementation to abstract modeling of domain and system aspects. In this way, models are raised to the level of primary development artifacts. Different aspects of complex software systems require different modeling languages to be expressed with. The UML [2], for instance, contains seven structure modeling languages, with class diagrams probably being the most famous, and also seven behavior modeling languages, such as statecharts and activity diagrams. Integration of modeling languages for a software project either requires composing the languages specifically for this project a priori, or designing the independent languages with composition in mind - but without prior assumptions of the actual composition. The former approach yields monolithic language aggregates that are hardly reusable for different projects.

We propose an approach to syntax-oriented black-box integration of grammar-based textual languages developed around the notions of language

© Springer International Publishing Switzerland 2015
P. Desfray et al. (Eds.): MODELSWARD 2015, CCIS 580, pp. 45–66, 2015.
DOI: 10.1007/978-3-319-27869-8_3

aggregation, language embedding, and language inheritance [3,4]. This approach addresses all aspects of syntax-oriented language integration, namely concrete syntax, abstract syntax, symbol tables, and context conditions. It is based on previous work on syntactic modeling language integration [5] and introduces new mechanisms to inter-language model validation. Different aspects of these new mechanisms were briefly introduced at the GEMOC workshop at MODELS 2013 [6] and at the MODELSWARD conference [7]. This contribution extends the concepts and provides an in depth discussion of their implementation with the language workbench MontiCore [8] in detail.

At first, we motivate the need for language integration in MDE on the example of a robotic system in Sect. 2. Afterwards, Sect. 3 explains the concepts for language integration, and Sect. 4 their support through a language integration framework. Section 5 discusses concepts related to our work. Section 6 concludes this contribution with an outlook on future work and a summary.

2   Motivation

To illustrate our approach we first motivate the concepts of language aggregation, language embedding, and language inheritance by the example of a robot that is described by various, heterogeneous models. The techniques employed in this example are described in detail in the following sections. Throughout the example, different needs for language integration arise that we categorize as follows:

- Language aggregation integrates different modeling languages by mutually relating their concepts such that their models can be interpreted together, yet remain independent.
- Language embedding denotes the composition of different modeling languages by embedding concepts of one language into declared extension points of another. Models of the new language thereby contain concepts of both languages.
- Language inheritance is the definition of new languages on the basis of existing languages through reuse and modification of existing language concepts.

Consider a robot exploring uncharted areas, identifying obstacles, and storing these in a map. Our aim is to specify this system by using models in a way detailed enough to generate a significant amount of its implementation automatically.

To this end, various system aspects, such as its overall architecture, the data it operates on, and its deployment onto a runtime infrastructure, need to be addressed individually by appropriate modeling languages, including architecture models, data models, and deployment models. Yet, many of those aspects are not independent, but mutually related. For instance, the components of a software architecture operate on inputs defined via data models and may employ component behavior models to describe output behavior. In addition, some aspects of the system are of a more general nature and apply to a wide

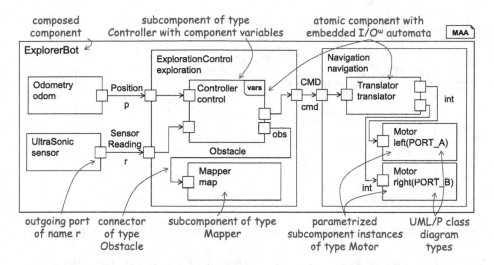

Fig. 1. The MontiArcAutomaton software architecture of the exploration robot uses modeling elements inherited from MontiArc, references aggregated UML/P CDs for data types, and embeds I/O$^\omega$ automata to describe component behavior.

range of system kinds. Conversely, other aspects are specific to the application domain at hand. For instance, architectural distribution is not only relevant in robotics, but also in web systems, whereas aspects such as graceful degradation are more specific to robotics. It is desirable to separate the language concepts for general aspects from those for specific aspects in order to facilitate the modularization of languages into reusable language components. Besides, such reuse of existing general languages reduces the need for developers to learn new notations and concepts.

In the following, we model the software architecture and the domain model of our system using multiple modeling languages. In doing so, we stress the different needs of language integration arising from our scenario.

2.1 Software Architecture

Robotic systems typically consist of different components for specific tasks, such as sensing, navigation, motion, or planning. We model the overall software architecture of the robot with the component and connector architecture description language (ADL) [9] MontiArcAutomaton [10–12] that is derived from the ADL MontiArc [13] and includes *extensions* to model component behavior with application-specific modeling languages [10].

Figure 1 shows the graphical representation of the robot's software architecture model, formulated in terms of hierarchically composed components. Components realize the system's functionality by interacting through directed connectors over which they exchange messages. They comprise of an interface of typed, directed ports, configuration parameters, and type parameters, and of a body containing component behavior. Composed components contain a

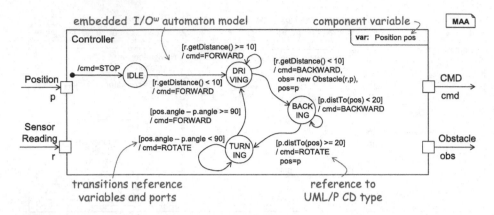

Fig. 2. Atomic component `ExplorationControl` with embedded I/O$^\omega$ automaton.

hierarchy of subcomponents and their behavior emerges from the behavior of these subcomponents. The behavior of atomic components is specified by source code artifacts. Connectors are at each end connected to typed ports that in sum represent a component's interface. While these elements are defined by MontiArc and reused in MontiArcAutomaton via language inheritance, MontiArcAutomaton also introduces new extensions, two of which are shown in the following example. First, atomic components can contain *embedded* behavior models of other languages instead of a reference to a implementation artifact. Second, atomic components may contain variables as well.

In our example, the software architecture model describes the logical software architecture of the exploration robot `ExplorerBot` (Fig. 1). The software architecture comprises of several atomic and composed components to provide sensor data (`Odometry`, `Ultrasonic`), control the robot (`Controller`), store obstacles on a map (`Mapper`), and propel the robot (`Navigation` with subcomponents `Translator` and two `Motors`). Components and connectors are inherited from MontiArc. To be reusable with multiple target platforms, the atomic components controller and translator employ behavior models. The extension points for behavior models are a feature of MontiArcAutomaton to describe the input-output behavior of atomic components. In this case, the behavior of both components is modeled with I/O$^\omega$ automata and embedded into MontiArcAutomaton. The component `Controller` is depicted in Fig. 2 that shows its embedded automaton. The automaton comprises of four states and eight transitions that react on messages received by the component's input ports, store values to variables, and emit messages on its output ports.

The language of I/O$^\omega$ automata was developed independently of MontiArcAutomaton and vice versa. Consequently, automata are unaware of component & connector concepts, such as components or ports while MontiArcAutomaton is unaware of the I/O$^\omega$ language. Nonetheless, automata reference to MontiArcAutomaton's ports and data types and efficient modeling requires that the well-formedness of such references is checked. Checking the validity of assignment `obs = new Obstacle(r,p)`, for instance, requires checking whether `obs` is an

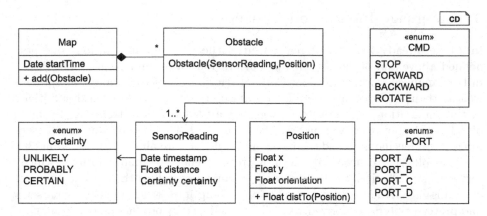

Fig. 3. Domain model `SensorData` for sensor measurements with data types `CMD` and `PORT` used by component type `Motor` and `Control`.

outgoing port or a variable, whether `obs` is of type `Obstacle`, and whether the data type `Obstacle` provides a constructor that accepts two arguments of types `SensorReading` and `Position`, respectively. This requires checking properties of three languages: the component & connector ADL, its behavior languages, and the language of its domain model. Before this is explained, the following section illustrates the domain model used by `Explorerbot`.

2.2 Domain and Data Modeling

Nearly all object-oriented systems operate in the context of a domain model. Such models describe the application's real world context in terms of classes and associations between classes. Their most prominent role is to serve as the basis for the application's fundamental data structures that are used for computation, communication, and persistence.

Class diagrams (CD) are the foundational modeling language in which domain models are described. We formulate them by means of a textual syntax defined by the UML/P [3,14,15], a variant of the UML focused on precise semantics and applicability to generative software engineering. Figure 3 shows a graphical representation of the domain model for our exploration robot example. It consists of classes representing the messages received by the system and the values they convey. A `Map` consists of a set of obstacles (class `Obstacle`), that may contain multiple `SensorReadings` for a specific `Position`. Each `SensorReading` is associated with a `Certainty` to reflect the reading's quality. The domain model furthermore contains the two enumerations `CMD` and `PORT` used by components of type `Motor` and `Control`. The types `Obstacle`, `SensorReading`, `Position`, `CMD`, and `PORT` are referenced directly by the `ExplorerBot` software architecture. It is evident that integration concepts between these different and heterogeneous models are required. In the following section we define such concepts on the language level.

3   Language Integration Concepts

In [6] we already gave a first realization of the language integration concepts defined above and outlined their implementation for grammar-based languages in the language workbench MontiCore [8]. Here, we describe these concepts as well as their application in detail. In particular, we give a detailed description of the integration concepts, the integrated abstract syntax trees (AST), and of references between AST nodes. Please note that the corresponding parser integration mechanisms and the resulting challenges are already discussed in [8].

The following concepts use MontiCore's extended grammar format, which serves to systematically derive both the concrete as well as the abstract syntax of a language. Additionally, language processing infrastructure such as parsers and pretty-printers are derived. Described briefly, every production of a grammar corresponds to a generated AST node class of the same name. The nonterminals of the production become the set of attributes forming the signature of that class. In addition, grammars can define abstract productions and interface productions which can be extended, or implemented respectively. Thus, these can be used anywhere the extended/implemented production's nonterminals are used. Abstract productions differ from normal productions since they have to be extended by at least one normal production. Interface productions are basically the same without defining concrete syntax. An in-depth description of the MontiCore grammar format is given in [8].

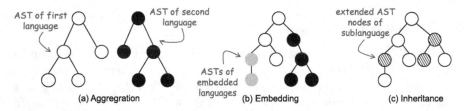

(a) Aggregration   (b) Embedding   (c) Inheritance

Fig. 4. The resulting ASTs for aggregation, embedding, and inheritance. Aggregation results in separate ASTs for each model. Embedding results in a single AST with subtrees embedded at the leaves of the host language. Inheritance results also in a single AST containing extended nodes of the sublanguage (cf. [6]).

3.1   Language Aggregation

Language aggregation integrates multiple languages into a so called *language family*, such that models of these languages are kept in seperate artifacts but interpreted together, enabling loose coupling but mutual referencing each others elements, as shown in Sect. 2.1. There, port declarations of the MontiArcAutomaton model reference type definitions given by the seperate class diagram.

Figure 5 shows how aggregation works on a conceptual level and how concrete aggregations can be defined within the MontiCore language workbench. The left half shows two grammars (MCG) while the right half shows a class diagram and part of a MontiArcAutomaton model that correspond to their respective

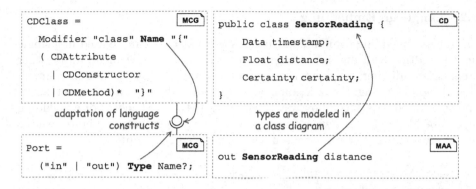

Fig. 5. The mechanism for aggregating languages. By adaptation between elements of two independent languages referencing between them is achieved. The right half of the figure shows concrete models of aggregated languages referencing each other.

grammar on the left. The upper left part shows an excerpt of the grammar for UML/P CDs. In particular, it shows the production of the CDClass nonterminal which defines a class as consisting of multiple subelements, especially a name defininf a possible identifier. Curly brackets enclose the possible subelements. The upper right part contains an instance of the production in concrete syntax in which a SensorReading class is defined. The lower left part shows an excerpt of the MontiArcAutomaton grammar in which the production for a component Port declaration is defined. Both Type and Name define possible identifiers for types and instances names similar to the naming scheme used in Java. As explained earlier, the Type of a port is a name interpreted as a reference to a data type. The lower right part shows an instance of the production referencing a SensorReading type.

Via language aggregation CD and ADL models can be combined such that the type references in the ADL model are interpreted as references to class definitions in the CD. The technical realization of language aggregation works in two steps. First, every model of every language is parsed individually, resulting in an AST for each model as shown in Fig. 4. In our example, the type reference in the AST of the architecture model is represented by an AST node of type Name containing the name of the reference, whereas the class definition in the AST of the CD is represented by an AST node of type CDClass. Second, the references are related to each other by a symbol table. Conceptually, the symbol table manages a kind of link between AST nodes. Technically, the links are implemented by adapter classes to allow for flexible linking to AST nodes from other languages. The details of this are described in Sect. 4.

Language aggregation is adequate for modeling different aspects of a system, each of which can be understood on their own. Each aspect is then described by individual model documents in specialized modeling languages. Through aggregation, these models are related to each other without infringing a tight coupling between them. Thereby, models can be reused in different combinations and in a modular way.

3.2 Language Embedding

Language embedding combines languages such that they can be used in a single model. To this end, an embedding language incorporates elements from other languages at distinguished extension points. Even though this gives the impression of tight coupling, the individual languages are still developed independently and integrated in a black-box way. References between elements of embedding and embedded languages work similarly to language aggregation. Figure 2 shows an example of MontiArcAutomaton with embedded I/O$^\omega$ automata.

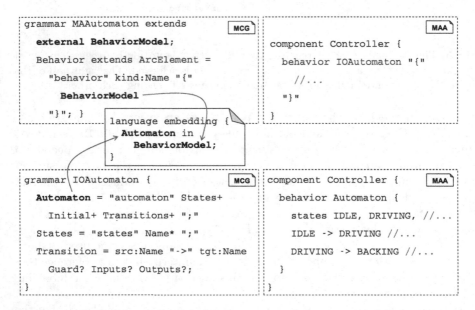

Fig. 6. The mechanism for embedding languages. By declaring an external nonterminal BehaviorModel and a separate mapping artifact, nonterminals of arbitrary languages, such as Automaton can be embedded. The right half of the figure shows a concrete model with the embedded element.

Figure 6 shows how the embedding is accomplished within the MontiCore language workbench. The upper left part again shows an excerpt of the MontiArcAutomaton grammar with the production of the nonterminal Behavior. The production describes a component behavior with a name followed by a BehaviorModel enclosed in curly brackets.

The BehaviorModel is defined as an external nonterminal. Such external productions act as the extensions points into which elements from other languages can be embedded. In fact, the language is incomplete as long as its external productions have not been bound to external language elements. Note that neither the grammar nor the external production contain any information about filling the external nonterminal, leaving the binding to a later stage. The lower left part shows an excerpt of the I/O$^\omega$ automaton grammar containing the definition of an Automaton nonterminal that comprises further nonterminals. Again, the

IOAutomaton grammar does omit any explicit reference to language embedding. This is specified in the language configuration model, shown in the middle part of Fig. 6, which maps Automaton to the external BehaviorModel.

It is also possible to embed several languages into a single external production by mapping several external nonterminals to it. After parsing, the resulting AST consists of different nodes of the different languages, as shown in Fig. 4. Nodes from embedded languages manifest as subtrees attached in place of the node representing the external production. Language embedding is especially useful when the language developer does not want to force the use of a specific language but allows choosing the sub-language later.

3.3 Language Inheritance

Language inheritance can be used to extend or refine an existing language. For this purpose, MontiCore allows to define new languages on the basis of existing languages by reusing, modifying and overriding their productions. The example in Sect. 2.1 illustrates how MontiArcAutomaton extends the MontiArc ADL and adds robotics-specific extensions.

Figure 7 illustrates how this extension is defined within MontiCore's grammar format. The upper left part shows a production (with details omitted) from the MontiArc grammar that specifies the nonterminal interface ArcElement, which all productions usable in a component body implement (cf. the production Ports that references the production Port introduced in Fig. 5). Each production that implements ArcElement thus can be used in a component's body.

The upper right part shows part of a model that conforms to the production shown in the upper left part, i.e., a component with name and a single port. The lower left part shows an excerpt of the textual MontiArcAutomaton grammar extending the MontiArc grammar. The name of the extended grammar is followed by the keyword extends and a reference to the extended grammar. The MontiArcAutomaton grammar introduces a new production Variable that also implements ArcElement, which is available due to inheritance. It is mandatory to keep all elements of a production that have been present in the parent production. Instead, it is also possible to leave some out, reorder them, add new elements in between, or even remove all elements. The lower right part shows a model element that corresponds to the production on the lower left.

Productions of extended languages (or "parent" language) are "virtually'" copied into the extending new language where they can be referenced from new productions. In addition, new productions can individually extend productions from the parent language and thereby inherit that production's interface. This means that the extending production can be used anywhere the nonterminal from the extended production is used. The resulting new AST nodes consequently implement the signatures of their parent counterparts.

The right part in Fig. 4 illustrates the structure of ASTs from inheriting languages. The generated parser for the sublanguage is able to parse text corresponding to the parent language as well as text corresponding to the sublanguage, and consequently creates an AST containing node types from both

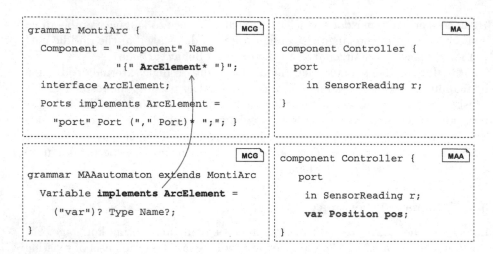

Fig. 7. The mechanism for inheritance between languages. By declaring an extension, languages can inherit from each other and are able to override or implement productions. The right half of the figure shows a concrete model using the inheritance.

languages. Since parent grammars and nodes are referenced by names, name collisions can occur. To prevent this, the language designer may use full qualified names formed by the respective grammar's package, the grammar's name and the name of the production.

Language inheritance is particularly useful for reusing existing concepts of languages while extending them with new concepts. It is applicable when the inheriting language is conceptually similar to the parent language.

3.4   Context Conditions

Context conditions are well-formedness rules for languages inexpressible by their context-free grammars, e.g., restraining a class in a CD from having two members with the same name. These context conditions can impose restrictions between multiple models of the same or different languages. Thus, we distinguish four types of context conditions [3] that have to be integrated differently:

1. **Language-internal Intra-model Context Conditions** only consider a single model of a single language, e.g., to check whether a class of a CD contains two members with the same name.
2. **Language-internal Inter-model Context Conditions** emerge from references between models of the same language, e.g., to check whether a class can instantiate another with certain parameters.
3. **Cross-language Intra-model Context Conditions** consider relations emerging from the embedding of one language's model into the model of another language, e.g., to check whether the return type of an embedded SQL statement matches the return type of the embedding method declaration (cf. Fig. 7).

4. **Cross-language Inter-model Context Conditions** check conditions between models of different languages, e.g., whether the type of a component's port is declared within the imported CDs.

4 Language Integration Framework

In this section, we describe a framework to (1) implement *symbol table infrastructures* that relate model elements in composed languages in a black-box way and to (2) configure them for concrete language compositions based on the concepts introduced above.

Section 3 described how language embedding and language inheritance manifest in the ASTs of processed models that are instances of combined languages (cf. Fig. 4). Both mechanisms make information about embedded or inherited model elements directly available in the AST for further model processing, such as code generation. However, this is not the case for models of aggregated languages in which elements of one language reference elements of another language by name. Here, the AST nodes only contain the raw name of the referenced model element. The same holds for embedding and embedded languages that refer to each other through raw names as well. Consequently, additional infrastructure is necessary to translate raw name references into information about referenced model elements.

In the following, we describe an infrastructure named symbol table that (a) allows to acquire information from referenced models as well as (b) to transparently interpret elements of one language as elements of another. Compared to traditional symbol table techniques, our realization must be able to translate these different kinds of concepts between languages. For example, automata know about states and input signals, whereas Java knows nothing about these. To integrate these languages nonetheless, the concept of a state must be translated into Java in a meaningful way. For instance, states could be mapped to an enumeration or also to subclasses (as, e.g., in the state pattern [16]). To keep both languages, independent, we cannot define this translation in either language. Instead, we need to define it as a separate artifact during language integration. The ability to do this is one key feature of our symbol table framework.

4.1 Symbol Table Concepts

A *symbol table* is a data structure that is used to store and to resolve identifiers within a language [4]. An identifier, such as a name, is associated with further information from the corresponding language element. In this way detailed information may be gathered from the symbol table by resolving an element using its name. The result of a name search is a symbol. In the following we define the core concepts of a symbol table structure[1].

---

[1] Please note that part of the nomenclature introduced in [7] was changed to reflect the refined concepts more precisely.

Definition 1 (Symbol and Kind). A symbol, i.e., an entry in the symbol table, is a representation of essential information about a (named) model element. It has a specific kind and a well defined signature determined by the model element it denotes, e.g., variable, method, state.

Every symbol has a name (resp. simple name), e.g., `SensorReading`, which usually is unique within the scope (see below) the symbol is defined in. The qualified name (resp. full name) of a symbol additionally includes, among others, its package name. For example, `de.se.SensorReading` is the qualified name where `de.se` is the package name and `SensorReading` the simple name. Above all, the qualified name of a symbol is important to resolve a *referenced symbol* that is defined in another model. Generally, every symbol is defined exactly once, but may be referenced several times. The symbol definition contains the whole information about the symbol, whereas a symbol reference only contains information needed to resolve the definition.

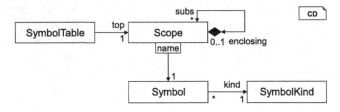

Fig. 8. Symbol table, hierarchical scopes and related symbols.

Definition 2 (Symbol Visibility). The visibility of a symbol is the region where the symbol is accessible through its name.

The visibility of a symbol can be shadowed by other symbols (*shadowing*). For example, a variable defined in a Java method shadows a same-named field defined in the enclosing class. Some languages provide *access modifiers* to set the visibility depending on the context, e.g., in Java, the access modifier `private` narrows the symbol visibility down to the class scope. Access modifiers determine whether specific model elements may be accessed *from outside*, i.e., from other models whereas shadowing is *within* a model or model hierarchy. A combination of both is also possible, for example, a Java field in a class can shadow protected and public fields of the super class.

Definition 3 (Scope). A scope holds a logical grouping of symbol definitions and limits their visibility. Usually, scopes are attached to nonterminals that open scopes and are thus organized hierarchically, which leads to a *scope-tree*. If a scope redefines (i.e., shadows) names from its enclosing scope(s), it is a *shadowing scope*, else, it is a *visibility scope*.

The structural relation of the symbol table elements is depicted in Fig. 8. A `Scope` associates symbols (`Symbol`) with their name. Scopes may have an arbitrary number of sub-scopes and an optional enclosing scope to represent a scope-tree.

The SymbolTable mainly consists of that scope-tree and points to its root. Every symbol has exactly one kind (SymbolKind).

The different symbol table kinds we described in [7] are now substituted by a combination of symbol shadowing and the aforementioned access modifiers:

1. **Encapsulated** symbol are only visible within their defining scope. For example, a local variable that is defined in a if-statement in Java, is only visible within that statement, not in the enclosing method or class.
2. **Imported** symbols are symbols that are imported from another scope in order to make them visible in the importing scope. Simply put, scopes can import symbols of their enclosing scope. For example, a field defined in a Java class is visible in all its methods (i.e., sub-scopes). If the enclosing scope is from another model, e.g., a super class in Java, not all symbols are visible, depending on what symbols the enclosing scope *exports*, as described next.
3. **Exported** symbols are defined in a corresponding scope and are publicized to their environment. Whether a symbol is exported can be set by access modifiers. In Java, for example, all non-private symbols are exported. However, those symbols may not necessarily be used from everywhere equally: a protected field symbol is exported, but can only be imported by sub-classes and classes in the same package.
4. **Forwarded** symbols are both imported and exported. For example, an imported symbol that represents a protected method inherited from a super-class is also exported, and hence, can be imported by the corresponding sub-classes.

4.2   Symbol Table Components

The previously described symbol table and scope structure has to be created for each language. The MontiCore language workbench [17] provides infrastructure for a uniform development of technical symbol table components for modeling languages. The most important classes and interfaces are depicted in Fig. 9.

Each concrete modular modeling language is presented by the interface ILanguage. It offers the technical components needed to create the symbol table with the scopes for an instance of that language. Its symbol creators (subclasses of ConcreteASTAndScopeVisitor) are used to set up the scope hierarchy of a model. Then, symbols for model elements are created and organized in the symbol table, i.e., in the corresponding scope. The registered IInheritedSymbolCalculatorClients are used to compute whether symbols from imported scopes are shadowed by locally defined symbols. An IQualifierClient has to be provided for each element kind of a language which instances may be referenced within the current or another model, such as a referenced type of a field. The concrete qualifier client is used to calculate the qualified name of a referenced symbol with the corresponding kind. Resolver clients (IResolverClient) have to be provided for each symbol kind that may be referenced within the current scope hierarchy. The registered deserializers

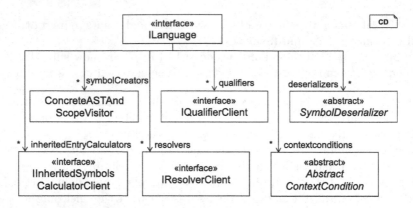

Fig. 9. Technical components of a symbol table (cf. [4]).

(`SymbolDeserializer`) load serialized symbols from externally referenced models. They are used to resolve the corresponding symbol definitions for symbol references that represent a referenced model element. Associated context conditions that extend the abstract class `AbstractContextCondition` are used to check if processed models are well formed.

This way a concrete `ILanguage` module offers all means to process models or model parts of a certain language and produce a corresponding symbol table. The provided infrastructure additionally alleviates inter-model relations that allow to resolve external information defined in related models. How to combine these components in several ways to realize the language integration concepts presented in Sect. 3 is described in the following subsection.

4.3   Configuration of Language Compositions

Language integration requires different effort depending on the type of integration. The composition takes place hierarchically to enable application of mechanisms in the best possible order. Figure 10 shows the different language concepts required to achieve this compositionality.

Language aggregation of two or more existing modeling languages is implemented in `LanguageFamily` instances. These gather the different independent `ModelingLanguages` together with the inter-language infrastructure, such as resolvers, qualifiers and adapters for symbol table integration, as well as factories and inter-language context conditions. Language families are used by MontiCore's `DSLTools` to process sets of heterogeneous but related models. The MontiArcAutomaton language family, for instance, comprises a modeling language for architecture models and a modeling language for CDs.

A `ModelingLanguage` is a black-box language and contains language-specific information such as the file ending. It may contain either a single language or a composition of embedded languages, such as MontiArcAutomaton components with embedded I/O$^\omega$ automata. Therefore, modeling languages contain a hierarchy of `ILanguage` interfaces. Based on this, MontiCore creates the infrastructure

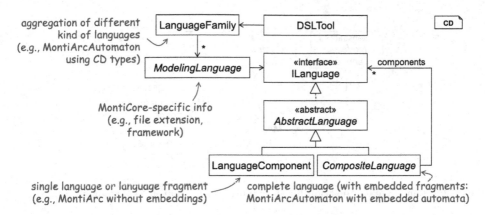

Fig. 10. Technical realization of MontiCore's language composition mechanisms (cf. [3,4]).

to parse model instances accordingly. This infrastructure contains the correct combination of parser and lexer for the model at hand.

For single languages, modeling languages contain only a single `Language Component` that contains the symbol table infrastructure and context conditions necessary. A `LanguageComponent` contains the information required to process symbols of the respective single language, i.e., how symbols are created, deserialized, qualified, resolved, which context conditions are available, and which symbol types are exported (see Sect. 4.2). For embedded languages, modeling languages contain a hierarchy of `CompositeLanguages`. These are composed of the embedded languages that themselves are represented by an implementation of `ILanguage`. Language components and composite languages are implemented as `AbstractLanguage` that provide common functionality used by language components and composite languages. They implement the interface `ILanguage` to allow utilization in a composite [16]. Using the composite pattern for embedding allows to reuse the resulting language combinations easily in different contexts, e.g., to embed activity diagrams and I/O$^\omega$ automata into components. Composite languages and language families can be considered as the glue between languages and their symbol tables as they hold the required adapters, resolvers, qualifiers, and context conditions for their specific composition.

Figure 10 also shows, that the order of language aggregation is arbitrary and depends on the language engineer. Whether a subset of the embedded languages should define a new `ModelingLanguage` solely depends on the desire to reuse this combination. It might, for example, be useful to combine MontiArcAutomaton and I/O$^\omega$ automata first, and to reuse the resulting combination with different, additional component behavior languages. Please note that language inheritance is not reflected in this structure, as the resulting combined abstract syntax does not necessarily require any interaction on symbol level. If this however is necessary, usually a new 'main' symbol has to be created that contains the additional information resulting from the language extension. Thus, MontiArcAutomaton

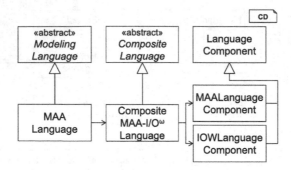

Fig. 11. Language composition for the MontiArcAutomaton `MAALanguage` (cf. [3]).

introduces a new component symbol to contain the new language features. To be reusable with existing language integration infrastructure of the inherited language, these need to be adapted to its symbols accordingly. Hence, MontiArcAutomaton component symbols need to be adapted to MontiArc component symbols. Similar to the development of the symbol table of a new language, symbols, symbol creators, qualifiers, and resolvers have to be registered for elements added by the inheriting language. The inheriting language can also reuse context conditions of the inherited language and add new ones.

Figure 11 illustrates the language composition mechanisms on the MontiArcAutomaton language `MAALanguage`. The language allows to model components with embedded I/O$^\omega$ automata illustrated in Sect. 2.2. As this embedding happens on the concrete syntax, there is no need to reference models of other languages by name. Therefore, the language is implemented as a modeling language that contains the composite language `CompositeMAAAutomata` which realizes the embedding. `CompositeMAAAutomata` is composed of language components for `MontiArc`, and `IOAutomaton` respectively, and contains adapters between the two languages as well as inter-language context conditions. Language-internal context conditions are defined in the language component. Cross-language inter-model context conditions are defined in language families, whereas cross-language intra-model context conditions are defined in composite languages. Adaptation between symbols of two languages, such as the types of automaton messages and ports of embedding MontiArcAutomaton, requires the composite language to provide adapters, qualifiers, and resolvers for type pairs. Adaptation between aggregated languages of a language family requires to configure these elements in the language family instead. Figure 12 shows the elements required to adapt type symbols of MontiArcAutomaton to type symbols of a CD language. Integration requires to provide a new adapter factory marked responsible to create symbols of a certain type (here MontiArcAutomaton type symbols for CD types). When a CD type needs to be qualified or resolved for embedded I/O$^\omega$ automata, the factory produces an adapter which behaves like a MontiArcAutomaton type symbol, but delegates all methods to the adapted CD type symbol.

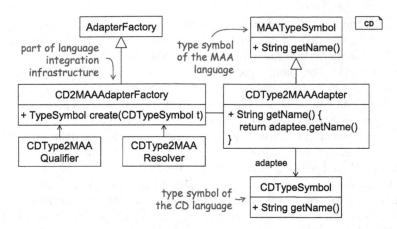

Fig. 12. Adaptation between type symbols of MontiArcAutomaton and those of the CD language.

Using adaptation on the levels of composite languages and language families allows to develop languages without consideration of a posteriori integration. As the languages are free from integration premises, they can be composed arbitrarily.

5 Related Work

We have presented three mechanisms for the integration of modeling languages. Integration takes place on the syntactical level and enables language aggregation, language embedding, and language inheritance. Related to our contribution are other studies and approaches on general syntax-oriented language integration. We do neither discuss language integration for specific language families [18, 19] as these are usually specifically created to be integrated, nor do we discuss semantic language integration [20–23].

A study on language composition mechanisms distinguishes the mechanisms: "language extension, language restriction, language unification, self-extension, and extension composition" [24]. The authors' notion of language extension also requires that languages can be composed a-posteriori and distinguishes language extension from language integration. Our approach to language extension allows to overwrite nonterminals from the extended language in order to reduce expressiveness. The proposed notion of "language unification" matches our definition of language aggregation, where two independent languages can be used "unchanged by adding glue code only". In their definition of "self-extension", the authors start from a different definition of "language embedding" than we do: there, language embedding is that a "domain-specific language is embedded into a host language by providing a host-language program that encapsulates the domain-specific concepts and functionality" [25], which defines the use of domain-specific programs and is hardly recognizable as language embedding.

Accordingly, the author's definition of "self-extension" requires that "the language can be extended by programs of the language itself while reusing the language's implementation unchanged"–which also allows to "embed" languages as strings into the host language, e.g., SQL queries or regular expressions in Java. MontiCore does not provide an explicit "self-extension" mechanism, but supports it by embedding action languages allowing definition of programs. MontiCore languages also support the language extension composition mechanisms denoted as incremental extension and language unification as defined in [24].

A recent study on language workbenches [26] provides an overview of existing tools and their features. In particular, Ensō [27], Más [28], MetaEdit+ [29], MPS [30], Onion [26], Rascal [31], Spoofax [32], SugarJ [33], Whole Platform [34] and XText [35] are reviewed. This review considers four dimensions: syntax, validation, semantics and editor services. According to the overview all of the presented tools are able to achieve syntactical composition via different mechanisms. Nevertheless the composition on the validation depends on the validation features of the respective workbench. Only MPS, SugarJ and XText provide validation for naming and type checking similar to our approach to syntax-oriented language integration, namely concrete syntax, abstract syntax, symbol tables, and context conditions. In [36] the composition of languages in MPS is shown in more detail. To compose types new type definition rules have to be applied to infer types via unification. Since MontiCore is not projectional and uses independent parsers we define these connections between AST elements via our adaptation mechanisms and not via generic type definition rules. Furthermore, [36] distinguishes between language combination, extension, reuse and embedding. While language combination and reuse are similar to our notion of aggregation, language extension corresponds to our language inheritance, and language embedding is congruent with our concept of embedding.

The authors of [37] highlight cross-language context conditions as an important source for errors, propose to develop reusable cross-language context conditions and sketch how these can be implemented with their language workbench. It remains to be discussed how context conditions checking semantic properties specific to a language family can be designed for reuse.

Another approach to deal with the complexity of language integration is to employ domain-specific embedded languages (DSELs) in a host language (e.g., Scala) [38]. Regarding our example, this circumvents the problems arising from using data types between languages and allows to reuse existing development infrastructure. These approaches focus on syntax-oriented integration as well, but language reuse is limited to languages of the same host language and often DSELs lack explicit meta-models usable for integration purposes.

Attribute grammars [39] allow to enrich grammar symbols with computation rules. Research in attribute grammars led to promising results regarding language integration, such as Forwarding [40], and produced capable language workbenches as well [23]. Using multiple inheritance of attribute grammars to integrate is another interesting approach [41] to language integration that suffices to fulfill the language composition mechanisms identified in [24].

The authors of [42] propose a semi-automatic lifting from meta models to ontologies to ease language integration. After constructing ontologies representing the languages' meta models, the authors suggest nine refactoring patterns to make concepts implicit in the meta models explicit in the ontologies. The resulting ontologies should reduce language integration to ontology matching. While this process could ease language aggregation, neither language extension, nor language embedding require matching of symbols.

6 Conclusion

Engineering of complex software systems requires MDE where language integration can help to deal with the heterogeneity of modeling languages involved. We introduced language aggregation, language embedding, and language inheritance by example. These language integration techniques allow integration of languages without stipulating possible integration partners or mechanisms a priori. This enables to compose languages with minimal effort.

We have illustrated how these integration mechanisms are implemented in MontiCore. To achieve cross-language resolution of names, the symbol table, language families, and modeling languages were introduced. Language families and modeling languages contain the glue to enable cross-language model usage. This glue is implemented in the form of adapters between entries of symbol tables. The presented concepts and framework have been evaluated with various languages for different domains, such as architectural modeling [13], modeling the evolution of such architectures [43] modeling variability and evolution in software product lines [44–47], modeling cloud architectures [48] and architectural as well as behavioral modeling for cyber-physical systems [10, 49, 50].

In order to use the symbol table infrastructure out-of-the-box, in the future, it could be extended by generic default implementations. Following the MDE approach, it should also be examined whether (language-specific) parts of the symbol table can be generated from the language and its models directly. Moreover, it should be investigated whether the different language integration definition mechanisms (e.g., grammars for embedding, symbol table for aggregation) can be unified. Furthermore, it might be possible to generate the cross language infrastructure from enriched models of the respective language as well.

References

1. France, R., Rumpe, B.: Model-driven development of complex software: a research roadmap. In: Future of Software Engineering (FOSE 2007) (2007)
2. Object management group: OMG unified modeling language (OMG UML), superstructure version 2.3 (2010). http://www.omg.org/spec/UML/2.3/Superstructure/PDF/. Accessed 05 May 2010
3. Schindler, M.: Eine Werkzeuginfrastruktur zur Agilen Entwicklung mit der UML/P. Aachener Informatik-Berichte, Software Engineering, Band 11. Shaker (2012)

4. Völkel, S.: Kompositionale Entwicklung domänenspezifischer Sprachen. Aachener Informatik-Berichte, Software Engineering Band 9. 2011. Shaker Verlag (2011)
5. Krahn, H., Rumpe, B., Völkel, S.: MontiCore: modular development of textual domain specific languages. In: Paige, R.F., Meyer, B. (eds.) Proceedings of Tools Europe. Lecture Notes in Business Information Processing, vol. 11. Springer, Heidelberg (2008)
6. Look, M., Navarro Perez, A., Ringert, J.O., Rumpe, B., Wortmann, A.: Blackbox integration of heterogeneous modeling languages for cyber-physical systems. In: Proceedings of the 1st Workshop on the Globalization of Modeling Languages (GEMOC), Miami, Florida, USA (2013)
7. Haber, A., Look, M., Mir Seyed Nazari, P., Navarro Perez, A., Rumpe, B., Voelkel, S., Wortmann, A.: Integration of heterogeneous modeling languages via extensible and composable language components. In: Proceedings of the 3rd International Conference on Model-Driven Engineering and Software Development, Angers, France, Scitepress (2015)
8. Krahn, H., Rumpe, B., Völkel, S.: MontiCore: a framework for compositional development of domain specific languages. Softw. Tools Technol. Trans. (STTT) **12**(5), 353–372 (2010)
9. Medvidovic, N., Taylor, R.: A classification and comparison framework for software architecture description languages. IEEE Trans. Softw. Eng. **26**(1), 70–93 (2000)
10. Ringert, J.O., Rumpe, B., Wortmann, A.: MontiArcAutomaton: modeling architecture and behavior of robotic systems. In: Workshops and Tutorials Proceedings of the IEEE International Conference on Robotics and Automation (ICRA), Karlsruhe, Germany (2013)
11. Ringert, J.O., Rumpe, B., Wortmann, A.: Architecture and behavior modeling of cyber-physical systems with MontiArcAutomaton. Number 20 in Aachener Informatik-Berichte, Software Engineering. Shaker Verlag (2014)
12. Ringert, J.O., Rumpe, B., Wortmann, A.: Multi-platform generative development of component and connector systems using model and code libraries. In: 1st International Workshop on Model-Driven Engineering for Component-Based Systems (ModComp 2014). CEUR Workshop Proceedings, Valencia, Spain, vol. 1281, pp. 26–35 (2014)
13. Haber, A., Ringert, J.O., Rumpe, B.: MontiArc - architectural modeling of interactive distributed and cyber-physical systems. Technical report AIB-2012-03, RWTH Aachen (2012)
14. Rumpe, B.: Modellierung mit UML, 2nd edn. Springer, Heidelberg (2011)
15. Rumpe, B.: Agile Modellierung mit UML: Codegenerierung, Testfälle, Refactoring, 2nd edn. Springer, Heidelberg (2012)
16. Gamma, E., Helm, R., Johnson, R., Vlissides, J.: Design Patterns: Elements of Reusable Object-Oriented Software. Addison-Wesley Professional, Boston (1995)
17. Grönniger, H., Krahn, H., Rumpe, B., Schindler, M., Völkel, S.: MontiCore 1.0 - Ein Framework zur Erstellung und Verarbeitung domänenspezifischer Sprachen. Technical Report Informatik-Bericht 2006–04, Software Systems Engineering Institute, Braunschweig University of Technology (2006)
18. Barja, M.L., Paton, N.W., Fern, A.A.A., Williams, M.H., Dinn, A.: An effective deductive object-oriented database through language integration. In: Proceedings of the 20th International Conference on Very Large Data Bases (VLDB) (1994)
19. Groenewegen, D., Visser, E.: Declarative access control for WebDSL: combining language integration and separation of concerns. In: Proceedings of the 8th International Conference on Web Engineering 2008 (ICWE 2008) (2008)

20. Grönniger, H., Rumpe, B.: Modeling language variability. In: Calinescu, R., Jackson, E. (eds.) Monterey Workshop 2010. LNCS, vol. 6662, pp. 17–32. Springer, Heidelberg (2011)
21. Hedin, G., Magnusson, E.: JastAdd - an aspect-oriented compiler construction system. Sci. Comput. Program. **47**(1), 37–58 (2003)
22. Wende, C., Thieme, N., Zschaler, S.: A role-based approach towards modular language engineering. In: van den Brand, M., Gašević, D., Gray, J. (eds.) SLE 2009. LNCS, vol. 5969, pp. 254–273. Springer, Heidelberg (2010)
23. Wyk, E.V., Bodin, D., Gao, J., Krishnan, L.: Silver: an extensible attribute grammar system. Electron. Notes Theor. Comput. Sci. **203**(2), 103–116 (2008)
24. Erdweg, S., Giarrusso, P.G., Rendel, T.: Language composition untangled. In: Proceedings of the 12th Workshop on Language Descriptions, Tools, and Applications (2012)
25. Hudak, P.: Modular domain specific languages and tools. In: Proceedings of the 5th International Conference on Software Reuse 1998 (1998)
26. Erdweg, S., et al.: The state of the art in language workbenches. In: Erwig, M., Paige, R.F., Van Wyk, E. (eds.) SLE 2013. LNCS, vol. 8225, pp. 197–217. Springer, Heidelberg (2013)
27. van der Storm, T., Cook, W.R., Loh, A.: The design and implementation of object grammars. Sci. Comput. Program. **96**, 460–487 (2014)
28. Más website. http://www.mas-wb.com
29. Kelly, S., Lyytinen, K., Rossi, M.: Metaedit+ a fully configurable multi-user and multi-tool case and came environment. In: Constantopoulos, P., Vassiliou, Y., Mylopoulos, J. (eds.) CAiSE 1996. LNCS, vol. 1080. Springer, Heidelberg (1996)
30. Dmitriev, S.: Language oriented programming: the next programming paradigm. JetBrains onBoard **1** (2004). https://www.jetbrains.com/mps/docs/Language_Oriented_Programming.pdf
31. Klint, P., van der Storm, T., Vinju, J.: Rascal: a domain specific language for source code analysis and manipulation. In: Proceedings of the 9th IEEE International Working Conference on Source Code Analysis and Manipulation 2009 (SCAM 2009) (2009)
32. Kats, L.C., Visser, E.: The spoofax language workbench: rules for declarative specification of languages and IDEs. SIGPLAN Not. **45**(10), 444–463 (2010)
33. Erdweg, S., Rendel, T., Kästner, C., Ostermann, K.: SugarJ: library-based syntactic language extensibility. ACM SIGPLAN Not. **46**(10), 391–406 (2011)
34. Solmi, R.: Whole platform. Ph.D. thesis, University of Bologna (2005)
35. Eysholdt, M., Behrens, H.: Xtext: implement your language faster than the quick and dirty way. In: Proceedings of the ACM International Conference Companion on Object Oriented Programming Systems Languages and Applications Companion (2010)
36. Voelter, M.: Language and IDE modularization and composition with MPS. In: Lämmel, R., Saraiva, J., Visser, J. (eds.) GTTSE 2011. LNCS, vol. 7680, pp. 383–430. Springer, Heidelberg (2013)
37. Tomassetti, F., Vetro, A., Torchiano, M., Voelter, M., Kolb, B.: A model-based approach to language integration. In: Proccedings of the 5th International Workshop on Modeling in Software Engineering (MiSE) (2013)
38. Hofer, C., Ostermann, K.: Modular domain-specific language components in scala. ACM SIGPLAN Not. **46**(2), 83–92 (2010)
39. Knuth, D.F.: Semantics of context-free languages. Math. Syst. Theory **2**(2), 127–145 (1968)

40. Van Wyk, E., de Moor, O., Backhouse, K., Kwiatkowski, P.: Forwarding in attribute grammars for modular language design. In: Nigel Horspool, R. (ed.) CC 2002. LNCS, vol. 2304, pp. 128–142. Springer, Heidelberg (2002)

41. Mernik, M.: An object-oriented approach to language compositions for software language engineering. J. Syst. Softw. **86**(9), 2451–2464 (2013)

42. Kappel, G., et al.: Lifting metamodels to ontologies: a step to the semantic integration of modeling languages. In: Nierstrasz, O., Whittle, J., Harel, D., Reggio, G. (eds.) Model Driven Engineering Languages and Systems. Lecture Notes in Computer Science, vol. 4199, pp. 528–542. Springer, Heidelberg (2006)

43. Haber, A., Hölldobler, K., Kolassa, C., Look, M., Rumpe, B., Müller, K., Schaefer, I.: Engineering delta modeling languages. In: Proceedings of the 17th International Software Product Line Conference (2013)

44. Haber, A., Rendel, H., Rumpe, B., Schaefer, I.: Evolving delta-oriented software product line architectures. In: Calinescu, R., Garlan, D. (eds.) Monterey Workshop 2012. LNCS, vol. 7539, pp. 183–208. Springer, Heidelberg (2012)

45. Haber, A., Kutz, T., Rendel, H., Rumpe, B., Schaefer, I.: Delta-oriented architectural variability using MontiCore. In: ECSA 2011 5th European Conference on Software Architecture: Companion Volume (2011)

46. Haber, A., Rendel, H., Rumpe, B., Schaefer, I.: Delta modeling for software architectures. In: Tagungsband des Dagstuhl-Workshop MBEES: Modellbasierte Entwicklung eingebetteterSysteme VII (2011)

47. Haber, A., Rendel, H., Rumpe, B., Schaefer, I., van der Linden, F.: Hierarchical variability modeling for software architectures. In: Proceedings of International Software Product Lines Conference (SPLC 2011) (2011)

48. Navarro Pérez, A., Rumpe, B.: Modeling cloud architectures as interactive systems. In: 2nd International Workshop on Model-Driven Engineering for High Performance and CLoud computing (MDHPCL) (2013)

49. Thomas, U., Hirzinger, G., Rumpe, B., Schulze, C., Wortmann, A.: A new skill based robot programming language using UML/P statecharts. In: Proceedings of the 2013 IEEE International Conference on Robotics and Automation (ICRA), Karlsruhe, Germany (2013)

50. Ringert, J.O., Rumpe, B., Wortmann, A.: From software architecture structure and behavior modeling to implementations of cyber-physical systems. In: Wagner, S., Lichter, H. (eds.) Software Engineering 2013 Workshopband. Volume 215 of LNI, GI, Köllen, pp. 155–170. Druck+Verlag GmbH, Bonn (2013)

A Model-driven Approach for the Generation of Customizable Model Migrations

Paola Vallejo$^{(\boxtimes)}$, Mickaël Kerboeuf$^{(\boxtimes)}$, and Jean-Philippe Babau

Lab-STICC - MOCS Team, University of Brest, Brest, France
{vallejoco,kerboeuf,babau}@univ-brest.fr

Abstract. Migrations are usually performed automatically as a reflect of the transformations applied at the metamodel level. Thus model-level specifics cannot be automatically taken into account by co-evolution.

This paper puts the focus on the generation of customizable model migrations. A dedicated formalism is introduced to combine *automatically-generated migrations* with *custom-made migrations*. We present a model-driven approach and a prototype engine in order to deal with the lack of model-level customization. Then, the prototype is applied on a case study. The prototype processes the migration specifications that have been automatically generated and then customized. The case study consists of the reuse of a mapping tool, in order to represent different sets of highlighted places. During the reuse process the migration specification is customized in order to produce different migrated models.

Keywords: Migration generation · Migration customization

1 Introduction

Reusing legacy tools allows to reduce the cost of producing the tooling for a Domain Specific Modeling Language. A legacy tool is defined by its specific metamodel (the *tool metamodel*): the tool metamodel contains only the elements needed by the tool to execute its functionalities. A common issue when trying to reuse a legacy tool is that the context in which the tool should be used (the *domain metamodel*) is different than the tool metamodel.

Even if these metamodels are different, we can suppose that they share a common subset of close concepts. Thus, the tool metamodel can be considered *an evolution* of the domain metamodel. From this point of view, the reuse of a legacy tool implies to put existing models under the scope of the legacy tool by means of *migration* techniques.

A well-known and rather obvious way to achieve this purpose relies on the principle of metamodel and model co-evolution. It basically allows the metamodel transformations to be automatically reflected at the model level. Thus, model-level specifics cannot be automatically taken into account by co-evolution. In order to overcome this lack of model-level customization, we present an approach to combine both automatically-generated model migrations with custom-made model migrations.

© Springer International Publishing Switzerland 2015
P. Desfray et al. (Eds.): MODELSWARD 2015, CCIS 580, pp. 67–81, 2015.
DOI: 10.1007/978-3-319-27869-8_4

This paper is structured as follows. Section 2 introduces a motivating example. Section 3 presents the principles of the *migration specification* which underlies our approach. A case study is presented in Sect. 4 to show the relevance of this approach. Related works are discussed in Sect. 5. The paper is concluded with an outlook on future work in Sect. 6.

2   Motivation

This section introduces a case used as running example throughout the rest of the paper. *MapView* is a legacy tool we aim at reusing. It displays a map in which the location of specific buildings is marked. The color and the label of the marker depend on the place's type. The tool has been implemented by using the Google Maps API.[1] An excerpt of the Ecore metamodel of the input data that can be processed by this tool is shown in Fig. 1. This metamodel introduces the concepts of City, Place, Address and Reference. There are different types of places (e.g. University, Dormitory, HealthFacility). Each place is located at a specific Address.

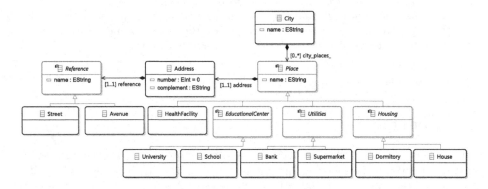

Fig. 1. Excerpt of MapView metamodel.

Figure 2 shows a variant of the metamodel on which *MapView* has been designed. This metamodel corresponds to an excerpt of a *City Information System* (CIS) which represents the population of a city. It contains information about the citizens, their job, theirs studies, their accommodation and theirs places in the city. These data are typically expected to be collected during a census. This metamodel can be seen as a variant of the *MapView* metamodel with additional elements (i.e. Neighborhood class and its features *name* and *places*; Citizen class with its features; *citizens, zipCode* and *country* features of the City class; NamedElement class). The reuse of *MapView* in this context requires the *deletion* of these extra-elements.

---

[1] https://developers.google.com/maps/.

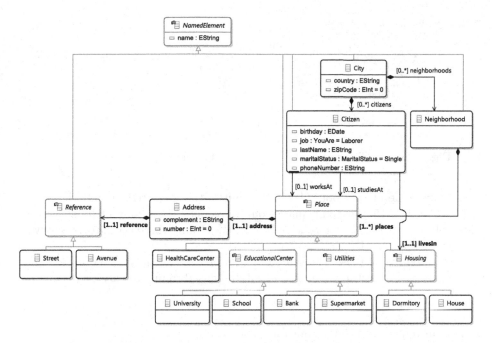

Fig. 2. Excerpt of CIS metamodel.

Figure 3 presents a model conforming to the CIS metamodel. To put it under the scope of *MapView*, we apply typical co-evolution operators like *remove* and *rename* [1] and complex co-evolution operators like *hide* and *flatten* [2].

The *modified metamodel* fully matches with the metamodel of *MapView*. Then, *MapView* can be applied on the migrated model. The migrated model is illustrated by Fig. 4, citizens Anne and Robert have been removed. Neighborhoods Bellevue and Recouvrance have been removed, however, the places of the neighborhoods still in the migrated model; it is because instead of applying the *remove* operator on the class Neighborhood, the *hide* operator was applied. Before giving details about this operator, we introduce the concept of reference path; a *reference path* is made up of a set of corresponding references and intermediate connected classes. In Fig. 2, (*neighborhoods*, Neighborhood, *places*) is a reference path between City and Place. *hide* is a weak implementation of the *remove* operator in which the hidden class and its features are removed, but the reference path involving the hidden class is preserved. *hide* removes the Neighborhood class, and the *places* reference, the *neighborhoods* reference is renamed into *neighborhoods_places_*, then the target of *neighborhoods_places_* is set to be Place. NamedElement was flattened, it means, NamedElement was removed, but the attribute *name* was propagated to each of its subclasses. Finally HealthCareCenter was renamed to HealthFacility and *neighborhoods_places_* was renamed to *city_places_*.

Fig. 3. Simple CIS model.   **Fig. 4.** Migrated model.

The outcome of the tool, when the input is the migrated model (Fig. 4), is depicted by Fig. 15. The map marks one university (blue marker labeled with U), one health facility (red marker labeled with H) and three dormitories (brown marker labeled with D).

In the context of reuse, the same tool can be used according to different and specific needs. For instance, *MapView* will be reused to provide a view of specific places:

1. Only dormitories;
2. The university and the dormitories near to it;
3. The health facility and the closest dormitory.

In case 1, model migration involves deletion of all instances of university and health facility. In cases 2 and 3, some instances of dormitory have to be kept and some others have to be removed. The way to select the dormitories to be kept depends on the notion of nearness.

A way to remove the unnecessary instances is by using co-evolution operators. In co-evolution of metamodel and models, if a class is removed at the metamodel level, all its instances are removed at the model level. If a class is kept, thus all its instances are kept too. There are tools as Edapt[2] that allows to manually specifying model migrations when they are so specific to the model context. Edapt generates migration code for instances affected by metamodel transformations. As in cases 1, 2 and 3 there are not metamodel transformations for Place or its subclasses, migration code is not generated, so it is not possible to specify specific model migrations.

In all cases, classes HealthFacility, University and Dormitory have to persist at the metamodel level for structural needs (modified metamodel must fully matches with tool metamodel). Co-evolution operators are not useful in these cases because it is not possible to define a model migration for instances whose corresponding class is not transformed.

Another way to handle cases 1, 2 and 3 is by using classical transformation languages, for example ATL.[3] ATL allows to define specific model migrations.

The code presented below is an excerpt of the ATL code that keeps only dormitories:

---

[2] http://www.eclipse.org/edapt/.
[3] http://www.eclipse.org/atl/.

```
-- @path City=/.../metamodel/cityis.ecore
-- @path Mapview=/.../metamodel/mapview.ecore
module city2mapview;
create OUT : Mapview from IN : City;
rule Dormitory2Dormitory {
   from
         c : City!Dormitory
   to    m : Mapview!Dormitory (name <- m.name ...)
}
rule deleteUniversity {
   from
         c : City!University
   to    drop
}
```

The code presented below is an excerpt of the ATL code that keeps only dormitories located near to the university:

```
create OUT : Mapview from IN : City;
rule Dormitory2Dormitory {
   from
         c : City!Dormitory(c.address.reference.name  = 'Lanredec' ||
                            c.address.refrence.name = 'Archives')
   to    m : Mapview!Dormitory (name <- m.name ...)
}
```

The code presented below is an excerpt of the ATL code that keeps the dormitory closest to the health facility:

```
create OUT : Mapview from IN : City;
rule Dormitory2Dormitory {
   from
         c : City!Dormitory(c.address.reference.name  = 'Lanredec' )
   to    m : Mapview!Dormitory (name <- m.name ... )
}
```

The difference between the three pieces of code is the constraint *c. address. reference.name* = . In the first case, there is not constraint because all instances of dormitory are kept. It is mandatory to specify the migration code for each case, which makes this solution model dependent, programming language oriented and not generic.

More generally, three cases can be encountered: (1) A class and all its instances have to be removed. For example, Citizen class. (2) A class is kept but *some* of its instances have to be removed. For example, Dormitory in cases 2 and 3. (3) A class is kept but all its instances have to be removed. For example, University in case 1.

In all cases, there are two concerns, the first one, related to the classes; the second one, related to model instances and specific contexts. There is a lack of a mechanism to ensure the separation of those concerns. Then, we propose to address the proposed cases by an approach able to generate model migrations and allowing customization of migrations without making modifications directly in the migration's code. It consists in promoting the *adaptation* of automatically generated model migration thanks to a *formal* and *generic migration specification*. For a given metamodel MM transformed into a new metamodel MM', and for a given model m conforming to MM: instead of *directly reflecting* the metamodel evolution at the model level by means of a generated migration mig such that mig(m) provides a migrated model conforming to MM', we suggest to generate a *migration specification* $\overrightarrow{m}$ such that provided to a dedicated and generic engine M, it produces the expected migration mig (*i.e.* M($\overrightarrow{m}$) = mig). As a consequence, the migration specification $\overrightarrow{m}$ is *editable* and *processable*. Even if it is automatically generated, it can be *modified* before being processed by the generic engine M. Then we can obtain an *adapted migration* mig.

The next section states the formal basis of this approach. The following section illustrates this approach with the reuse of *MapView*.

3   Formal Framework for Adaptable Model Migrations

The formal specification of model migration is a major issue to ensure safe reuse of the tools. The formalization of our approach relies on graph-based denotational semantics of models as in [3]. Due to a lack of space, it is not detailed here. See [4] for more details about this formalization and the properties it enables to ensure. A *migration specification* relies on *formal model denotations*, which are *oriented and labeled graphs*. These notions are detailed in the first part of this section. They underlie the prototype presented in the second part.

3.1   Migration Specification Foundations

Model Graph. A model graph is a *graph-based denotation* of a model, *i.e.* a labeled graph composed of *vertices* denoting *instances* and *scalar values*, and *edges* denoting *references* and *attributes*. The *namespaces* corresponding to instances, scalar values, attributes and references are defined by the following *alphabets*, (*i.e.* non-empty finite set of symbols):

I : instances, S : scalar values, A : attributes, R : references.

We call *model* and note m a triplet composed of a set of instances corresponding to vertices noted V, and two sets of edges noted E_a and E_r. The first set of edges denotes attributes. It relates instances to scalar values through attribute names. The second one denotes references. It relates instances to other ones through reference names:

$$m \triangleq (V, E_a, E_r) \quad \text{with} \quad \begin{cases} V \subseteq I \\ E_a \subseteq V \times A \times S \\ E_r \subseteq V \times R \times V \end{cases}$$

We note $m.V$, $m.E_a$ and $m.E_r$ the V, E_a and E_r components of a given model m. As an illustration, Fig. 5 depicts an excerpt of the CIS model with its model graph.

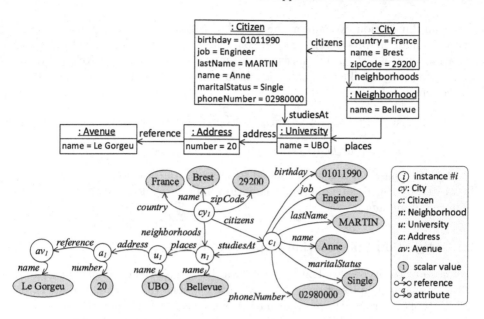

Fig. 5. Model and model graph.

Migration Specification. For a given model m, we call *migration specification* and note $\overrightarrow{m}$ a quadruplet composed of m and of three sets noted D_i, D_a and D_r. These sets specify the instances, attributes and references of m that are intended to be *removed*:

$$\overrightarrow{m} \triangleq (m, D_i, D_a, D_r) \quad \text{where} \quad \begin{cases} D_i \subseteq m.V \\ D_a \subseteq m.V \times A \\ D_r \subseteq m.V \times R \end{cases}$$

We note $\overrightarrow{m}.D_i$, $\overrightarrow{m}.D_a$ and $\overrightarrow{m}.D_r$ the D_i, D_a and D_r components of a given migration specification $\overrightarrow{m}$. The migration specification is intended to be used together with the model to produce a *migrated model*. This migration specification is *computed* from co-evolution (i.e. *Modif specification* [2]). A specification makes it possible to state the deletion of a class, an attribute or a reference (corresponding to D_i, D_a and D_r at the model level).

Migration Engine. We call *migrator* and note M the tool aiming at producing a *migrated model* from a *migration specification*. According to the following algorithm, it commits the *deletion* of instances and of features (attributes and references) on the source model to produce a target model:

$m' = M(\overrightarrow{m})$
$m'.V = m.V \setminus \overrightarrow{m}.D_i$
$m'.E_a = m.E_a \setminus \{(i,a,s) \in I \times A \times S \mid i \in \overrightarrow{m}.D_i \vee (i,a) \in \overrightarrow{m}.D_a\}$
$m'.E_r = m.E_r \setminus \{(i,r,i') \in I \times R \times I \mid i \in \overrightarrow{m}.D_i \vee i' \in \overrightarrow{m}.D_i \vee (i,r) \in \overrightarrow{m}.D_r\}$

As an illustration, we note m the model of Fig. 5 and $\vec{m}$ its migration specification aiming at producing a model conforming to the a metamodel of Fig. 1, *i.e.* a model in which all instances of Citizen and all instances of Neighborhood have been removed. This specification is formally and explicitly defined by its components:

$$\vec{m}.D_i = \{c_1, n_1\} \qquad \vec{m}.D_a = \{zipCode, country\}$$

$$\vec{m}.D_r = \{studiesAt, citizens, places\}$$

Once the migrator has been applied to $\vec{m}$, we obtain the migrated model m_m illustrated by Fig. 6. The migration is performed at the model level. It does not require any *metadata*.

3.2 Migration Specification Implementation

A *migrator* prototype based on Ecore and Modif [2] has been developed according to the formal principles of *migration specification*. The refactoring, the migrator and the tool to be reused form a toolchain depicted by Fig. 7 and detailed as follows. The tool is available at http://lab-sticc.univ-brest.fr/babau/modif/modif.htm

Refactoring (Re). The first step is the application of co-evolution operators at the metamodel level. Consider a domain metamodel MMd.ecore in Fig. 7. On it, co-evolution operators are applied to obtain an evolved metamodel that

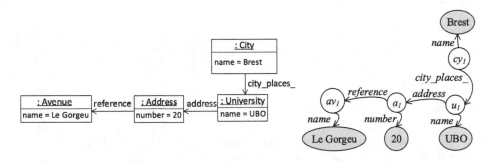

Fig. 6. Model and model graph of a model without Citizen and Neighborhood.

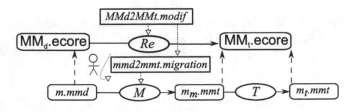

Fig. 7. Typical toolchain including the *migrator*.

matches with the tool metamodel (MMt.ecore). The prototype uses a *Modif Specification* to indicate the operators to be applied, but some other metamodel transformation tool or language can be used as well (e.g. COPE [5], ATL [6], QVT [7]).

Migration Specification Generation. The second step is the automatic generation of a *by default* migration specification conforming to the metamodel of Fig. 8. The *by default* migration specification is derived from the co-evolution operators applied at the Refactoring step. It contains the URIs of source and target models and metamodels. The instances that must be updated by the migration are identified by a unique identifier (UUID). When a class is removed at the metamodel level, deleteInstance is set to *true* for each Instance of the removed class. Otherwise, it is set to *false* and then, the modification is related to *features*. When a class is hidden at the metamodel level, for each reference pointing to the class, a derived reference is added. The migration specification is typically generated from Modif, but it can be defined from other sources, including a model editor generated from the metamodel of Fig. 8.

Specification Edition. The third step is the edition of the migration specification. In order to take into account some model specifics in the generated migration specification. It is therefore possible to produce migrated models according to specific needs without having to generalize it at the metamodel level. And without modifying any source code.

Migration Engine (M). In the fourth step, the Migration Engine is executed to obtain a migrated model according to the modifications indicated in the migration specification. It takes an MMd input model (m.mmd) and produces a migrated MMt output model (m$_m$.mmt). The Migration Engine is independent of the input model. It means, it can be reused for different input models. And it is not overloaded with unnecessary metadata.

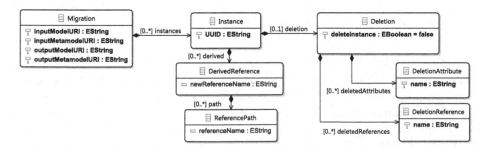

Fig. 8. Graphical view of Migration metamodel.

Use of a Legacy Tool (T). Before reusing the legacy tool, the migrated model coming from the migrator is validated. Finally, the legacy tool is applied on the migrated validated model.

4   Experiment

We present in this section the results of the application of the prototype to the *MapView* case study introduced in Sect. 2.

An excerpt of the Modif Specification is illustrated by Fig. 9. The features *citizens, zipCode* and *country* of the class City are removed, *neighborhoods* reference is renamed. The class Citizen with all its features is removed, NamedElement is flatten, Neighborhood is hidden, HealthCareCenter is renamed. Figure 10 depicts the *by default* migration specification generated from the Modif Specification and the model of Fig. 3 (this specification allows to produce the map of Fig. 15). The left column contains the instances and the features that have to be removed. The right column contains the instances that have to be kept.

Fig. 9. cityis2mapviewer.modif file.

Once the *by default* migration is generated, it can be edited allowing the specification of customized model migrations. Just by selecting one instance of the *Keep* column and clicking on the *To Delete* button, it will be placed on the *Delete* column. By selecting one instance of the *Delete* column and clicking on the *To Keep* button, it will be placed on the *Keep* column. The (gray colored) instances and features of the top of the *Delete* column are there to indicate they were remove because of the application of *remove* or *hide* co-evolution operators

 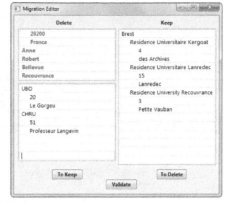

Fig. 10. By default migration specification.

Fig. 11. Migration specification of case 1.

at the metamodel level, it can not be moved to the other column because it will result in a model not conform with the tool metamodel. By means of the EcoreValidate method, *Validate* button verifies that the instances and features of the *Keep* column produce a model conform to the tool metamodel.

Figure 11 presents the customized migration specification allowing to keep only dormitories (case 1 of Sect. 2), the model graph is shown by Fig. 12.

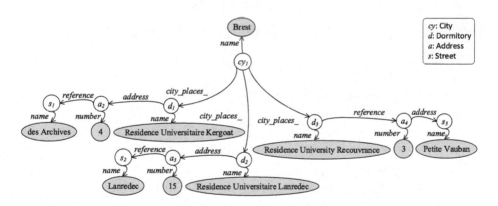

Fig. 12. Model graph of case 1.

Figure 13 presents the migration specification allowing to keep the university and the dormitories near to it (case 2 of Sect. 2).

Figure 14 illustrates the migration specification allowing to keep the health facility and the closest dormitory (case 3 of Sect. 2), the model graph is also depicted by this figure.

From a model and the *by default* migration specification, some *customized* migration specifications can be produced. After customizing the migration

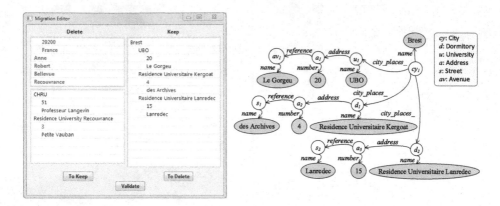

Fig. 13. Customized migration specification and model graph of case 2.

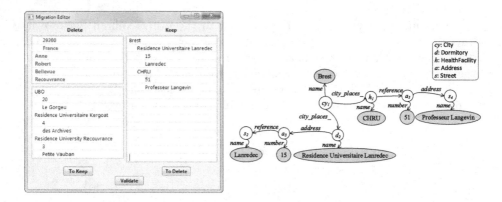

Fig. 14. Customized migration specification and model graph of case 3.

Fig. 15. MapView outcome.

Fig. 16. D near to the U.

specification, the Migration Engine is executed to produce a model conforms to the legacy tool metamodel. Finally, *Map View* is applied. Figure 16 illustrates the specific outcome when the migration specification is that of Fig. 13.

Our approach is able to generate model migrations and allows customization of migrations. Thanks to the migration editor, a same migration specification can be used as a common basis to generate quickly and efficiently various migrated models. Any knowledge about transformation or programming languages is required to customize model migrations.

5   Current and Related Works

The necessity of providing automatic co-evolution of metamodels and models was identified as an important challenge in software evolution by Mens and et al. [8]. With the growing importance of model transformations, much work is intended to improve the definition and the verification of such transformations by providing adapting formalism and tooling.

Wachsmuth [9] proposes a transformational approach to assist metamodel evolution by stepwise adaptation. Ciccheti et al. [10] present a classification of metamodel and model changes. They propose an approach for performing co-evolution automatically, based on dependencies between different kinds of modifications. In those works the migration of models is based on reusable operators, automated and non adaptable. It allows to reduce the effort associated with building a model migration. As a complement, we allow to define customize model migrations by means of a *Migration Specification*. It is possible to generate it from the history of co-evolution operators applied to transform a metamodel.

The authors of [11,12] evoke the need of methods and tools to automate and speed up the process of migrating models. However, some metamodel changes require information during migration which is not available in the model, these migration inherently cannot be fully automated. They enable user interaction during migration only when missing information has to be provided. Epsilon Flock language [13] uses a migration strategy that can be extended by adding constraints. COPE [14] provides a library of reusable co-evolution operators which produces model migrations automatically. Only in case no reusable operators are available, the user defines custom operators by manually encoding a model migration. When using those approaches, additional effort is necessary to learn a new language for model migrations. In general, the definition of custom migrations is tedious and error-prone. Unlike those approaches, our approach allows user interaction even if migration is fully automated. Definition of new operators is not needed and knowledge about a particular language is not required. MOLA [15] is a graphical model transformation language whose main goal is to describe model transformations in a natural and easy readable way. It focuses on easy readability and customization of transformations. This approach is not related to co-evolution, it means that they not include the notion of co-evolution operators and it works only at the model level.

6   Conclusion and Future Works

The paper outlines an approach for supporting the co-evolution of metamodels and models. The proposition combines the automatic generation nature of co-evolution approaches with user interactions. In this way, part of the definition of model migrations is achieved automatically, but it still possible update them manually. We experimented the approach by performing adaptable model migrations combining automaticallygenerated migration with custom-made migrations. Those model migrations allows to reuse the *MapView* tool according to specific user needs.

Our perspective is to extend the approach to perform adaptable model migrations with others co-evolution approaches. We are working on the definition of other co-evolution operators at model level (*change value*). This approach will be used for generate different migrated models in the Orcc domain. Orcc is an open-source Integrated Development Environment based on Eclipse and dedicated to dataflow programming.[4]

References

1. Herrmannsdoerfer, M., Vermolen, S.D., Wachsmuth, G.: An extensive catalog of operators for the coupled evolution of metamodels and models. In: Malloy, B., Staab, S., van den Brand, M. (eds.) SLE 2010. LNCS, vol. 6563, pp. 163–182. Springer, Heidelberg (2011)
2. Babau, J.-P., Kerboeuf, M.: Domain specific language modeling facilities. In: 5th MoDELS Workshop on Models and Evolution, pp. 1–6 (2011)
3. Ziemann, P., Hölscher, K., Gogolla, M.: From UML models to graph transformation systems. In: Proceedings of the Workshop on Visual Languages and Formal Methods, pp. 17–33 (2005)
4. Kerboeuf, M., Vallejo, P., Babau, J.-P.: Research report: formal framework of recontextualization by means of dependency graphs (2015). http://hal.univ-brest.fr/hal-01140107/file/ModifKeysGraph.pdf
5. Herrmannsdoerfer, M., Benz, S., Juergens, E.: COPE - automating coupled evolution of metamodels and models. In: Drossopoulou, S. (ed.) ECOOP 2009. LNCS, vol. 5653, pp. 52–76. Springer, Heidelberg (2009)
6. Jouault, F., Kurtev, I.: Transforming models with ATL. In: Bruel, J.-M. (ed.) MoDELS 2005. LNCS, vol. 3844, pp. 128–138. Springer, Heidelberg (2006)
7. Object Modeling Group: MOF QVT Final Adopted Specification (2007)
8. Mens, T., Wermelinger, M., Ducasse, S., Demeyer, S., Hirschfeld, R., Jazayeri, M.: Challenges in software evolution. In: Proceedings of the 8th IWPSE, pp. 13–22. IEEE (2005)
9. Wachsmuth, G.: Metamodel adaptation and model co-adaptation. In: Ernst, E. (ed.) ECOOP 2007. LNCS, vol. 4609, pp. 600–624. Springer, Heidelberg (2007)
10. Cicchetti, A., Di Ruscio, D., Pierantonio, A.: Managing dependent changes in coupled evolution. In: Paige, R.F. (ed.) ICMT 2009. LNCS, vol. 5563, pp. 35–51. Springer, Heidelberg (2009)

---

[4] orcc.sourceforge.net.

11. Rüegg, U., Motika, C., von Hanxleden, R.: Interactive transformations for visual models. In: 3rd Workshop Methodische Entwicklung von Modellierungswerkzeugen. Lecture Notes in Informatics (LNI) (2011)
12. Agrawal, A., Karsai, G., Shi, F.: Graph transformations on domain-specific models. Institute for Software Integrated Systems (2003)
13. Rose, L.M., Kolovos, D.S., Paige, R.F., Polack, F.A.C.: Model migration with epsilon flock. In: Tratt, L., Gogolla, M. (eds.) ICMT 2010. LNCS, vol. 6142, pp. 184–198. Springer, Heidelberg (2010)
14. Herrmannsdoerfer, M., Ratiu, D.: Limitations of automating model migration in response to metamodel adaptation. In: Ghosh, S. (ed.) MODELS 2009. LNCS, vol. 6002, pp. 205–219. Springer, Heidelberg (2010)
15. Kalnins, A., Barzdins, J., Celms, E.: Model transformation language MOLA. In: Proceedings of Model-Driven Architecture: Foundations and Applications, pp. 14–28 (2004)

Parallel Application Development Using Architecture View Driven Model Transformations

Ethem Arkın[1]([✉]) and Bedir Tekinerdogan[2]

[1] Aselsan A.Ş., Ankara, Turkey
earkin@aselsan.com.tr
[2] Information Technology Group, Wageningen University, Wageningen, The Netherlands
bedir.tekinerdogan@wur.nl

Abstract. To realize the increased need for computing performance the current trend is towards applying parallel computing in which the tasks are run in parallel on multiple nodes. On its turn we can observe the rapid increase of the scale of parallel computing platforms. This situation has led to a complexity of parallel application development that is not scalable and tractable anymore for manual processing, and therefore automated support is required to design and implement parallel applications. To this end, we present a model-driven transformation chain for supporting the automation of the lifecycle of parallel computing applications. The model-driven transformation chain adopts metamodels that are derived from architecture viewpoints. The transformation chain is defined as a logical sequence consisting of model-to-model transformations. We present the tool support that implements the metamodels and transformations.

Keywords: Model driven software development · Parallel computing · High performance computing · Domain specific language · Tool support

1 Introduction

To increase the performance that is required from large scale applications, the current trend is towards applying parallel computing on multiple nodes. Here, unlike serial computing in which instructions are executed serially, multiple processing nodes are used to execute the program instructions simultaneously. To benefit from the parallel computing power, usually parallel algorithms are defined that can be executed simultaneously on multiple nodes. As such, increasing the processing nodes will increase the performance of the parallel programs. Different studies have been carried out on the design and analysis of parallel algorithms to support parallel computing [1, 6, 10]. These studies have provided useful results and further increased the performance of parallel computing. Several important challenges have been identified and tackled in parallel computing related to activities such as the analysis of the parallel algorithm, the definition of the logical configuration of the platform, and the mapping of the algorithm to the logical configuration platform. The research on parallel algorithms and its mapping to parallel computing platforms is still ongoing.

We can identify two important trends in parallel computing. First of all, the scale of parallel computing platforms is rapidly increasing. Over the last decade the number of

© Springer International Publishing Switzerland 2015
P. Desfray et al. (Eds.): MODELSWARD 2015, CCIS 580, pp. 82–96, 2015.
DOI: 10.1007/978-3-319-27869-8_5

processing nodes has increased dramatically to tens and hundreds of thousands of nodes providing processing performance from petascale to exascale levels [8]. The second trend includes the increasing complexity and variety of current software systems. Here the design problem goes beyond the notion of algorithms and data structures of the computation, and the design of the overall system or application of the parallel computing systems emerges as an important problem. Hence, the challenge then becomes not only analyzing, deploying and mapping parallel algorithms but requires considering the overall analysis and mapping of parallel applications to parallel computing platform.

These two trends have led to a complexity that is not scalable and tractable anymore for manual processing, and therefore automated support is required to design and implement parallel applications. In this context, we present a model-driven transformation chain for supporting the automation of the lifecycle of parallel computing applications. The model-driven transformation chain adopts metamodels that are derived from architectural viewpoints. The architecture viewpoints have been defined in our earlier work for modeling the mapping of parallel applications to parallel computing platforms [13]. In essence, the viewpoints can be used to derive architectural views that serve as blueprints for realizing the system. The viewpoints are in essence visual and do not support the automated processing. In this paper we map the viewpoints to domain specific languages to represent architecture views as textual executable descriptions that can be used in model transformations to automate the steps of the life cycle of parallel computing. The transformation chain is defined as a logical sequence consisting of model-to-model transformations. We present the tool support that implements the metamodels and transformations.

The remainder of the paper is organized as follows. In Sect. 2, we shortly describe the viewpoints which form the basis for the domain specific languages and the model transformations. Section 3 presents the model transformation approach and the model transformations. Section 4 describes the implementation and the toolset. Section 5 presents the related work and finally we conclude the paper in Sect. 6.

2 Preliminaries

2.1 Modeling Parallel Applications

A close analysis of parallel computing research shows that the well-defined concept of *algorithm* is prevailing and the broader consideration of software *application* and its mapping to parallel computing platform does not seem to have got much attention. Given the current architectural modeling approaches no direct and integrated support is provided to model these concerns. Some approaches focus on a particular concern but to the best of our knowledge none of the approaches provide an integrated approach for architectural modeling of the mapping of parallel applications to parallel computing platforms. In principle we can identify the following important concerns in the life cycle for modeling parallel applications:

- Identifying parallel and serial modules in the application

Depending on the application semantics, while some modules can run in parallel others can only run in serial. Typically serial modules will be mapped to a single node, while parallel modules need to be mapped to multiple nodes. For the architect it is important to depict these explicitly and as such help to identify the proper selection of parallel module.

- Modeling of the physical computing platform

The application will run on a selected or to be selected physical configuration platform that consists of multiple nodes. The architect needs to be able to model the physical computing platform for smaller but also for very large computing platforms (e.g. exascale computing).

- Mapping of modules and algorithms to physical nodes

The mapping of the modules to the computing platforms can be done in different ways. The mapping can be usually done in many different alternative ways and each alternative will typically behave differently with respect to quality metrics such as speedup and efficiency. The architecture needs to be able to communicate the decision on which mapping is made. Based on this the optimal design decision can be made.

- Defining the interaction patterns among parallel modules

Parallel modules and algorithms will typically exchange information to perform the requested tasks. In general it is important to define the proper interaction patterns not only for functional reasons but also to optimize the parallelization overhead and as such increase efficiency.

- Modeling Multiple Computer Architectures

When considering application instead of algorithm only it appears that we cannot reduce the problem to one of the computing platforms as defined in the Flynn's taxonomy. Typically, multiple of these categories are integrated in the overall application. That is, for example, both the SIMD and MISD could be needed for realizing the application. For complex applications all the four kinds of computing architectures might be required. The Order Management case is such an example.

2.2 Architecture Viewpoints for Modeling Parallel Applications

Based on the above concerns we have proposed an architecture framework consisting of a coherent set of viewpoints which addresses the different concerns for supporting the design of parallel applications [3, 12]. These six viewpoints are as follows:

- Application Decomposition Viewpoint

The viewpoint is used to indicate the modules from which the application is composed, and on the other hand defines the parallelism property for each module. The application can consist of modules or algorithms which can be serial or parallel. Hence we have defined four different types of modules, *Serial Module, Parallel Module, Serial Algorithm,* and *Parallel Algorithm.* A serial module and a serial algorithm module is the implementation of a set of instructions or algorithm which is executed on a single processing unit. A parallel module is a module with the instruction set that run on multiple processing units simultaneously. *Package* is the conventional grouping module for grouping a set of modules together.

- Algorithm Decomposition Viewpoint

Each module in the application decomposition viewpoint has a separate behavior for the deployment of the application. A parallel algorithm module includes serial or parallel sections that determines the behavior of the algorithm and must be decomposed into sections that will be executed serial or parallel. Since parallel algorithms are considered as consisting of multiple instructions it is important to analyze the algorithm first and define the serial and parallel sections.

- Physical Configuration Viewpoint

Physical configuration viewpoint includes the hardware configuration for the parallel computing platform including nodes, network, processing units, memory and bus. The physical configuration can be defined as shared memory that has multiple processing units that use the same memory, distributed memory in which each node has its own memory, or hybrid memory that has also multiple nodes as distributed memory and each node has multiple processing units with a shared memory.

- Component Viewpoint

According to the decomposition of the parallel application, a component view includes serial components, serial algorithm components, parallel components and parallel algorithm components. The types of the components are determined by the module that is compiled to the component. Each component can provide an interface for another component and each component can require an interface from another component. The interface relations are defined between the components.

- Deployment Viewpoint

The components defined in the component view must be deployed on processing units defined in the physical configuration. Here, a serial module or a serial algorithm module can be deployed on a single processing unit. A parallel module or a parallel algorithm module can be deployed on different processing units. The parallel module runs the same instruction sets on multiple processing units and provides output to other components. The parallel algorithm module runs different instruction sets and coordinate data between themselves to calculate a specific algorithm using different processing units.

- Logical Configuration Viewpoint

The logical configuration is a view of the physical configuration that provides the logical communication structure among the physical nodes. Typically, for the same physical configuration we can have many different logical configurations. To represent the mapping of the parallel algorithm to the logical configuration, the cores are identified using the identification values of nodes and processing units. The number of cores should be equal to the selected processing units in the deployment view. As stated before for each parallel algorithm a corresponding algorithm view is provided. In addition, a logical configuration view needs to be defined to present the communication structures of the physical nodes to realize the parallel algorithm. This viewpoint is used to represent the logical communication patterns and the dynamic behavior of the algorithm. Logical configuration is generated according to the tile and communication pattern definitions which are described in our earlier study [13].

3　Architecture View Driven Transformations

To illustrate the problem we will use the Order Management Application architecture as an example. The Order Management application is typically a critical part of commercial systems including, for example, packages like Order Entry, Financial and Inventory. To increase the performance of such a system several modules need to be run in parallel.

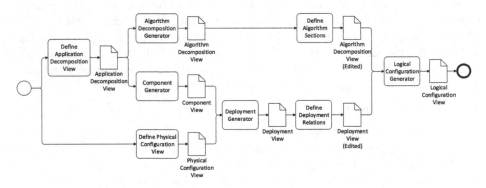

Fig. 1. Transformation chain for supporting the lifecycle of parallel applications.

The architecture viewpoints of the previous section can be used to realize the mapping of parallel applications to parallel computing platforms. However, the viewpoints are mainly visual and not appropriate for automated support. In this section we present the approach for automating the overall process using the architecture viewpoints. Figure 1 represents the transformation chain including views and transformations between the views for parallel computing architectures. Four transformation processes represented as generators are defined including *Algorithm Decomposition Generator*, *Component Generator*, *Deployment Generator*, and *Logical Configuration Generator*. In the following subsections we discuss each generator in detail. In addition to the generators the transformation chain includes two manual activities to define algorithm sections and to define deployment relations. Both activities are used to enhance additional details to the generated views. In the activity *Define Algorithm Sections* the preliminary generated Algorithm Decomposition View is manually edited for identifying the parallel and serial sections of the algorithm [2]. In the activity *Define Deployment Relations* the parallel components are manually assigned to physical configuration processing units.

3.1　Algorithm Decomposition Generator

Algorithm Decomposition Generator transforms the ParallelAlgorithmModule elements of application decomposition view to Algorithm elements of algorithm decomposition view. Figure 2 shows the metamodels of the application decomposition viewpoint and algorithms decomposition viewpoint. Application Decomposition metamodel (Fig. 2a) has a main Application element. Application includes the Module Elements which can be either a Package or a Module. Package contains other module elements that can be either ParallelModule, SerialModule, ParallelAlgorithmModule or SerialAlgorithm-Module. Algorithm Decomposition metamodel (Fig. 2b) contains parallel algorithms used for the parallel application. Algorithm includes Sections, Parallel Sections and Serial Sections. Each section can contain other sections. A parallel application is related to a parallel Operation that is defined in the parallel library. This library is used for defining reusable parallel operations using tiles and communication patterns which are described in detail in [2].

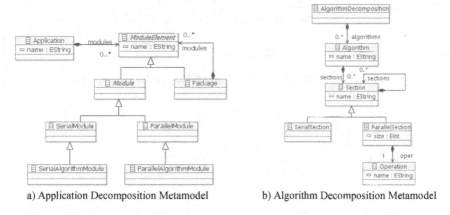

a) Application Decomposition Metamodel   b) Algorithm Decomposition Metamodel

Fig. 2. Metamodels for algorithm decomposition generator.

The Algorithm Decomposition Generator searches for the Parallel Algorithm Modules in the application decomposition view and generates the algorithm decomposition view. Figure 3 shows the transformation rules of Algorithm Decompostion Generator.

The main transformation rule iterates over the modules of the application and calls the operation generateAlgorithm for the module (lines 4–7). The generateAlgorithm operation (lines 9–22) first checks the module whether it is a ParallelAlgorithmModule or a Package. If the module is a Parallel Algorithm Module, then a new algorithm instance is created and added to algorithm list (lines 12–16). If the module is a Package, then generateAlgorithm operation is recursively called for each submodule (lines 17–21).

3.2   Component Generator

Component Generator transforms modules of application decomposition view to components for component view. The transformation uses Application Decomposition Meta-model (Fig. 2a) and Component Metamodel (Fig. 4). Component metamodel includes Application element as main element. Application consists of Packages and Components. Similarly, components can be either Parallel Component, Serial Component, Parallel Algorithm Component or Serial Algorithm Component. Each component has an Interface relation with another component. A component has required and provided interfaces.

```
1.   rule AlgorithmDecompositionGenerator
2.        transform app : applicationdecomposition!Application
3.        to algs : algorithmdecomposition!AlgorithmDecomposition {
4.      algs.algorithms = Sequence{};
5.      for (module in app.modules) {
6.        generateAlgorithm(algs, module);
7.      }
8.   }
9.   operation generateAlgorithm(
10.       algs: algorithmdecomposition!AlgorithmDecomposition,
11.       module: applicationdecomposition!ModuleElement) {
12.     if(module.isTypeOf(applicationdecomposition! ParallelAlgorithmModule)) {
13.       var alg = new algorithmdecomposition!Algorithm;
14.       alg.name = module.name;
15.       algs.algorithms.add(alg);
16.     }
17.     if(module.isTypeOf(applicationdecomposition!Package)) {
18.       for (m in module.modules) {
19.         generateAlgorithm(algs, m);
20.       }
21.     }
22.   }
```

Fig. 3. Algorithm decomposition generator transformation rules.

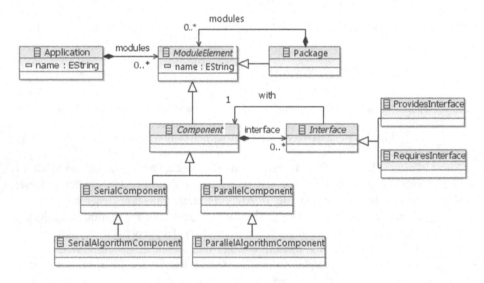

Fig. 4. Component metamodel.

The transformation rules for Component Generator are shown in Fig. 5. The main transformation rule is shown from lines 2 to 10. The application decomposition view modules are transformed into component view modules. The transformModule operation is defined to implement this transformation. The transformed module is added to component view in lines 7–8. In the transformModule operation, the type of the application decomposition module is checked. Each module type is transformed to the counter component. If the module is ParallelModule, then a new ParallelComponent instance is created with the same name (lines 13–16). If the module is SerialModule, then a new SerialComponent instance is created (lines 17–20). In lines 21–25, ParallelAlgorithmComponent is created from ParallelAlgorithmModule and in lines 26–30, SerialAlgorithmComponent is created from SerialAlgorithmModule. If the module is a Package, then the transform-Module operation is called for its submodules (lines 31–38).

```
1.  rule ComponentGenerator
2.      transform app : applicationdecomposition!Application
3.      to capp : component!Application {
4.      capp.name = app.name;
5.      capp.modules = Sequence{};
6.      for (module in app.modules) {
7.        capp.modules.add(transformModule(module));
8.      }
9.  }
10. operation transformModule(
11.     module:applicationdecomposition!ModuleElement) : component!ModuleElement
    {
12.     var comp;
13.     if(module.isTypeOf(applicationdecomposition!ParallelModule)) {
14.       comp = new component!ParallelComponent;
15.       comp.name = module.name;
16.     }
17.     if(module.isTypeOf(applicationdecomposition!SerialModule)) {
18.       comp = new component!SerialComponent;
19.       comp.name = module.name;
20.     }
21.     if(module.isTypeOf(
22.         applicationdecomposition!ParallelAlgorithmModule)) {
23.       comp = new component!ParallelAlgorithmComponent;
24.       comp.name=module.name;
25.     }
26.     if(module.isTypeOf(
27.         applicationdecomposition!SerialAlgorithmModule)) {
28.       comp = new component!SerialAlgorithmComponent;
29.       comp.name = module.name;
30.     }
31.     if(module.isTypeOf(applicationdecomposition!Package)) {
32.       comp = new component!Package;
33.       comp.name = module.name;
34.       comp.modules = Sequence{};
35.       for (m in module.modules) {
36.         comp.modules.add(transformModule(m));
37.       }
38.     }
39.     return comp;
40. }
```

Fig. 5. Component generator transformation rules.

3.3 Deployment Generator

Deployment Generator merges and transforms the component view and physical configuration view to deployment view. The transformation uses the Component Metamodel (Fig. 4), Physical Configuration Metamodel (Fig. 6a) and Deployment Metamodel (Fig. 6b). The Physical Configuration metamodel is adopted from [13] which includes Network, Node, Processing Unit, Bus and Memory elements. Deployment metamodel is a composition of component metamodel and physical configuration metamodel which has a relation of «deployed on» from component to processing unit.

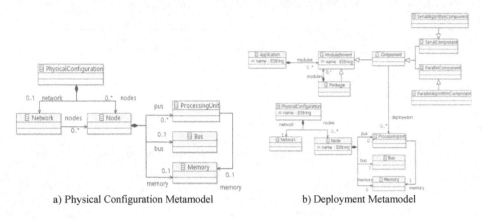

a) Physical Configuration Metamodel   b) Deployment Metamodel

Fig. 6. Metamodels for deployment generator.

The transformation rules as shown in Fig. 7 have two main rules. The first rule transforms the physical configuration elements to deployment view elements. The Physical Configuration Transform rule transforms the physical configuration to deployment configuration in which the network and nodes are transformed to deployment instances. Each node of the physical configuration is transformed to deployment node calling transformNode operation in line 8. The transformNode operation creates a new node instance and transforms the memory, bus and processing unit elements in the node (lines 12–19). The second rule transforms the component application elements into deployment application elements. Here, the modules of the component view are transformed using transformModule operation (lines 30–51), which checks the type of the module and transforms to the counter element in the deployment view.

3.4   Logical Configuration Generator

Logical Configuration Generator transforms an algorithm decomposition view to a logical configuration view using the information of the deployment of parallel algorithm components to processing units. The metamodel for logical configuration is adopted and is used to generate the dynamic behaviour of the algorithm using tiles, communication patterns and operations. The transformation rules to generate the logical configuration is defined in Fig. 8. The transformation rules consist of three main parts. In the first part, tiles that will be used according to deployment view and algorithm sections are found from the base library (lines 20–31). The prime factorization method is used to find the tile size of appropriate tiles. In the second part, patterns are selected to generate the communication patterns for the tiles with respect to the operations for the algorithm sections (lines 32–44). Subsequently, these selected patterns are added to the patterns list of the corresponding operation. Later on when it is needed the pattern can be reused in the last section in which the final logical configuration is generated (lines 45–54).

```
1.   rule PhysicalConfigurationTransform
2.       transform pc : physicalconfiguration!PhysicalConfiguration
3.       to dpc : deployment!PhysicalConfiguration {
4.       dpc.name = pc.name;
5.       dpc.network = new deployment!Network;
6.       dpc.nodes = Sequence{};
7.       for (node in pc.nodes) {
8.               dpc.nodes.add( transformNode(node) );}
9.   }
10.  operation transformNode
11.      (node: physicalconfiguration!Node) : deployment!Node {
12.      var n = new deployment!Node;
13.      n.memory = new deployment!Memory;
14.      n.bus = new deployment!Bus;
15.      n.pus = Sequence{};
16.      for (pu in node.pus) {
17.              var p = new deployment!ProcessingUnit;
18.              p.memory = n.memory;
19.              n.pus.add(p);}
20.      return n;
21.  }
22.  rule ApplicationTransform
23.      transform app : component!Application
24.      to dapp : deployment!Application {
25.      dapp.name = app.name;
26.      dapp.modules = Sequence{};
27.      for (module in app.modules) {
28.              dapp.modules.add(transformModule(module));}
29.  }
30.  operation transformModule
31.      (module: component!ModuleElement) : deployment!ModuleElement {
32.      var comp;
33.      if(module.isTypeOf(component!ParallelComponent)) {
34.              comp = new deployment!ParallelComponent;
35.              comp.name = module.name;}
36.      if(module.isTypeOf(component!SerialComponent)) {
37.              comp = new deployment!SerialComponent;
38.              comp.name = module.name;}
39.      if(module.isTypeOf(component!ParallelAlgorithmComponent)) {
40.              comp = new deployment!ParallelAlgorithmComponent;
41.              comp.name = module.name;}
42.      if(module.isTypeOf(component!SerialAlgorithmComponent)) {
43.              comp = new deployment!SerialAlgorithmComponent;
44.              comp.name = module.name;}
45.      if(module.isTypeOf(component!Package)) {
46.              comp = new deployment!Package;
47.              comp.name = module.name;
48.              comp.modules = Sequence{};
49.              for (m in module.modules) {
50.                      comp.modules.add(transformModule(m));}}
51.      return comp;
52.  }
```

Fig. 7. Deployment generator transformation rules.

```
1.    operation library!Pattern isDominating(tile:library!Core) : Boolean
2.    operation logicalconfiguration!Pattern getTile
3.        (i:Integer, j:Integer) : logicalconfiguration!Tile
4.    operation logicalconfiguration!Pattern setCommunication
5.        (from_i:Integer, from_j:Integer, to_i:Integer, to_j:Integer,
6.         patternList:Sequence, level:Integer)
7.    operation logicalconfiguration!Pattern setCommunication
8.        (ft:logicalconfiguration!Tile, tt:logicalconfiguration!Tile)
9.    operation createPattern
10.        (main:logicalconfiguration!Pattern, i:Integer, j:Integer,
11.         patternList:Sequence, commLevel:Integer, level:Integer,
12.         parentSize:Integer, scaling:Any)
13.
14.   rule LogicalConfigurationGenerator
15.     merge base : library!AssetBase
16.     with algorithm : algorithm!Algorithm
17.     into lc :  logicalconfiguration!LogicalConfiguration {
18.     for(parallelSection in
19.          algorithm!ParallelSection.all) {
20.     //FIND TILES
21.     var n = coreSize;
22.     while (i<=n) {
23.       while ((n - (n/i * i)) = 0) {
24.         factors.add(i);
25.         n = n / i;}
26.       i = i + 1;}
27.     var operationName=parallelSection.oper.name;
28.     var sizeList = Sequence{};
29.     i = 0;
30.     while(i < factors.size()){
31.       sizeList.add(factors.get(i)); i = i + 1;}
32.     //FIND PATTERNS
33.     var patternList = Sequence{};
34.     for(factor in sizeList){
35.       for(oper in base.operations) {
36.         if(oper.name == operationName) {
37.           for(pattern in oper.uses) {
38.             if(pattern.size == factor) {
39.               //pattern.name.println();
40.               //commLevel.println();
41.               patternList.add(pattern);}}}}}
42.     var commLevel = 0;
43.     if(scaling == base!ScalingType#UP) {
44.       commLevel = patternList.size - 1; }
45.     //GENERATE LOGICAL CONFIGURATION
46.     for(pattern in patternList) {
47.       var mainPattern = new
48.               logicalconfiguration!Pattern;
49.       createPattern(mainPattern, 0, 0, patternList,
50.               commLevel, 0, 1, pattern.scaling);
51.       var patternOperation = new
52.               logicalconfiguration!Operation;
53.       mainPattern.implements = patternOperation;}
54.     lc.tiles.add(sectionPattern);}}
```

Fig. 8. Logical configuration generator transformation rules.

4   Implementation and Toolset

To assist the architect for applying the architecture views and transforming using the transformation chain, we have developed the toolset that implements each architecture viewpoint metamodel and defined transformation rules. For this we have used the Epsilon [4] toolset for Eclipse IDE that is used to represent the notation (concrete syntax) of the viewpoints. For each viewpoint we have defined the corresponding metamodel. The metamodels are defined in the Eclipse Modeling Framework (EMF) using Emfatic language in Epsilon.

Figure 10 shows the architecture views for the earlier defined case study, which are generated by the transformation chain in the toolset. In Fig. 10a a test computer is defined with four nodes and a network among nodes. Each node has four processing units, a bus and a memory. Application decomposition for Order Management Application, which is shown in Fig. 10b, is composed of three packages and each package includes modules. In Fig. 10c, Algorithm Decomposition View is generated using application decomposition viewpoint, where parallel algorithm module ShippingCalculations is defined. Component viewpoint (Fig. 10d) is generated using application decomposition. Deployment view (Fig. 10e) includes test computer definition (physical configuration), order management components and «deployedon» relation property for each component. Logical configuration (Fig. 10f) is generated from algorithm decomposition using parallel mapping library and the information that the parallel algorithm component is deployed on which processing units.

Moreover, in the toolset we have implemented view editors for the architecture view definitions. The Eclipse Graphical Modeling Framework (GMF) models are generated from the EMF models using EuGENia tool in Epsilon. Figure 9 shows a snapshot of the toolset with the example for Physical Configuration Editor. The user interface of the editor provides four panels: (1) Project Explorer, (2) Outline Overview, (3) Editor Panel and (4) Palet Panel. Project Explorer shows the projects to define different physical configuration models. Outline Overview shows the outline of the editing physical

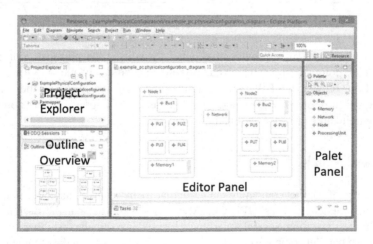

Fig. 9.   Physical configuration editor.

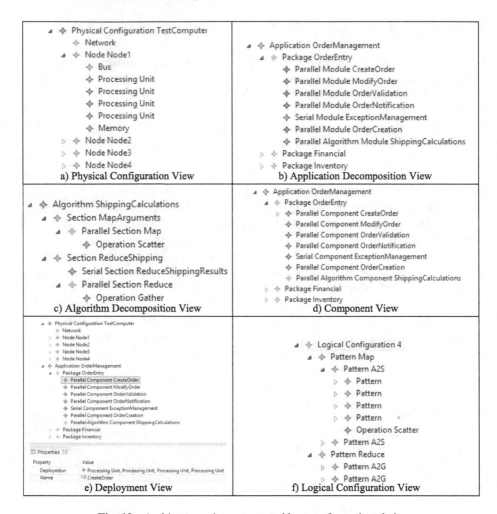

Fig. 10. Architecture views generated by transformation chain.

configuration. Editor Panel, provides the panel for editing the physical configuration using the Viewpoint structures which can be selected and easily added to the model by drag and drop. Finally, the Palet Panel includes the view structures. In the example a physical configuration with two nodes and a network is given. Each node has 4 processing units and a memory with a bus.

5   Related Work

In the literature of parallel computing the particular focus seems to have been on parallel programming models such as MPI, OpenMP, CILK etc. [11] but the design and the modeling got less attention. Several papers have focused in particular on higher level design abstractions in parallel computing and the adoption of model-driven development.

Palyart et al. [9] propose an approach for using model-driven engineering in high performance computing. They focus on automated support for the design of a high performance computing application based on abstract platform independent model. The approach includes the steps for successive model transformations that enrich progressively the model with platform information. The approach is supported by a tool called Archi-MDE. Gamatié et al. [7] represent the Graphical Array Specification for Parallel and Distributed Computing (GASPARD) framework for massively parallel embedded systems to support the optimization of the usage of hardware resources. GASPARD uses MARTE standard profile for modeling embedded systems at a high abstraction level. MARTE models are then refined and used to automatically generate code. Our approach can be considered an alternative approach to both GASPARD and Archi-MDE. The difference of our approach is the particular focus on optimization at the design level using architecture viewpoints.

In our earlier studies [3, 12, 13], we have proposed an architecture framework for mapping parallel algorithms to parallel computing platforms. In these studies we only focused on parallel algorithms and did not consider the broader concept of application. Also we assumed a distributed memory model in which each node has its own memory unit and, as such, targeted the MISD architecture of the Flynn's taxonomy. The current approach is more general and detailed in the sense that it focuses on software application, supports both modules and algorithms, can represent different memory models, supports modeling different computing architectures, and most importantly, supports the generation of the views.

6   Conclusion

We have applied model-driven transformation techniques to support the automation of the mapping of parallel applications to parallel computing platforms. We have mainly focused on the practical aspects and showed that this is indeed possible. We could define the required views without substantial problems and use these in the generators that we implemented. The overall approach provides a substantial support for the scalability problem in parallel computing and increases the productivity and quality. In our future work we will go further than modeling and focus also on supporting design aspects for optimizing the deployment configurations of parallel applications.

References

1. Amdahl, G.M.: Validity of the single processor approach to achieving large scale computing capabilities. In: Reprinted from the AFIPS Conference Proceedings, vol. 30, Atlantic City, NJ, 18–20 April 2007. AFIPS Press, Reston, VA, 1967, pp. 483–485, Solid-State Circuits Newsletter, IEEE, vol. 12, no. 3, pp. 19–20 (Summer, 2007)
2. Arkin, E., Tekinerdogan, B., Imre, K.: Model-driven approach for supporting the mapping of parallel algorithms to parallel computing platforms. In: Proceedings of the ACM/IEEE 16th International Conference on Model Driven Engineering Languages and System (2013)

3. Arkin. E., Tekinerdogan, B.: Architectural view driven transformations for supporting the lifecyle of parallel applications. In: 3rd International Conference on Model-Driven Engineering and Software Development (MODELSWARD 2015) (2015)

4. Epsilon. http://www.eclipse.org/epsilon

5. Flynn, M.: Some computer organizations and their effectiveness. IEEE Trans. Comput. **C-21**(9), 948–960 (1972)

6. Frank, M.P.: The physical limits of computing. Comput. Sci. Eng. **4**(3), 16–26 (2002)

7. Gamatié, A., Le Beux, S., Piel, E., Ben Atitallah, R., Etien, R., Marquet, P., Dekeyser, J.: A model-driven design framework for massively parallel embedded systems. ACM Trans. Embed. Comput. Syst. **10**(4), 1–36 (2011)

8. Kogge, P., Bergman, K., Borkar, S., Campbell, D., Carlson, W., Dally, W., Denneau, M., Franzon, P., Harrod, W., Hiller, J., Karp, S., Keckler, S., Klein, D., Lucas, R., Richards, M., Scarpelli, A., Scott, S., Snavely, A., Sterling, T., Williams, R.S., Yelick, K., Bergman, K., Borkar, S., Campbell, D., Carlson, W., Dally, W., Denneau, M., Franzon, P., Harrod, W., Hiller, J., Keckler, S., Klein, D., Williams, R.S., Yelick, K.: Exascale computing study: technology challenges in achieving exascale systems. In: DARPA (2008)

9. Palyart, M., Ober, I., Lugato, D., Bruel, J.: HPCML: a modeling language dedicated to high-performance scientific computing. In: Proceedings of the 1st International Workshop on Model-Driven Engineering for High Performance and CLoud computing (MDHPCL 2012), Article 6, 6 p. ACM, New York, NY, USA (2012)

10. Pllana, S., Fahringer, T.: UML based modeling of performance oriented parallel and distributed applications. In: Simulation Conference, Proceedings of the Winter, vol. 1, pp. 497–505, 8–11 (2002)

11. Talia, D.: Models and trends in parallel programming. Parallel Algorithms Appl. **16**(2), 145–180 (2001)

12. Tekinerdogan, B., Arkin. E.: Architecture framework for modeling the deployment of parallel applications on parallel computing platforms. In: 3rd International Conference on Model-Driven Engineering and Software Development (MODELSWARD 2015) (2015)

13. Tekinerdogan, B., Arkin, E.: Architecture framework for mapping parallel algorithms to parallel computing platforms. In: MDHPCL@ MoDELS, pp. 53–62 (2013)

Runtime Translation of Model-Level Queries to Persistence-Level

Xabier De Carlos[1], Goiuria Sagardui[2], Aitor Murguzur[1],
Salvador Trujillo[1], and Xabier Mendialdua[1(✉)]

[1] IK4-Ikerlan Research Center, P.J.M. Arizmendiarrieta, 2, 20500 Arrasate, Spain
{xdecarlos,amurguzur,strujillo,xmendialdua}@ikerlan.es
[2] Mondragon Unibertsitatea, Goiru 2, 20500 Arrasate, Spain
gsagardui@mondragon.edu

Abstract. Different studies have proved that XMI (default persistence in Eclipse Modelling Framework) has some limitations when operating with large models. Recent approaches propose databases for persistence of models. Therefore, persistence level languages could be used to efficiently query models. While persistence level languages increase performance as they take advantages of underlying databases, they compromise usability for model engineers. Model engineers are familiar with model-level query languages (e.g. EOL or OCL). We present MQT (Model Query Translator), a runtime translation of model-level to persistence-level queries. Thus, we provide model engineers the usability of a model level language but also take advantage of performance optimization of databases. We have performed an empirical study of the approach using the GraBaTs 2009 case study (models from 8.8 MB to 646 MB) and results indicate that persisting models in a database, and combining it with runtime query translation provides a promising alternative for querying large models.

1 Introduction

Model Driven Development (MDD) raises the level of abstraction from code to models and makes the latter first-class citizens of the development process. To effectively operate with large models, scalable model persistence mechanisms are essential. Unfortunately, this is not the case for the standard XML Metadata Interchange (XMI), which the Eclipse Modelling Framework (EMF) uses as its default persistence format [1].

To overcome scalability problems several approaches have been proposed to leverage relational and non-relational databases to facilitate scalable model persistence and loading [1–4]. These approaches provide persistence-level query languages that leverage the capabilities of these databases (e.g. SQL, MorsaQL [5], etc.). Persistence-level queries are specific and dependent on a particular persistence mechanism. This results in queries that are expressed at a low level of abstraction and tightly couples the queries with the specific model persistence mechanism. By contrast, model-level queries are closer to model engineers since

© Springer International Publishing Switzerland 2015
P. Desfray et al. (Eds.): MODELSWARD 2015, CCIS 580, pp. 97–111, 2015.
DOI: 10.1007/978-3-319-27869-8_6

they are expressed in languages focused on interacting with models, independently of the persistence mechanism (e.g. IncQuery, Epsilon Object Language (EOL), etc.). The main disadvantage of model-level query languages is that they typically require to load models into memory before queries can be executed.

This paper focuses on the scalable querying of persisted models. We present the Model Query Translator (MQT) approach in order to translate at runtime queries expressed in the Object Constraint Language (OCL)-based EOL to SQL. MQT supports read-only EOL queries and we plan to add support for modification query expressions in a next version. General overview of MQT was presented in [6]. As a quantitative evaluation, we have performed an empirical study using five models of different sizes (from 45.3 MB to 403 MB). Each model has been persisted using both XMI and an embedded relational database. Then we have executed the *GraBaTs'09 Reverse Engineering Contest* query (singleton extraction). In our experiments, models persisted using our approach take up more storage space but consistently outperform their XMI counterparts in terms of memory footprint and query execution time.

Sections 2 and 3 describe MQT approach and the translation process. An empirical study is performed in Sect. 4 and then Sect. 5 reviews related work. Paper concludes with conclusions and future work in Sect. 6.

2   MQT: Overview

MQT is an approach that supports querying models with a model-level language but also takes advantage of the persistence-level query language. MQT translates at runtime model-level (EOL) queries to persistence-level (SQL) queries.

We have chosen EOL as model-level query language. Main reasons for choosing EOL are that (i) EOL is a OCL-like language that besides read-only queries it also provides queries for model modification; (ii) other languages such as Epsilon Validation Language (EVL), Epsilon Transformation Language (ETL), Epsilon Comparison Language (ECL) are built on top of EOL [7] and provide model validation, transformation or comparison features. On the persistence-level, we have chosen SQL since it is a structured and mature language used to query information from relational databases (and also some NoSQL databases). EOL is imperative and cannot be directly mapped to SQL. For this reason, MQT performs partial translation of EOL queries into equivalent SQL queries. Partial translation is suitable when the model-level query language provides constructs that have no direct mapping in the target language. Approaches such as [8,9] perform OCL to SQL translation at compilation-time, but the translation on MQT is executed at runtime. Runtime-translation facilitates translation of languages that have not direct mapping (e.g. EOL and SQL).

The translation mechanism provided by our approach is based on the Epsilon Model Connectivity Layer (EMC) [7]. EMC is an API that provides abstraction facilities over modelling and data persistence technologies. It defines the IModel interface that provides methods that enable querying and modifying model elements. MQT provides, EDBObject class (described in Sect. 2.2) that implements the IModel interface of EMC. Using instances of this class, MQT is able to interact with models conforming to an Ecore metamodel and persisted in a relational database. Our approach is based on [10], where the naive translation provided by EMC is used to query large datasets stored on a single-table relational database. By contrast, MQT provides: (i) a metamodel-agnostic data-schema that is able to persist models conforming to any Ecore metamodel; and (ii) customized translation of queries from EOL to SQL. At this stage, although translation of read-only EOL query expressions is supported, MQT does not support query expressions that modify model.

2.1 Data-schema

The relational data schema is metamodel-agnostic so persistence of models in the database is independent of metamodels they conform to. In case metamodel evolves, no changes are required in the schema. We have defined different indexes within the schema that allow running the translated SQL queries faster. Figure 1 illustrates the schema. The EOL to SQL translation process of MQT is dependent on this data-schema. Tables, relations and indexes shown on the schema are discussed below:

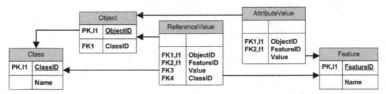

Fig. 1. Specified metamodel-agnostic database schema.

- **Object** table: Contains the identifier (ObjectID, indexed primary key) of each model element and the identifier of the meta-class that the element conforms to (ClassID, foreign key).
- **Class** table: Contains the identifier (ClassID, indexed primary key) and the name of all meta-classes existing in the model.
- **Feature** table: Contains the identifier (FeatureID, indexed primary key) and the name of all attributes and references existing in the model.
- **AttributeValue** table: It contains the attribute values of model elements. They are identified by the ObjectID and a the FeatureID (indexed foreign keys). Value column contains the value of the attribute.
- **ReferenceValue** table: It contains the reference values of model elements. They are identified by the ObjectID and a the FeatureID (indexed foreign keys). Value and ClassID columns contain the identifier and the class of the referenced element.

Although the schema is metamodel-agnostic,the users should provide it in the execution. The approach uses the metamodel at runtime to: (i) identify superclasses and subclasses of model elements; (ii) obtain the default values of attributes; (iii) identify whether a feature is an attribute or a reference; or (iv) obtain bounds of features.

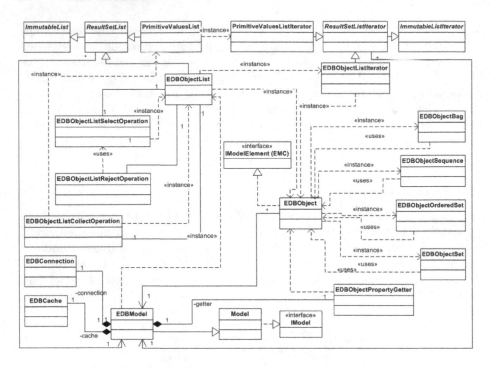

Fig. 2. Class-diagram of MQT.

2.2   Conceptual Model

Figure 2 illustrates a UML class diagram of MQT, where the conceptual model of MQT is specified. Next, each class is described one-by-one:

- **EDBConnection.** This class is responsible for connecting with the database and it is used to execute queries and get results from the database.
- **EDBCache.** This class supports loading in memory names and identifiers of the existing classes and features. Using this class the approach is able to avoid some *joins* on the translated SQL queries. Identifiers and names of classes and features are accessible using the methods getClassID(name), getFeatureID(name), getClassName(id) and getFeatureName(id).
- **EDBModel.** This is the main class of MQT and it extends the Model class of EOL (which implements the IModel of EMC). This class is responsible for interacting with model elements persisted in the database. The EDBModel class overrides Model methods that query models (modification methods are not supported).
- **EDBObjectPropertyGetter.** It extends the AbstractProperty Getter class of EOL and is invoked when a feature value is queried.
- **EDBObject.** This class implements the IModelElement interface of EOL and it is used to represent model elements that are persisted in the database. EDBObject class is instantiated by classes such as EDBObjectList, EDB-ObjectIterator or EDBModel to return elements of the model. Instances

of EDBObject class are able to get attribute and reference values of the model object that they represent. Attribute and reference values are obtained through the method getValue(String featureName). It also provides other methods to obtain other information about the model element: equals(Object object) compares the model element with another object and returns if it is equal; getEClass() returns the EClass of the represented model element; getOwningModel() returns the model where the element is contained; getObjectID() returns the ID that identifies the model element within the database; etc.

- **EDBObjectBag, EDBObjectSequence, EDBObjectSet, EDBObject OrderedSet**. These classes extend different collection type classes of EOL (EolBag, EolSequence, EolSet and EolOrderedSet). These classes are instantiated and returned in the execution of the method getValue(feature) of the class EDBObject.
- **ImmutableList.** An abstract class that implements the interface java.util.List and provides support for read-only lists.
- **ResultSetList.** An abstract class that extends the previously described ImmutableList. This class is used to provide a List that is able to work with results returned by the database (ResultSet) after executing a SQL query.
- **EDBObjectList.** This class extends ResultSetList and specifies a list composed by EDBObjects. It is instantiated when the translated and executed SQL query returns a list of model elements. To support runtime adaptation of queries the EDBObjectList class implements the interface IAbstractOperationContributor and an implementation of getAbstractOperation(String operation) method is provided. Depending on the translated operation (select, collect, etc.) it returns an instance of class EDBObjectSelectOperation, EDBObjectCollect Operation or EDBObjectRejectOperation.
- **PrimitiveValuesList.** This class extends ResultSetList and is similar to the previously described EDBObjectList. In this case, this class is instantiated when the translated and executed SQL query returns a list of primitive values (instead of model elements).
- **ImmutableListIterator.** An abstract class that implements the interface java.util.ListIterator and provides an implementation for read-only list iterators.
- **ResultSetListIterator.** Abstract class extending the previously described ImmutableListIterator. This class is used to provide a ListIterator that is able to work with results returned by the database (ResultSet) after executing a SQL query.
- **EDBObjectListIterator.** It extends the ResultSetListIterator class and implements methods of IteratorList but returning results (EDBObjects) based on a database (ResultSet). This class is instantiated when the method listIterator() of the EDBObjectList class is executed.

- **PrimitiveValuesListIterator.** Implements the same methods of the previous class but in this case it is adapted to work with a ResultSet containing primitive values. The class is instantiated when the method listIterator() of the PrimitiveValuesList class is executed.
- **EDBObjectSelectOperation, EDBObjectCollectOperation** and **EDBObjectRejectOperation.** These classes extend different EOLOperations, overriding the execute() method and providing more performant and adapted translated select, collect and reject queries. EMC provides a naive translation where each expression is translated and then executed one-by-one. For example, the expression "Elem.all.collect(n | n.name)" returns a list containing names of all model elements of type Elem. In the case of the EMCs' naive translation and execution of the query, first "Elem.all" is executed, getting a EDBObjectList containing all Elem type elements. Then, one SQL query is generated and executed to get the name of each element returned on the list. By contrast, extending EOLOperations, more performant queries are constructed when translating select, reject and collect expressions. For example, in case of "Elem.all.collect(n | n.name)", we can construct a SQL query that returns in one execution all Elem type elements' name. We compared query execution times of the naive and of the extended translation in [6].

3 MQT: EOL to SQL Translation

This section describes the translation process by analysing how MQT translates EOL query expressions. The EOL query parsing and execution is driven by the *EOL Module* and our approach is able to interact with it since MQT is based on the EMC. Figure 3 illustrates the sequence diagram of the translation of the most noteworthy EOL expressions. Following, the translation and execution process of the expressions illustrated in the Fig. 3 and of other EOL expressions is described. We have extracted from [7] the description of each EOL expression.

3.1 Query Model Elements

The model itself is the input of EOL expressions of this type. The starting point of the translation are the methods located on the EDBModel class instance and they are executed by the *EOL Module*. First step of the Fig. 3 illustrates the translation process of an EOL query of this type. Next, the translation process for EOL expressions of this type is described:

- **allOfKind(), allInstances(), all():EDBObjectList:**
  EOL Description: allOfKind() returns an EDBObjectList containing all the model elements (EDBObject instances) that are instances either of the type itself or of one of its subtypes. Methods allInstances() and all() are aliases of allOfKind() and the execution and result is the same.

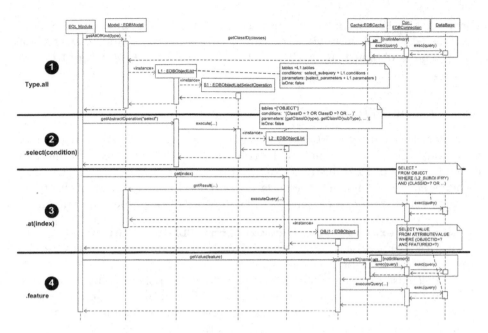

Fig. 3. Sequence diagram of a MQT execution.

MQT Translation: returned EDBObjectList is able to construct a SQL query that obtains model elements that are instances of the type or subtypes: (SELECT * FROM OBJECT WHERE (OBJECT.CLASSID = getClassID(type) OR OBJECT. CLASSID = getClassID(subtype) OR ...)), but the query is not executed until the result is required. As step 1 of Fig. 3 illustrates, when allOfKind() EOL query is executed, the EOLModule executes the getAllOfKind(String type) method of the EDBModel class instance (*Model* in the figure). In this method, summarizing, first classIds of the type and subtypes (if exist) are obtained from memory through the EDBCache class instance. If the queried class is loaded in memory, it returns the ID directly. If it is not yet loaded, the ID of the class is obtained through a SQL query that is executed by an EDBConnection instance. Next, an EDBObjectList is instantiated (*L1*) and it is able to construct the SQL query when results are required.

– **allOfType():EDBObjectList**:
EOL Description: returns an EDBObjectList containing all the elements in the model (represented using EDBObject instances) that are instances of the type.
MQT Translation: returned EDBObjectList is able to construct a query that obtains from the database model elements that are instances of the type (SELECT * FROM OBJECT WHERE (OBJECT.CLASSID = getClassID(type))) and the query is not executed until the result is required. The process to get the EDBObjectList is similar to the

expression `allOfKind()`. In this case, the `getAllOfType(type)` method of the `EDBModel` instance is executed. In this method, first, `classId` of the type is obtained using `EDBCache` instance. Then `EDBObjectList` is instantiated.

3.2 Element Filtering

A previously instantiated `EDBObjectList` is the input of EOL expressions of this group. The starting point of the translation is the execution of a method of the `EDBObjectList` instance, and it is performed by the *EOL Module*. The second step in Fig. 3 illustrates translation of a select, an expression of this type. Next, translation process of some EOL expressions of this type is described:

- **select(iterator:Type | condition):EDBObjectList:**
  EOL Description: getting an `EDBObjectList` as input, it returns all elements of the list satisfying the condition.
  MQT Translation: returned `EDBObjectList` is able to query from the database elements of the input `EDBObjectList` satisfying specified condition (`SELECT * FROM OBJECT WHERE (L2_SUBQUERY) AND (CLASSID=? OR ...)`). But the query is not executed until the result is required.
  Step 2 of Fig. 3 illustrates the translation process and it is explained below: First, the *EOL Module* executes the `getAbstractOperation("select")` method of the corresponding `EDBObjectList` (previously instantiated on the translation of another expression; e.g. *L1* of the figure). Then, the `execute()` method of the `EDBObjectListSelectOperation` class instance (*S1*) is executed. It returns a new instance of the `EDBObjectList` class (*L2*). In this case, constructor parameters are completed with attributes of L1 and with the condition of the select. With this information, the `EDBObjectList` instance is able to construct the SQL expression that gets model elements that meet previous conditions and also the condition of the select.
- **reject(iterator:Type | condition):EDBObjectList:**
  EOL Description: getting an `EDBObjectList` as input, it returns all elements of the list that do not satisfy the condition.
  MQT Translation: returned `EDBObjectList` is able to query from the database model elements of the input `EDBObjectList` that do not satisfy the condition.
  When this expression is parsed, as with the select expression, the *EOL Module* executes the `getAbstractOperation("reject")` method of the corresponding `EDBObjectList`. It uses a `EDBObjectListRejectOperation` instance (based on a `EDBObjectListSelectOperation`) to instantiate the returned `EDBObjectList`.
- **collect(iterator:Type | condition):**
  EOL Description: getting an `EDBObjectList` as input, it returns a `EDBObjectList` or a `PrimitiveValueList`. The returned list contains values of the specified condition for each element of the input list.

MQT Translation: if the specified condition is based on an attribute, the returned `PrimitiveValueList` contains values of the feature for each element of the input `EDBObjectList`. Else, if the feature is based on a reference, an `EDBObjectList` is returned.

When this expression is parsed, the *EOL Module* executes the `getAbstractOperation("collect")` method of the corresponding `EDBObjectList`. To return the computed list, first, SQL queries should be executed and then results obtained from the database are used to populate returned list. The executed query is based on the input `EDBObjectList`, but it is re-factorized to return in one execution all the required values.

- **selectOne(...), closure(...), aggregate(...), exists (...), etc.:**
  The approach makes use of the previously described methods' to get the result of these methods.

3.3 Query Results (EDBObjectList)

These EOL query expressions return a result from a given `EDBObjectList`. The translation starting point is a method of the `EDBObjectList` instance that is executed by the *EOL Module*. It is important to note that as this type expressions require to return the result, SQL expression constructed by the input `EDBObjectList` should be executed. The SQL query expression is only executed once, since in the following execution of methods of the same `EDBObjectList` instance same ResultSet is used. Then, based on the `ResultSet` returned by the database, required result is prepared and returned. Third step of the Fig. 3 illustrates translation of an expression of this type: at(2) that returns the second `EDBObject` of the list.

Next, translation process of some EOL expressions of this type are described:

- **at(index: Integer):EDBObject:**
  EOL Description: returns the `EDBObject` of the collection at the specified index.
  MQT Translation: returns a new instance of EDBObject based on the result located in the `ResultSet` (returned by the database) at the specified index. As step 3 of the Fig. 3 illustrates, the *EOL Module* executes the method get(2) of the `EDBObjectList` (L2). To get the result, first the SQL expression constructed by the *L2* is executed through the `EDBConnection` instance (*Con*) located at the `EDBModel` instance (*Model*). The database returns a `ResultSet` that is stored on *L2*. Finally, it is used to return results, in this case creating a new `EDBObject` instance based on the second row of the `ResultSet`.
- **first(), second(), third(), fourth(), last(): EDBObject:**
  EOL Description: returns the first, second, third, fourth and last `EDBObject` of the `EDBObjectList` respectively.
  MQT Translation: these expressions make use of the previously described method at(index) (e.g. at(0) in case of first()).

- **size():Integer**:
  EOL Description: returns how many EDBObjects are contained in the
  EDBObjectList.
  MQT Translation: first, ResultSet is obtained (as previously described) and
  then returns the number of rows that it contains.
- **includes(obj: EDBObject):Boolean**:
  EOL Description: returns true if the EDBObjectList includes the
  EDBObject.
  MQT Translation: the *EOL Module* executes the contains(obj) method
  of the EDBObjectList. This method iterates all the rows of the previously
  obtained ResultSet analysing if the specified obj is in the list. *ObjectID* is
  used to compare EDBObjects and if it is equal once, the method returns *true*.
- **includesAll(objCol: Collection):Boolean**:
  EOL Description: returns true if the EDBObjectList includes all the
  EDBObjects objCol.
  MQT Translation: the *EOL Module* executes the containsAll(col)
  method of the EDBObjectList. This method iterates all EDBObjects of
  col, executing for each one the previously described includes(obj).

3.4   Query Results (EDBObject)

These EOL query expressions return a result from a given EDBObject. The
translation starting point is a method of the EDBObject instance that is executed by the *EOL Module*. Next, the translation process of some EOL expressions
of this type is described:

- **.feature** (e.g. *obj.name*):
  EOL Description: returns the value of the specified feature of the given
  EDBObject.
  MQT Translation: constructs and executes the SQL expression getting the
  features' value from the database. As shown on the fourth step of Fig. 3, to
  translate the EOL expression to SQL, first, the *EOL Module* executes the
  getValue(feature) method of the EDBObject instance. This method,
  constructs and executes the SQL query. Finally, the results returned by the
  query are returned.
- **type(): Type**:
  EOL Description: returns the type of the EDBObject.
  MQT Translation: the *EOL Module* executes the getEClass() method that
  returns EClass of the EDBObject. The EClass is obtained directly from
  the EDBObject instance (it is specified in the instantiation through the
  constructor).

4   Empirical Study

This section presents an empirical study of MQT. We have executed a query over
five models (Set0...Set4) of different sizes. We have evaluated storage size, query

execution time and memory footprint. The query is based on the *GraBaTs'09 Reverse Engineering Contest*, and identifies singletons within a Java project. The query has been implemented using EOL, and it is illustrated in Listing 1.1. First all instances of `TypeDeclaration` (abstraction of source-code classes) are obtained (line 1). Then, a `select` query-expression is specified to filter elements satisfying singleton conditions. The conditions are the existence of a method (line 2), which being public (line 3), static (line 4) and of type `SimpleType` (line 5), returns same type as the class that contains it (line 6). The number of existing singleton classes are displayed at line 7.

```
1  var t = TypeDeclaration.all.select(td|
2  td.bodyDeclarations.exists(md:MethodDeclaration|
3    md.modifiers.exists(mod:Modifier|mod.public==true)
4    and md.modifiers.exists(mod:Modifier|mod.static==true)
5    and md.returnType.isTypeOf(SimpleType)
6    and md.returnType.name.fullyQualifiedName == td.name.
   fullyQualifiedName));
7 t.size().println();
```

Listing 1.1. GraBaTs 2009 case study query.

We have used models from the Grabats 2009 Case Study[1]. The models have been persisted in the native XMI and also in a single-file, embedded database using H2 v.1.3.168 and a metamodel agnostic schema (previously described in Sect. 2.1). Table 1 summarizes different properties of the GraBaTs models. The size of models ranges from 8.8 MB, containing 14 java classes and 70447 model elements (set0), to 646 MB, containing 5984 java classes and 4961779 model elements (set4).

The query has been executed 100 times over each model and using both persistence formats (XMI and embedded DB). We have measured storage size, memory footprint and query execution time. All tests have been executed under an Intel Core i7-3520M CPU at 2.90 GHz with 8 GB of physical RAM running 64 bits Windows 7 SP1, JVM 1.8.0 and the Eclipse Luna (4.4.0) distribution configured with 6 GB of maximum heap size.

Table 1. Details of the GraBaTs models.

	XMI size	Java classes	Model elem.	Query results
Set0	8,8	14	70447	1
Set1	27	40	198466	2
Set2	271	1605	2082841	41
Set3	598	5796	4852855	155
Set4	646	5984	4961779	164

---

[1] "http://www.emn.fr/z-info/atlanmod/index.php/GraBaTs_2009_Case_Study".

4.1   Results

This section shows and discusses obtained results: storage size, execution time and memory footprint. Storage size and memory footprint are shown in Megabytes (MB) and query execution time in milliseconds (ms).

Storage Size. As is illustrated on Fig. 4 models persisted using our approach are bigger than models persisted using XMI. The main reason is that besides model information, it also contains information related to the database management system (e.g. indexes).

Memory Footprint. As is shown in Fig. 5, memory usage is similar in both options (175–159 MB) for set0. In case of set1, while the maximum memory increases for XMI (an increase of 130 MB), the memory usage has the same value for MQT. The model size has higher impact over memory usage in set2 if XMI is used and it is increased to around 1.1 GB. By contrast, memory usage impact is lower if MQT is used and it increases 140 MB. In set3, while memory usage is duplicated respect to set2 if XMI is used (using around 2.3 GB), MQT only requires 318 MB. The trend is similar in set4 where XMI requires more than 2.4 GB and MQT only uses 345 MB.

Results show that XMI does not scale well in terms of memory when models are large. However, MQT does not require upfront memory loading, and consequently it scales better than XMI (increasing from 159 MB of set0 to 345 MB of set4).

In MQT, the memory usage increases, but the growth is slower: comparing with M1, memory usage is 2.79 times higher in M5, while in the case of XMI the use of memory is 6.27 bigger. Being so, although model size has impact over used memory in MQT, it scales better than XMI.

Query Execution Time. As is shown in Fig. 5, size of the model has a great impact over the time required to execute the GraBaTs query if XMI is used (querying the smaller model takes around 4.5 s while around 60 s are required for the largest model. Using MQT, the required execution time grows more

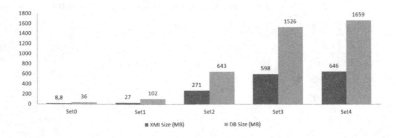

Fig. 4. Comparison of storage size (MB) between XMI and Embedded DB.

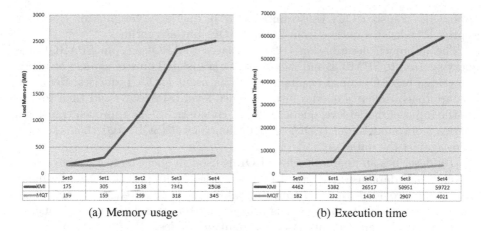

	Set0	Set1	Set2	Set3	Set4
XMI	175	305	1138	2342	2508
MQT	159	159	299	318	345

(a) Memory usage

	Set0	Set1	Set2	Set3	Set4
XMI	4462	5382	26517	50951	59722
MQT	182	232	1430	2907	4021

(b) Execution time

Fig. 5. Comparison between XMI and MQT.

slowly: from 182 ms to query Set0 to 4 s to query Set4. Main reason of this difference is that using XMI models have to be completely loaded, and it is a time consuming task. By contrast, if MQT is used, only the required information is loaded, avoiding the entire model loading time.

In case of MQT, the number of queries to be translated and executed has direct impact over the execution time result and it is dependent on the nature of the model. However, in this case, model size has not significant impact over the result.

Threats to Validity. Used memory and execution time results, show that our approach is promising in terms of scalability with respect to XMI. A more intensive evaluation should be performed analysing the impact of the nature of the model and of the query program over the execution time and memory footprint.

5   Related Work

We have identified other approaches that are focused on the generation of queries based on OCL-like languages:

[11] proposes an approach focused on generating SQL queries from invariants that are specified using OCL. This approach supports mapping between Unified Modelling Language (UML) models and databases. Then, the approach generates queries that allow to evaluate invariants using SQL. [8] describes an approach that generates views using OCL constraints. Then it uses views to check the integrity of the persisted data. The approach has been implemented in OCL2SQL[2], a tool that generates SQL queries from OCL constraints. [9] proposes another similar approach for integrity checking. While previously described

---

[2] Read more at http://dresden-ocl.sourceforge.net/usage/ocl22sql/.

approaches translate OCL constraints into SQL queries at compilation-time, our approach translates queries from EOL to SQL, but at runtime.

The approach described in [12], translates SPARQLAS (an SPARQL-like query syntax) to SPARQL and then executes translated queries against an OWL knowledge base. Obtained results are used as input for OCL queries. Being so, this approach executes queries in persistence-level (SPARQL) and then results are the input of model-level queries (OCL). By contrast, our approach translates queries from model-level (EOL) to persistence-level (SQL) and then executes them against the database.

[10] describes an approach where EOL is used to query large datasets stored on relational databases composed by one table. This approach uses the naive translation provided by EMC to query information persisted in a single-table database. By contrast, our approach provides custom translation of SQL queries to be executed against a database with multiple tables.

6   Conclusions and Further Work

In this paper, we have presented MQT, a prototype that is able to query models persisted in a relational database at model-level (same level of abstraction used for querying models persisted with XMI) but exploring the advantages of a persistence-level language (SQL). While existing approaches which are able to translate OCL-like languages statically at compilation time, our approach provides runtime translation of queries from EOL to SQL. Performing the translation at runtime eases to translate languages that have not direct mapping, and this is the case of EOL and SQL. We plan to add support for modification queries in a future prototype.

We have performed an empirical study where querying using both MQT and XMI is compared. The preliminary results show that our approach scales better than XMI on the execution of the *GraBaTs'09 Case Study*. While model size has a substantial impact on the memory footprint and loading time using XMI, the impact is softer in the case of MQT. However, results show that number of queries to be translated and executed has direct impact over the execution time. The number of queries is dependent on the nature of the model.

For future work, we plan to perform a complete study that will involve: (i) experimenting with different database configurations and with different in-memory caching strategies; (ii) experimenting with queries of different types; and (iii) comparing results with other persistence approaches.

Acknowledgements. This work is partially supported by the EU Commission with project MONDO (FP7-ICT-2013-10), no. 611125. Authors wish to thank Dr. Dimitris Kolovos.

References

1. Pagán, J.E., Cuadrado, J.S., Molina, J.G.: A repository for scalable model management. Softw. Syst. Model. **14**, 219–239 (2013)

2. Eike Stepper: CDO Model Repository Overview (2014). http://www.eclipse.org/cdo/documentation/. Accessed 17 March 2014
3. Benelallam, A., Gómez, A., Sunyé, G., Tisi, M., Launay, D.: Neo4EMF, a scalable persistence layer for EMF models. In: Cabot, J., Rubin, J. (eds.) ECMFA 2014. LNCS, vol. 8569, pp. 230–241. Springer, Heidelberg (2014)
4. Scheidgen, M.: Reference representation techniques for large models. In: Proceedings of the Workshop on Scalability in Model Driven Engineering. BigMDE 2013, pp. 5:1–5:9. ACM, New York (2013)
5. Pagán, J.E., Molina, J.G.: Querying large models efficiently. Inf. Softw. Technol. **56**, 586–622 (2014)
6. De Carlos, X., Sagardui, G., Trujillo, S.: MQT, an approach for runtime query translation: from EOL to SQL. In: Proceedings of the 14th International Workshop on OCL and Textual Modeling Applications and Case Studies. OCL 2014 (2014)
7. Kolovos, D., Rose, L., García-Domínguez, A., Paige, R. (eds.): The Epsilon Book, Enterprise Systems. University of York (2014)
8. Demuth, B., Hussmann, H., Loecher, S.: OCL as a specification language for business rules in database applications. In: Gogolla, M., Kobryn, C. (eds.) UML 2001. LNCS, vol. 2185, pp. 104–117. Springer, Heidelberg (2001)
9. Marder, U., Ritter, N., Steiert, H.: A dbms-based approach for automatic checking of ocl constraints. In: Proceedings of Rigourous Modeling and Analysis with the UML: Challenges and Limitations. OOPSLA (1999)
10. Kolovos, D.S., Wei, R., Barmpis, K.: An approach for efficient querying of large relational datasets with OCL-based languages. In: XM 2013-Extreme Modeling Workshop, p. 48 (2013)
11. Heidenreich, F., Wende, C., Demuth, B.: A framework for generating query language code from ocl invariants. ECEASST 9 (2008)
12. Parreiras, F.S.: Semantic Web and Model-Driven Engineering. Wiley, Hoboken (2012)

Integration of Handwritten and Generated Object-Oriented Code

Timo Greifenberg[1], Katrin Hölldobler[1], Carsten Kolassa[1], Markus Look[1],
Pedram Mir Seyed Nazari[1], Klaus Müller[1 (✉)], Antonio Navarro Perez[1],
Dimitri Plotnikov[1], Dirk Reiss[2], Alexander Roth[1], Bernhard Rumpe[1],
Martin Schindler[1], and Andreas Wortmann[1]

[1] Software Engineering, RWTH Aachen University, Aachen, Germany
{greifenberg,hoelldobler,kolassa,look,nazari,mueller,
perez,plotnikov,roth,rumpe,schindler,wortmann}@se-rwth.de
[2] Institute for Building Services and Energy Design, TU Braunschweig,
Braunschweig, Germany
reiss@sse-tubs.de

Abstract. In many development projects models are core artifacts used
to generate concrete implementations from them. However, for many
systems it is impossible or not useful to generate the complete software system from models alone. Hence, developers need mechanisms for
integrating generated and handwritten code. Applying such mechanisms
without considering their effects can cause issues in projects, where model
and code artifacts are essential. Thus, a sound approach for the integration of both forms of code is needed.

In this paper, we provide an overview of mechanisms for integrating
handwritten and generated object-oriented code. To compare these mechanisms, we define and apply a set of criteria. The results are intended to
help model-driven development (MDD) tool developers in choosing an
appropriate integration mechanism. In this extended version, we additionally discuss essential integration aspects including the protection of
generated code and elaborate on how to use action languages to extend
generated code.

1 Introduction

The vision to create complex software systems from abstract models by systematically transforming these into concrete implementations [1] is pursued by
model-driven development (MDD) [2]. The prevailing conjecture, however, is
that deriving a non-trivial, complete implementation from models alone is not
feasible [3]. Thus, current MDD techniques require tool developers to integrate
generated and handwritten code. Various mechanisms can be used to perform
this code integration. However, there is no ultimate integration mechanism that
should always be used. Instead, it depends on the context in which this code integration has to be carried out and on the concrete requirements which integration
mechanisms are best suited to be applied.

K. Hölldobler is supported by the DFG GK/1298 AlgoSyn.

© Springer International Publishing Switzerland 2015
P. Desfray et al. (Eds.): MODELSWARD 2015, CCIS 580, pp. 112–132, 2015.
DOI: 10.1007/978-3-319-27869-8_7

We examined existing mechanisms to integrate handwritten and generated object-oriented code to support MDD tool developers in selecting integration mechanisms. Additionally, we created a set of criteria focusing on different properties of code integration mechanisms to assess and compare these mechanisms. The presented criteria are based on a decade of experiences in object-oriented software engineering and MDD research [4,5], code generator development and code integration research [6,7], and experiences with MDD processes within various domains including automotive [8], cloud computing [9], robotics [10], and smart buildings [11].

We introduce eight handwritten code integration mechanisms and evaluate each with respect to our criteria. Their strengths and weaknesses are shown in the evaluation results. By means of this, we seek to increase the comparability between the integration mechanisms. In particular, this overview is intended to be used by MDD tool developers to find a proper integration mechanism on a case-by-case basis.

The list of integration mechanisms and evaluation criteria presented in this paper does not claim to be complete. However, if further integration mechanisms need to be compared or the mechanisms need to be evaluated with respect to additional evaluation criteria, this paper can be used as a basis easily.

In summary, the contributions of this paper are:

- A list of evaluation criteria for code integration mechanisms.
- A collection of mechanisms to integrate generated and handwritten code.
- An evaluation of the integration mechanisms based on the list of evaluation criteria.

In previous work, we have already presented different mechanisms to integrate handwritten and generated code for object-oriented programming languages [12]. This article is an extension of our previous work. It presents action languages as a further approach to customize generated code in addition to integrating handwritten code. Additionally, we provide an extended discussion on protecting generated code from being overridden.

The remainder of this article is structured as follows. We begin by introducing criteria to assess the code integration mechanisms (Sect. 2). The mechanisms are separated into mechanisms based on specific concepts in programming languages (Sect. 3) and mechanisms free of such requirements (Sect. 4). Subsequently, we summarize and discuss the evaluation results (Sect. 5). After that we elaborate on related work (Sect. 6) before we briefly present action languages as an alternative to extend generated code. Finally, we conclude this contribution (Sect. 8).

2   Evaluation Criteria

The following criteria concern different properties of integration mechanisms and aim at helping developers in selecting a suitable mechanism. These criteria are based on existing literature [13,14], best practices in software development [15,16], and our experience [4–11]. This list does not claim to cover all aspects of handwritten code integration. Nonetheless, it can be used as an initial list of criteria which can be adapted to fit personal needs. The presented criteria are not weighted on purpose since a weighting is highly subjective and also tailored to an application scenario, which is not intended.

C1: Separation of Generated and Handwritten Code. - Can generated and handwritten code be separated into different files?

Separation of concerns is an essential design practice in software development [15] and has been proposed as a criterion to evaluate integration mechanisms for handwritten code by [13,14]. One crucial benefit of separating generated and handwritten code into different files is that it can be ensured that the generator does not overwrite handwritten code. In case of mixing generated and handwritten code in one file, the handwritten code might not always be preserved.

C2: Support for Overriding Generated Parts. - Can developers add handwritten parts that are used instead of particular generated parts?

Depending on the developer's requirements it can be necessary to adapt particular parts of the generated functionality. This can be done by integrating handwritten code that refines these parts. A benefit of such handwritten code refinements is that the code generator does not have to be changed to fit different requirements.

C3: Extendability of the Generated Interfaces. - Can the generated interfaces be extended with handwritten methods?

Hiding implementation details is accepted as common practice in software development [15,16]. Accordingly, we assume that functionality of the generated system is provided to developers through dedicated generated interfaces and that the system's functionality is only accessed by using these. Obviously, these generated interfaces are oblivious to handwritten code. Consequently, the generated interfaces need to be extended to allow access to handwritten functionality.

C4: Independence of Handwritten Code at Generation-time. - Is the generator independent of the existence of handwritten code at generation-time?

In some handwritten code integration mechanisms the generated code needs to be adapted if handwritten code is present. In this case the handwritten code is processed by the generator and the generated code is adapted accordingly. For instance, the handwritten code is merged into the generated code and one artifact is produced. If this functionality is not provided by the generator framework, a generator developer has to extend the generator with such functionality. This additional effort might not be desired and can be avoided by choosing a generator framework with support for handling handwritten code. However, then the choice of an integration mechanism influences the choice of the generator framework. This is not always feasible.

C5: Independence of Additional OOP Language Constructs. - Can the integration mechanism be realized using only default OOP language constructs?

Some of the existing handwritten code integration mechanisms are tailored to a particular type of OOP language that provides specific language constructs.

Consequently, such integration mechanisms are restricted to generators that generate code in one of these languages. The benefit of handwritten integration mechanisms using default OOP language constructs is that no additional tooling is required and the generator is not tailored to a specific type of language. The following language constructs are regarded as the default OOP language constructs in this work: (abstract) classes, inheritance, interfaces, object creation facility and message-passing capability. Except for interfaces this understanding complies with [17]. We are aware that not all OOP languages provide the concept of interfaces but interfaces can be realized using classes with empty method bodies and inheritance.

3   Integration Mechanisms Based on Language Concepts

In this section, we present a catalog of integration mechanisms that presuppose certain concepts in the target language, for instance, inheritance known from object-oriented programming. Each presented mechanism is described and evaluated with the following scenario:

Assume the input model for the code generator is an UML class diagram (CD) containing the class Editor. As CDs do not model class behavior, implementations of Editor methods can be developed manually and the resulting handwritten code needs to be integrated with the code generated for Editor.

The same problems arise whenever modeling languages do not support modeling of all aspects of a system and these parts have to be developed manually. The mechanisms presented in the remainder of this publication are not limited to CDs and a particular type of code generation. We only use CDs to give an illustrative example.

3.1   Generation Gap

The generation gap mechanism [13, 18, 19] assumes that an interface and a default implementation are generated for each class in the input model. For instance, the interface Editor and the default implementation EditorBaseImpl are generated for the class Editor. Manual extensions of specific methods or behavior different from the default implementation are defined in the handwritten class EditorImpl. Figure 1 depicts this pattern for the class EditorImpl. Please note, that here and in the following «gc» denotes generated code and «hc» denotes handwritten code.

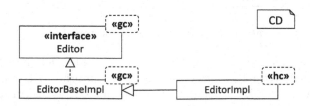

Fig. 1. Generation gap pattern for the Editor example.

In this case, `EditorImpl` is the implementation that will be used by both the generated code as well as manually written code that uses the interface `Editor`.

Please note, that the generation gap mechanism requires developers to create the handwritten class, no matter whether handwritten code is inserted into that class or not. In projects in which handwritten extensions are rarely needed, this leads to bloated projects with an unnecessary high number of artifacts.

Evaluation

C1: Separation of Generated and Handwritten Code. Fulfilled. This criterion holds by definition of the pattern, as the handwritten code has to be stored in separate classes.

C2: Support for Overriding Generated Parts. Fulfilled. The possibility to override generated methods is a crucial feature of the pattern.

C3: Extendability of the Generated Interfaces. Unfulfilled. This approach does not provide means to reflect added methods in the generated interface. The extended generation gap mechanism (see Sect. 3.2) addresses this issue.

C4: Independence of Handwritten Code at Generation-time. Fulfilled. Whether or what handwritten code exists does not influence the code generation in any way.

C5: Independence of Additional OOP Language Constructs. Fulfilled. This mechanism does not require additional OOP language constructs.

3.2   Extended Generation Gap

A mechanism that addresses two disadvantages of the basic generation gap mechanism (see Sect. 3.1) - the inability to extend the generated interface and the necessity to create an implementation class - is the extended generation gap mechanism, as shown in Fig. 2. Since this mechanism has been developed for our particular needs, its name is not a well-known term in MDD.

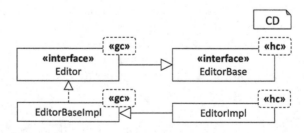

Fig. 2. Extended generation gap pattern with an additional handwritten Interface.

The first disadvantage is addressed by allowing to add a handwritten interface on top of the generated interface. As the generated interface `Editor` extends the handwritten interface `EditorBase`, all methods added to `EditorBase` are also available when accessing `Editor`. However, developers do not have to add this handwritten interface. Instead, the generator checks at generation-time whether it exists. If it does exist, the generated interface will extend the handwritten interface. Consequently, the generator needs to be executed again after adding a handwritten interface to reflect this change in the generated code.

When a developer adds a handwritten interface, the handwritten implementation class (EditorImpl in Fig. 2) has to be provided as well. If no handwritten interface is present, the generator generates a concrete class EditorBaseImpl by default and an additional implementation class does not have to be added by developers. In this way, developers are not forced to integrate their own implementation class. However, if a developer adds the handwritten class EditorImpl, which has to extend the generated base class EditorBaseImpl, this class is used in the generated code and EditorBaseImpl becomes abstract. This integration of handwritten code requires the generator to be executed again, as it checks at generation-time whether developers added their own implementation classes.

Other variations of the generation gap mechanism are possible. For instance, assuming that a handwritten interface always exists. A detailed discussion is neglected because the variations are very similar and, as shown in the example, differ in technical details.

Evaluation

C1: Separation of Generated and Handwritten Code. Fulfilled. See Sect. 3.1.

C2: Support for Overriding Generated Parts. Fulfilled. See Sect. 3.1.

C3: Extendability of the Generated Interfaces. Fulfilled. The API of the generated class can be extended easily by adding a handwritten interface which is extended by the generated interface. Thus, method signatures which are added to the handwritten interface are also available in the generated one. The actual implementations of these methods have to be added to the handwritten implementation class.

C4: Independence of Handwritten Code at Generation-time. Unfulfilled. The generator has to check whether a handwritten interface or implementation class was introduced, as this influences the structure of the generated code.

C5: Independence of Additional OOP Language Constructs. Fulfilled. See Sect. 3.1.

3.3 Delegation

Delegation is a pattern of object composition in object-oriented programming. In essence, the pattern consists of two objects taking the roles of one delegator and one delegate, respectively. The delegator delegates parts of its functionality to the delegate by invoking methods of the delegate. To this end, the delegate provides an interface declaring the method signatures that can be invoked. Figure 3 gives an overview of the objects and relationships involved. Here, Editor is the delegator and EditorDelegateImpl is the delegate implementing the methods defined in the EditorDelegate interface.

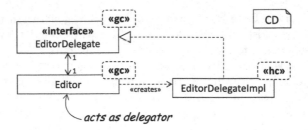

Fig. 3. Delegation pattern requires a delegator for regarding handwritten implementations.

The delegator is responsible for instantiating the delegate. `EditorDelegate-Impl` is the implementation that will be used by both the generated code as well as manually written code that uses the interface `EditorDelegate` in this case.

In essence, the purpose of delegation is to outsource functionality to a distinct object with an explicit interface specific to this functionality. This purpose makes delegation naturally applicable to the integration of handwritten and generated code. The roles of the delegators are taken by generated classes while the roles of the delegates are taken by handwritten classes. All functionality that cannot be generated is delegated to the handwritten delegates. The delegate interfaces, thus, are well-defined and distinct interfaces between generated and handwritten code. It can be generic and handwritten or specific and generated. The choice depends on whether the delegated functionality depends on the model or not. For instance, to delegate the implementation of method signatures in class diagrams to a delegate, it is appropriate to generate the delegate interface based on the method signatures defined by the CD.

In general, delegation provides a higher degree of encapsulation and cohesion compared to alternative patterns. Moreover, it avoids inheritance in handwritten classes since delegates only have to implement an interface. In programming languages without support for multiple inheritance delegation allows developers to use inheritance with handwritten classes.

Evaluation

C1: Separation of Generated and Handwritten Code. Fulfilled. The pattern separates generated and handwritten code by putting them into different classes and interfaces.

C2: Support for Overriding Generated Parts. Unfulfilled. In this mechanism, only designated delegators can be implemented to provide handwritten code. It is not possible to override other generated parts.

C3: Extendability of the Generated Interfaces. Unfulfilled. The generated interface can be extended by subinterfaces and concrete delegators according for the extended subinterface. However, the generated delegator is not aware of these extensions.

C4: Independence of Handwritten Code at Generation-time. Fulfilled. The existence of handwritten delegate classes does not influence the code generation.

C5: Independence of Additional OOP Language Constructs. Fulfilled. The default OOP language constructs suffice to implement this mechanism.

Alternatives. The cardinalities of the delegation relationship are not necessarily restricted. Thus, an implementation of the pattern may associate one delegator with exactly one delegate, or one delegator with many delegates, or many delegators with one delegate. The choice between these variants depends heavily on whether the delegate is stateful or stateless. Stateless delegates can generally be shared by many delegators and do not need to be instantiated repeatedly.

3.4 Include Mechanism

Include mechanisms are based on dedicated language constructs which allow to define that a certain file should be included into another file at a specific point. This idea can be easily used to integrate generated and handwritten files as either a generated file includes handwritten files (see Fig. 4) at designated places or vice versa. In general, the effect of using an include statement is equivalent to injecting the content of the included file to the corresponding location in the including file. Specific languages may offer include mechanisms with different meanings, but this will not be discussed in the following as the focus is on the general idea of include mechanisms.

By including handwritten files in generated files, the generator can define the required structure of the files and developers merely need to introduce selected handwritten files, which are included properly without the developer having to worry about it. This is advantageous if developers should not be able to deviate from this generated structure, as they can only provide the handwritten files which are included. Thus, developers are guided in which files to provide. On the other hand, if developers need more flexibility and should be able to deviate from such a generated structure, including generated files in handwritten files is more appropriate. This variant is, of course, accompanied by the risk that developers forget to include the proper generated files at the proper places.

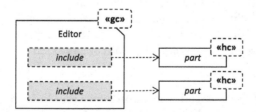

Fig. 4. The include mechanism adds include statements to the generated file to consider handwritten artifacts.

Evaluation

C1: Separation of Generated and Handwritten Code. Fulfilled. No matter whether generated files include handwritten files or vice versa, generated and handwritten parts are separated into different files.

C2: Support for Overriding Generated Parts. Unfulfilled. It is not possible to integrate handwritten code which is used instead of generated code as handwritten code can only be included and, therefore, added.

C3: Extendability of the Generated Interfaces. Conditionally fulfilled. To fulfill this criterion, a programming language has to allow include statements inside of interfaces to extend the signature. Even though we are not aware of a language that supports this, the concept itself does not forbid it. Therefore this criterion might be fulfilled, depending on the specific target language.

C4: Independence of Handwritten Code at Generation-time. Fulfilled. The generation of the include functionality does not depend on the existence of handwritten code.

C5: Independence of Additional OOP Language Constructs. Unfulfilled. The mechanism requires include constructs which do not belong to the default OOP language constructs.

3.5   Partial Classes

Partial classes facilitate splitting class implementations into several source code files. These parts are merged in a pre-compilation phase. The result contains the union of all methods, fields and super types of all its partial definitions. In contrast to aspect-oriented programming (see Sect. 3.6), partial classes are concerned with only one class rather than multiple. In Fig. 5 this approach is illustrated.

The partial classes mechanism suits well for integrating handwritten and generated code. Each generated partial class can be extended by adding handwritten code in its own partial class in a separate source file. The resulting generated and handwritten code is integrated automatically by merging them. This merging can either be done by applying naming conventions, i.e., partial classes with the same name are merged, or by explicit notations. How and which partial classes are merged is defined by the used language.

The CD in Fig. 5 illustrates the partial class mechanism. In this case, the generated code is stored in the partial class `EditorBaseImpl` and the handwritten code is stored in a separate partial class `EditorBaseImpl`.

Evaluation

C1: Separation of Generated and Handwritten Code. Fulfilled. The handwritten and generated partial classes can be located in different source code files.

C2: Support for Overriding Generated Parts. Conditionally fulfilled. In general, the partial classes mechanism does not forbid to override methods' implementations. However, depending on the used programming language that supports partial classes, this criterion may not be fulfilled.

C3: Extendability of the Generated Interfaces. Conditionally fulfilled. The concept of the partial classes mechanism can be applied to interfaces, too.

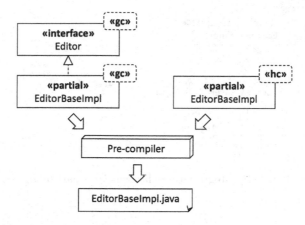

Fig. 5. Partial classes mechanism merges the handwritten and the generated implementation to one single artifact.

Thus, the additional method signatures can be added to the handwritten partial interface which is merged with the generated partial interface. However, if a realization of the partial class mechanism supports partial classes but not partial interfaces, this criterion is not fulfilled.

C4: Independence of Handwritten Code at Generation-time. Fulfilled. Handwritten code does not have to exist at generation-time, because its existence does not influence the code generation process. Handwritten code only has to be available when the pre-compiler merges the generated and handwritten code.

C5: Independence of Additional OOP Language Constructs. Unfulfilled. This mechanism requires support for partial classes which is not regarded as a default OOP language construct in this work.

3.6 Aspect-Oriented Programming

Aspect-oriented programming (AOP) [20] addresses crosscutting concerns - functionality or features scattered across several classes causing duplication - by encapsulating duplicated code in one place. Although integrating handwritten code with generated code does not necessarily deal with crosscutting concerns, AOP can be used for this integration [7]. One advantage in this context is that the generated code does not need to offer a specific architecture to be extendable by handwritten code. Instead, the handwritten code is added by so called *aspects*, as shown in Fig. 6.

An aspect reacts to a predefined event (*pointcut*) during the program execution. Such a predefined event can be, for instance, a method call of a specific method in a specific class. The action that is executed when a pointcut is reached is implemented in an *advice*. Such an advice can be executed before, after or instead of the according event.

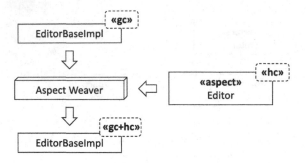

Fig. 6. Overview of an AOP integration mechanism for a part of a generated software system.

The integration of handwritten code can be performed by implementing an advice that is executed instead of, before or after a specific generated method. All these cases, of course, require the generator to create at least a dummy implementation of the corresponding method so that the handwritten advice can be executed instead of that generated method.

Figure 6 illustrates the idea underlying the integration of handwritten code using AOP. In this case, handwritten code is added to an advice in an aspect. An aspect weaver then takes the instructions given in the aspect and produces a combined artifact (e.g. a source code file) in which the advice implementation is woven into the code of the generated classes. This means that the advice instructions are introduced into the proper locations in the generated classes. In the example given in Fig. 6, the implementation of a generated method in `EditorBaseImpl` would be replaced by the advice implementation, if the aspect contains one advice for one method.

Besides the additional overhead of weaving the aspects into the source code, a major drawback of AOP is that it is more difficult to understand the program flow as it is influenced by aspects. Moreover, refactorings in the source code may lead to invalid aspects, known as the fragile pointcut problem [21].

Evaluation

C1: Separation of Generated and Handwritten Code. Fulfilled. AOP offers a clear separation of the handwritten and the generated code. The generated code is not aware of the aspects, which contain the handwritten code and which are stored in separate files.

C2: Support for Overriding Generated Parts. Fulfilled. As described above, an advice can be implemented such that it is called instead of a particular event in the generated class. By means of this, the execution of a generated method can be prevented and instead the handwritten implementation is executed.

C3: Extendability of the Generated Interfaces. Fulfilled. Concepts in AOP allow to extend interfaces and classes. Consequently, the API can be extended.

C4: Independence of Handwritten Code at Generation-time. Fulfilled. The generator and the generated code is not aware of handwritten code at all.

C5: Independence of Additional OOP Language Constructs. Unfulfilled. In order to be able to use this mechanism, the generated code needs to conform to a programming language that supports AOP or contains aspect-oriented extensions. This is not provided by OOP languages by default.

Alternatives. If the target language does not support aspect-orientation, hook points can be created in the generated code. Every hook point is called at the beginning and end of a method execution. By using inheritance, these hook points can be used to add behavior before or after the actual method execution. The behavior can be changed completely by overriding the method representing the hook point (see generation gap in Sect. 3.1). To some extent, this mechanism simulates aspects in AOP but it is not able to extend the API.

4 General Integration Mechanisms

Besides integration mechanisms that rely on language concepts, integration approaches free of this restriction are presented in this section. In compliance with Sect. 3, these approaches are evaluated with respect to the criteria described in Sect. 2.

4.1 PartMerger Mechanism

A PartMerger is a component that is capable of merging multiple files of a specific type, e.g., Java files, into one file. Obviously, this idea fits well to integrate handwritten and generated parts, as these parts can be separated into different files and later be merged by the PartMerger as shown in Fig. 7.

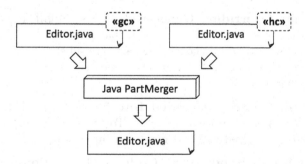

Fig. 7. The PartMerger mechanism merges source code artifacts (e.g. Java source code) to one artifact.

The PartMerger mechanism is a generalization of the partial classes mechanism (see Sect. 3.5). In contrast to partial classes, the PartMerger can also deal with non-source code artifacts. For instance, the DSL tool bench Monti-Core [22, 23] uses this mechanism to merge generated and handwritten Eclipse plugin.xml files and Eclipse manifest files.

Without any restriction on how to merge files, the PartMerger mechanism is very flexible. To consider handwritten code, a PartMerger can give higher priorities to handwritten extensions when merging two files. Furthermore, there are different strategies for invoking the PartMerger and for defining the files to be merged. A simple strategy is to invoke the PartMerger automatically for files conforming to a specific naming convention on the artifact level, e.g., files with the same file name in specific folders or files with a common pre- or postfix. Another strategy is to let the developers configure which files should be merged.

A drawback of the PartMerger mechanism is the lack of tool support when integrating handwritten code. Common functionalities such as code completion are not directly available to access parts of the generated code due to the strict separation of the generated and the handwritten source code files. Instead, developers need to implement such tooling on their own. This is an advantage of applying partial classes (see Sect. 3.5). The according tooling does not have to be implemented by the developer but it is already provided.

The PartMerger mechanism is very similar to the partial classes mechanism. The main difference is rooted in the language support for partial classes. In other words, a language that supports partial classes provides concepts to define what language parts are merged. The compiler takes care of the merging. In contrast, the PartMerger approach is based on a dedicated configurable tool that merges different artifacts, e.g. Java source code artifacts. Consequently, the PartMerger mechanism is not tailored to a particular language. However, the realization of the PartMerger might be tailored to particular languages.

Evaluation

C1: Separation of Generated and Handwritten Code. Fulfilled. The separation of artifacts is a precondition for this approach.

C2: Support for Overriding Generated Parts. Fulfilled. A PartMerger component can be implemented in such a way that it assigns a higher priority to handwritten parts so that certain generated parts are substituted by handwritten parts in the merged artifact. In this way, the handwritten code will be executed instead of the generated code.

C3: Extendability of the Generated Interfaces. Fulfilled. Extending the API of a generated interface is easily possible. To accomplish this, a handwritten interface needs to be merged with the generated interface.

C4: Independence of Handwritten Code at Generation-time. Fulfilled. Handwritten artifacts do not have to exist at generation-time, because they do not influence the generation-process. Instead, handwritten artifacts only have to be available when the PartMerger merges the generated and handwritten artifacts. This takes place after the code generator has finished.

C5: Independence of Additional OOP Language Constructs. Fulfilled. This mechanism does not require any kind of OOP language construct at all.

4.2 Protected Regions

Protected regions are designated regions located in generated code that allow to add handwritten code (see Fig. 8). A common use case for applying protected regions is to generate method signatures from input models and to insert protected regions into the corresponding method bodies.

Each protected region is typically surrounded by comments comprising a unique identification string. In this way, it can be differentiated between different protected regions. Before (re)generating code, the generator identifies protected regions in the generated code and manages the code contained in these regions based on the identification strings. While generating code, it reinserts the code previously contained in a particular protected region. As a consequence, the identification string associated with a protected region is crucial to be able to preserve the handwritten code in subsequent generator executions.

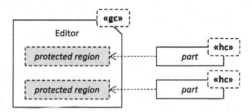

Fig. 8. The protected regions mechanism requires predefined regions that contain handwritten code.

Different model-to-text transformation languages provide built-in support for declaring protected regions, including XPand [24], Acceleo [25], Epsilon Generation Language [26], JET [27] and MOFScript [28]. Some of these languages have different names for the protected region mechanism, e.g., protected area [13], user code block in Acceleo, user region in JET, and unprotected block in MOFScript.

A major drawback of protected regions is that it cannot be guaranteed that the generator preserves handwritten implementations. The reason for this is that handwritten code is mixed with generated code. In addition, to support this mechanism, a guarantee has to be given that the identification string is unique and stable. Otherwise, handwritten code may get lost in some situations.

Evaluation

C1: Separation of Generated and Handwritten Code. Unfulfilled. The handwritten and generated parts are mixed within the same files, therefore there is no separation according to our criterion.

C2: Support for Overriding Generated Parts. Unfulfilled. It is not possible to override generated code. Only explicitly designated parts can be extended.

C3: Extendability of the Generated Interfaces. Fulfilled. An extension of the API can be achieved by generating in such a way that protected regions are introduced into the generated interfaces. Then, methods can be added to that protected region.

C4: Independence of Handwritten Code at Generation-time. Unfulfilled. The generator has to analyze the previously generated code·to extract handwritten code from protected regions. Otherwise the generator would not be able to inject that code from the protected regions back into the generated code.

C5: Independence of Additional OOP Language Constructs. Fulfilled. This mechanism does not require any kind of OOP language construct at all.

Alternatives. The Eclipse Modeling Framework (EMF) [29] applies a mechanism to integrate handwritten code which is different to protected regions described so far, but conceptually comparable. In EMF, every class, method etc. that is generated, includes a Javadoc comment that contains a generated tag [30]. By removing the generated tag the generated implementation can be changed. Hence, removing the generated tag corresponds to introducing a protected region.

5   Discussion

In this section, we summarize and discuss the evaluation results shown in Table 1. A plus sign in a table cell indicates that the approach fulfills the corresponding criterion, whereas a minus sign expresses that the criterion was not satisfied. Parentheses denote that the criterion is fulfilled under certain conditions.

All approaches, except for protected regions, separate generated and handwritten code on the basis of files. Thus, it is ensured that the handwritten code is not overwritten because only the generated files are overwritten. However, the protected regions approach combines generated and handwritten code. Consequently, this approach does not protect handwritten code from being overwritten.

Table 1 also shows that the extended generation gap approach, the AOP approach and the PartMerger approach provide the most flexibility when overriding generated parts and extending the generated interfaces. For partial classes, it depends on the actual programming language being used whether it is possible to override generated parts or not. Moreover, it also depends on the programming language, if besides partial classes also partial interfaces are supported. The situation is different for include mechanisms. Here, we are not aware of any language allowing for includes in interfaces to extend the generated interfaces. However, the concept itself does not forbid such behavior. Therefore, its applicability also depends on the used language.

All approaches but the extended generation gap mechanism and protected regions do not need to check for the existence of handwritten code at generation-time. The extended generation gap approach demands the generator to check for the existence of a handwritten interface or implementation class. In case of protected regions, the generator has to extract the handwritten code from the generated code before (re)generating to be able to reinsert it into the generated code.

Table 1. Overview of integration mechanisms and results of analysis with respect to the criteria.

	Generation Gap	Extended Gen. Gap	Delegation	Include Mechanism	Partial Classes	AOP	PartMerger	Protected Regions
C1: Separation of Generated and Handwritten Code	+	+	+	+	+	+	+	-
C2: Support for Overriding Generated Parts	+	+	-	-	(+)	+	+	-
C3: Extendability of the Generated Interfaces	-	+	-	(+)	(+)	+	+	+
C4: Independence of Handwritten Code at Generation-time	+	-	+	+	+	+	+	-
C5: Independence of Additional OOP Language Constructs	+	+	+	-	-	-	+	+

Moreover, Table 1 illustrates that only the following approaches can be used without requiring other language constructs than the default OOP language constructs: generation gap, extended generation gap, delegation, PartMerger and protected regions. All other mechanisms depend on additional language constructs which are not provided by default by OOP languages, e.g., include functionality or partial classes.

A topic that should be discussed when allowing to add handwritten code is the support for restricting what parts of the generated code can be overridden. If it needs to be ensured that specific generated code is executed in the software system, it should not be possible to override such parts. This is mostly true for parts of the software system that define a static and fix behavior without any chance of adaptation. Approaches that do not support overriding generated parts such as delegation, include mechanisms and protected regions ensure this property by construction. This means that handwritten code can only be introduced in designated regions. For generation gap and the extended generation gap, generated methods have to be generated using specific modifiers (e.g. private modifier) of the underlying OOP language to prevent that these methods can be overridden. For the PartMerger approach, it has to be ensured that the PartMerger can be configured in a way to not override generated code. This protected code may be marked in a specific way. When applying AOP, it depends on the programming language used whether it can be restricted that handwritten code is executed instead of specific other generated code. Finally, the partial classes mechanism is generally not designed in a way that parts of the generated code are protected, because the different parts are merged. However, it depends on the compiler and programming language, which may support such a mechanism.

6   Related Work

To the best of our knowledge, no other publication exists which gives a comparable overview and evaluation of different integration mechanisms. However, as most of the presented mechanisms have been described by other authors, we give an overview of existing work in this section.

Pietrek et al. [14] list guidelines on how to integrate generated and handwritten artifacts including generation gap, protected regions, as well as include mechanisms. These mechanisms are also covered in [31].

Similarly, Stahl et al. [13] describe the adaptation of different design patterns - in particular delegation - to integrate handwritten and generated code. These mechanisms are also discussed in [32,33]. The latter covers aspect-oriented methods as well. This concept is also employed in [34–36]. Additionally, a brief overview of integration mechanisms is given in [19]. It includes different variations of the generation gap, partial classes and protected regions mechanisms.

Approaches that specifically target .NET as the target platform and thus allow special language features including partial classes are covered in [37,38]. Both also cover protected regions, as well as generation gap and delegation.

The mechanisms supported in MetaEdit+ [39] are protected regions, functionality externalized in files (similar to the include approach in our paper) as well as the direct inclusion of handwritten code in model files and are described in [40]. Direct inclusion of handwritten code in model files has been left out, because we put the focus on integrating handwritten code in generated code.

The different approaches that affect the implementation of model-driven architecture are presented in [41]. They range from the unidirectional code inclusion to complete round-trip engineering, where code portions of handwritten code are traced and reflected back into the model.

The code generator LLBLGen Pro [42] supports different target infrastructures and allows the integration of handwritten code through protected regions, user-specific templates that are included during the generation process, as well as language-specific features such as partial classes.

The approach described in [43] supports the concept of partial classes for generated object-oriented code and protected regions for code that does not support this mechanism. Additionally, Brückmann et al. [44] advocate patterns such as delegation to incorporate manually written code in generated parts.

7   Extend Generated Code with Action Languages

The integration of handwritten code into generated code is mainly done by using mechanisms provided by the target language. A different approach to extend generated code is to embed an action language into the used modeling language.

An action language can be a (restricted) expression language (e.g., a boolean expression language), a DSL for behavior description (e.g., statecharts), or even a general-purpose language such as Java. For instance, UML provides a designated action language [45]. The main idea is to describe the implementation of specific model parts within the model by using the action language [40]. A code generator is finally responsible for merging this embedded code into the generated code. For instance, the body of a method in a UML class diagram could be described in Java and the generator can merge this Java code into the method body part of the generated code.

The major drawback of this approach is that the models are polluted with technical implementation details. In addition to that, the tool support to implement code within models is typically less sophisticated than the tool support for implementing code in a typical IDE. Mainly, the difference to the integration mechanisms described so far is that the code to be integrated is embedded in the model and not implemented separately in an external source code file. Moreover, the action language may require a code generator to map it to a concrete implementation. Nevertheless, additional code can be added to the generated code quite easily.

There are three variants of applying action languages that are not based on a direct embedding in a modeling language. Figure 9 shows all three variants. The first approach is to embed references to the action language code into the model instead of embedding the complete action language code directly into the model [40]. Even though this decreases the level of pollution of the models, the models are still polluted with technical details. Another variant is that the action language code references the modeling language element where it is to be used. Finally, a configuration can be used to link action language code and the modeling language element. The commonality of all variants is that an infrastructure is required to merge the action language code and the generated code.

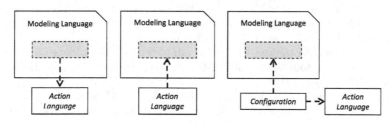

Fig. 9. Three variants of applying action languages.

8 Conclusion

Current model-driven development (MDD) techniques require tool developers to integrate generated and handwritten code to create a complete software system. In this journal paper, we presented eight integration mechanisms useful for OOP languages: generation gap, extended generation gap, delegation, include mechanisms, partial classes, AOP, PartMerger, and protected regions. These mechanisms are compared with respect to a set of five evaluation criteria that aim to address essential aspects of handwritten and generated code integration. For instance, if generated and handwritten code can be separated or if it is possible to override generated parts. Our evaluation results are summarized in Table 1 and show that no mechanism is the best solution.

Essentially, choosing a suitable mechanism for integrating handwritten and generated code depends on the concrete use case and the associated requirements. The catalog of integration mechanisms and evaluation criteria presented in this paper provides an overview for MDD-tool developers that can be used to find an appropriate integration approach on a case-by-case basis. In this extension of our previous work, we present action languages as another approach to integrate handwritten and generated code and discussed issues related to restricting parts that can be overridden to emphasize concerns that have to be regarded when choosing the right mechanism.

The proposed evaluation criteria are not complete and may not be sufficient to choose an appropriate mechanism in special cases. Nevertheless, the approaches and criteria shown in this paper can be used as a foundation that can be adapted and extended to fit specific requirements.

References

1. France, R., Rumpe, B.: Model-driven development of complex software: a research roadmap. In: Future of Software Engineering, ICSE 2007, pp. 37–54. IEEE Computer Society (2007)
2. Kleppe, A.G., Warmer, J., Bast, W.: MDA Explained: The Model Driven Architecture: Practice and Promise. Addison-Wesley Longman Publishing Co., Inc., Boston (2003)
3. Wile, D.S.: Lessons learned from real DSL experiments. In: Proceedings of the 36th Annual Hawaii International Conference on System Sciences, HICSS 2003, pp. 265–290. IEEE Computer Society (2003)
4. Rumpe, B.: Modellierung mit UML, 2nd edn. Springer, Heidelberg (2011)
5. Rumpe, B.: Agile Modellierung mit UML: Codegenerierung, Testfälle, Refactoring. Springer, Heidelberg (2012)
6. Rumpe, B., Schindler, M., Völkel, S., Weisemöller, I.: Generative software development. In: Proceedings of the 32nd International Conference on Software Engineering, ICSE 2010, pp. 473–474. ACM (2010)
7. Schindler, M.: Eine Werkzeuginfrastruktur zur agilen Entwicklung mit der UML/P. Ph.D. thesis, RWTH Aachen University (2012)
8. Grönniger, H., Hartmann, J., Krahn, H., Kriebel, S., Rothhardt, L., Rumpe, B.: Modelling automotive function nets with views for features, variants, and modes. In: Proceedings of Embedded Real Time Software and Systems, ERTS 2008 (2008)
9. Navarro Pérez, A., Rumpe, B.: Modeling cloud architectures as interactive systems. In: 2nd International Workshop on Model-Driven Engineering for High Performance and CLoud computing, MDHPCL 2013, Miami, Florida, CEUR Workshop Proceedings, pp. 15–24 (2013)
10. Ringert, J.O., Rumpe, B., Wortmann, A.: From software architecture structure and behavior modeling to implementations of cyber-physical systems. In: Software Engineering 2013 Workshopband, GI, pp. 155–170. Köllen Druck+Verlag GmbH, Bonn (2013)

11. Kurpick, T., Pinkernell, C., Look, M., Rumpe, B.: Modeling cyber-physical systems: model-driven specification of energy efficient buildings. In: Proceedings of the Modelling of the Physical World Workshop, MOTPW 2012, pp. 2:1–2:6. ACM (2012)

12. Greifenberg, T., Hölldobler, K., Kolassa, C., Look, M., Mir Seyed Nazari, P., Müller, K., Navarro Perez, A., Plotnikov, D., Reiss, D., Roth, A., Rumpe, B., Schindler, M., Wortmann, A.: A comparison of mechanisms for integrating handwritten and generated code for object-oriented programming languages. In: Proceedings of the 3rd International Conference on Model-Driven Engineering and Software Development, Angers, France, pp. 74–85. Scitepress (2015)

13. Stahl, T., Völter, M.: Model-Driven Software Development: Technology, Engineering, Management. Wiley, UK (2006)

14. Pietrek, G., Trompeter, J., Niehues, B., Kamann, T., Holzer, B., Kloss, M., Thoms, K., Beltran, J.C.F., Mork, S.: Modellgetriebene Softwareentwicklung. MDA und MDSD in der Praxis. Entwickler.Press (2007)

15. Parnas, D.L.: On the criteria to be used in decomposing systems into modules. Commun. ACM **15**(12), 1053–1058 (1972)

16. Gamma, E., Helm, R., Johnson, R., Vlissides, J.: Design Patterns: Elements of Reusable Object-Oriented Software. Addison-Wesley Professional, Boston (1995)

17. Eliens, A.: Principles of Object-Oriented Software Development. Addison-Wesley Longman Publishing Co., Inc., Boston (1994)

18. Vlissides, J.: Pattern Hatching: Design Patterns Applied. Addison-Wesley, UK (1998)

19. Fowler, M.: Domain Specific Languages. Addison-Wesley, Boston (2010)

20. Kiczales, G., Lamping, J., Mendhekar, A., Maeda, C., Lopes, C., Loingtier, J.-M., Irwin, J.: Aspect-oriented programming. In: Akşit, M., Matsuoka, S. (eds.) ECOOP 1997. LNCS, vol. 1241, pp. 220–242. Springer, Heidelberg (1997)

21. Kellens, A., Mens, K., Brichau, J., Gybels, K.: Managing the evolution of aspect-oriented software with model-based pointcuts. In: Thomas, D. (ed.) ECOOP 2006. LNCS, vol. 4067, pp. 501–525. Springer, Heidelberg (2006)

22. Grönniger, H., Krahn, H., Rumpe, B., Schindler, M., Völkel, S.: MontiCore: a framework for the development of textual domain specific languages. In: 30th International Conference on Software Engineering, ICSE 2008, pp. 925–926. ACM (2008)

23. Krahn, H., Rumpe, B., Völkel, S.: MontiCore: a framework for compositional development of domain specific languages. Int. J. Softw. Tools Technol. Transf. **12**, 353–372 (2010)

24. XPand website, May 2014. http://www.eclipse.org/modeling/m2t/?project=xpand#xpand. Accessed on 13 May 2015

25. Acceleo website, May 2014. http://www.eclipse.org/acceleo/. Accessed on 13 May 2015

26. Rose, L.M., Paige, R.F., Kolovos, D.S., Polack, F.A.C.: The epsilon generation language. In: Schieferdecker, I., Hartman, A. (eds.) ECMDA-FA 2008. LNCS, vol. 5095, pp. 1–16. Springer, Heidelberg (2008)

27. JET website, May 2014. http://www.eclipse.org/modeling/m2t/?project=jet#jet. Accessed on 13 May 2015

28. Oldevik, J., Neple, T., Grønmo, R., Aagedal, J.Ø., Berre, A.-J.: Toward standardised model to text transformations. In: Hartman, A., Kreische, D. (eds.) ECMDA-FA 2005. LNCS, vol. 3748, pp. 239–253. Springer, Heidelberg (2005)

29. Budinsky, F., Steinberg, D., Merks, E., Ellersick, R., Grose, T.J.: Eclipse Modeling Framework, 2nd edn. Addison-Wesley, Boston (2008)

30. Gronback, R.C.: Eclipse Modeling Project: A Domain-Specific Language (DSL) Toolkit. Addison-Wesley, Boston (2009)
31. Petrasch, R., Meimberg, O.: Model-Driven Architecture: Eine praxisorientierte Einführung in die MDA. Dpunkt Verlag, Heidelberg (2006)
32. Völter, M.: A Catalog of Patterns for Program Generation, Version 1.6, April 2003. http://www.voelter.de/data/pub/ProgramGeneration.pdf. Accessed on 13 May 2015
33. Völter, M., Bettin, J.: Patterns for Model-Driven Software-Development, Version 1.4, May 2004. http://www.voelter.de/data/pub/MDDPatterns.pdf. Accessed on 13 May 2015
34. Groher, I., Voelter, M.: Aspect-oriented model-driven software product line engineering. In: Katz, S., Ossher, H., France, R., Jézéquel, J.-M. (eds.) Transactions on Aspect-Oriented Software Development VI. LNCS, vol. 5560, pp. 111–152. Springer, Heidelberg (2009)
35. Völter, M., Groher, I.: Handling variability in model transformations and generators. In: Proceedings of the 7th OOPSLA Workshop on Domain-Specific Modeling, DSM 2007. ACM (2007)
36. Kang, K.C., Sugumaran, V., Park, S.: Applied Software Product Line Engineering. Auerbach Publications, Boston (2009)
37. Dollard, K.: Code Generation in Microsoft .NET. Apress, Berkley (2004)
38. Greenfield, J., Short, K., Cook, S., Kent, S.: Software Factories: Assembling Applications with Patterns, Models, Frameworks, and Tools. Wiley, New York (2004)
39. Tolvanen, J.P., Kelly, S.: MetaEdit+: defining and using integrated domain-specific modeling languages. In: Proceeding of the 24th ACM SIGPLAN Conference Companion on Object Oriented Programming Systems Languages and Applications, OOPSLA 2009, pp. 819–820. ACM (2009)
40. Kelly, S., Tolvanen, J.P.: Domain-Specific Modeling: Enabling Full Code Generation. Wiley, New York (2008)
41. Frankel, D.S.: Model Driven Architecture: Applying MDA to Enterprise Computing. Wiley, New York (2003)
42. LLBLGen Pro website, May 2014. http://www.llblgen.com/. Accessed on 13 May 2015
43. Warmer, J., Kleppe, A.: Building a flexible software factory using partial domain specific models. In: Proceedings of the 6th OOPSLA Workshop on Domain-Specific Modeling, DSM 2006, pp. 15–22. ACM (2006)
44. Brückmann, T., Gruhn, V.: An architectural blueprint for model driven development and maintenance of business logic for information systems. In: Babar, M.A., Gorton, I. (eds.) ECSA 2010. LNCS, vol. 6285, pp. 53–69. Springer, Heidelberg (2010)
45. Object Management Group website: Concrete Syntax for a UML Action Language: Action Language for Foundational UML (ALF) Version 1.0.1 (2013–09–01), May 2014. http://www.omg.org/spec/ALF/1.0.1/PDF/

A Framework for Metamodel Composition and Adaptation with Conformance-Preserving Model Migration

Ingrid Chieh Yu[✉] and Henning Berg

Department of Informatics, University of Oslo, Oslo, Norway
{ingridcy,hennb}@ifi.uio.no

Abstract. Metamodels are important artefacts in Model-Driven Engineering. Composition and adaptation of metamodels have been studied thoroughly during the last decade. However, there are still challenges concerning how to co-evolve modelling artefacts as metamodels are changed. Specifically, conformant models will no longer be valid instances of their changed metamodel. In this paper, we propose a formal analysis-based framework for composition and adaptation of metamodels. The framework enables an arbitrary number of metamodels to evolve based on adaptation strategies. During the analysis we accumulate information that are used to re-establish conformance between existing models and the metamodels. We prove how model conformance is ensured based on the accumulated information from the analysis.

1 Introduction

From a broad view, software engineering is the process of understanding a system and representing it as a set of models that can be understood by computers. The models allow reasoning about the system and perform various analyses and evaluation of system-specific data; whether the system already exists or is to be built. Modelling is the process of creating abstractions of a system. A system may itself be a model [5,25], something that has given us the notion of *metamodelling*. Metamodelling is the process of formalising models by indentifying their structure and semantics. The result of such a process is one or more metamodels.

Metamodelling is a key process in several *Model-Driven Engineering (MDE)* [13] disciplines including language design, product line engineering, variability management and domain modelling. The promised benefits of using model-oriented approaches are increased efficiency, quality and consistency in software. Using models also supports code generation, multi-view modelling and improved verification of system properties. There are clear incentives in the industry for applying MDE approaches, as shorter time to market for software products and mechanisms that support variability are needed.

A metamodel is defined according to the rules and constraints of a metamodelling architecture or metamodelling framework. The prominent metamodelling architecture in the industry is the *Object Management Group (OMG)* standardised *MetaObject Facility (MOF)* [21], and a variant based on *Essential MOF*

© Springer International Publishing Switzerland 2015
P. Desfray et al. (Eds.): MODELSWARD 2015, CCIS 580, pp. 133–154, 2015.
DOI: 10.1007/978-3-319-27869-8_8

(EMOF) implemented in the *Eclipse Modeling Framework (EMF)* named *Ecore* [28]. Both MOF and Ecore have concepts for creating standalone metamodels of arbitrary domains. However, the architectures do not have built-in mechanisms that address co-evolution of models as metamodels change. One such change or adaptation is composition of metamodels. Composition may be used to increase a metamodel's expressiveness or to weave in variability [4,6,15,17,18].

A model is said to conform to its metamodel when all elements in the model are legal instances of structural elements found in the metamodel. Changing the metamodel typically causes the conformance relation to be broken. Consequently, the models are no longer valid according to the changed metamodel. This is unfortunate as it creates system inconsistencies.

There are three main categories of approaches available that address how models, transformations and tools may adapt to changes of evolving metamodels [23]. These are *manual specification, operator-based co-evolution* and *metamodel matching*, where the latter category may be further divided into *change recording* and *differencing*. In this paper we present a novel approach of model migration by using analysis as a core process. Specifically, our approach is a hybrid between operator-based co-evolution and metamodel matching, where information required to re-establish model conformance is generated automatically during the analysis step. All model migration approaches we have come across are limited to what we refer to as *serial evolution*, i.e. model migration is only addressed for evolution of one metamodel at a time, where the metamodel is evolved from an initial version to a revised version independently of other metamodels. However, this is an ideal case. In practice, metamodels may evolve in parallel due to dependencies that exist or are introduced *between* the metamodels. We refer to this as *parallel evolution*. Examples of dependencies that may be introduced are when metamodels are composed, e.g. by merging or interfacing classes. In the general case, there may be an arbitrary number of metamodels for which dependencies are introduced. Hence, evolving one metamodel should be reflected on the other metamodels as well. Furthermore, the evolution of the metamodels should be propagated to all existing models of all the metamodels. That is, existing models conforming to the metamodels must *all* be updated to conform to the new metamodel versions or resulting composite metamodel. This is not trivial due to the dependencies introduced, and is the reason why analysis is required. The proposed analysis framework is able to process an arbitrary number of metamodels simultaneously, and accumulates information about changes performed on the metamodels. The information is later used as input to model-to-model transformations that update existing models.

Changing or adapting metamodels do not only impact the models. Changing a metamodel also severely impacts other artefacts in the metamodelling ecosystem that are defined relative to the metamodel. Such artefacts include editors, concrete syntaxes, transformations and interpreters. Changing or altering a metamodel results in co-evolution issues with these artefacts, as the metamodel and artefacts do not evolve in a synchronised manner. Our approach is also applicable for co-evolution of artefacts. Specifically, the information generated indicates what changes that must be performed in the artefacts for these to be valid with respect to evolved metamodels. In this paper we limit our scope to describing how the conformance between models and metamodels may be re-established as the metamodels are changed or adapted. We exemplify the approach by studying how two metamodels are composed (we view metamodel composition as an adaptation).

We formalise an analysis framework based on a set of *basic adaptation operations*. The adaptation operations are fine grained and can be traced back to the catalogue of operators presented in [11]. The analysis framework systematically generates information which is needed for re-establishing conformance between the adapted metamodels and existing models. We focus on model structure and leave semantics for future work. We do not consider matching of metamodels using heuristics [3], as this is outside of our scope. However, we give our thoughts on this topic with respect to our approach in Sect. 6 where we briefly describe how to incorporate the use of ontologies in the analysis.

The contribution of this paper is two-fold. First, we discuss a new approach for model migration and how conformance between models and metamodels can be re-established as metamodels are adapted or composed. The approach is applicable to other artefacts in the metamodelling ecosystem, e.g. it supports metamodel-tool co-evolution. Second, we present a thorough formalisation of the analysis that is used in our approach. The formalisation not only describes our approach in details, but it gives a formalisation of how model conformance may be re-established as metamodels evolve, i.e. metamodel-model co-evolution. There is not much work available that formalises metamodel-model co-evolution. As far as we know, the only formalisations on this topic is in the form of typed graphs and category theory [16,27].

Paper overview. Section 2 gives a motivating example, Sect. 3 introduces adaptation operations for metamodel evolution, Sect. 4 addresses model conformance, Sect. 5 discusses related work, and Sect. 6 concludes the paper.

2   Motivating Example

We will motivate and explain our approach using a simplified example in the domain of ecommerce. The example will be developed throughout the paper. Ecommerce is an industry concerned with sale and purchase of products and services using Internet technologies. Ecommerce is a multi-facetted concept comprising e.g. financing and payment, pricing and marketing analysis, logistics, product modelling, business modelling and business strategies. All of these concerns are modelled in some way - either informal or in a more formal manner using e.g. a set of UML models. An increasingly popular approach is to create a set of domain-specific languages (DSLs) for each of the major concerns. This approach allows stakeholders to model their solution directly at the level of ecommerce domain concepts. That is, each domain-specific language contains a set of constructs for modelling of one explicit concern. An ecommerce solution is then the sum of all the models that describe it.

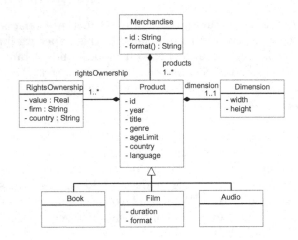

Fig. 1. Metamodel for modelling of products/merchandise.

To keep our example manageable, we will only focus on two aspects of an ecommerce solution: product modelling and business context modelling. Product modelling, as we use the term here, is the process of describing a product intended for sale - including all its metadata. Business context modelling deals with concerns such as ownership, regions where a given product or group of products should be available, price and such.

We assume that the conceptual domain of our example is sale of media products like books, films and audio. That is, our target software solution is that of an online retailer like Amazon. A product, see Fig. 1, has attributes like year of publication or release, title, genre, etc. A product has a dimension and a set of copypright owners (note that most attribute types and attribute multiplicites are excluded for clarity reasons). A product model describes either one specific product or a product group. The product model does not describe any aspects related to sale of this product.

The trading perspective is covered by the business context model, see Fig. 2, which describes the business dimension of a product or product group. That is, the business model puts a product in a business context. This includes describing the price of the product, availability, fees and eventual discounts. A product may have several business contexts. As an example, a product may have different prices and discounts depending on the region of sale.

The two metamodels, supporting modelling of concerns in two different domains, may be combined to form a new metamodel for ecommerce, see Fig. 3. The new metamodel has a class named MBC that is a combination of the Merchandise and BusinessContext classes. The metamodel is also extended with a new ProfitShare concept. In the subsequent sections, we will demonstrate how the new metamodel is systematically derived.

3   Metamodel Adaptations

We base our analysis framework and example on an excerpt of the MOF structural concepts [21, 26]. The excerpt represents the most essential concepts of MOF:

$$
\begin{aligned}
Metamodel &::= \text{package } P \; \{\overline{ClassDecl}\} \\
ClassDecl &::= \text{class } C \text{ extends } \overline{C}' \; \{\overline{PropDecl \; OpDecl}\} \\
PropDecl &::= t \; P \; (Multi)? \; (containment)? \; (\# \; P')? \\
Multi &::= [lower \; .. \; upper] \\
OpDecl &::= t \; O(\overline{t_i \; P_i}) \\
t \in Type &::= Primitive \mid C \mid set\langle C\rangle \mid \text{Void} \\
Primitive &::= \text{Boolean} \mid \text{Integer} \mid \text{Real} \mid \text{String}
\end{aligned}
$$

A metamodel consists of a package with one or more classes. (In general a metamodel may have several packages, which can be easily accommodated by our approach.) A class may have an arbitrary number of properties and operations. Properties do either have primitive types or class types. Hence, they either act as attributes or references. *containment* takes the values true or false, whereas *lower* and *upper* are natural numbers. In this paper, we use the term *well-typed metamodel* as a model satisfying the requirements in [21]. Specifically we have the following typing restrictions on property and operation definitions in MOF metamodels that inherently affect the proposed adaptation rules:

– A property name can only occur once in a class hierarchy.
– Operations may be overloaded in the same class, but only occur once with the same signature.
– Overloaded operations in a class hierarchy that have the same parameter types require the same return type.

We formalise metamodel adaptations in terms of *basic adaptation operations*. We consider constructive operations, where the adaptation operations do not

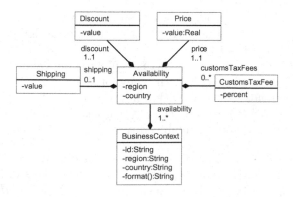

Fig. 2. Metamodel for modelling of business contexts.

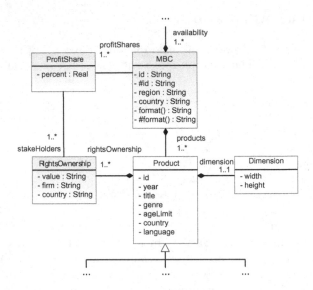

Fig. 3. The metamodel resulting from composing the metamodels for product and business context modelling.

remove classes, properties, or operations. The operations are not neccessarily model-preserving [11] and can be combined to form more complex adaptation strategies. We do not aim at theoretical completeness but rather focus on common practical adaptations. The framework is structured in such a way that it can easily be extended by adding more operations.

Metamodels can be adapted using the following basic adaptation operations, where N and N' are class names, C a class term, P a property definition, O an operation definition, and $\mathcal{R}$ a tuple $\langle N, \overline{P} \rangle$:

- *merge*(N, N') creates a new class by merging two classes named N and N'
- *addClass*(C) adds a new class definition
- *addSuperClass*(N, N') extends the class named N with a new superclass N'
- *addInterfaceClass*$(C, \mathcal{R})$ adds a class C that serves to bridge classes according to the relations specified in $\mathcal{R}$
- *override*(N, N') overrides the class named N with the definition of N'
- *addProp*(N, P) extends class N with a new property P
- *addOp*(N, O) extends a class N with a new operation O
- *addBiProp*(N, P, N', P') extends class N with a property P and N' with a property P', where P and P' combined describe a bi-directional relation.

Note that the *merge*, *addSuperClass* and *override* operations differ from other operations in the sense that existing models may have objects that relate to the structure of the operands (i.e. the classes). That is, *addClass*, *addInterfaceClass*, *addProp*, *addOp* and *addBiProp* deal with adding new metaelements for which no existing objects relate to. Still, it may be required to generate default objects of added structure. We will return to this later.

A sequence of adaptation operations, $\varphi_1 \cdot \varphi_2 \cdot \cdots \cdot \varphi_n$, defines an *adaptation strategy* Φ for a particular metamodel adaptation. An adaptation strategy can be seen as a description that differentiates one metamodel variant from another. The adaptation strategy and sequence of operations are given by the user, e.g. as provided using a graphical tool (i.e. not specified textually). Figure 4 gives a conceptual overview of the analysis framework and how two metamodels are composed by using the *merge* operation. Specifically, the classes represented by filled boxes are merged according to a merge strategy specified by the user. Notice the references to the classes marked with x. The multiplicities have a lower bound equal to 1, which indicates that objects of the classes need to be created to have conformant models. We will later see how this is addressed by the framework.

3.1 The Analysis Environment

The analysis environment for metamodel adaptations consists of a tuple $\langle \mathcal{E}, \sigma, \delta \rangle$:

Definition 1. *The environment mapping $\mathcal{E}$ maps class names Nc to class definitions: $\mathcal{E} : Nc \rightarrow Class$, where Class is a set of classes $\langle Nc, Inh, Prop, Op \rangle$. Nc is the name of the class. Inh is a list of class names defining class inheritance (direct superclasses). Prop is a set of properties $\langle Type, Np, Multi, Cont, Opp \rangle$ where Type is a type, Np a property name, Multi the property's multiplicity comprising a lower and upper bound, Cont describing whether the property is of containment type, and Opp the name of an optional opposite relation. Op is a set of class operations $\langle Type, No, Param \rangle$ where Type is the operation's return type, No is the operation's name and Param is a list of input parameter declarations.*

Dot notation is used to access the elements of tuples such as properties and operations; e.g. $(C, \overline{I}, \overline{P}, \overline{O}).Prop = \overline{P}$, where we use overlines to denote sets or list structures. $Prop(N)$ denotes a subset of properties in $Prop$ with name N and $Prop.Np$ gives all property names in $Prop$. Similar notation is used for Op. The empty list is denoted ϵ.

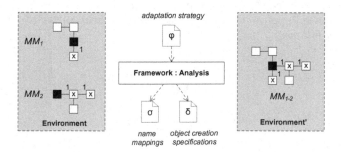

Fig. 4. Illustration of the analysis and the *merge* operation.

Definition 2. *The environment mapping* σ *consists of a family of mappings* $\langle \sigma_c, \sigma_p, \sigma_o \rangle$:

$$\sigma_c : Nc \;\rightarrow\; Nc$$
$$\sigma_p : Np \;\overset{Nc}{\rightarrow}\; Np$$
$$\sigma_o : No \;\overset{Nc}{\rightarrow}\; No$$

where Nc, Np *and* No *are class, property and operation names, respectively. For* σ_p *and* σ_o, Nc *(above the arrow) specifies the containing class of the property and operation.*

The family of mappings contains substitutions accumulated during the analysis of classes, properties and operations, respectively. Substitutions are introduced in the adaptation analysis to resolve conflicts associated with overlapping metamodel definitions and will be used to ensure conformance for the underlying models. A mapping family σ is built from the empty mapping family $\emptyset$.

Default objects have to be created of a property's type if the lower bound of its multiplicity is unequal to zero. This is required to preserve conformance. It is irrelevant if the property has a class type or primitive type. A property implicitly has a multiplicity of $0..1$ if no multiplicity is stated. δ contains tuples of the form $\langle Nc, Np, Nat \rangle$ which maintain information of what objects that have to be created in the existing models as a consequence of new properties. Nc is the name of the class whose objects will contain or refer objects of Np's type[1]. The number of objects that need to be created is described by the natural number Nat, e.g. a property with multiplicity $3..4$ requires the creation of three default objects to preserve conformance.

The adaptation analysis of a syntactic construct D is formalised by a deductive system for judgements $\langle \mathcal{E}, \sigma, \delta \rangle \vdash D \; \langle \mathcal{E}', \sigma', \delta' \rangle$, where $\langle \mathcal{E}, \sigma, \delta \rangle$ is the analysis environment *before* and $\langle \mathcal{E}', \sigma', \delta' \rangle$ is the environment *after* the analysis of D, where $\mathcal{E}'$ represents a package containing the derived metamodel. For updating the analysis environment, we use the associative operator $+$ on mappings with the identity element $\emptyset$. Let $\mathcal{E} + \mathcal{E}'$ denote $\mathcal{E}$ *overriden* by $\mathcal{E}'$. Mappings are now formally defined.

Definition 3. *Let* n *be a name,* d *a declaration,* $i \in I$ *a mapping index, and* $[n \overset{c}{\mapsto}_i d]$ *the binding of* n *to* d *indexed by* i. *A mapping family* σ *is built from the empty mapping family* $\emptyset$ *and indexed bindings by the constructor* $+$. *The extraction of an indexed mapping* σ_i *from* σ *and application for the mapping* $\mathcal{E}$, *are defined as follows*

$$
\begin{aligned}
\emptyset_i &= \varepsilon \\
(\sigma + [n \overset{c}{\mapsto}_{i'} d])_i &= \text{if } i = i' \text{ then } \sigma_i + [n \overset{c}{\mapsto}_i d] \\
&\quad\; \text{else } \sigma_i \\
\varepsilon(n) &= \bot \\
(\mathcal{E} + [n \mapsto d])(n') &= \text{if } n = n' \text{ then } d \\
&\quad\; \text{else } \mathcal{E}(n')
\end{aligned}
$$

---

[1] The exact realisation of object containment is dependent on the underlying implementation.

Assume given two well-typed metamodels, $\mathcal{MM}_1$ and $\mathcal{MM}_2$. Since the meta-models are from two different domains, we assume unique class names (otherwise, this can easily be resolved by package annotations on class names). The environment $\mathcal{E}$ will initially contain well-typed class definitions from $\mathcal{MM}_1$ and $\mathcal{MM}_2$ and through a series of *adaptation operations*, we adapt or compose $\mathcal{MM}_1$ and $\mathcal{MM}_2$, causing modifications to $\mathcal{E}$ and σ, and additions to δ. The final environment that is returned after the analysis is the adapted metamodel(s) and the mappings constructed during the analysis for resolving name conflicts (i.e. substitutions generated by the framework) in addition to a specification of objects that need to be created due to property multiplicities with a non-zero lower bound.

3.2   The Adaptation Rules

Metamodels are adapted given an adaptation strategy Φ, $\mathcal{E}$ of initial metamodel definitions, an empty mapping σ, and an empty set of object creation specifications δ. Thus if $\mathcal{E}, \emptyset, \emptyset \vdash \Phi \langle \mathcal{E}', \sigma', \delta' \rangle$, then we derive the resulting environment $\langle \mathcal{E}', \sigma', \delta' \rangle$. The adaptation rules are given in Figs. 5 and 6. The involved operations are applied in a sequential manner as illustrated in Rule (SEQ):

The analysis environment propagates throughout the analysis, i.e. $\overline{\varphi_2}$ is analysed in the context resulting from the analysis of φ_1. Note that the substitution, denoted $[\varphi]_\sigma$, rewrites φ into normal form in Rule (SEQ). σ is accumulated through sequential analysis of the adaptation operations, thus the substitution is deterministic; the rule substitutes input class, property and operation names by mappings in σ before retrieving or updating class information and thus ensures that class definitions from the latest environment are used in each basic rule application. By transitivity a sequence of class mergings is possible, e.g. $[X]_{[X \mapsto_c Y] + [Y \mapsto_c Z] + [Z \mapsto_c V]}$ maps the class named X to V. Rules for metamodel composition and class addition are given in Fig. 5. In Rule (ADD CLASS) the analysis environment is extended with a new class definition that is previously not defined. Rule (CLASS MERGE) merges two classes C and C' into a class given a fresh name D, represented by *fresh(D)*. The new class will replace C and C' in the analysis environment, hence the rule redirects references by creating mappings from the old classes to D. We assume that metamodels are well-typed prior to adaptation. However, it is likely that overlapping definitions occur when classes are merged, which introduce type errors. Consequently, the rule will consider and *resolve* overlapping definitions that exist between the classes, i.e. C and C', and their superclasses. The auxiliary functions *anProp* and *anOp* (given in Fig. 7) traverse the inheritance tree and resolve conflicts so that all property names are unique within the resulting class hierarchy, and that equally named operations with the same input types have the same return type. Mappings containing information of resolved conflicts are returned from the application of the rule (σ''). Finally, the class definition for D is constructed by specifying the superclasses of both C and C', and adding sets of conflict-free properties and operations, i.e. $[\overline{P; P'}]_{\sigma''}$ and $[\overline{O; O'}]_{\sigma''}$, respectively. The class D is added to $\mathcal{E}'$ whereas C and C' are removed. As other classes in $\mathcal{E}$ may still have old

$$(\text{Add Class})$$

$$\mathcal{E}(C) = \bot \qquad \mathcal{E}' = \mathcal{E} + [C \mapsto \langle C, \epsilon, \emptyset, \emptyset \rangle]$$
$$\forall P \in \overline{P} \cdot \mathcal{E}', \emptyset, \emptyset \vdash addProp(C, P)\langle \mathcal{E}'', \emptyset, \delta' \rangle$$
$$\forall O \in \overline{O} \cdot \mathcal{E}'', \emptyset, \emptyset \vdash addOp(C, O)\langle \mathcal{E}''', \emptyset, \emptyset \rangle \qquad \delta'' = \bigcup \delta'$$
$$\overline{\mathcal{E}, \sigma, \delta \vdash addClass(\langle C, \epsilon, \overline{P}, \overline{O} \rangle)\langle \mathcal{E}''', \sigma, \delta \cup \delta'' \rangle}$$

$$(\text{Class Merge})$$

$$\mathcal{E}(C) = \langle C, \overline{B}, \overline{P}, \overline{O} \rangle \qquad \mathcal{E}(C') = \langle C', \overline{B'}, \overline{P'}, \overline{O'} \rangle \qquad C \neq C'$$
$$fresh(D) \qquad \sigma' = \sigma + [C \mapsto_c D] + [C' \mapsto_c D]$$
$$\sigma_p = anProp(\mathcal{E}, C, C') \qquad \sigma_o = anOp(\mathcal{E}, \sigma', C, C') \qquad \sigma'' = \sigma' + \sigma_p + \sigma_o$$
$$\mathcal{E}' = [(\mathcal{E} \setminus \{C, C'\})]_{\sigma''} + [D \mapsto \langle D, \overline{B}; \overline{B'}, [\overline{P}; \overline{P'}]_{\sigma''}, [\overline{O}; \overline{O'}]_{\sigma''} \rangle]$$
$$\delta' = createInst(C, [\overline{P'}]_{\sigma''}; flatten(\mathcal{E}', \overline{B'})) \qquad \delta'' = createInst(C', [\overline{P}]_{\sigma''}; flatten(\mathcal{E}', \overline{B}))$$
$$\overline{\mathcal{E}, \sigma, \delta \vdash merge(C, C')\langle \mathcal{E}', \sigma'', \delta \cup \delta' \cup \delta'' \rangle}$$

$$(\text{Add Superclass})$$

$$C \neq C' \quad \mathcal{E}(C) = \langle C, \overline{B}, \overline{P}, \overline{O} \rangle \quad \mathcal{E}(C') = \langle C', \overline{B'}, \overline{P'}, \overline{O'} \rangle$$
$$\sigma_p = anProp(\mathcal{E}, C, C') \qquad \sigma_o = anOpInh(\mathcal{E}, C, C')$$
$$\sigma' = \sigma_p + \sigma_o \qquad \delta' = createInst(C, \overline{P'}; flatten(\mathcal{E}_{\sigma'}, \overline{B'}))$$
$$\overline{\mathcal{E}, \sigma, \delta \vdash addSuperClass(C, C')\langle [\mathcal{E}]_{\sigma'} + C \mapsto \langle C, C'; \overline{B}, [\overline{P}]_{\sigma_p}, [\overline{O}]_{\sigma_o} \rangle, \sigma + \sigma', \delta \cup \delta' \rangle}$$

$$(\text{Add Interface Class})$$

$$isPrimitive(\overline{P}) \qquad \mathcal{E}, \sigma, \delta \vdash addClass(\langle C, \epsilon, \overline{P}, \overline{O} \rangle)\langle \mathcal{E}', \sigma, \delta \rangle \qquad opposite(\mathcal{R})$$
$$\forall (C', \overline{P''}) \in \mathcal{R} \cdot \mathcal{E}'(C') = \langle C', \overline{B}, \overline{P'}, \overline{O'} \rangle \wedge \overline{P''}.Np \cap \overline{P'}.Np = \emptyset \wedge createInst(C', \overline{P''}) = \delta''$$
$$uniqueProp(\mathcal{E}', \overline{P''}, \overline{B}) \qquad \mathcal{E}'' = \bigcup [C' \mapsto \langle C', \overline{B}, \overline{P'}; \overline{P''}, \overline{O'} \rangle] \qquad \delta''' = \bigcup \delta''$$
$$\overline{\mathcal{E}, \sigma, \delta \vdash addInterfaceClass(\langle C, \epsilon, \overline{P}, \overline{O} \rangle, \mathcal{R})\langle \mathcal{E}' + \mathcal{E}'', \sigma, \delta \cup \delta''' \rangle}$$

$$(\text{Class Override})$$

$$\mathcal{E}(C) = \langle C, \overline{B}, \overline{P}, \overline{O} \rangle \quad \mathcal{E}(C') = \langle C', \overline{B'}, \overline{P'}, \overline{O'} \rangle \quad \forall P \in \overline{P} \cdot P \in \overline{P'} \quad \forall O \in \overline{O} \cdot O \in \overline{O'}$$
$$\sigma' = [C \mapsto_c C'] \quad \sigma_p = anProp(\mathcal{E}, C', \overline{B}) \quad \sigma_o = anOpInh(\mathcal{E}, \sigma', C', \overline{B})$$
$$\sigma'' = \sigma' + \sigma_p + \sigma_o \quad \mathcal{E}' = [(\mathcal{E} \setminus C)]_{\sigma''} + [C \mapsto \langle C', \overline{B}; \overline{B'}, [\overline{P'}]_{\sigma''}, [\overline{O'}]_{\sigma''} \rangle]$$
$$createInst(C, [\overline{P'} \setminus \overline{P}]_{\sigma''}; flatten(\mathcal{E}', \overline{B'})) = \delta' \qquad createInst(C', flatten(\mathcal{E}', \overline{B})) = \delta''$$
$$\overline{\mathcal{E}, \sigma, \delta \vdash override(C, C')\langle \mathcal{E}', \sigma + \sigma'', \delta \cup \delta' \cup \delta'' \rangle}$$

Fig. 5. Definitions of the adaptation operations (rules) for class merging and additions. C and C' are class names.

references to C and C', these classes must also be updated. Consequently, we apply the substitution mapping σ'' on $\mathcal{E}$ when creating the new environment (e.g. $\langle N, \overline{I}, (C', P, m, c, P_i); \overline{P}, \overline{O} \rangle_{[C' \mapsto_c D]} \rightarrow \langle N, \overline{I}, (D, P, m, c, P_i); \overline{P}, \overline{O} \rangle$). Moreover, σ'' also contains information of resolved conflicts in superclasses, thus these superclasses must also be updated to ensure well-typedness of the modified class hierarchy. *createInst* is a function that builds specifications of default objects that need to be created to preserve conformance. We have to ensure that existing models with objects of C or C' will have required objects as imposed by properties with a lower bound unequal to zero as reachable through D. That is, properties of D, $\overline{B}$ and $\overline{B'}$. *createInst* does only specify the smallest number of required default objects needed to ensure conformance. *flatten* returns a set of all properties found in the set of classes given as argument and their respective superclasses. The environment after the application of (Class Merge) is $\langle \mathcal{E}', \sigma'', \delta \cup \delta' \cup \delta'' \rangle$. Note that we can not merge attributes with the same names

$$(\textsc{Add Property})$$

$$\frac{isPrimitive(P) \vee \mathcal{E}(P.Type) \neq \bot \quad \mathcal{E}(C) = \langle C, \overline{B}, \overline{P}, \overline{O}\rangle \quad uniqueProp(\mathcal{E}, P, C)}{\mathcal{E}, \sigma, \delta \vdash addProp(C, P)\langle \mathcal{E}', \sigma, \delta \cup \delta'\rangle}$$
$$P.Opp = \epsilon \quad \mathcal{E}' = \mathcal{E} + [C \mapsto \langle C, \overline{B}, P; \overline{P}, \overline{O}\rangle] \quad createInst(C, P) = \delta'$$

$$(\textsc{Add Bi-directional Property})$$

$$P.Type = C' \quad \mathcal{E}(C) = \langle C, \overline{B}, \overline{P}, \overline{O}\rangle \quad uniqueProp(\mathcal{E}, P, C)$$
$$P'.Type = C \quad \mathcal{E}(C') = \langle C', \overline{B}', \overline{P}', \overline{O}'\rangle \quad uniqueProp(\mathcal{E}, P', C')$$
$$\frac{P.Opp = P'.Np \quad P'.Opp = P.Np \quad \mathcal{E}' = \mathcal{E} + [C \mapsto \langle C, \overline{B}, P; \overline{P}, \overline{O}\rangle] + [C' \mapsto \langle C', \overline{B}', P'; \overline{P}', \overline{O}'\rangle]}{\mathcal{E}, \sigma, \delta \vdash addBiProp(C, P, C', P')\rangle\langle\mathcal{E}', \sigma, \delta \cup \delta' \cup \delta''\rangle}$$
$$createInst(C, P) = \delta' \quad createInst(C', P') = \delta''$$

$$(\textsc{Add Operation})$$

$$\frac{\forall t \in \{O; O.Param\} \cdot isPrimitive(t) \vee \mathcal{E}(t) \neq \bot \quad \mathcal{E}(C) = \langle C, \overline{B}, \overline{P}, \overline{O}\rangle}{\mathcal{E}, \sigma, \delta \vdash addOp(C, O)\langle\mathcal{E}', \sigma, \delta\rangle}$$
$$uniqueOp(\mathcal{E}, O, C) \quad \mathcal{E}' = \mathcal{E} + [C \mapsto \langle C, \overline{B}, \overline{P}, O; \overline{O}\rangle]$$

Fig. 6. Adaptation operations for adding new properties and operations. P and O are property and operation definitions and C is used for class names.

$anProp(\mathcal{E}, C; \overline{C}, \overline{B}) =$ $\quad an(\mathcal{E}, C, \mathcal{E}(C).Prop, \overline{B}) + anProp(\mathcal{E}, \overline{C}; \mathcal{E}(C).Inh, \overline{B})$

$an(\mathcal{E}, C, P; \overline{P}, \overline{B}) =$ $\quad an(\mathcal{E}, C, P, \overline{B}) + an(\mathcal{E}, C, \overline{P}, \overline{B})$

$an(\mathcal{E}, C, P, \epsilon) =$ $\quad \epsilon$

$an(\mathcal{E}, C, (t, P, m, c, P_i), B; \overline{B}) =$ $\quad$ if $\mathcal{E}(B).Prop(P) \neq \emptyset$ then $[P \overset{\mathcal{C}}{\mapsto}_p P'] \wedge fresh(P')$
$\quad$ else $an(\mathcal{E}, C, (t, P, m, c, P_i), \overline{B}; \mathcal{E}(B).Inh)$

$anOp(\mathcal{E}, \sigma, C, C') =$ $\quad anMerge(\mathcal{E}, \sigma, C', C, \mathcal{E}(C).Op, C') + anOpInh(\mathcal{E}, \sigma, \mathcal{E}(C).Inh, C')$

$anOpInh(\mathcal{E}, \sigma, C; \overline{C}, \overline{B}) =$ $\quad anCl(\mathcal{E}, \sigma, C, \mathcal{E}(C).Op, \overline{B}) + anOpInh(\mathcal{E}, \sigma, \overline{C}; \mathcal{E}(C).Inh, \overline{B})$

$anCl(\mathcal{E}, \sigma, C, O; \overline{O}, \overline{B}) =$ $\quad anCl(\mathcal{E}, \sigma, C, O, \overline{B}) + anCl(\mathcal{E}, \sigma, C, \overline{O}, \overline{B})$

$anCl(\mathcal{E}, \sigma, C, O, \epsilon) =$ $\quad \epsilon$

$anCl(\mathcal{E}, \sigma, C, (t, O, \overline{(t_i P_i)}), B; \overline{B}) =$ $\quad$ if $[type(\mathcal{E}(B).Op(O).Param)]_\sigma = [\overline{t_i}]_\sigma$ then
$\quad\quad$ if $[\mathcal{E}(B).Op(O).Type]_\sigma = [t]_\sigma$ then ϵ
$\quad\quad$ else $[O \overset{f}{\mapsto}_o O'] \wedge fresh(O')$
$\quad$ else $anCl(\mathcal{E}, \sigma, C, (t, O, \overline{(t_i P_i)}), \overline{B}; \mathcal{E}(B).Inh)$

$anMerge(\mathcal{E}, \sigma, C', C, O; \overline{O}, \overline{B}) =$ $\quad anMerge(\mathcal{E}, \sigma, C', C, O, \overline{B}) + anMerge(\mathcal{E}, \sigma, C', C, \overline{O}, \overline{B})$

$anMerge(\mathcal{E}, \sigma, C', C, O, \epsilon) =$ $\quad \epsilon$

$anMerge(\mathcal{E}, \sigma, C', C, (t, O, \overline{(t_i P_i)}), B; \overline{B}) =$ if $[type(\mathcal{E}(B).Op(O).Param)]_\sigma = [\overline{t_i}]_\sigma$ then
$\quad\quad$ if $B = C'$then $[O \overset{f}{\mapsto}_o O'] \wedge fresh(O')$
$\quad\quad$ else if $[\mathcal{E}(B).Op(O).Type]_\sigma = [t]_\sigma$ then ϵ
$\quad\quad$ else $[O \overset{f}{\mapsto}_o O'] \wedge fresh(O')$
$\quad$ else $anMerge(\mathcal{E}, \sigma, C', C, (t, O, \overline{(t_i P_i)}), \overline{B}; \mathcal{E}(B).Inh)$

Fig. 7. Definition of the auxiliary functions $anOp$ and $anProp$.

because these attributes may not represent the same concept from an ontological perspective, i.e. the attributes may describe different domain entities.

Rule (Add Superclass) extends class C with a new superclass C' and overrides the old class definition. Similar to Rule (Class Merge), the class hierarchy is traversed and conflicting definitions are resolved. The resulting environment contains an updated version of C that replaces the previous version of the class. In particular, C additionally inherits from C'.

Rule (Add Interface Class) creates a new class (by Rule (Add Class)) and constructs references between this and existing classes in the environment. *opposite* verifies that bi-directional relationships are correctly specified in $\mathcal{R}$. As there are no name conflicts, the mapping σ remains unchanged after the analysis. *isPrimitive* verifies that the type of the input, e.g. a property, is primitive. Rule (Class Override) allows a class C' to override a class C if C' subsumes C. Finally, rules for extending classes with new operations and properties are given in Fig. 6.

The operations *addClass*, *addInterfaceClass*, *addProp*, *addOp* and *addBiProp* add new metaelements, therefore there are no existing models that refer to these elements. Consequently σ, which is later used to update existing models, remains unchanged for these operations. Rule (ADD PROPERTY) adds a new primitive- or class-typed property to an existing class. In contrast to Rule (ADD BI-DIRECTIONAL PROPERTY), this rule addresses properties without an opposite relation. Rule (ADD BI-DIRECTIONAL PROPERTY) adds a bi-directional relationship between two classes and verifies that its constituent uni-directional relationships are correct. Rule (ADD OPERATION) adds a new operation to a class. For the rules in Fig. 6, *uniqueProp* ensures that the new property is not previously defined within super- or sub-classes in the class hierarchy and *uniqueOp* verifies correct overloading of the new operation. See the requirements for well-typedness stated in Sect. 3. Notice that we do not resolve conflicts when new structure is added to the environment. As before, *createInst* creates a set of specifications for objects that need to be created to ensure conformance.

3.3   Example Revisited

We revisit the example introduced in Sect. 2 and show how the analysis framework addresses composition of the metamodels, resulting in the metamodel in Fig. 3. We show the intermediate analysis steps and use the following abbreviations for class names: M for Merchandise, ROS for RightsOwnership, BC for Business-Context and PS for ProfitShare. In the example we will consider the adaptation strategy given in Fig. 8. The adaptation strategy comprises two operations: a *merge* operation and an *addInterfaceClass* operation.

$$
\begin{aligned}
\varPhi = \ &merge(M, BC) \cdot \\
&addInterfaceClass(\langle PS,\ \epsilon,\ \langle(Real,\ percent,\ (1,1))\rangle,\ \epsilon\rangle, \\
&\qquad (M,\ \langle(PS,\ profitShares,\ (1,*))\rangle), \\
&\qquad (PS,\ \langle(ROS,\ stakeholders,\ (1,*))\rangle)))
\end{aligned}
$$

Fig. 8. The adaptation strategy used in the example.

$$
\begin{aligned}
\mathcal{E} = \ &\langle\langle M, \epsilon, \langle(String,\ id)\rangle, \langle(String,\ format)\rangle\rangle, \\
&\langle BC, \epsilon, \langle(String,\ id), (String,\ region), (String,\ country, (1,1))\rangle, \\
&\qquad \langle(String,\ format)\rangle\rangle, \\
&\langle ROS, \epsilon, \langle(Real,\ value), (String,\ firm), (String,\ country), \epsilon\rangle\rangle, ...\rangle \\
\sigma = \ &\delta = \emptyset
\end{aligned}
$$

Fig. 9. The initial environment.

Figure 9 gives the initial environment which consists of all classes from the two metamodels, e.g. the M, BC and ROS classes. As can be read from the figure, M has no superclass, an attribute id of type String and an operation format with type String as well. The BC class has no superclass, three attributes and one operation. Notice the lower bound in the multiplicity for the country attribute, which is 1. This means that an object of the BC class needs to have a value for this attribute. The other two attributes in the class have a 0..1 multiplicity by default. Finally, the ROS class has no superclass and three attributes.

The first operation in the adaptation strategy specifies that the M and BC classes should be merged. Merging the two classes yields a new class with the name MBC[2]. Merging of classes requires collecting information about the constituent classes of the merging operation. In this case, two mappings are created and stored, see Fig. 10.

$$\mathcal{E}, \sigma, \delta \vdash merge(M, BC)\langle \mathcal{E}', \sigma', \delta' \rangle$$
$$\mathcal{E}' = \langle\langle MBC, \ \epsilon, \langle (String, \ \#id), (String, \ id), (String, \ region),$$
$$(String, \ country, \ (1,1))\rangle, \langle (String, \ \#format), (String, \ format)\rangle\rangle,$$
$$\langle ROS, \epsilon, \langle (Real, \ value), (String, \ firm), (String, \ country)\rangle, \epsilon\rangle, ...\rangle$$

$$\sigma' = [M \mapsto_c MBC] + [BC \mapsto_c MBC] + [id \overset{M}{\mapsto}_p \#id] +$$
$$[format \overset{M}{\mapsto}_o \#format]$$
$$\delta' = \langle\langle M, country, 1\rangle\rangle$$

Fig. 10. The result of analysing the merge operation.

The first mapping binds the name M with MBC and the other mapping binds the name BC with MBC. Furthermore, equally named properties in the two classes need to be addressed, otherwise, this will result in a name conflict. The classes M and BC both have a property named id. Hence, the id property in the M class is given the new name #id by the *anProp* function (#id represents the new name for the id property). This renaming is also reflected by creating a new name mapping. The two classes also have an equally named operation. This name conflict is handled in a similar manner as for the id property. We use the notation $id \overset{M}{\mapsto}_p \#id$ for specifying that the name of the property id is mapped to the name $\#id$ in the M class.

Notice how an object creation specification is constructed since BC has an attribute country whose lower bound is 1. Hence, existing product models need to be updated with a value for this attribute in objects of MBC (previously M). Finally, a new environment is constructed and superfluous classes, that is M and BC, are removed. Note that the new environment still contains the remaining unaffected classes of the two metamodels.

---

[2] The name chosen is decided by the implementation.

$$\mathcal{E}', \sigma', \delta' \vdash addInterfaceClass(\langle PS,\ \epsilon,\ \langle(Real,\ percent)\rangle, \epsilon\rangle,$$
$$\langle\langle MBC,\ \langle(PS,\ profitShares,\ (1, *))\rangle\rangle,$$
$$(PS, \langle(ROS,\ stakeholders,\ (1, *))\rangle\rangle\rangle\rangle\langle\mathcal{E}'', \sigma'', \delta''\rangle$$

$$createInst(MBC, \langle(PS,\ profitShares,\ (1, *))\rangle) =$$
$$\langle MBC, profitShares, 1\rangle$$
$$createInst(PS, \langle(ROS,\ stakeholders,\ (1, *))\rangle) =$$
$$\langle PS, stakeholders, 1\rangle$$
$$\mathcal{E}'' = \langle\langle MBC, \epsilon, \langle(String,\ id), (String,\ \#id), (String,\ region),$$
$$(String,\ country, (1, 1)), (PS,\ profitShares,\ (1, *))\rangle,$$
$$\langle(String,\ \#format), (String,\ format)\rangle\rangle,$$
$$\langle ROS, \epsilon, \langle(Real,\ value), (String,\ firm), (String,\ country),$$
$$(PS,\ stakeholders,\ (1, *))\rangle, \epsilon\rangle\rangle, \langle PS,\ \epsilon,\ \langle(Real,\ percent)\rangle, \epsilon\rangle, ...\rangle$$

$$\sigma'' = [M \mapsto_c MBC] + [BC \mapsto_c MBC] + [id \overset{M}{\mapsto}_p \#id] +$$
$$[format \overset{M}{\mapsto}_o \#format]$$
$$\delta'' = \langle\langle M, country, 1\rangle, \langle MBC, profitShares, 1\rangle, \langle PS, stakeholders, 1\rangle\rangle$$

Fig. 11. The final environment, mappings and object creation specifications.

The next step is analysis of the *addInterfaceClass* operation, refer Fig. 8 for details on how the *addInterfaceClass* operation is specified. First, a new class named PS is added to the environment. The purpose of this class is to bridge the MBC and RightsOwnership classes, see Fig. 3. Second, a selection of classes in the environment is revised. Specifically, the classes relating to the PS class, and potentially the PS class itself, are updated with class references. Notice how the accumulated mapping of $[M \mapsto_c MBC]$ has been applied (by SEQ) before the analysis by the (ADD INTERFACE CLASS) rule. Thus, even though the *addInterfaceClass* operation refers to M, the name mapping ensures that the MBC class is used in the analysis. Also, pay note of how the *createInst* function is applied to specify generation of default objects of the PS and ROS classes, which is required since these classes are related to by the references profitShares and stakeholders, respectively. Both of these references have a non-zero lower bound in their multiplicity.

The final environment, $\langle\mathcal{E}'', \sigma'', \delta''\rangle$, can be seen in Fig. 11. The enviroment $\mathcal{E}''$ corresponds to the metamodel in Fig. 3 and contains updated versions of the classes MBC and ROS, the new PS class, and all remaining unaltered classes of the constituent metamodels. δ has been updated to indicate that a default object has to be created by both PS (profitShares is typed with PS) and ROS (stakeholders is typed with ROS) for all existing models that contain objects of MBC (M and BC). Notice that it does not exist any models with objects of PS (since this is a new class), however, since MBC has a property typed with PS whose lower bound is 1, this requires creation of an object of PS in all existing models previously conforming to either of the two metamodels. This in turn requires creation of default objects of ROS since PS has a property typed with ROS whose lower bound is 1 as well.

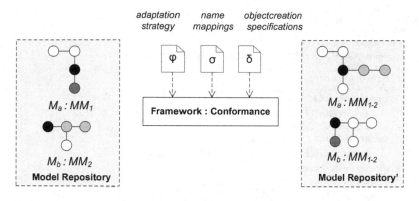

Fig. 12. Illustration of how conformance is re-established.

4   Conformance

We use the definition of conformance as given in [9]. A model $\mathcal{M}$ conforms to a metamodel $\mathcal{MM}$ if all objects in the model are classified by one concept in the metamodel. A concept is described by a class. Γ denotes a classification abstraction. The extension of a concept, $\epsilon(C)$, is defined by a set of predicates that characterise the same elements. The set of these predicates is known as the intension of the concept - $\iota(C)$.

Definition 4. *A model $\mathcal{M}$ conforms to a metamodel $\mathcal{MM}$, denoted conformsTo $(\mathcal{M}, \mathcal{MM})$, iff. $\mathcal{MM}$ is well-typed and:*

$$\forall_i o_i \in \mathcal{M}, \exists_j C_j \in \mathcal{MM} \; such \; that \, o_i \; \Gamma \; C_j, \; where$$
$$o_i \; \Gamma \; C_j \; \Leftrightarrow \; o_i \in \; \epsilon(C_j), \; and$$
$$\epsilon(C) \; = \; \{x | P(x)\} \; where \; P \; = \; \iota(C)$$

Based on the definition of conformance we have the following property:

Lemma 1. *Let $\mathcal{MM}_1$ and $\mathcal{MM}_2$ be well-typed metamodels, $\mathcal{M}$ a model, and $\mathcal{E}$ contains all classes in $\mathcal{MM}_1$ and $\mathcal{MM}_2$. If conformsTo$(\mathcal{M}, \mathcal{MM}_1)$, then conformsTo$(\mathcal{M}, \mathcal{E})$. Similarly, if conformsTo$(\mathcal{M}, \mathcal{MM}_2)$, then conformsTo$(\mathcal{M}, \mathcal{E})$.*

We show that with an adaptation strategy Φ for metamodel adaptation and the accumulated effects σ and δ, the associated models can be updated so that they conform to the altered metamodel. Figure 12 illustrates this for the *merge* operation. The figure contains a model of each of the metamodels given in Fig. 4. The circles illustrate model objects. Notice how default objects are created to satisfy conformance according to non-zero lower bound multiplicities in the meta-models. Thus, two default objects are required to be added to the M_a model for this model to conform to the MM_{1-2} metamodel. Similarily, a default object has to be added to the M_b model for this to conform to MM_{1-2}.

```
transform(M, φ₀ ··· φₙ, σ, δ) : M
  let transform(φᵢ ··· φₙ)
    for each object ⟨oid : N, (P, v)⟩ ∈ M do
      if φᵢ == addClass(⟨C, ε, P̄, Ō⟩) // No action − no objects exist
      if φᵢ == merge(C, C')
        σ' = projc(σc); projc'(σc)
        if N == C then
          update(M, ⟨oid : [C]projc(σc),
                 createObj((P, v), projc(δ)); [(P, v)]projc(σp);σ'⟩)
        else if N == C' then
          update(M, ⟨oid : [C']projc'(σc),
                 createObj((P, v), projc'(δ)); [(P, v)]projc'(σp);σ'⟩)
        else if (C subClassOf N) or (C' subClassOf N) then
          update(M, ⟨oid : N, [(P, v)]projN(σp);σ'⟩
        else update(M, ⟨oid : N, [(P, v)]σ'⟩)

        [φᵢ₊₁ ··· φₙ]σ'

      if φᵢ == addInterfaceClass(⟨C, ε, P̄, Ō⟩, (D, P̄') ∪ R)
        if N = D then
          update(M, ⟨oid : N, createObj(P̄', projD(δ)); (P, v)⟩)

      if φᵢ == addProp(C, P)
        if N = C then
          update(M, ⟨oid : N, createObj(P, projN(δ)); (P, v)⟩)
      ...
    endfor
    tranform(φᵢ₊₁ ··· φₙ)
  in
    transform(φ₀ ··· φₙ)
  end
return M
```

Fig. 13. The transform function.

The semantics of model evolution is described by the *transform* function, see Fig. 13. Let $proj_c(\sigma_p)$ return property mappings for class C, i.e., $[Np \overset{c}{\hookrightarrow} Np]$ and $proj_c(\delta)$ object creation specifications, i.e. $\overline{\langle C, Np, Nat \rangle}$. *createObj* produces objects as specified by δ. Object creation is only performed if the containing object does not already contain/refer these objects. A class may have a reference with a non-zero lower bound that is typed with a class that contains a reference with a non-zero lower bound to the first class. That is, there are two references between a pair of classes where both references have a non-zero lower bound. In this case, and in similar more comprehensive cases, the algorithm/function will not terminate. This may be addressed by reusing already created objects of the classes. *update* creates a new version of the given object. We show an excerpt of the function, the rest is defined in a similar manner.

Theorem 1. *Let $\mathcal{MM}_1$ and $\mathcal{MM}_2$ be well-typed metamodels, and let $\mathcal{E}$ contain all classes in $\mathcal{MM}_1$ and $\mathcal{MM}_2$, and $\mathcal{M}$ an arbitrary model such that conformsTo $(\mathcal{M}, \mathcal{MM}_1)$ or conformsTo$(\mathcal{M}, \mathcal{MM}_2)$. Let Φ be an adaptation strategy such that $\mathcal{E}, \emptyset, \emptyset \vdash \Phi \langle \mathcal{E}', \sigma, \delta \rangle$, then we have conformsTo(transform$(\mathcal{M}, \Phi, \sigma, \delta), \mathcal{E}')$.*

Proof. The proof is by induction over the length of the adaptation strategy Φ and then by cases. By Lemma 1 we have $conformsTo(\mathcal{M}, \mathcal{E})$ and we show that if $\mathcal{E}, \emptyset, \emptyset \vdash \varphi_0 \cdots \varphi_i \langle \mathcal{E}', \sigma, \delta \rangle$ and $conformsTo(transform(\mathcal{M}, \varphi_0 \cdots \varphi_i, \sigma, \delta), \mathcal{E}')$ then if $\mathcal{E}', \sigma, \delta \vdash \varphi_{i+1} \langle \mathcal{E}'', \sigma', \delta' \rangle$, then $conformsTo(transform(\mathcal{M}, \varphi_0 \cdots \varphi_{i+1}, \sigma', \delta'), \mathcal{E}'')$. Let o be an object in $\mathcal{M}$. We show that o remains a valid instance of its class after each adaptation step that modifies $\mathcal{E}$. We show that properties and operations are analysed which yields name mappings specified in σs. The mappings are used to update affected slots in o. Hence, renamings, as a consequence of resolving name conflicts, are reflected upon the objects of these classes. Values for properties with a non-zero lower bound need to be created, and this is ensured by *createInst*, where the required type of objects and their respective counts are determined based on information in δs. We consider each adaptation operation:

- Rule (SEQ). This follows directly from the induction hypothesis.
- Rule (ADD CLASS) adds a new class to $\mathcal{E}'$ yielding $\mathcal{E}''$. By the induction hypothesis, $conformsTo(transform(\mathcal{M}, \varphi_0 \cdots \varphi_i, \sigma, \delta), \mathcal{E}')$. Rule (ADD PROPERTY) ensures that properties are unique with respect to the class hierarchy and verifies that they have valid types. Similarily, Rule (ADD OPERATION) ensures that the operations and their parameters have correct types. Therefore, we have that $\mathcal{E}''$ is still well-typed. Since C is new, there are no existing objects of C in $\mathcal{M}$ and $conformsTo(transform(\mathcal{M}, \varphi_0 \cdots \varphi_i \cdot addClass(\langle C, \epsilon, \overline{P}, \overline{O} \rangle), \sigma', \delta'), \mathcal{E}'')$.
- Rule (CLASS MERGE). Assume that o is an object of either $\mathcal{E}'(C)$ or $\mathcal{E}'(C')$. For o to be a valid instance of $\mathcal{E}''(D)$ (where D is the new composite class) all properties found in $\mathcal{E}'(C)$ and $\mathcal{E}'(C')$ must be included in D. In the rule, properties and operations are analysed which yields name mappings specified in σs, which are used to update the environment yielding $\mathcal{E}''$. The mappings are later used to ensure that slots in o bind to the correct attributes and references. Hence, renamings in C or C', as a consequence of name conflicts, are reflected upon the objects of these classes. Since mappings are transitively defined in σ we ensure that the lastest defined name for a given property is used to update the objects. In addition, values for properties with a non-zero lower bound need to be created. This is achieved by *createInst*.
- Rule (ADD SUPERCLASS). The proof is similar to (CLASS MERGE).
- Rule (ADD INTERFACE CLASS). Assume o is an object of C' and that $(C', \overline{P}) \in \mathcal{R}$. The rule ensures that the new references are uniquely defined in the class hierarchy, so $\mathcal{E}''(C')$ remains well-typed after adding references $\overline{P}$ to this class (C already exists in $\mathcal{E}''$ when analysing the new references, thus any reference typed with this class is well-typed). We show that o remains a valid object of $\mathcal{E}''(C')$; objects for non-zero lower-bounded references are created by the *transform* function as a result by the analysis of $createInst(C', \overline{P})$ where $createInst(C', \overline{P}) \subseteq \delta'$.
- Rule (CLASS OVERRIDE). The rule requires C' to contain all properties and operations that are defined in C. There are two cases: Case 1. Assume o is an object of class C'. By Rule (CLASS OVERRIDE), class $\mathcal{E}''(C')$ extends the definition of $\mathcal{E}'(C)$ with new superclasses. For o to be a valid instance

of $\mathcal{E}''(C')$, a set objects has to be created for each $p \in flatten(\mathcal{E}'', \overline{B})$ where $p.Multi.lower \neq 0$. The required type of objects and their respective counts are specified in δ'. Case 2. Assume o is an object of class C. By Rule (CLASS OVERRIDE), we have that $\forall P \in \overline{P} \cdot P \in \overline{P'}$ and $\forall O \in \overline{O} \cdot O \in \overline{O'}$ where $\mathcal{E}'(C') = \langle C', \overline{B'}, \overline{P'}, \overline{O'} \rangle$ and $\mathcal{E}'(C) = \langle C, \overline{B}, \overline{P}, \overline{O} \rangle$. Consequently, in order for o to be a valid instance of $\mathcal{E}''(C')$ the object must be updated to point to the new class C' and a set of objects has to be created for each $p \in \overline{P'} \setminus \overline{P}; flatten(\mathcal{E}'', \overline{B'})$. Information needed to respecify o can be aquired from $\sigma + [C \mapsto_c C']$. Similar to case 1, required objects of non-zero bounded references are also specified in δ'. Consequently, we have that $conformsTo(transform(\mathcal{M}, \varphi_0 \cdots \varphi_i \cdot override(C, C'), \sigma', \delta', \mathcal{E}''))$.

– Rule (ADD PROPERTY) adds a property P to a class C. It is trivial that if o is not an object of class C, then o remains a valid instance of its class C'. Let o be of C. In order for o to be a valid instance of $\mathcal{E}''(C)$, a set of objects of the property's type has to be created if $Multi.lower \neq 0$. The number of objects to be created is $Multi.lower$ as spcified in δ'. The objects are either contained in o or referenced by o, as facilitated by the implementation. Hence we have that $conformsTo(transform(\mathcal{M}, \varphi_0 \cdots \varphi_i \cdot addProp(C, P), \sigma', \delta'), \mathcal{E}'')$.

– Rule (ADD BI-DIRECTIONAL PROPERTY). The proof for adding opposite references is similar to (ADD PROPERTY).

– Rule (ADD OPERATION). Assume o is an object of class $\mathcal{E}'(C) = \langle C, \overline{B}, \overline{P}, \overline{O} \rangle$. The rule ensures $unique_{Op}(\mathcal{E}', O, C)$ so classes in $\mathcal{E}''$ remains well-typed after adding O to C, o remains a valid instance of $\mathcal{E}''(C)$, and we have that $conformsTo(transform(\mathcal{M}, \varphi_0 \cdots \varphi_i \cdot addOp(C, O), \sigma', \delta'), \mathcal{E}'')$.

4.1 Example Revisited

In Sect. 3.3 we showed how the product/merchandise metamodel and business context metamodel were combined by applying a simple adaptation strategy Φ involving merge and interfacing operations. Consequently, all existing product and business context models should now be considered as models of the composite metamodel. In order to re-establish conformance between existing models and the composite metamodel, existing models must be updated as specified by the mappings in σ'', and default object specifications in δ''.

Figure 14 shows how two existing models of the product and business context metamodels, respectively, are updated to ensure conformance with the composite metamodel. In particular, $transform(\mathcal{M}, \Phi, \sigma'', \delta'')$ updates objects of M and BC to be valid instances of MBC, values of the attribute id in M to be values of #id, and creates a default value for country in all objects that were previously instances of class M, as well as default objects for PS and ROS in all existing models. As the objects do not contain any references to operations, no changes are required for the renaming of the format operation in M. Clearly, we are aware that the default values and objects may have to be updated to reflect the domain, e.g. a correct value of country has to be specified. However, such considerations are outside the scope of our work.

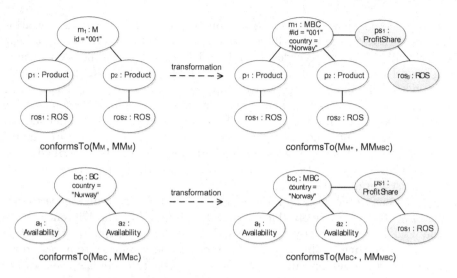

Fig. 14. Evolution of models to ensure conformance.

5   Related Work

One approach for automatic metamodel evolution is discussed in [29]. The work is inspired by object-oriented refactoring, and is based on a stepwise adaptation of metamodels using transformations. Three different types of transformations are used to achieve this: refactoring (e.g. renaming of an element), construction (e.g. adding a new class or property) and destruction (e.g. removing a class or property). The paper also discusses how models may be co-adapted by defining transformations that work on models. The work of our paper resembles that of [29]. We have defined a set of basic operations that can be combined arbitrarily to define adaptation strategies. We take things a step further by formally defining all operations and proving that conformance are preserved after adaptation. Also, our approach uses analysis as a prerequisite for supporting parallel evolution of an arbitrary number of metamodels.

[24] discusses how artefacts in the metamodelling ecosystem are impacted when metamodels evolve. In particular, the paper discusses how adaptation of artefacts should be facilitated inherently by the metamodel definition. This way, artefacts evolve directly as a consequence of metamodel evolution. It is argued that this perspective on co-evolution is important in order for metamodels to freely evolve without being constrained by required modifications to other artefacts, which may be both complex and expensive to perform. In our paper, we have seen how the accumulated effects can be used to update existing models. However, the effects are structured in a way that supports co-adaptation of other artefacts in the metamodelling ecosystem. Hence, our work addresses the concerns put forward in [24].

The proposed analysis of our paper can be supported by model migration processes such as the one described in [8]. The adaptations to be analysed can be provided by a change recorder [8] and model migrations can be implemented using model transformation languages such as QVT [20], ATL [12] and ETL [14,22] where the analysis effects give mappings/rules for how model elements from a input model can be mapped to elements in a target model. When creating an element, a transformation may fail if a target metaclass is not defined [8]. Our static analysis prevents this and ensures that execution of generated model transformations will succeed. Metamodel evolution can also be described using visual languages such as the one proposed in [19] where migration rules are defined with a graphical syntax.

[2,10] discuss mechanisms for addressing co-evolution using difference models and transactions, respectively. The work of [1] discusses how a difference model can be used to automatically create transformations that support co-evolution of models. According to this work, a difference model conforms to an extended KM3 meta-metamodel. Specifically, the KM3 meta-metamodel has been revised with classes for expressing atomic modifications, e.g. *reference added*, *attribute changed* or *class added*. By substracting one metamodel from another it is possible to derive a difference model which gives all the changes required to derive the one metamodel from the other. The discussion differentiates between *parallel independent* and *parallel dependent* modifications. Parallel dependent modifications can, as the name suggests, not be performed in parallel since the modifications depend on each other. A difference model is decomposed into breaking resolvable and unresolvable changes. This in turn yields two types of transformations: transformations that can be automatically generated and transformations that must be completed with input from the user. An implementation is available for difference models containing parallel independent changes, whereas a solution for parallel dependent changes is sketched in the paper. The latter is addressed by an iterative process that splits the difference models into submodels that only contain parallel independent changes. Our approach resembles that of [1]. However, there are some significant differences. First, our approach derives effects directly from the analysis. The effects are used as input for the transform function or for generating model-to-model transformations; instead of a difference model. Second, we support adaptation operations that create dependencies between an arbitrary number of metamodels, yet ensure that conformance is preserved for all existing models of all metamodels. We have focused on breaking resolvable adaptations. We support both parallel independent and parallel dependent adaptation operations. The analysis verifies that dependent operations are applied in an appropriate sequence, as given by the user, which can be supported by an interactive editor.

The work of [7] resembles that of [1]. The main difference is how metamodels are matched using heuristics in order to derive the difference model.

[16,27] formalise metamodel evolution and model co-evolution using category theory and graph transformations. In contrast, we formalise the low-level operations that typically emerge in metamodel/model co-evolution senarios based on MOF-metamodels which are the most common metamodel formalisation used

in industry. Hence, our approach is closer to existing frameworks and tools. We have not found any work that formalises metamodel/model co-evolution and metamodel composition in a similar manner as our approach.

6 Conclusion and Future Work

In this paper we have discussed a mechanism for metamodel adaptation and showed how model conformance can be preserved when metamodels are adapted and modified, e.g. composed. We formalised metamodel adaptation operations and addressed co-evolution of models. We also proved that conformance can be re-established between models and their altered metamodels.

In the proposed framework, conflicts during merging of classes are remedied by renaming and not resolved from an ontological perspective. We foresee that considering ontological knowledge as part of the analysis would refine the adaptation mechanism, where adaptation of metamodels can be tuned by utilising domain knowledge, e.g. classes representing the same type of domain concepts may be merged, etc. This way we would also address matching of classes prior to merging.

We addressed how the accummulated effects can be used to update models. These effects can also be used to update existing tools and model-to-model transformations that are defined according to the constituent metamodels. This can be achieved by defining a similar algorithm as described for model co-evolution by the *transform* function. We have focused on model structure, and not considered adaptation of language semantics, which we consider as future work.

References

1. Cicchetti, Λ., Di Ruscio, D., Eramo, R., Pierantonio, A.: Automating co-evolution in model-driven engineering. In: Proceedings of the Enterprise Distrubuted Object Computing Conference (EDOC 2008) (2008)
2. Cicchetti, A., Di Ruscio, D., Eramo, R., Pierantonio, A.: Meta-model differences for supporting model co-evolution. In: Proceedings of the 2nd International Workshop on Model-Driven Software Evolution (2008)
3. Del Faḥro, M.D., Valduriez, P.: Semi-automatic model integration using matching transformations and weaving models. In: Proceedings of the 2007 ACM Symposium on Applied Computing, pp. 963–970. ACM (2007)
4. Didonet Del Fabro, M., Bzivin, J., Valduriez, P.: Weaving models with the eclipse amw plugin (2006)
5. Favre, J.-M.: Towards a basic theory to model model driven engineering. In: 3rd International Workshop on Software Model Engineering (WISME 2004) (2004)
6. Fleurey, F., Baudry, B., France, R.B., Ghosh, S.: A generic approach for automatic model composition. In: Giese, H. (ed.) MODELS 2008. LNCS, vol. 5002, pp. 7–15. Springer, Heidelberg (2008)
7. Garcés, K., Jouault, F., Cointe, P., Bézivin, J.: Managing model adaptation by precise detection of metamodel changes. In: Paige, R.F., Hartman, A., Rensink, A. (eds.) ECMDA-FA 2009. LNCS, vol. 5562, pp. 34–49. Springer, Heidelberg (2009)
8. Gruschko, B., Kolovos, D.S., Paige, R.F.: Towards synchronizing models with evolving metamodels. In: Workshop on Model-Driven Software Evolution (2007)

9. Henderson-Sellers, B.: On the Mathematics of Modelling, Metamodelling, Ontologies and Modelling Languages. Springer, Heidelberg (2012)
10. Herrmannsdoerfer, M., Benz, S., Juergens, E.: COPE - Automating coupled evolution of metamodels and models. In: Drossopoulou, S. (ed.) ECOOP 2009. LNCS, vol. 5653, pp. 52–76. Springer, Heidelberg (2009)
11. Herrmannsdoerfer, M., Vermolen, S.D., Wachsmuth, G.: An extensive catalog of operators for the coupled evolution of metamodels and models. In: Malloy, B., Staab, S., van den Brand, M. (eds.) SLE 2010. LNCS, vol. 6563, pp. 163–182. Springer, Heidelberg (2011)
12. Jouault, F., Kurtev, I.: Transforming models with ATL. In: Bruel, J.-M. (ed.) MoDELS 2005. LNCS, vol. 3844, pp. 128–138. Springer, Heidelberg (2006)
13. Kent, S.: Model driven engineering. In: Butler, M., Petre, L., Sere, K. (eds.) IFM 2002. LNCS, vol. 2335, pp. 286–298. Springer, Heidelberg (2002)
14. Kolovos, D.S., Paige, R.F., Polack, F.A.C.: Eclipse development tools for epsilon. In: Eclipse Summit Europe, Eclipse Modeling Symposium (2006)
15. Kolovos, D.S., Paige, R.F., Polack, F.A.C.: Merging models with the epsilon merging language (EML). In: Wang, J., Whittle, J., Harel, D., Reggio, G. (eds.) MoDELS 2006. LNCS, vol. 4199, pp. 215–229. Springer, Heidelberg (2006)
16. Mantz, F., Rutle, A., Lamo, Y., Rossini, A., Wolter, U.: Towards a formal approach to metamodel evolution. In: Nordic Workshop on Programming Theory (2010)
17. Morin, B., Klein, J., Barais, O.: A generic weaver for supporting product lines. In: 13th International Workshop on Early Aspects (EA 2008), pp. 11–18. ACM Press (2008)
18. Morin, B., Perrouin, G., Lahire, P., Barais, O., Vanwormhoudt, G., Jézéquel, J.-M.: Weaving variability into domain metamodels. In: Schürr, A., Selic, B. (eds.) MODELS 2009. LNCS, vol. 5795, pp. 690–705. Springer, Heidelberg (2009)
19. Narayanan, A., Levendovszky, T., Balasubramanian, D., Karsai, G.: Automatic domain model migration to manage metamodel evolution. In: Schürr, A., Selic, B. (eds.) MODELS 2009. LNCS, vol. 5795, pp. 706–711. Springer, Heidelberg (2009)
20. ObjectManagementGroup. MOF QVT Final Adopted Specification. OMG (2007)
21. ObjectManagementGroup. Meta object facility (mof) core specification (2014)
22. Rose, L.M., Kolovos, D.S., Paige, R.F., Polack, F.A.C.: Model migration with epsilon flock. In: Tratt, L., Gogolla, M. (eds.) ICMT 2010. LNCS, vol. 6142, pp. 184–198. Springer, Heidelberg (2010)
23. Rose, L.M., Paige, R.F., Kolovos, D.S., Polack, F.A.C.: An analysis of approaches to model migration. In: Proceedings of the Models and Evolution Workshop. ACM (2009)
24. Di Ruscio, D., Iovino, L., Pierantonio, A.: Evolutionary togetherness: how to manage coupled evolution in metamodeling ecosystems. In: Ehrig, H., Engels, G., Kreowski, H.-J., Rozenberg, G. (eds.) ICGT 2012. LNCS, vol. 7562, pp. 20–37. Springer, Heidelberg (2012)
25. Seidewitz, E.: What models mean. IEEE Softw. 20(5), 26–32 (2003)
26. Steel, J., Jzquel, J.-M.: On model typing. Softw. Syst. Model. 6(4), 401–413 (2007). Springer
27. Taentzer, G., Mantz, F., Lamo, Y.: Co-transformation of graphs and type graphs with application to model co-evolution. In: Ehrig, H., Engels, G., Kreowski, H.-J., Rozenberg, G. (eds.) ICGT 2012. LNCS, vol. 7562, pp. 326–340. Springer, Heidelberg (2012)
28. TheEclipseFoundation. Eclipse modeling framework (emf) (2014)
29. Wachsmuth, G.: Metamodel adaptation and model co-adaptation. In: Ernst, E. (ed.) ECOOP 2007. LNCS, vol. 4609, pp. 600–624. Springer, Heidelberg (2007)

A Textual Domain-Specific Language Based on the UML Testing Profile

Johannes Iber[✉], Nermin Kajtazović, Georg Macher, Andrea Höller,
Tobias Rauter, and Christian Kreiner

Institute for Technical Informatics, Graz University of Technology,
Inffeldgasse 16, Graz, Austria
{johannes.iber,nermin.kajtazovic,georg.macher,andrea.hoeller,
tobias.rauter,christian.kreiner}@tugraz.at

Abstract. Model-Driven Development (MDD) is a well-established area in software engineering. Today, it is applied in many sectors of industry to support various activities in systems lifecycle, from requirements to verification and validation. One of the first, and most notable modeling languages for specifying test cases for complex software systems is the UML Testing Profile (UTP). Unfortunately, the problem with such a language is that the scope of concepts and modeling elements is too broad in order to solve specific problems. In this paper, we introduce a textual domain-specific language, the UTP-based Testing Language (Ubtl) that allows specifying test cases from UTP. This approach eases the use of UTP, because only particular aspects are captured within the language and a test engineer is obligated to use transformable constructs only. The remainder of this paper consists of an application of Ubtl on a system and a test architecture from the automotive domain.

Keywords: UML Testing Profile · UML · Textual domain-specific language · Test specification language · Software testing · Model-Driven Development

1 Introduction

Numerous industrial sectors are currently confronted with massive challenges originating from managing the complexity of system engineering. The automotive industry, for instance, has an annual increase rate of software-implemented functions of about 30 %. This development is even higher for avionics systems [1,2]. In addition, the complexity is driven by several other dimensions, including the number of devices that run software functions and the inter-connections among those devices. As a consequence of this several organizations are participating in the development in some sectors, thus raising additional issues related to system integration (e.g., suppliers and manufacturers in the automotive development landscape). This all poses an enormous problem for verification and validation activities, since the aforementioned class of systems needs to be rigorously tested and quality-assured.

© Springer International Publishing Switzerland 2015
P. Desfray et al. (Eds.): MODELSWARD 2015, CCIS 580, pp. 155–171, 2015.
DOI: 10.1007/978-3-319-27869-8_9

Model-driven Development (MDD) is a promising engineering discipline for addressing the challenges outlined above. Industry is currently utilizing MDD in many aspects of the system lifecycle, by putting models in focus of the development [3]. To date many MDD products (i.e., meta-models, languages, tools, etc.) have been developed, to support the development of complex technical systems in various fields [1]. A sub-set of these products (specifications) is tailored to testing systems of this kind and allows developers to define and to synthesize various types of tests required for their systems. One of these products is the UML Testing Profile (UTP), which is a meta-model commonly used to specify and to synthesize tests based on a computational model of UML [4]. The test model in UTP provides a generic architecture tailored to perform various types of black-box tests, and allows UTP to be used in general for embedded system engineering, as shown in several studies [5,6].

Unfortunately, there are a number of issues, which make the application of UTP within a well-known V-model[1] cumbersome for test engineers or software architects.

First, the *representation*: the graphical notation of test suites is not necessarily optimal for all types of tests within a V-model. For instance, module tests usually have a strong focus on a functional behavior of a single module, and capture merely a portion of system behavior (e.g., a software component). Such a test may consist of many primitive statements, for example value assignments, loops and use of test data from external files. In many cases, specifying such tests with textual notation would be more practical for test engineers.

Second, the *scope*: UML, which is used to specify a system under test in UTP, provides a large and complex set of elements and features. The main problem here is that the same concepts can often be defined in UML in many different ways. This poses a grand challenge to synthesizing the concrete test code, because explicit checks need to be performed in order to ensure that test engineers are prevented from specifying tests which include fragments of UML that cannot be technically synthesized.

In this paper, we propose a textual domain-specific language (DSL) that allows the specifying of tests from the UML Testing Profile (UTP) – UTP-based Testing Language, Ubtl. The main contribution here is that only particular aspects of UTP are captured, thereby allowing the MDD process to be narrowed to specific needs, such as supporting code generation facilities for certain types of tests or even specific statements within tests for example. In response, by using the proposed DSL, the test engineer is obligated to work with only a sub-set of UTP and UML features for which the corresponding synthesis (code generation) functionality is provided. We report at the end of the paper on the applicability of the DSL within a MDD synthesis process.

The remainder of this paper is structured as follows: the next section provides a brief overview over relevant related studies. In Sect. 3, the proposed DSL (Ubtl) with the main language features is introduced. Subsequently, a use case demonstrating the applicability of Ubtl in the automotive domain is described in Sect. 4. Finally, concluding remarks are given in Sect. 5.

---

[1] A common lifecycle model for safety-critical systems [7].

2   Related Work

We briefly summarize some relevant studies that focus in particular on models and languages for testing complex technical systems in the following.

One of the first, and most notable models for software and system testing is the UML Testing Profile (UTP). UTP is standardized by the Object Management Group, [4], and offers well-thought-out concepts for specifying test cases in UML [8]. Although the underlying test model is based on UML, UTP is not restricted to object-oriented design. For instance, it has been used in the context of resource-constrained real-time embedded systems [6] for testing web applications running in web browsers [9] or for testing protocols [10]. The key concept is the usage of UML classes tagged with the stereotype *TestContext*, as entry point and container for test cases and optional test configuration, while the concrete test cases are specified as UML interactions, which could be visualized for example as sequence diagrams. UTP is mainly used with the graphical syntax of UML in order to specify the different parts of its elements and features. As explained previously, UTP can be used on all levels of the well-known V-Model [5], but with some difficulties, however, in modelling and code synthesis.

UTP is strongly influenced by the Testing and Test Control Notation version 3 (TTCN-3), which is a DSL similar to our Ubtl. However, the main difference between Ubtl and TTCN-3 is that TTCN-3 test cases are meant to be used by the (domain-specific) standardized test architecture, [11]. It is not foreseen here to translate a TTCN-3 test case to other test platforms, for instance JUnit. Furthermore, there is no standardized meta-model as an intermediate representation. A possible meta-model has been discussed by [12]. However, it depends on the tool vendors how the transformation is actually implemented and which programming languages or platforms are supported.

The abstract syntax of the Test Description Language (TDL) has been released recently and standardized by ETSI, [13]. TDL offers concepts similar to UTP, but with a simpler meta-model than UML. This limits the possible interpretations of the concepts and semantics, which is a problem with UML due to the complexity and different ways possible for specifying the same thing. There is currently an implementation of the TDL meta-model based on the Eclipse Modeling Framework (EMF, [14]) provided by ETSI, [13]. It is planned to standardize a concrete graphical syntax [15]. Depending on the maturity of TDL, i.e. if the standardized meta-model is used more intensively by the industry in future and if that results in the emergence of several compatible tools, it should be theoretically possible in our opinion to transform the generated UML/UTP models automatically to TDL models.

In the literature, several other approaches for specifying test cases have been proposed based on models (e.g. [16–19]). In summary, these approaches have a common limitation in their focus on a specific domain, and, in addition, they do not rely on simplifying use of external standard models, as in our case – the UTP, but rather on generating code out of models in a conventional way.

3   Test Specification Language – Ubtl

In this section we introduce the proposed test specification language Ubtl. We first provide general information to highlight some benefits of the language. We then show the possible uses of Ubtl in terms of different system configurations (e.g., IDE tools using Ubtl, software and system models, etc.). Furthermore, we describe the realized software architecture and tools used to compile Ubtl into concrete test cases. Finally, we outline the main Ubtl elements and features, and their mappings to UTP.

3.1   General

Ubtl offers a concise textual language. This textual language is automatically compiled to UML in conjunction with UTP. The benefit of using Ubtl for a code generator is that related UML and UTP models are always generated in the same way, i.e. they do not contain UML and UTP concepts a code generator cannot know beforehand, which in response simplifies the development of code generation functionality. Another advantage is that a test engineer engaged in developing tests is prevented from providing specifications that contain UML or UTP elements and features not supported by the underlying code generators. For this purpose, we provide a powerful Eclipse IDE for Ubtl, which automatically validates whether the code contains errors or missing properties. Furthermore, the IDE provides content assistance. For a test engineer this "feels" like any other textual programming language.

3.2   Applications

As mentioned above, Ubtl code is always compiled to UML models. We identify the following four Ubtl use applications from the viewpoint of a test engineer responsible for the definition of tests:

Application One: Figure 1(a) illustrates the first application. A test engineer could specify test cases with the Ubtl IDE inside Eclipse. After the Ubtl compiler generates an UML model, a test engineer can manipulate this model with a compatible UML tool when necessary. Furthermore, a test engineer could trigger a code generator by using the UML model. This can occur within Eclipse or by leveraging an external tool which is compatible with the Eclipse UML2 project. The generated test cases can then be used by the target test environment. These final test cases can be written in any programming/testing language or format such as XML. In the final step the test engineer obtains the test results of the final test platform. The benefit of this approach is that the test engineer does not have to know how the test cases must look like on the test platform. Supporting another test environment is easy, because all that has to be developed is a different generator. Another benefit is that the test cases do not have to be written over and over again for every platform. Ubtl might be useful even when there is only one target

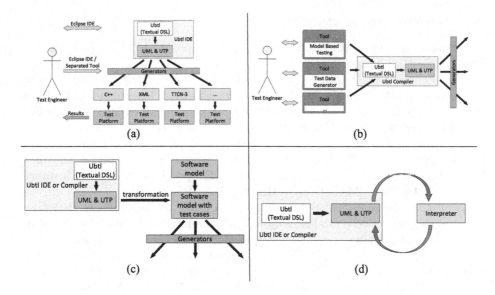

Fig. 1. Four different possible applications of using Ubtl.

platform. For example when the platform expects an XML file as a test input, it may be easier to specify it with Ubtl rather than using XML.

Application Two: Ubtl could be used by other tools (see Fig. 1(b)). For instance, a MDD tool could specify resulting test cases or test data in Ubtl. The advantage of this is that a tool does not have to be aware of any dedicated platform except Ubtl. It would be easy to add other test platforms without changing the front tools, because the corresponding generators work with the UML model. The Ubtl compiler can be leveraged as Java library in such an automatic process.

Application Three: Ubtl can be used in conjunction with models of software (see Fig. 1(c)). The test cases would be specified with Ubtl, while the resulting UML models could be transformed to test cases part of the software model, or specified in the same modeling language as the model. The advantage is that it could be easier to specify test cases with Ubtl than with the target modeling language. Ubtl may be simpler and easier to understand. Ideally, the generators for the model of the software could be reused for the test cases. This variant could be especially useful for component-based system engineering, where the interfaces of components are often modeled, for instance with the EAST-ADL UML2 profile, [20]. It would be easy to merge test cases and components, and to synthesize concrete code and test cases. Additionally, components could be configured for testing purposes.

Application Four: The resulting UML models do not have to be used by code generators (see Fig. 1(d)). An interpreter could use an UML model as input to stimulate test components or SUTs.

3.3   Software Architecture

We chose to develop Ubtl based on Java and Eclipse projects for two reasons: The Eclipse UML2 project and the Xtext project.

The Eclipse UML2 project [21] is part of the Model Development Tools project and implements the OMG UML 2.x meta-model based on EMF. This project *serves as the de facto "reference implementation" of the specification and was developed in collaboration with the specification itself,* [22].

Several commercial or open-source UML modeling tools can import/export Eclipse UML2 compatible models [23]. This makes it a viable target for Ubtl. Prominent commercial tools, which support Eclipse UML2, are for instance Enterprise Architect, MagicDraw UML, and IBM RSM/RSA.

Note that the graphical representations of UML models can not generally be interchanged between modeling tools. For example, a diagram (concrete syntax) drawn with Papyrus cannot be opened by Enterprise Architect, but the underlying Eclipse UML2 model (abstract syntax) is supported. In this case a user would have to create a new diagram based on the model with Enterprise Architect. This is an issue which the OMG attempts to solve with the UML 2.5 specification. We thus only generate Eclipse UML2 models currently, but no corresponding diagrams.

The Xtext project [24] is part of the Concrete Syntax Development project of the Eclipse Modeling Project. It is a so-called language workbench [25] for designing textual languages, ranging from domain-specific languages to general-purpose languages. Concerning Ubtl, we use an Xtext version based on version 2 for creating a compiler and a corresponding Eclipse IDE.

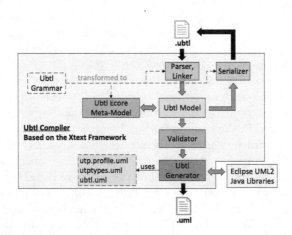

Fig. 2. Ubtl compiler architecture based on the Xtext framework.

Figure 2 shows a simplified view of the relevant components of the Ubtl compiler architecture. These components are:

- The **Ubtl Grammar**, specified with the Xtext grammar, is automatically transformed to the Ubtl meta-model, parser, linker, and serializer.
- The **Parser** and **Linker** are responsible for reading an Ubtl file and generating an Ubtl model. Internally only the Ubtl model is used.
- The **Serializer** is responsible for transforming an Ubtl model back to the textual representation.
- The **Validator** contains our restrictions of Ubtl.
- The **Ubtl Generator** is used to transform an Ubtl model to an UML model. It leverages the Eclipse UML2 libraries for this task. Additionally, it uses the predefined UML models utp.profile.uml, utptypes.uml, and ubtl.uml. We develop the generator, as is the case for all other parts, with the Xtend programming language [26].

All these compiler components seamlessly integrate into the EMF environment and can be used separately. The Ubtl IDE, which is automatically generated by the Xtext framework, also leverages the compiler components. A difference to the compiler is that the IDE uses a different parser for the content assist, which in this case is faster. We customized the IDE slightly in the context of the behavior of the content assist and the visual appearance.

3.4   Language Elements

We separate the elements of the textual DSL into *declarations* and *definitions*. Declarations are defined by the test platform designers and may relate to types, interfaces, and classes, which a code generator can know in advance. A test engineer on the other hand can use these declarations to define the actual test data, runtime objects, and test cases. The declarations, definitions and test cases are always transformed correctly to UML according to the UML and UTP semantics. All these elements must be grouped in Ubtl packages, which are mapped to UML packages. They can exist side-by-side in a package.

Declarations. Table 1 enumerates the available declarations of the textual DSL and their mappings to UML. Exemplary declarations can be found in Listing 1.1, which is part of our presented use case.

The basic declarations, consisting of primitive, array, and record, allow the restricting of the possible usages for corresponding Ubtl objects. Primitives provide for restricting that the name of a variable must be specified when it is defined inline. Arrays can be restricted to require names of contained primitive variables or not allowing a reference to a variable multiple times. All basic declarations have in common that they can be configured to be referenceable only once, which means that only one variable can refer to such a restricted object.

Test Context allows the restricting of the available statements within test cases (see Table 3).

All adjustable configurations/restrictions of the Ubtl declarations, which are only relevant for the Ubtl code, are mapped to UML as comments. It is thus

Table 1. Declarations in Ubtl and their mapping to UML.

Declaration	Description	Mapping
Primitive	Primitive types are used to declare types like integer, float, string, and boolean	Class realizing interface *Primitive*
Array	Array types can be used to define collections of primitives, arrays, records, or component and interface types.	Class realizing interface *Array*
Record	Record types are used to define containers which can hold several objects of specified types as attributes.	Class realizing interface *Record*
Interface	Interfaces can hold attributes and signatures. Interfaces can be used by code generators, to identify what type a component is	Interface generalizing from interface *Component*
SUT	SUTs can hold attributes and signatures. They represent the targets of test cases	Class realizing interface *Component*. When a SUT definition becomes a property of a UML test context, the property is tagged with the UTP stereotype *SUT*
Test component	Test components are similar to SUT declarations. They can be used to provide helper signatures or represent mock objects	Class realizing interface *Component* and tagged with the stereotype *TestComponent*
Test context	Test contexts can disable specific statements inside a test case. They are necessary to specify the name of the UTP test context for the Ubtl test cases	Class tagged with the stereotype *TestContext*

possible to transform the UML models back to Ubtl including the Ubtl specific configurations.

Signatures and attributes, specifiable by interface, SUT, and test component, are mapped to UML operations (without a corresponding interaction) and attributes.

Table 2. Definitions in Ubtl and their mapping to UML.

Definition	Description	Mapping
Variable	Variable definitions are runtime instances of primitive, array, and record declarations.	Instance specification.
Component	Component definitions represent runtime instances of SUT and test component declarations.	Instance specification. If a signature is called, it also becomes a property of a test context which refers to the instance specification.
Testcase	Testcases hold the actual test logic	Interaction and operation of test context according to the UTP semantics. Test context is generated on the same package level

Table 3. Statements which can be used inside a test case.

Statement	Description and Mapping
Variable	This is the same variable definition as in Table 2. The difference is that the scope is narrowed to the test case
Assignment	We only allow the assigning of values to primitive variables. Such variables can be part of records or arrays. This concept is mapped to UML as call operation action on a predefined assignment class
Signature call	Signature calls are mapped to synchronous calls to operations of component definitions which become part of the enclosing test context. We allow the assigning of a return parameter, which is mapped to a reply message
Set verdict	Set verdict is mapped to UML according to the UTP semantics
Assertion	Assertions allow the evaluating of primitive variables. They are mapped to call operation actions on a predefined assertion class
Loop	Loops are used to repeat a sequence of statements for a defined limit of iterations. They are mapped to combined fragments with the interaction operator *loop*
Foreach loop	Foreach loops allow the iteration through one or several arrays of the same size. UML does not offer a dedicated concept for this kind of loop. They are thus mapped to combined fragments with the interaction operator *loop*, but the specification of the guard owns references to the instance specifications of the foreach variables and arrays as operands. The name of the fragment is *foreach*
If Else	If statements can only use primitive variables. They are mapped to combined fragments with the interaction operator *alt*
Log	Log statements are mapped according to the UTP semantics

Definitions. Table 2 illustrates the available definitions, which can implement declarations. Listing 1.2, part of the use case, shows how definitions and statements are used.

Table 3 lists the statements which can be used in test cases. With test components it is possible to provide signatures, which offer additional functionality, for example arithmetical, test platform or time related operations. Code generators may need to know such signatures in advance.

Currently, we do not offer an Ubtl concept for UTP test configurations.

4   Use Case

In our preceding work [27], we demonstrated Ubtl in an industrial setup to conduct the functional testing and qualification of component-based safety-critical systems. We showed how a test case for an IEC61131-like component [28], implementing a simple cosine function (in Function Block Diagram notation), is specified with Ubtl. Further we explained in detail the transformation and the resulting executable test case. Additionally, we measured the performance of the transformation and the memory usage.

In this work we demonstrate a use case from a somewhat different domain. We present Ubtl in the context of the automotive industry, where it is common to specify components via Simulink models and to leverage the code generation facilities of Matlab to produce executable code. In the following subsection, we discuss the context of the presented use case. Subsequently, we provide an overview of the system under test. The remainder of this section consists of a description how the example Ubtl test case is specified, a short explanation of the transformation and the resulting Matlab script.

4.1   Context of the Use Case

A typical software development process in the automotive domain involves the previous specification of requirements and corresponding test cases. These test cases are usually described by software architects on system level in a non-executable form [29, 30]. A software engineer, who creates e.g. a Simulink model based on the requirements, must manually transform the predefined test cases into Simulink models that stimulate the system under test model. The problem with this approach is, that one cannot be sure if a software engineer preserved and transformed the non-executable test case correctly. We believe that Ubtl could either fill the gap, or at least minimize the problem. A software architect acting on the system level would specify test cases with Ubtl in advance. The Ubtl compiler generates a UTP model based on the Ubtl information. A software engineer (referred to in the following as test engineer) who implements the Simulink model, would, with the help of a code generator, automatically transform the UTP test case to Simulink in order to verify the system under test model. In our opinion, Ubtl is abstract enough to specify test cases without knowing the implementation details, but expressive enough to generate executable test cases.

4.2   System Under Test

The example target of our use case is to test an electronic throttle control (ETC) system which is specified as Simulink model. An ETC system is responsible for electronically controlling the throttle based on accelerator pedal sensor data. In principle, it replaces the mechanical linkage between the accelerator pedal and the throttle inside a car with an electronic solution.

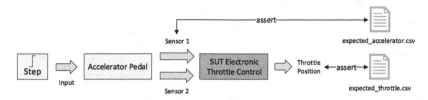

Fig. 3. Overview of the ETC test case.

Listing 1.1. Predefined component types for testing Simulink models.

```
package automotive_types {                              1        attribute output_1: float32              33
import datatypes                                        2    }                                            34

declare testcontext automotive {                        4    declare testcomponent to_workspace realizes  36
 umlName = "Automotive TestContext"                     5        simulink_component {
 disableAssertion = true                                6     umlName = "Sinks/To Workspace"              37
 disableAssignment = true                               7     required attribute VariableName: string     38
 disableForEachLoop = true                              8     required attribute SaveFormat: string       39
 disableIf = true                                       9     attribute input_1: float32                  40
 disableLoop = true                                    10    }                                            41
 disableSetVerdict = true                              11
 disableVariableDefinition = true                      12    declare testcomponent accelerator realizes   43
}                                                      13        provided_component {
                                                             umlName = "Accelerator"                     44
declare interface simulink_component {                 15     attribute input_1: float32                  45
 umlName = "Simulink Component"                         16     attribute output_1: float32                 46
}                                                      17     attribute output_2: float32                 47
                                                         }                                                48
declare interface provided_component {                 19
 umlName = "Provided Component"                         20    declare testcomponent framework_controller { 50
}                                                      21     umlName = "Framework Controller"            51
                                                             signature connect(from: float32, to: float32) 52
declare interface custom_component {                   23     signature simulate(output_name: string)     53
 umlName = "Custom Component"                           24     signature loadConfiguration(file: string)   54
 attribute configuration: string                       25     signature                                    55
}                                                      26         assertWorkspaceVectorsEqual(vector1:
                                                                 string, vector2: string, tolerance:
declare testcomponent step realizes                    28         float32)
     simulink_component {                                    signature importCsvData(name: string, file:  56
 umlName = "Sources/Step"                               29         string)
 required attribute Time: float32                       30    }                                            57
 required attribute Before: float32                     31  }                                              58
 required attribute After: float32                      32
```

Figure 3 illustrates the setup of the ETC test case. It uses the Simulink *Step* component to generate the accelerator input data. The predefined *Accelerator* component takes this data and calculates two inverse accelerator pedal sensor data. This needs to be done for safety reasons, since at least two different and independent accelerator sensors are used in a car. The calculated accelerator sensor data are used as input for the ETC system. Finally, we compare if the observed accelerator and the calculated throttle positions equal corresponding expected values. The expected values are specified beforehand by a software architect with any suitable tool and loaded as CSV data into Matlab.

Listing 1.2. Electronic Throttle Control test case.

```
package etc_test {                                  1
                                                    
import automotive_types                             3
                                                    
comp step st {                                      5
  Time = 1.0                                        6
  Before = 0.0                                      7
  After = 90.0                                      8
  output_1 = 0.0                                    9
}                                                  10
                                                    
comp accelerator acc {                             12
  input_1 = 0.0                                     13
  output_1 = 0.0                                    14
  output_2 = 0.0                                    15
}                                                  16
                                                    
declare sut sut_etc realizes custom_component {    18
  umlName = "sut/Electronic_Throttle_Control"       19
                                                    
  attribute input_1: float32                        21
  attribute input_2: float32                        22
  attribute output_1: float32                       23
}                                                  24
                                                    
comp sut_etc etc {                                 26
  configuration = "etc_config.m"                    27
  input_1 = 0.0                                     28
  input_2 = 0.0                                     29
  output_1 = 0.0                                     30
}                                                  31
                                                    
comp to_workspace workspace1 {                     33
  input_1 = 0.0                                     34
  SaveFormat = "Array"                              35
```

```
      VariableName = "Acc_Pos1"                    36
    }                                              37
                                                    
    comp to_workspace workspace2 {                 39
      input_1 = 0.0                                40
      SaveFormat = "Array"                          41
      VariableName = "Throttle"                    42
    }                                              43
                                                    
    comp framework_controller framework           45
                                                    
    testcase automotive test0 {                    47
      log("Specify Model")                          48
      framework.connect(st.output_1, acc.input_1)  49
      framework.connect(acc.output_1,              50
          workspace1.input_1)
      framework.connect(acc.output_1, etc.input_1) 51
      framework.connect(acc.output_2, etc.input_2) 52
      framework.connect(etc.output_1,              53
          workspace2.input_1)
      log("Simulate Model")                         54
      framework.loadConfiguration("automotive_config.m")55
      framework.simulate("simOut")                  56
      log("Assert Data")                            57
      framework.importCsvData("expected_accelerator", 58
          "expected_accelerator.csv")
      framework.assertWorkspaceVectorsEqual("Acc_Pos1", 59
          "expected_accelerator", 0.1)
      framework.importCsvData("expected_throttle",  60
          "expected_throttle.csv")
      framework.assertWorkspaceVectorsEqual("Throttle", 61
          "expected_throttle", 0.0000001)
      log("Finished!")                              62
    }                                              63
  }                                                64
```

4.3 Specifying Test Case

Listing 1.1 illustrates predefined component types for constructing test cases based on Simulink. These types are available to a software architect in advance and must be known by a code generator. We omit the declarations of primitive datatypes because of the page limit (see our recent work [27] for an example). Inside the test context (lines 4 to 13), we disable several kinds of statements because we only want to call *framework_controller* signatures. The interfaces *simulink_component* (lines 15 to 17) and *provided_component* (lines 19 to 21) are used to distinguish between the Simulink and our predefined library of helper components. The *custom_component* interface (lines 23 to 26) is used for components which are not predefined. Such components can use the *configuration* attribute in order to configure the component with a Matlab script. We use this interface for the *etc* component. The test component *step* (lines 28 to 34) represents the corresponding Simulink component. The required attributes *Time*, *Before* and *After* are options, while the attribute *output_1* (line 33) represents the first outgoing port of the component. We use the convention *input_** and *output_** to select the corresponding ingoing and outgoing ports. The test component *to_workspace* (lines 36 to 41) is used to make observed data accessible through the workspace. The test component *accelerator* (lines 43 to 48) is a provided component that calculates two inverse accelerator sensor values. These two values are used as inputs for the ETC system. Last but not least, we declare the test component *framework_controller* (lines 50 to 58), which offers signatures to construct (line 52) and simulate (line 53) the Simulink model. Note that it is only necessary to connect component ports in order to construct a model. The rest is automatically added by the code generator. Furthermore, it provides signatures to apply Simulink configurations to assert that two vectors are equal and to import CSV files to the workspace (lines 54 to 56).

Based on these declared test components, interfaces and test context, a software architect can specify actual test cases that are transformable to Matlab scripts. Listing 1.2 illustrates the ETC test case.

First an instance of the *step* component is defined, including the parameters and output port (lines 5 to 10). In Ubtl it is obligatory to define default values for properties in order to use them. The *step* component is used to generate input values for the *accelerator* component (lines 12 to 16) inside Simulink. Next, the ETC system is declared as system under test component (lines 18 to 24). It offers two input ports for the inverse accelerator positions and one output port, which represents the calculated throttle position. Following on from this the ETC system is instantiated (lines 26 to 31). It uses a Matlab script to configure the ETC model (line 27). Two *to_workspace* components are defined to observe an accelerator position and the calculated throttle position (lines 33 to 43). Inside the test case (lines 47 to 63), the defined *framework_controller* instance (line 45) and the log statement provided by Ubtl only are called. The log statement (lines 48, 54, 57, 62) is used to print useful information for a test engineer. As mentioned above, the *connect* signature of the *framework_controller* is used to construct a model. It links the input and output ports of the different components. In line 49 the output port of the step component is connected with the accelerator input port. Next the first accelerator output port is connected with the *to_workspace* component *workspace1* to collect the accelerator position (line 50). After that, both accelerator output ports are linked with the corresponding ETC input ports (lines 51 to 52). Finally, the throttle output port of the ETC system is observed by *workspace2*. So far the model is constructed. In line 55 a predefined automotive configuration is applied to the Simulink model. Line 56 simulates the model. Last but not least the observed accelerator position and the resulting throttle values are compared with the predefined expected data (lines 58 to 61).

4.4   Transformation to Matlab Code

A code generator for this use case is quite simple. A generator searches inside the resulting UML model for test contexts named *Automotive TestContext* and generates for each containing test case a separate Matlab script. The *Framework Controller connect* calls are transformed to Simulink *add_line* calls. When a component has not been connected before, corresponding Simulink *add_block* and *set_param* calls are added. A *Custom Component configuration* property is represented as Simulink *run* operation. The other *Framework Controller* signatures are transformed to their semantically equivalent Simulink calls. Log statements are represented as Matlab *disp* calls.

Listing 1.3. Resulting Matlab Code.

```
sys = 'sys_test0';                                    1
sys_handle = new_system(sys); % Create the model      2
% End Matlab Script Header                            3

disp('Specify Model');                                5
add_block('simulink/Sources/Step', [ sys             6
'/st']);
set_param([ sys '/st'], 'Time', '1.0');              7
set_param([ sys '/st'], 'Before', '0.0');            8
set_param([ sys '/st'], 'After', '90.0');            9
add_block('provided_components/Accelerator', [      10
sys '/acc']);
add_line(sys,'st/1', 'acc/1');                       11
add_block('simulink/Sinks/To Workspace', [ sys      12
'/workspace1']);
set_param([ sys '/workspace1'], 'SaveFormat',        13
'Array');
set_param([ sys '/workspace1'], 'VariableName',      14
'Acc_Pos1');
add_line(sys,'acc/1', 'workspace1/1');               15
add_block('sut/Electronic_Throttle_Control', [      16
sys '/etc']);
run('etc_config.m');                                 17
add_line(sys,'acc/1', 'etc/1');                      18
add_line(sys,'acc/2', 'etc/2');                      19

add_block('simulink/Sinks/To Workspace', [ sys      20
'/workspace2']);
set_param([ sys '/workspace2'], 'SaveFormat',        21
'Array');
set_param([ sys '/workspace2'], 'VariableName',      22
'Throttle');
add_line(sys,'etc/1', 'workspace2/1');               23
disp('Simulate Model');                              24
Simulink.BlockDiagram.loadActiveConfigSet(sys,       25
'automotive_config.m');
simOut = sim(sys);                                   26
disp('Assert Data');                                 27
expected_accelerator =                               28
csvread('expected_accelerator.csv');
assert(all(abs(Acc_Pos1 - expected_accelerator)     29
<= 0.1));
expected_throttle =                                  30
csvread('expected_throttle.csv');
assert(all(abs(Throttle - expected_throttle) <=     31
0.0000001));
disp('Finished!');                                   32

% Begin Matlab Script Footer                         34
save_system(sys);                                    35
close_system(sys);                                   36
```

4.5   Resulting Matlab Script

Listing 1.3 illustrates the generated Matlab code. The header (lines 1 to 3) creates a new Simulink model, while the footer (lines 34 to 36) saves the constructed model. These two parts are automatically generated for every test case. In the context of the component *Accelerator* provided, the system under test *Electronic Throttle Control*, and the Matlab configuration scripts, we assume that a test engineer adds the surrounding folders inside Matlab to the search path. Lines 6 to 23 are the transformed *framework.connect* calls of Listing 1.2. The code generator adds the used components to the model when necessary. Line 26 simulates the constructed model. Lines 28 to 31 are responsible for asserting the observed values with the expected values. The constructed model can be graphically viewed and adjusted by a test engineer.

5   Conclusion

In this paper, we presented a textual domain-specific language (DSL) for the specification of tests based on the UML Testing Profile (UTP). With the introduced DSL, we addressed two very important problems of applying UTP in systems engineering: (a) the representation: the use of a graphical notation to define tests is not always optimal from the viewpoint of modelling for different types of tests, and (b) the scope: the complexity of UML and UTP poses severe challenges to both modelling and code synthesis. Both specifications offer the possibility to express the same concepts within a test specification in many different ways. To consistently synthesize the concrete tests, the modelling support must prevent the engineers from providing tests that cannot be synthesized.

Using the proposed DSL, a (necessary) sub-set of both specifications is captured for test specifications so that the process of synthesis is narrowed to only considered elements and features of UML and UTP.

This means of constricting the complex meta-models such as UML and UTP can help to better use and align them for specific purposes, i.e., for different types of tests within a V-lifecycle model for example, and to more simply realize the synthesis process.

We showed the application of the proposed DSL using a representative example of the automotive domain where the system under test represents an electronic throttle control. We presented how an Ubtl test case would be specified by a software architect on system level. Such a test case can be transformed to a Matlab script, which constructs a Simulink model and performs the verification tasks. The advantage is that such a workflow would automatically preserve the test case logic in contrast to a process where a test engineer manually transforms a textual specification to a Simulink model. Another advantage is that the test case logic could be transformed to alternative modeling languages or programming languages. Therefore, an Ubtl test case would not be limited to Simulink.

As part of our ongoing work, we are focusing on extensibility and re-usability aspects of the DSL. Some parts have been already discussed in this paper, such as declarations of elements and their use. We further plan to investigate the possibilities of applying the Ubtl approach to realize mappings or integrations between different models. For instance, we will enable linking between UTP test cases and evidence from EAST-ADL2 in order to improve traceability on system level and to simplify activities related to safety engineering.

References

1. Feiler, P., Hansson, J., de Niz, D., Wrage, L.: System architecture virtual integration: An industrial case study. Software Engineering Institute, Carnegie Mellon University, Pittsburgh, Pennsylvania, CMU/SEI-2009-TR-017 (2009)
2. Ebert, C., Jones, C.: Embedded software: facts, figures, and future. Computer 42(4), 42–52 (2009)
3. BITCOM: a study to relevance of embedded systems in germany. BITKOM Germany (2008)
4. Object Management Group (OMG): UML Testing Profile (UTP) Version 1.2 (2013)
5. Baker, P., Dai, Z.R., Grabowski, J., Haugen, O.Y., Schieferdecker, I., Williams, C.: Model-Driven Testing: Using the UML Testing Profile. Springer, Heidelberg (2008)

6. Iyenghar, P., Pulvermueller, E., Westerkamp, C.: Towards model-based test automation for embedded systems using UML and UTP. In: ETFA2011. IEEE (2011)
7. Smith, D., Simpson, K.: A Straightforward Guide to Functional Safety, IEC 61508 (2010 Edition) and Related Standards, Including Process IEC 61511 and Machinery IEC 62061 and ISO 13849. Elsevier Science (2010)
8. Object Management Group (OMG): Website of the Unified Modeling Language (2014). http://uml.org/
9. Bagnato, A., Sadovykh, A., Brosse, E., Vos, T. E.: The OMG UML testing profile in use-an industrial case study for the future internet testing. In: 2013 17th European Conference on Software Maintenance and Reengineering. IEEE (2013)
10. Kumar, B., Jasperneite, J.: Industrial communication protocol engineering using UML 2.0: a case study. In: 2008 IEEE International Workshop on Factory Communication Systems. IEEE (2008)
11. ETSI: TTCN-3: TTCN-3 Runtime Interface Version 4.6.1 (2014)
12. Schieferdecker, I., Din, G.: A Meta-model for TTCN-3. In: Núñez, M., Maamar, Z., Pelayo, F.L., Pousttchi, K., Rubio, F. (eds.) FORTE 2004. LNCS, vol. 3236, pp. 366–379. Springer, Heidelberg (2004)
13. ETSI: Methods for Testing and Specification (MTS); The Test Description Language (TDL); Specification of the Abstract Syntax and Associated Semantics Version 1.1.1 (2014)
14. Eclipse Foundation: Website of the EMF Project (2014). http://www.eclipse.org/modeling/emf/
15. Ulrich, A., Jell, S., Votintseva, A., Kull, A.: The ETSI test description language TDL and its application. In: MODELSWARD. SciTePress (2014)
16. Guduvan, A.R., Waeselynck, H., Wiels, V., Durrieu, G., Fusero, Y., Schieber, M.: A meta-model for tests of avionics embedded systems. In: Proceedings of the 1st International Conference on Model-Driven Engineering and Software Development. SciTePress (2013)
17. Arpaia, P., Buzio, M., Fiscarelli, L., Inglese, V., La Commara, G., Walckiers, L.: Measurement-domain specific language for magnetic test specifications at CERN. In: 2009 IEEE Intrumentation and Measurement Technology Conference. IEEE (2009)
18. Hernandez, Y., King, T.M., Pava, J., Clarke, P.J.: A meta-model to support regression testing of web applications. In: SEKE (2008)
19. Mews, M., Svacina, J., Weißleder, S.: From AUTOSAR models to co-simulation for MiL-Testing in the automotive domain. In: 2012 IEEE Fifth International Conference on Software Testing, Verification and Validation. IEEE (2012)
20. Debruyne, V., Simonot-Lion, F., Trinquet, Y.: EAST-ADL An Architecture Description Language. In: Architecture Description Languages SE - 12. IFIP The International Federation for Information Processing, vol. 176. Springer, US (2005)
21. Eclipse Foundation: Website of the UML2 Project (2014). http://www.eclipse.org/modeling/mdt/
22. Gronback, R.C.: Eclipse Modeling Project: A Domain-Specific Language (DSL) Toolkit, 1st edn. Addison-Wesley Professional, Upper Saddle River (2009)
23. Eclipse Foundation: MDT-UML2-Tool-Compatibility (2014). http://wiki.eclipse.org/MDT-UML2-Tool-Compatibility
24. Eclipse Foundation: Website of the Xtext Project (2014). http://www.eclipse.org/Xtext/
25. Fowler, M.: Domain-Specific Languages. Addison-Wesley Signature Series (Fowler). Pearson Education, Upper Saddle River (2010)

26. Eclipse Foundation: Website of the Xtend Project (2014). http://www.eclipse.org/xtend/
27. Iber, J., Kajtazovic, N., Höller, A., Rauter, T., Kreiner, C.: Ubtl - UML testing profile based testing language. In: Proceedings of the 3rd International Conference on Model-Driven Engineering and Software Development. SciTePress (2015)
28. John, K.H., Tiegelkamp, M.: IEC 61131–3: Programming Industrial Automation Systems Concepts and Programming Languages, Requirements for Programming Systems, Decision-Making Aids, 2nd edn. Springer Publishing Company Incorporated, Heidelberg (2010)
29. Lovric, T., Schneider-Scheyer, M., Sarkic, S.: SysML as backbone for engineering and safety - practical experience with TRW braking ECU. In: SAE International, SAE Technical Paper (2014)
30. Marinescu, R., Saadatmand, M., Bucaioni, A., Seceleanu, C., Pettersson, P.: A model-based testing framework for automotive embedded systems. In: 2014 40th EUROMICRO Conference on Software Engineering and Advanced Applications (SEAA) (2014)

Metamodel and Model Composition by Integration of Operational Semantics

Henning Berg[✉] and Birger Møller-Pedersen

Department of Informatics, Faculty of Mathematics and Natural Sciences,
University of Oslo, Oslo, Norway
{hennb,birger}@ifi.uio.no

Abstract. Several metamodel composition mechanisms have been proposed during the course of the last decade. However, most of the composition mechanisms do not consider existing models or other artefacts like editors, transformations and semantics which are defined relatively to a metamodel. Consequently, the models and the artefacts typically become invalid as metamodels are composed. Moreover, very few of the available metamodel composition mechanisms support composition of metamodels' operational semantics. In this paper we discuss an approach for composing metamodels, and their models, by integrating their operational semantics. This is achieved by using a placeholder mechanism; classes in one metamodel may represent classes of other metamodels. We have validated our approach by the construction of a framework.

Keywords: Model composition · Languages · Domain-specific modelling · Runtime

1 Introduction

Metamodel composition is an important operation in metamodelling. In the course of the last decade, several mechanisms for composition of models and metamodels have been devised, e.g. [1–4]. However, most of the mechanisms work either on the model or on the metamodel level, and do not consider composition of both kinds of models simultaneously. Specifically, metamodel composition mechanisms do not address how existing models can be combined as their metamodels are composed. A consequence of this is that the models are rendered invalid as they are not valid instances of the composite metamodel resulting from the composition process. Other artefacts in the metamodelling ecosystem like editors (concrete syntax), semantics (including constraints), transformations and code generators are also impacted when metamodels are composed. The reason is that these artefacts are defined relatively to a metamodel. Typically, each of these artefacts needs to be refactored to comply with a composed metamodel. Ideally, artefacts in the ecosystem should be aligned with new metamodel variants automatically by utilising information from the composition process. Similar considerations are discussed in [5–7].

© Springer International Publishing Switzerland 2015
P. Desfray et al. (Eds.): MODELSWARD 2015, CCIS 580, pp. 172–189, 2015.
DOI: 10.1007/978-3-319-27869-8_10

A natural evolution of composition mechanisms is the ability to consider model composition both at the metamodel and model levels. Put differently, a composition mechanism should govern the composition of metamodels *and* their models. This requires the composition mechanism to work explicitly on two abstraction levels where composition-specific directives, as required to compose (meta)models, are propagated and utilised for composition of models.

Meta Object Facility (MOF) [8] is the most prominent architecture for classification of models according to abstraction levels. In this architecture, metamodels reside on the M_2 level, whereas the models reside on the M_1 level. A model contains objects which are instances of classes in its metamodel. Thus, a model is classified by its metamodel. In the literature, this is typically referred to as the *conformsTo* relationship. A mechanism that supports composition of metamodels and the conforming models would work on both the M_2 and M_1 levels, respectively.

In this paper, we discuss how metamodels and models may be composed virtually *non-intrusively*. What this means is that metamodels and models are kept separate, yet they are composed through a set of implicitly defined mappings which allow specifying proxy classes. A proxy class in one metamodel represents a class in another metamodel. The approach only requires a minimal refactoring of existing artefacts which may be performed automatically or semi-automatically. The essence of our approach is the ability to integrate or link the operational semantics of languages, so that models/programs of different languages can interact at runtime. The ideas presented are applicable to metamodelling environments that allow expressing the operational semantics of a metamodel/language using an object-oriented action language, e.g. the *Eclipse Modeling Framework (EMF)* [9] and *Kermeta* [10]. The approach has been validated by the construction of a prototypical framework on top of EMF. We will use this framework and show how the behaviour of classes/objects in a *General-Purpose Language (GPL)* can be defined by models expressed in a domain-specific *State Machine Language (SML)*.

The paper is organised as follows. In Sect. 2 we define our non-intrusive composition mechanism. We then introduce an example in Sect. 3 and use it to illustrate the ideas and the mechanics of the framework in Sect. 4. An evaluation of the composition mechanism follows in Sect. 5, and in Sect. 6 we discuss our approach in relation to existing work in the field. Finally, in Sect. 7 we summarise and conclude the paper.

2   Definitions

Traditional (meta) model composition mechanisms are *explicit* in the sense that structural elements from different constituent models are interwoven, e.g. two classes from different metamodels may be merged or a class may be made a subtype of another class. As motivated, this has consequences with respect to other entities in the metamodelling ecosystem. The mechanism presented in this paper works by establishing mappings between metamodels and models in a practically non-intrusive manner. This means that the composition is lifted away from the modelling space and established using a separate specification. There are two types of mappings: M_2-mappings and M_1-mappings. The names reflect the MOF level on which the mappings occur. That is, M_2-mappings are created between metamodel structures, whereas M_1-mappings are created between model structures (objects of the classes in the metamodels). Both types of mappings can be expressed by non-injective partial functions. M_2-mappings are described in a *Unification Model (UM)*, while M_1-mappings are described in a *Linking Model (LM)*.

Definition 1. *An M_2-mapping is a uni-directional or bi-directional binding between two structural elements, τ_x and π_y, in two different metamodels. A structural element is a package, class, attribute, operation or parameter*[1]. *A bi-directional binding may be decomposed into two uni-directional bindings. For uni-directional bindings, τ_x is the source element and π_y is the target element. For bi-directional bindings, τ_x and π_y are both source and target elements corresponding to decomposition of the bi-directional binding into two uni-directional bindings.*

$$: \langle \tau_1 \mapsto \pi_1 \rangle (uni - directional)$$
$$: \langle \tau_1 \leftrightarrow \pi_1 \rangle (bi - directional)$$

where τ_x and π_x are on either of the forms (N being a name):

$$: \langle N_{package}, N_{class} \rangle$$
$$: \langle N_{package}, N_{class}, N_{attribute} \rangle$$
$$: \langle N_{package}, N_{class}, N_{operation} \rangle$$
$$: \langle N_{package}, N_{class}, N_{operation}, N_{parameter} \rangle$$

Definition 2. *A unification point is a collection of M_2-mappings between two classes in two different metamodels. A unification point is either asymmetric or symmetric. The source class of an asymmetric unification point is referred to as a proxy as it represents a placeholder for the target class. The two classes of a symmetric unification point represent compatible types. A unification point is only valid if both classes share a common equivalent structure. A class may be part of an arbitrary number of unification points. A unification point χ can be modelled as a set of mappings:*

$$\chi_a : \langle \tau_1 \mapsto \pi_1, \tau_2 \mapsto \pi_2, ..., \tau_n \mapsto \pi_n \rangle \ (asymmetric)$$
$$\chi_s : \langle \tau_1 \leftrightarrow \pi_1, \tau_2 \leftrightarrow \pi_2, ..., \tau_n \leftrightarrow \pi_n \rangle \ (symmetric)$$

Definition 3. *The (partial) equivalent structure of a unification point is a set of attributes, operations and operation parameters that both related classes of the unification point need to have. Two classes C_1 (proxy) and C_2 (classes are*

---

[1] References are not currently supported.

considered as sets of attributes, references and operations) of two metamodels may be unified if:

$$\forall s_1 \in \mathcal{C}_1 \cdot \exists s_2 \in \mathcal{C}_2 \ \rightarrow \ s_1 \sim s_2$$

where $\sim \ : \mathcal{S} \times \mathcal{S} \rightarrow Bool$ *is a recursive partial function that is true if its two arguments have an identical structure. For symmetric unification points,* $\mathcal{C}_1$ *and* $\mathcal{C}_2$ *have to be equipotent, that is:* $\mid \mathcal{C}_1 \mid = \mid \mathcal{C}_2 \mid$. $\mathcal{S}$ *is a set of structural elements:* $\mathcal{S} = \{Class, Attribute, Operation, Parameter\}$.

Definition 4. *A Unification Model (UM) unifies an arbitrary number of meta-models. It consists of one or more unification points. Two given metamodels may be unified with one or more unification points. The Unification Model comprises a set of unification points:*

$$UM : \langle \chi_1, \chi_2, ..., \chi_n \rangle$$

Definition 5. *An* M_1-*mapping* φ *is a bi-directional binding between two model elements (objects), with identifiers* i *and* j, *in two models* x *and* y. *An identifier encompasses both the class name for which the object is an instance and a unique integer designator.*

$$\varphi : O_i^x \leftrightarrow O_j^y, \ i, j \in \mathcal{I}$$

where $\mathcal{I}$ *is a set of tuples on the form:* $\langle ClassName, NaturalNumber \rangle$. *Inheritance of attributes and operations (including overriding) is supported (e.g. binding to an operation specified in a superclass to ClassName).*

Definition 6. *The Linking Model comprises a set of* M_1-*mappings between an arbitrary number of models:*

$$LM : \langle \varphi_1, \varphi_2, ..., \varphi_n \rangle$$

Figure 1 illustrates non-intrusive composition. The figure has three metamodels and models of these. The C_4 (proxy) class in MM_1 is unified asymmetrically with the D_1 class in MM_2, whereas the (proxy) class D_3 in MM_2 is unified asymmetrically with the class E_1 in MM_3. The classes C_3 and D_4 are unified symmetrically. That is, C_3 and D_4 represent a structure-wise identical type. A key feature of the mechanism is the ability to specify the exact models (and objects) that should be linked, e.g. the M_1 model of MM_2 is linked with the M_2 model of MM_3.

The χ_1 and χ_3 unification points are illustrated in Fig. 2.

For the sake of the illustration, we assume that the C_4 class contains an operation O_c with a parameter P_c. The operation and its parameter are unified with equivalent structure in D_1. M_2-mappings bind instance names of metamodel structure, e.g. the parameter named P_c is bound to the parameter named P_d. However, for structural equivalence, attribute and parameter names are irrelevant. What is relevant is the types of attributes or parameters (and their sequence). Hence, the types of P_c and P_d need to be structural equivalent for the two classes to form a valid unification point.

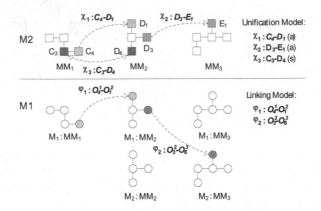

Fig. 1. Conceptual overview of non-intrusive composition (class names are omitted for object identifiers).

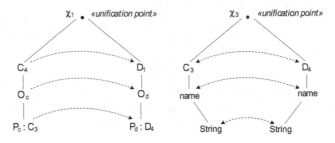

Fig. 2. The χ_1 (asymmetric) and χ_3 (symmetric) unification points.

By looking at the χ_3 unification point in the Unification Model it is clear that the types C_3 and D_4 are structural equivalent, as both only contain a String attribute, as can be seen by the rightmost unification point. (The two classes represent an identical concept as seen from an ontological perspective.) At runtime this implies that an object of C_3 may be converted to an object of D_4 and used in a type-safe invocation of the O_d operation. By construction, all unification points can be represented as tree structures as seen in the figure.

The idea of non-intrusive composition is based on the principle of partial representation. Structural commonalities allow for a proxy class to represent another class, as long as both classes have a set of common structure (as dictated by the proxy class). Hence, the proxy class mimics the structure and meaning of another class.

3   Example

We will illustrate the approach by exemplifying how the behaviour of classes/objects in a GPL may be defined using a state machine.

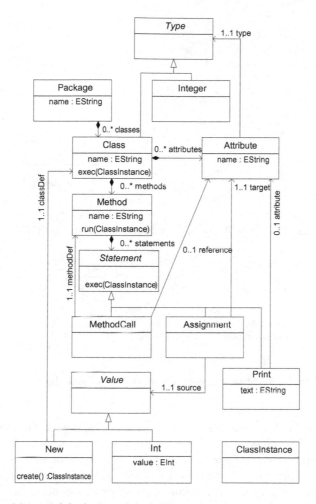

Fig. 3. Metamodel of a simplified General-Purpose Language (GPL).

Specifically, we will see how the state of an object can be maintained by a state machine and how methods in the class of the object may be invoked as a consequence of a state change in the state machine model. To the best of our knowledge, no composition mechanism available can handle simultaneous composition at both the metamodel and model levels in the situation where the behaviour of classes/objects are defined by a state machine.

Figure 3 gives an overview of the metamodel of the GPL. The metamodel allows creating very simple programs. We have kept the number of statement types to a bare minimum, yet they suffice to model interesting enough programs for the purpose of illustrating our framework. We will not consider other language artefacts like concrete syntax in detail and merely use such to visualise models.

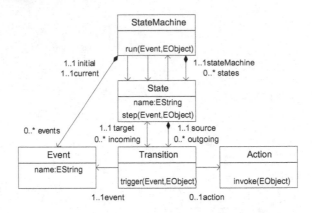

Fig. 4. Metamodel of a State Machine Language (SML).

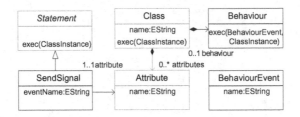

Fig. 5. Additional classes for modelling of signals/events.

Briefly explained, a program consists of a package with an arbitrary number of classes. The classes may have attributes and methods. An attribute is either of the primitive type Integer or class-typed. Methods have no return type or parameters. They may be defined using a combination of assignments, print statements and method calls. A method may either invoke other methods defined in the same class or methods in any other class defined within the same package by using references (class-typed attributes). ClassInstance represents a (runtime) object of a class. Notice how Method and Statement both have operations with a ClassInstance parameter. This allows invoking methods and executing statements for one particular object (class instance). A ClassInstance is constructed by invoking the operation create() in the New class.

The metamodel for the SML is given in Fig. 4. The StateMachine class has an operation named run that takes two arguments. The first parameter is of type Event, the other is of the more generic type EObject. The latter allows sending an object of an EObject subtype as an optional argument when a new event is raised. The Transition class has an operation named trigger which causes a state change if the event received matches the event associated with any of the outgoing transitions. The metamodel includes a class Action with an operation named invoke. The invoke() operation has to be overridden in a subtype of Action in order to provide a custom action semantics (when using the language by itself).

Both metamodels are defined in EMF. The operational semantics of the classes has been added by building on the code generated using the built-in code generator of the EMF framework. Thus, the models/programs of the two languages may be run standalone. In order to model the behaviour of objects we need to extend the GPL metamodel with concepts for sending signals/events. In particular, we want to add a new kind of statement that allows sending signals from within methods. Figure 5 shows how this can be achieved.

Behaviour is intended to be a proxy class for the StateMachine class in the SML metamodel, whereas BehaviourEvent is intended to represent the Event class. Notice that using send signal statements and creating Behaviour objects are optional, which means that existing models and tools are not impacted significantly, e.g. existing models of the GPL metamodel are still valid. That is, classes in the extended GPL language may have behaviour externally defined if required. The only required update to e.g. a model editor is to support creating instances of a proxy class, if such is added to a metamodel to facilitate composition (existing classes in a metamodel can also be used as proxy classes).

The next step is to compose the metamodels and models in the two languages. The behaviour of the objects of a class may be modelled by a state machine. An object's state thus depends on the current state of the state machine and what signals (events) that have been received. The source of such signals is irrelevant in this case, but we assume there is some kind of sensor. An example program in the extended GPL is given in Fig. 6. A send signal statement takes two arguments; an event name and the object on which to send the signal. The signalling concept could have been defined to wait for an external event from e.g. a sensor. A behaviour is associated to the C2 class by setting a flag named behaviour (resulting in the creation of a Behaviour object). To keep things manageable, what we set out to do can be summarised by these main points:

```
package Example {
  class C1 {
    attribute c2 : C2

    main() {
      c2 = new C2();
      c2.print();
      sendSignal( "On", c2 );
      c2.print();
      sendSignal( "Off", c2 );
      c2.print();
      sendSignal( "On", c2 );
      c2.print();
    }
  }

  class C2 [behaviour = true] {
    attribute a : Int

    setA0() { a = 0; }
    setA1() { a = 1; }
    print() { _print( "Value:" + a ); }
  }
}
```

Fig. 6. An example GPL program.

- Program execution starts by invocation of main
- An "On" signal/event is sent to an object of the C2 class
- The event is forwarded to the specified SML model (utilising the framework)
- The current state of the state machine changes from Idle to On
- The state change causes invocation of setA1() in C2 (utilising the framework)
- The value of a is printed to screen

The simple scenario above suffices to underline the mechanics of our framework.

4   The Framework

We have implemented a prototypical framework that realises the concepts of this paper. The framework builds on top of EMF. This means that it works with all EMF-compatible metamodels and their operational semantics (model code).

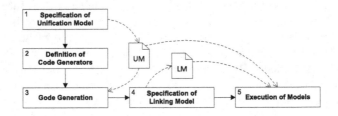

Fig. 7. The five phases of non-intrusive model composition.

Non-intrusive composition using the framework corresponds to the five phases illustrated in Fig. 7. We will discuss each phase in detail using the example.

4.1   Specification of Unification Model

In order to specify the behaviour for the Class concept using a state machine model we have to create a set of unification points that relate the classes of the two metamodels. The Behaviour class in the GPL metamodel is going to represent the StateMachine class in the SML metamodel, whereas Action will be representing Method. Furthermore, the BehaviourEvent class of the GPL metamodel will be unified with the Event class of the SML metamodel. Four unification points are required to achieve this.

Behaviour is intended to be a proxy class for StateMachine. Hence, all the structure of Behaviour needs to be matched by equivalent structure in StateMachine, since code generated for the Class concept will implicitly refer to such structure. Behaviour contains an operation with two parameters; one of type BehaviourEvent and one of type ClassInstance. StateMachine contains an operation as well with parameters of type Event and EObject. The only way that Behaviour and StateMachine can be unified is if the BehaviourEvent class can be unified with the Event class and the ClassInstance class can be unified with the EMF built-in EObject interface. BehaviourEvent consists of an attribute with a String type. Event has a String attribute as well. Hence, BehaviourEvent and Event can be unified by a symmetric unification point since BehaviourEvent and Event are structurally equivalent. Moreover, ClassInstance can be unified with EObject. ClassInstance is not a subtype of EObject. However, the Java counterpart of ClassInstance, ClassInstanceImpl, will be generated as a subtype of the EObjectImpl Java class by the built-in EMF code generator. EObjectImpl implements the EObject interface. As a result, Behaviour and StateMachine may indeed be unified by an asymmetric unification point. The purpose of the EObject parameter in the run() operation is to allow sending an optional argument. In the example, a ClassInstance object of the C2 class, whose behaviour is modelled by the state machine model, is passed as an argument. It is later used to know what object on which to invoke the setA1() operation. Action contains an operation named invoke with an EObject parameter, whereas Method contains an operation run() with a parameter of type ClassInstance. We have already seen that ClassInstance and EObject are type-compatible, thus, Action and Method can be unified. Notice that additional structure in StateMachine with respect to Behaviour, and additional structure in Method with respect to Action, would have been ignored as it is not required for the partial representation whose requirements are specified by the proxy classes (Behaviour and Action). Figure 8 gives the complete Unification Model. The nodes representing parameters are replaced with types instead of parameter names to improve the readability of the figure.

4.2   Definition of Code Generators

The framework supports the automatic generation of reflective code for linking the operational semantics of two metamodels non-intrusively. By also using subtyping and overriding of methods we ensure that the existing operational semantics does not need to be changed.

In the example, the added Behaviour class in the GPL metamodel is intended to represent the StateMachine class in the SML metamodel. This means that the operational semantics of the Class concept of the GPL metamodel needs to be revised to reflect this. This is achieved by creating a code generator which outputs a subtype of ClassImpl. ClassImpl is the Java class generated by EMF which defines the Class concept's operational semantics. The subtype will contain the necessary code for interacting with the operational semantics of the StateMachine class. The code will be defined in an operation named signal. The signal() operation has a parameter typed with BehaviourEvent and one typed with ClassInstance. It will be invoked from the operational semantics of the SendSignal class, i.e. an overridden version of the exec() operation as defined in Statement. See Fig. 9.

Similarly, Action is intended to represent Method. Thus, a code generator that generates a subtype of the TransitionImpl class needs to be constructed. The code generators may be simple Java classes or utilise emitter templates. Code

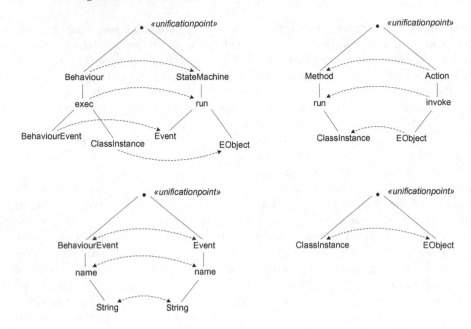

Fig. 8. The four unification points between classes in the GPL and SML metamodels.

```
public class ClassImplCustom extends ClassImpl
{
    public void signal( BehaviourEvent be,
        ClassInstance ci )
    {
        ...
    }
}
```

Fig. 9. The subtype of ClassImpl.

generators are used as tools for simplifying specification of glue code. It is possible to define the subtypes manually and utilise the framework directly, though this requires writing a lot more code.

4.3   Code Generation

The code generators are run to generate code required for linking the operational semantics of two or more metamodels. The new code is added to the existing code defining a metamodel's operational semantics by using inheritance. A build script also ensures that the EMF factories are updated to create objects of the generated subtypes. The subtypes are still compatible with EMF. The generated subtypes contain manually defined domain-specific code and automatically produced reflective code. There are two types of reflective code that may be generated: code for accessing attributes and/or code for invoking operations. The reflective code may be tailored by using a set of simple options/flags, e.g. it may be required to clone a set of objects at runtime or send objects as operation arguments that will later be returned in a callback fashion. The framework will take care of forwarding invocations between two metamodels' operational semantics and convert parameter types at runtime (corresponding to symmetric unification points). That is, it eliminates the need for a common type (used in the definitions of both metamodels) when sending non-primitive values.

4.4 Specification of Linking Model

The Linking Model allows pin-pointing what (proxy) object of a given model that should be linked to a (target) object in another model. The Linking Model is built by referring to objects of different models and building pairs of two objects. In principle, there is no restriction to what objects that may be linked. However, only pairs that reflect unification points in the Unification Model are valid.

Figure 10 gives a state machine model whose definition captures the intended class/object behaviour, and the objects of the GPL program previously introduced. Notice the event names that trigger the transitions, e.g. "On" for the transition between the Idle and On states. What we want to achieve is that each signal/event from the GPL program is forwarded to the state machine model. Hence, we need to create an M_1-mapping between the Behaviour object and the object of the StateMachine class. An important point is that each instance of the C2 class needs a unique set of runtime objects representing the state machine model, since their behaviour is independent. This is achieved by setting a flag when utilising the generateOperationCall() method of the framework[2]. However, it is still possible to specify the Linking Model with only one state machine model (at M_1). The state machine model contains two Action objects. These objects need to be linked to the Method objects representing the setA0() and setA1() methods. By creating these mappings, we complete the definition of the Linking Model.

4.5 Execution of Models

By linking model objects we are able to ensure that the corresponding runtime objects (Java objects) are linked as well. This is essential for the operational semantics of different metamodels to work in concert. The framework forwards operation invocations and deals with conversion of runtime objects used as arguments. It utilises the Unification Model to find the correct pairing of classes and creates objects using reflective code. Figure 11 details how the operational semantics of the two languages work together. It also summarises how non-intrusive composition works. To avoid confusion we use the term *object* for an M_1-object, e.g. the object C1 resulting from instantiating the Class concept in the GPL metamodel. For a runtime object of C1 we use the term *instance*. Furthermore, invocations of operations (language semantics) are in a regular font, whereas invocations of methods (in GPL programs) are in an italic font.

---

[2] The method generates reflective code for invocation of an operation.

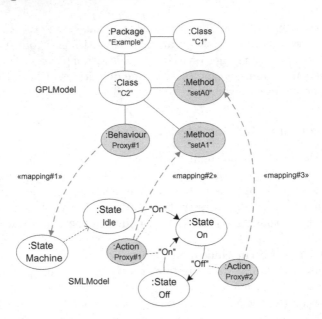

Fig. 10. Linking of the objects in the GPL and SML models (graphical representation of the Linking Model).

The execution starts by invoking the exec() operation on the Class object that represents C1 in the GPL model (1). A instance of C1 (represented by a ClassInstance object) is passed as argument to the operation (manually chosen). The semantics of the exec() operation invokes the main() method as defined in the C1 class (2). The print() method of the C2 class is then invoked after instantiating this class (3). The next statement of the main() method is a send signal statement (4). The semantics of this statement creates a BehaviourEvent instance and invokes the signal() operation on the C2 object (5). The BehaviourEvent and C2 instances are passed as arguments to the operation. signal() invokes the exec() operation on the associated Behaviour object (6). More precisely, the invocation of exec() does not result in the actual operation in the Behaviour class to be invoked. Instead the operation invocation is sent to the framework where it is resolved and forwarded as an invocation of the run() operation on the StateMachine object in the SML model (7). This includes converting the BehaviourEvent instance passed as argument to an Event object. Notice how the ClassInstance object, representing the instance of C2, is sent as the second argument. The Event object causes the transition between the Idle and On state to be triggered (9). This results in the invoke() operation on the Action object to be invoked (10), or more precisely, the invocation of the operation is resolved by the framework, which forwards the invocation to the run() operation on the designated Method object (11). The argument to run() is the ClassInstance object that was initally passed via the call to the run() operation on the StateMachine object. The setA1() method is then invoked on the ClassInstance object, i.e. the instance of the C2 class. Finally, the

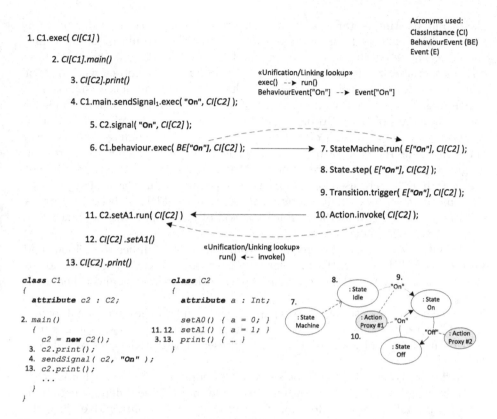

Fig. 11. Illustration of how a object's behaviour is executed at runtime. Acronyms used: ClassInstance (CI), BehaviourEvent (BE), Event (E).

print() method is invoked and the value 1 is printed to screen. Notice how the Unification Model and Linking Model are queried for information at runtime.

5   Evaluation

The key problem arising when composing metamodels is how existing tools and models are rendered invalid. The approach of this paper addresses this. Specifically, we wanted to show that it is possible to combine two languages' operational semantics by defining mappings between the languages' concepts and objects in the models of these languages in a separate manner. By using reflective code we are able to forward operation invocations and convert parameter types. The key advantage with our approach is that the metamodels' structures are not woven together. Hence, there are minimal impacts on modelling artefacts that are defined relative to the metamodels. Even though the approach is flexible, it may be required to design a metamodel in a way that allows it to be composed with another metamodel. As an example, it may be required to add a proxy class to an existing metamodel in order to create the structural bridge between metamodels. That said, an object of such a proxy class would be optional and therefore not impact existing tools or models significantly. The proxy class is only instantiated when the metamodel is intended to be composed with another metamodel. An interesting observation is that the object of a class changes role depending on whether the class is part of a unification point or not. Consider the Method class of the GPL metamodel in Fig. 3. Let us assume that we have a metamodel for modelling of methods - an expression language. The Method class may thus represent a proxy for the top node class of such an expression language. In such case, an object of the Method class does now have a different purpose. It is merely used to establish an M_1-mapping in the Linking Model. This means that its contained statement objects would have been ignored. A class may have several methods. Each method object would thus be linked to a distinct expression language model.

Evolution of metamodels requires evolution of the Unification Model and Linking Model. However, the complexity concerned with changing these models are significantly lower than addressing co-evolution of models and other modelling artefacts.

The mechanism described in this paper focuses on how the operational semantics of different languages can work together. The M_1- and M_2-mappings may also be used by tools, e.g. by editors, to present integrated views of different languages.

Reflective code is known to be slower than non-reflective code. The mechanism discussed in this paper uses reflective code to decouple different metamodels' operational semantics. However, the reflective code is only active when the operational semantics of the metamodels interact. For the example in this paper, this adds up to two operation invocations (with instantiation of arguments) per new signal/event received. That is, most of the operational semantics being executed is based entirely on non-reflective code.

In the example, we saw how the Behaviour class is a placeholder for the StateMachine class. Consequently, it appears that an object of Class contains a StateMachine object via the behaviour containment reference. This is an important point, because the containment reference dictates the type of composition between the GPL and SML metamodels. That is, the association represents a composition relation.

We have not discussed tool support for creating the Unification Model and Linking Model. In an industrial context, a reflective graphical editor (created using e.g. GMF) may greatly simplify the process of specifying these models by allowing to draw the M_2- and M_1-mappings directly between metamodel and model structure. The graphical models can then be used to generate the Unification Model and Linking Model automatically. A graphical editor may also provide a simple way of specifying the manual code required to realise unification of two classes' operational semantics. An editor may also implement functionality for addressing co-evolution of the models.

6   Related Work

We have not been able to find much related work concerned directly with the implicit nature of our composition approach. That is, the literature mainly covers explicit model composition and adaptation strategies using migration techniques and transformations. Most of the available related work addresses composition of structure and does not directly consider composition of operational semantics.

Methods for automatic co-evolution of metamodels and models are necessary to further model-driven engineering. The work of [11] describes how models may be migrated as a consequence of metamodel adaptations. This is achieved using coupled transactions. A coupled transaction is constructed using a set of primitives. There are two types of primitives: primitives for querying a metamodel or model, and primitives for modifying such artefacts. A coupled transaction preserves both metamodel consistency and metamodel-model conformance. The work has been validated by implementing a language on top of EMF. With respect to the work of our paper, the method for coupled co-evolution works on metamodels and models by changing these explicitly. Hence, other modelling artefacts are impacted by the changes, i.e. co-evolution of tools are not addressed.

Another similar approach for metamodel-model co-evolution is discussed in [12]. The work is based on the application of transformations both on the metamodel and model level. Co-evolution of metamodels is described using a set of relations between metamodels, in which are used to ensure semantics and instance preservation for the transformations.

The authors of [13,14] discuss how model migration steps can be generated directly from a difference model that encorporates information on the evolutionary changes of a metamodel. The difference model is used as basis for a higher-order transformation in which produces a transformation that is capable of re-establishing conformance between models and their metamodel. The work addresses concerns related to parallel dependent metamodel manipulations which may cause conflicts as they work on the same metamodel elements. These can be resolved in an iterative process, which yields a set of parallel independent modifications.

The work of [15] presents a catalogue of (coupled) operators for achieving automated migration of models as a consequence of evolving metamodels. The operators are classified according to several dimensions: language preservation, model preservation and bi-directionality.

The work discussed in our paper does not utilise coupled operators. However, the M_1-mappings carefully reflect the M_2-mappings. Specifically, only objects whose classes are related using M_2-mappings may safely be related using M_1-mappings.

Another approach utilising higher-order transformations is discussed in [16]. The approach is based on defining bi-directional transformations between modelling artefacts, and uses higher-order transformations on the specifications of the bi-directional transformations. This ensures that also the transformations between the modelling artefacts co-evolve correctly.

An approach for defining reusable metamodel behaviour is discussed in [17]. The approach is based on generic concepts which allow adding the same behaviour to unrelated metamodels. This is achieved by using pattern matching according to the parameters and requirements of the concept. A similar approach, in the form of model types, is discussed in [18].

7   Conclusion and Future Work

Composition mechanisms that work on both the metamodel and model level are important to ensure consistency in the metamodelling ecosystem. In this paper, we have illustrated how metamodels and models can be composed in a practically non-intrusive manner in order for their operational semantics to be linked together. Non-intrusive composition is achieved by utilising a set of mappings, both at the metamodel level and at the model level. By building on the principle of partial representation we are able to specify proxy classes. A proxy class is a placeholder for another class. Its attributes and operations represent structural requirements that need to be supported by the class for which the proxy class is a placeholder. Non-intrusive composition allows for metamodels and models to be composed without rendering models, editors and other modelling artefacts invalid.

An interesting next step is to see whether the mappings may be realised in a different form and incorporated more closely into a language's definition, and to study whether non-intrusive composition brings value also for non-executable models. Future work also includes solidification of the framework to industry standard, with the inclusion of a graphical editor.

References

1. Morin, B., Perrouin, G., Lahire, P., Barais, O., Vanwormhoudt, G., Jézéquel, J.-M.: Weaving variability into domain metamodels. In: Schürr, A., Selic, B. (eds.) MODELS 2009. LNCS, vol. 5795, pp. 690–705. Springer, Heidelberg (2009)
2. Fleurey, F., Baudry, B., France, R.B., Ghosh, S.: A generic approach for automatic model composition. In: Giese, H. (ed.) MODELS 2008. LNCS, vol. 5002, pp. 7–15. Springer, Heidelberg (2008)
3. Kolovos, D.S., Paige, R.F., Polack, F.A.C.: Merging models with the Epsilon Merging Language (EML). In: Wang, J., Whittle, J., Harel, D., Reggio, G. (eds.) MoDELS 2006. LNCS, vol. 4199, pp. 215–229. Springer, Heidelberg (2006)
4. Groher, I., Voelter, M.: Xweave - models and aspects in concert. In: 10th International Workshop on Aspect-Oriented Modeling (AOM 2007), pp. 35–40. ACM Press (2007)
5. Di Ruscio, D., Iovino, L., Pierantonio, A.: Evolutionary togetherness: how to manage coupled evolution in metamodeling ecosystems. In: Ehrig, H., Engels, G., Kreowski, H.-J., Rozenberg, G. (eds.) ICGT 2012. LNCS, vol. 7562, pp. 20–37. Springer, Heidelberg (2012)
6. García, J., Diaz, O., Azanza, M.: Model transformation co-evolution: a semi-automatic approach. In: Czarnecki, K., Hedin, G. (eds.) SLE 2012. LNCS, vol. 7745, pp. 144–163. Springer, Heidelberg (2013)

7. Demuth, A., Lopez-Herrejon, R.E., Egyed, A.: Supporting the co-evolution of metamodels and constraints through incremental constraint management. In: Moreira, A., Schätz, B., Gray, J., Vallecillo, A., Clarke, P. (eds.) MODELS 2013. LNCS, vol. 8107, pp. 287–303. Springer, Heidelberg (2013)
8. OMG: Meta object facility (mof) core specification (2014)
9. EMF: Eclipse modeling framework (emf) (2014)
10. Muller, P.-A., Fleurey, F., Jézéquel, J.-M.: Weaving executability into object-oriented meta-languages. In: Briand, L.C., Williams, C. (eds.) MoDELS 2005. LNCS, vol. 3713, pp. 264–278. Springer, Heidelberg (2005)
11. Herrmannsdoerfer, M., Benz, S., Juergens, E.: COPE - Automating coupled evolution of metamodels and models. In: Drossopoulou, S. (ed.) ECOOP 2009. LNCS, vol. 5653, pp. 52–76. Springer, Heidelberg (2009)
12. Wachsmuth, G.: Metamodel adaptation and model co-adaptation. In: Ernst, E. (ed.) ECOOP 2007. LNCS, vol. 4609, pp. 600–624. Springer, Heidelberg (2007)
13. Cicchetti, A., Di Ruscio, D., Eramo, R., Pierantonio, A.: Automating co-evolution in model-driven engineering. In: Enterprise Distributed Object Computing Conference (2008)
14. Cicchetti, A., Di Ruscio, D., Eramo, R., Pierantonio, A.: Meta-model differences for supporting model co-evolution. In: Proceedings of the 2nd Workshop on Model-Driven Software Evolution (2008)
15. Herrmannsdoerfer, M., Vermolen, S.D., Wachsmuth, G.: An extensive catalog of operators for the coupled evolution of metamodels and models. In: Malloy, B., Staab, S., van den Brand, M. (eds.) SLE 2010. LNCS, vol. 6563, pp. 163–182. Springer, Heidelberg (2011)
16. Hoisl, B., Hu, Z., Hidaka, S.: Towards co-evolution in model-driven development via bidirectional higher-order transformation. In: Proceedings of the 2nd International Conference on Model-Driven Engineering and Software Development. Springer (2014, to appear)
17. de Lara, J., Guerra, E.: From types to type requirements: genericity for model-driven engineering. Softw. Syst. Model. 12, 453–474 (2011). Springer
18. Steel, J., Jzquel, J.M.: On model typing. Softw. Syst. Model. 6(4), 401–413 (2007). Springer

Computability Assurance for UML Template Binding

José Farinha[1]([⊠]) and Pedro Ramos[2]

[1] ISTAR, ISCTE-IUL Lisbon University Institute, Av. Forças Armadas, Lisbon, Portugal
jose.farinha@iscte.pt
[2] IT-IUL, ISCTE-IUL Lisbon University Institute, Av. Forças Armadas, Lisbon, Portugal
pedro.ramos@iscte.pt

Abstract. Binding to a template in UML encompasses the substitution of that template's parameters by compatible domain elements. However, such compatibility is scarcely verified by a minimal set of rules in the UML metamodel. As a consequence, binding to a template can result in badly-formed models. Such option in the design of UML was certainly intentional, since more stringent rules could prevent the development of richer semantics for the *Bind* relationship. But, while such semantics are not in place, problems may arise in several parts of a model just because of a bad, yet valid, template parameter substitution. This paper proposes a new set of validation rules for UML templates, introducing the requirement of *Functional Conformance*. Functional Conformance guarantees well-formedness and computability for elements bound to a template, consistently with the default semantics of the Bind relationship. It is formulated as OCL constraints on top of the OMG's UML metamodel.

Keywords: UML · Templates · Verification · Computability

1 Introduction

Through the concept of Template, UML allows the definition of generic solutions to recurring problems. An UML template is a model element embodying a patterned solution that can be reproduced within any domain model where the addressed problem is observed. This is achieved by binding a model element of that domain to the template, through a *Bind* relationship. In order to have a template reproduction contextualized to the target (domain) model, a template is a parameterized element. A template parameter marks an element participating in the template's specification that, in a reproduction of that template, must be substituted by an actual element in the target model. Only when all of the template's parameters are substituted, it becomes an actual, fully integrated solution in the target model.

Aiming at getting consistent specifications out of a template reproduction, UML enforces a set of constraints to template parameter substitutions. One such constraint imposes that a substitute element must be of the same metaclass as the parametered element: an attribute must be replaced by an attribute, an operation by an operation, etc. Another constraint ensures that if a parameter exposes a typed element, its substitute must have a type that conforms to that parametered element's type.

© Springer International Publishing Switzerland 2015
P. Desfray et al. (Eds.): MODELSWARD 2015, CCIS 580, pp. 190–212, 2015.
DOI: 10.1007/978-3-319-27869-8_11

Yet, the set of validations falls short in guaranteeing the well-formedness of the element resulting from the template. For instance, UML allows an operation *Op1* be substituted by an operation *Op2* whose signature is not compatible with the former's. If *Op1* is substituted by *Op2*, every call to *Op1* in the template's code will be reproduced as a call to *Op2*...with a set of arguments aligned to *Op1*'s signature, which makes calls to *Op2* badly-formed. Also, UML allows the specification of a set of substitutions that are not mutually consistent. For instance, having a class and one of its attributes exposed as parameters in a template, UML allows the former being replaced by a class *C'* and the latter by an attribute that is not a member of *C'*. Merely considering the semantics and constraints that UML declares for the concept of template, according to version 2.1.4 of the standard [6], it seems the language greatly relies on the modeler's skills and prudence.

In spite of the permissive set of validations, a bad substitution will generally be prevented by some well-formedness rule, associated to some element within the bound element that will try to use the bad substitute. In the example above, the substitution of *Op1* by *Op2* will generate errors raising from the calls to *Op2*, which will actually prevent the substitution. However, the error that will be reported will be detuned from the real source of the problem. The problem will be reported somewhat like "Arguments to *Op2* do not match that operation's signature". But the cause of the problem is the substitution of *Op1* by *Op2*. Hence, although UML is not really trusting in the prudence of the developer, it certainly trusts in his/her ability to diagnose.

This paper proposes an additional set of constraints for the concept of Template, aiming at removing the aforementioned disadvantages. The set of constraints was designed with the following purposes: (1) Guaranteeing the well-formedness and computability of any element resulting from the application of a template; (2) Reporting problems resulting from incorrect usages of a template to their real causes, i.e., to inadequate bindings and/or substitutions.

In (1), 'well-formedness' means that none of the components of an element resulting from the template will violate any constraint imposed by the UML metamodel. 'Computability' means that every expression within the template or within the bound element can be processed and evaluated to a value (including *Null*), i.e., the expression successfully compiles in the scope of the model it belongs to. For simplicity, in this text, the term 'computability' will be used meaning 'well-formedness' as well.

To accomplish (2), the proposed constraints establish conformance criteria between every parametered element and its substitute. The way a parametered element is used by the template does not participate in the criteria. In that way, any error may be reported exclusively in terms of the adequacy of a substitute to a parameter, in the context of a specific binding to the template.

The constraints put forth in this text formulate a concept named *Functional Conformance*, a term that aims at denoting the equivalence between two elements, from a third-party, client perspective. An element (the substitute) conforms functionally to another element (the parameter) if its characteristics and scope allow it being used instead of the latter. Functional Conformance is presented through its definition and several illustrating examples, which should provide an intuitive perception of its effectiveness as a guarantee of computability. A formal demonstration of that effectiveness is postponed to a future paper.

The structure of the paper is as follows: Sect. 2 provides a brief introduction to the concept of Template in UML; Sect. 3 points out some problems in assuring that elements resulting from templates are well-formed and computable; Sect. 4 proposes the concept of Functional Conformance to ensure computability; Sect. 5 presents related work; Sect. 6 draws some conclusions on an empirical evaluation of functional conformance and outlines some prospective benefits of the concept; the appendix includes a set of OCL constraints that assesses functional conformance.

2   An Introduction to UML Templates

In UML, a template is a parameterized model element that can be replicated and have its replicas contextualized to the models they are put into. Model elements of several kinds may be qualified as templates. For instance, classes, packages and operations are allowed to be declared as templates and, therefore, be reproduced as concrete classes, packages and operations, respectively.

The complete set of model element types that can be declared as templates – called templateable elements – is comprehended by the following metaclasses: *Classifier*, *Package*, *Operation* and *StringExpression*. *Classifier* encompasses all kinds of element that may have instances: Class, Datatype, Association, Use Case, Activity, etc. Package templates should be used when a model fragment encompassing two or more classifiers is meant to form a single template and be replicated as a whole. Operation templates lack of graphical notation but are supported by the UML metamodel. Finally, *String-Expression* templates are used to derive concrete element names or literal strings by concatenating the values of a template's parameters. *StringExpression* templates do not pose computability problems; therefore, they will not be referred from now on.

In this paper, the term "target" is used to refer to a model, package or class that gives context to a replica of a template.

Figure 1 shows a class and a package template. A template element is recognized graphically through the dashed rectangle on the top-right corner, whose purpose is to declare the template's parameters.

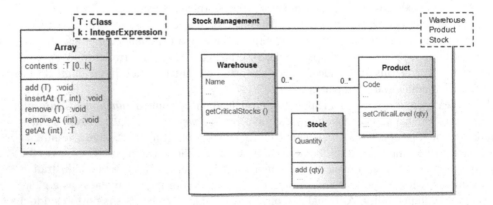

Fig. 1. Examples of class and package templates.

Template parameters declare some of the elements participating in the specification of the template as parametered. Such elements are said *exposed as parameters*. When applying a template, its parametered elements must be replaced by elements of the target model in order to obtain a fully functional and contextualized reproduction of the template. If any of the parametered elements is not replaced, the reproduction of the template is also a template – this allows the incremental definition of templates.

In this text, for clarity reasons, *parametered element* will sometimes be referred simply as *parameter*. However, it should be noted this is use of "parameter" in the broad sense, since there is a strict difference in UML between the parameter and the element it exposes: the parameter is a "mark" superimposed to the element, which qualifies it as replaceable when applying the template, and it can supply a default in case such element is not explicitly replaced.

The UML concept for assigning a target element to a template parameter is *Substitution*. It is said that the target element *substitutes* the parameter. The former is often called *actual parameter* and the latter *formal parameter*. In this text, for simplicity, an actual parameter will be referred as the *substitute*.

In Fig. 1, class *Array* is a template with two parameters, T e k. T's kind is *Class*, meaning it must be substituted by a class. k's kind is *IntegerExpression* and therefore must be substituted by such expressions, including one with a plain literal value. The package *StockManagement* is a template with three parameters – *Warehouse*, *Product*, and *Stock* – all of them exposing classes. When applied to a target package, its parameters require picking three target classes as substitutes. These substituting classes will receive the specifications of their respective parametered classes, and any relationships between these.

Both the name and the kind of a parameter are determined by the element the parameter exposes. In the example in Fig. 1, parameter T exposes a class named 'T' (not shown in the figure) and parameter k exposes an integer expression named 'k'. Parameters adopt the names of the elements they expose.

Any model element accessible from a template may be exposed as a parameter. For instance, in Fig. 2 *AlphabeticList* is a class-template with one parameter that exposes another class. The dashed line labeled "exposes" is merely illustrative; there is no graphical notation in UML that links a parameter to the element it exposes.

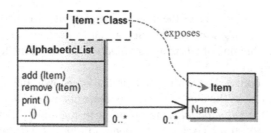

Fig. 2. Definition of a template with a class-parameter.

A template may be used to specify elements from scratch or to add specifications to elements having specifications of their own. For instance, a class-template may be used to create a class as a replica of itself, as well as to add all its members (features, constraints, etc.) to an existing class. The application of a template is specified through a *Bind* relationship. A Binding is a directed relationship from a *bound element* to a template. By means of the Bind relationship, everything specified for the template is also valid for the bound element.

Figure 3 shows a binding to the *AlphabeticList* template, by class *AlphabeticList<Person>*, which is said anonymous. In that binding, the template parameter (*Item*) is substituted by class *Person*. The UML notation for a substitution is textual, in the form 'parameter –> substitute', placed next to the graphical representation of the binding. The figure also shows (on the right) the semantics of that binding: class *AlphabeticList<Person>* receives a reproduction of *AlphabeticList*'s specification (of all its features, behaviors, constraints, etc.) with all references to *Item* replaced by references to *Person*. It's worth noting that, among the features inherited by *AlphabeticList<Person>*, this class receives a copy of the association-end connected to *Item*; such copy will connect to *Person*, since this class substitutes *Item*. Strictly, the association-end is reproduced as a property and such property will not be part of any association. Nevertheless, the association symbol linking to *Person* is shown for a question of clarity.

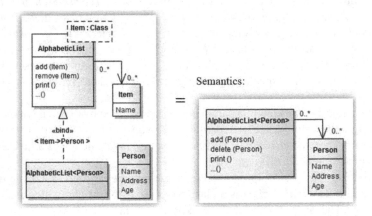

Fig. 3. A bind and its semantics, producing an anonymous class.

Figure 4 shows another bind to the same template, with a bound class that is not anonymous, but named *Glossary*. Strictly according to the semantics of UML for the Bind relationship, the binding of *Glossary* to *AlphabeticList* is equivalent to the diagram on the right of that figure.

Figure 5 shows a bound class with specifications of its own. In such cases, the bind merges the specification of the template with the contents of the bound class.

The purpose of the *AlphabeticList* template is to maintain a list of items sorted alphabetically. To perform such ordering, its operations use an attribute called *Name* in class *Item* (the use of *Name* is not observable in the figure). Since the code of *AlphabeticList* is copied to its bound classes, these will also use a *Name* attribute. Being *Item* substituted by another class, *Name* must also exist in this class. If it doesn't, the code of the bound class will not be compilable. (Notice that class *Item* is not part of the template;

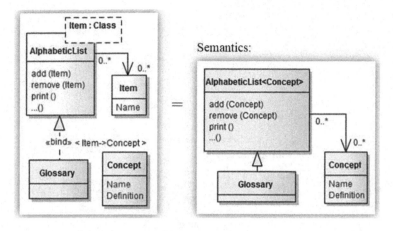

Fig. 4. Another example of binding to a template.

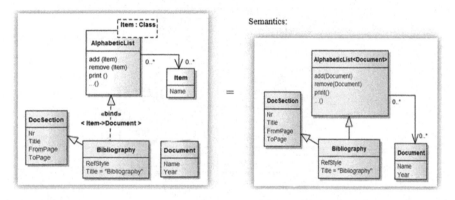

Fig. 5. A bound class with contents of its own.

thus, *Item*'s contents will not be copied to the substituting class; this class must have a *Name* attribute of its own.) The situation is exemplified in Fig. 6: since *Document* doesn't have a *Name* attribute (but one called 'Title', instead), every expression in the template referring to *Item::Name* will not be computable once reproduced in class *Bibliography*. For instance, expressions 'it.name' and 'iter.name' will not be computable in *Bibliography*.

Situations such as in Fig. 6 require flexibility regarding the attribute corresponding to *Name*, in the substituting class. This is achieved exposing *Name* as another template parameter. The definition of the template becomes as in Fig. 7.

Since the new parameter in Fig. 7 exposes an attribute, it must be substituted by an attribute in the target model. For attribute-parameters, UML establishes also that the type of the substitute must conform to the type of the parametered attribute. Thus, *Name* must be substituted by an attribute whose type is *String* or a subtype of it.

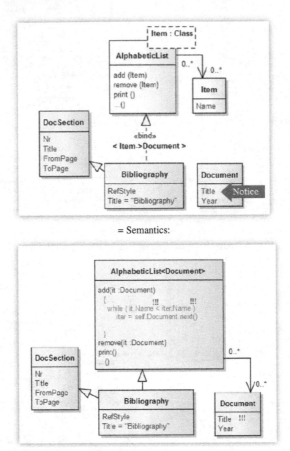

= Semantics:

Fig. 6. A bind that produces non-computable code.

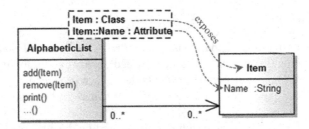

Fig. 7. Definition of a template with a class parameter and an attribute parameter.

Note: Although the UML notation for a substitution is textual, in this paper, for clarity reasons, sometimes it is shown graphically, draw as a dashed arrow (similar to a dependency) linking the parametered element to its substitute and labeled "substitution".

3   Some Limitations of UML Templates

Conformance of kind (class, attribute, package, etc.) and conformance of type (this for typed elements) are the only restrictions that apply to the substitution of UML template parameters. Consequently, not computable specifications such as the one previously shown in Fig. 6 and the one in Fig. 8 are considered valid bindings by UML.

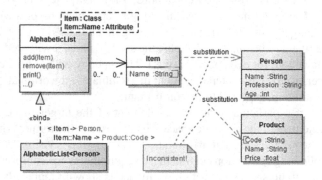

Fig. 8. A bind that produces non-computable code.

Since the referred situations lead to badly-formed elements or non-computable expressions, some error will be reported. However, that error will not refer the binding, nor the substitutions it contains, as the source of the problem. Instead, it will refer problems within the bound element that are not immediately recognized as consequences of an erroneous binding or substitution.

For instance, the problem with Fig. 6 is that template *AlphabeticList* is not applicable to classes *Bibliography* and *Document*. An error message should report that. More specifically, it could mention that it is because the substitution of *Item* by *Document* cannot be done. Instead of that, the error that is raised by the UML metamodel is about variables *it* and *iter* being unable to access an attribute called 'Name'.

Similarly, the error raised in Fig. 8 will mention that variables *it* and *iter* can't access an attribute (*Code*), instead of the real cause: the incorrect substitution of the attribute *Name* of *Item* by an attribute not pertaining to the substitute of *Item* (*Person*). The rule that would signal correctly the problem would be: considering two parametered elements P_{child} and P_{parent} being both substituted in a binding, if P_{child} belongs to P_{parent} then the substitute of P_{child} must belong to the substitute of P_{parent}. Such rule should be a constraint to substitutions, but no such constraint exists in UML.

Similar problems will arise if a single-valued property is substituted by a multivalued one, or if an operation is substituted by another with incompatible signature.

The examples given so far show that there are some reasonable constraints missing in UML templates. Although not strictly necessary to prevent badly-formed elements resulting from a template, their absence increases the risk of ill-specified binds and causes a parallax problems in error-reporting. Next section proposes a set of constraints that would remove these shortcomings of UML templates while ensuring the computability of bound elements.

4   Functional Conformance

The concept of *Functional Conformance* between two model elements is used to express that if one is used successfully by a template the other will also be used successfully in a reproduction of that template, if used in the same circumstances and with the same goals. Taking an example from a domain other than computer science, it can be said that a piano is functionally conformant to a clavichord, for the purpose of playing a classical piece of music. The piano may be used in today's reproductions of a Mozart piece, substituting the long ago used clavichord. Providing that it is used to play the keyboard line of the piece (it won't be functional to play the strings' part), it will produce the same results as the clavichord (or even better results). The analogy with template-based software development is: the parametered element in a template is the original "instrument" to which its substitute is expected to be conformant.

In the scope of a particular binding, an element of the target space functionally conforms to an element of the template space if it conforms to the former regarding type, multiplicity, contents, and static nature (is static?), and also if it is visible from the bound element. The following subsections define these requirements for conformance.

Note: In some figures of this paper conformance is shown graphically as a dashed arrow, from the parametered element to its substitute, meaning that the latter conforms to the former. This graphical representation uses the reversed direction of that of the phrase "conforms to" for the sake of consistency with the direction of the UML notation for substitution (parametered – > substitute).

4.1   Type Conformance

Type conformance applies to every typed element: properties, expressions, constants, operation parameters, action pins, etc. This conformity criterion is already partially enforced by UML, which states that the type of a substituting element must be the same or a subtype of that of the parametered element. However, this UML rule is incomplete, for two reasons: (1) UML only applies it to properties and value specifications (expressions and constants) (see constraints of *TemplateParameterSubstitution* and operation *isCompatibleTo()*, in [6]); (2) this rule should be applied only if the type of the parametered element is not substituted.

Full type conformance should be: (1) imposed on all typed elements; (2) formulated considering two different scenarios:

- If parametered element e^P has a type that is not substituted: element e^S conforms in type to e^P if its type is the same or a subtype of e^P's. This is the original UML rule.
- If e^P's type is substituted: element e^S conforms in type to e^P if its type is the same or a subtype of the substitute of e^P's type.

The second scenario is exemplified in Fig. 9.

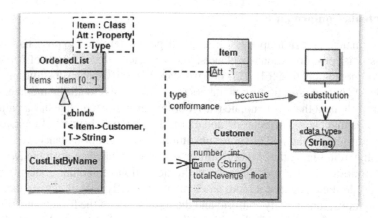

Fig. 9. Type conformance when the type is substituted.

4.2   Multiplicity Conformance

UML imposes no constraints on template parameter substitution regarding the multiplicity of the involved elements. We propose the criteria of multiplicity conformance. This rule checks if two elements involved in a substitution are both single valued (upper multiplicity = 1) or both multivalued (upper multiplicity > 1) and, for the second case, both elements must have the same kind of ordering (ordered/not-ordered).

The single/multiple valued is important for computability because code that uses a multivalued element does it through flow control structures and operations that act upon collections of values (e.g.: foreach x in obj.feature, obj.feature.size(), etc.), while code using a single-valued element accesses it directly. Therefore, a computable piece of code that uses a single-valued element becomes non-computable if that element is replaced by a multivalued one, and vice versa.

For multivalued elements, the ordered/not-ordered nature may also impact computability. On ordered elements one can apply operations that assume an ordering of values, such as the OCL operations *first()*, *last()*, and *at()*.Calls to such operations will not compute if the ordered element is replaced by a non-ordered one. Similarly, some operations on non-ordered elements are not applicable to ordered ones, e.g. the OCL operation *intersection()*.

Strictly, computability would be compromised only if the code of the template includes any of these operations depending on ordered/not-ordered. This aspect opens the possibility for establishing two levels of conformity enforcement – say, strict and flexible – a subject for future discussion.

It is also worth explaining that the reason why this conformance criteria doesn't take into account concrete values of multiplicity, other than 1 and *, is because it is considered a matter of semantic equivalence, not a requisite for computability. Albeit a legitimate concern, it is also postponed for future discussion.

4.3 Contents Conformance

This conformance criterion applies to template parameters that expose namespaces: classes, associations, operations, packages, and all other sub constructs of *Namespace* in the UML metamodel (see [6]). This rule is meant to certify that a substituting element (e.g., a class) contains substituting members (e.g., attributes) to all the members of the parametered element that the template uses. For instance, if a template has a parameter-class and uses that class' attributes *a1* and *a2* of, then every substitute of the class must also have attributes *a1* and *a2* or some substitutes for these. For instance, recalling the template shown in Fig. 2, the class substituting *Item* must have an attribute *Name*.

The definition of this criterion requires the definition of another concept: *Implicit Substitution*. In the context of a bind, an element implicitly substitutes another if they are homonymous, functionally conform and the namespace of the former substitutes the namespace of the latter. In this definition, "homonymous" refers to having the same proper name, i.e., the elements have the same identification within the corresponding namespaces. For example, attributes *Item::Name* and *Person::Name* are (properly) homonymous. The same is true between the operations *Item::setName (String)* and *Person::setName (String)*. But not between *::setName (String)* and *::setName (String, String)*, because in UML an operation is identified by its signature (name and parameters). If two properly homonymous elements e^T and $e^\varnothing$ are also conformant in type, multiplicity, etc. (note the recursive definition) and the namespace of e^T is substituted by the namespace of $e^\varnothing$, then e^T is substituted implicitly by $e^\varnothing$. Notice that this definition is assuming that, even if the bind under consideration doesn't include an explicit substitution of e^T by $e^\varnothing$, such substitution will be made. For example, recalling Fig. 4, previous statement implies that, even though the modeler doesn't specify the substitution of *Item::Name* by *Concept::Name*, such substitution is done. Thus, the concept of implicit substitution is an assumption regarding the semantics of the Bind relationship, regarding an aspect that UML's official documentation is silent about. Such assumption certainly deserves further discussion, yet postponed for another text. For the current purpose, implicit substitutions are assumed, just on the basis that the automatic substitution of an element by another with the same characteristics and name (or signature) is a reasonable option.

Thus, *Contents Conformance* is defined as: in the context of a template binding, namespace $NS^\varnothing$ conforms in contents to a namespace NS^T if every element in NS^T referenced by the template is substituted, explicitly or implicitly, by elements in $NS^\varnothing$.

This rule would detect problems such as the one previously shown in Fig. 6. The substitution of *Item* by *Document* would be refused because those elements do not have conforming contents, since *Item::Name* is neither substituted nor homonymous of any attribute in *Document* (Fig. 10).

The contents conformance requirement assumes two particular forms:

- A corollary named *Membership Conformance*, preferable to the general rule in certain, well-known situations;
- A specialisation applicable to operations, named *Signature Conformance*;

These more specific rules are analyzed in the following subsections.

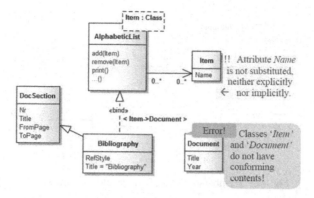

Fig. 10. A violation of contents conformance.

Membership Conformance. Erroneous binds such has the one previously show in Fig. 8 would be prevented by the contents conformance rule. In that figure, *Person* will not be accepted as a substitute for *Item* because its contents don't fully substitute those of *Item* used by the template. Yet, the inadequacy of *Person* would be reported in a more specific way rephrasing that violation of contents conformance as: the substitution of *Item* by *Person* is not possible because one of *Item*'s attributes, *Name*, is not substituted by an attribute of *Person*. Or the problem could be imputed to the substitution of *Name* by *Code*: *Code* cannot substitute *Name* because its owning class does not substitute *Name*'s owning class. This last report exemplifies the application of the corollary *Membership Conformance*, defined as:

An element $e^{\odot}$ conforms in membership to an element e^{T} if at least one of its namespaces substitutes one of e^{T}'s namespaces, either explicitly or implicitly.

Membership conformance is a sub-rule of (part of) contents conformance. It assesses the adequacy of a namespace's member instead of the adequacy of the namespace as a whole.

In the definition, the use of the plural "namespaces" is because an element may be inherited or imported and, consequently, be a member of several namespaces. Membership conformance is satisfied if the namespace substitution required by the rule occurs for any of these multiple namespaces, a detail that is not so apparent in the general rule (contents conformance). This is explained bellow.

Figure 11 shows a situation of membership conformance, involving inheritance. Since *Person* inherits *Name*, this attribute is member of *Entity* and *Person*, its namespaces. It is required that any of these classes substitutes *Item* in order to have membership conformance between *Att* and *Name*. It is so indeed (*Person* substitutes *Item*).

An element that is member of a template also acquires namespaces by means of bind relationships. This is due to the fact that the semantics of the bind relationship includes a generalization (see Fig. 4). Consequently, every element bound to a template becomes namespace of any non-private member of that template. Figure 12 shows a situation where membership conformance verifies, involving a bind. In that case, *Aged::Date* may substitute *Item::Att* because that attribute is member of Person and this class substitutes *Item*.

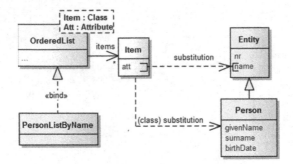

Fig. 11. Membership conformance and inheritance.

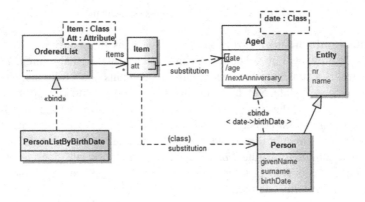

Fig. 12. Membership conformance and binding.

As a guideline to choose whether a problem should be reported by contents or by membership conformance, it should be checked whether contents conformance doesn't hold due to a missing substitution or due to an incorrect substitution. For instance, in Fig. 13 *att* may not be substituted by *wage* because that would lead to *PersonList* sorting *Person* objects by wage, while not every object of *Person* has a *wage* attribute. This problem will be detected by the contents conformance requirement (the contents of *Person* do not fully substitute those of *Item*) as well as by membership conformance (none of the namespaces of *att* is substituted by a namespace of *wage*). This problem would be more appropriately reported as a membership problem: *wage* cannot substitute *att* because the class it belongs to (*Employee*) doesn't substitute the class *Att* belongs to (*Item*). In this situation contents conformance doesn't hold due to a bad substitution.

When contents conformance is not observed due to a missing substitution, explicit or implicit, of members of the parameter-namespace, then the problem is be better reported by the general rule (contents conformance). For instance, Fig. 14 would raise an error message such as: *Person* cannot substitute *Item* because their contents do not conform. The problem could be further diagnosed, more specifically: *att* is not substituted. But this is not a violation of membership conformance. Such corollary is not even evaluable in the situation, since there is no prospective substitution for *att*.

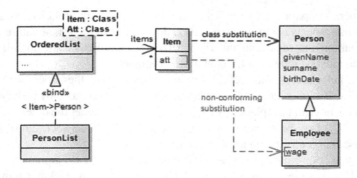

Fig. 13. A situation where reporting by membership conformance is better than by contents conformance.

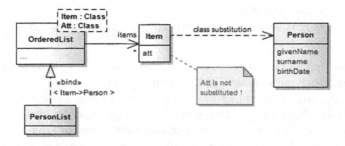

Fig. 14. A situation where reporting by contents conformance is preferable to membership conformance.

Signature Conformance. In UML, an operation is a special case of namespace. An operation's parameters are the members of that namespace. Thus, contents conformance converts to signature conformance when it comes to operations. Signature conformance checking is intended to assure that, when an operation foo_A $(p_{A1}, ...)$ is substituted by foo_B $(p_{B1}, ...)$, the computability of calls 'foo_A $(arg_{A1}, ..., arg_{An})$' in a template is preserved when such calls are replaced by 'foo_B $(arg_{B1}, ..., arg_{Bn})$' in the bound element.

Since UML doesn't consider the concept of substitution between operation parameters, only implicit substitutions occur between elements of such kind. When foo_A $(p_{A1}, ...)$ is substituted by foo_B $(p_{B1}, ...)$, p_{A1} is implicitly substituted by p_{B1}.

The definition of implicit substitution also assumes a particular form, derived from the way operation calls in UML identify parameters when passing arguments: by their position in the signature of the operation, taking into account the direction of the parameters. I.e., when substituting operation OPp by OPs, the ith parameter in the list of parameters of OPp having direction *in* or *inout* will be substituted by the ith parameter of the same list of OPs. The same applies to the ordered list of *out*, *inout* and *return* parameters, according to the semantics of *CallAction* ([6], pp. 250–251). Therefore, to ensure computability of calls to OPs, the ith *in/inout* parameter of OPs must be functionally conformant to the ith *in/inout* parameter of OPp. The same applies to *out/inout/return* parameters.

Since operation parameters are elements with type and multiplicity, conformance regarding those aspects is required. However, due to the contravariant nature of *in*, *out* and *inout* parameters regarding inheritance (*return* parameters are covariant), type conformance must be redefined for operation parameters.

Contravariance means that if class *C* is specialized by *C'*, then operation *Op (C)* is generalized by *Op' (C')*. I.e., while instances of C may be replaced by instances of C', calls to *Op (C)* may not be replaced by calls to *Op' (C')*, but rather the other way around: calls to *Op' (C')* may be replaced by calls to *Op (C)*. Refer to Sect. 2.6 of [1], for a thorough discussion on covariance and contravariance.

Hence, type conformance between *in*, *out* or *inout* operation parameters is defined as follows. If *pp* is an *in*, *out* or *inout* parameter of an operation used by a template and *ps* is a prospective substitute for *pp*, *ps* conforms in type with *pp* if:

- In case *pp*'s type is not substituted (in the binding under consideration), *ps'* type is *pp*'s type or a supertype of it;
- In case *pp*'s type is substituted, *ps'* type must be the substitute of *pp*'s type or a supertype of it.

This rule is the opposite of the general rule of type conformance, previously presented in Sect. 4.1 and applying all other typed elements in UML.

Additionally, conforming operations must have the same number of parameters. Indeed, while for other types of namespaces having more members than those that will participate in the substitution doesn't spoil computability, that isn't true for operations. In Fig. 15, attribute *a3* in class *Cs* does not affect the conformance of *Cs* to *Cp*. On the contrary, parameter *p3* makes *OPs* non-conformant to *OPp*.

Fig. 15. The number of operation parameters is relevant for functional conformance.

Figure 16 shows examples of signature conformance. Only two operations of *Customer* are prospective substitutes to the operation *search()*: *find()* and *selectBy-Name()*. Since UML considers the return of an operation as a parameter (with *return* direction), it is part of the operation's signature. That's why operation *setAddress()* is not signature-conformant to *search()*.

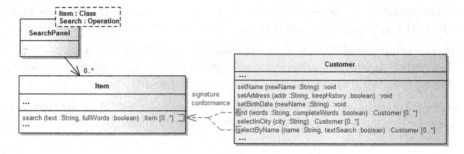

Fig. 16. Signature conformance, examples.

4.4 Staticity Conformance

Since static features are executed by the classifier and non-static by instances of the classifier, staticity clearly affects computability. Therefore, functional conformance between two features requires they are both static or both non-static.

4.5 Visibility Requirement

Finally, there is a requirement relevant to computability that doesn't involve the pair substitute/substituted, but rather the pair substitute/bound element. That's why it is not called "conformance".

An element may substitute a parameter only if that element is visible from the bound element.

This requirement is easily understood since the substitutions are done in the code of the bound element: since the bound element will refer to substitute elements, it needs visibility of such elements.

4.6 Computability Assurance

An element bound to a template is computable if the template itself is computable and if, for every parameter substitution, the substitute functionally conforms to the parametered element.

A formal demonstration is required to prove such statement. This can be done by demonstrating that every computable expression and statement in a template will be reproduced as a computable element if all substitutions verify the criteria for conformance. For lack of space, such demonstration will be provided in a future paper. Appealing to the reader's intuition, the following explanation is provided:

According to the semantics of the bind relationship, the template element will be equal to the bound element except at the points it references a substituted parameter. At the reproduction of such points, the bound element will be referencing the substitute. Let's call those "points of difference". If the template is computable, only at the points of difference the bound element could be non-computable. If every substitute functionally conforms to its parametered element, that substitute will:

- Be successfully used in contexts that are reproductions of its parameter's contexts;
- Respond successfully to services that are reproductions of its parameter's services;
- Yield results that are reproductions of its parameter's results.

Therefore, if at the points of difference the substitutes are doing well, the bound element is computable at those points and, consequently, fully computable.

5   Related Work

Research aiming at improving the UML Template model is scarce. References [2, 7] are the pieces of work most affine to the one presented in this paper.

Like current paper, [2] also propose a set of well-formedness rules, additional to that of standard UML, aiming at strengthen the notion of template as a means to enforce the correctness of elements bound to a template. [2] is not very specific on the level and/or kind of correctness that is ensured by the proposed set of constraints. If it were to ensure computability, it overlooks some important aspects, such as multiplicity, staticity, and visibility. There are also minor inaccuracies, probably by lapse (for instance, the imposition that a parametered element must be owned by the template).

Reference [7] proposes the concept of Aspectual Templates (AT) to enforce structural conformance between a template and the model it is applied to. [7] states that ATs have only one parameter, which is a model, and defines a set of constraints to enforce structural conformance between the parameter and its substitute. Generally speaking, structural conformance has the same goal as functional conformance in current paper. But our concept is more complete and comprehensive. More complete because ATs omit some UML concepts and, by doing so, become too strict on the one hand and too indulgent on the other hand. For instance, by omitting inheritance ATs forbid substitutions by an inherited feature (too strict). By omitting multiplicity ATs allow a multivalued property be substituted by a single-valued one (too indulgent). Our approach is also more comprehensive because it works for any kind of templateable and parameterable element in UML. Finally, the *Apply* operation proposed by [7] is roughly the same as binding to a package-template.

Although with a goal different from current paper's, [5] also introduces a technique to validate structural conformance between a template and its bound elements. Although the proposed extension to UML put some added value in terms of expressiveness, the conformance verification method overlooks several aspects essential to computability, such as multiplicity and signature conformance.

Considering the field of Aspect Oriented Modeling, one can find plenty of methods with the same goal as current paper: how to obtain concrete, correct solutions from generic ones. Because those methods use approaches and formalisms other than UML templates, the comparison would be somewhat pointless. The only exception we are aware of is the Theme/UML approach [3], which uses UML package templates to model crosscutting functionalities. Theme/UML extends the concept of template to incorporate aspect-oriented capabilities. Although it supports the definition of parameters with owner-member relationships, which resembles contents/membership conformance in the current paper, it is not clear if substitute elements (which are also organized in owner-member relationships) are checked against parameters. For further exploration of the Aspect-Oriented Modeling field a good starting point could be the survey in [8].

6   Conclusions and Future Work

The concept of functional conformance proposed in this paper has been experimentally applied to a reasonably large set of templates (approximately 50) and application domains (12, some of them with alternative models). Such experiments showed a success rate of 100 %, which provides some empirical evidence of the effectiveness of the approach.

However, the authors believe that a more reliable demonstration should be provided. With that goal, a formal demonstration is being developed, and will soon be proposed for publication. Although under development, such demonstration has already yielded results. Namely, it showed that a previous definition of type conformance for operation parameters, presented in [4], was not fully accurate. The definition in the current paper reformulates it. The fact that none of the empirical experiences revealed the problem clearly endorses formal demonstrations over empirical ones.

The aforementioned experiments also suggested that, when sorting out substitutes for a parameter, taking into account functional conformance may leverage automatic or semi-automatic substitution. Therefore, additionally to computability assurance, automatic binding is a potential benefit of functional conformance. This is a line of work to develop.

Another perception instilled by these experiments is that UML templates, to some extent, lack of flexibility. For instance, if a template exposes an association as parameter it would be useful if one could substitute that association by a chain of two connected associations, whenever that is the setting in the application domain.

Appendix: OCL Formulation of Functional Conformance

Auxiliary definitions

```
context TemplateBinding
def: substituteOf (p: ParameterableElement)
     : ParameterableElement
   = self.parameterSubstitution.any (
                  formal.parameteredElement = p).actual


context Operation
def: inputParameters
   : OrderedSet (Parameter)
   = self.ownedParameters.select (direction = #in or
                                  direction = #inout)


context Operation
def: outputParameters
   : OrderedSet (Parameter)
   = self.ownedParameters.select (direction = #out or
                                  direction = #inout or
                                  direction = #return)
```

Type conformance

```
context TypedElement
def: typeConformsTo
     ( p: ParameterableElement,
       b: TemplateBinding) : Bool
   = let allTypes = p.type.allParents()
                        .including (p.type) in
     allTypes.forAll ( tp |
        let tpSubs = b.substituteOf (tp)
        in
          if tpSubs = null then
            self.type.conformsTo (tp)
          else
            self.type.conformsTo (tpSubs) )
```

Multiplicity conformance

```
context MultiplicityElement
def: multiplicityConformsTo
        (p: MultiplicityElement) : Bool
  = self.upper = 1 and p.upper = 1
    or
    (self.upper > 1 and p.upper > 1 and
     self.isOrdered = p.isOrdered)
```

Contents conformance

```
context TemplateBinding
def: implicitSubstituteOf
        ( p: NamedElement) : NamedElement
  = let subsNs
    = p.elementNamespaces
      ->collect (ns| self.substituteOf (ns))
      ->union (p.elementNamespaces
      ->collect (ns | self.implicitSubstituteOf (ns)))
      ->asSet()->excluding (e | e = null)
    in
      if subsNs.isEmpty() then
        implicitSubstituteOf = null
      else
        subsNs.collect (members)->any (
          not isDistinguishableFrom (p, ns))
```

```
context Namespace
def: contentConformsTo
      ( p: Namespace,
        b: TemplateBinding ) : Bool
  = let elemsNotSubstituted
    = p.member
      ->intersection (b.signature.template.usedElements)
      ->excluding (p | b.substituteOf (p) <> null)
      ->excluding (p |
                      b.implicitSubstituteOf (p) <> null)
    in
      elemsNotSubstituted->isEmpty()
```

Membership conformance

```
context ParameterableElement
def: membershipConformsTo
        ( p: ParameterableElement,
          b: TemplateBinding ) : Bool
   = p.memberNamespace
      ->collect (ns | b.substituteOf (ns))
      ->intersects (self.memberNamespace)
```

Signature conformance

```
context Operation
def: signatureConformsTo
        ( p: Operation,
          b: TemplateBinding ) : Bool
   = (self.parameter->size = p.parameter->size)
     and
     Sequence {1..self.inputParameters->size}
        ->forAll ( i |
             self.inputParameters ->at(i)
             .conformsTo (p.inputParameters ->at(i), b))
     and
     Sequence {1..self.outputParameters->size}
        ->forAll ( i |
             self.outputParameters->at(i)
             .conformsTo (p.outputParameters->at(i), b))


context Parameter
  def: conformsTo
        ( p: Parameter,
          b: TemplateBinding ) : Bool
   = self.typeConformsTo (p, b) and
     self.multiplicityConformsTo (p) and
     self.direction = p.direction
```

```
context Parameter
  def: typeConformsTo
          ( p: Parameter,
            b: TemplateBinding ) : Bool
      = if self.direction = #return then
            self.oclAsType (TypedElement).typeConformsTo (p, b)
        else
            p.oclAsType (TypedElement).typeConformsTo (self, b)
```

Staticity conformance

```
context Feature
def: staticityConformsTo ( f: Feature ) : Bool
  = self.isStatic = f.isStatic
```

Visibility requirement

```
context TemplateableElement
def: hasVisibilityOf ( e: NamedElement ) : Bool
  = self.allNamespaces()->first().hasVisibilityOf (e)
-- By default, an element forwards
-- the query to its closest namespace,
-- until it gets a namespace that
-- redefines this operation.
```

```
context Classifier
def: hasVisibilityOf ( e: NamedElement ) : Bool
  = if e = self then
      hasVisibilityOf = true
    elseif self.allParents().member->includes (e) then
      hasVisibilityOf = (e.visibility <> #private)
    else
      hasVisibilityOf = (e.visibility = #public)
```

```
context Package
def: hasVisibilityOf ( e: NamedElement ) : Bool
  = if e = self or self.allOwnedMembers()->includes (e)
    then hasVisibilityOf = true
    else hasVisibilityOf = (e.visibility = #public)
```

References

1. Abadi, M., Cardelli, L.: A theory of objects. Syst. Res. 1–130 (1996)
2. Caron, O., Carré, B.: An OCL formulation of UML2 template binding. In: Baar, T., et al. (eds.) UML' 2004 — the Unified Modeling Language. Modeling Languages and Applications. Lecture Notes in Computer Science, vol. 3273, pp. 27–40. Springer, Berlin, Heidelberg (2004)
3. Clarke, S., Walker, R.J.: Generic aspect-oriented design with THEME/UML. In: Aspect-Oriented Software Development, pp. 425–458 Addison-Wesley, Boston (2005)
4. Farinha, J., Ramos, P.: Extending UML templates towards computability. In: Modelsward 2015, 3rd International Conference on Model-driven Engineering and Software Development, SCITEPRESS (2015)
5. France, R.B., et al.: A UML-based Pattern specification technique. IEEE Trans. Softw. Eng. **30**(3), 193–206 (2004)
6. OMG Consortium: OMG Unified Modeling Language (UML), Superstructure, v2.4.1. http://www.omg.org/spec/uml/2.4.1/ (2012)
7. Vanwormhoudt, G., et al.: Aspectual templates in uml (2013)
8. Wimmer, M., et al.: A survey on UML-based aspect-oriented design modeling. ACM Comput. Surv. **43**(4), 1–33 (2011)

Challenging a Transformation-Wise Architecture Framework in a Comparative Case Study

Fabian Gilson[✉] and Vincent Englebert

PReCISE Research Center, University of Namur, Namur, Belgium
{fabian.gilson,vincent.englebert}@unamur.be

Abstract. The maintenance and evolution of software architecture models may become tricky when design rationale is lost over time. Lots of requirements and decisions must be taken into account when dealing with software architecture, such that proper traceability mechanisms should be used all over the system life-cycle. In a previous work, we specified an architectural framework based on domain specific languages meant to address this traceability problem. We now relate a comparative case study we conducted over a simulated project where participants had to develop an online book store in two phases, the second phase imitating a system evolution. We evaluated the functional completeness of the software they built as well as the traceability of design decisions and rationale. The participants were also asked to criticize the design method and language they used in a feedback report and through a questionnaire. Even if the size of the case study is rather limited, it clearly highlights the advantages of our approach regarding, among others, its expressiveness and decisions traceability (The present paper is a revised version of *SA design by stepwise transformations* [8]).

1 Introduction

Software engineering methods offer guidelines and tool-support to structure the creation process of software systems. As the complexity of such systems increases, the need for iterative methods has been widely expressed [2]. In drawing the architecture model of the *system-to-be*, many decisions are taken and a large part of the knowledge resides in the reasons that lead to a particular model. Besides, architectural knowledge must be maintained all over the architecture life-cycle by appropriate traceability mechanisms [19].

An increasing number of companies are moving to *Agile* design methods that offer benefits like time-overrun reduction and a higher developer productivity [5]. With faster release frequencies, the amount of design decisions logically increases. Without an appropriate tracing mechanism, the architectural knowledge is often lost, even by the practitioners in charge of the impacted models or code [23]. However, one of the most crucial piece of information is the link between a requirement and its implementation in a model or in the code [12].

We integrated both aspects into an *architecture framework* [11]. On the one hand, we use structural models iteratively enriched through model transformations, and on the other hand, an ad-hoc requirement modeling language with

© Springer International Publishing Switzerland 2015
P. Desfray et al. (Eds.): MODELSWARD 2015, CCIS 580, pp. 213–229, 2015.
DOI: 10.1007/978-3-319-27869-8_12

explicit traceability mechanisms for design decisions and rationale. In this comparative case study, we confronted the Domain Specific Languages (DSL) we formalized in our framework to the OMG's SysML^{TM} modeling language [18]. We evaluated the feasibility and advantages of using such languages in an iterative approach (common to both groups under study) to build a web-based software from scratch. We identified that the functional completeness and correctness were slightly higher under our framework. The *decision documentation rate*, *i.e.* the amount of documented design decisions, was also evaluated. During the two phases of the evaluation, we counted a median rate of *0.945* and *1* documented decision under our framework where only *0.215* and *0.285* on the other side. Aside, we conducted a paper-based survey and analyzed feedback reports to capture the participants' feelings regarding the languages they used. This survey highlighted a significant improvement regarding modeling expressiveness.

The present paper starts with an overview of some related work in Sect. 2. Afterwards, in Sect. 3, we give a quick description of the proposed languages. The protocol of the comparative case study is then presented in Sect. 4. Next, the teams' deliverables and feedbacks are detailed in Sect. 5. We discuss the outcomes of the case study in Sect. 6 where we evaluate the research method itself and identify the potential threats to validity. Finally, the research perspectives and conclusions are presented in Sect. 7.

2   Related Work and Motivation

Numerous architecture description languages have been proposed like ACME [6] or AADL [22], but most of them do not provide decision-making traceability, even if their long-term added-value is widely recognized [17].

Many decision and rationale recording methods have also been defined. A case study was recently conducted on documentation of architectural decisions and highlighted that an explicit recording of these decisions empowers a more systematic exploration of design alternatives [9]. However, these techniques require to maintain extra traceability models.

Within model-driven approaches, model-to-model transformation languages play a key role. Hybrid imperative and declarative languages, like ATL [14], usually do not support incremental model transformations with change propagations. Triple Graph Grammars offer such a feature, but make it difficult to define transformations where operational semantics is needed [16]. Also, abstract syntax-based techniques require to learn another language, such that extra expertise is needed.

In our approach, we believe in a fully integrated framework where any change in an architecture will be fully traceable as documented model transformations, together with their design rationale. Explored alternatives may also be recorded, again as concrete transformations. Last, reusable solutions, *i.e.* architectural patterns, may be documented as dedicated transformations too.

3   Design Method in Short

The design method is supported by three DSL, being depicted in dedicated publications[1]. We illustrate their main principles in the following sections.

3.1   Requirement Listing

A simple language has been defined to list requirements with their design decisions. We focus on *architecturally-significant requirements* (ASR), i.e., requirements that have *"a measurable impact on the software system's architecture"* [3].

A requirement model gathers a list of ASR for a specific architecture model. Every requirement must be assigned to an architectural construct in charge of satisfying it. Listing 1 depicts a simplified ASR model with one functional requirement that will be implemented as a transformation.

```
1  asrmodel clientserver {
2    func SayHello assigned Server {
3      description "The Server shall print 'Hello World!' to the console.";
4      realisation implementSayHello {
5        assessment "Functionality is trivial, a unique service should make the
             trick.";
6        strength "Very simple implementation with unique service without parameters
             .";
7      }
8    }
9  }
```

Listing 1. Simplified ASR model.

Decisions can be taken on requirements, such as *refinements, implications, conflicts,* alternative *selections* or *realization* through model transformations. Any decision must be at least justified by an *assessment*, but can be further refined by other design rationale like *strengths* or *constraints* for example.

3.2   Architecture Description and Transformations

An architecture description language has been defined to represent the structure of software systems at different levels of abstraction. Listing 2 depicts an empty Client-Server *Definition Assemblage Deployment* (DAD) model.

```
1  dadmodel clientserver {
2    definition {
3      componenttype Client { }
4      componenttype Server { }
5    }
6  }
```

Listing 2. Simplified DAD model.

The set of transformation rules, referred as the *realization* documented in Listing 1, is illustrated in Listing 3.

---

[1] The complete list can be found in [7].

```
1  transformationset implementSayHello concerns SayHello {
2    create interface Hello { sync void hello(); }
3    alter componenttype Client{ uses Hello as hello; }
4    alter componenttype Server { implements Hello as hello; }
5    create connectortype One2One { mode one2one; }
6    create linkagetype from Client.hello to Server.hello with One2One;
7  }
```

Listing 3. Simplified transformations set.

Concretely, a binding is created between the `Client` and the `Server` through their *facets* typed by the `Hello` *interface*.

More modeling elements are available in the DAD language to express a software architecture from *(i)* an abstract *definition*, *(ii)* a *runnable assemblage* with, among other, particular communication protocol constraints, and *(iii)* a *deployment* specification with (user-defined) infrastructure properties. Listing 4 shows a more complete, though simplified, overview of all stages of a DAD model.

```
1   dadmodel dadsample {
2     definition { // building blocks
3       interface Hello { sync void hello (); }
4       componenttype Client { uses Hello as h; }
5       componenttype Server { implements Hello as h; }
6       protocol TCP { layer transport; }
7       connectortype Con { mode one2one; }
8       linkagetype from Client.h to Server.h with Con;
9       nodetype Computer { Ethernet eth; }
10      mediumtype RJ45 { supports TCP; }
11    }
12    assemblage { // concrete instances
13      soi c : Client { Client.h as h on TCP; }
14      soi s : Server { Server.h as h on TCP; }
15      linkage from c.h to s.h with Con;
16    }
17    deployment { // possible deployment
18      node comp[2] : Computer;
19      deploy client on comp[0]; open c.h on comp[0]::eth;
20      deploy server on comp[1]; open s.h on comp[1]::eth;
21      plug RJ45 from comp[0]::eth to comp[1]::eth;
22    }
23  }
```

Listing 4. All DAD model stages.

Note that all stages are optional so that, for example, reusable building blocks can be specified separately in dedicated library-models or different *assemblage* or *deployment* stages for the same *definition* can be defined.

3.3 A Transformational Approach

Our design approach is transformation-centric, i.e., changes made in the architecture model must be expressed by model transformations. As illustrated in Listing 3, it provides rules to create, delete and modify any type of construct. A software architecture is created in an iterative way where designers start from a model with a list of ASR (possibly incomplete), a set of basic constructs and make successive decisions. Figure 1 depicts the typical design process, based upon Hofmeister's *general model* [10].

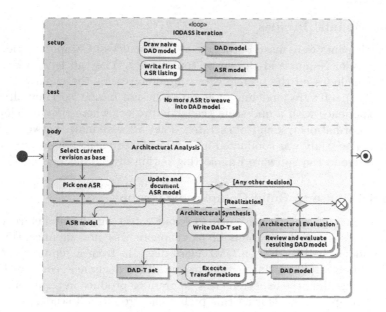

Fig. 1. IODASS Design process with *general model*'s activities.

4   Case Study Protocol

We conducted our study on a group of master students, following recognized guidelines [20,21,24]. We planned to evaluate *(i) the feasibility and benefits of a transformation-centric approach to build a software system* and *(ii) the expressiveness of our modeling languages and their impacts on model documentation.*

For the first goal, we had to integrate this *design by transformation* approach in a common iterative design process where participants may pick one requirement at a time, refine or implement it and evaluate the resulting model. As identified by Hofmeister *et al.* in their general model and in Fig. 1, this iterative process is very common and somewhat intuitive [10]. This way, participants followed the same methodological framework that only differed on the set of languages they used.

Regarding the languages themselves, we decided to compare them to the OMG's SysML. On top of structural modeling facilities at variable levels of abstraction, requirements, traceability and rationale-related information can be added into SysML models. It allows to define building blocks in a similar fashion as in our architectural language, with infrastructure-related objects too. Also, the participants had no knowledge of both modeling languages, even if they all were familiar with UML modeling, such that previous knowledge in one or the other language would not have biased the study.

Finally, we also had to take care of the development environment. Our languages are implemented as Eclipse plugins, and a couple of plugins for SysMl also exist. All participants could thus work in the same environment, which reduces the possible bias regarding the tool's takeover.

4.1 Participants' Profiles

The 24 participants were master students of the Faculty of Computer Science at the University of Namur and chosen by convenience. They all have a Bachelor degree that includes all the prerequisite competencies for the experiment concerning (UML) software modeling or iterative design methods. They all had a previous experience with a mid-scale academic project where they developed a web-based information system from scratch. They all were males between 21 and 25 year old. The study was conducted from mid-March until end of May 2013 as part of a course in the Software Engineering option of the Master's curriculum.

4.2 Initial Phase to Build Comparable Groups

This preliminary phase was designed to avoid a too significant heterogeneity between groups since the amount of participants was not significantly large enough. Students had to draw a UML class diagram from a requirement document describing a vehicle inspection system. This document contained clear instructions regarding the expected class diagram to produce in terms of level of details and completeness. During this preliminary round, all students received exactly the same remarks at the beginning of the lecture and were spread into a room wide enough to minimize cheating possibilities.

At the end of the lecture, we gathered their models and classified them using a *judging* method inspired from the work of Jones [13]: three researchers, all familiar with UML modeling, were asked to categorize the diagrams (from syntacticly and semantically incorrect to correct). From this classification, we created four *hats* based on the judges categories to equalize as much as possible the modeling competences of the future teams. We fairly distributed the students between the hats assigned to SysML (*S-Teams*) and to our languages (*I-Teams*) from which the participants could choose their team mates.

4.3 Case Study Startup

Prior to give to the students the description of the system to develop, they separately followed a 2 h lecture where SysML was presented to the *S-Teams*, and our framework to the *I-Teams*. Both lectures were organized the same way and given by the same person. Two *screencasts* were realized to explain how to install the plugins and how to create a *helloworld model*.

The remaining of the study was realized by the participants outside classroom, per teams of two, except for one session dedicated to general questions and for the final demonstration of their prototypes. The study was organized in two phases, the first one dedicated to the realization of a prototype from scratch, the second one to modify part of the system, with a notable impact at the architectural level. For each phase, the students received a separate document explaining the system requirements only for the concerned phase, so that they had no idea of the nature of the future evolutions. After the first phase, we had an individual 15 min discussion with all teams to answer their questions and debrief about their deliverables.

4.4   Case Description

We specified a fictitious library system where customers can order books from different stores. Each time a book is sold, an auction is organized between all stores. At the end of the auction, the library contacts a delivery system to pick up the book and deliver it to the customer. For this first phase, the library was leading the overall process. The participants received a document with the list of the expected functionalities and qualities for all three subsystems, specified in ten very detailed requirements. Some simplifying hypotheses and methodological aspects regarding the iterative design method to follow and the expected deliverables were also specified.

For the second phase, the participants received another document with new requirements. They were expressed at a higher abstraction level, though still complete and unambiguous, in order to compare the decision traceability mechanisms of both languages. They also received detailed guidelines on how to write their own evaluations of the language(s) they used. In the modified system *(i)* the auction had to be taken in charge by the book stores, *(ii)* the customer could withdraw his purchase, and *(iii)* the catalog had to be exposed also as a web service.

At the end of both phases, aside to their prototypes, the teams delivered a set of models representing the system with its rationale and the description of the design process they followed. At the end of the second phase, the teams also submitted an evaluation report on the language expressiveness, the documentation and traceability facilities, and models' maintainability.

4.5   Evaluation Method

We use a *Goal-Question-Metric* approach for our evaluation metrics [1] detailed hereafter with the *Purpose/Issue/Object/Viewpoint* template (PIOV).

GOAL 1. *Evaluate the feasibility of a transformational architecture design method to design a software system*

PIOV. Evaluate / the feasibility of iteratively transform a / software architecture model / from the project manager's viewpoint.

Question 1. Is it effective to implement a software based on an architecture model created from stepwise formal model transformations?

Metric 1. Number of top-level functionalities correctly implemented.

GOAL 2. *Evaluate the quality of architecture and requirement models using DAD-ASR languages*

PIOV. Evaluate / the functional completeness of a / software architecture model regarding the expected model elements / from the architect's viewpoint.

Question 2. Does the produced architecture models contain all expected components and interfaces to fulfill the software's requirements?

Metric 2. Number of requirements without any responsible component/part.

Question 3. Are the newly introduced subrequirements correctly documented with their rationale?

Metric 3. Number of decisions regarding subrequirements with a meaningful explanation of their purposes (rationale).

GOAL 3. *Evaluate the traceability of a transformational method regarding the history of the development process (planning-evaluation)*
PIOV. Evaluate / the actual implementation order of the / architecturally significant requirements / from the architect's viewpoints.
Question 4. Does all development iterations have been *backlogged* for evaluation and traceability purposes?
Metric 4. Number of iterations reported with corresponding implementation plans.

GOAL 4. *Evaluate the feasibility of a transformational method in maintenance and evolution activities of a software system*
PIOV. Evaluate / the feasibility of iteratively transform an / existing software architecture model / from the architect's viewpoints.
Question 5. Is it effective to incorporate new functionalities in a software based on an architecture model modified by stepwise formal model transformations?
Metric 5. Number of impacted functionalities correctly implemented.

5   Case Study Results

We now detail the results gathered from the deliverables produced by all teams.

5.1   Functional Correctness and Quality of Deliverables

At the end of the first phase, we deployed their prototypes, following their `readme` files. To test their systems, we ordered a book and checked if the auction completed as expected, as well as if the delivery was correctly done (happy scenario). We also analyzed their decision making processes, *i.e.* the recorded (sub-)requirements and rationale. Table 1 summarizes the results for all teams. Some columns have been directly linked to the metrics identified in the previous section. We also provide the median values for each groups.

Regarding the happy scenario, our framework produced slightly better results. One more *I-Team* provided a fully functional prototype than the *S-Teams*. Two *S-Teams'* prototypes did not implement correctly any requirement, where one *I-Team* did so. Moreover, a *median* value $(Q_2)^2$ of *3.5* requirements were correctly implemented by the *I-Teams*, where *2.5* for the *S-Teams*. Even if the difference is not significant, we can notice than, except for the *I6-Team*, all other five *I-Teams* implemented at least *3* requirements where three *S-Teams* completed similar functional results.

Concerning the number of produced requirements and their traceability as structural elements, the results show a better result for the *S-Teams*, where only *0.5* requirement remained untraced against *2.5* for *I-Teams*. However,

---

[2] We use median instead of arithmetic means because the sampling is rather small and we are mainly interested in *central tendencies*.

Table 1. Evaluation of the deliverables of phase 1.

Team	Happy scenario	Impl.(M1)	Req.	Untr.(M2)	Decis.	Rat.(M3)	Iter.(M4)
S1	Stopped during auction	2	19	1	17	10	4
S2	No possibility to order	0	15	2	11	2	0
S3	Fully functional	4	10	0	10	1	0
S4	Fully functional	4	10	0	11	8	3
S5	Stopped after auction	3	11	1	16	4	0
S6	No possibility to order	0	10	0	12	2	3
Q2_S	n/a	2.5	10.5	0.5	11.5	3	1.5
I1	Fully functional	4	23	1	15	15	1
I2	No book delivery	3	30	1	28	28	5
I3	Fully functional	4	10	10	0	0	0
I4	Stopped after auction	3	14	2	9	8	8
I5	Fully functional	4	41	3	29	29	4
I6	Compilation failure	0	27	3	24	21	5
Q2_I	n/a	3.5	25	2.5	19.5	18	4.5

the amount of sub-requirements identified within our framework is significantly higher with a median of *25* requirements against *10.5* on the other side. Half of the *S-Teams* listed only the ten requirements found in the initial document and did not refine any of them. This was also the case for the *I3-Team* that did not provide any traceability information or even design rationale.

Similarly to the amount of produced requirements, the amount of rationale is significantly higher for *I-Teams* than for *S-Teams*. To identify the decisions and their rationale, we analyzed the design reports given by the students, where they were asked to justify the decisions (and alternatives) they made to build the online library system. A median of *11.5* decisions could be found in the models and documents produced by the *S-Teams*, from which *3* were documented. On the other side, *I-Teams* typically produced *19.5* decisions from which *18* were justified by non-empty *rationale* fields with non-fuzzy justifications. The comparison of the documentation rates is illustrated in Figs. 2 and 3.

At the end of the second phase, we evaluated the functional correctness of their prototypes in a different way. Each team had a 10 min slot to demonstrate the full scenario, from the book purchase to the withdrawal at the delivery. We especially evaluated *(i)* the user feedback, *(ii)* the new auction mechanism, *(iii)* the withdrawal with credit note and *(iv)* the catalog as a web service (not shown in the table). Table 2 summarizes the results of this second phase.

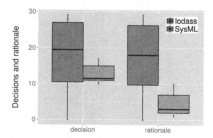

Fig. 2. Number of decisions and rationale.

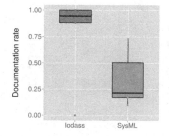

Fig. 3. Documentation rates.

Each new requirement received a value corresponding to the amount of sub-requirements that should have been produced at least (*Feedback* values from *0* to *3*, *Auction* from *0* to *2* and *Credit* note from *0* to *2*).

Table 2. Evaluation of the final prototypes and deliverables.

Team	Feedback	Auction	Credit	M5	Req.	M2	Decis.	M3	M4
S1	2	2	1	**5**	23	2	19	12	0
S2	0	1	2	**3**	17	1	13	2	0
S3	2	2	1	**5**	15	0	13	4	0
S4	1	2	2	**5**	14	0	24	7	0
S5	1	2	0	**3**	15	1	18	5	0
S6	1	1	2	**4**	18	1	16	4	2
Q2 S	n/a	n/a	n/a	4.5	16	1	17	4.5	0
I1	2	2	2	**6**	27	3	24	24	1
I2	1	2	2	**5**	35	1	31	31	3
I3	2	2	2	**6**	17	14	3	3	1
I4	1	2	0	**3**	17	3	11	11	2
I5	1	2	2	**5**	56	5	51	48	3
I6	3	2	2	**7**	38	4	34	28	7
Q2 I	n/a	n/a	n/a	5.5	31	3.5	27.5	26	2.5

As for the first phase, the overall amount of requirements implemented successfully is very close for both groups. Qualitatively, we may note that all six *I-Teams* implemented correctly the modification of the *Auction* mechanism, which was more intrusive and used as an evaluation criterion for GOAL 4, where four *S-Teams* provided the same functional completeness for that requirement. However, even if this result is promising, the difference is not significant enough to claim our framework lead to a more efficient system design.

The same tendencies as during the first phase are also observed concerning the requirement traceability, design decisions and rationale. The amount of identified requirements increased in a comparable manner in both groups, confirming a significantly more systematic decomposition of requirements under our framework. The proportion of documented decisions by meaningful rationale stays at a very high level too (median of *1* against *0.285*), as depicted in Figs. 4 and 5.

The last metric we are interested in concerns the number of iterations needed by the participants to implement the system. For the first phase, We could not

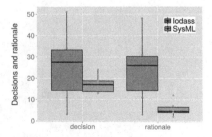

Fig. 4. Number of decisions and rationale.

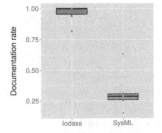

Fig. 5. Documentation rates.

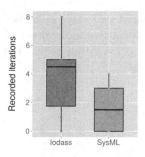

Fig. 6. Iterations for the first phase.   **Fig. 7.** Iterations for the final phase.

Table 3. Questionnaire (statements to be rated).

1. The languages constructs allow to represent:
1.a. the expected functionalities of the system.
1.b. the technological and communication constraints.
1.c. the physical constraints related to the deployment.
1.d. the non-functional requirements.
2. The modeling language coupled to an agile development method as the one used during this laboratory offers an added value :
2.a. to manage the complexity of the system-to-be.
2.b. for the traceability of the requirements in terms of functionalities to implement.
2.c. for the correctness and completeness of the implementation (code) of the system.
3. The structural constructs impacted by a modif. of a requirement can be identified *quickly*.
4. The structural constructs impacted by a modif. of a requirement can be identified *at a glance*.
5. The language offers the necessary constructs and mechanisms to write an accurate documentation.
6. The written documentation allows to efficiently comprehend the system within the framework of a modification of the system.
7. During the second phase:
7.a. a major work was necessary to re-understand the architectural concepts of the system.
7.b. the modeling languages eased the structural changes linked to new functionalities to implement.

retrieve any information regarding the implementation order of the functionalities for three *S-Teams* and two *I-Teams*. For the second phase, those iteration explanations dropped significantly for the *S-Teams* where only one team actually reported the design steps they followed, as depicted in Figs. 6 and 7.

5.2 Paper-Based Survey

In order to complement the above metrics, we gathered the participants' *feelings* about the case study and the modeling languages they used. Questionnaire were filled in anonymously to encourage them to freely express their opinions. The survey evaluated *(i)* the language expressiveness, *(ii)* the added value of the language (implicitly regarding UML), *(iii)* the evolution capabilities and *(iv)* the documentation support for model evolution, as detailed in Table 3.

We used a non-graduated scale only indexed by *fully disagree* (0) and *fully agree* (5) marks, inspired from [15]. The participants could draw a line wherever they estimated it appropriate. This technique suits particularly when comparing different approaches because answers are expressed on a continuous interval that can be measured with a ruler. It also lets more freedom to the respondents and usually avoid them to backtrack to previous answers because they want to order them within related questions. Besides, we dissimulated two very close questions (Q3 and Q7b.) that concern the evolution phase to evaluate more precisely the impact of our framework on model maintenance and evolution tasks. Figure 8 shows the average rankings given by the respondents.

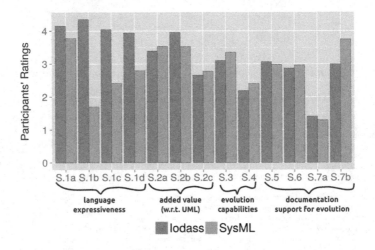

Fig. 8. Results of the questionnaire-based survey.

The collected answers show notably better results in our framework regarding constructs expressiveness (Q1), especially for communication facilities. The ratings for the added value and evolution capabilities are very close, so we cannot say anything on that. Model evolution seems a bit more complicated in our approach since the impacted elements can be identified almost as rapidly than for SysML diagrams (Q3), but requires more effort (Q4, Q7).

But, for all questions except Q7a. that was formulated in a dissimulated *negative* manner and Q4, the IODASS ratings are upper to *2.5* which is a rather satisfactory result.

6   Discussion

We will now summarize the observations we made and discuss the results regarding our four goals introduced at the end of Sect. 4. We will afterwards evaluate the protocol itself.

We decided to discuss the results of the study and survey outside a statistical framework because we did not have a statistically significant sample since the amount of software engineers is very large (which requires then a large sample) and we were conducting the study over students *in a vacuum* (which limits the generalization possibilities). We then preferred to stick to objective metrics and discuss only over very large differences.

6.1   Evaluation of the Approach

As a first goal, we wanted to evaluate the feasibility of our approach. After both phases, the functional correctness (M1 and M5) was slightly higher for the *I-Teams*. The changes in the *Auction* mechanism was correctly implemented by the six *I-Teams*, against four *S-Teams*. Two more *I-Teams* also implemented the *Credit Note* with the expected level of details. Even if the small amount of involved teams does not allow us to claim the difference is statistically significant, we may claim *it is feasible for master students in software engineering to successfully implement a system that have been modeled with the* IODASS *framework under our controlled environment.*

The second goal concerned the quality of architecture and requirement models regarding their completeness (M2) and traceability of design decisions (M3). The amount of unrelated requirements is higher in our framework than in the produced SysML models. These unrelated requirements were mostly the ones that were not related to other requirements or formally linked to a model transformation. However, in an ASR model, a requirement is always *assigned* to a structural element which is equivalent to the *satisfy* relation in SysML. Since this feature is mandatory in ASR models, we looked for other types of formal relations, where the SysML *satisfy* relationship was considered as an explicit link and counted accordingly. So we may observe that *there seems to be a positive influence of our decomposition of requirements, but more requirements stay unrelated to architecture model constructs.*

About the traceability of design decisions (M3), the results are significantly higher. As median documentation rates, we observed *0.945* and *1* for IODASS teams where only *0.215* and *0.285* for SysML teams. However, from the questionnaire, we observed that the perceived readability of models is slightly lower for our languages, so we may say then that *the systematic recording of design decisions increases the amount of design rationale, but its positive impact on model comprehension is unsure.* Also, as part of this third goal, we wanted to evaluate the reporting of the design process with the number of iterations necessary to draw the architecture model (M4). Even if we explicitly asked for such details, the number of *S-Teams* that provided their development plan dropped at only one team for the second phase. We could not find any explicit or implicit explanations in the final reports from the *S-Teams* and we can reasonably think they did not implement the whole second phase at once, such that part of the design history is lost. Since this aspect only concerns our framework, we may conclude that *in most cases, the participants follow an iterative design process and the history of the successive changes are completely recorded.*

Last, we wanted to evaluate the evolution capability of our languages. We introduced new requirements for the second phase with various impact at the architectural level, the new auction mechanism being quite intrusive. At the sight of the functional results, we may answer to this fourth goal that *it is feasible for master students in software engineering to successfully modify an existing functionality with noticeable impact at the architectural level and add new functionalities to an existing system specified and documented within the* IODASS *framework under our controlled environment.*

6.2   Threats to Validity

We now discuss the threats to validity that are relevant to our study [4, 24].

Conclusion Validity. Because the amount of participants is rather small and the *randomness* between profiles could not be ensured, we intentionally did not use a statistical framework to analyze our results. We focused on metrics where the differences in the results were very high and could be interpreted *as-is*.

All *measures* have been made on quantitative aspects easily observable. The only tricky part resides in the rationale that had been extracted from the SysML teams' reports. However, we analyzed multiple times those reports, and even if we cannot guarantee we did not miss any of them, the difference is so large regarding the IODASS teams that the results would not have been insignificant.

The main part of the study was conducted outside classroom. But even if the participants had *communicate*, we could not find any clones in code or models. Also, we do believe such a communication would not have influenced the results.

Internal Validity. No student had previous knowledge regarding one or the other languages, so we may reasonably think the participants' *history* had no influence. Regarding the *maturation* effect, since the study was conducted also as a teaching goal, we do hope the students learned something from it.

The *instrumentation* is probably the most tendentious aspect. A visual bug affected the commercial SysML plugin we used (that appeared in a release between we analyzed the tool and we gave it to the students). The *satisfy table* were not displayed correctly. This may have had a discouraging effect for the SysML teams. On the other hand, the IODASS tool was at early stage of development, though stable, but it has not the *professional look-and-feel* of a commercial tool.

We especially took care of acting *socially* fairly between teams, without favoring one or the other. Some students may have been too gentle, or harsh regarding our method. The impact of this *good-looking* effect is hardly identifiable and must be kept in mind aside our conclusions.

Construct Validity. The size of the case study and the amount of *measures* are other threats, even if the case sounds realistic, and the final prototype was evaluated by all authors in a *client demo*-like setup. We crosschecked our findings with the results of the questionnaire and the participant's evaluation reports.

External Validity. *Selecting* students represents a significant threat to external validity. They all were students from the University, but with different backgrounds and experiences. They were almost equally coming from the first and the second year of the Master's degree. During the preliminary phase, we particularly paid attention to build comparable groups regarding their former experiences and modeling skills to equalize as much as possible the competencies between both groups.

Regarding the *setting*, the target software was more than a toy sample, since it involved various technologies, analysis and programming skills. We may then reasonably consider a valid extrapolation of our results to junior analysts.

7 Conclusions

The present work detailed a comparative case study that evaluated the feasibility of using model transformations in a highly iterative design method. The study was conducted on a group of students as part of a Software Engineering course. The participants were split in two groups and composed pair-teams to develop a library system in two phases. Half of the teams used SysML models, the other half used a set of languages we defined in previous publications. Both teams were required to follow an *Agile* method and to document the design rationale and decisions during the project. We tested their prototypes after each phase and evaluated the quality of the produced models. We also conducted a paper-based survey in order to collect their feedbacks in a structured way.

At the sight of this study, it appears that our transformation-centric approach produces software with at least an equivalent rate of functional correctness and completeness, even sometimes better. Also, the amount of design rationale was significantly higher (median documentation rate of *0.945* and *1* against *0.215* and *0.285*). However, the study was rather small, so the scalability of our approach should be definitely evaluated on a bigger project.

A critical feature requested by the participants concerned a graphical editor, combined to the textual syntax, in order to enhance model visualization. Combined textual and graphical representations of the same model, but focusing on different aspects, may be a very effective tool support and should be investigated.

References

1. Basili, V.R.: Software modeling and measurement: the goal/question/metric paradigm. Technical report, University of Maryland at College Park, College Park, MD, USA (1992)
2. Bosch, J., Molin, P.: Software architecture design: evaluation and transformation. In: IEEE International Conference on the Engineering of Computer-Based Systems, pp. 4–10 (1999)
3. Chen, L., Ali Babar, M., Nuseibeh, B.: Characterizing architecturally significant requirements. IEEE Softw. **30**(2), 38–45 (2013)
4. Cook, T.D., Campbell, D.T.: Quasi-Experimentation: Design & Analysis Issues for Field Settings. Houghton Mifflin Company, Boston (1979)
5. Dybå, T., Dingsøyr, T.: Empirical studies of agile software development: a systematic review. Inf. Softw. Technol. **50**(9–10), 833–859 (2008). http://www.sciencedirect.com/science/article/pii/S0950584908000256

6. Garlan, D., Monroe, R.T., Wile, D.: ACME: an architecture description interchange language. In: Conference of the Centre for Advanced Studies on Collaborative Research (CASCON 97), Toronto, Ontario, pp. 169–183, November 1997

7. Gilson, F.: Transformation-Wise Software Architecture Framework. Presse Universitaire de Namur, Namur (Belgium), ph.D. Thesis, March 2015

8. Gilson, F., Englebert, V.: Software architecture design by stepwise model transformations : a comparative case study. In: Proceedings of the 3rd International Conference on Model-Driven Engineering and Software Development, pp. 134–145. SciTePress (2015)

9. van Heesch, U., Avgeriou, P., Tang, A.: Does decision documentation help junior designers rationalize their decisions? a comparative multiple-case study. J. Syst. Softw. **86**(6), 1545–1565 (2013). http://www.sciencedirect.com/science/article/pii/S0164121213000228

10. Hofmeister, C., Kruchten, P., Nord, R.L., Obbink, H., Ran, A., America, P.: A general model of software architecture design derived from five industrial approaches. J. Sys. Softw. **80**(1), 106–126 (2007)

11. ISO/IEC/IEEE: Systems and software engineering – architecture description. ISO/IEC/IEEE 42010:2011(E) (Revision of ISO/IEC 42010:2007 and IEEE Std 1471-2000), January 2011

12. Jansen, A., Bosch, J.: Software architecture as a set of architectural design decisions. In: Proceedings of the 5th Working Conference on Software Architecture, pp. 109–120. IEEE Computer Society, Washington, DC (2005)

13. Jones, S.: Stereotypy in pictograms of abstract concepts. Ergonomics **26**(6), 605–611 (1983). http://www.tandfonline.com/doi/abs/10.1080/00140138308963379

14. Jouault, F., Kurtev, I.: Transforming models with ATL. In: Model Transformations in Practice (MTIP) Workshop at ACM/IEEE 8th International Conference on Model Driven Engineering Languages and Systems (2005)

15. Krosnick, J.A., Presser, S.: Question and questionnaire design. In: Marsdenand, P.V., Wright, J.D. (eds.) Handbook of Survey Research, 2nd edn, pp. 263–313. Emerald Group Publishing Limited, Bingley (2010)

16. Leblebici, E., Anjorin, A., Schürr, A., Hildebrandt, S., Rieke, J., Greenyer, J.: A comparison of incremental triple graph grammar tools. In: Proceedings of the 13th International Workshop on Graph Transformation and Visual Modeling Techniques (GTVMT'14). Electronic Communications of the EASST, vol. X (2014)

17. Malavolta, I., Lago, P., Muccini, H., Pelliccione, P., Tang, A.: What industry needs from architectural languages: a survey. IEEE Trans. Softw. Eng. **39**(6), 869–891 (2013)

18. Object Management Group: OMG Systems Modeling Language (OMG SysML^{TM}), version 1.3, oMG document formal/2012-06-01, June 2012

19. Parnas, D.L., Clements, P.C.: A rational design process: how and why to fake it. IEEE Trans. Softw. Eng. **12**, 251–257 (1986). http://portal.acm.org/citation.cfm?id=9794.9800

20. Pfleeger, S.L.: Experimental design and analysis in software engineering. Ann. Softw. Eng. **1**, 219–253 (1995)

21. Runeson, P., Höst, M.: Guidelines for conducting and reporting case study research in software engineering. Empirical Softw. Eng. **14**(2), 131–164 (2009). http://dx.doi.org/10.1007/s10664-008-9102-8

22. Society of Automotive Engineers: Architecture Analysis & Design Language (AADL), standard number AS5506 Revision: B (2012). http://standards.sae.org/as5506b/

23. Tang, A., Ali Babar, M., Gorton, I., Han, J.: A survey of architecture design rationale. J. Syst. Softw. **79**(12), 1792–1804 (2006). http://www.sciencedirect.com/science/article/pii/S0164121206001415
24. Wohlin, C., Runeson, P., Höst, M., Ohlsson, M.C., Regnell, B., Wesslén, A.: Experimentation in Software Engineering. Springer, Heidelberg (2012)

Meta Model Extensibility of BPMN: Current Limitations and Proposed Improvements

Richard Braun[(✉)]

Chair of Wirtschaftsinformatik, esp. Systems Development,
Technische Universität Dresden, 01062 Dresden, Germany
`richard.braun@tu-dresden.de`

Abstract. The Business Process Model and Notation (BPMN) is the prevalent conceptual modeling language for business process modeling and process analysis. BPMN benefits from its expressiveness and the well-defined meta model, which is defined by the Meta Object Facility (MOF). The emergence of BPMN entails an increasing demand for language extensions in order to both benefit from the dissemination and apposite concepts. Although BPMN is one of very few languages that explicitly provides capabilities for its extension, the proposed mechanism reveals some shortcomings and inaccuracies concerning model abstractions, specificity and semantical clarity. A list of improvable aspects is hence provided based on an in-depth analysis of the extension mechanism. The analysis has a special focus on the abstract syntax (BPMN meta model). Several techniques for enhanced BPMN extension design are proclaimed by adapting alternative mechanisms for language extensibility: Profiling, under specification (hooking) and annotation (plug-ins and add-ons). The stated mechanisms are partly adapted from other modeling languages (profiling) or the field of Software Engineering (hooking, plug-ins, add-ons). Each approach is described by its core concepts, its application and by some examples. The approaches are finally compared regarding several criteria.

Keywords: Conceptual modeling · Business process modeling · Meta model extensions · Extension mechanisms · Language dialects · MOF

1 Introduction

The Business Process Model and Notation (BPMN) is the prevalent conceptual modeling language for business processes modeling and widely used in academia and professional practice [1,2]. BPMN provides a range of generic business process model types, which can be applied in various domains. BPMN is defined by the Object Management Group (OMG) and specified as ISO standard [1]. Prevalence and dissemination of (de facto) standard modeling languages like BPMN imply several benefits such as a common understanding of syntactical rules and semantical interpretations as well as a certain level of quality management. The emergence of BPMN as standard language entails an increasing

© Springer International Publishing Switzerland 2015
P. Desfray et al. (Eds.): MODELSWARD 2015, CCIS 580, pp. 230–247, 2015.
DOI: 10.1007/978-3-319-27869-8_13

demand for extensions [3]. Similar effects can be observed for comparable languages like UML or BPEL [4,5]. Extending a stable and rather mature modeling language seems to be more reasonable instead of expensively building individual modeling languages in order to both benefit from the language capabilities and the integration of concepts from a particular domain or problem context [6,7].

In contrast to the vast majority of modeling languages [8], BPMN explicitly provides a dedicated meta model extension mechanism for the generic definition of BPMN extensions [1]. BPMN defines four meta model classes for extension definition (*Extension, ExtensionDefinition, ExtensionAttributeDefinition* and *ExtensionAttributeValue*). However, a recent study reveals that only few BPMN extensions are built on the base of these meta classes [3]. Instead, the most extensions are designed in an ad-hoc manner by dedicated meta model alterations. While this might be unproblematic within single projects, an unsystematic extensibility hampers interoperability, comprehensibility and negates the general compliance to the language standard. It is supposed, that the BPMN extension mechanism itself provokes missing application due to several syntactical shortcomings or inaccuracies [3,6]. For instance, the BPMN extension mechanism suffers from some abstraction conflicts, which violate the immanent four-layer architecture of OMG [1]. In addition, BPMN struggles with the concrete specification of those meta classes that are extended and reveals limitations regarding to the integration of more complex extensions [8].

Against the background of these scientifically relevant issues, the main objective of this research article is the analysis and description of alternative extension mechanisms for BPMN by adapting techniques from comparable modeling approaches (profiling) and from Software Engineering (hooking, add-ons, plug-ins). The secondary research objective is the analysis of shortcomings and inaccuracies of the current BPMN extension mechanism. Thereby, the research article solely addresses issues of the abstract syntax in the form of the BPMN meta model (cf. [9]). Neither the concrete syntax nor procedural aspects are considered due to the limited space of this paper. The remainder of this article is as follows: Sect. 2 provides some fundamentals concerning extensibility. Section 3 presents implicit and explicit capabilities of BPMN for meta model extension design and outlines several limitations. Sections 4, 5 and 6 introduce the techniques of profiling, under specification (hooking) and meta model annotation (plug-ins and add-ons). The characteristic functionality and immanent concepts of each approach are therefore briefly introduced and the potential adaptation for BPMN is elaborated by some examples. Section 7 compares the proposed approaches and provides a short conclusion.

2   Fundamentals

2.1   Extensibility of Conceptual Modeling Languages

Conceptual modeling languages combine aspects of formal languages and natural languages: The syntax of semi-formal modeling languages is defined formally within a meta model and can be divided into abstract syntax and concrete syntax [9, 10]. The semantics of language types is defined by textual, informal statements, their particular configuration and their naming [11]. A conceptual modeling language should be further embedded into a modeling method which outlines procedures for the guided application of particular language concepts and constructs [12]. Consequently, language extensibility can affect several parts: syntax, semantics and procedure [13]. Current research primarily considers the syntax part as it constitutes as mainstay of a language [6] and also this research article solely investigate extensibility of the meta model. Extending the meta model can be realized by ad-hoc modifications (customization or redefinition [13]) or by applying explicitly defined mechanisms [6]. The first one serves as proprietary approach and should not be applied due to missing standardization and interoperability. Explicit mechanisms for meta model extension usually affect the meta model layer (referred as M3 in the OMG environment [14]) in order to provide appropriate meta model concepts for language enhancement. As BPMN is defined by the MOF, each elaboration of BPMN meta model extensibility must also consider the M3 layer in order to comply the separation of abstraction layers and clear type-instance relations.

In a wider sense, an *extension* is defined as enhancement of expressiveness and functionality of a conceptual modeling language by introducing new types, properties or by specifying existing elements in order to represent purpose-specific concepts, which are not provided by the original language. In the narrower sense, an extension must conform to a possibly defined extension mechanism in order the ensure integrity with the original meta model (sometimes referred as core [1] or host [7]). An *extension mechanism* is thereby understood as the specification of elements, rules and constraints within a language meta model as well as the provision of methodical support for their application. [5] states that an extension is neither useful nor functional on its own. However, this view is not shared with respect to the concepts of plug-ins, which can be defined independently.

2.2   Excursus: Extensibility of Programming Languages

The consideration of unforeseen program extensions is perceived as important but non-trivial task within Software Engineering [15, 16]. An extensible program is defined as program that can be adapted to new tasks without accessing the source code [17]. An extensible program should provide explicit concepts and mechanisms for customization on the one side, but needs to ensure high cohesion within an extension and low coupling between extension and the host software on the other side [18, 19]. Several techniques and mechanisms can be used for program extensibility. First, *plug-ins* serve as adaptable components providing additional functionality to a host system [20–22]. Second, *add-ons* describe punctual annotations of a host system but do not provide explicit new functionality. Third, *hooks* can be used for the specification and refinement of particular code segments[1]. The stated approaches are adapted for the extension of BPMN in Sects. 5 and 6.

---

[1] Hooking is similar the instantiation and specification technique from reference modeling [23, 24].

3   BPMN Extensibility

3.1   Implicit Capabilities

BPMN provides some concepts for language customization, which do not require specific extension classes. Particularly, *Artifacts* and *External Relationships* can be used for the integration of domain-specific or additional information. BPMN provides three *Artifact* types by default: *Groups, Text Annotations* and *Associations* [25, p. 67]. BPMN explicitly allows modelers and modeling tools to add additional *Artifacts* for specific purposes [25, p. 28]. This opportunity allows augmentation of the BPMN [7] in the sense of specific domain concepts or constructs for operations on BPMN models such as model transformations. New types can be added to a BPMN diagram, if sequence flow rules and message flow connection rules are respected [25, p. 66]. From a language point of view, rules and constraints of BPMN are not affected by this simple extension option.

Problem Notice 1: It remains unclear what level of complexity a custom *Artifact* should have. This especially addresses the issue of attributed *Artifact* types and relations between them. Actually, *Artifacts* are supposed to be very simple objects getting their semantics primarily from their assigned name. Second, it also remains open, whether custom *Artifacts* should be integrated on meta layer (M2) or model layer (M1).

BPMN also allows the integration of *Artifacts* and "elements expressed in any other addressable domain model" [25, p. 62]. This is enabled by the *External Relationship* element which represents associations between *Artifacts* an external model elements. This simple mapping mechanism is intended to facilitate traceability, model derivation and model integration [25, p. 63]. Thereby, the BPMN meta model remains unmodified, but techniques like model weaving need to be applied in order to realize model integration [26].

3.2   Explicit Capabilities

BPMN provides an extension by addition mechanism that aims to ensure the validity of the BPMN meta model while specifying additional constructs [25, p. 44]. Due to the fact, that the majority of BPMN extensions is not designed in conformity to the BPMN meta model [3], an analysis of BPMN extension capabilities is conducted by analyzing both syntactical and semantical aspects of the four BPMN extension classes. Based on a rational discourse, some problematic or am aspects are stated within problem notices.

Extension: This meta model class binds and imports the entire extension definition and its attributes to a BPMN model definition. By doing so, all extension elements become accessible for BPMN elements [1, p. 58]. If the semantics of an *Extension* need to be understood by a BPMN adopter in order to process a BPMN model correctly, the *mustUnderstood* attribute is set to true. Otherwise, the *Extension* remains optional to BPMN definitions. Any BPMN definition can be associated to multiple *Extensions*. Further, an *Extension* consists of exactly one *Extension Definition*, that defines its actual content.

Semantically, the *Extension* class is only the outermost definition layer, without any concrete domain-specific information.

Extension Definition: This meta model class is a named group of new attributes that can be used by BPMN elements. An *Extension Definition* is not inevitably a new element, since it can also be intended as a single additional attribute of a BPMN element. The only attribute of the class is the *name* attribute that denotes the group. The particular characteristics of the new element or attribute are defined by *Extension Attribute Definitions*. A *Base Element* can reference an *Extension Definition* multiple times. On the contrary, it is not intended to specify, *what* specific BPMN element can access the *Extension Definition*. Thus, actually all extensions are accessible for *all* BPMN elements since each element is a sub class of *Base Element*. A navigation from the *Extension Definition* to the *Base Element* is not possible. Semantically, this class servers as named container of the extension. Due to the fact, that the *Extension* is associated with exactly one *Extension Definition*, an extension actually can be seen as exactly one new element in the sense of a concept having attributes or a concept that only stands for an additional attribute of some BPMN element (a differentiation is only possible in context of the application). This additional element then can be referenced by several BPMN standard elements what emphasizes the additional character of the extension mechanism.

Problem Notice 2: Due to the stated constellation, it is quite inconvenient to add complex extensions, since it is necessary to first design all *Extension Definitions* singularly and than add the relationships between them subsequently. Therefore, it remains unclear, whether an *Extension Definition* can also have an *Extension Attribute Definition* that is typed by another new *Extension Definition*. Actually, that should be possible, since the type is specified as String. However, the specification should make this more clearer, because a domain extension with - for instance - a set of five elements requires a preloading of all five *Extension Definitions* in order to make the corresponding *Extension Attribute Definitions* available. Moreover, it would be better, to explicate the conceptual interrelations between the new elements in one model. Currently, each of the exemplarily five elements would cause a particular extension model and their conceptual interrelations would be barely obvious. Further, it is currently not possible to depict more complex relations between single extension elements such as aggregations or inheritances what hampers expressiveness and the representation of domain rules.

Problem Notice 3: Each BPMN element can access all *Extension Definitions*. This causes both to missing separation of concern and to semantic irregularities, as also elements that are not intended to be related to an *Extension Definition*, can be related to them technically. In order to avoid such situations, it needs to be specified, to which element an *Extension Definition* can be associated.

Problem Notice 4: In the current version, BPMN does not make an unambiguous conceptual difference between element-wise extensions (in the sense of definable classes with own attributes that can be referenced by other classes) and attribute-wise extensions (in the sense of adding some attributes to standard BPMN classes). While this is syntactically correct, it might provoke some conceptual confusion.

Extension Attribute Definitions: This meta model class defines the actual characteristics of an extension. An *Extension Attribute Definition* is specified by the name and the type of the attribute. The corresponding type must be given as string reference to the identifier of the corresponding class. The *isReference* attribute indicates whether the attribute value is set directly or by reference to the referred element. Semantically, the class provides a list of attributes of a new element or attribute.

Extension Attribute Value: This meta model class can be used for the specification of concrete attribute values. If the corresponding *isReference* attribute of the *Extension Attribute Definition* is set of false, the attribute value is given directly. Otherwise, a reference to the targeted class needs to be given [1, p. 59]. A specific meta model *Element* is addressed in both cases. The stated *Element* class is one of the most generic classes within the Complete Meta Object Facility (CMOF) on level M3. Thus, both complex types (e.g., BPMN elements) and primitive data types (e.g., Strings) can be referenced by the defined attribute values (cf. [14]). Thus, the class semantically serves for typed attributes of new elements.

Problem Statement 5: By using the *Element* class, the current BPMN meta model violates the separation of abstraction layers (type instance relation), as the stated class is located on the M3 layer and not on the M2 layer as BPMN is. Further, BPMN does not provide clear evidences regarding to the instance-of relation between BPMN classes and corresponding meta meta classes. Nonetheless, this is quite clear for the most classes (e.g., namespaces or associations), it is confusing regarding the potential application of MOF-based extension classes [14, p. 23].

BPMN defines elements that should facilitate the design of vertical or domain-specific extensions. By providing elements on meta level M2 the instantiated extensions are actually located on model level M1 due to the instance-of relation between model layers. However, an application of the extension requires an instantiation step in order to generate the defined extension elements and make them usable on level M1. Hence, a new "intermediate layer" is created, which contains the standard meta model and its new extension meta model elements. Nevertheless, the BPMN mechanism is principally feasible, its application should be clearly explained. If BPMN aims to provide an extension on level M2, the problems are getting more severe, since BPMN is defined on level M2 and cannot provide any mechanism of the level it is defined on. Rather, there either needs to be an application of MOF extension capabilities in the form of clear instances or any kind of overwriting of the M3 definitions regarding extensibility.

Problem Notice 6: Currently, it is not clear whether BPMN aims to provide an extension mechanism similar to the lightweight UML profile mechanism (M1) or a heavyweight meta model extension (M2). Evidences for both approaches can be found.

3.3   Problematic Aspects of Extending the BPMN Meta Model

Based on the above stated analysis of the abstract syntax of BPMN and its extension capabilities, the following problem notices can be summarized[2]:

1. Allocation of *Artifacts* within the model layer architecture.
2. Missing complexity of extension models.
3. Missing specification of the concrete meta model class which its extended.
4. Unclear differentiation between element extension and attribute extension.
5. Abstraction conflicts regarding to the *CMOF::Element* class.
6. Extension instantiation enforces intermediate layer between M2 and M1.

The list of current shortcomings, inaccuracies and limitations can be further condensed into two main aspects for improving BPMN meta model extensibility: Separation of abstraction and specificity. The first aspect covers the exact and unambiguous usage of model elements regarding to their original abstraction layer. Also, instance-of relations between abstraction layers need to be implemented clearly and the issue of intermediate layers, resulting fromextension instantiation, should be addressed. It is further necessary to specify exactly, which meta model classes are extended by particular extensions in what kind (by attributes or by new types). Thereby, the creation of more complex extensions with a considerable number of interrelations should be also feasible.

Despite the high relevance of BPMN and its extensibility at all, guidance on BPMN extension design and the underlying constructs is little analyzed so far [3, 8]. [27] proposes a model transformation based approach for the derivation of valid BPMN extension models and XML definitions from conceptual domain models. [28] extends this approach by an ontology-based pre-processing in order to substantiate real need for extension. However, both approaches build on the current BPMN extension architecture and its peculiarities. The research works do not discuss any alternatives regarding to the revision of the extension syntax. Hence, the following Sections outline and discuss potentially applicable techniques for extending the abstract syntax of the BPMN.

4   Profiling

4.1   Modus Operandi

UML provides a lightweight extension mechanism, which allows the extension and specification of UML meta models by applying so-called *Stereotypes* to UML meta classes [4]. Profiling serves as means for the specification of existing meta classes or the annotation of additional properties without the modification of a particular meta model. [29] adapts the principle of profiling to BPMN by reusing relevant profile classes from UML and MOF.

---

[2] In contrast to the previous work in [8], only extensibility of the abstract syntax is considered. Neither the concrete syntax, procedural aspects or issues regarding extension exchangeability are considered due to space limitations.

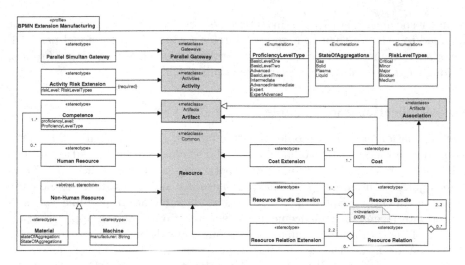

Fig. 1. Application of the profile technique for the integration of resource-related concepts by specifying *Parallel Gateways, Activities, Artifacts* and *Resources* (extracted and adapted from [29,30]).

4.2 Modeling Concepts

Stereotypes are fundamental concepts in order to enable the assignment of additional properties (*Tag Definitions*) to meta classes. Further, [29] proclaims the application of *Stereotypes* for the definition of entirely new types as well as sub types of original meta classes. Therefore, a single BPMN meta class is extended by a specific *Stereotype*, owning respective *Tag Definitions* (attributes). An *Extension* edge links both model types in order to enable a later application. Contextually interrelated *Stereotypes* are encapsulated within a *Profile*, which serves as organizational container, that can be applied by meta model parts. This architecture also facilitates multiple profile application to one meta model class. Within a *Profile*, complex model structures and interrelations between original classes and extension classes are feasible [14].

However, it is important to emphasize, that any kind of profiling leads to the previously stated "intermediate layers" within the model layer architecture, as the defined *Profile* first needs to be instantiated on layer M2. Only then, a subsequent, conjoint instantiation of the original meta model and the extension is possible. An other aspect for consideration is the strong dependency of *Stereotypes* on meta classes [29]. This condition limits the freedom of modeling, as *each* new concept must be semantically similar to an original meta class, as *Stereotypes* can be understood as class specifications [1]. This aspect is less important in UML, as the *Class* concept is extremely generic and can be specified in various kinds. In contrast, BPMN is not that generic, as it covers specifically the process domain. Hence, additional concepts actually must conform to that domain. For the integration of concepts from vertical domains, [29] recommends the usage of under specified meta classes like *Artifacts* or *Data Objects*. *Profiles* are not intended to exist on their own and must refer a concrete meta model part. On the other side, meta model classes are generally independent from single *Profiles*, although *Extensions* can be declared as required [29].

4.3 Application and Example

The application of BPMN profiles is rather simple, as the original BPMN meta model does not need to be modified. Particular *Profiles* can be defined separately, only with a reference to the extended meta classes. If a particular *Profile* is than applied, containing *Stereotypes*, *Constraints* and *Constraints* extend the BPMN meta classes. Based on the above stated examination, profiling serves as appropriate means for enhancement and specification [7,8]. An application for reasons of augmentation remains possible but depends on the reasonable usage of appropriate meta classes.

Figure 1 depicts a profiling exemplar, which extends four BPMN meta classes. The *Artifact* meta class was conducted as base for specification of *Competences*, *Costs* and *Resource Bundles*. Those new concepts are assigned to the extended BPMN meta classes by particular stereotypes realizing the property-wise extension. If such a property-wise extension is mandatory (e.g., *Activity Risk Extension*), then it is necessary to label the extension as *required*. Further, some enumerations with domain-specific value specifications are defined. Also relations between stereotypes should be considered. It is possible to define generalizations (cf. *Material* and *Machine*) and both simple and complex associations with respective multiplicities (e.g., an aggregation between *Resource Relation* and *Resource Bundle*). More complex relations and restrictions can be specified by constraints which can be annotated to any meta model element within the profile.

5 Under Specification (Hooking)

5.1 Modus Operandi

The concept of *hooking* is adapted from Software Engineering and stands for leaving open parts of a program in order to define and specify those parts later in accordance with specific requirements[3]. Usually, the implementation of hooks is rather optional (referring to [31]). In the conceptual modeling domain, some reference modeling techniques provide similar capabilities [23]. The following hooking options are proposed: On *model level*, single meta model classes are left open for filling in specific constructs. A hook always relates to one original meta model element by specifying it or just referring to it. However, original BPMN meta classes can only be referenced; extensions in the form of new dependencies or existential constraints are not permitted. On the *level of concepts*, single BPMN meta classes can be specialized by user-specific subtypes. On the *level of attributes*, several hooks are possible: First, it is feasible to leave open the

---

[3] Hooks are alternatively referred as *extension points* [22] or *hot spots* [31].

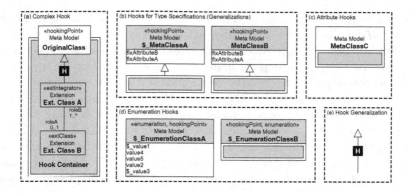

Fig. 2. Graphical notation for modeling any kind of hooks on the M2 layer.

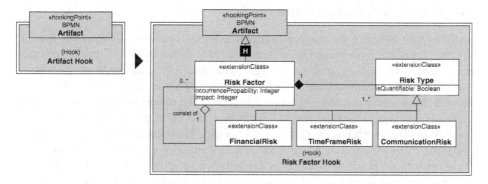

Fig. 3. Application of the hooking technique for specifying *Artifacts* (extracted and adapted from [33]).

entire attribute body of a class at all. Further, it should be possible to specify the types of attributes. With regard to reference modeling [23], it is also allowed to *rename* a model element if it is a hooking point.

5.2   Modeling Concepts

Realizing hooking operations in a meta model requires several additional concepts on the M3 layer. A current research project of the author defines those meta model modifications by extending the MOF with a *Hooking* package [32]. Basically, [32] divides into *Original Classes* (BPMN meta classes), *Extension Classes* and *Extension Integrator Classes*. Integrator classes are responsible for the specification of BPMN meta classes by sub class building or simple referencing, whereby the original class is independent of the extending class. BPMN meta classes can be referenced by extension classes, but must remain independent of them [32]. Further, *Classes*, *Properties* and *Enumerations* can be specified if they are marked as *Hooking Point*. Renaming is possible if a particular property is set. It is also possible to specify property types, cardinalities and enumeration literals [32].

Figure 2 introduces different notational supplements for general meta modeling [32]. *Hook Containers* are represented as grey filled rectangles with a double lined border. The particular *extensionClass* is positioned at its border (cf. Fig. 2a). Figure 2b depicts hooking classes which can be specified by added subtypes (represented by grey rectangles at the bottom). The left class indicates a required renaming of the class by the special notation of the class-name (*$_MetaClassA*). Figure 2c depicts the notation for a hooking class with an attribute body that needs to be filled by individual attributes. Figure 2d represents extensible enumerations. The left enumeration owns both fixed (e.g., *value2*) and changeable enumeration literals (e.g., *$_value1*). The right enumeration leaves out the specification of enumeration literals completely. Figure 2e depicts the specialized generalization edge.

5.3   Application and Example

Applying the hooking techniques requires several revisions of the meta model: The first version represents the original BPMN meta model. The second version contains the assignment and integration of all intended hooking points by instantiating the proposed meta model extension. This version is than filled with different hook elements, leading to subsequent meta model versions, until a final version is reached. This final meta model version is than instantiated in order to enable modeling with the extended meta model. Hooking is an useful extension technique if the skeleton and structure of a meta model are rather fixed and only single aspects need to be specified in accordance to a domain or some peculiarities. Hooking can be both used for language enhancement [7] and customization (also referred as specification [6]).

Figure 3 represents an example hook for specifying the *Artifact* meta class with concepts from the risk management domain. The example was constructed in dependence on the proposed BPMN extension of [33]. The *Risk Factor* class acts as extension integrator class and specifies the original meta class. All other classes constitute as extension classes and relate directly or indirectly to this integrator class.

6   Annotation (Plug-ins and Add-Ons)

6.1   Modus Operandi of Plug-Ins

Plug-ins are functional extensions of a host system through well-defined interfaces [20, 34]. In contrast to hooks and add-ons, plug-ins are usually able to exist on their own, which means that plug-ins are separately executable. The interface of a plug-in is realized by the definition of several *extension points*. Extension points can be understood as code spots, where the executing program asks a central registration unit for plug-ins which want to execute own code. A plug-in as meta model extension is understood as consistent, coherent and independent model, which can enhance the conceptual expressiveness of a modeling language [32]. This implies

the same level of abstraction and a concrete relation to an area of discourse (referring [34]). Consequently, a meta model plug-in is characterized by an ample level
of complexity in regard of its concepts and interdependencies.

6.2   Modus Operandi of Add-Ons

Add-ons are extensions with rather limited capabilities and a small conceptual
scope. Their existence strictly depends on the host system and add-ons cannot
be executed separately. While plug-ins enhance the capabilities of the host and
even provide mandatorily functions, add-ons merely provide optional features,
which are not that important for the host system. Add-ons have the same basal
architecture as plug-ins, excepting two points: The inner complexity of add-ons
is limited and an add-on cannot be instantiated or executed alone. With regard
to meta models, we propose add-ons for primarily incremental, attribute-wise
extensions of meta models. Thereby, new attributes and concepts have a strong
dependency on original concepts, while the original meta class is never dependent
on any extension class. Add-ons can further specify original classes. Both aspects
are neither possible nor reasonable within plug-ins.

6.3   Modeling Concepts

Similar to under specification, the implementation of plug-ins and add-ons in
the BPMN meta model requires the extension of the MOF, which is realized by
adding a *Add-Ons and Plug-Ins* package to the EMOF [32]. Similar to hookings,
BPMN meta classes are divided into *Original Classes* and *Extension Classes*.
Extension Containers are package-like classes for encapsulating and grouping
related extension classes. An *Interface* defines the interface between the BPMN
meta model and the particular extension (plug-in or add-on). Also, the *Extension Integrator Class* enables the integration of original BPMN meta classes and
extension classes. Therefore, a specific association is defined (*Adapter Association*) [32]. An *Adapter Association* is assessed as *dependent*, if the lower bound
is greater than 0 or if the relation constitutes as aggregation or composition.

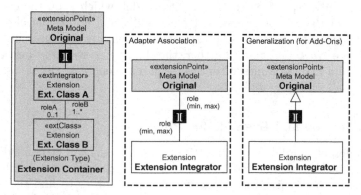

Fig. 4. Graphical notation for the introduced extension concepts.

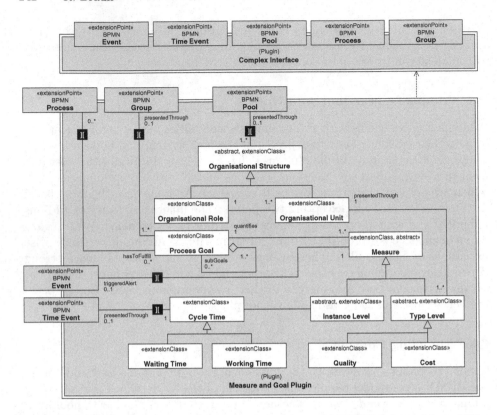

Fig. 5. Plug-in for the annotation of costs and measures in BPMN (adapted from [35]).

A distinction between plug-ins and add-ons is possible by analyzing both *Adapter Association* and relations within the proposed extension. In plug-ins, BPMN meta model classes depend on particular extension classes. However, neither simple relations (associations) nor generalizations between BPMN classes and extension classes are allowed within an extension container, as plug-ins are independent and separated. In contrast, add-ons may contain such constructs, as add-ons highly depend on the host meta model, which is on the other hand independent of the add-on. Figure 4 depicts additional notational elements for plug-in and add-on modeling. The *Extension Container* is represented in the same kind as a *Hook Container*. Further, the *Adapter Association* between original classes and extension integrator classes is represented as simple association with a special icon in the middle.

6.4   Application and Example for Plug-Ins

Initially, different interfaces within a BPMN meta model can be defined in order to declare which classes or sets of classes can be extended at all. Thereafter, it is necessary to examine the respective plug-in in order to find the mapping and integration points (cf. [32]). If the plug-in conforms to the defined interface,

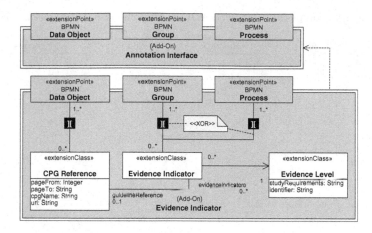

Fig. 6. Annotation of concepts for evidence-based medicine by applying the add-on technique (adapted from [36]).

than both parts can be unified. The plug-in technique is appropriate for enhancement and augmentation of a host meta model as it adds conceptually new elements [6,7]. As plug-ins are generally understood as rather domain-oriented components, they are *not* useful for analytical purposes (e.g., model analysis [6]). Further, they are also not useful for specification as they do not provide respective concepts.

Figure 5 represents an example of a meta model plug-in by leveraging (and slightly altering) a BPMN extension [35]. The plug-in aims to provide cost and time aspects by BPMN. The group of added concepts fulfills the criteria of plug-ins: A certain level of complexity can be stated, the plug-in can be instantiated on its own and is not dependent of the host meta model. Merely, the interface classes slightly depend on the plug-in.

6.5 Application and Example for Add-Ons

The procedure for application is equivalent to plug-in applications. Due to the additional nature of add-ons, they can be leveraged for the element-wise annotation of further attributes or single aspects in the form of a small set of new concepts. Hence, add-ons are appropriate for model analysis, specification and minimal augmentation [6,7]. Figure 6 presents an exemplary add-on as BPMN extension for evidence-based medicine, extracted from [36]. The extension has a rather limited complexity (only three concepts) and depends on original BPMN concepts (not vice versa!). Further, an isolated instantiation of the add-on makes only little sense.

7 Comparison and Conclusion

7.1 Comparison of Extension Approaches

Table 1 presents a comparison of the adapted techniques. Especially, the dependency directions between original classes (extension points) and extension classes

Table 1. Comparison of the approaches (OC = original class, EP = extension point).

Criterion	Profiling	Hooking	Add-Ons	Plug-Ins
Problem solving (cf. Sect. 3.3)				
Artifact spec.	(+)	(+)	(+)	(+)
Complexity	(+)	+	+	+
Element spec.	+	+	+	+
Type vs. attribute	o	+	+	o
Separation of abstraction	+	+	+	+
Intermediate layer	–	–	–	–
Relation to the Original Meta Model				
Host to extension	N - M	1 - N	N - M	N - M
Dependency	Strongly dependent	Strongly dependent	Dependent	Independent
Separate instantiation	Neither possible nor reasonable	Neither possible nor reasonable	Rarely possible, but not reasonable	Possible and reasonable
Inner complexity	Various	Low	Low	Rather high
Impact and Purpose				
Effected element types	Classes	Classes, properties, property values, etc	Classes	
Technical purpose	Specification	Specification	Adding	Extending functionally
Practical purpose [6, 7]	Specification, enhancement	Specification	Model operations, specification	Enhancement, augmentation
Architecture and Syntax				
Extension interface	De facto specification of multiple EPs	Specification of one EP	Specification of/ association to multiple EPs	Association to multiple EPs
Within the extension	Referencing OCs, specification of OCs (by stereotyping)	Referencing OCs, specification of OCs	Referencing OCs, specification of OCs	No referencing and specification of OCs

are focussed for emphasizing. It is further important to keep in mind, that hooks, add-ons and profiles are rather weaved with an original meta model, whereas plug-ins constitute as isolated, separately defined model components.

Table 1 also represents the problem solving capabilities of the approaches. All approaches solve the first issue, as each meta model class can be extended (cf. element specification). Complex extension models can be provided by nearly all approaches. Profiles are rather limited in this regard, as each extension class must specify an original meta class. Separation of abstract layers is satisfied by each approach. However, the issue of intermediate layers remains unsolved, as each extension technique requires a multi-step procedure within the M2 layer.

First, the general extension interface is declared (e.g., by setting the hooking points). Second, the intended extension is specified. And finally, host and extension model are integrated (or merged) in order to instantiate it and generate the extended BPMN version. Hence, it is extremely important to provide further methodical support for extension design (see below).

7.2   Conclusion and Further Research

This research article addresses extensibility of the BPMN and presents an extended version of a previous paper (cf. [8]), with a special focus on the abstract syntax of BPMN. Based on a summary of problematic aspects and limitations of the current BPMN extension mechanism, four alternatives were elaborated. All approaches reveal benefits and limitations, which requires the purpose-specific selection of a particular approach against the backdrop of a specific problem. For instance, the plug-in approach is very useful for den integration of separated meta models of a vertical domain (e.g., organizational modeling). Hooks are appropriate for scenarios, were some very specific aspects of a meta model should be configured and specialized. Add-ons are useful for the annotation of separated concepts, which are primarily used for model analysis or operations. Profiles are well suited means for the definition of particular dialects (specifications) of existing BPMN meta classes.

Nevertheless, several issues have to be investigated in further research. As this article focusses the abstraction syntax, it is important to further examine semantical aspects in detail, as syntax and semantics are extremely interrelated. For instance, it seems to be reasonable to conduct several semantical check routines in order to avoid contradictions between the meta model and the added extension. It is also required to provide integrated methodical support for the creation of single extensions based on specific domain requirements and for the selection of the most appropriate extension technique.

References

1. OMG: Unified Modeling Language, Infrastructure, Version 2.4.1. OMG (2011)
2. Chinosi, M., Trombetta, A.: Bpmn: an introduction to the standard. Comput. Stand. Interfaces **34**(1), 124–134 (2012)
3. Braun, R., Esswein, W.: Classification of domain-specific bpmn extensions. Lect. Notes of Bus. Inf. Process. **147**, 42–57 (2014)
4. Pardillo, J.: A systematic review on the definition of UML profiles. In: Petriu, D.C., Rouquette, N., Haugen, Ø. (eds.) MODELS 2010, Part I. LNCS, vol. 6394, pp. 407–422. Springer, Heidelberg (2010)
5. Kopp, O., Görlach, K., Karastoyanova, D., Leymann, F., Reiter, M., Schumm, D., Sonntag, M., Strauch, S., Unger, T., Wieland, M., et al.: A classification of bpel extensions. J. Syst. Integr. **2**(4), 3–28 (2011)
6. Braun, R.: Towards the state of the art of extending enterprise modeling languages. In: Proceedings of the 3rd International Conference on Model-Driven Engineering and Software Development (2015)

7. Atkinson, C., Gerbig, R., Fritzsche, M.: Modeling language extension in the enterprise systems domain. In: 17th IEEE International Enterprise Distributed Object Computing Conference, pp. 49–58 (2013)
8. Braun, R.: Behind the scenes of the bpmn extension mechanism - principles, problems and options for improvement. In: Proceedings of the 3rd International Conference on Model-Driven Engineering and Software Development (2015)
9. Wand, Y., Weber, R.: Research commentary: information systems and conceptual modeling–a research agenda. Inf. Syst. Res. **13**(4), 363–376 (2002)
10. Frank, U.: Conceptual modelling as the core of the information systems discipline-perspectives and epistemological challenges. In: Proceedings of the Fifth Americas Conference on Information Systems (AMCIS 1999), pp. 695–697 (1999)
11. Pfeiffer, D., Gehlert, A.: A framework for comparing conceptual models. In: Proceedings of the Workshop on Enterprise Modelling and Information Systems Architectures (EMISA 2005), pp. 108–122. Citeseer (2005)
12. Greiffenberg, S.: Methodenentwicklung in Wirtschaft und Verwaltung. Kovač (2004)
13. Braun, R., Esswein, W.: A generic framework for modifying and extending enterprise modeling languages. In: 17th International Conference on Enterprise Information Systems (2015)
14. OMG: Meta Object Facility (MOF) Core Specification, Version 2.4.2 (2014)
15. Parnas, D.L.: Designing software for ease of extension and contraction. IEEE Trans. Softw. Eng. **SE–5**(2), 128–138 (1979)
16. Rytter, M., Jørgensen, B.N.: Independently extensibile contexts. In: Babar, M.A., Gorton, I. (eds.) ECSA 2010. LNCS, vol. 6285, pp. 327–334. Springer, Heidelberg (2010)
17. Krishnamurthi, S., Felleisen, M.: Toward a formal theory of extensible software. In: ACM SIGSOFT Software Engineering Notes, vol. 23, pp. 88–98. ACM (1998)
18. Bass, L., Clements, P., Kazman, R.: Software Software Architecture in Practice. Addison Wesley Professional, Reading (2003)
19. Martin, R.C.: Design principles and design patterns. Object Mentor **1**, 34 (2000)
20. Wolfinger, R.: Plug-in architecture and design guidelines for customizable enterprise applications. In: Companion to the 23rd ACM SIGPLAN Conference on Object-oriented Programming Systems Languages and Applications, pp. 893–894. ACM (2008)
21. Mayer, J., Melzer, I., Schweiggert, F.: Lightweight plug-in-based application development. In: Akşit, M., Mezini, M., Unland, R. (eds.) NODe 2002. LNCS, vol. 2591, pp. 87–102. Springer, Heidelberg (2003)
22. Birsan, D.: On plug-ins and extensible architectures. Queue **3**(2), 40–46 (2005)
23. Becker, J., Delfmann, P., Knackstedt, R.: Adaptive reference modeling: integrating configurative and generic adaptation techniques for information models. In: Becker, J., Delfmann, P. (eds.) Reference Modeling, pp. 27–58. Springer, Heidelberg (2007)
24. Becker, J., Delfmann, P.: Reference Modeling. Springer, Heidelberg (2007)
25. OMG: Business Process Model and Notation (BPMN) - Version 2.0. Object Management Group (OMG) (2011)
26. Del Fabro, M.D., Valduriez, P.: Towards the efficient development of model transformations using model weaving and matching transformations. Softw. Syst. Model. **8**(3), 305–324 (2009)
27. Stroppi, L.J.R., Chiotti, O., Villarreal, P.D.: Extending BPMN 2.0: method and tool support. In: Dijkman, R., Hofstetter, J., Koehler, J. (eds.) BPMN 2011. LNBIP, vol. 95, pp. 59–73. Springer, Heidelberg (2011)

28. Braun, R., Schlieter, H.: Requirements-based development of bpmn extensions - the case of clinical pathways. In: 1st International Workshop on the Interrelations between Requirements Engineering and Business Process Management (2014)
29. Braun, R.: Bpmn extension profiles - adapting the profile mechanism for integrated bpmn extensibility. In: Proceedings of the 17th IEEE Conference on Business Informatics (2015)
30. Braun, R., Esswein, W.: Extending bpmn for modeling resource aspects in the domain of machine tools. WIT Trans. Eng. Sci. **87**, 450–458 (2014)
31. Kulesza, U., Alves, V., Garcia, A., de Lucena, C.J.P., Borba, P.: Improving extensibility of object-oriented frameworks with aspect-oriented programming. In: Morisio, M. (ed.) ICSR 2006. LNCS, vol. 4039, pp. 231–245. Springer, Heidelberg (2006)
32. Braun, R.: Adaptation of Software Engineering Techniques for the Extension of Conceptual Modeling Languages (to be published) (2015)
33. Marcinkowski, B., Kuciapski, M.: A business process modeling notation extension for risk handling. In: Cortesi, A., Chaki, N., Saeed, K., Wierzchoń, S. (eds.) CISIM 2012. LNCS, vol. 7564, pp. 374–381. Springer, Heidelberg (2012)
34. Marquardt, K.: Patterns for plug-ins. In: EuroPLoP, pp. 203–232 (1999)
35. Korherr, B., List, B.: Extending the epc and the bpmn with business process goals and performance measures. In: ICEIS (3), pp. 287–294 (2007)
36. Braun, R., Schlieter, H., Burwitz, M., Esswein, W.: Bpmn4cp: design and implementation of a bpmn extension for clinical pathways. In: IEEE International Conference on Bioinformatics and Biomedicine (BIBM), pp. 9–16. IEEE (2014)

An Approach to Define and Apply Collaboration Process Patterns for Software Development

Thuan Tan Vo, Bernard Coulette[✉], Hanh Nhi Tran, and Redouane Lbath

Institut de Recherche en Informatique de Toulouse, Toulouse, France
vtthuan89@gmail.com, {bernard.coulette,hanh-nhi.tran,
redouane.lbath}@irit.fr

Abstract. Complex system developments are more and more collaborative. Collaboration strategies largely depend on the development context at modelling, instantiation or enactment time. To put collaboration in action, we propose collaboration process patterns to define, reuse and enact collaborative software development processes. In this paper we describe the definition and application of collaboration patterns. Our patterns, inspired from workflow patterns of Van der Aalst, are described in CMSPEM, a Process Modelling Language developed in our team in 2014. In this paper, we briefly describe the CMSPEM metamodel and focus our presentation on two collaboration patterns: Duplicate in Sequence with Multiple Actors, Duplicate in Parallel with Multiple Actors and Merge. The approach is illustrated by a case study concerning the collaborative and representative process "Review a deliverable".

Keywords: Model driven engineering · Software development process · Collaboration · Collaboration pattern

1 Introduction

Nowadays, software systems are more and more complex, and development processes are usually collaborative. Indeed, these processes are enacted by several actors, possibly deployed on several sites, who work together on collaborative tasks with shared artifacts to achieve a common goal. To facilitate project management and improve the coherence during software process execution, collaboration must be identified, modeled and assisted. Once defined and approved, generic collaboration situations can be reused for further projects [12].

An efficient way to put reuse in action is to define and apply collaboration patterns. Some research works can be found in the literature about collaboration patterns (such as [7, 14, 23]), but very limited work has been done about their automatic application during software development.

In this paper, extension of [25], we propose an approach to define and apply collaboration patterns. More precisely, we describe a set of generic collaboration software patterns and propose a way to apply them automatically during a software development. This work is a continuation of our previous works on process patterns [21] and on collaborative software processes [15–17]. In the first work we proposed a language to

© Springer International Publishing Switzerland 2015
P. Desfray et al. (Eds.): MODELSWARD 2015, CCIS 580, pp. 248–262, 2015.
DOI: 10.1007/978-3-319-27869-8_14

represent process patterns and a mechanism to apply patterns at modeling time. In the second work, we defined the meta-model CMSPEM as an extension of the OMG standard SPEM for describing collaborative software processes. The work described here uses CMSPEM to represent collaboration patterns which are inspired from work-flow patterns [22], and proposes mechanisms to apply collaborative patterns not only at modeling but also at instantiation or enactment time.

This paper is structured as follows. Section 2 presents the essential concepts of collaborative software process modeling. Section 3 presents a way to represent collaboration patterns. Section 4 shows how collaboration patterns can be applied at modeling, instantiation or enactment time. Section 5 presents a case study and a brief overview of the supporting tool prototype. Section 6 concludes this paper and proposes a short discussion and some perspectives.

2 Modelling Collaborative Processes

Several studies can be found in the literature about notions of process modeling and collaboration. In this section, we put the emphasis on Software process modeling languages, on the notion of collaboration in process enactment, and on the CMSPEM meta-model that was elaborated in our team, and finally on workflow patterns which are reference solutions mainly used in business process modeling.

2.1 Software Process Modelling

A software process is defined as a set of activities for developing, administrating and maintaining a software product [2, 8, 9, 11]. A software process model describes process elements and relationships among them. Process elements can be classified in two categories; primary elements are activities, roles, work products; secondary elements provide additional information on organizational and qualitative aspects of a process. Figure 1a shows the primary process elements and basic relations among them.

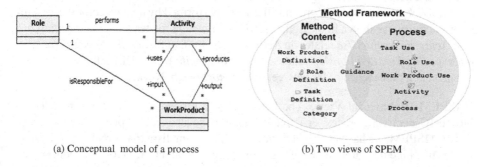

(a) Conceptual model of a process   (b) Two views of SPEM

Fig. 1. Key concepts of SPEM 2.0.

Among existing Software Process Modeling Languages (SPML), we decided to put the focus on the OMG standard SPEM 2.0 which is probably the richest modeling language for software process designers, in the sense where it favors reusability and is open for execution expression [6]. Main primary concepts of SPEM 2.0 are *Role*, *Task* and *WorkProduct* which may have two views: definition and use (Fig. 1b). In the definition view, we find process elements (*Method Content*) which are intended to be reused into several processes; in the use view (*Process*), we find instances of those process elements in the context of real processes. For example, a *TaskDefinition* describes a reusable task whereas a *TaskUse* represents an instance of *TaskDefinition* in a given process.

2.2 Collaboration in Software Process Modeling

A process is said to be collaborative when it contains at least one collaborative activity, i.e. an activity which is performed by two or more human actors targeting the same goal. A collaborative activity is defined as a coordinated and synchronous task whose goal is to build and maintain a shared design of a problem [18, 20]. Collaboration has been largely studied in the literature as shows the review provided by [23]. In [19], the authors propose a classification of collaboration approaches based on prescriptive and descriptive formalisms.

CMSPEM meta-model is a prescriptive process modeling language defined by our team in the context of the GALAXY ANR project [17] whose objective was to propose a framework for supporting collaborative model driven development. CMSPEM is an extension of SPEM which allows defining collaborative software processes. CMSPEM supports both dynamic and static aspects of a process, allowing to enact process models with an appropriate tool. In the following of this section, we briefly present the structural and behavioral views of CMSPEM.

CMSPEM: Structural View. From a structural view, we added in CMSPEM a new package, called *CollaborationStructure*, that introduces the following concepts – *Actor*, *ActorSpecificWork* and *ActorSpecificArtifact* – and a set of related relationships. An *Actor* is a human participant who plays one or several roles in a process. An *ActorSpecificWork* represents the contribution of an *Actor* into a given *TaskUse*. An *ActorSpecificArtifact* represents a copy of a *WorkProductUse* for a given *Actor*.

Figure 2 below shows an extract of the CMSPEM metamodel concerning the *ActorSpecificWork* concept which represents the work performed by a given actor in a collaborative activity. As shown in the figure, a *TaskAssignment* relates an *ActorSpecificWork* to an *Actor*; an *ArtifactUse* relates an *ActorSpecificArtifact* to an *ActorSpecificWork*; an *ActorSpecificWorkRelationship* relates two *ActorSpecificWork*. This latter can be used to represent a precedence order between two *ActorSpecificWork*.

CMSPEM: Behavioral View. The behavior of a process must also be modeled to rigorously specify the process enactment (that may be also called "process execution"). In CMSPEM, we have chosen the state-machine formalism to express this behavior. A state-machine describes states of a given process element (activity or product), and transitions between them. We distinguish two types of transition: manual and automatic. A manual transition – called *OperatorEvent* – is triggered by an actor. An automatic transition is either a *ProcessStateChangeEvent* or a *ConditionalEvent*. Figure 3 shows the kernel of the behavioral part of CMSPEM. Each enactable process element is associated a state-machine.

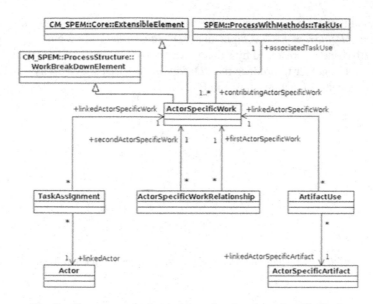

Fig. 2. Concepts and relationships related to *ActorSpecificWork*.

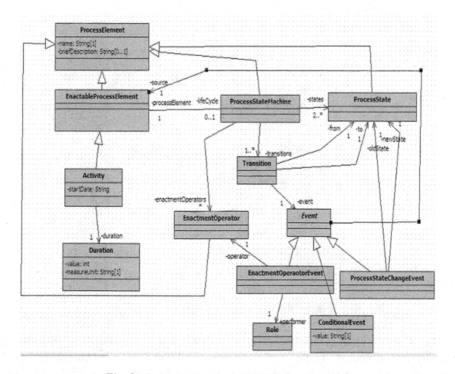

Fig. 3. Behavioral part of CMSPEM meta-model.

Figure 4 illustrates, in a concrete syntax of CMSPEM, a simple example of *"Design"* activity with *"Requirements"* as input, and *"Design Model"* as output. This activity is a collaborative one (represented by a double rectangle) in the usual case where several designers work together to produce the *"Design model"*. Design activity's behavior is described as the state machine shown in Fig. 5.

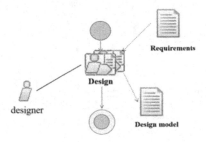

Fig. 4. Collaborative *"Design"* activity expressed in CMSPEM.

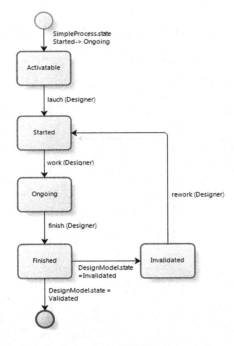

Fig. 5. Behaviour of the Design activity.

The states through which the *Design* activity passes are *Activatable*, *Started*, *Ongoing* and *Finished*. These states are reached by means of *«OperateurEvent»* transitions—launch, work or finish—triggered by a designer. From Finished state, depending on the current state of *DesignModel*, a *«ConditionnalEvent»* transition determines whether the next state will be the terminal state (corresponding to the fact that *DesignModel* is validated) or the Invalidated state which means that the design is not validated and thus should be reworked.

2.3   Workflow Patterns

Patterns have been highly used for software process modelling [1, 3, 5, 10, 13]. Workflow patterns are reusable generic process fragments which are of high interest for describing collaborative processes. Thus, we studied the workflow patterns proposed in [22] which are reference patterns. It is a set of 42 generic patterns grouped into 8 parts: *Basic Control Flow Patterns, Multiple Instance Patterns, State-based Patterns, Cancellation and Force Completion Patterns, Iteration Patterns, Termination Patterns, Trigger Patterns*. Figure 6 illustrates, as an example, the *Synchonization* pattern which is a basic control flow pattern.

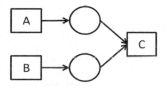

Fig. 6.   Synchronization workflow pattern.

3   An Approach to Collaboration Patterns

3.1   Introduction

Collaboration process patterns are development strategies that can be applied either at modeling time or later at instantiation or enactment time. As any pattern, a collaboration pattern can be defined by a recurrent problem, a solution and an application context. We decided to derive in a first time a set of collaboration patterns from elementary workflow patterns that have proven to be efficient in process modeling [21]. Indeed, most of collaboration strategies can be described by means of control flows such as sequence, parallelism, merging, concatenation, etc.

We have defined a set of collaboration patterns that can be found in [24]. In the following of this section, we illustrate two of them that we consider as representative of collaboration strategies: *DuplicateInSequenceWithMultipleActors, DuplicateInSequenceWithMultipleActorsAndMerge*. They are described in a graphical syntax associated to CMSPEM. For each pattern, we briefly present below the recurring problem, the application context, and a solution described as an activity diagram.

3.2   Pattern "Duplicate in Sequence with Multiple Actors" (DSMA)

Problem and Context. This pattern represents a collaboration in sequence among actors playing the same role in a given activity. The recurring problem is the one where human resource is limited in a given enterprise, but constraint time is not too strong. So in this context, it is possible to apply a sequence-based pattern.

Solution. The same activity (cloned) is done by different actors playing a given role. They work in sequence on a product elaborated by another actor. The resulting product becomes the input for the next actor. Figure 7 shows this pattern as an activity diagram in CMSPEM for two abstract actors called *Actor1* and *Actor2*.

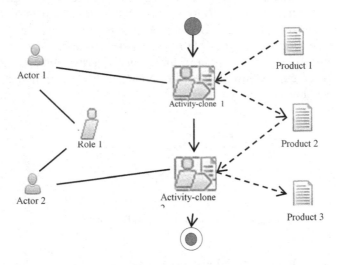

Fig. 7. Pattern *Duplicate In Sequence With Multiple Actors* (DSMA).

It contains abstract cloned activities having one input product and one output product. Each activity is enacted in sequence by different actors playing the same role. For example, this pattern could be used for enacting activities such as *Design a software*, *Review a document*, *Test a program*, etc.

3.3 Pattern "Duplicate in Parallel with Multiple Actors and Merge" (DPMAM)

Problem and Context. This pattern represents a collaborative situation where several actors work on the same cloned activity with the same role. The problem occurs whenever outputs are specific of each actor. In other words, each actor has his own point of view on the activity. This pattern is suitable when several actors are available at the same time, meaning that activities can be enacted in parallel. One of the actors is then in charge of merging the output products into a unique one. This merging activity may be hard to perform in case of conflicting products.

Solution. Cloned activities are enacted in parallel with the same product (cloned) as input. Their termination is synchronized and then followed by a merging activity performed by one of the actors. Figure 8 shows this pattern with two actors working on the same cloned activity, with abstract names.

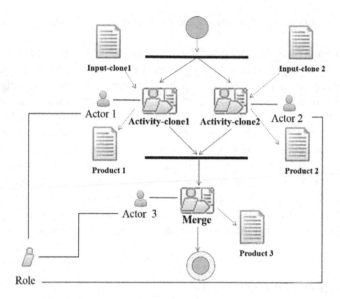

Fig. 8. Pattern *Duplicate in Parallel With Multiple Actors and Merge* (DPMAM).

This pattern could be used for enacting activities such as: *Test a software component, Review a deliverable, Evaluate a submission*, etc.

This pattern has a specific variant where the *Merge* activity is replaced by a *Concatenate* one. Indeed, the concatenation can be seen as a particular case of merging. This variant may be used whenever *Product1* and *Product2* are disjoint.

3.4 Conclusion

We have put the emphasis in this section on two representative collaboration patterns derived from elementary workflow patterns. However, as discussed in Sect. 6 there are many collaboration strategies so that the set of collaboration process patterns is potentially very big.

4 Application of Collaboration Patterns

Whenever a collaborative activity is identified, one can search for patterns to apply. These patterns are supposed to be stored into a repository. One can note that pattern application can be done at modeling time and/or at instantiation time and/or at enactment time. At modeling time, the application of a collaboration pattern consists in identifying a collaborative activity, choosing a collaboration pattern without instantiating it and refining the activity diagram by unfolding the activity. Unfolding is based on the structural solution (activity diagram) of the pattern which serves as a template. The result of the application of patterns is a refined process model. The choice of the best collaboration pattern to apply is an important issue but it is out of the scope of this paper. To apply such patterns at modeling time, one must know in advance that an activity will be enacted as a collaborative one. It is not always the case since this information may be known later.

At instantiation time, the goal is to take into consideration the real resources that will be used in a given project, that is to say products in input and output, actors playing a given role on a given activity, etc. For each collaborative activity, one must choose a collaboration pattern to apply, thus identify and instantiate the actors (real persons) that will collaborate, define the products to clone, and unfold the activity as explained above.

At enacting time, the goal is to enact (execute) the process which can be seen as its root activity. Execution of the process must respect the behavioral description of the process (as explained in Sect. 2.2), and in particular the lifecycles that are assigned to process elements. Actors participate in the execution of some manual tasks. It is possible and even necessary to differ the application of collaboration patterns until this enacting time. Indeed, some decisions depend on dynamic information (availability of actors, time constraints, etc.). The principle of the pattern application is the same as for the two previous cases.

5   Realization and Case Study

We describe in this section the case study that we performed and the tool prototype developed as a proof of concept.

5.1   Case Study

We have applied our approach to the process "Review a Deliverable" intensively applied during the ANR Galaxy project (see Fig. 9).

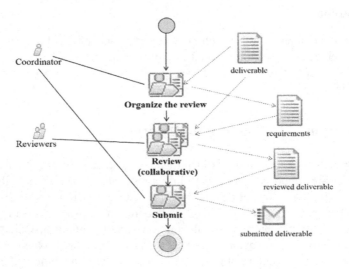

Fig. 9. Process model "Review a deliverable" of the Case Study.

Though it is a quite simple process, it is a real one and it is representative of collaborative processes. This process is made of 3 activities: *Organize the review, Review the deliverable, Submit the reviewed deliverable*. The second one – *Review the deliverable*, done by several reviewers, is a collaborative one. The reviewing process is organized by a coordinator who specifies requirements to be satisfied by the reviewers. Let us suppose that the collaborative activity *Review the deliverable* is done by 3 reviewers: *Peter, Paul* and *Tracy*.

In the following, we present 2 strategies of collaboration corresponding to the application of the 2 collaboration patterns presented in Sect. 3: DSMA, DPMAM. We address the modeling phase, and only consider here the structural solution proposed by collaboration patterns.

Application of Pattern DSMA (Duplicate in Sequence with Multiple Actors). This pattern is applicable in the case where the 3 reviewers can work in sequence one after the other, and whenever there is enough time to achieve the reviewing activity (Fig. 10). It was the case during the Galaxy project.

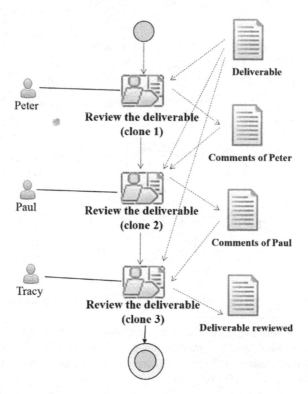

Fig. 10. Activity diagram resulting of DSMA application.

The order in which the reviewers must work is important because the last one finishes the reviewing work. We suppose here that the same input deliverable is in entry of the 3 cloned activities, which means that a reviewer does not update the deliverable. *Peter* produces comments on the deliverable. *Paul* adds his own comments to those of Peter. *Tracy* produces the reviewed deliverable by analyzing *Paul's* comments.

Application of Pattern DPMAM (Duplicate in Parallel with Multiple Actors and Merge). This pattern is applicable in the case where the reviewers are available at the same time and thus can work in parallel. Figure 11 shows the activity diagram of the pattern's solution. The same deliverable (clone) is in input of each *Review* activity (cloned activity). Each reviewer – that is *Peter*, *Paul* or *Tracy* – produces his proper review by updating the deliverable. *Peter*, is also in charge of the merging activity, whose goal is to merge the results of the 3 reviews included his own. This merging task cannot be automated since conflicts may appear among the reviewed deliverables. It is up to Peter to solve such conflicts in collaboration with the other reviewers.

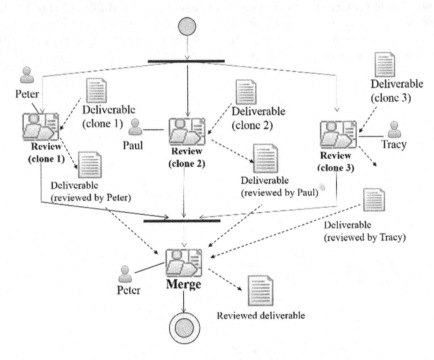

Fig. 11. Activity diagram resulting from DPMAM application.

A variant of this pattern is the following one: each reviewer produces a document containing his comments without modifying the deliverable. In this case, the merger (*Peter*) would have to analyze the three documents produced by the reviewers and to update the deliverable accordingly.

5.2 Supporting Tool Prototype

We have developed a tool prototype for supporting collaborative processes enactment. It is written in Java JEE. To represent a process, we first developed a textual Process

Modeling Language (PML). A process model – described with this PML – is then represented as a tree.

So far, we have implemented the *Duplicate in Sequence with Multiple Actors* pattern (DSMA) described above. Other patterns are being implemented. To illustrate the tool, we have chosen a very simple software process composed of 2 classical activities: *Design* and *Coding*. Figure 12 shows the process model in tree representation.

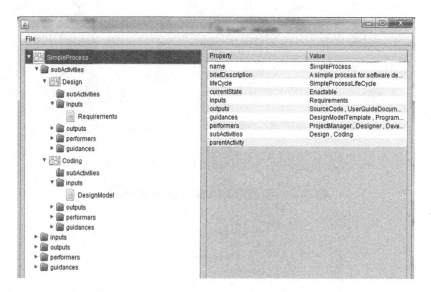

Fig. 12. Example of collaborative simple process.

Enactment of this process is based on the state machines associated to its process elements, including the *Design* activity. At any time of the process enactment, a set of actions is proposed to the current actor depending on the current state.

In the following, we consider the *Design* activity which may be seen as a collaborative one. Let us suppose that this activity is performed in an iterative way by a set of 3 designers. Figures 13 shows the actions proposed to each designer at the beginning of the process; one can notice that only the *launch* action is executable.

To perform the collaborative *Design* activity, one can choose one collaboration pattern in an existing repository, for instance the DSMA pattern. As shown in Fig. 14, three Design activities are performed in sequence in conformity with DSMA's solution. The first one, *Design 1*, done by *Bob*, takes *Requirements* as input and produces *Design-ModelBob* as output. This latter product becomes the entry of the second activity, done by Marc, and so one.

It is obvious that this simple process is not a significant case study that would demonstrate the scalability of our approach. However we do not really have any scalability issue with our approach because the number of collaborative activities is always limited in a given process. So the size of the process model is not a significant criterion for the proof of concept.

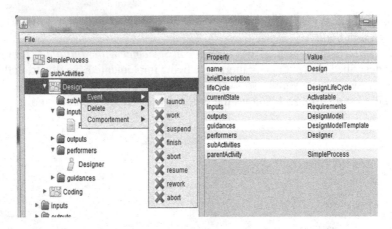

Fig. 13. Interface of the tool: manual action triggering.

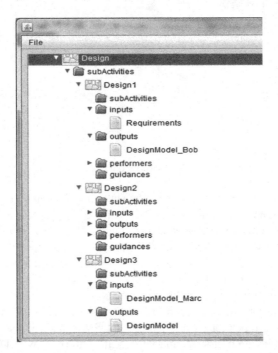

Fig. 14. Process model resulting from DSMA pattern application.

6   Conclusion

We have been working for years on software process modeling and enactment. In the
GALAXY ANR project, we defined a new metamodel, extended from SPEM, to model
and enact model-based collaborative processes [17]. But putting collaboration in action
is very hard and human-dependent, so we decided to provide process designers and

developers with means to perform collaborative tasks. For that sake, we defined a methodology to represent and apply collaboration patterns.

Work Done. In this paper, we have proposed an approach to firstly (1) model collaboration patterns in CMSPEM, and secondly (2) apply them at modeling time (by a process designer) or during software development (by chief projects). So far our process patterns are inspired from workflow ones [22] but our proposition may be applied to any kind of patterns. Our proposition has been validated (as a proof of concept) on a simple but realistic case study. A prototype supporting the approach has been also developed.

Discussion and Perspectives. At short time, our future work will target the supporting tool. First we intend to enrich the set of collaboration patterns available and to organize them through a repository. It is also necessary to improve the tool prototype, to automate the application of collaboration patterns, and to apply our approach to larger collaborative software development processes.

Collaboration is a complex and non-deterministic task which depends on several parameters: availability of human resources, time and budget constraints, etc. Without any guidance for choosing collaboration patterns, the project chief may have big difficulties to do optimal choices. So we are thinking of introducing the notion of collaboration strategy and heuristics for assisting process designer (at modelling time) and project chief (at instantiation and enactment times). The idea is to consider a strategy as a meta-pattern that is a coherent set of collaboration patterns which may be applied in a given context. To represent collaboration strategies, we are working on the definition of a metamodel which is an extension of the one proposed in [4].

References

1. Beck, K., Cunnimgham, W.: Using pattern languages for object-oriented programs. In: Proceedings of OOPSLA 1987 (1987)
2. Benali, K., Derniame, J.C.: Proceedings of the European Workshop on Software Process Technology, Norway (1992)
3. Buschmann, F., Meunier, R., Rohnert, H.: Pattern-Oriented Software Architecture - A System of Patterns. Wiley, New York (1996)
4. Cánovas Izquierdo, J.L., Cabot, J.: Enabling the collaborative definition of DSMLs. In: Salinesi, C., Norrie, M.C., Pastor, Ó. (eds.) CAiSE 2013. LNCS, vol. 7908, pp. 272–287. Springer, Heidelberg (2013)
5. Coad, P., North, D., Mayfield, M.: Object Models – Strategies, Patterns and Application. Yourdon Press Computing Series, Prentice-Hall (1995)
6. Diaw, S., Lbath, R., Coulette, B.: Specification and implementation of SPEM4MDE, a metamodel for MDE software processes. In: SEKE, pp. 646–653. USA Knowledge Systems Institute, Miami (2011)
7. Erikson, T.: Lingua Francas for Design: Sacred Places and Pattern Languages. ACM Press, New York (2000)
8. Feiler, P., Humphrey, W.: Software process development and enactment: concepts and definitions. In: Second International Conference on the Software Process, Continuous Software Process Improvement, pp. 28–40. IEEE (1993)

9. Finkelstein, A., Kramer, J., Nuseibeh, B.: Software Process Modelling and Technology. Wiley, New York (1994)
10. Fowler, M.: Analysis Patterns, Reusable Object Models. Addison-Wesley, Boston (1997). 1997
11. Fuggetta, A., Woft, A.: Software Process. Wiley, New York (1996)
12. Gallardo, J., Bravo, C. Redondo, M.A.: A model-driven development method for collaborative modeling tools. J. Netw. Comput. Appl. Arch. **35**(3), 1086–1105 (2012). ACM.
13. Gamma, E., Helm, R., Johnson, R., et al.: Design Patterns: Elements of Reusable Object-Oriented Software. Addison Wesley, Boston (1994)
14. Herrmann, T., et al.: Concepts for usable patterns of groupware applications. In: Proceedings of the 2003 International ACM SIGGROUP Conference on Supporting Group Work. ACM, Florida, 9–12 November 2003
15. Kedji, K.A., Coulette, B., Nassar, M., Lbath, R., Tran, H.N., Ton That, M.T.: Collaborative processes in the real world: embracing their essential nature (regular paper). In: International Symposium on Model Driven Engineering: Software & Data Integration, Process Based Approaches and Tools - colocated with ECMFA, Birmingham (2011)
16. Kedji, K.A., Ton That, M.T., Coulette, B., Lbath, R., Tran, H.N., Nassar, M.: A tool-supported approach for process modeling: application to collaborative processes. In: 18th Asia Pacific Software Engineering Conference (APSEC), Hochiming City (2011)
17. Kedji, K.A., Lbath, R., Coulette, B., Nassar, M., Barrese, L., Racaru, F.: Supporting collaborative development using process models: a tooled integration-focused approach. J. Softw. Evol. Process (JSEP), February 2014. doi:10.1002/smr.1640, Wiley Online Library
18. Mehra, A., Grundy, J., Hosking, J.: A generic approach to supporting diagram differencing and merging for collaborative design. In: ACM (2005)
19. Poltrock, S., Handel, M.: Modeling collaborative behavior: foundations for collaboration technologies. In: 42nd Hawaii International Conference in System Sciences (2009)
20. Roschelle, J.: The construction of shared knowledge in collaborative problem solving. In: O'Malley, C. (ed.) Computer Supported Collaborative Learning. NATO ASI Series F computer and Systems Sciences, vol. 128. Springer, Heidelberg (1994)
21. Tran, H.N., Coulette, B., Tran, D.T., Vu, M.H.: Automatic reuse of process patterns in process modeling. In: ACM Symposium on Applied Computing (SAC 2011), Taiwan (2011)
22. Van der Aalst, W.: Workflow patterns. http://workflowpatterns.com/
23. Verginadis, Y., Papageorgio, N., Apostolou, D., Mentzas, G.: A review of patterns in collaborative work. In: GROUP 2010, pp. 283–292 (2010)
24. Vo, T.T.: Application de patrons de collaboration lors de la mise en œuvre de procédés collaboratifs. Master thesis, Toulouse, June, 2013
25. Vo, T.T., Coulette B., Tran H.N., Lbath R.: Defining and using collaboration patterns for software development. In: International Workshop on Cooperative Model Driven Development, Colocated with MODELSWARD 2015. SciTe Press, February 2015

An Ontology-Based Process Editor
for Generating Model Mapping
in Tool Integration

Hanh Nhi Tran[1]([⊠]), Chanh Duc Ngo[2], and Joel Champeau[3]

[1] Institut de Recherche En Informatique de Toulouse (IRIT), Toulouse, France
hanh-nhi.tran@irit.fr
[2] University of Science of HoChiMinh (HCMUS), Ho Chi Minh City, Vietnam
ncduc@fit.hcmus.edu.vn
[3] Ecoles Nationales Supérieures de Techniques Avancées de Bretagne (ENSTA),
Brest, France
joel.champeau@ensta-bretagne.fr

Abstract. Tool integration is an important issue in collaborative process to enable interoperability among various tools employed during the development. Model Driven Development uses transformation technique to realize the data exchange between tools. In general, such transformations are defined manually and separately with the development process. Thus, they are rarely reusable and not well integrated with respect to process steps. This paper presents a solution for identifying tool-incompatible points in a process and generating the mappings between artefacts produced by two different tools. To this end, we proposed to integrate a process ontology with a process editor to allow reasoning about the semantics of process models. The idea is using ontology to store process assets from various sources so that the relations between similar elements in different technical spaces can be established automatically. The process editor enriches the ontology by process elements captured from modelling activities. Then the integrated ontology helps the editor detect tool integration points as well as generate the mappings between concerned process elements.

Keywords: Process modelling · Model transformation · Tool integration · Collaborative process

1 Introduction

Modern software and system process involves various teams in different development phases. Often, each team uses specific tools in their domain of expertise that are not always compatible with other teams in the global process. This diversity makes tool integration an important issue in collaborative process to enable exchanges of artefacts during the development [19]. Model Driven Development (MDD) uses model transformations to deal with tool integration. So far, process's participants identify themselves the incompatible points in their process and then develop needed transformations to bridge the gaps. One problem with this solution is the manual definition of mappings between models which hinders transformation reuses.

© Springer International Publishing Switzerland 2015
P. Desfray et al. (Eds.): MODELSWARD 2015, CCIS 580, pp. 263–277, 2015.
DOI: 10.1007/978-3-319-27869-8_15

We seek to remedy this problem by adding semantics to process models in order to allow the reasoning on the equivalence between different process's elements. Our objective is detecting tool-incompatible points in a process and generating the mapping among similar process elements from various technical spaces.

We proposed an extension of the *Software and System Process Engineering Meta-model* standard (SPEM 2.0) [9] to describe process elements at different levels of abstraction, from domain-dependent to tool-dependent. We developed a process editor supporting this multilevel modeling and used ontology to store process assets. On the one hand, the refinement of abstraction level allows reusing more pertinent process elements for a given context. On the other hand, the use of process ontology brings out the semantics relationships among process elements. An algorithm was developed to analyze a process model and identify the non-matching points on artefacts formats (i.e. tool integration points); another algorithm was used to reason the process ontology storing these artefacts to deduce the equivalence relations between them and create transformation rules.

The paper begins with an example illustrating the process modeling and tool integration issues addressed by our work. Section 3 presents our main propositions on: (1) an extension of SPEM 2.0 enriched with tool-related process elements; (2) an ontology to stock and to reason reusable process elements. We report in Sect. 4 the iSPEM process editor and its use to detect tool-integration points in a process model and to generate transformation rules for the detected points. A case study used to validate the iSPEM editor is also presented in this section. In the conclusion we resume our contribution compared to some related works.

2   Illustrating Example

Figure 1 shows an example of a process fragment used in the development of a lift.

In this example, the first activity *Design System by MoPCoM* uses MoPCom [18], a system design methodology dedicated to co-design, and the tool Rhapsody-UML to

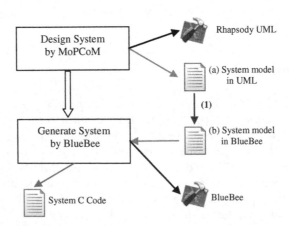

Fig. 1. Two activities of a lift development process, extracted from the project iFest [3].

produce the UML design model (a) *System model in UML*. The second activity *Generate system by BlueBee* takes the design model as input to generate the *System code in C*. However, this activity uses BlueBee tool [2], a compiler generating the application code for a given hardware architecture, thus requires the design model (b) *System model in BlueBee* as an annotated C code in order to describe the mapping onto hardware.

Semantically, the artefacts (a) and (b) in this process present the same design model of system but represented in different languages: one is modelled in UML and the other is in annotated C. We can say (a) is equivalent to (b).

Our first remark was that if the equivalence relation (1) between these two artefacts is modelled, it will be possible to detect the point of tool integration from the process model. However, currently, SPEM 2.0 does not allow modelling the relation (1).

Secondly, if we can distinguish the abstract artefacts of a domain (e.g. *System Model*) from their representations in different technical spaces (e.g. *System model in UML* and *System model in BlueBee*), we can deduce the equivalence relation between two technique-dependent artefacts presenting the same domain artefact. For example, at the technical space level we have artefact (a) in MoPCom UML and (b) in BlueBee C. These artefacts both have a relation to their domain artefact system design model; thus the relation between (a) and (b) can be deduced.

We think that a reasonable approach to enhance the process modelling and facilitate the tool integration issue could be refining the modelling language and using a semantics network to store process elements and their inter-relations at different levels. The next sections present in details these propositions.

3 iSPEM – A Multilevels Process Modeling Language

This section is divided into two parts: the first one recalls some basic concepts of SPEM; the second resumes iSPEM, our extension of SPEM 2.0.

3.1 SPEM 2.0

A *Process* in SPEM is composed of several *Activities*; an *Activity* is described by a set of linked *Tasks*, *WorkProducts* and *Roles*. A *Role* can *perform* a *Task*; a *WorkProduct* can be the input or output of a *Task*. A *WorkProduct* can *be managed* by a *Tool* and a *Task* can *use* a *Tool*.

To support process reuse, SPEM 2.0 separates the definition of process elements from their uses (Fig. 2). *Method Content* regroups reusable element's definitions (*Task Definition*, *Work Product Definition* and *Role Definition*) which can be instantiated several times as element's use (*Task Use*, *Work Product Use* and *Role Use*) in one or many concrete processes.

3.2 Multi-level Process Elements

We proposed iSPEM [14] based on our previous works on process modelling [7, 16, 20]. The two key features of iSPEM are: (1) adding into SPEM new concepts describing

Fig. 2. SPEM 2.0 process elements in two viewpoints.

tool-related elements to prepare tool integration; (2) distinguishing reusable method content elements at different abstraction levels to allow a better context-based reusability and to make semantic relationships emerge.

iSPEM extends the SPEM 2.0's package *ProcessWithMethods*. Three abstraction levels were defined: *Engineering Domain*, *Development Method*, and *Language*.

- **Engineering Domain:** this level represents the working context where the elements are defined. Thus, each element at this level has a consensus semantic in a given engineering domain, independently with any development method or modelling language.
- **Development Method:** this level represents the elements defined in a concrete development method which are used to realize one *Engineering Domain element*. Therefore, an *Engineering Domain element* can be realized by various *Method elements*.
- **Representation Language**[1]**:** this level characterizes method content elements according to the modelling language used to represent them. Once again, a *Method element* can be represented by various *Language elements*.

Thanks to the above distinction of abstraction levels, the semantical equivalence relation between two elements can be defined as followed:

- **Equivalence Relation:** two elements at the same abstraction level are equivalent if they are in relation with the same element in a higher abstraction level.

Thus, two different *Method elements* realizing the same *Domain element* are equivalent; two *Language elements* representing the same *Method element* are equivalent.

For example, Fig. 3 shows that the *Domain WorkProduct A* can be implemented in the first method as an aggregation of *Method WorkProduct A1* and *Method WorkProduct A2*, but it will be implemented in the second method as *Method WorkProduct A*. In this example, the method element representing the aggregation of *A1* and *A2* is equivalent with the method element *A*. In the same way, at *Language level*, the equivalent relation between *WorkProduct AX* and *WorkProduct AY* can be

---

[1] At this stage of our study, the *Representation Language* level is associated to tools. In practical, each tool can define its own format for implement a given language. In that case, the artefacts represented in the same language but by different tools may be lightly different.

deduce since they both represent the method *WorkProduct A* in two different languages.

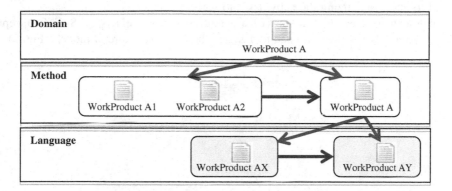

Fig. 3. Equivalence relation between two elements at the same abstraction level in **iSPEM.**

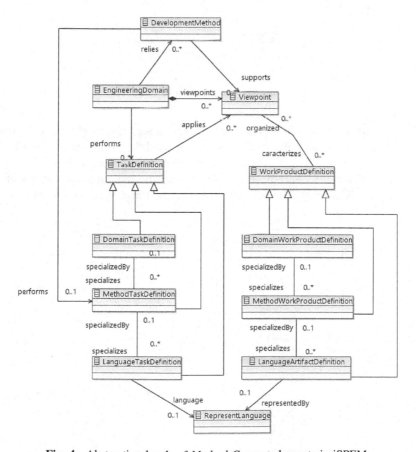

Fig. 4. Abstraction levels of *Method Content* elements in iSPEM.

Figure 4 gives the extraction of iSPEM meta-model refining the *Method Content* elements, including *Task Definition* and *Work Product Definition*, for three abstraction levels. The *EngineeringDomain*, *DevelopmentMethod* and *Viewpoint* concepts were added to allow organizing the activities into various categories.

In order to generate the mappings between the aggregate artefacts, the SPEM concept *WorkProductDefinition* was refined to describe the inside structure of models (Fig. 5).

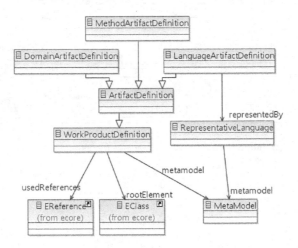

Fig. 5. *WorkProductDefinitions* in iSPEM.

The concept *MetaModel* was introduced and linked to *WorkProductDefinition* element, then associated to the *ArtifactDefinition* on different abstraction levels. The meta-meta-model Ecore was reused to construct the structure of *ArtifactDefinitions*.

We also refined the concepts *Process* and *Activity* and associate them with the *Engineering Domain* level. The new element *ArtifactTransformation* is used to model

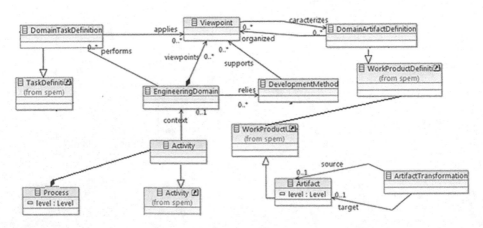

Fig. 6. iSPEM process elements.

the tool integration points where a model transformation is needed to enable the exchange of artefacts between two tasks (Fig. 6).

4 Combining Process Editor and Ontology

This section presents the use of a process ontology to store process assets and to reason about semantics of process elements' inter-relations.

4.1 Reusable Process Ontology

To enable reasoning about process elements, we didn't use a simple database to store reusable process elements captured from different processes but an ontology. The structure of the ontology then defined in respect of the iSPEM meta-model as shown in Table 1.

Table 1. Mapping between the OWL class of *Process Ontology* and *EClass of iSPEM*.

Reusable process ontology	iSPEM
(Domain/method/language) process activity	(Domain/method/language) task definition
(Domain/method/language) artifact	(Domain/method/language) artifact
(Domain/method/language) artifact definition	(Domain/method/language) artifact definition
Role	Role definition
Tool	Tool definition
Engineering domain	Engineering domain
Viewpoint	Viewpoint
Development method	Development method
Representation language	Representation language
Meta model	Meta model

Our *Reusable Process Ontology* is represented in OWL [11] as shown in Fig. 7.

The existing Ecore ontology in OWL from ModelCVS [6] which has a full mapping with MOF version was reused to describe meta-models. The other concepts related the refinement of *Work Product Definition* such as *EReferencesRelation*, *EclassesRelation* were also defined on the ontology. In this paper, we suppose that the content of the *Process Ontology* was defined during process modeling sessions. Describing the solution to realize this task is out of scope of this paper.

4.2 Generation of Transformation Rules for a Tool Integration Point

We developed two algorithms for reasoning about the process ontology. Algorithm 1 identifies the tool integration points in a process model. Algorithm 2 generates the needed mapping rules between two equivalent artefacts at an identified tool integration point.

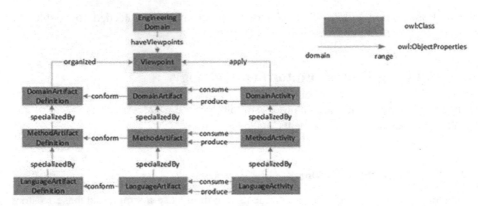

Fig. 7. An extract of *Process Ontology*.

Algorithm 1. Identify Artefacts to be transformed at a tool integration point.

Input: List of artefacts at the Language level – artifactList.

Output : List of artefacts to be transformed – artifactTransformationList.

```
for each (artifact1, artifact2) ∈ artifactList
  if artifact1 is created before artifact2
  and artifact1.tool!=artifact2.tool then
      if artifact1.domain == artifact2.domain then
        var t = new Transformation(artifact1,artifact2);
        artifactTransformationList.add(t);
      endif
    endif
endfor
return artifactTransformationList;
```

Algorithm 2. Generate Mappings between two meta-models of the artefacts in the transformation list identified by Algorithm 1.

Input : Source Meta-model MM-in, Target Meta-model MM-out
Output: List of mappings between elements of MM-in and MM-out – mappingList

```
for each e1 ∈ MM-in
  for each e2 ∈ MM-out
    if e1.specializedBy == e2.specializedBy then
      var rep1 : e1.representedBy;
      var rep2 : e2.representebBy;
      mappingList.addMapping(rep1, rep2);
    endif
  endfor
endfor
return mappingList;
```

The idea is from the actual abstraction level of a source artefact; go up one level of the ontological relationship *specializedBy* to find out its upper-class. From the found upper-classe we can go down again one level to find out an equivalence of our source artefact but represented in another technical space.

The above algorithms were formalized in SWRL [4]. They can be reasoned by ontologies reasoners.

5   iSPEM Process Editor

This section presents the implementation of the iSPEM process editor and a case-study used to validate the system.

5.1   Implementation of iSPEM System

Figure 8 shows the structure of the iSPEM system which is composed of two components: a process editor for process modelling and an ontology to store reusable process elements.

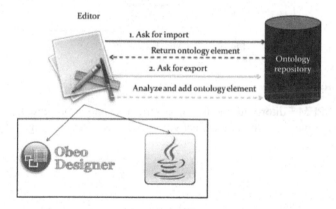

Fig. 8. Structure of iSPEM process editor.

Process Ontology: First, we used Protégé (Protégé Ontology Editor) [13] to define the following ontologies:

- *Ontology of Meta models* based on the existing ontology ModelCVS project [6] and added with additional properties such *specializedBy*, *representedBy*, etc.
- *Process Ontology* supporting the iSPEM meta-model.

In the first time, we enrich manually these ontologies with the data come from our case-studies. For storing ontologies, we use OWLIM-Lite [10], a RDF database management system. The algorithms presented in Sect. 4.2 are implemented as SWRL rules.

Process Editor: the iSPEM editor was implemented an extension of the SPEM-Designer editor of Obeo [8] which provided basic process modeling functionalities. Then we developed the editor's additional functionalities in Java to enable:

- An EMF-based framework for creating and manipulating iSPEM models.
- Modeling process by reusing relevantly the *Method Contents* in a specific context.
- Connect to the ontology repository and importing the *Method Contents* from the *Reusable Process Ontology* repository into iSPEM models.
- Identifying automatically the tools integration points. OWL API was used for manipulate the ontology and Pellet reasoner [12] helped us on reasoning the rules implementing the Algorithms 1 and 2 (c.f. Sect. 4.2).
- Generating the textual transformation rules for each the tools integration point.

Figure 9 presents the Java classes for iSPEM editor's enhanced functionalities.

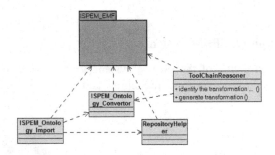

Fig. 9. iSPEM's Java classes.

5.2 Case-Study

We validate iSPEM Editor with the lift development example presented in Sect. 1 (c.f. Fig. 1) this time with details on each activity's tasks as shown in Fig. 10.

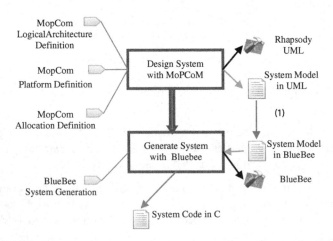

Fig. 10. Lift development process's activities in Design & Implementation Engineering Domain.

This process fragment contains two activities in the *Design & Implementation Domain*: *Design System* for producing *System Model* and *Generate System* for generating the *System Code* for a given hardware architecture. By using specific methods and languages to implement the *Lift Development Process*, these domain-dependent elements can be specialized into method-dependent elements which, in their turn, can be also specialized into language-dependent elements. Here, the process in Fig. 10 is realized with the development methods and languages MoPCoM in UML and BlueBee in C.

A system model designed by MoPCoM methodology is split up into 3 sub-models: a functional specification of the system, a representation of the platform and an allocation of the functional element onto the platform. Thus the MoPCom method refines the *Design System* activities into three tasks: *MoPCom Logical Architecture Definition*, *MoPCom Platform Definition* and *MoPCom Allocation Definition*) to produce respectively *Architecture Model*, *Application Model* and *Mapping Model* which together compose the *System Model in UML*.

The *Generate System* activity is realized with the Bluebee toolchain. Concretely, the task *System Generation with Bluebee* takes a Bluebee comprehensible *System Model* to generate the *System Code* for the target architecture. A Bluebee comprehensible model is composed of an annotated C code, the pragmas that define the C function mapping onto the computing elements and a XML file that describes features about the target architecture.

While MoPCoM allows describing both functional and hardware elements in UML elements, Bluebee makes a distinction with hardware elements represented in XML and functional ones represented in C. So we need to transform the *System Model in UML* into the format required by Bluebee (relation (1)). For instance, the platform model in MoPCom actually corresponds to the architecture specification by XML in BlueBee.

In this case study, we assume that the necessary reusable process elements are already stored in the *Process Ontology*. Concretely, first we created the ontology in Protégé and added into it the *Design and Implementation Domain* process package containing activities, tasks, artefact definitions, artefacts and also the related metamodels of the domain. Then the more specialized packages including *MoPCoM* method package, *MoPCoM with UML* lanuguage package, *MoPCoM with SysML* language package, *Bluebee* method package, *Bluebee with C* language package are added.

Figures 11 and 12 show the process elements of the *D&I Domain* stored in the *Process Ontology* at three levels: *Domain*, *Method* and *Language* and the specialization relations between them.

Now we can use iSPEM to model the process in Fig. 10. To do so we import the *Process Ontology* into the iSPEM editor and create corresponding iSPEM method content elements. These elements then are used to create the lift development process. Then we use the functionality *Identify Transformation Points*, which implements the Algorithm 1 in Sect. 4.2, to detect the tool integration points. The complete model is shown in Fig. 14.

The generation of transformation rules for each tool integration point is realized by using the Algorithm 2 in Sect. 4.2. For example, Fig. 13 shows the mappings deduced between the artefact *LogicalArchitechPackage* in MoPCom (represented as an UML package) and the artefact *SourceCode* in BlueBee (represented by a C program) thanks to the links from these artefacts to the common artefact *Application Model Definition* at

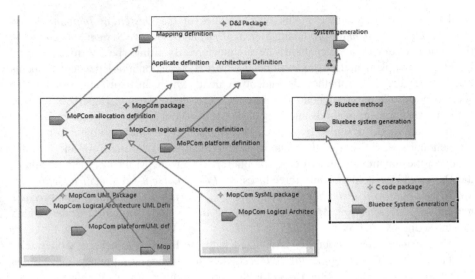

Fig. 11. Specialization of tasks in D&I domain.

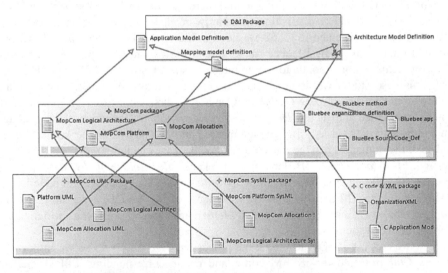

Fig. 12. Specialization of artefacts in D&I domain.

the *Domain Level*. Similarly, we can deduce that the *Platform Model* in MoPCom (an UML package) actually corresponds to the *Organization Specification* (XML code) in BlueBee. Figure 15 shows the generated transformation rules based on this mappings.

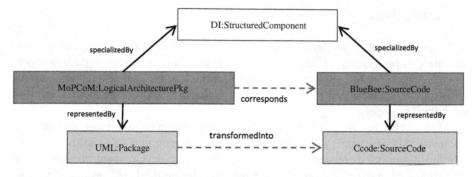

Fig. 13. Mappings deduced from the ontology.

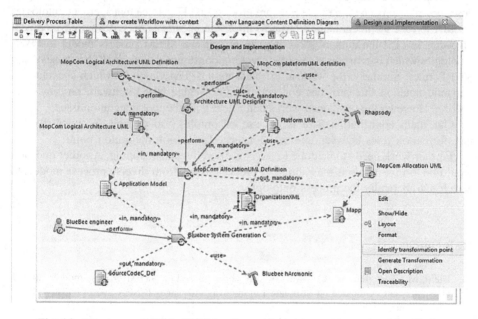

Fig. 14. Process modeled in iSPEM editor with tool integration points identified.

```
1    <UML:Package>
2        <role>
3        <MopCom:LogicalArchitecture_pkg/></role>
4        <TransformTo>
5            <CSourceCode:EClass_CSourceCode"/>
6            <role>
7            <Bluebee:SourceCode/></role>
8        </TransformTo>
9        <Reference>
10           <UML:Package_packagedElement type="UML:Package">
11               <role>
12               <MopCom:LogicalArchitecturePkg_system type="MopCom:System"/></role>
13               <TransformTo>
```

Fig. 15. Extraction of the generated transformation rule.

6 Conclusions

This paper presents a combination of ontology and process modelling technique to facilitate tool integration. Lifting the process elements up to ontology space enhances the capacity of process editors in reasoning about the semantical relation between process assets accumulated from different process and thus could be more helpful for collaborative processes.

Some works also use SPEM to describe the information on tool integration as in [1] which uses SPEM process models for creating the skeleton of a tool chain. This work identifies a number of relationship patterns between the development process and its supporting tool chain and show how the patterns can be used for constructing a tool chain which is aligned with the process. But they don't use ontology technique.

Some works combine ontology with process techniques as [5, 15, 17]. The work in [17] describes an approach to integrate Sofware Process and IT service management ontologies in order to ease the integration of business information early in the software development lifecycle. In [15] the authors show how to translate a SPEM process model to OWL ontologies which in turn can be used for checking constrains defined in the processes using SWRL rules. Similarly, the work in [5] presents a SPEM Ontology which constitutes a semantic notation that provides concepts for knowledge based software process engineering. However the mentioned works don't deal with the tool integration issue.

Our main contribution here is the use of ontology to deduce automatically the transformation rules between artefacts concerned in a tool integration point.

Further work needs to be done to develop more precise mapping. Another question would be to investigate is the capture of process assets from diverse process models to enrich automatically the process ontology.

References

1. Biehl, M., Törngren, M.: Constructing tool chains based on SPEM process models. In: 7th International Conference on Software Engineering Advances ICSEA 2012 (2012)
2. Bluebee. http://www.bluebeetech.com
3. European iFEST project: Industrial framework for embedded systems tools. http://www.artemis-ifest.eu/home
4. Horrocks, I., Patel-Schneider, P.F., Boley, H., Tabet, T., Grosof, B., Dean, M.: SWRL: a semantic web rule language, combining OWL and RuleML (2004). http://www.w3.org/Submission/SWRL
5. Líška, M.: Extending and Utilizing the Software and Systems Process Engineering Metamodel with Ontology. Inf. Sci. Technol. Bull. ACM Slovakia 2(2), 8–15 (2010)
6. Kappel, G., Kramler, G., Kapsammer, E., Reiter, T., Retschitzegger, W., Schwinger, W.: ModelCVS - a semantic infrastructure for model-based tool integration. Technical report (2005)
7. Koudri, A.: MODAL: a SPEM extension to improve co-design process models. In: New Modeling Concepts for Today's Software, pp. 248–259 (2010)
8. Obeo: SPEM designer (2012). http://marketplace.obeonetwork.com/module/spem

9. Object Management Group: Software and systems process engineering meta-model 2.0 (2008)
10. OWLIM-Lite. http://owlim.ontotext.com/display/OWLIMv50/OWLIM-Lite
11. OWL API. http://owlapi.sourceforge.net/
12. Pellet: OWL 2 Reasoner for Java. http://clarkparsia.com/pellet/
13. Protégé Ontology Editor and Knowledge Acquisition System. http://protege.stanford.edu/
14. Ngo, C.D.: Master thesis at Ensta-Bretagne (2012)
15. Rodríguez, D., García, E., Sánchez, S., Nuzzi, C.R.-S.: Defining software process model constraints with rules using Owl and Swrl. Int. J. Software Eng. Knowl. Eng. **20**(04), 533–548 (2010)
16. Tran, H.N., Coulette, B., Dong, B.T.: A UML-based process meta-model integrating a rigorous process patterns definition. In: Münch, J., Vierimaa, M. (eds.) PROFES 2006. LNCS, vol. 4034, pp. 429–434. Springer, Heidelberg (2006)
17. Valiente, M.-C., Garcia-Barriocanal, E., Sicilia, M.-A.: Applying ontology-based models for supporting integrated software development and IT service management processes. IEEE Trans. Syst. Man Cybern. Part C Appl. Rev. **42**(1), 61–74 (2012)
18. Vidal, J., de Lamotte, F., Gogniat, G., Soulard, P., Diguet, J.-P.: A co-design approach for embedded system modeling and code generation with UML and MARTE. In: Design, Automation and Test in Europe Conference and Exhibition, 2009 (DATE 2009) (2009)
19. Wasserman, A.I.: Tool integration in software engineering environments. In: Long, F. (ed.) Software Engineering Environments. LNCS, vol. 467, pp. 137–149. Springer, Heidelberg (1990)
20. Zhang, W., Leilde, V., Moller-Pedersen, B. Champeau, J., Guychard, C.: Towards tool integration through artifacts and roles. In: Proceedings of 19th Asia-Pacific Software Engineering Conference (APSEC 2012) (2012)

Using Model Driven Engineering to Support
Multi-paradigms Security Analysis

Rouwaida Abdallah[✉], Anas Motii, Nataliya Yakymets, and Agnes Lanusse

CEA, LIST, Laboratory of Model Driven Engineering for Embedded Systems,
Gif-sur-Yvette, France
{Rouwaida.Abdallah,Anas.Motii,Nataliya.Yakymets,
Agnes.Lanusse}@cea.fr

Abstract. Nowadays, security analysis of complex systems has become a major concern. Many works have been achieved to reduce vulnerabilities in such systems. However, existing methods used to perform security assessment as a holistic approach are still poorly instrumented and limited in scope. In this work, we propose methodology and associated framework for security analysis. The methodology relies upon model-driven engineering approach and combines two types of methods: a qualitative method named EBIOS that is usually simple and helps to identify critical parts of the system; then a quantitative method, the Attack Trees method, that is more complex but gives more accurate results. We present the automatic generation of Attack trees from EBIOS analysis phase. We show on a SCADA system case study how our process can be applied.

Keywords: Security · Model-driven engineering · UML profiles · EBIOS · Attack trees · Papyrus

1   Introduction

Model Driven Engineering (MDE) has proven its efficiency to cope with the ever-growing system complexity [1, 2]. In particular, there has been substantial research on model-based security analysis [3]. The use of models in security engineering offers more focused views of complex systems, and several levels of abstraction to assist experts to implement security efficiently.

Several risk management methods have been established to improve the security of information systems. Most of the methods are usually based on security standards like ISO 27005 [4] or others. These methods identify areas of focus within the project that need special attention and security and privacy measures. These methods can be broken down mainly into two essential types: qualitative (e.g. NIST SP 800-30 [5], CORAS [6], OCTAVE [7], EBIOS [8], etc.) and quantitative (e.g. CORA [9], ISRAM [10], AttackTree [11], etc.). Some approaches can be applied to all types of risks, while others are specific to particular risks like for instance risks related to information security. Qualitative methods implement no complex mathematical computations in general and thus they are considered as simpler but less precise than quantitative methods. Then, if an organization is concerned with simplicity rather

© Springer International Publishing Switzerland 2015
P. Desfray et al. (Eds.): MODELSWARD 2015, CCIS 580, pp. 278–292, 2015.
DOI: 10.1007/978-3-319-27869-8_16

than accuracy, qualitative methods are good fit, otherwise the choice will be quantitative methods [12].

In this paper, we present the first steps towards a model-driven methodology for risk analysis in order to get accurate results but in a simpler way. The methodology is twofold: First, we proceed by a qualitative method to assess the risks that we consider as dangerous or unacceptable relatively to the threshold we have preliminary fixed for the system. This step will reduce the perimeter of the risk analysis. Then we apply a quantitative method considering only the reduced perimeter to get more precise and accurate results for all the system. The methodology itself is applied on the basis of a system model described using standards of system engineering languages such as SysML.

Our approach presents many advantages: First, as it is a model driven approach we can benefit from the architecture of the system realized at the design phase to apply the risk analysis methods. Second, having the two methods in the same environment allows us to reuse information which is complicated when we use special methods dedicated tools. Most existing risk analysis methods rely on separate tools or models etc. Using separate tools requires a lot of experience and extra effort and may lead to inconsistencies between the different analyses. Similar challenges have been solved in software engineering by model-driven approaches. The core idea is to reuse as much information as possible from earlier design stages in later stages of the development cycle. This idea is already very successfully used for the development of software intensive systems [13].

In this paper we present the first steps towards a model-driven process for security analysis. It is structured as follows: Sect. 2 provides the background of this work. Section 3 describes the framework and associated framework. Section 4 presents related works. Finally, the conclusions are in Sect. 5.

2 Background

In this section, we present first the two security analysis methods supported by the framework: EBIOS and Attack Tree. Then we give the motivation of this work.

2.1 EBIOS Method

One of the well-known qualitative methods dedicated to manage risks in information systems operating in steady environments is called EBIOS (Expression of Needs and Identification of Security Objectives). EBIOS is used by many organizations in both public and private sectors to conduct Information System Security (ISS) risk analyses. EBIOS method [8] provides uniform vocabulary and concepts that allows attending security objectives. It can be adapted to the context of each organization (its tools and methodologies) and then used to develop either a complete global study of the information system or a detailed study of a particular system. Some efforts have been made to automate the EBIOS method. It helps the user to perform risk analysis and management steps according to the five EBIOS phases and to automatically generate reports:

- Phase 1 deals with context analysis. It establishes the environment, purpose and operation of the target system and identifies the essential elements (assets) on which they are based.

- Phase 2 conducts the security needs analysis. The identified security needs of the essential elements are evaluated in terms of availability, integrity and confidentiality, etc. In other terms we identify the Feared Events of the system. We also define a severity level to this Feared Event based on the harm that it may induce.
- Phase 3 consists of identifying and describing the threats affecting the system. We identify their origin called threat sources, and the vulnerabilities of the systems' elements that can be exploited to apply each attack method. We associate to each threat the likelihood of occurrence.
- Phase 4 contributes to risk evaluation and treatment. It formalizes the real risks affecting the system by comparing the threats with the security needs.
- Phase 5 determines how to specify security countermeasures allowing the security objective to be fulfilled and how to validate these measures and the residual risk. Actually, for each Feared Event we associate a risk level. This level is computed based on the severity "*sev*" (possible values for *sev*: *Negligible, Limited, Important*, etc.) of the Feared event concerned by the risk and the maximal value "*lik*" (possible values for *lik*: *Minimal, Significant, Heavy*, etc.) between the likelihoods of the threats that lead to this Feared Event (possible values for the risk level: *Negligible, Significant, Intolerable*, etc.). The risk level is deduced from a predefined matrix *RiskLevel(sev,lik)*. A residual risk is the risk level computed after application of existing or new countermeasures that may decrease the severity and/or the likelihoods of Feared Events.

Some efforts have been made to automate the EBIOS method. For instance, the French ANSSI (Agence Nationale de la Sécurité des Systèmes d'Information) proposes a free tool that helps the user to perform risk analysis and management steps according to the five EBIOS phases and to automatically generate reports. However, such tools are disconnected from the design model and do not provide an overview of the system or its layers. Besides, they do not offer the possibility to perform any further security analysis methods which can be important to get a more complete security analysis of the system.

Although EBIOS is dedicated to ISS, it can be adapted to different contexts such as [14]. Besides, EBIOS meets the risk management described in ISO 27001 and supports entirely ISO 27005 and ISO 31000 [8] (Fig. 1).

2.2   Attack Tree Quantitative Method

Attack trees (the term is introduced by Schneier in [11]) can be used to model potential attacks on a system and corresponding risks associated with each attack path.

Attack trees describe attacks towards any system as a logical function of atomic attacks. The top node of an Attack tree is the ultimate goal (goal of the attacker) with combinations of sub-goals for achieving the goal. Children of a node are refinements of this goal, and leaf nodes therefore represent attacks that can no longer be refined.

An Attack (or Intrusion) Scenario is the combination (based on the node connectivity associated with each leaf node) of attack leaves that lead to the top node. We have two types of node connectivity: "OR" nodes represent different ways to achieving the same

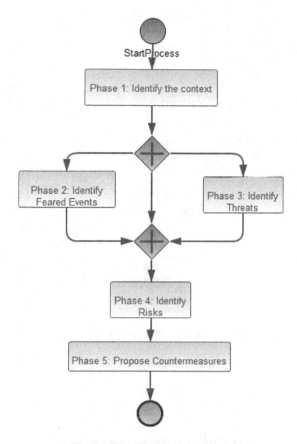

Fig. 1. EBIOS analysis method.

goal (in Fig. 2 the top node is an OR node). "And" nodes represent different steps (not ordered) in achieving a goal (in Fig. 2 the node labeled by "Eavesdrop" is an AND node).

Figure 3 presents the procedure that we follow in general in an Attack tree based analysis inspired from [15]. Once a tree is created, we can compute all the scenarios that lead to its top node. Moreover, Attack trees allow several parameters values to be associated to leaf nodes (cost, time to achieve, likelihood of occurrence, etc., or qualitative statements such as "possible" "impossible", etc.). These parameters are used to compute the value of the vulnerability index (or index) associated to an Attack tree.

We distinguish between three types of indices: First, the index v (l_i) associated to a leaf node l_i which is computed based on a formula F that we choose and the set of parameters values P_i of this as shown in (1). Second, the index $V(s_m)$ of an Attack scenario s_m concerning a subset $L_m = \{l_1, l_2, ..., l_p\}$ of p leaf nodes is computed as shown in (2). Finally, the index of a top node V_t is determined from the scenarios as shown in (3) where $S = \{s_1, s_2, ..., s_k\}$ is the set of the scenarios and k is the total number of scenarios.

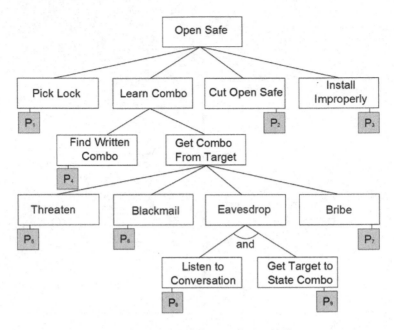

Fig. 2. Example of an attack tree [11].

$$v\left(l_i\right) = F(P_i) \tag{1}$$

$$V\left(s_m\right) = \prod_{j \leq p, lj \in Lm} v\left(lj\right) \tag{2}$$

$$V_t = \max\{V\left(s_1\right), V\left(s_2\right), \dots, V\left(s_k\right)\}. \tag{3}$$

2.3   Motivation

In many engineering disciplines, model building is at the heart of any system design. But model building is not an end in itself and certainly does not come for free. There is an important added value so that this effort becomes worthwhile. In [3], the authors summarize in four activities what models can be used for in the development of secure systems: (1) Precisely documenting security requirements together with design requirements; (2) Analyzing security requirements; (3) Model-based transformation, such as migrating security policies on application data to policies for other system layers or artifacts; (4) Generating code, including complete, configured security infrastructures. These four activities can be used to automate EBIOS and Attack trees in the following way.

(1) Models, especially graphical ones, give a clear overview of the system or a part of it. The core idea is to reuse as much information as possible from earlier design stages in later stages of the system development cycle. Existing EBIOS tools do not present any graphical representation of the system, the security analysis

performed with EBIOS is not based on any other document or support used in the system design phase. Moreover, the contextual information about the system and its environment are entered from scratch. For Attack trees we find several graphical tools (e.g. SecureITree [16]) however they are not related to the design phase either.

(2) EBIOS presents a very robust process for analyzing security requirements. However, we believe that a global overview and several viewpoints of the system, or subsystems can offer to the security engineer a better recognition of the hazards. Attack trees method is not as robust as the EBIOS method at this point.

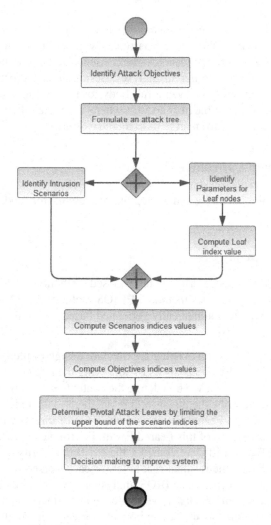

Fig. 3. General attack tree analysis process.

(3) To perform a robust security analysis we need to run several analysis security methods. Each method has its own and independent model. Consequently, to

conduct several methods, model transformation facilities remain very important. Model transformation plays a key role in model-based software development. It describes the relationship between models, more specifically the mapping of information from one model to another which allows traceability. This traceability allows tracking changes in models and how it affects other models.

(4) Some model-based environments (for instance, Papyrus [17]) offer the possibility of code generation. Thus we can for instance implement the propagation of proposed countermeasures to the system model and proceed by code generation, etc.

On the other side, implementing several methods in the same environment allows the reuse of information. This remains particularly difficult, when we use separate method dedicated tools as it requires a lot of experience and extra effort and may lead to inconsistencies between the different analyses. Besides, this approach allows to automatically generating skeletons or even a full body for the next methods to be applied. This is what we will show in the next section where we explain how to automatically generate partial Attack trees from an EBIOS analysis study.

3   Model Driven Approach

Next we propose a methodology and associated framework for model-driven security analysis.

3.1   Process Description

Figure 4 presents the process describing our proposed methodology that consists mainly in applying two security analysis methods: EBIOS method, then Attack tree method. Partial Attack trees will be automatically generated based on the results of the EBIOS analysis.

- Phase 1: We design or use an existing architecture design of the system.
- Phase 2: We apply the EBIOS analysis by following the five phases described in the previous section (Sect. 2.1): We first define the context. Second we define the Feared Events. Third, we describe the threats and relate them to the existing Feared Events so that for each defined Feared Event we have a list of threats where each of them can lead to the occurrence of this Feared Event. Fourth we appreciate the risk level for each Feared Event. Fifth, we consider the existing security countermeasures in the system to compute the residual risk level for each Feared Event. At this phase, we do not only apply a classical EBIOS analysis but we also relate it to the design architecture of the system. Actually, we relate the Feared Events, threats and vulnerabilities to the concerned assets (a component in the system architecture: function, software, hardware, etc.) in the system architecture. This allows visualizing the critical components in a system, and keeps the traceability between all the phases.
- Phase 3: We automatically retrieve the Feared Events that have the residual risk level higher than a threshold that we have already fixed.

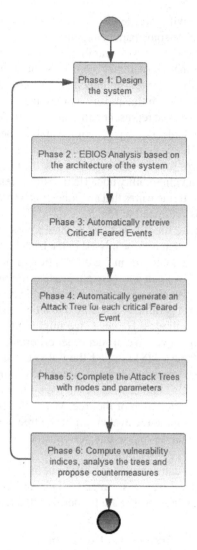

Fig. 4. The structure of a generated attack tree.

- Phase 4: We generate an Attack tree for each Feared Event as follows:
  - The top node of the tree is the Feared Event. This node is an OR node, and its children are the threats that lead to this Feared Event as defined in the EBIOS Analysis step (It is an OR node because as it is defined in EBIOS method any of these threats can lead to the Feared Event).
  - Then those threats nodes are AND nodes based on the description in the EBIOS Analysis: Each Threat can exploit one or several vulnerabilities of an asset.
  - Vulnerabilities exploited by a threat will be the leave nodes related to this threat node.

We get an attack tree with three levels. Besides the generation of the structure of the tree we also generate some parameters that might help in the evaluation of the Attack tree: First, for each vulnerability corresponding node we keep the concerned asset information (parameter A). This allows us to keep the traceability of the Attack tree with the system architecture. Second, in the EBIOS analysis we associate likelihood for each threat. But, as in Attack trees, parameters are associated only to leaf nodes that represent vulnerabilities in our case, we will associate to each vulnerability node a new parameter which is the set of likelihoods of all threats that can exploit this vulnerability (parameter P). Finally, another parameter is the countermeasures that are related to the assets in the EBIOS analysis. Then, as in an Attack tree, a vulnerability node (leaf node) is related to one asset, we can deduce the set of countermeasures that are concerned (parameter M). The structure of a generated tree is presented in Fig. 5.

- Phase 5: We can complete the tree in three manners. First we might add some new nodes: to add new threats that may be missed in the EBIOS Analysis step, or to detail some nodes, or maybe to go deeper in the description of the Attack tree (more than 3 levels depth). Second, we can add new parameters to the nodes. Actually, in the EBIOS analysis level the evaluation of risk is computed as described in Sect. 2. It is based on the severity level parameter associated to a Feared Event and the likelihood parameters associated to threats. However we might define new formulas to have more precise evaluation or even to consider other criteria to evaluate the Attack tree. For instance, in the Magerit [18] method they also consider a third parameter to compute the risk which is vulnerability level, as for [15] their evaluation of the Attack tree is based on the existing countermeasures in the system only. Third we define the formula to compute the evaluation of the tree. We notice that we didn't define any formula by default to compute the evaluation of the tree we only extract the parameters from the EBIOS analysis phase that we consider that might be useful for the evaluation.
- Phase 6: At this level we can compute the different indices based on the Attack tree and the parameters that we have associated to their nodes. Then we propose countermeasures to minimize indices that are higher than the threshold we decided.

3.2 Model-Based Security Framework Description

We implement a framework that allows integrating security analysis methods into Papyrus environment. Papyrus is an Eclipse based environment supporting UML and SysML modeling standards from the OMG (Object Management Group). Besides, Papyrus can serve as a modelling platform for other tools dedicated to different analysis and specific domains and this by using UML profile (e.g. RobotML [19]). Profile is a powerful extension mechanism for UML that allows introducing specific concepts to the model.

This framework includes profiles and tools to automate typical security analysis methods. We implement EBIOS method and Attack Tree method based on UML profiles. We can also generate tables and documents as in the EBIOS Tool. Besides the complete analysis study and the architecture of the system can also be generated in customizable documents.

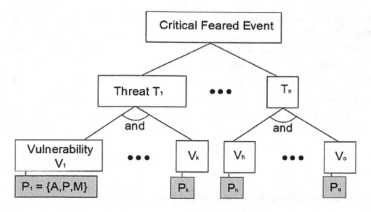

Fig. 5. Generated attack tree structure.

Figure 6 presents the simplified EBIOS meta-model with the main concepts that we have implemented in the EBIOS profile:

- We distinguish between two types of assets composing the system: Primary Assets defined as process or data for which some security criteria (like availability, integrity or confidentiality, etc.) has to be protected. Supporting Assets are assets on which some Primary Assets rely. Supporting assets can be hardware, software, networks, people, paper, transmission channels, etc.

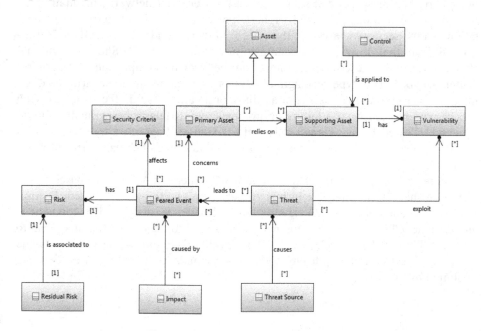

Fig. 6. Simplified EBIOS meta-model.

- Vulnerability is a characteristic of a Supporting Asset that can be used to allow the occurrence of a threat.
- Feared Event is an incident that affects security criteria of a Primary Asset. Feared Events are caused by Threats and lead to Impacts.
- Threat Sources can be a person or non-human source that can cause a risk, accidentally or deliberately.
- The Risk associated to a Feared Event is estimated in terms of severity of the Im-
- pacts and the likelihood of the Threats. The Residual Risk is the risk remaining after considering the existing/recommended Controls.

4   Cyber-Power System Case Study

We validate the methodology and framework described in the previous sections by analyzing several use case studies developed in the scope of the SESAM Grids [20] and RISC [21] projects. In this work, we use a case study based on Control and Data Acquisition (SCADA) systems. SCADA systems and other similar control systems are widely used by utilities and industries that are considered critical to the functioning of countries around the world. They are also found in Smart Grids.

The case study we consider is inspired from the two projects but mainly from the cyber-power with SCADA system described in [15]. This system describes the cyber network environment of a control center. The control center network is connected to other corporate networks and substation and power plant networks maintained by information technology personnel. Figure 7 presents some aspects of the implementation and the security analysis of the system in Papyrus: (1) shows a Block Definition Diagram that describes the composition of the system. (2) Shows an Internal Block Diagram that describes the connections between the components of the control center network. This type of diagrams allows us to apply some security analysis method (propagating the impacts of a failure or an attack within the system, search for the possible causes of a failure or an attack, etc. (3) describes a small scenario of attack (Feared Event, Threats, Risk, etc.). Similar diagrams allow focusing on specific scenarios. (4) Shows some generated table (table of threats, table of risks, etc.).

Figure 8 shows an excerpt of an automatically generated Attack Tree based on the results of the EBIOS analysis. In this Attack Tree, the top node "System Disruption" corresponds to a critical Feared Event in the EBIOS analysis. This top node is an OR node. Children nodes of top node correspond to the threats that may lead to the Feared Event. These nodes are AND nodes (In this Figure we only present some of those threats). Finally, leave nodes corresponds to vulnerabilities that are exploited by threats.

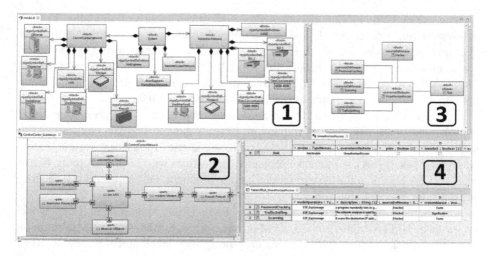

Fig. 7. Security analysis with EBIOS profile within Papyrus tool.

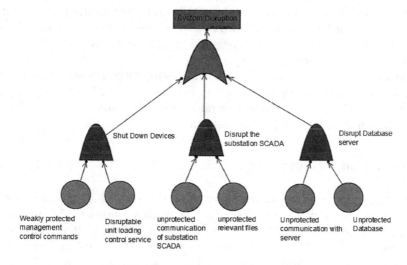

Fig. 8. Extract of a generated attack tree.

5   Related Work

There are several model-based technologies and tools for security analysis in general. For instance, Coras, Magerit, Mehari, these methods similar to EBIOS, propose a model based analysis of the system. However, with these tools we can only model security concepts and Attack scenarios, but not the design of the system. For Attack trees, we can find several graphical tools, but the analysis is still independent of the system architecture and of other security analysis methods.

The use of UML Profiles becomes very widespread in several domains: In [22], authors provide a generalizable and tool-supported solution to support the verification of compliance to safety standards IEC 61508. The Object Management Group (OMG) has standardized the UML Profile for Modelling and Analysis of Real-time and Embedded Systems (MARTE) [2]. In [23], authors present a UML Profile for modelling QoS and Fault Tolerance Characteristics and Mechanisms (QFTP), etc.

An existing framework named Sophia [24] based on UML Profiles, presents a similar approach but for safety. Sophia framework extends generic Papyrus environment to safety domain. Sophia includes facilities (i) to automatically perform various Safety Analysis methods (SA), (ii) to make semantic connections with formal SA tools, (iii) to represent SA results in the system modelling environment. Our approach is a security approach for Sophia framework.

Our framework considers a part of the RMF (Risk Management Framework) proposed by NIST SP 800-160 [25]. RFM provides a process that integrates information security and risk management activities into the system development life cycle. RFM considers 6 steps: (1) Categorize information system, (2) Select security controls, (3) Implement security controls, (4) Assess security controls, (5) Authorize information system, (6) Monitor security controls. In our framework, we consider steps (1) and (2). Phases 1 to 5 in our Process are included in step (1): we describe the system, and the existing security controls (or countermeasures) of the system (Fig. 4 - Phase 2: we consider these existing controls to compute the residual risk in the EBIOS analysis), and we compute the risk level. Phase 6 is included in step (2) where based on the previous step results we select the controls to apply. Documents related to the security plan considered by RFM can be partially generated as we don't have for the moment the implementation related to process management.

6   Conclusion, Perspectives

In this work, we propose the methodology and framework which provide a support for security engineers by integrating security techniques within a model-driven engineering process. The methodology relies on the well-known methods: EBIOS and Attack Trees. The use of the proposed methodology aims to fill the gap between system modeling and security analysis tools and helps to better cope with system engineering time and cost constraints. Indeed, the results of preliminary qualitative security analysis with EBIOS method can reveal the most security-critical parts of the system which should be mitigated. EBIOS presents many advantages and is widely used. Besides it supports entirely ISO 27005 standard. Then Attack Tree quantitative method allows getting more accurate results. Attack trees are automatically generated from the EBIOS analysis phase. These generated Attack trees can then be completed (adding parameters, formulas, etc.).

This work presents several perspectives: One perspective is to merge this framework with Sophia to provide both safety and security analysis support. One should consider the impacts that security considerations can have on a safety case and vice versa. Another perspective is to try achieving an approach that can deal with the safety and security properties of a system in an integrated way and ensure that the system is safe and operable in a given environment, against a specific set of security threats.

Acknowledgements. The work in this paper is funded by SESAM Grids project [20] and RISC project [21]. Tools developed have been experimented on use cases from these two projects.

References

1. Bernardi, S., Merseguer, J., Petriu, D.: Model-Driven Dependability Assessment of Software Systems. Springer, Berlin (2013)
2. Bran, S., Gérard, S.: Modeling and Analysis of Real-Time and Embedded Systems with UML and MARTE. Elsevier, Amsterdam (2014)
3. Basin, D., Clavel, M., Egea, M.: A decade of model-driven security. In: Proceedings of the 16th ACM Symposium on Access Control Models and Technologies, pp. 1–10. ACM (2011)
4. ISO/IEC: Information technology - security techniques - information security risk management. ISO/IEC 27005, International Organization for Standardization (ISO) and International Electrotechnical Commission (IEC) (2008)
5. Stoneburner, G., Goguen, A., Feringa, A.: Risk management guide for information technology systems. Nist Special Publication, 800(30), 800-30 (2002)
6. den Braber, F., Hogganvik, I., Lund, M.S., Stølen, K., Vraalsen, F.: Model-based security analysis in seven steps—a guided tour to the CORAS method. BT Technol. J. **25**(1), 101–117 (2007)
7. Alberts, C., Dorofee, A., Stevens, J., Woody, C.: Introduction to the OCTAVE Approach. Carnegie Mellon University, Pittsburgh (2003)
8. Secrétariat Général de la Défense Nationale. EBIOS- Expression des Besoins et Identification des Objectifs de Sécurité, Méthode de Gestion des risques. http://www.ssi.gouv.fr/IMG/pdf/EBIOS-1-GuideMethodologique-2010-01-25.pdf (2010)
9. International Security Technology (IST): A brief history of CORA (2002). http://www.ist-usa.com. Accessed 16 June 2013
10. Karabacaka, B, Songukpinar, I.: ISRAM: Information security risk analysis method. In: Computer and Security, pp. 147–169 (2005)
11. Schneier, B.: Attack trees: modeling security threats. Dr. Dobb's J. **12**(24), 21–29 (1999)
12. Behnia, A., Rashid, R.A., Chaudhry, J.A.: A survey of information security risk analysis methods. Smart CR **2**(1), 79–94 (2012)
13. Gudemann, M., Ortmeier, F.: Towards model-driven safety analysis. In: 3rd International Workshop on Dependable Control of Discrete Systems (DCDS), pp. 53–58. IEEE (2011)
14. Mcdonald, J., Decroix, H., Caire, R., Sanchez, J., Chollet, S., Oualha, N., Puccetti, A., Hecker, A., Chaudet, C., Piat, H., et al.: The SINARI project: security analysis and risk assessment applied to the electrical distribution network (2013)
15. Ten, C.W., Liu, C.C., Manimaran, G.: Vulnerability assessment of cybersecurity for SCADA systems. IEEE Trans. Power Syst. **23**(4), 1836–1846 (2008)
16. Saini, V., Duan, Q., Paruchuri, V.: Threat modeling using Attack trees. J. Comput. Small Coll. **23**(4), 124–131 (2008)
17. Gérard, S., Dumoulin, C., Tessier, P., Selic, B.: 19 Papyrus: a UML2 tool for domain-specific language modeling. In: Giese, H., Karsai, G., Lee, E., Rumpe, B., Schätz, B. (eds.) Model-Based Engineering of Embedded Real-Time Systems. LNCS, vol. 6100, pp. 361–368. Springer, Heidelberg (2010)

18. Ministerio de Administraciones Publicas: Magerit - version 2 - Methodology for Information Systems Risk Analysis and Management - Book I - The Method, Madrid, 20 June 2006
19. Dhouib, S., Kchir, S., Stinckwich, S., Ziadi, T., Ziane, M.: RobotML, a domain-specific language to design, simulate and deploy robotic applications. In: Noda, I., Ando, N., Brugali, D., Kuffner, J.J. (eds.) SIMPAR 2012. LNCS, vol. 7628, pp. 149–160. Springer, Heidelberg (2012)
20. The consortium Sesam-Grids, The Sesam-Grids Project (2012). http://www.sesam-grids.org/
21. The consortium RISC, The RISC Project (2013). http://risc.sec4scada.com/
22. Panesar-Walawege, R.K., Sabetzadeh, M., Briand, L.: Supporting the verification of compliance to safety standards via model-driven engineering: approach, tool-support and empirical validation. Inf. Softw. Technol. **55**(5), 836–864 (2013)
23. OMG, U.: Profile for modeling quality of service and fault tolerance characteristics and mechanisms. Revised submission, Object Management Group (2003)
24. Yakymets, N., Dhouib, S., Jaber, H., Lanusse, A.: Model-driven safety assessment of robotic systems. In: 2013 IEEE/RSJ International Conference on Intelligent Robots and Systems (IROS), pp. 1137–1142 (2013)
25. National Institute of Standards and Technology: Systems Security Engineering, An Integral Approach to Building Trustworthy Resilient Systems. NIST Special Publication 800–160 (2014)

Designing Safe and Secure Embedded and Cyber-Physical Systems with SysML-Sec

Ludovic Apvrille[1] and Yves Roudier[2]([⊠])

[1] CNRS LTCI, Telecom ParisTech, Institut Mines-Telecom, Sophia Antipolis, France
ludovic.apvrille@telecom-paristech.fr
[2] EURECOM, Sophia Antipolis, France
yves.roudier@eurecom.fr

Abstract. The introduction of security flaws into a system may result from design or implementation mistakes. It entail far-reaching consequences for connected embedded or cyber-physical systems, including physical harm. Security experts focus either on finding out and deriving security mechanisms from more or less explicitly defined security requirements or on the a posteriori assessment of vulnerabilities, namely pentesting. These approaches however often miss the necessary iterations between security countermeasures and system functionalities in terms of design and deployment. Worse, they generally fail to consider the implications of security issues over the system's safety, like for instance the adverse effect that security countermeasures may produce over expected deadlines due to costly computations and communications latencies. SysML-Sec focuses on these issues throughout design and development thanks to its model-driven approach that promotes exchanges between system architects, safety engineers, and security experts. This paper discusses how SysML-Sec can be used to simultaneously deal with safety and security requirements, and illustrates the methodology with an automotive use case.

1 Introduction

Embedded systems and cyber-physical systems progressively pervade an increasing part of our daily lives, information systems, and industrial systems. Because these systems are by essence connected, they are strongly exposed to attacks. To give but a few examples, researchers have reported attacks over the Microsoft XBox [17], ADSL routers [8], mobile and smartphones [1,15,22], avionics [34] or automotive systems [21], and even medical appliances as recently demonstrated [33]. Such attacks also target industrial systems whose sensors are increasingly commonly connected with vulnerable information systems, as demonstrated by the Stuxnet, Flame, or Duqu [23] attacks. The motivations of attackers are very diverse, ranging from terrorism to extortion.

The complexity of such systems in terms of code size, distribution, and heterogeneity, among other features, is a major factor for the risks they face. We contend that taking into account security from the very first design and development

© Springer International Publishing Switzerland 2015
P. Desfray et al. (Eds.): MODELSWARD 2015, CCIS 580, pp. 293–308, 2015.
DOI: 10.1007/978-3-319-27869-8_17

phases, and including both software and hardware components, could lower the risk those systems face, both in terms of security and safety. We also think that safety and security should be designed and jointly validated, that is, from the same models. Likewise, the impact of the security mechanisms execution over the safety-related functions should be clearly established. Our solution relies on a model-driven environment named SysML-Sec. SysML-Sec targets the capture and analysis of security and safety requirements, the description of the attacks envisioned, the modeling of system functionalities, the hardware/software partitioning, the design of software components, and the validation of both safety and security properties. SysML-Sec also aims at a comprehensive validation performed since the partitioning and design stages. The objective is to assess the effectiveness of the selected hardware/software architecture for supporting both safety and security requirements, and for mitigating the identified attacks. The validation should also closely investigate whether the design choices adhere to the safety and security requirements.

This paper discusses how SysML-Sec [4] can be used to evaluate the impact of the security mechanisms introduced to prevent attacks over embedded or cyber-physical systems with strong critical aspects or whose attack may lead to strong economical losses. It is organized as follows. Section 2 focuses on the impact of attacks on safety-critical systems. Section 3 discusses different modeling approaches to efficiently take into account both the system architecture and the requirements in the development process of a safe ad secure system. We then present the methodology and the validation process of the SysML-Sec framework in Sects. 4 and 5, respectively, with a strong emphasis on the relationship between safety and security properties and features. An automotive-based case study is given in Sect. 6. Section 7 concludes the paper.

2   Impact of Attacks

Performing attacks relies on the exploitation of either low-level vulnerabilities (e.g., buffer overflows) or design weaknesses. Low-level vulnerabilities can often be handled with good programming skills, or by using efficient security tests, e.g., different kinds of fuzzing. On the contrary, design errors generally come from a bad requirement and attack capture, or from a bad partitioning of hardware/software components, including security mechanisms that those components implement, or even a faulty deployment of the secrets that they contain and rely upon for cryptographic mechanisms. Unfortunately, those errors are more difficult to correct once the system has been released. Moreover, security tools commonly used by security experts, like for instance ProVerif [12] or AVISPA [7], do not take into account the hardware/software partitioning.

Classical information systems are still widely targeted by attackers. Nonetheless, the integration of communicating embedded equipments into systems makes those embedded systems even more "interesting" targets for attackers. At least three issues make these systems distinctly more difficult to secure than plain information systems:

- If an attack relies on a hardware vulnerability, it can be difficult, or even impossible, to correct (i.e., patch) the system via a software update, in particular if functions have been implemented mostly with hardware components, e.g., with hardware accelerators or network filtering techniques. In the case of usual information systems, a "simple" software update and a system reboot can generally solve the problem.
- Updating software in embedded systems is far more complex than for personal computers. Patching the software of a vehicle for instance requires sending a letter to the owner, who must later on bring his car to a garage for maintenance. Over-The-Air (OTA) updates have started to be used but are nonetheless complex and themselves subject to attacks. Users of embedded systems are also less used to updating their systems, as recently demonstrated with IP cameras. On the contrary, updating a PC or a server has become a common practice (e.g., the famous "Tuesday patch"), and can be handled remotely and automatically.
- The impact of attacks over safety critical systems, and therefore the risk associated with an attack, can be much higher than for other kinds of systems. This was for instance recently demonstrated by new critical vulnerabilities found in healthcare equipment, like infusion pumps [33]. Moreover, the growing interconnection between information systems and smart objects gives more chances to attackers to illegally breach into those systems, once they managed to compromise one of the interconnected elements.

3 The Fundamental Role of the System Architecture for Security

From our own experience, we claim that modeling the architectural elements of the system has to be undertaken in the first place, even if only partially specified, in order to better capture and analyze potential attacks on the system. This modeling, as described below, is progressively and iteratively refined together with the safety and security analyses we describe further in the paper.

3.1 Software/Hardware Partitioning

Software-centric systems are commonly designed with a V-cycle comprising the following stages: requirements elicitation, software analysis, software design, implementation. Each of these stages is then followed with a corresponding verification state, that commonly relies on testing, simulation, and formal verification techniques. In the case of embedded systems, that approach is obviously applicable only once functions that should be software implemented have been specified. In other words, the V-cycle can start only once the hardware/software partitioning has been performed.

System partitioning (a.k.a. Design Space Exploration) is a process to analyze various functionally equivalent implementations of a system specification. It usually relies on the Y-chart approach [9] depicted in Fig. 1:

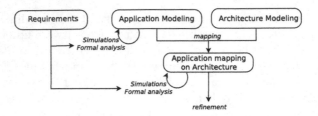

Fig. 1. The Y-chart methodology.

1. *Applications* are first described as abstract communicating tasks: tasks represent functions independently from their implementation form.
2. Targeted *architectures* are independently described from tasks. They are usually described with a set of execution nodes (e.g., CPUs), communication nodes (e.g., buses), and storage nodes (e.g., memories).
3. A *mapping* model defines how application tasks and abstract communications are assigned to computation and communication/storage devices, respectively. For example, a task mapped on a hardware accelerator is a hardware-implemented function whereas a task mapped on a CPU is a software implemented function.

Ideally, the result of the Y-chart approach shall be an optimal hardware / software architecture with regards to criteria at stake for that particular system (e.g., cost, area, power, performance, flexibility, reliability, etc.). This process can be manually performed by experimented engineers, or can be automated by specific toolkits like Metropolis [9]. This partitioning step is of utmost importance. Indeed, if critical high-level design choices are invalidated afterwards because of the late discovery of issues (performance, power, etc.), then it may induce prohibitive re-engineering costs and late market availability.

3.2   Model-Driven Engineering

Model-Driven Engineering is probably the main contribution of the last decade in modeling approaches. MDE targets system analysis, design, simulation, code generation, and documentation. MDE generally relies on the UML language, and on meta-modeling techniques in order to define Domain-Specific Languages. OMG's Model Driven Architecture for instance specifically targets two abstraction levels, namely the Platform-Independent Model (PIM), and the Platform Specific Model (PSM): embedded systems are thus clearly targeted by MDE. Profiles have also been defined by the OMG to more specifically address embedded systems: SPT [26] and MARTE [36], but none of them addresses requirements modeling. Conversely, the SysML OMG profile [27] clearly takes into account requirements with explicit modeling capabilities and diagrams, but ignores some concerns inherent to embedded systems, e.g., the partitioning question.

Other methodologies, like for example *Extreme programming* (XP) [10] or *Agile Software Development* [38] have also been proposed for software-oriented systems. However, their software focus means that they totally ignore the partitioning issue. They also make traceability and refinement extremely hard to achieve, also because requirements are mostly separate from the design process.

4 Specifying the Security Requirements

Security and privacy are too often the last concern in the design of connected and distributed information systems (e.g., cloud services) and embedded system, contrary to safety that is generally better anticipated. Security requirements thus appear after the system has already been released, generally when security vulnerabilities are discovered. Nonetheless, those vulnerabilities have a critical aspect whenever they can be exploited to impact economical or safety-related components.

4.1 Security Goals and Threats

Many researchers have already addressed the modeling and analysis of security requirements and threats, mostly in the scope of information systems. Nhlabatsi et al. [24] classify them in four categories: goal-oriented approaches, model-driven approaches, process-oriented approaches and last problem-oriented approaches. The two first are the closest to SysML-Sec. KAOS is a well-known goal-oriented approach [35] that relies on the explicit model of security goals and anti-goals. TwinPeaks [25] also follows a goal-oriented approach with an agile iterative process between goals and system architecture. UMLSec is a model-oriented approach. It includes tools for the specification and verification of distributed systems with security mechanisms, including cryptographic protocols. Model-oriented approaches are considered as more adapted to the design of security mechanisms, but goal-oriented approaches offer a better way to analyze security requirements during the first design iterations.

4.2 SysML-Sec: A SysML-Based Model-Oriented Approach

The first objective of SysML-Sec [4] is to foster the collaboration and communication between experts in system design and experts in system security and privacy. Moreover, SysML-Sec intends to cover all the methodological stages of the design and development of these systems. SysML-Sec combines a goal-oriented approach for capturing requirements, and a model-oriented approach for system architecture and threats. In contrast to TwinPeaks [25], SysML-Sec follows the Y-chart scheme [9] and its underlying allocation techniques. The latter facilitates the identification of resources to be protected and the link between resources, safety requirements, and security requirements.

4.3   Methodology

The SysML-Sec methodology is first based on an Y-Chart-based system analysis, and then on a software design phase following the well-known V-cycle. This methodology is given at Fig. 2.

The analysis stage intends to identify and analyze both requirements and attacks altogether with the identification of the main functions ("application") and of candidate hardware architectures, and with the mapping of the main functions over execution nodes (mapping). Simulations and (formal) verifications are used in order to identify safety-related issues, e.g., deadlock situations, non-reachability of states, etc. Functional models are untimed, which means that no performance study can be conducted on their behavior. However, the mapping of functions over execution nodes gives the former a logical and physical execution time. Post-mapping simulations and formal verifications are thus intended to demonstrate the system's performance on the selected hardware architecture, including the study of latencies, the load of processors and buses, and communication time. Obviously, the results are due to the logical parts of the application, to the way the underlying hardware behaves, but also to the security mechanisms. For example, a given security protocol may impact a bus load, and a cryptographic function may impact a processor load: both can consequently increase the overall system latency. The mapping scheme, for example, mapping a cryptographic function over a hardware accelerator, or on a general-purpose processor, also impacts system latencies. The performance study thus really intends to assess altogether both the safety and security of mapped functions. The result of this study is a hardware/software architecture that complies with both safety and security requirements, and that can withstand attacks, according to a given risk level.

The goal of the design stage is to design the software components, that is, functions mapped onto processors at the previous stage. During design, software components are progressively refined to the point where executable code generation is feasible. This refinement also includes security-related functions, e.g., cryptographic protocols. During the first refinements, simulations can be used to "debug" the models. When the model is moderately sized, formal verification, which relies on model-checking and is thus size-sensitive, can also be used to assess safety properties (e.g., the reachability of a given state, or its liveness), and security properties (e.g., the confidentiality of a given block attribute, or the authenticity of a message). When the model is too large to be verified, model-to-code transformations are used to perform security and safety tests. This paper does not address the design stage, which is described in [4].

4.4   Toolkit

The free and open-source TTool software supports all SysML-Sec methodological stages, including model capture, model simulation, and model verification. TTool is a multi-profile toolkit whose main strength is to offer a press-button approach for performing simulations and formal proofs from models. Proofs can

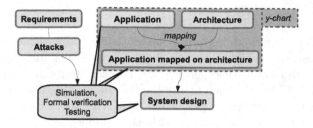

Fig. 2. The SysML-Sec methodology.

be performed automatically for both safety and security properties. For the partitioning stage, TTool relies on the DIPLODOCUS UML profile [3], even if security aspects presented in this paper are specific to SysML-Sec. Requirements, attacks, software design are all captured and analyzed with an environment called AVATAR [2] which covers the V development cycle of software components. Formal verifications and simulations can be performed either with TTool's integrated model checkers and simulators, or with external formal verification toolkits, e.g. UPPAAL [11], CADP [16] and ProVerif [12].

5   Safety- and Security-Oriented Validations

Model-oriented approaches favor the early validation of models. SysML-Sec supports such validations, either from partitioning models, or from design models. Once the validation results have been obtained (property is satisfied, property is not satisfied, property cannot be proved), the model is back-annotated with the results. Formal validation is more likely to be used to prove specific and precise safety and security properties, e.g., that a given data is confidential. Simulation is more likely to be used whenever the impact of a security mechanism over safety properties (e.g., latency-related properties) must be studied. This impact is mostly studied at partitioning stage.

5.1   Safety Properties

Safety validations relate to the following models: functional models, partitioning models, and design models. Properties can be proved with the use of simulation techniques [5], of formal verification techniques [2,11], or by generating an executable code (only from refined design models) and performing tests on that code [6]. From design diagrams, safety proofs take into account both safety and security mechanisms, because the latter impact the behaviour of software components, e.g., following a given execution path.

The system architecture and behavior are commonly modeled with graphical languages. On the contrary, languages used for expressing properties still mostly rely on textual languages, e.g. LTL/CTL, or derived languages from those ones. It is however possible to model all logical and timing properties with SysML parametric diagrams [20].

5.2   Security Properties

At the design stage, formal proofs of confidentiality and authenticity properties can be obtained. If possible, security requirements must first be refined into confidentiality and authenticity properties modeled as pragmas in SysML-Sec block diagrams. TTool can then transform the design diagrams into a security-oriented formal specification in pi-calculus [28]. This specification can be given as an input to ProVerif [12], along with the confidentiality and authenticity properties to be proved.

5.3   Safety and Security, Safety vs. Security

It is not a common practice to assess the relationship between safety and security at the partitioning stage. We believe however that such an assessment should be undertaken as early as possible in the development cycle. Eames and Moffet [14], and more recently Piètre-Cambacédès and Bouissou [29] as well as Raspotnig and Opdahl [30] have proposed ways to relate safety and security properties. More precisely, [29,30] aim at explicitly describing conflicts between such requirements, and also to provide "reinforcements", that is, requirements with different scopes that drive the architecture models into the same direction.

As we show in the next section, SysML-Sec makes it possible to assess the compatibility of security mechanisms with regards to safety properties at the partitioning stage as well as at the design stage. During the partitioning stage, mechanisms are evaluated according to the system latency and the usage of the platform, e.g., the necessary computation power, the load of buses, and the respect of real time deadlines. Partitioning models are typically validated by generating a known average traffic in the system, and then introducing security mechanisms so as to evaluate the impact of the latter on the former. The refinement of SysML-Sec models leads to introduce fine-grained cryptographic functions and security protocols. Thus, at design stage, we also rely on provers so as to assess the consistency of requirements and the coverage of attacks.

6   Example: Safety and Security Analysis of a Communicating Vehicle

This section illustrates the use of SysML-Sec for the identification of requirements and attacks and for the definition of safe and secure system architectures. The automotive system that serves as case a study is taken from the European FP7 EVITA project [19]. EVITA has defined the first generic security architecture for automotive communicating systems. This architecture contains safety critical Electronic Control Units (ECUs) interconnected with CAN or Flexray buses. Automotive systems are likely to be attacked either for economical reasons (activating optional features for free) or for criminal purpose. The interconnection of automotive systems with information systems (roads signs, tolls, etc.) and the Internet offers new ways to conduct attacks over these systems.

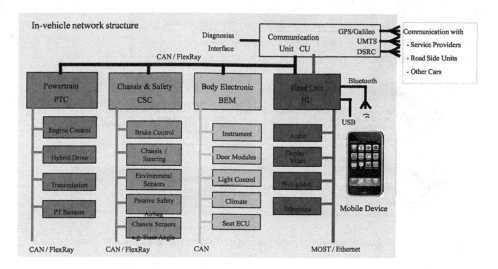

Fig. 3. EVITA automotive reference architecture.

A reference automotive architecture is given in Fig. 3. It comprises several domain (Powertrain, Chassis & Safety, Communication Unit, Head Unit, etc.). A domains contains several subdomains, each of them comprising several buses and processors. A main CAN/FlexRay bus interconnects all ECU bridges together. The Communication Unit and Head Unit also have external interfaces (Bluetooth, LTE, etc.).

We now apply the SysML-Sec methodology to satisfy authentication and confidentiality requirements in this setting. A key distribution mechanism is defined to derive cryptographic session keys between domains and sub-domains. An ECU1 asks a "Key Master" to generate a session key so as to communicate in a secure way with other domain ECUs (ECUN) of this session.

6.1 Security Requirements

Security requirements are captured within SysML requirements diagrams whose semantics are extended in SysML-Sec. Security requirements are stereotyped $<<$ $SecurityRequirement >>$ and contain an extra *kind* field (*confidentiality, access control, integrity, freshness*, etc.). Usual SysML relations between requirements (*containment, derive*) can be used, in particular to trace requirements throughout the different abstraction levels. Figure 4 presents an excerpt of the EVITA security requirements dealing with the environment-related security requirements, e.g., to prevent the use of manipulated data coming from the environment. The main requirement is composed of two subrequirements (data origin authenticity, and freshness). Two other requirements on integrity are derived from the two sub requirements.

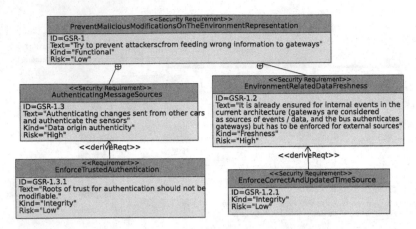

Fig. 4. Security requirements (excerpted from the EVITA use case).

6.2   Threats and Attacks

Attack trees [31] have become a rather well-known approach to capture attacks. Such trees allow an efficient decomposition of attacks into sub-attacks. However, they are not really adapted to the description of complex scenarios in which the attacker follows an opportunistic approach, in contrast to capturing an instance of an attack. For instance, attacks currently performed over embedded systems generally involve retrieving information from one or multiple alternate sources and sometimes depend on the timed execution of attack phases, like for instance the Zeus/Zitmo attack, which exploits a time-limited authentication token. The use of attack trees to express such scenarios would result in the implementation of multiple attack trees, often with a lot of duplicate branches, as we experienced in the EVITA use case. Furthermore, defining alternative scenarios would require coordinating the execution of all those trees.

We instead used a more compact attack model based on graphs (an even older approach for describing attacks [13] that has received some attention lately due to its conciseness [37]). We combined the graph based description of dependencies between attacks with the SysML parametric diagram in order to achieve a better integration with the architectural description of the system. The graph also captures "properties" of SysML blocks. Indeed, blocks represent resources of the system, a representation which highlights the architectural elements to be protected. Constraints are used to relate attacks together. Among other things, attacks can be composed like in attack trees to build more complex attacks. However, an attack can also establish a dependency with multiple other attacks in our graphs, meaning that this attack is used in other attacks, the equivalent of multiple trees. Attack equations are used to describe details of the set of constraints expressed on the graph. They correspond to logical operators like $<< OR >>$, $<< AND >>$, and $<< XOR >>$, or to temporal operators like $<< SEQUENCE >>$, $<< BEFORE >>$, and $<< AFTER >>$ that explicitly state how attacks are temporally constrained. Each constraint has a denotational correspondence: for instance, the equation of a $<< OR >>$ between two attacks $a1$ and $a2$ is $a = a_1 \lor a_2$, with a being the resulting attack. The connector ports on constraints are also used in equations to describe temporal relationships about the occurrence of attacks. Finally, attacks can also be linked to requirements through specific attributes.

Figure 5 depicts a simplified attack of our case study. A main resource *AutomotiveECUsAndBuses* is the target of an attacker wishing to steal the car (*Steal_car* root attack). To successfully perform that attack, the attacker first needs to access the system bus so as to be able to open the doors and then start the engine. To access the system bus, the attacker can either connect through a remote interface (Bluetooth, Internet) or through a diagnosis interface (OBD-II plug). Those are alternative solutions as indicated by the XOR in the sense that the attacker will opportunistically adopt the first solution that works and will not try to get hold of another connection means. In all cases, once connected, he then needs to bypass the automotive system firewall.

Attack graphs are formally defined by a *model-to-uppaal* transformation. More precisely, this transformation takes into account attacks and relations between attacks, thus ignoring blocks whose purpose is mostly to link attacks to resources. This process allows to formally verify the reachability and liveness of a given attack. Also, it is possible to check whether a given attack a_1 is eventually followed by another attack a_2 ("leads to" property). In TTool, attacks to be verified must first be selected: one may notice the small red cross on attacks Plug_on_OBD, bypass_internal_firewall and Steal_Car (Fig. 5). All of these attacks are reachable.

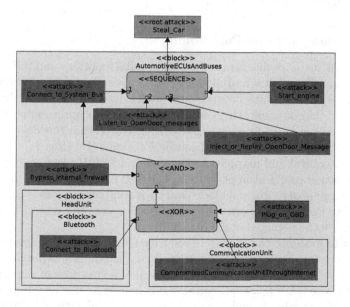

Fig. 5. An attack described with a SysML parametric diagram (Color figure online).

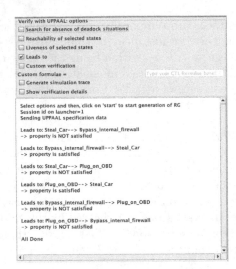

Fig. 6. Results of the "leads to" verification performed on the graph of Fig. 5.

The liveness holds only for the last two, but not for Plug_on_OBD since Steal_Car can occur by other means, e.g., through via Bluetooth. At last, Fig. 6 presents the results given by TTool for the "leads to" property. Steal_Car does not lead to any attack. Plug_on_OBD and bypass_internal_firewall both lead to Steal_Car. Finally Plug_on_OBD and bypass_internal_firewall do not lead to each other. Indeed, there is no ordering between those two attacks, and thus, when one of them occurs, the other one can already have occurred.

6.3   Hardware/Software Partitioning

A SysML block instance diagram is used to describe functions and their relations. Data and event flows between functions can be described with ports and links. Semantically speaking, data flows do not model data values, but only the data exchanges and their amount: this vastly simplifies proofs and simulations at that level of abstraction. In addition, we have demonstrated that this does not impact partitioning decisions in the scope of complex systems [18] (Fig. 7).

The architectural and mapping models rely on a UML deployment diagram, but the allocation mechanism of SysML or MARTE could be used for that purpose. The mapping of functional blocks and their communications is based on artifacts added to deployment nodes the latter being assets to protect. Those assets are also likely to be depicted in the attack diagrams.

In order to evaluate the impact of security mechanisms, two simulations are performed with two different partitionings. A first simulation is performed on the automotive system with no security mechanism. The purpose of that simulation is to evaluate the CAN bus load, because it is in charge of conveying urgent and non-urgent messages between domains. The average load with no security is 40 %.

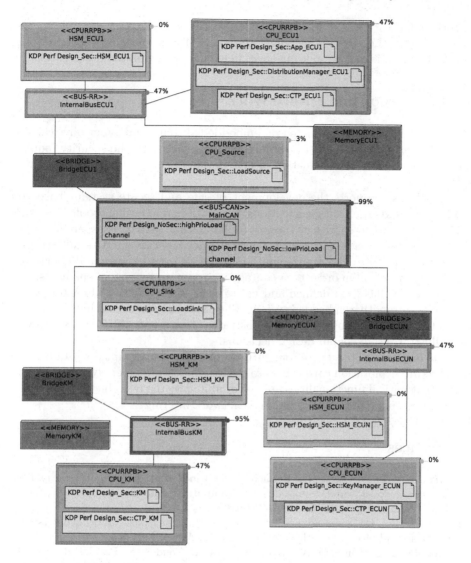

Fig. 7. Simulation with the key distribution mechanism.

A second simulation evaluates how the performance of the previous system is impacted by the key distribution protocol. For that purpose, a subset of the automotive system is modeled: cryptographic hardware accelerators (HSM - Hardware Security Module), the ECU asking for a session key (ECU1), the Key Master (KM), and the ECUs that will participate to the session and thus need the session key. The simulation shows a much higher load on the main CAN bus during a key distribution, and a much higher latency was observed for all classes of traffic not related to the key distribution [32]: this security mechanism does impact the safety of the system. To solve that issue, one solution we experimented with was to use a unique authentication token for multiple successive messages, thereby trading some storage at the recipient and an additional delay for validating those split messages in exchange of additional bandwidth.

7   Conclusion and Future Work

Many attacks are now conducted on embedded systems and cyber-physical systems. A short time-to-market combined with strong safety and security requirements encourages the introduction of new development methodologies for those systems.

SysML-Sec supports the development of safe and secure systems based on semi-formal and graphical specifications. Simulations and formal proofs on models can easily be conducted with its support toolkit TTool, so as to assess architectural choices and design choices, in terms of performance, safety properties, and security properties. Moreover, our environment is based on a well known and recognized language in the field in order to encourage its adoption by system engineers.

SysML-Sec has been defined and used in the scope of the EVITA project to secure an automotive embedded system. The case study presented in this paper is extracted from this project, and demonstrates the interest of SysML-Sec as well as it illustrates some of our design decisions.

One important objective of our future work is to add complex reasoning and architecture exploration capabilities to SysML-Sec. More precisely, our goal is to verify that critical functionalities are not inhibited by the introduction of security mechanisms, e.g. message encryption or network filtering.

References

1. Apvrille, A., Strazzere, T.: Reducing the window of opportunity for android malware Gotta catch 'em all. J. Comput. Virol. **8**(1–2), 61–71 (2012). http://dx.doi.org/10.1007/s11416-012-0162-3
2. Apvrille, L., De Saqui-Sannes, P.: Requirements analysis. Embedded Systems: Analysis and Modeling with SysML, UML and AADL (2013)
3. Apvrille, L., Muhammad, W., Ameur-Boulifa, R., Coudert, S., Pacalet, R.: A UML-based environment for system design space exploration. In: 13th IEEE International Conference on Electronics, Circuits and Systems, ICECS 2006, pp. 1272–1275, December 2006
4. Apvrille, L., Roudier, Y.: SysML-Sec: a SysML environment for the design and development of secure embedded systems. In: APCOSEC 2013, Yokohama, Japan, September 2013
5. Apvrille, L., De Saqui Sannes, P.: AVATAR/TTool: un environnement en mode libre pour SysML temps réel. Génie Logiciel (98), 22–26, September 2011
6. Apvrille, L., Becoulet, A.: Prototyping an embedded automotive system from its UML/SysML models. In: ERTSS 2012, Toulouse, France, February 2012
7. Armando, A., et al.: The AVISPA tool for the automated validation of internet security protocols and applications. In: Etessami, K., Rajamani, S.K. (eds.) CAV 2005. LNCS, vol. 3576, pp. 281–285. Springer, Heidelberg (2005)

8. Assolini, F.: The Tale of One Thousand and One DSL Modems, kaspersky lab, October 2012. http://www.securelist.com/en/blog/208193852/The_tale_of_one_thousand_and_one_DSL_modems
9. Balarin, F., Watanabe, Y., Hsieh, H., Lavagno, L., Passerone, C., Sangiovanni-Vincentelli, A.: Metropolis: an integrated electronic system design environment. Computer **36**(4), 45–52 (2003)
10. Beck, K., Andres, C.: Extreme Programming Explained: Embrace Change, 2nd edn. Addison-Wesley Professional, New York (2004)
11. Bengtsson, J., Yi, W.: Timed automata: semantics, algorithms and tools. In: Desel, J., Reisig, W., Rozenberg, G. (eds.) ACPN 2003. LNCS, vol. 3098, pp. 87–124. Springer, Heidelberg (2004)
12. Blanchet, B.: Automatic verification of correspondences for security protocols. J. Comput. Secur. **17**(4), 363–434 (2009)
13. Dacier, M., Deswarte, Y., Kaâniche, M.: Information systems security. In: Models and Tools for Quantitative Assessment of Operational Security, pp. 177–186. Chapman & Hall Ltd., London (1996). http://dl.acm.org/citation.cfm?id=265514.265530
14. Eames, D.P., Moffett, J.D.: The integration of safety and security requirements. In: Felici, M., Kanoun, K., Pasquini, A. (eds.) SAFECOMP 1999. LNCS, vol. 1698, pp. 468–480. Springer, Heidelberg (1999)
15. Esser, S.: Exploiting the iOS Kernel. In: BlackHat 2011 (2011)
16. Garavel, H., Mateescu, R., Lang, F., Serwe, W.: CADP 2006: a toolbox for the construction and analysis of distributed processes. In: Damm, W., Hermanns, H. (eds.) CAV 2007. LNCS, vol. 4590, pp. 158–163. Springer, Heidelberg (2007)
17. Huang, A.: Keeping Secrets in Hardware: the Microsoft XBox Case Study, AI Memo 2002–008, Massachusetts Institute of Technology, Artificial Intelligence Laboratory. Technical report (2002)
18. Jaber, C.: High-Level SoC Modeling and Performance Estimation Applied to a Multi-CoreImplementation of LTE EnodeB Physical Layer. Ph.D. thesis, Telecom ParisTech (2011)
19. Kelling, E., Friedewald, M., Leimbach, T., Menzel, M., Säger, P., Seudié, H., Weyl, B.: Specification and Evaluation of e-Security Relevant Use cases. Technical report Deliverable D2.1, EVITA Project (2009)
20. Knorreck, D., Apvrille, L., De Saqui-Sannes, P.: TEPE: a SysML language for time-constrained property modeling and formal verification. ACM SIGSOFT Softw. Eng. Notes **36**(1), 1–8 (2011)
21. Koscher, K., Czeskis, A., Roesner, F., Patel, S., Kohno, T., Checkoway, S., McCoy, D., Kantor, B., Anderson, D., Shacham, H., Savage, S.: Experimental security analysis of a modern automobile. In: Proceedings of the 2010 IEEE Symposium on Security and Privacy, SP 2010, pp. 447–462. IEEE Computer Society, Washington, DC (2010). http://dx.doi.org/10.1109/SP.2010.34
22. Maslennikov, D.: Russian cybercriminals on the move: profiting from mobile malware. In: The 20th Virus Bulletin International Conference, Vancouver, Canada, pp. 84–89, October 2010
23. Maynor, D.: Scada security and terrorism: We're not crying wolf! In: Invited presentation at BlackHat BH 2006, USA (2006). https://www.blackhat.com/presentations/bh-federal-06/BH-Fed-06-Maynor-Graham-up.pdf
24. Nhlabatsi, A., Nuseibeh, B., Yu, Y.: Security Requirements Engineering for Evolving Software Systems: a survey. Technical report 1, The Open University (2010)
25. Nuseibeh, B.: Weaving together requirements and architectures. IEEE Comput. **34**(3), 115–117 (2001)

26. OMG: OMG Profile for Scheduling, Performance and Time (2005). http://www.omg.org/spec/SPTP/

27. OMG: OMG Systems Modeling Language (2012). http://www.sysml.org/specs/

28. Pedroza, G.: Assisting the design of secured applications for mobile vehicles. In: Ph.D. of Ecole doctorale informatique, télécommunications et électronique of Paris, January 2013

29. Pietre-Cambacedes, L., Bouissou, M.: Cross-fertilization between safety and security engineering. Reliab. Eng. Syst. Saf. **110**, 110–126 (2013)

30. Raspotnig, C., Opdahl, A.L.: Comparing risk identification techniques for safety and security requirements. J. Syst. Softw. **86**(4), 1124–1151 (2013)

31. Schneier, B.: Attack Trees: Modeling Security Threats, December 1999

32. Schweppe, H., Roudier, Y., Weyl, B., Apvrille, L., Scheuermann, D.: C2x communication: securing the last meter. In: The 4th IEEE International Symposium on Wireless Vehicular Communications, WIVEC 2011, San Francisco, USA, September 2011

33. SCIP: VulDB: Hospira Lifecare PCA Infusion Pump 412 Telnet Service weak authentication, April 2015. http://www.scip.ch/en/?vuldb.75158

34. Teso, H.: Aircraft Hacking. In: HITB Security Conference, Amsterdam, The Netherlands (2013)

35. Van Lamsweerde, A.: Engineering requirements for system reliability and security. Softw. Syst. Reliab. Secur. **9**, 196–238 (2007)

36. Vidal, J., de Lamotte, F., Gogniat, G., Soulard, P., Diguet, J.P.: A co-design approach for embedded system modeling and code generation with UML and MARTE. In: Design, Automation and Test in Europe Conference and Exhibition, DATE 2009, pp. 226–231, April 2009

37. Vigo, R., Nielson, F., Nielson, H.: Automated generation of attack trees. In: 2014 IEEE 27th Computer Security Foundations Symposium (CSF), pp. 337–350, July 2014

38. Waters, K.: All About Agile: Agile Management Made Easy!. CreateSpace Independent Publishing Platform, Seattle (2012)

Methodologies, Processes and Platforms

Architecture Optimization with SysML Modeling: A Case Study Using Variability

Patrick Leserf[1](✉), Pierre de Saqui-Sannes[2], Jérôme Hugues[2], and Khaled Chaaban[1]

[1] ESTACA-Lab, 53000 Laval, France
{patrick.leserf,khaled.chaaban}@estaca.fr
[2] ISAE-SUPAERO, University of Toulouse, 31055 Toulouse, France
{pdss,jerome.hugues}@isae-supaero.fr

Abstract. Obtaining the set of trade-off architectures from a SysML model is an important objective for the system designer. To achieve this goal, we propose a methodology combining SysML with the variability concept and multi-objectives optimization techniques. An initial SysML model is completed with variability information to show up the different alternatives for component redundancy and selection from a library. The constraints and objective functions are also added to the initial SysML model, with an optimization context. Then a representation of a constraint satisfaction problem (CSP) is generated with an algorithm from the optimization context and solved with an existing solver. The paper illustrates our methodology by designing an Embedded Cognitive Safety System (ECSS). From a component repository and redundancy alternatives, the best design alternatives are generated in order to minimize the total cost and maximize the estimated system reliability.

Keywords: Architecture optimization · SysML · Embedded systems · Model variability

1 Introduction

Embedded system design has become an important development activity, due to the industrial demands for new functions integration and design. These systems are mainly composed of software. However hardware components such as sensors, CPU and embedded networks have to be considered too. The designer must implement an architecture that fulfills the functionalities according to the requirements, but numerous indicators such as cost, weight and reliability have to be optimized too. These indicators typically compete with one another. Improving one of them often leads to degrading another one. In this context, this paper considers that the designer has a twofold objective: to obtain the set of optimal architecture designs and to obtain it using a Model-Based System Engineering approach that seamlessly unifies system modeling in SysML [1] with architecture optimization. Such an optimization may be automated using architecture models and transformations. Then the designer can select the appropriate design alternative, according to his or her preferences. These activities shall be integrated into Model-Based System Engineering (MBSE).

© Springer International Publishing Switzerland 2015
P. Desfray et al. (Eds.): MODELSWARD 2015, CCIS 580, pp. 311–327, 2015.
DOI: 10.1007/978-3-319-27869-8_18

The expected benefits of MBSE include the capacity to simulate and formally verify models in order to detect design errors as soon as possible in the life cycle of systems. A great number of papers present tools (e.g. TOPCASED [2], TTool [3]) that enable simulation and verification of SysML models. By contrast, little work has been published on SysML modeling as a front-end to come up with and compare different design alternatives. Current approaches such as [4, 5] address design optimization from SysML models but differ from our approach for they focus on component parameters tuning, such as CPU frequency or memory size. In this paper, we propose to take into account hardware component selection, the component redundancy level and the component connection in order to optimize the system cost and reliability.

The paper is organized as follows. Section 2 introduces the methodology we propose for model-based system design optimization in the context of embedded systems. Sections 3 and 4 respectively address SysML modeling and architecture optimization. An algorithm for Pareto front extraction is proposed in Sect. 5 with results from the case study. Section 6 surveys related work. Section 7 concludes the paper and outlines future work.

2   Methodology

2.1   Design Flow with MBSE

We consider architecture design in the context of systems engineering activities with MBSE, as described in [6]. The output of systems engineering activities is a system model written in SysML language (Fig. 1).

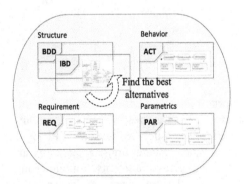

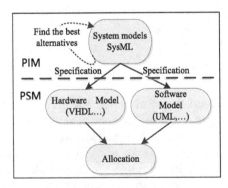

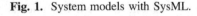

Fig. 1. System models with SysML.   **Fig. 2.** Design flow with MBSE.

The model can be divided into a Platform Independent Model (PIM) and a Platform Specific Model (PSM). The PIM and PSM concepts come from the Model Driven Architecture standard of the Object Management Group [7]. Figure 1 uses the model of the system to specify both hardware and software components requirements. During the PIM stage, the hardware platform is not yet selected. The designer has to consider a set of candidate platforms in order to find the best alternatives. After the specification step, the execution platform is selected. In SysML, the model of the system is defined by a set of diagrams (Fig. 2). The requirement diagram (REQ) describes the requirements. The activity diagram (ACT) represents the behavior of the system. The Block Definition Diagram (BDD) and the Internal Block Diagram (IBD) describe the structure of the system. Finally the parametric diagram captures relationships among properties. An important activity of system engineering is to find the best design alternatives for the whole system. However the exploration space is very large, especially, with current approach such as [10] that does exploration on PSM. In this paper, we focus on system model optimization issues (dashed elements in Figs. 1 and 2) because it comes first in the design activity and it will substantially restrict the design space exploration (DSE). With this approach, the DSE can be done in a stepwise manner, exploring the system model first, and then the software, hardware and allocation alternatives with current DSE approaches. The system structure is also a key point for metric evaluation (i.e. cost, weight and reliability). In this context, the objective for the designer using MBSE and SysML is to obtain the best trade-off system structure, in order to optimize objective functions such as cost and reliability. This multi-objective optimization problem can be described by mathematical terms:

$$min[f_1(\boldsymbol{x}), f_2(\boldsymbol{x}), \dots f_n(\boldsymbol{x})] with \ x \in S$$

Above, f is the objective function vector and S the set of constraints. Our approach is to suggest the best configurations to the designer, that is, to find the Pareto-optimal solutions. Pareto-optimal solutions have the lowest (or equivalently low) values for all objective functions. The set of solutions is presented to the decision-maker by the designer for the selection of optimal solutions. The methodology we propose is presented by next sub-section. The requirement and structure models are adapted for the optimization, including objective function definition, variability and constraints. We assume that the system design is done using the SysML language. Also, a component repository is available including the parameters for the objective functions.

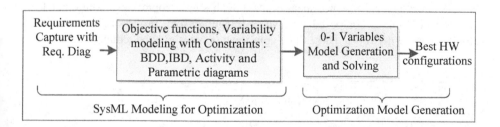

Fig. 3. Methodology overview.

Note: The SysML diagrams of this paper have been edited using the Papyrus tool from CEA [8].

2.2 Our Proposal

Figure 3 presents the methodology we propose for optimizing system architecture, showing the activities and the produced artifacts. The first stage is the SysML modeling for optimization (cf. Sect. 3). In a preliminary step, the requirements are captured using requirement diagrams. Architecture requirements are taken into account. This allows to express constraints and to add traceability between requirements and architecture elements. Then the SysML model is completed for optimization, by adding objective function definitions in parametric diagrams and by adding model variability. The model variability expresses the different design alternatives the designer wants to explore. The model variability is represented by several degrees of freedom from the model, using variability variables inserted into comments. We distinguish between the instance variability variable (IVV), meaning that we may have several instances of the same component in the model, and component variability variable (CVV), meaning that a component instance may be replaced. The second stage, described in Sects. 4 and 5, is the optimization model generation and solving. To do this, the variability variables of the SysML model are transformed into a new set of 0-1 variables in the optimization model. By re-using the constraints from the SysML model, the problem can be resolved as a Constraint Satisfaction Problem (CSP), using a standard solver. Then the designer can select among the trade-off solutions the ones that best fit to his or her needs.

3 SysML Modeling for Optimization

This section presents the Embedded Cognitive Safety System (Fig. 4) that serves as a running case study throughout the paper, and step-by-step discusses how to model the ECSS in SysML.

3.1 Case Study

The ECSS system can be integrated in an on-board vehicle digital system or in aeronautics systems such as drones. Typical features for an ECSS are line detection, obstacle detection and distance measurement with stereoscopic view. The embedded hardware platform is composed of CMOS image sensors, processing elements and vehicle interface networks. These three components types may be redundant, for safety

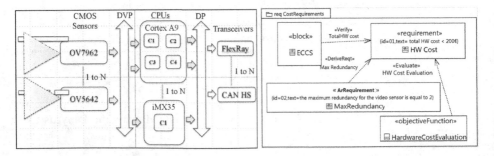

Fig. 4. ECSS system.   **Fig. 5.** Requirements for optimization.

purposes or stereoscopic processing. CMOS image sensors support auto focus engine and image stabilization. Image sensors are connected to processing elements through Digital Video Port (DVP), a type of parallel bus interface. Processing elements are CPU supporting image processing such as Cortex A9 or iMX35. The vehicle interface is an embedded serial bus such as CAN High Speed or FlexRay. The vehicle interface is integrated into the ECSS system with a transceiver component, connected to the processing element with a digital port (DP) which is a parallel bus interface.

3.2 Requirements Capture

SysML provides modeling constructs to capture and represent textual requirements, and to link the requirements to other modeling elements. The requirement diagram (Fig. 5) depicts requirements, but a requirement may also appear on other diagrams to show its relationship to other modeling elements. A standard requirement includes a unique identifier and a text requirement. The *"Satisfy"* and *"Verify"* relationships relate requirements to other model elements such as blocks and test cases. In our context of architecture optimization, specific requirements for the architecture, so-called the "architecture requirements," are derived from standard requirements. To clearly identify architectural requirements, a stereotype *"ArRequirement"* extends the standard SysML requirement. On the other hand, a standard requirement is evaluated by an objective function. The objective function is a stereotype extending the standard SysML constraint block. This objective function is related to a requirement with a stereotype "evaluate" extending the basic UML-2 dependency relationship. A dependency is a design-time relationship between definitions. In Fig. 5, the *"MaxRedundancy"* architecture requirement limits the sensor component redundancy to two for cost reason, and the system cost requirement is evaluated.

3.3 MDO Context and Objective Functions Definition

To integrate multi-domain optimization (MDO) into the system model design, we propose to define a MDO context, a type of analysis context. The MDO context is represented by a BDD diagram and a parametric diagram, both including constraint blocks. The parametric diagram captures the internal structure of a constraint block, in term of parameters and connectors between parameters. The BDD defines constraint blocks and their relationships. This BDD diagram contains a top-level constraint block, named *"ECSS MDO Context"* in Fig. 6. This constraint block has a reference to the block representing the system under analysis and including the variability for representing the alternatives. The MDO context diagram also contains the objective functions and the optimization model representation. The Pareto frontier, a result of the MDO context, is used to present alternatives to the designer. The MDO context can be passed to an external optimization solver, and the result can be provided back as Pareto frontier values of the MDO context. The objective function block extends the standard SysML Constraint Block and contains an optimization goal parameter (i.e. maximize or minimize). A constraint provides a description of the analytical function supporting the

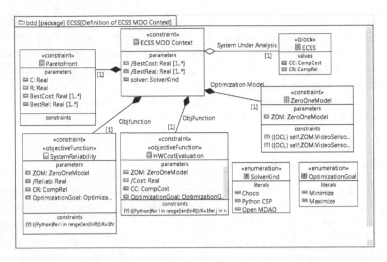

Fig. 6. BDD diagram for ECSS MDO context definition.

objective function. Other parameters specify the interaction points between the objective function and the system under analysis, and between the objective functions and the optimization model. Figure 6 shows the MDO context definition for our case study, in a BDD. The MDO context is called ECSS MDO Context, to perform a multi-objective optimization of the ECSS system. The ECSS MDO Context constraint block has two value vectors, /BestCost[1..*] and/BestRel[1..*], representing the Pareto frontier. The *ParetoFront* constraint block produces these value vectors from the two objectives functions. It is intended that the equations are solved by an external optimization solver for these two vectors, so they are shown as derived.

The result values obtained with an external CSP solver are presented later in Sect. 4. As indicated by its associations, ECSS MDO context contains two constraint properties, both typed by an objective function, namely *HWCostEvaluation* and *SystemReliability*. A precision to the modeling of the objective function is added, with a constraint. The two constraints describe the equation underlying the total cost and the reliability calculation. In this case, the Python language can be used as constraint language, because it is used by the CSP solver [14]. For the *SystemReliability* function, the system reliability R is calculated with parameters coming from the system under analysis (the components reliability) and from the Zero One Model. The ECSS MDO context also contains one reference property typed by ECSS, the system under analysis including variability. Finally, ECSS MDO contains a constraints property Zero One Model, representing the optimization model described in Sect. 4. The Zero One Model has a parameter and a set of constraints deduced from the ECSS system (see Sect. 4, Eq. 2) and from the model itself. These constraints can be expressed using the Object Constraint Language (OCL). Figure 7 shows a parametric diagram. Its frame represents the ECSS MDO context constraint block. This diagram is similar to an internal block diagram but uses binding connectors to link constraints parameters.

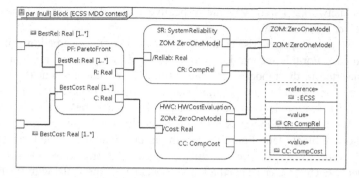

Fig. 7. Parametric diagram for MDO context definition.

3.4 System Composition and Redundancy Modeling

The architecture modeling represents the set of hardware resources available for the execution of the application. The hardware system is made up of several components and described by a block definition diagram (see Fig. 8). In our optimization problem, the composition is known, but the redundancy level of each component is not. The redundancy level is the first degree of freedom for the optimization problem. At this step, we specify instance variability variables (IVV) in comments. Each IVV is related to a composition association, between the top-level component and the low-level component. The ECSS system in Fig. 8 contains one or two sensors, processing

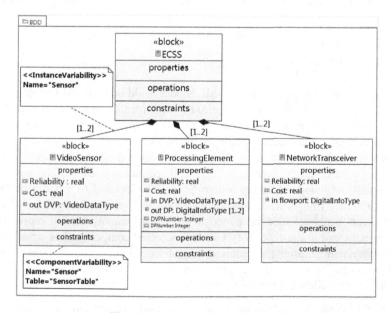

Fig. 8. BDD for HW composition.

elements and networks. Three IVVs are respectively related to the sensor, the CPU and the Transceiver composition.

The hardware components selection is the second degree of freedom for the optimization process. For this second degree of freedom, a Component Variability Variable (CVV) is inserted in the model as a comment. A CVV indicates that the component instance can be replaced by another hardware component specification. The hardware component specification is provided by the designer, and belongs to a component repository. The repository includes a set of tables. Each table is associated with one component of the block definition diagram. In our example, we define three tables and three CVV, respectively associated with the sensor, the processing element and the network block. Each table contains the list of available components, with their cost and reliability (see Table 2). The user, in addition to the SysML model, provides these tables.

3.5   Component Interface Modeling

Component interface modeling is useful for the optimization problem, because new constraints arise during this stage. These constraints will be added to the computational model for the problem solving. The Internal Block Diagram in SysML captures the internal structure of a block in terms of properties and connectors between properties. If we consider the IBD depicted by Fig. 10, we have one or two sensors with one output DVP port connected to one or two processing elements for video data transmission. At this step, the goal is to retain the valid configurations with a constraint used by the optimization process. In our case and for the digital video port (DVP), the sum of input ports for processing elements shall be greater than or equal to the sum of output port for video sensors. This constraint may be expressed in OCL and attached to the VideoData connection.

4   Problem Statement

Previous section has shown how the SysML model could be prepared for optimization. But a mathematical representation is required to perform the optimization with suitable algorithms. In this section we propose a representation and show how to obtain it from the SysML model. This representation is based on zero-one variables, and can be solved as a constraint satisfaction problem. Optimization models have been developed to select software or hardware components and redundancy levels. The system (see Fig. 9) consists of independent subsystem Si. Si is associated to a given block with instance variability (the *VideoSensors* aggregation in Fig. 9). Subsystem Si is composed of components selected in a repository of components Ci. Cij represents the component number j in the repository Ci. Each selected component has a position k in the final subsystem Si, after the problem resolution. Figure 9 shows there exists two possible positions for a selected component in the final subsystem Si.

We define the following sets and parameters:

- S_i the set of components with position k. C_i the set of components available in the component repository

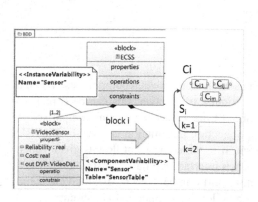

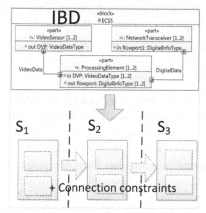

Fig. 9. From BDD to problem formulation.

Fig. 10. From IBD to connection constraints.

- c_{ij} the cost of component C_{ij} and θ_i an interconnection cost for any component
- r_{ij} the reliability of component C_{ij}
- e_{ij} and s_{ij} the input and output port numbers of component C_{ij}. For sensors (the first block) we have no input port and one output port, so we have: $e_{1j} = 0$ and $s_{1j} = 1$

Table 1. Association between SysML model elements and optimization model.

Sets	SysML model element
S and S_i	S is the system, modeled by the top-level block in the BDD. The ECSS block in Fig. 9 represents the system. One sub-system S_i per sub-block in the BDD with instance variability variable (IVV)
C_i, e_{ij} s_{ij}	One C_i per block associated to component variability variable (CVV), from BDD diagram. In Fig. 9, C_i is the set of video sensor components, with cost and reliability in video sensor table (Table 2). e_{ij} and s_{ij} are deduced from the IBD diagram

These sets and parameters are deduced from the SysML model, as it is shown in Table 1.

In Fig. 9, the range of k is given by the SysML aggregation multiplicity in the BDD, the range of i by the system composition in the BDD and the range of j by the component table size. The following zero-one programming formulation of this problem defines decision variables:

$$\forall i \in S,\ j \in C_i,\ k \in S_i\ a_{ijk} = \begin{cases} 0 & \text{if component } C_{ij} \text{ is used in position } k \text{ of } S_i \\ 1 & \text{otherwise} \end{cases} \quad (1)$$

Seen as constraints applied to the system, the first set of constraints comes from the decision variable definition.

At any position of the final subsystem S_i we can have only one component in position k:

$$\forall i,j \sum_k a_{ijk} \leq 1 \tag{2}$$

Other constraints can be expressed such as exclusion between components. When a CPU component is not compatible with a particular transceiver, this can be expressed as a constraint, such as a sum lower than one. In the same way, a sum comparison is used to express a component dependency. Connection information is given by the IBD diagram (see Fig. 10). First, the place of each Si in the component flow is given. Then the connection constraints are provided. At each interface we have constraints between the total input port number and the total output port number. In Fig. 10, for *VideoData* connection, the sensors and CPUs satisfy the following connection constraint:

$$\sum_{j,k} a_{1jk}s_{1j} \leq \sum_{j,k} a_{2jk}e_{2j} \tag{3}$$

For *DigitalData* connection, each transceiver input is connected to one CPU, and each CPU has at least one connected output:

$$\sum_{j,k} a_{3jk}e_{3j} \leq \sum_{j,k} a_{2jk}s_{2j} \text{ and } \sum_{j,k} a_{2jk}s_{2j} \leq \sum_{j,k} a_{3jk}e_{3j} \tag{4}$$

The objective functions are included in the parametric diagram. In our example, the goal is to minimize the cost and to maximize reliability. The total system cost including interconnection cost is given by Eq. (5). The system reliability to be maximized, using serial-parallel interconnection model, can be calculated by Eq. (6).

$$\min C = \sum_{i,j,k} c_{ij} \left[a_{ijk} + exp\left(\theta_i \sum_k a_{ijk} \right) \right] \tag{5}$$

$$\max R = \prod_i \left[1 - \prod_{j,k} \left[1 - a_{ijk}r_{ij} \right] \right] \tag{6}$$

5   Model Transformation

In this section, CSP problems are presented, and a formalization for the system under analysis (SuA) is proposed.

5.1   CSP Problem

The problem defined in Sect. 4 including variables and constraints can be seen as a constraint satisfaction problem (CSP). A CSP, as defined in [13] consists of a set of n variables $X = \{x_1, x_2, \ldots x_n\}$, a set of n domains $D = \{D_1, D_2, \ldots D_n\}$ with $x_i \in D_i$, a set of constraints and a set of objective functions $F = \{f_1, f_2, \ldots f_i\}$. A function f_i is an objective function which maps every solution to a numerical value.

Researchers in artificial intelligence usually adopt CSP to solve problems such as scheduling or decision problems. CSP problems are combinatorial by nature. They are NP-complete or NP-hard (Karp [17]). An efficient algorithm (i.e. with polynomial time for all inputs) does not exist, but some heuristics produce good approximate solutions. A feasible solution for the problem consists in an assignment of values from its domain to every variable, in such a way that each constraint is satisfied. When a feasible solution exists, we may want to find just one solution, all solutions or an optimal solution. In our case we want to find optimal solutions. An optimal solution is given by the objective functions defined in the SysML model. The selected approach in this paper consists in finding all solutions of the CSP problem and then to evaluate the different solutions with objective functions, to determine the optimal solutions. Algorithms for solving CSP use to systematically search through the possible assignments of values to find a solution. Brailsford et al. [13] show that a simple algorithm is the backtracking algorithm, and others are forward checking and the MAC algorithm. These algorithms use a search tree, as it would be done in a branch and bound algorithm. In the backtracking algorithm, the current variable is assigned to a value from its domain. This assignment is checked against the current partial solution. If any of the constraints is violated, another value for the current variable is chosen. If all the values have been tried, the algorithm backtracks to the previous variable and assigns it with another value. A CSP solver typically uses a problem description file to define the problem. This file is written in high level programming language such as Python and contains several sections. The first one is the variables definition, including the variable names, the data types and variables bounds. Depending on the solver, data types can be integer, Boolean, choice or real. The second section is the constraints section, with relationships of equality or inequality between variables. The problem to solve is created with a particular command, and the previous variables and constraints are added to the problem. Lastly, a resolution command is used to invoke the solver algorithm for the problem solving.

5.2   Creation of CSP Variables

The appropriate variables are created in the CSP description file, from the SuA including variability. When a combination between component and instance variability is found, as it is described in Fig. 9, we create a two dimensional array of Boolean variables, corresponding to the $a_{ijk}, \in \{0, 1\}$ coefficients described in Eq. (1).

We obtain the following lines of code in the first section of the CSP problem description file. These lines create a two dimensional array of Boolean variables a_{ij} for the problem, corresponding to the sensors variability. The variability is a combination of single or dual redundancy, and a list of two sensors:

```
problem.addVariables(["a"+str(i)+str(j)         for    j    in
range(1,3) for i in range(1,3)], [0,1])
```

5.3 Constraints and CSP Resolution

The second section of the CSP problem description file includes the constraints coming from the SysML model and from the representation of variables. For the representation of variables, when a combination between component and instance variability is found, the constraint expressed by Eq. (2) is inserted in the problem description file. The following lines of code correspond to the sensors representation in the case study:

```
problem.addConstraint(lambda   a11,a12,   :   a11+a12   <=   1,
("a11","a12"))

problem.addConstraint(lambda   a21,a22,   :   a21+a22   <=   1,
("a21","a22"))
```

The other constraints come from constraint blocks in the SysML model. The Internal Block Diagram in Fig. 10 provides constraints between the total input port number and the total output port number, for the sensors, the CPUs and the transceiver. These constraints are expressed by Eqs. (3) and (4), given in Sect. 4. In Eq. (3), one sensor shall be connected to one CPU having one or two inputs. This corresponds to the following lines of code in the CSP problem description file of our case study:

```
problem.addConstraint(lambda
a11,a12,a21,a22,b11,b12,b21,b22   :   2*b11+b12+2*b21+b22   >=
a11+a12+a21+a22,
["a11","a12","a21","a22","b11","b12","b21","b22"])
```

After the variable definition and the constraints instantiation, the CSP problem can be solved and the solutions are sorted with the following lines:

```
solutions   =   sorted(sorted(x.items())   for   x   in   pro-
blem.getSolutions())
```

Regarding the case study, as a first experiment, we obtain a CSP problem with Boolean variables, a_{ij}, b_{ij}, c_{ij} with $i, j \in \{1, 2\}$ for the sensors, the CPUs and the transceivers. The resolution of this constraint problem provides seventy-four CSP solutions, after the filtering of equivalent configurations due to the Boolean representation.

5.4 Evaluation of the CSP Solutions

After obtaining the CSP solutions, each solution can be evaluated with the objective functions. An objective function is expressed with an algorithm included in a constraint block of the optimization context. In Fig. 6, the "*SystemReliability*" and the "*HWCostEvaluation*" constraint blocks contain Python code of the objective functions given by Eqs. (5) and (6).

The input parameters for the algorithms are the a_{ij}, b_{ij}, c_{ij} coefficients and the cost and reliability of each component in the repository (see Table 2). The $a_{ij}, b_{ij}, b_{ij} \in \{0, 1\}$ coefficients are defined in Eq. (1) and correspond to the decision variables. By applying the algorithm of the objective functions (Cost and reliability) to each solution of the CSP problem, we get results in the following form:

Table 2. Component repository extract.

Component	Reliability min-max	Cost min-max (€)
Sens. 1–3	0.99997–0.99998	16.9–20.2
Sens. 4–6	0.999976–0.999985	21.5–25.7
CPU 1–3	0.99996–0.99998	12.6–21.2
CPU 4–6	0.99997–0.999985	28.4–34.5
Trans. 1–3	0.9934–0.9969	12.8–13.1
Trans. 4–6	0.9971–0.9995	13.8–15.4

```
Solution 39
a11 a12 = 01 b11 b12 = 01 c11 c12 = 01
a21 a22 = 01 b21 b22 = 01 c21 c22 = 10
Fail. R.=0.00001484  Cost=95
```
This result means that the solution #39 to the CSP problem has a hardware cost of
€95 and a failure rate of 14.8 failures per million. This solution is obtained by using
two identical sensors of type 2, two identical CPUs of type 2, and two transceivers of
type 1 and 2.

5.5   Pareto Frontier

From the set of solutions obtained in previous section, it is possible to extract the Pareto
frontier. Each solution represents an alternative for the system design. Generally
speaking, the Pareto frontier consists of all alternatives that are not dominated by
another one. In Fig. 11, the A alternative dominates C because A is both cheaper and
more reliable than C. But A and B do not dominate each other.

For a minimization problem, an alternative named A dominates another one named
C if and only if:

$$\begin{cases} \forall i \in \{1 \ldots n\}\, f_i(a) \leq f_i(c) \\ \exists i \in \{1 \ldots n\}\, f_i(a) < f_i(c) \end{cases}$$

with $f(x) = (f_1(x), f_2(x), \ldots f_n(x))$ is an array of n objective functions. x is the array of
decision variables. In the context of our case study, we have: $x = \{a_{11}, a_{12}, \ldots, b_{11}, b_{12}, \ldots, c_{11}, c_{12}, \ldots\}$ with $a_{ij}, b_{ij}, c_{ij} \in \{0, 1\}$ defined in Eq. (1),
$f_1(x)$ is the failure rate and $f_2(x)$ is the system cost. After solving the CSP problem in
previous section, we obtained an array S of n solutions with a cost and failure rate
estimation. In order to obtain the Pareto frontier P, we apply Algorithm 1. In line 2, the
solutions are sorted according to their increasing cost (primary sort key) and according
to their increasing failure rate (secondary sort key). We obtain a second S' array of
solutions. In line 4, the cheapest solution (first solution of S') is added to the Pareto
Frontier. Then we skip the successive alternatives until we find one with a lower or
equal failure rate (line 7 and 8). This alternative is added to the Pareto frontier and the
search is restarted from this alternative.

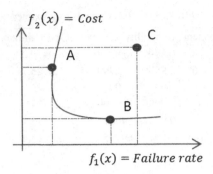

Fig. 11. Pareto frontier.

With this algorithm, when several alternatives have the same cost and the same failure rate, they are all added to the Pareto frontier, if they are not dominated by another solution.

Algorithm 1. Pareto frontier extraction from a solution set.

---

1. $P \leftarrow \emptyset$, $index \leftarrow 1$, $ItemFound \leftarrow True$
2. Sort S array in order of increasing cost and increasing failure rate, we obtain $S' = (S_1, S_2, \dots S_n)$
3. **$While$**$(ItemFound = True)$
4. **Add** S'_{index} **to** P
5. $ItemFound \leftarrow False$
6. **For**$(j = index + 1 \text{ to } n)$
7. **if**$(FailureR(S'_j) \leq FailureR(S'_{index}))$
8. $index \leftarrow j$, $ItemFound \leftarrow True$
9. **$EndFor$**
10. **$EndWhile$**
11. **$Return$** P

5.6 Results

We consider the case study with a maximum redundancy of two and four connection constraints between sensors, processing elements and network transceivers. A repository of 18 components is specified in Table 2. We obtain a 36-decision variables problem to be solved. With the CSP solver using a backtracking algorithm implemented in Python, and a posteriori objective function evaluation, we obtain 13,500 solutions in 36 min of computation time (Fig. 12). The X-axis displays the Failure rate (1-Rs) instead of reliability Rs. The figure is obtained with a MATLAB [16] implementation of algorithm 1 running on an Intel i5 3 GHz machine with 4 GB RAM. Each

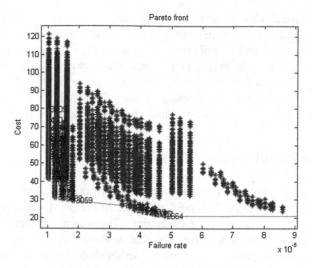

Fig. 12. Pareto frontier with CSP solver.

Table 3. Three best trade-off configurations.

Solution #	Sensors	CPUs	Transceivers	Cost (€)	FR (10-5)
1	S1 + S1	CPU1	T4 + T1	73	1.48
2	S1 + S3	CPU1	T1 + T1	75.3	1.22
3	S1 + S3	CPU1 + CPU1	T1 + T1	87.9	1.02

point figures a solution to the CSP problem obtained with the Python labix solver [14]. The solid line figures the Pareto frontier.

For a maximum cost of €90 and a failure rate < 0.00002, Table 3 presents the three best trade-off configurations selected by the user.

6   Related Work

In recent literature, there are approaches such as [4, 5, 15] on the architecture optimization at the system level with SysML. In [15], the authors have demonstrated the adaptability of SysML by extending the language to provide integration with mathematical solver for optimization. However this approach lacks support of multi-criteria optimization that would help designers to perform design space exploration and trade-off analysis. The approach proposed by Van Huong and Binh [4] and Spyropoulos and Baras [5] allows the user to perform multiple analyses in the same environment. These approaches are adapted to the component parameters optimization such as CPU frequency or memory size, not to the architecture composition and redundancy problem we want to address. In [9] an optimization technique is proposed for a microwave module design, with combination of alternatives for part modules, but without redundancy constraint. In the Design Space Exploration (DSE) approach [10], the problem to solve is related to the hardware/software partitioning and the mapping of application onto hardware elements. Our approach comes earlier in the design flow and is complementary, providing a limitation of the design space exploration. The redundancy allocation problem (RAP [11, 12]) deals with component selection, for cost and reliability optimization at system level. In these approaches (DSE, RAP), the problem is formalized as an optimization problem, and not with the MBSE approach. Similarly, in the RAP formulation the connection topology is fixed as a serial-parallel model.

7   Conclusions and Future Work

The paper presents a methodology for multi-objective optimization of system architecture. Starting from a SysML model, we add information concerning objective functions, variability and architecture constraints. The redundancy level and the component alternatives are tagged with variables that describe variability. Then the SysML model can be further exploited to generate a mathematical representation, based on integer variables, linear constraints and objective functions. The problem can be solved using a CSP solver. Finally, the ECSS case study shows that there exists three best configurations, minimizing cost and maximizing reliability, from a repository of 18 components. Ongoing work includes the integration of two steps in the methodology, the deployment and the system configuration. The deployment is the allocation of software components onto hardware components. The configuration is the determination of the best values for model attributes such as ECSS position in the vehicle. For the deployment and configuration, the variability concept shall be extended. In particular, for the system configuration, the variables can be either discrete or continuous. That is why in addition to instance and component variability, the value variability, relative to component attributes, will be integrated too. The CSP problem generation shall be adapted too, to cope with the resolution of these mixed problems, including discrete and continuous variables.

References

1. OMG Systems Modeling Language (OMG SysML™), V1.3. http://www.omg.org/spec/SysML/1.3/PDF
2. TOPCASED. The open source toolkit for critical systems. http://www.topcased.org/
3. TTool. The TURTLE Toolkit. http://labsoc.comelec.telecom-paristech.fr/ttool
4. Van Huong, P., Binh, N.: Embedded system architecture design and optimization at the model level. IJCCE 1(4), 345–349 (2012). IAP, San Bernardino
5. Spyropoulos, D., Baras, J.S.: Extending design capabilities of SysML with trade-off analysis: electrical microgrid case study. Procedia Comput. Sci. 16, 108–117 (2013). Elsevier, Amsterdam
6. Friedenthal, S., Moore, A., Steiner, R.: A Practical Guide to SysML. The MK/OMG Press, San Francisco (2009)
7. MDA, the Model Driven Architecture. http://www.omg.org/mda/
8. Papyrus tool from CEA. http://www.eclipse.org/papyrus/

9. Meyer, J., Ball, M., Baras, J., Chowdhury, A., Lin, E., Nau, D., Trichur, V.: Process planning in microwave module production. In: 1998 Artificial Intelligence and Manufacturing: State of the Art and State of Practice (1998)
10. Apvrille, L.: TTool for DIPLODOCUS: an environment for design space exploration. In: Proceedings of the 8th International Conference on New Technologies in Distributed Systems, p. 28. ACM (2008)
11. Coit, D.W., Smith, A.E.: Optimization approaches to the redundancy allocation problem for series-parallel systems. In: 4th Industrial Engineering Research Conference Proceedings, pp. 342–349. Citeseer (1995)
12. Limbourg, P., Kochs, H.D.: Multi-objective optimization of generalized reliability design problems using feature models—a concept for early design stages. Reliab. Eng. Syst. Saf. **93** (6), 815–828 (2008). Elsevier, Amsterdam
13. Brailsford, S.C., Potts, C.N., Smith, B.M.: Constraint satisfaction problems: algorithms and applications. Eur. J. Oper. Res. **119**(3), 557–581 (1999). Elsevier, Amsterdam
14. Niemeyer, G.: Python-constraint. http://labix.org/doc/constraint/
15. Schamai, W., Fritzson, P., Paredis, C., Pop, A.: Towards unified system modeling and simulation with ModelicaML: modeling of executable behavior using graphical notations. In: Proceedings 7th Modelica Conference, Como (2009)
16. Mathews, J.H., Fink, K.D.: Numerical Methods Using MATLAB, vol. 31. Prentice Hall, Upper Saddle River (1999)
17. Karp, R.M.: Reducibility among combinatorial problems. In: Miller, R.E. (ed.) Complexity of Computer Computations, pp. 85–103. Springer, Berlin (1972)

Knowledge Modeling in the Health Care Domain: Capturing Semantics to Bridge the Gap Between Complex Data Models and Object Models

Thomas Reichherzer$^{(\boxtimes)}$, John Coffey, Bilal Gonen, and Irad Gillett

Department of Computer Science, University of West Florida, 11000 University Pkw., Pensacola, FL 32503, USA

{treichherzer,jcoffey,bgonen}@uwf.edu, ipg2@students.uwf.edu

Abstract. This article contains a description of a knowledge elicitation effort and representation pertaining to the modeling of conceptual knowledge in the health care field. The project has the goal of building a conceptual model of data in the Military Health System Data Repository, a large DoD/VA aggregation of databases that can be used in the implementation of software. The goal is to create a just-in-time conceptual model of the data to facilitate software development and foster software developer understanding of the domain.

Keywords: Knowledge modeling · Concept mapping · Software engineering · Health information systems

1 Introduction

Health care information systems play a critical role in providing information about patients, insurers, and service providers. Modern systems have become huge, complex, and difficult-to-understand with no real consistency in the use or meanings of the vocabularies that describe the health care data. Better integration among health care systems is critical to the goals of cost containment and improved health care delivery. With vast amount of health care data becoming accessible it is important that the transmitted data are well understood by end users and machines in order to support decision making and automatic processing respectively.

Concept mapping [1] is a proven technology that helps people express and visualize their knowledge [2–4]. Concept maps are graphical representations of propositional knowledge based upon concepts and linking phrases that make explicit the relationships between concept pairs. The goal of this project was to develop a knowledge model using concept mapping [4–6] as a means to capture domain knowledge pertaining to the concept of "health care provider" as a proof-of-concept to show that:

1. a concept map-based knowledge model can be an effective tool to develop a domain vocabulary that describes data streams and services generated by health care systems,

P. Desfray et al. (Eds.): MODELSWARD 2015, CCIS 580, pp. 328–338, 2015.
DOI: 10.1007/978-3-319-27869-8_19

2. an improved understanding on data models can assist software developers to build and maintain integrated systems that can deliver desired services to end users.

The remainder of this paper contains a brief review of literature pertaining to concept mapping and knowledge modeling, and a description of the research. Included in the research description is the motivation for the work, the activities and results that have been achieved to date, and a scheme to assess the utility of the work to the sponsors of the project. The paper closes with a description of anticipated future work.

2   Concept Mapping and Knowledge Modeling

Concept maps represent knowledge as a two-dimensional graph capturing concepts and their relationships on a specific topic. In this graph, concepts are visualized as labeled nodes and relationships as labeled links. A concept can be a word or phrase that describes a perceived regularity in events or objects, or records of events or objects [1]. A labeled link is comprised of any word or phrase so that the two concepts connected by a link give rise to a meaningful statement about the concepts. Such a statement is also known as a proposition or a semantic unit that captures human knowledge on a specific topic. For example, the proposition "humans require food" is comprised of two concepts, "humans" and "food", and the linking phrase "require". Fully developed concept maps include a cohesive set of concepts and their relationships to address a specific question that focuses the discussion in the map. Furthermore, a single concept at the top of the map known as the root concept serves as a starting point to explore the captured knowledge of the map.

Concept maps elucidate an individual's conceptualization on a domain, which can be useful to track the individual's learning progress. Novak *et al.* [1, 3] originally conceived of Concept Maps as a means to externalize conceptual knowledge of science students in service of uncovering what they knew, as well as misapprehensions they held. Subsequently, several groups have embraced Concept Mapping for knowledge elicitation (KE). McNeese *et al.* [7, 8] used Concept Maps to externalize expert knowledge over a variety of knowledge domains. These included the expertise of pilots regarding their decision-making strategies and to create conceptual designs of cockpits, and that of managers, for internal information management systems and procedures. Novak and Gowin [1] described knowledge elicitation with Concept Maps as a means of idea generation in groups of people. Beyond the use of concept maps as a learning and teaching tool, successful applications of concept mapping include institutional memory preservation [4, 5], sharing of domain expertise for public outreach [2], visualization of artifacts in Service-Oriented Architecture (SOA) composite applications [9], and representation of software security assurance cases [10].

Electronic concept mapping offers the prospect of connecting concept maps via navigational links and annotating concepts with multimedia resources such as video clips, images, and links to Web sites to provide additional information and examples on the concepts in a map. A set of closely-related and interconnected concept maps and their multi-media resources are organized into a knowledge model [11–13], a hypermedia representation of domain knowledge. CmapTools [14] is a publicly available software tool for creating knowledge models and publishing them on the Web for knowledge sharing purposes. It offers special drawing and labeling operations for constructing maps as well as a suite of tools for annotating nodes in a map with multimedia resources or links to other concept maps in the same knowledge model. Cmap-Tools is extensively used for research involving concept maps and, generally, as a learning and teaching tool by teachers and students alike [15].

Snider *et al.* [10] describe a study in which concept maps were elicited as a means of efficiently developing security assurance cases. They describe a two-phase process based upon concept map-based knowledge elicitation and modeling. In the first phase, the security expert performs the preliminary work with a KE to identify the critical security concerns, creating a "skeleton" concept map containing nodes for each critical concern. In the second phase, the security expert and KE interview the software developers who demonstrates how he or she has addressed those security concerns. In the process, the skeleton concept map from the first phase is elaborated to document program files, other documentation, and other application responsibilities (such as the server software being configured to produce logs) that address the concerns. The concept map of the software assurance case is augmented with links to the actual files that address the security concerns.

3   The Research Project

Creating knowledge models typically involves a domain expert and knowledge engineers interviewing the expert, eliciting his/her knowledge, and representing it as concept maps (a concise, unambiguous format). The goal of the current project is to conduct a case study that answers questions regarding how knowledge elicitation of domain knowledge via concept mapping might be useful to assist software developers in creating data definitions for programs in an efficient manner. For the project, a new knowledge model was built to help understand the semantics of a complex data model of an actual Department of Defense (DOD) medical information system. The model was then used to develop data type definitions in the form of UML diagrams and Enterprise Java Beans. Software developers and the domain expert evaluated the process and artifacts that were produced for this case study for usability and completeness.

Motivation for the project comes from the fact that bottlenecks in communication between the domain expert and software developers threaten the timely development of software. The communication problem comes from the differences in expertise between the software developers and domain expert and the inherent complexity and ambiguity of the medical domain in general. Medical terms that label data in health care systems lack standardization, requiring interpretation for proper use. The domain expert has deep knowledge about the data and their origin and application in the medical field, while the software engineer understands how to organize data into logical units for efficient access and processing. There is a tremendous amount of information that has to be exchanged to capture and understand data used in health care information systems. The lack of knowledge of the software engineer about the domain makes the interpretation of data models very difficult. A concept map-based knowledge model can be an effective tool to develop a domain vocabulary that describes data stored in complex data models. We attempt to show that concept maps can be an effective vehicle for communication between the domain expert and software engineer, giving the engineer relevant information to interpret the data from the data models, alleviating the knowledge gap between software engineer and domain expert. In addition, the possible reuse of built maps may help in breaking down bottlenecks in communication.

4   Research Methods

Researchers collaborated with a domain expert who understood the Military Health System Data Repository (MDR) along with its associated databases. The MDR is a "centralized data repository that captures, archives, validates, integrates and distributes Defense Health Agency (DHA) corporate health care data worldwide." [16] The MDR is comprised of more than 95 database tables, each with 50 to 300 attributes, keeping health care records to support 9.6 million military and related beneficiaries world-wide.

The current case study involves information retrieval pertaining to providers. The provider topic is of particular interest to this study because of the ambiguities in the representation of provider information. Two simple but realistic scenarios were created around the general problem of matching patients to providers (e.g. finding a family practitioner or finding a surgeon and facility). From this initial effort, two use cases for software development were created:

- Use Case 1: *Determine the simple provider workload given the patient history.* Background: The user gives the system a provider name and the system returns the workload of that provider. The system answers the question: What work load does a given provider have with his current enrollment panels?
- Use Case 2: *Given the workloads of the members of a group of providers, assign a patient to a provider.* Background: The user gives the system patient name and pertinent other information (geographic location, health care needs, personal preferences, etc.) and the system recommends a physician in a way that balances physician workload. Patients might need to be assigned to a new provider because they have not yet seen a provider in the area due to relocation, the previous provider leaving the network, etc.

One-sentence summaries of the use cases were recast as focus questions (a question intended to keep the concept map creation effort focused on one particular topic so as to avoid inclusion of extraneous information). A concept map-based knowledge elicitation effort aimed at building conceptual models of data from the MDR was completed. The goal of this activity was to provide the necessary knowledge to understand a small subset of data from the MDR that are relevant for the implementation of the use cases. The output of this phase was three concept maps providing a semantic description of relevant data in the MDR database. Concepts in the maps were annotated with links to the MDR database schema to identify the relevant data for the use cases.

After the knowledge model was developed, the software developers set about creating UML diagrams and Java beans to implement the use cases. An initial goal was to link the Java beans back to the knowledge models and the use cases from which they were created. This was to be achieved by including URLs and a list of relevant concepts at the top of each bean referring to the Web-exported concept map. The software developers presented questions about the information in the knowledge model to the domain expert and the KE for clarification. A transcript was used to capture ongoing conversations among these participants.

5   Data Analysis

A goal of the initial modeling attempt was to determine what information was needed in the concept maps in order to: (1) identify and link to data elements in the MDR that were needed to develop the software described by the use cases, (2) provide conceptual information to help developers understand the application domain, (3) identify base elements that might be in a skeleton concept map for such data modeling activities. The initial knowledge modeling effort produced a total of three concept maps, two concept maps for Use Case 1 and one additional concept map for Use Case 2. The concept map developed for Use Case 2 links back to the concepts maps produced for Use Case 1 taking advantage of prior elicited knowledge. Figure 1 illustrates the relationships among the use cases and the three concept maps.

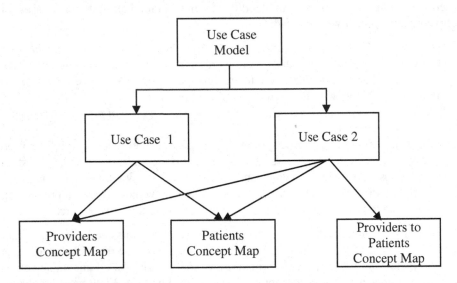

Fig. 1.   The relationships among the use cases and the concept maps.

Concept maps for each use case were built over two 1-hour modeling sessions that produced progressively more refined maps. The resulting concept maps for Use Case 1 had an average of 16 concepts and 17 connections and for Use Case 2 a total of 15 concepts and 16 connections. The initial concept maps were further revised in a follow-up knowledge modeling session after deficiencies in the elicited knowledge were identified during the creation of Java Beans by the software developers. The revised maps increased in size by an average of 10 concepts and 8 connections for Use Case 1 and by 4 concepts and 7 connections for Use Case 2. Figure 2 shows one of the three concept maps from the knowledge model created for Use Case 2. Figure 3 shows a portion of a concept map developed for Use Case 1.

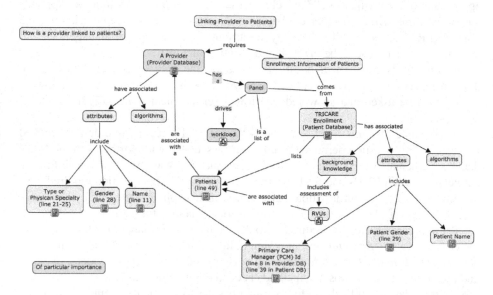

Fig. 2. A concept map from the knowledge model describing how providers are linked to patients.

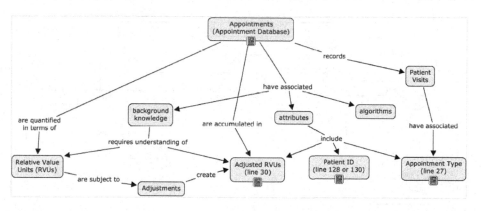

Fig. 3. An excerpt of a larger concept map created for Use Case 1 with links into the MDA.

In the course of the knowledge modeling effort several conventions were developed. The first was to indicate when nodes in the concept map pertain to databases. Such a node can be seen at the top of Fig. 2, "TRICARE Enrollment (Patient Database)." The icon at the bottom of that node links to a database schema that describes all elements of that table in the MDR, the element's data type and format, and some explanatory information.

When specific elements within the database were identified as necessary to the data definitions in the use case, their line numbers were indicated in the concept map. For instance, "Adjusted RVUs," seen at the bottom of the concept map in Fig. 3, is an important field pertaining to the amount of credit the physician receives for handling an appointment. The "Adjusted RVUs" element is found on line 30 within the Appointments database. The remainder of the concept map contains conceptual knowledge regarding RVUs, specifically, that they are assigned on the basis of management and procedure codes that describe the type and duration of a visit.

As previously mentioned, questions asked by the software developers and the domain expert's answers were captured. Analysis reveals that two general categories of questions were asked and answered: (1) low-level technical issues, (2) higher level conceptual issues.

An example of a low-level question is "What kind of data value does Num(5,3) describe?" This question pertained to notations associated with attributes in the MDR database schema. An example of a high-level question was "What is the difference between Adjusted RVUs and RVUs in the concept map?" This question required clarification of conceptual information that was not made explicit in the initial knowledge model. A total of 11 questions and answers were exchanged for the two use cases.

The software developers produced initially a total of three classes to address the two use cases: *Provider*, *Appointment*, and *Patient*. In addition to the three classes, a manager class named *ProviderPatientManagement* was created to manage providers, patients, and appointments and to host the methods needed to implement the use cases (to determine a provider's workload and to assign a provider to a patient). Figure 4 contains a UML diagram produced on the basis of the knowledge modeling activity.

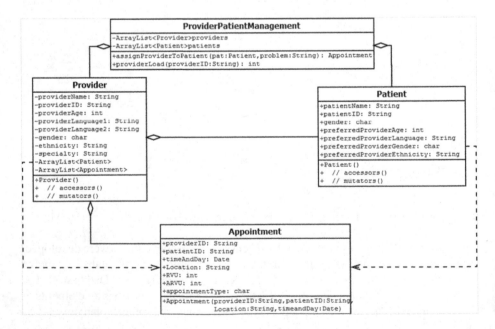

Fig. 4. UML diagram of the classes derived from the knowledge model.

The *ProviderPatientManagement* class is composed of providers and patients and that relationship is indicated in the UML. The *Provider* class is composed of patients and appointments. The *Appointment* class depends upon the *Provider* and *Patient* classes with the dependencies indicated in the diagram. The attributes declared in the *Provider*, *Patient* and *Appointment* classes all came from the knowledge model. No attempt was made to define utility methods or classes that might be needed in implementing the use cases since the focus in this study is on basic data definitions.

The domain expert (who in our case also has knowledge of software development) was asked to judge the quality of the data definitions according to the following criteria:

1. All necessary data is defined to address the use case *or*
2. Some data is missing *and*:
   (a) the elements were missing from the conceptual model or,
   (b) the elements were in the conceptual model but not made explicit enough for the software developers to notice them or,
   (c) the elements were included in the conceptual model, made explicit, but simply missed by the software developers.

The domain expert judged the data definitions to be sufficient for Use Case 1. However, for Use Case 2, the software developers had created two attributes that were not part of the conceptual model, due to a somewhat idiosyncratic approach to the implementation of containers for the Patient and Provider classes. However, all needed (and specified) attributes were present both in the conceptual model and in the data definitions produced by the software developers. Accordingly, the knowledge modeling work proved to be sufficient to define data definitions in UML and Java Beans. Although beyond the scope of the current work, the knowledge model would also prove sufficient to form necessary queries to populate instances of the Java Beans that would implement the use cases, as depicted in Fig. 5.

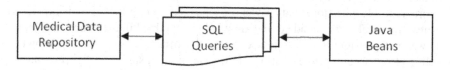

Fig. 5. SQL Queries tying together the MDR to the Java Beans.

6   Related Work

The work described in this paper proposes a new process to support software development and maintenance. It applies concept mapping to capture semantic information of selected health care concepts in a just-in-time knowledge modeling effort to address questions related to new use cases. The captured domain knowledge provides context for interpreting information in large-scale, complex health care data models. This work differs from a number of other approaches discussed in the literature that use conceptual modeling techniques for system development. Widely used conceptual modeling techniques are the

Extended Entity Relationship (EER), the Unified Modeling Language (UML), and variations of it [17]. They produce visual data models directly from the narrative of a business
use case as abstractions of real-world phenomena of interest. In all cases a specific
language must be used to translate the mental representation of a problem domain into a
physical diagram. However, as several authors have pointed out in their research [18, 19],
experience in building models, domain expertise, and expressiveness of the modeling
language can have a significant effect on the modeling outcome and the usefulness of the
resulting model for system development. In contrast, concept mapping requires little
training experience for building models and interpreting them. It allows a domain experts
to participate in and shape the modeling effort eliminating the need for the software developers as the model builder to have knowledge of the modeling domain or perform interpretation of a narrative that could introduce ambiguity or errors into the model.

In more closely related work, concept mapping has been used to efficiently develop
security assurance cases in which pre-built maps were used to facilitate and structure
ongoing conversations between software developers and security experts and build
comprehensive knowledge models on security assurance cases [10]. The resulting maps
provide evidence as a set of statements and annotations that the software product meets
the necessary security requirements prior to its release. However, in the current work
concept mapping was used to capture relevant semantic information about health care
data from a domain expert that is needed by the software developers to create new data
definitions and algorithms for processing health care data and develop new services.

7   Conclusions

Several conclusions can be drawn from the current work. First and most important, it
was possible to develop the data definitions from the models. An evaluation of the data
definitions produced by the software developers revealed that all attributes needed to
implement the Use Cases were present. This result was achieved with a minimal amount
of information (11 questions and answers) exchanged among the domain expert, KEs
and software developers outside of the knowledge contained in the conceptual model.

It was not possible to calibrate accurately the time efficiency of the knowledge
modeling effort because quite a bit of initial time was consumed in figuring out what
elements should be in a baseline map and how to make the data items in the MDR explicit
in the concept maps. Now that these elements are known, future work can include an
evaluation of efficiency.

Some conclusions can be drawn regarding the effectiveness of the representation.
As evidenced by the questions exchanged among the domain expert, KEs and software
developers, the initial knowledge models failed to convey some information both of a
high-level, conceptual nature and low-level technical nature. No significant effort was
made to address the latter problem. However, KE and domain expert conducted a follow-
up knowledge modeling session to address the issue of missing conceptual, high-level
information in the initial model, which enabled the software developers to complete the
data definitions for the two use cases. While it seems unavoidable that some conceptual
knowledge of interest to the developers might be missed, given the limited amount of
time devoted to knowledge elicitation in this study, it would likely have occurred in any

representation. The representation used here is well known to be more concise and less ambiguous than textual descriptions. Further, on the basis of the exchanges between the domain expert and the developers it can be determined that, while gaps in the model's conceptual knowledge representations existed, the developers at least knew the right questions to ask.

Acknowledgements. Partial funding for this project was provided by Blue-Cross Blue-Shield through the Security and Software Engineering Research Center (http://www.serc.net).

References

1. Novak, J., Gowin, D.: Learning How to Learn. Cambridge University Press, New York (1984)
2. Briggs, G., Shamma, D., Cañas, A.J., Scargle, J., Novak, J.D.: Concept maps applied to Mars exploration public outreach. In: Cañas, A.J., Novak, J.D., González, F. (eds.) Concept Maps: Theory, Methodology, Technology. Proceedings of the First International Conference on Concept Mapping, pp. 125–133, Pamplona, Spain. (2004)
3. Novak, J.D., Musonda, D.: A twelve-year longitudinal study of science concept learning. Am. Educ. Res. J. **28**(1), 117–153 (1991)
4. Coffey, J.W., Eskridge, T.: Case studies of knowledge modeling for knowledge preservation and sharing in the U.S. nuclear power industry. J. Inf. Knowl. Manage. **7**(3), 173–185 (2008)
5. Coffey, J.W., Hoffman, R.R., Cañas, A.J.: Concept map-based knowledge modeling: perspectives from information and knowledge visualization. Inf. Vis. **5**, 192–201 (2006)
6. Turns, J., Atman, C.J., Adams, R.: Concept maps for engineering education: a cognitive motivated tool supporting varied assessment functions. IEEE Trans. Educ. **43**(2), 164–173 (2000)
7. McNeese, M., Zaff, B.S., Brown, C.E., Citera, M., Selvaraj, J.: Understanding the context of multidisciplinary design: establishing ecological validity in the study of design problem solving. In: Proceedings of the 37th Annual Meeting of the Human Factors Society, Santa Monica, CA, pp. 1082–1086 (1993)
8. McNeese, M., Zaff, B.S., Citera, M., Brown, C.E., Whitaker, R.: AKADAM: eliciting user knowledge to support participatory ergonomics. Int. J. Ind. Ergon. **15**, 345–363 (1995)
9. Coffey, J., Reichherzer, T., Wilde, N., Owsnicki-Klewe, B.: Automated concept-map generation from service-oriented architecture artifacts. In: Proceedings of the 5th International Conference on Concept Mapping, Valetta, Malta (2012)
10. Snider, D., Coffey, J., Reichherzer, T., Wilde, N., Terry, C., Vandeville, J., Heinen, A., Pramanik, S.: Using concept maps to introduce software security assurance cases. CrossTalk J. Defense Softw. Eng. **27**(5), 4–9 (2014)
11. Ford, K.M., Cañas, A.J., Jones, J., Stahl, H., Novak, J., Adams-Webber, J.: ICONKAT: an integrated constructivist knowledge acquisition tool. Knowl. Acquisition **3**, 215–236 (1991)
12. Ford, K.M., Cañas, A.J., Coffey, J.W.: Participatory explanation. In: Proceedings of the Sixth Florida Artificial Intelligence Research Symposium, Ft. Lauderdale, FL, pp. 111–115 (1993)
13. Ford, K.M., Bradshaw, J.M.: Beyond the repertory grid: new approaches to constructivist knowledge acquisition tool development. Int. J. Intell. Syst. **8**, 287–333 (1995)
14. Cañas, A.J., Hill, G., Carff, R., Suri, N., Lott, J., Eskridge, T., Gómez, G., Arroyo, M., Carvajal, R.: CmapTools: a knowledge modeling and sharing environment. In: Cañas, A.J., Novak, J.D., González, F. (eds.) Concept Maps: Theory, Methodology, Technology. Proceedings of the First International Conference on Concept Mapping, Pamplona, Spain (2004)
15. Walker, J.M.T., King, P.H.: Concept mapping as a form of student assessment and instruction. In: Proceedings of the 2002 ASEE Annual Conference and Exposition (2002)

16. Health.Mil, The Official website of the Military Health System and Defense Health Agency. http://www.health.mil/Military-Health-Topics/Technology/Clinical-Support/Military-Health-System-Data-Repository
17. Combi, C., Oliboni, B.: Conceptual modeling of XML data. In: Proceedings of the 2006 ACM Symposium on Applied Computing, Dijon, France (2006)
18. Aguirre-Urreta, M., Marakas, G.M.: Comparing conceptual modeling techniques: a critical review of the EER vs OO empirical literature. DATA BASE Adv. Inf. Syst. **39**(2), 9–32 (2008)
19. Castro, L., Baião, F., Guizzardi, G.: A semantic oriented method for conceptual data modeling in OntoUML based on linguistic concepts. In: Jeusfeld, M., Delcambre, L., Ling, T.-W. (eds.) ER 2011. LNCS, vol. 6998, pp. 486–494. Springer, Heidelberg (2011)

The Interface-Modular Method for Global System Behaviour Specification

Urooj Fatima[✉] and Rolv Bræk

Department of Telematics, Norwegian University of Science and Technology (NTNU),
Trondheim, Norway
{urooj,rolv.braek}@item.ntnu.no

Abstract. Traditionally, the global behaviour of distributed reactive systems has been considered hard to specify completely, and therefore many details are left to the designers to decide. The challenge addressed in this paper is how this situation can be improved. Is it possible to specify the global behaviour of distributed reactive systems in a way which eases comprehension of the system without compromising the specification's correctness, completeness, modularity and readability? Instead of defining the global behaviour models in a monolithic way, we approach the problem by decomposing the specification into interface functionality and core functionality. The resulting interface-modular method for system specification is presented and discussed in this paper using a *TaxiCentral* as case study. The novelty of this method lies in the clear separation of interfaces from core functionality, and the use of activity diagrams in combination with collaborations to express and compose the specifications. Given a set of core functionality and interface functionalities, the core functionality and interface functionalities are composed into a specification of the complete global behaviour. The prospects for automatic design synthesis from such a specification are discussed.

Keywords: Model-driven Engineering · Behaviour specification · Interface behaviour · Activity diagrams

1 Introduction

Normally in system development, after requirements have been captured and analysed, the desired system behaviour is first specified from a global, cross-cutting, perspective involving several entities and then mapped to a design structure of components with precisely defined local component behaviours. The global behaviour emerging from the joint local component behaviours shall of course correspond to the specified global behaviour. Such correspondence can be assured in two ways: (1) by a process of verification, that is verifying after a design has been developed, that the local behaviours of the designed components are in accordance with the specification; or (2) by a process of design synthesis (transformation) whereby the local designs are derived from specifications in such a manner that correctness is guaranteed. Most current system design

© Springer International Publishing Switzerland 2015
P. Desfray et al. (Eds.): MODELSWARD 2015, CCIS 580, pp. 339–355, 2015.
DOI: 10.1007/978-3-319-27869-8_20

methods follow the first approach because fully automated design synthesis has not been practically feasible. There are two main reasons for this:

a. it is normally very difficult and/or impractical to completely specify global behaviours.
b. the global behaviour emerging from a direct mapping to a distributed design may contain undesired behaviours that follow from the nature of a distributed design and not from the specification itself. This kind of behaviour, sometimes referred to as implied scenarios, is the cause of so-called realizability problems.

In order to solve problem 'b' mentioned above it is necessary that all realizability problems can be identified and resolved as part of the design synthesis process. In [8] the authors provide a classification of the various causes of such problems and explain how problems can be detected on the level of global behaviour and subsequently resolved during design. Based on this foundation [12] has proposed some refinements to the analysis while [10, 14] presented a method for design synthesis using activity diagrams for both global (source) and local (target) behaviour where the resulting local behaviour is in a form of activity diagrams that can be subject to extensive analysis before generating product quality (Java) code using a tool called Reactive Blocks [19]. Thus, there is now a systematic way to overcome problem 'b' and principal solutions to enable highly automated design synthesis.

In this paper, we focus on problem 'a' mentioned above - how to achieve the necessary completeness, rigour and modularity in global behaviour specifications to enable highly automatic design synthesis in practice?

Sequence diagrams of some sort are probably the most used notations for global behaviour. They define behaviour in terms of interactions taking place among different components of a system and/or its environment, either in the form of asynchronous message passing or in the form of synchronous invocations. They are well suited for specifications since they consider systems and components from the outside and describe only their externally visible behaviour. Purely sequential behaviours are easy to specify completely using sequence diagrams. It is concurrency that causes problems. The service provided by a distributed reactive system normally involves several concurrent parts. The number of possible and relevant interaction orderings is then often beyond what is practically feasible to specify, and therefore completeness is not achieved. The general countermeasure for this kind of problem is to factor out concurrency and thereby reduce the number of interaction orderings needed to be represented in a complete specification. Rather than considering cross-cutting service behaviours involving many concurrent parts, the complexity can be reduced by considering only one interface connecting two parts at the time. This interface may possibly be decomposed further into smaller and more manageable sub-behaviours. Such decomposition is well supported by UML 2 collaborations as we shall see in the following. However, the resulting separately defined interface behaviours are normally not sufficient to fully define the services. The remaining problem is to model the dependencies and global ordering among the interface behaviours.

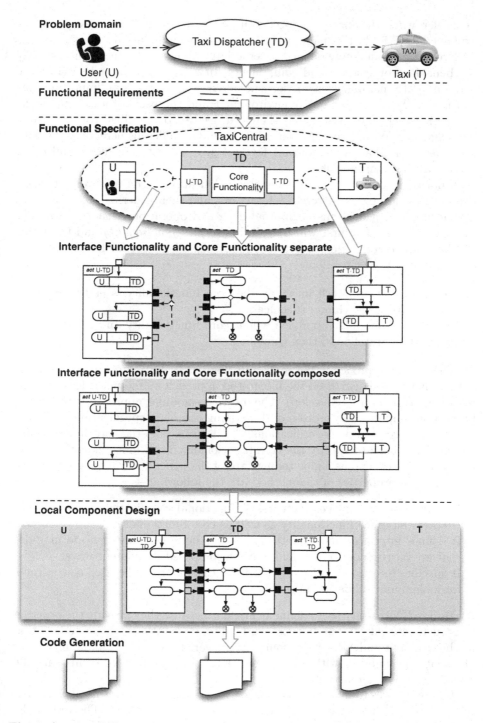

Fig. 1. An overall illustration of the proposed method. 'Functional Specification' is the focus of this paper.

In earlier work this has been accomplished using a global choreography as explained in [7,8]. In this paper we present a different solution.

Even when completely defined, interactions are not sufficient to fully specify the behaviour of systems and components. In many systems and services the data and data manipulation carried out by the system plays an important role and is equally important to the environment and the users of a system as the interactions across interfaces and therefore need to be specified to fully define the behaviour. We are not considering internal design details here, only the data and operations that are important for and give value to end users and other entities in the environment.

From this we assert that a complete specification needs to cover (at least) two related aspects: the external interactions and their ordering; and the information processing in terms of internal data and operations that give value to the environment. The first will be called *interface functionality* and the latter will be called *core functionality* in the following. There are (at least) two ways to organise such specifications:

1. the integrated approach in which the core functionality is embedded with interactions in one (large) specification,
2. the interface-modular approach where core functionality and interfaces are specified separately and then combined.

The second approach is the topic and main contribution of this paper (The authors have previously used the integrated approach and found it feasible, but hard and error prone to develop). The interface-modular approach is promising because it simplifies the process of developing complete specifications and also results in more modular specifications. As it turns out, the core functionality models serve both to specify the core functionality itself independently of particular interfaces, and as a glue taking care of the dependency among interfaces.

The main properties of the method are the following:

− It simplifies achieving completeness in functional specifications.
− It covers interface functionality as well as core functionality.
− It defines interface functionality and core functionality in separate modules that are partly independent and may be composed in different ways.
− It specifies interface behaviours in a form that later can be used as contracts for lookup and validation purposes.

We use UML activities to define behaviour because they provide the ordering constructs needed for our purpose and allow us to stay within one notation for both global and local behaviours. Moreover, they support building blocks of variable granularity with well defined interfaces suitable for composing the interfaces and core functionality.

Figure 1 serves to illustrate the approach in terms of a *TaxiCentral* that shall be used as a running example throughout the rest of the paper. The rest of the paper is organized as follows. The functional requirements of the *TaxiCentral* are presented in Sect. 2. In Sect. 3, we present the interface-modular method by explaining the guidelines and applying them on the *TaxiCentral*. Section 4 explains our method validation. We discuss related work in Sect. 5 and conclude in Sect. 6.

2   Functional Requirements

Functional requirements normally contain an informal textual specification of the core functionality (in terms of events, data and operations).

In the *TaxiCentral*, *Users* can book *Taxis* by placing taxi-booking requests to a *TaxiDispatcher*. *Taxis* inform the *TaxiDispatcher* about their availability. The *TaxiDispatcher* keeps an overview of available *Taxis* and assigns *Taxis* to *Users* as fairly as possible. Once a *Taxi* is assigned to a *User*, it can establish a voice session with the *User*. Clearly the core functionality needs to keep track of available *Taxis* and requesting *Users*, and assign *Taxis* to *Users* according to some queue discipline. Hence, it will need to hold a queue of available *Taxis* and a queue of requesting *Users*[1]. The precise queue discipline to use is clearly an important part of requirements and specification, that must be determined in cooperation with stake holders.

The *TaxiDispatcher* is driven by events generated by users and taxis and communicated across the interfaces as messages represented by the tokens in the activity diagrams. The functional requirements given below are organized according to the external events and specify the actions to be taken in response. Italicized items represent important domain entities and data. Italicized bold items represent important domain events.

A. ***TaxiRequest:*** The *User* initiates a taxi-booking request by sending a request to the *TaxiDispatcher*. As a result, either of the following two responses shall be generated:

   A1. ***TaxiAssign:*** If a *Taxi* is available, the *Taxi* shall be taken out of the *taxi queue* by the *TaxiDispatcher* and assigned to the *User*.

   A2. ***UserWait:*** If a *Taxi* is not available, the *User* shall be entered in a *user queue* and receive wait notification from the *TaxiDispatcher*, indicating the position in queue.

B. ***TaxiAvailable:*** The *Taxi* updates its availability status to the *TaxiDispatcher*. As a result, either of the following two responses shall be generated:

   B1. ***UserAssign:*** If a *User* is waiting in the *user queue*, the *User* shall be taken out of the *user queue* and assigned to the available *Taxi*.

   B2. ***TaxiWait:*** If no *User* is waiting in the *user queue*, the *TaxiDispatcher* shall insert the *Taxi* reference in a *taxi queue* and send wait notification to the *Taxi*. The *Taxi* may receive its queue position.

C. ***UserWithdraw:*** The *User* can withdraw its request while waiting in the *user queue*. Its reference shall then be removed from the queue by the *TaxiDispatcher*.

---

[1] The data structures needed may not necessarily be queues, but we refer to them as queues here for simplicity.

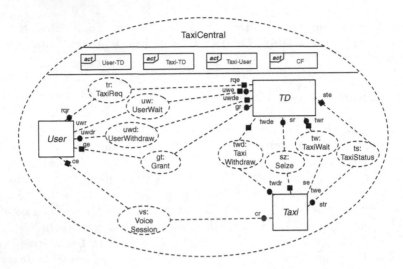

Fig. 2. UML collaboration diagram showing roles and collaboration uses in interfaces of *TaxiCentral* service.

D. ***TaxiWithdraw:*** The *Taxi* can withdraw while waiting in the *taxi queue*. The *TaxiDispatcher* shall then remove its reference from the *taxi queue*.

The *TaxiCentral* is not a trivial example since it has to deal with: (1) the multiplicity of taxis and users; (2) the queues and other data needed in order to coordinate users and taxis; (3) all the possible ways that events generated by taxis and users may interleave.

3 Functional Specification

We consider a service generally as a collaborative behaviour that may involve several components and more than one interface. In the interface-modular method, a service provided by a distributed reactive system is specified in four steps: (1) the service structure is defined using UML collaboration diagrams; (2) the interface functionality is defined using UML activity diagrams; (3) the core functionality is defined using UML activity diagrams; (4) the interface and core functionality is connected. Each of these steps are illustrated in this section using the *TaxiCentral*.

3.1 Service Structure

The method guidelines for creating the service structure (SS) are as follows:

SS1: *Use UML collaboration diagrams to define the structure of a service.*
SS2: *Identify the participants and interfaces of the service from the functional requirements document. Represent the participants as roles in the collaboration diagram.*

SS3: *Decompose the service behaviour into collaboration-uses, where each collaboration-use encapsulates the interactions needed to carry a domain event mentioned in the requirements.*

SS4: *Bind the roles of each collaboration-use to the roles of the main collaboration.*

SS5: *Indicate the initiating role of each collaboration-use with a filled circle and the terminating role with a filled square[2].*

SS6: *Add references to activity diagrams that will define the core functionality and the behaviours of the interfaces identified in 'SS2' (detailed in Sect. 3.2).*

By inspecting the functional requirements given in Sect. 2, three main roles are identified in the *TaxiCentral*: the *User*, the *Taxi* and the *TD* (*TaxiDispatcher*). Likewise, three interfaces are identified namely: *User-TD*, *Taxi-TD* and *Taxi-User*. The UML collaboration diagram of *TaxiCentral* is shown in Fig. 2. Each collaboration-use, for instance *TaxiReq*, *UserWait*, etc. encapsulates interactions needed to carry the events of the *TaxiCentral*. The decomposition of collaborations into roles and collaboration-uses is one important step towards mastering complexity. Each elementary[3] collaboration involves only two roles and has a limited complexity making a complete definition of its behaviour practically feasible.

3.2   Interface Functionality

The method guidelines for interface functionality (IF) are as follows:

IF1: *Develop activity diagrams of each interface identified in 'SS2' and referenced in 'SS6'.*

IF2: *Map the domain events, related to an interface, from the requirements to pins[4] on the boundary of that interface activity. The name of a pin should correspond to a particular event.*

IF3: *Add a 'CallBehaviourAction' for each collaboration-use performed on the interface.*

IF4: *Add partitions on each 'CallBehaviourAction' to indicate the participating roles. Mark the initiating and terminating roles with filled circles and squares, respectively.*

IF5: *Make flows and activity nodes to define the ordering of the CallBehaviourActions identified in 'IF3' that can be enforced locally in the interface. This may include interrupting regions and interrupting flows, forks, joins, merges, choices and other elements of UML activities.*

---

[2] Filled circles and squares are not standard UML notations, but can be provided by profiling. They represent information needed during subsequent behaviour analysis and design synthesis.

[3] We consider collaborations that are not further decomposed as elementary collaborations.

[4] The activity diagrams can have all types of pins that UML allows, i.e. initiating, terminating, streaming and alternative pins.

IF6: *For the ordering that is enforced externally, make flows to and from the corresponding pins.*

IF7: *Represent external dependencies using external flows connected to the external pins of the activity. External flows represent the external dependency on 'data', 'events' and 'flows' performed by external activities connected through the pins. Flow dependencies are represented by dashed flow-lines and nodes. Data dependency is represented by dashed choices and event dependency by dashed receive event actions, as illustrated in Fig. 3.*

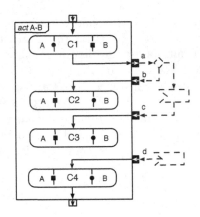

Fig. 3. Modelling of external flows that represents *data*, *event* and *flow* dependencies.

The resulting interface functionality models for the *TaxiCentral* are depicted in Fig. 4. Note that an interruptible region and interrupting flows have been used to specify that the *UserWait* collaboration-use shall be terminated when a *Taxi* becomes available or the *User* withdraws. The interruptible activity region is depicted by a dashed rectangle.

The dashed external flows in Fig. 4 represent essentially how the responses to incoming events shall be ordered by the core functionality depending on its data and events on the other interface. In the *TaxiCentral*, the arrival of an available *Taxi* on the *Taxi-TD* interface shall lead to actions on the *User-TD* interface, taking the user out of queue and assigning the *Taxi* if there is a waiting *User*. This case of *event dependency* is taken care of by the input pin *TaxiAvailable* connected with an event reception symbol on the *User-TD* interface. A corresponding event therefore has to be generated by the core functionality, or received on the *Taxi-TD* interface.

The case of combined data and event dependency does not exist in this *TaxiCentral* example. This case of dependency represents the situation when responses to events on one interface depend on both the data of the core functionality and events occuring on another interface. For instance, suppose it is required by the *TaxiCentral* to allow the available *Taxis* to accept and reject the

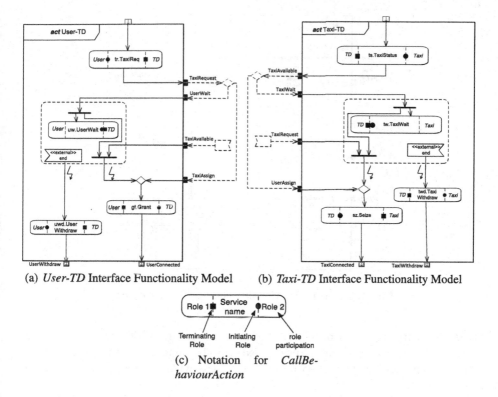

(a) *User-TD* Interface Functionality Model   (b) *Taxi-TD* Interface Functionality Model

(c) Notation for *CallBehaviourAction*

Fig. 4. Interface functionality models of *TaxiCentral*.

assignment of a *User* (a tour). If a *Taxi* is available, the core functionality of the *TaxiCentral* will forward the request to the *Taxi-TD* interface and depending on the accept/reject event on the *Taxi-TD* interface the core functionality will respond to the *User-TD* interface. Hence, in this case the core functionality orders the responses to the events on one interface by using the data and capturing the events from other interfaces.

By developing interfaces and core functionality as separate modules, the development task gets decomposed into simpler and more manageable tasks than when developing a complete behaviour monolithically using the integrated approach. Consider the two interfaces presented in Fig. 4 as an example. They are relatively simple and easy to understand even for a non-technical person (with a little explanation) and therefore useful for discussions and validation with end users and other stakeholders. A key to this is the simplified representation of external flow dependencies provided by the (dashed) external flows. They represent and help to understand the essence of external dependencies without needing to go into all the details of actual flows in the rest of the system (the core functionality and other interface functionalities). When later composing the interface functionalities with an actual core functionality, one must validate that the actual core functionality indeed satisfy the external flows required of it.

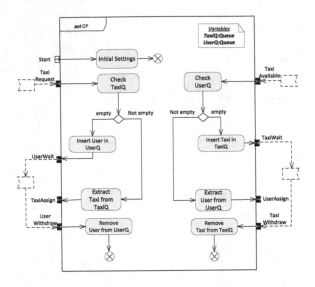

Fig. 5. The core functionality model of *TaxiCentral*.

Hence the external flows provide a key to internal flow validation whereas the interface functionality itself defines an external behaviour contract among components that can be used to validate interfaces when actual components are linked together.

3.3   Modelling the Core Functionality

In most systems the core functionality will be distributed over many components. Hence, it may make sense to define and analyse the core functionality on a global level separately from particular interface functionality. This can be accomplished using activity diagrams where partitions are used to represent components. The so-called swim-lane notation is a well known example of such notation, much used in business process modelling. One might well start without taking distribution into account at all if this is considered useful, and from there gradually introduce partitions and partition boundaries to define distribution. Token flows crossing partition boundaries represent events and information that needs to be carried using interactions in the distributed system. Once the partitions have been identified the core functionality of each component is defined by the part of the activity diagram contained within the corresponding partition with suitable pins added at the edges. For each partition boundary between two components the token flows must be refined to using the corresponding interface functionality with pins to connect to the core functionality in the two components, as illustrated for the Taxi Central in the following.

The method rules for core functionality (CF) are as follows:

CF1: *Define the activity that contains the core functionality of each component by using a UML activity diagram.*

CF2: *Map the domain events from the requirements to streaming pins on the edge of the activity that defines the core functionality. The name of each pin should correspond to the name of an event defined in the requirements.*

CF3: *Define local variables in the activity that can hold the data it shall handle according to the requirements.*

CF4: *For each domain event to be handled (represented by a streaming pin) define an internal activity flow that performs the actions given in the corresponding requirement.*

CF5: *If necessary add pins to start and stop the activity.*

CF6: *Add external flows to the pins to specify external data, event and flow dependencies.*

The resulting core functionality of the *TaxiCentral* is illustrated in Fig. 5. The functional requirements of the *TaxiCentral* given in Sect. 2 tells that the core functionality needs to maintain a user queue (*UserQ*) and a taxi queue (*TaxiQ*) to coordinate multiple users and taxis. The variables are indicated by a note on the upper right corner of the activity diagram as shown in Fig. 5 since UML does not have any specific notation to represent variables in activity diagrams.

Although this model may appear to be very internal, it actually specifies the core behaviour which is of main importance for end-users, and therefore very relevant in a specification. In purely interface oriented specifications this functionality is completely missing.

3.4   Composing the Core and Interface Functionality

Once the interface functionality and core functionality models are defined, one needs to ensure their correct alignment and coordination in order to compose the complete service behaviour. The method rules for composing the complete service behaviour (CSB) are as follows:

CSB1: *Find matching pins on the core functionality model and the interface functionality models. Connect the matching pins.*

CSB2: *If a matching output pin cannot be found in the core functionality, look into the core functionality model to identify the appropriate flow where the required event is represented. Add a fork to the flow identified and an output pin. Connect the fork to the pin.*

The resulting complete behaviour of the *TaxiCentral* is shown in Fig. 6. It also illustrates the rule 'CSB2' where the matching *TaxiAvailable* and *TaxiRequest* output pins are not found originally on the core functionality model. They are then added to the core functionality model and connected to the newly added fork on the corresponding flow.

Note that the interface functionality and core functionality are defined in separate modules, that are partly independent and may be modified separately as long as their interface remains unchanged. This is one of the advantages of the interface-modular approach.

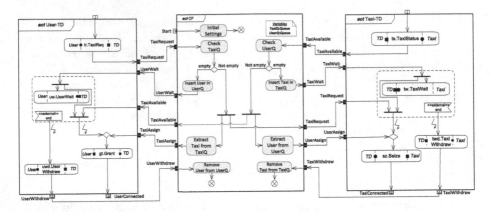

Fig. 6. Composition of core functionality and interface functionalities resulting in global behaviour model of the *TaxiCentral* (Note that the core functionality of the *User* and *Taxi* components have been omitted here for simplicity.)

4   Method Validation

First we comment that the development of a global interface-modular specification may not be quite as straight forward as suggested in the presentation above. In practice one may need to iterate in order to discover and resolve all dependencies and to develop the interface and core functionalities to the level presented in Fig. 6. In order to achieve sufficient completion to enable (semi-)automatic design synthesis, it is necessary that each component be specified with core and interface functionality to a level of detail corresponding to what is illustrated for *TaxiDispatcher* (TD) in Fig. 6.

As stated in the introduction the main goal when developing the interface-modular method was to enable sufficient completeness in global behaviour specifications so that automatic design synthesis becomes feasible. Almost as a side effect it turned out that the method also helps to structure and simplify the task of developing global specifications and increases the modularity of specifications. To see if the main goal is achieved, it is necessary to discuss the prospects for automatic design synthesis from interface-modular specifications.

In design synthesis the local behaviours shall be derived from global behaviour specifications in such a manner that correctness is guaranteed. The separation of core functionality from interface functionality splits this problem into two sub-problems: core functionality and interface functionality. Since the core functionality of a given component is a local behaviour it can be directly used in the component design. Using activities to specify core functionality is common practice in business process modeling. For this purpose activities seem both well suited and general enough. From the domain of reactive systems there is now extensive experience using activities to design components using a tool such as Reactive Blocks [15,19]. This tool can be directly used to define the core functionality to a level of detail that enable extensive analysis as well as to generate corresponding code (currently Java). From this we conclude that our goal can be achieved for the core functionality simply by expressing it using state-of-the-art tools such as Reactive Blocks.

However, as far as we know, there is no tool available that support the global definition of interface functionality in the form proposed here and automatic synthesis of local interface activities. Therefore, design synthesis for the interface-functionality part has presently to be performed by manual design steps. The challenge when defining the global interface functionality, is to make the definition complete in the sense that all relevant event orderings are defined and that realizability problems (implied scenarios) can be identified and resolved as part of design synthesis. Completeness is primarily achieved by the interface focus which reduces the concurrency to only two involved parts, the decomposition into elementary collaboration-uses, the ordering constructs provided by activity diagrams, the separation of interface functionality and core functionality into separate modules and the use of external flows to simplify external dependencies among modules.

Design synthesis for the interface functionality part involves several steps that have been described in previous publications [10, 13]:

1. Localizing the flows to the two participating components of the interface
2. Designing local activities for each collaboration role
3. Detecting and resolving realizability problems

The first two steps result in a local interface activity for each interface of a component with local *CallBehaviourActions* defining the local activity performed by the component in the collaboration-uses of the interface. In the *Taxi-Central*, for instance, the local behaviour of the *User* derived from the global interface behaviour is composed of activities for the *User* roles participating in different collaboration-uses: *User.TaxiRequest*; *User.UserWait*; *User.Grant*; and *User.UserWithdraw* as sketched in Fig. 7. The resulting local behaviour may however, contain undesired behaviour that follows from the nature of a distributed design, the so-called realizability problems. These can be detected using the principles presented in previous publications [8, 12]. To resolve such problems additional resolution activities and flows need to be added, as indicated in Fig. 7 which is part of our ongoing work. The result will be local interface activities that can be represented in a tool like Reactive Blocks and combined with core functionality into a complete component design ready for analysis and code generation.

Activity diagrams in the form supported by Reactive Blocks have been validated on numerous case studies including several different versions of the *TaxiSystem* and numerous IoT applications that include both the core functionality and the local interface functionality with communication interfaces using a variety of protocols. This suggests they are general enough and enable sufficient completeness to serve as a suitable target formalism for design synthesis. Presently the synthesis process for the interface functionality part is manual, but the prospects for automation are promising based on the rules developed so far.

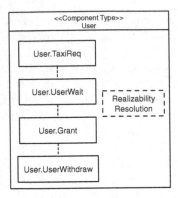

Fig. 7. The local role activities derived in the process of design synthesis of *TaxiCentral*.

We are currently working to develop detailed solutions to resolve the known realizability problems. Some manual input will probably be needed to select the most appropriate resolution method for cases, such as mixed initiatives, where this cannot be determined automatically.

5   Related Work

Expressing the core functionality using activity diagrams is similar to the common practice in work-flow modelling used in the business process development. Factoring out interfaces in separate interface contracts is also according to common practice in the same domain as seen in web services and SOA. What is not so common is to define the two aspects in modules that can be directly composed using pins. Within the embedded and reactive systems domain, it is common to specify interface functionality using sequence diagrams, but less common to specify core functionalities separately. It is more common to map (incomplete) sequence diagrams to state machines that integrate interface and core functionality during (manual) design.

In the literature, one can find many proposals to represent high-level service specification such as sequence diagrams and Use Case Maps (UCM) [5,6]. Interactions, for instance UML sequence diagram, are commonly used to express collaborative behaviour using messages which are exchanged between components. But sequence diagrams can normally be used for limited scenarios only and contain other drawbacks mentioned in [7,22].

The WSCI specification [1] describes the interface of a web service participating in a choreographed interaction using XML-based language. Unlike our approach, a WSCI interface describes only one partner's participation. The WSCI does not describe how a web service manages message ordering which in our approach is explicitly handled. Other approaches have been proposed [2,3,17] to define interface behaviours, but none of them models interface behaviour as activities ordering elementary collaborations. The problem addressed in the multi-view point approach proposed in [9] is similar to ours. But, there are important differences that sets our work apart from their approach. Interface behaviours for instance are one-sided in their approach. Moreover, their approach does not factor out internal tasks as we do in the core functionality.

Deriving interface contracts by projection from complete component behaviours have been much studied and several approaches exist [4,11,21]. However, the opposite problem of specifying interfaces first, and then composing the complete component behaviours has not been so well researched in the past.

The interface behaviours we develop, define the behaviour that is visible on each particular interface. This may be considered as a *projection* of the complete behaviour of a component or a system. One of the original methods of projections is proposed in [16] to reduce the complexity of analyzing non-trivial communication protocols. The method breaks up the protocol analysis problem into smaller problems by constructing a smaller image protocol system using refinement algorithms that preserves properties of the original protocol system. Our method is inspired by similar reduction of complexity by constructing smaller interface behaviours as projections. In doing this we seek to precisely define the visible interface behaviour that users and other entities in the environment will observe, while hiding other interfaces and details of the core functionality.

Various mathematical approaches have been proposed to define choreography semantics for example Labelled Transition System [20]. Activity traces are used by [18] to represent choreography. Most of these proposals lead to manual synthesis of the components. Whereas, once the system is specified using our interface-modular approach, synthesis of the components can be automated to a large degree as outlined in Sect. 4, based on the rules published in [10].

6   Conclusion and Future Work

We have presented an interface-modular method for system specification which is suitable to become the source of highly automated design synthesis. The method is demonstrated by a non-trivial case study, the *TaxiCentral*. Our method approaches the complexity of global behaviour specification problem by factoring out two separate aspects of a system i.e. 'core functionality' and 'interface functionalities'. Interface behaviours are decomposed using collaborations and defined as activities ordering elementary collaborations expressed using activity diagrams. This separation allows interfaces and core functionality to be combined in different ways as long as their internal interfaces are unchanged.

To our knowledge, the interface-modular method we have presented is original in the way it defines interface behaviour, separates the interface behaviour and core functionality, and composes interfaces and core functionality.

Currently, we are working on the process of design synthesis with detailed realizability resolution. The Reactive Blocks tool is being used to validate the derived components.

References

1. Arkin, A., Askary, S., Fordin, S., Jekeli, W., Kawaguchi, K., Orchard, D., Pogliani, S., Riemer, K., Struble, S., Takacsi-Nagy, P., et al.: Web service choreography interface (WSCI) 1.0. Standards proposal by BEA Systems, Intalio, SAP, and Sun Microsystems (2002)
2. Beyer, D., Chakrabarti, A., Henzinger, T.A.: An interface formalism for web services. In: Proceeding of the First International Workshop on Foundations of Interface Technologies (2005)
3. Beyer, D., Chakrabarti, A., Henzinger, T.A.: Web service interfaces. In: Proceedings of the 14th International Conference on World Wide Web. ACM, New York (2005)
4. Bræk, R., Haugen, Ø.: Engineering Real Time Systems. Prentice Hall, Hertfordshire (1993)
5. Buhr, R.J.A.: Use case maps as architectural entities for complex systems. IEEE Trans. Softw. Eng. 24(12), 1131–1155 (1998). IEEE Press
6. Castejón, H.N.: Synthesizing state-machine behaviour from UML collaborations and use case maps. In: Prinz, A., Reed, R., Reed, J. (eds.) SDL 2005. LNCS, vol. 3530, pp. 339–359. Springer, Heidelberg (2005)
7. Castejón, H.N.: Collaborations in Service Engineering: Modeling, Analysis and Execution. PhD Thesis, Department of Telematics, NTNU (2008)
8. Castejón, H.N., Bræk, R., Bochmann, G.V.: Realizability of collaboration-based service specifications. In: Proceedings of the 14th Asia-Pacific Software Engineering Conference (APSEC07). IEEE Computer Society Press (2007)
9. Dijkman, R., Dumas, M.: Service-oriented design: a multi-viewpoint approach. Int. J. Coop. Inf. Syst. 13, 337 (2004)
10. Fatima, U., Bræk, R.: On deriving detailed component design from high-level service specification. In: Haugen, Ø., Reed, R., Gotzhein, R. (eds.) SAM 2012. LNCS, vol. 7744, pp. 142–159. Springer, Heidelberg (2013)
11. Floch, J., Bræk, R.: Using projections for the detection of anomalous behaviours. In: Reed, R., Reed, J. (eds.) SDL 2003. LNCS, vol. 2708, pp. 251–268. Springer, Heidelberg (2003)
12. Kathayat, S.B., Bræk, R.: Analyzing realizability of choreographies using initiating and responding flows. In: Proceedings of the 8th International Workshop on Model-Driven Engineering, Verification and Validation, MoDeVVa, pp. 6:1–6:8. ACM, New York (2011). http://doi.acm.org/10.1145/2095654.2095662
13. Kathayat, S.B., Bræk, R.: From flow-global choreography to component types. In: Kraemer, F.A., Herrmann, P. (eds.) SAM 2010. LNCS, vol. 6598, pp. 36–55. Springer, Heidelberg (2011)
14. Kathayat, S.B., Le, H.N., Bræk, R.: A model-driven framework for component-based development. In: Ober, I., Ober, I. (eds.) SDL 2011. LNCS, vol. 7083, pp. 154–167. Springer, Heidelberg (2011)
15. Kraemer, F.A., Slåtten, V., Herrmann, P.: Tool support for the rapid composition, analysis and implementation of reactive services. J. Syst. Softw. 82(12), 2068–2080 (2009)
16. Lam, S.S., Shankar, A.U.: Protocol verification via projections. IEEE Trans. Softw. Eng. 10(4), 325–342 (1984)
17. Mencl, V.: Specifying component behavior with port state machines. Electron. Notes Theor. Comput. Sci. 101, 129–153 (2004)

18. Qiu, Z., Zhao, X., Cai, C., Yang, H.: Towards the theoretical foundation of choreography. In: Proceedings of the 16th International Conference on World Wide Web, WWW '07, pp. 973–982. ACM, New York (2007). http://doi.acm.org/10.1145/1242572.1242704

19. ReactiveBlocks: Reactive blocks - the tool for professional java developers (2014). http://www.bitreactive.com. Accessed on 14 May 2015

20. Salaün, G., Bultan, T., Roohi, N.: Realizability of choreographies using process algebra encodings. IEEE Trans. Serv. Comput. 5(3), 290–304 (2012)

21. Sanders, R.T., Bræk, R., Bochmann, G.V., Amyot, D.: Service discovery and component reuse with semantic interfaces. In: Prinz, A., Reed, R., Reed, J. (eds.) SDL 2005. LNCS, vol. 3530, pp. 85–102. Springer, Heidelberg (2005)

22. Zaha, M.J., Dumas, M., Hofstede, A.H.M., Barros, A., Decker, G.: Bridging global and local models of service-oriented systems. IEEE Trans. Syst. Man Cybern. 38(3), 302–318 (2008). IEEE Press

Identifying Code Generation Candidates Using Software Categories

Pedram Mir Seyed Nazari$^{(\boxtimes)}$ and Bernhard Rumpe

Software Engineering, RWTH Aachen University, Aachen, Germany
nazari@se-rwth.de
http://www.se-rwth.de

Abstract. Code generators are a crucial part of the model-driven development (MDD) approach. They systematically transform abstract models to concrete executable source code. Typically, a generator developer determines the code parts that should be generated and separates them from handwritten code. Since performed manually, this task often is time-consuming, labor-intensive, difficult to maintain and may produce more code than necessary. This paper presents an iterative approach for identifying candidates for generated code by analyzing the dependencies of categorized code parts. Dependency rules are automatically derived from a predefined software category graph and serve as basis for the categorization process. Generator developers can use this approach to systematically identify code generation candidates. The ideas and concepts of this paper were introduced at the MODELSWARD conference [1] and are extended in this contribution.

Keywords: Model-Driven Development · Generators · Software categories

1 Introduction

Models are at the center of the model-driven development (MDD) [2] approach. They abstract from technical details [3], facilitating a more problem-oriented development of software. In contrast to conventional general-purpose languages (GPL, such as Java or C), the language of models is limited to concepts of a specific domain, namely, a domain-specific language (DSL). To obtain an executable software application, code generators systematically transform the abstract models to instances of a GPL [4] (e.g., classes of Java). However, code generators are software themselves and need to be developed as well. There are different development processes for code generators. One that is often suggested (e.g., [5,6]) is shown in Fig. 1.

The approach includes four steps. First, a reference model is created, which ultimately serves as input for the generator. Depending on this reference model, the generator developer (resp. tool developer [7]) creates the reference implementation. Next, it has to be determined which code parts need to be or can

© Springer International Publishing Switzerland 2015
P. Desfray et al. (Eds.): MODELSWARD 2015, CCIS 580, pp. 356–372, 2015.
DOI: 10.1007/978-3-319-27869-8_21

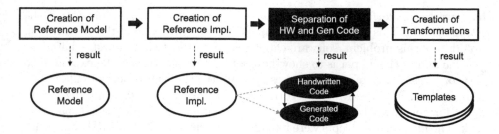

Fig. 1. Typical development steps of a code generator.

be generated and which ones should remain handwritten. Finally, the transformations are defined to transform the reference model to the aforementioned generated code.

Often, the third step, i.e., 'separation of hand-written and generated code' is not explicitly mentioned in the literature. This separation is implicit part of the last step, i.e., 'creation of transformations', since the transformations are only created for code that ought to be generated. However, the separation of handwritten and generated code ought to be distinguished as a step on its own, since it is not always obvious which classes need to be generated.

In general, every class can be generated, especially when using template-based generators. In an extreme case, a class can be fully copied into a template containing only static template code (and, thus, is independent of the input model). This is not desired, following the guideline that only as much code should be generated as necessary [5,8,9]. Optimally, most code is put into the domain framework (or domain platform), increasing the understandability and maintainability of the software. The generated code then only configures the domain framework for specific purposes [10] through mechanisms, e.g., as described in [11].

One important criterion for a code generator to be reasonable is the existence of similar code parts, either in the same software product or in different products (e.g., software product lines [12,13]). Typically, generation candidates are similar code parts that are also related to the domain. For example, in a domain about cars, the classes Wheel and Brake would be more likely generation candidates than the domain independent and thus unchanged class File. This, of course, is the case, since the information for the generated code is obtained by the input model which, in turn, is an instance of a DSL that by definition describes elements of a specific domain. Of course, the logical relation to the domain is not a necessary criterion, because if the DSL is not expressive enough, the generated code is additionally integrated with handwritten code. Nevertheless, the generated code often has some bearing on the domain.

In most cases, the generator developer manually separates handwritten code from generated code. This process can be time-consuming, labor-intensive and may impede maintenance. Furthermore, when using a domain framework, this separation is insufficient, since the handwritten code needs to be separated into handwritten code for a *specific project* and handwritten code concerning the *whole domain*. This separation also impacts the maintenance of the software [8]. To address this problem, software categories, as presented in [14], are suited.

The aim of this paper is to show how software categories can be exploited to categorize semi-automatically classes and interfaces of an object-oriented software system. The resulting categorization can be used for determining candidates for generated code, supporting the developer performing this separation task. The ideas and concepts were introduced at the MODELSWARD conference [1] and are extended in this contribution.

This paper is structured as follows: Sect. 2 introduces software categories and the used terminology. In Sect. 3, these software categories are adjusted for generative software. Section 4 presents the allowed dependencies derived by the previously defined software categories. The general categorization approach is explained in Sect. 5 and exemplified in Sect. 6. Section 7 outlines further possible dependencies. Concepts related to our work are discussed in Sect. 8. Finally, Sect. 9 concludes the paper.

2   Software Categories

Software systems, especially larger ones, consist of a number of components that interact with each other. The components usually belong to different kinds of categories, such as *persistence*, *gui* and *application*. Therefore, [14] suggests using software categories for finding appropriate components. In the following this idea is demonstrated by an example.[1]

Suppose that a software system for the card game Sheepshead[2] should be developed. The following categories then could be created (see Fig. 2):

- *0* (Zero): contains only global software that is well-tested, e.g., `java.lang` and `java.util` of the JDK.
- *CardGame:* contains fundamental knowledge about card games in general. Hence, it can be used for different card games.
- *SheepsHead:* Contains rules for the Sheepshead game, e.g., whether a card can be drawn.
- *CardGameGUI:* determines the design of the card game, independent of the used library, e.g., that the cards should be in the middle of the screen.
- *CardGameGUISwing:* extends Swing by illustration facilities for cards.
- *Swing:* contains fundamental knowledge about Java Swing.

---

[1] The example is taken from [14] and reduced to only the aspects required to explain our approach.

[2] This game (in German called *Schafkopf* or *Schaffkopf*) is a popular and complex Bavarian card game with thirty-two cards where four players play in dynamic alliances. The English translation *Sheepshead* is actually wrong as it comes from ancient times where the game was played on top (*kopf*) of a barrel (*schaff*). It has nothing to do with sheep.

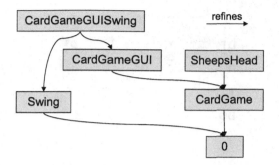

Fig. 2. Software categories for virtual *SheepsHead* [14] (shortened).

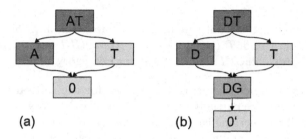

Fig. 3. Software categories (a) in general [14] and (b) adjusted for generative software.

An arrow in Fig. 2 represents a refinement relation between two categories. Classes that are in a category *C1* that refines another category *C2* may use classes of this category *C2*. The other way around is not allowed. Every category - directly or indirectly - refines the category *0* (arrows in Fig. 2). Hence, software in *0* can be used in every category without any problems. *CardGame* is refined by *SheepsHead* and *CardGameGUI* which means that code in these categories can also use code in *CardGame*. Note that a communication between *CardGameGUI* and *SheepsHead* is not allowed directly, but rather by using *CardGame* or *0* interfaces. Since the category *CardGameGUISwing* refines both *CardGameGUI* and *Swing*, it is a mixed form of these two categories.

Now, having these categories, appropriate components can be found. For example, a component `SheepsHeadRules` in the category *SheepsHead*, `CardGameInfo` and `VirtualPlayer` in *CardGame*, `CardGameInfoPresentation` for *CardGameGUI*.

Considering this example, it can be seen that beside the *0* category, three other categories can be identified that exist in most software systems (see Fig. 3a):

– *Application* (*A*): containing only application software, i.e., *CardGame*, *SheepsHead* and *CardGameGUI*.

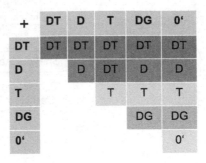

+	DT	D	T	DG	0'
DT	DT	DT	DT	DT	DT
D		D	DT	D	D
T			T	T	T
DG				DG	DG
0'					0'

Fig. 4. Addition of software categories.

- *Technical* (*T*): containing only technical software, e.g., Java *Swing* classes.[3]
- Combination of *A* and *T* (*AT*): e.g., *CardGameGUI-Swing* since it refines both an *A* (*CardGameGUI*) and a *T* (`Swing`) category.[4]

[14] summarizes the characteristics and rules for the software categories as follows: the categories are partially ordered, i.e., every category can refine one or more categories. The emerging category graph is acyclic. The category *0* (Zero) is the root category, containing global software. A category *C* is pure, if there is only one path from *C* to *0*. Otherwise, the category is impure. In Fig. 3a only the category *AT* is impure, since it refines the two categories *A* and *T*. All other categories are pure.

Terminology. We call a class that has the category *C* a *C*-class. Following from the category graph in Fig. 2 there are: *AT*-classes, *A*-classes, *T*-classes and *0*-classes. For the sake of readability, we do not explicitly mention interfaces, albeit what applies to classes applies to interfaces as well.

3   Categories for Generative Software

While [14] aims for finding components from the defined software categories, the goal of this paper is to determine whether a specific class should be *generated or not* by analyzing its dependencies to other classes.

To illustrate this, consider the following example. When having a class `Book` and a class `Jupiter`, which of these classes are generation candidates? Of course, it *depends on the domain*. If the domain is about planets, probably `Jupiter` is a candidate. In a carrier media domain, `Book` would be a candidate. So, we can say,

---

[3] Note that `Swing` classes are global (belonging to the JDK) and well-tested; hence meet the criteria of the category *0*. But –as usually the user-interface should be exchangeable– `Swing` classes are not necessarily global in a specific software system.

[4] In [14] also the *Representation* (*R*) category is presented. This category contains only software for transforming *A* category software to *T* and vice versa. It is a kind of cleaner version of *AT*. To demonstrate our approach, the *R* category can be neglected.

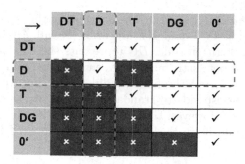

Fig. 5. Allowed dependencies between categories.

that a generation candidate somehow relates to the domain. But this condition is not enough. In a library domain where different books exist, Book would rather be general for the *whole domain* and should probably not be generated at all. Hence, additionally to the domain affiliation, a generation candidate *is not general for the whole domain.* Technically speaking, the class or interface should depend on a specific model (or model element). Consequently, a change in the model can imply the change of the generated class. Usually, classes that are global for the whole domain are not affected by changes in a model.

We adjusted the category model in Fig. 3a to better fit in with the domain. Figure 3b shows the modified category model.

The category A from Fig. 3a is renamed to D (Domain), to emphasize the domain. Consequently, the mixed form AT (Application and Technical) becomes DT (Domain and Technical). Category T remains unchanged. The new category DG (domain global) indicates software that is global for the whole domain and helps to differentiate from D-classes that are specific to the domain (a particular book, e.g., CookBook).

Resulting from the introduction of DG, the characteristic of the 0 category changes somewhat. It contains only global software that is well-tested and *independent of the domain*, e.g., java.lang and java.util of the JDK. To highlight the difference to the initial 0 definition, $0'$ is used.

With the above objective in mind and upon searching for generation candidates, in particular, classes of the category D are interesting, i.e., D itself and DT, refining the category of both D and T (see Fig. 3b).

The matrix in Fig. 4 underscores which software category results if two categories are combined. A usage of $0'$ has no effect, e.g., $D + 0' = D$. The same is true for DG, as we defined it to be like $0'$ (global for the whole domain). Hence, $D + DG = D$, e.g., if the D-class CookBook extends the DG-class Book it still remains a D-class. Only the combination of D and T leads to an (impure) mixed form, concretely DT. Any combination with DT results in DT, i.e., $* + DT = DT$.

The aim of this paper is not to define an architecture for generative software, but rather to use both the semantics of the software categories and the dependencies between the classes to find candidates for generated code. Nevertheless, this kind of categorization conforms to the concepts of the architecture reference model suggested by [8]. D, T and DT are what [8] call *Application*, consisting of generated and handwritten code. DG represents the *Business* and *Technical Platform*. Here, we do not distinguish between technical and domain platform, since this would not improve the final candidate list, but only complicate the category graph. $0'$ corresponds to standard libraries of the programming language mentioned in [8]. However, the categories need not be as abstract as the architecture. They could be further divided if this improved finding generation candidates.

4   Dependency Rules for Categories

A total of four categories (plus the mixed form DT) have been suggested for a general classification of code in generative software (Fig. 3b). Classes of a particular category are only allowed to depend on classes of the same category and classes that are on the same path to $0'$. Consequently, based on these categories, the dependency matrix in Fig. 5 can be derived automatically.

The matrix can be read in two ways: line-by-line or column-by-column. The former shows the allowed dependencies *of* a category, whereas the latter shows the categories that may depend *on* a category. The first row in Fig. 5 shows that a DT-class may depend on classes of any of the categories. A D-class can only depend on D-, DG- and $0'$-classes[5] (Fig. 5, second row). A D-class must not depend on a DT-class. Only the other direction is allowed. Analogous to D-classes, a T- class may only depend on T-, DG- and $0'$-classes. A class from category DG cannot depend on any of the categories but DG and $0'$; otherwise it would contradict the definition of DG being global for the whole domain. For example, in the library domain, the (abstract) class Book (DG) would not know anything about the single books (such as CookBook (D) or MDDBook (D)). Of course, $0'$-classes can only communicate among each other. For instance, classes in the java.lang package ($0'$) do not have any dependencies to a class of any of the other categories.

As mentioned before, the columns in Fig. 5 show those categories that can depend on a specific category. It can be seen that this is somehow antisymmetric to the previously described allowed dependencies of a category.

In the following, we briefly describe the categorization in a formal way. $\mathbb{C}$ is a set containing the categories illustrated in Fig. 3b, i.e., $\mathbb{C} = \{DT, D, T, DG, 0'\}$. A pair (a, b) with $a, b \in \mathbb{C}$ means category a *directly* refines category b. Consequently, possible pairings are $\Re = \{(DT, DT), (DT, D), (DT, T), (D, D), (D, DG), (T, T), (T, DG), (DG, DG), (DG, 0'), (0', 0')\}$. For every category c, $\varphi(c)$ returns a set of categories which are directly refined by c. $\varphi(c)$ is defined as: $\varphi(c) = \{b | (c, b) \in \Re\}$ with $\varphi : \mathbb{C} \to P(\mathbb{C})$, where $P(\mathbb{C})$ is the power set of $\mathbb{C}$. $\varphi^*(c)$ is the corresponding *transitive closure*. The following listing shows the resulting set of $\varphi^*(c)$ for every category $c \in \mathbb{C}$:

---

[5] Note that a D-class that depends on a T-class is rather a DT-class.

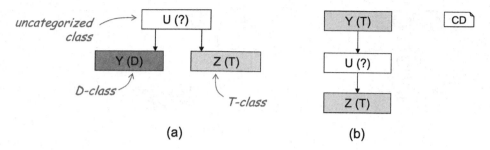

Fig. 6. (a) Uncategorized class depends on two categorized classes. (b) Uncategorized class in-between two categorized classes.

(1) $\varphi^*(DT) = \{DT, D, T, DG, 0'\}$
(2) $\varphi^*(D) = \{D, DG, 0'\}$
(3) $\varphi^*(T) = \{T, DG, 0'\}$
(4) $\varphi^*(DG) = \{DG, 0'\}$
(5) $\varphi^*(0') = \{0'\}$.

Analogously, $\varphi^{-1} : \mathbb{C} \to P(\mathbb{C}), \varphi^{-1}(c) = \{a | (a, c) \in \Re\}$ represents the set of categories that directly refine c, with $\psi^* = (\varphi^{-1})^*$ being its transitive closure:

(1) $\psi^*(DT) = \{DT\}$
(2) $\psi^*(D) = \{DT, D\}$
(3) $\psi^*(T) = \{DT, T\}$
(4) $\psi^*(DG) = \{DT, D, T, DG\}$
(5) $\psi^*(0') = \{DT, D, T, DG, 0'\}$.

With the help of these sets classes can be categorized. Figure 6a shows an example. The uncategorized class U depends on both the D-class Y and the T-class Z. Formally, the category of U is $\psi^*(D) \cap \psi^*(T) = \{DT, D\} \cap \{DT, T\} = \{DT\}$.

In Fig. 6b the uncategorized class U depends on a T-class. Additionally, a T-class depends on U. From this it follows that $\varphi^*(T) \cap \psi^*(T) = \{T, DG, 0'\} \cap \{DT, T\} = \{T\}$.

If two classes depend on each other, and thus, a circular dependency exists, they always have the same category. The reason is that $\varphi^*(c) \cap \psi^*(c) = \{c\}$ holds true for every category $c \in \mathbb{C}$, since the software category graph is acyclic.

In the above cases, the classes can be categorized unambiguously. Figure 7a demonstrates an example where the categorization is ambiguous. A DT-class depends on the uncategorized class which itself depends on a T-class: $\varphi^*(DT) \cap \psi^*(T) = \{DT, T\}$. Consequently, the category of U is either DT or T. In such a case, the class must be categorized manually. In general, the more classes are categorized, the better the categorization. For instance, if the class U additionally depends on a D-class (see Fig. 7b), its category will be determined unambiguously, since $\varphi^*(DT) \cap \psi^*(T) \cap \psi^*(D) = \{DT\}$.

Dependencies in Java. Up to now, we included the term dependency, but we did not define it so far. This is mainly because what a dependency ultimately

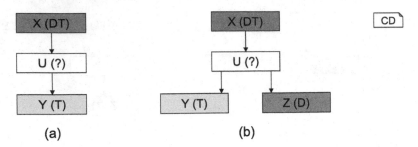

Fig. 7. (a) Ambiguous categorization. (b) Categorization becomes unambiguous by adding new classes.

is, depends on the (target) programming language. Java, for example, provides different kinds of dependencies between classes and interfaces. The following shows one possible classification, where the class A depends on the class B and the interface I, respectively:

- Inheritance: `class A extends B`
- Implementation: `A implements I`
- Import: `import B`
- Instantiation: `new B()`
- ExceptionThrowing: `throws B`
- Usage: field access (e.g., `b.fieldOfB`), method call (e.g., `b.methodOfB()`), declaration (e.g., `B b`), use as method parameter (e.g., `void meth(B b)`), etc.

These are dependencies in Java that are mostly manifested in keywords (e.g., `extends` and `throws`), and hence, hold for any Java software project. However, not all of these dependencies are always desired. It is important to determine first of all what a dependency ultimately is. For example, an unused import, i.e., a class that imports another class without using it, is not necessarily a dependency.

5   Categorization Approach

The suggested approach for the categorization of the source code is demonstrated in Fig. 8. Three inputs are needed for the categorization: the source code to be categorized (from which a dependency graph is derived), the category graph (such as in Fig. 3b) and an initial categorization of some of the classes and interfaces (usually done by hand). Using these inputs, a categorization tool analyzes the dependencies of the uncategorized classes and interfaces to the already categorized ones. With the information obtained from the category graph some of the uncategorized classes and interfaces can be categorized automatically. For example, if a class C depends on a D- and a T-class and the category graph in Fig. 3b is given, the category of class C is definitively DT, since only this category refines both D and T.

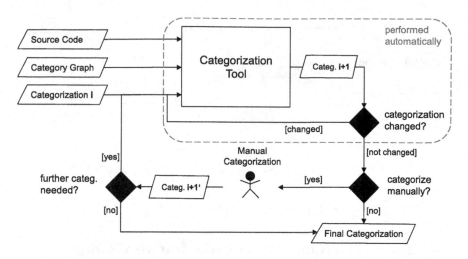

Fig. 8. Overview of the categorization approach.

In some cases the order of the categorization process matters. For example, if a class A only depends on a class B (and no categorized class depends on A), A will not be categorized until B is categorized. To prevent that the order has an effect on the final categorization, the categorization is performed iteratively. The output of iteration i serves as input for the next iteration $i+1$. This is repeated until a fixpoint is reached, that means, no further classes and interfaces could be categorized. These iteration steps can be conducted fully automatically. If there are still uncategorized classes left, some of them can be categorized by hand (Sect. 6 illustrates this case by an example). This updated categorization, again can serve as input. The process can be repeated until the whole source code is categorized or no further categorization is needed. Finally, classes and interfaces with a specific categorization serve as candidates for code to be generated. Here, this applies to the categories D and DT. The user now can decide which of these candidates will become generated code.

Concept Realization. The categorization tool consists of two domain-specific languages developed with the MontiCore language workbench [15–17]. The first DSL allows to specify a software category graph. The restrictions defined in Sect. 2 (e.g., acyclic graph) are checked by intra-model context conditions [6]. With the second DSL the source code can be categorized by mapping the defined categories to Java classes. The DSLs are composed through mechanisms described in [18–20].

As described in Sect. 6, the categories are iteratively extended. Technically, this means, the mapping model is extended after each iteration. Using an explicit DSL to categorize the classes has several advantages. First, when the developer initially categorizes the classes by hand, static checks can be performed to support the user, for example, that a class cannot be categorized with more than one category. Second, the developer can use the same tools and user-friendly syntax for the initial categorization of the classes as well as the manual categorization after each iteration.

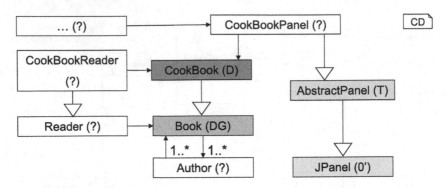

Fig. 9. Initially categorized classes.

6   Analyzing Usefulness on an Illustrative Example

Now, with the help of the allowed dependencies defined in Sect. 4, given some classes, the category of each of the classes can be derived semi-automatically, following the approach presented in the previous section.

Consider the case in Fig. 9. The figure depicts overall ten classes, whereby four are pre-categorized (CookBook, AbstractPanel, Book and JPanel) and six are not. The category is in parentheses beside the class name. Uncategorized classes are marked with a question mark (?). Let us assume that the four categorized classes already exist and are categorized (e.g., manually by an expert) and the six other classes are newly created. This situation can arise, for instance, when software evolves. In the following, the categorization process is illustrated.

The class CookBookPanel communicates with both a D-class (CookBook) and a T-class (AbstractPanel). Following Fig. 5, only a DT-class may communicate with a D as well as with a T class (marked by a check mark in the D and T column). Thus, CookBookPanel is definitively a DT-class. Moreover, any other class depending on CookBookPanel (represented by the three dots), is also a DT-class. In the column DT in Fig. 5 there is only a check mark for DT.

Next, CookBookReader depends on the D-class CookBook and the not yet categorized class Reader. If Reader is a DT- or T-class, CookBookReader will be definitive a DT-class, for it would depend on a D-class and either a DT- or T-class. With regard to Fig. 5, this only fits for DT-classes. If Reader is of any of the other categories, CookBookReader will be a D-class. However, when trying to categorize Reader, we encounter a problem. Reader only depends on Book, a DG-class. According to Fig. 5 this can apply to any category except $0'$. So, in this iteration, Reader cannot be categorized automatically. Consequently, the exact categorization of CookBookReader cannot be determined.

Analogous to the class Reader, the class Author only depends on the DG-class Book. So, except $0'$, it can be of any category. Unlike the previous case, Book also has a dependency to Author, which means that Author is either DG or $0'$. We have already excluded $0'$; hence, only DG remains as a possible category for Author. Figure 10 shows the extended categorization after this iteration.

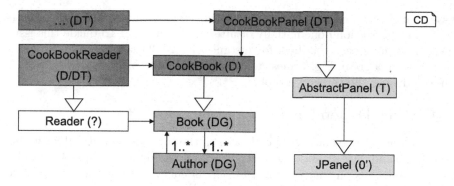

Fig. 10. Categorized classes after the first iteration.

Two classes could not be categorized exactly after the first iteration: Reader and CookBookReader. Recalling that our goal is to find generation candidates, we are above all interested in classes of the category D. So, the approximate categorization of CookBookReader (D or DT) is sufficient, since both D and DT are of the category D. In contrast, Reader is still completely uncategorized which hampers the categorization of classes depending on it. There are two options to categorize Reader in the next iteration: either manually by the expert or automatically by adding new classes and dependencies limiting the possible categories of Reader.

Note that the order of the categorization of CookBookPanel and the classes depending on it (marked by "...") is important for the first iteration. The "..." classes could not be categorized if they were considered *before* CookBookPanel. However, the order has no impact on the final result, since after the first iteration CookBookPanel is surely categorized, and thus, the "..." classes can be categorized in the next iteration.

Finally, three candidates (plus the "..." classes) for generated code are identified: CookBook (D), CookBookReader (D/DT) and CookBookPanel (DT). All of these classes belong to the category D directly or indirectly (i.e., DT), and hence, are somehow related to the domain. Having these candidates, the generator developer has to decide which of these classes in the end need to be generated and which remain handwritten. Of course, this decision is restricted above all by the information content of the input model. The generator developer must be aware of this restriction.

Please note that without knowing anything about the intrinsic properties of the uncategorized classes, the classes can be categorized by only analyzing the dependency graph. Of course, this is not always possible. Yet the more classes are already categorized, the better the proposed categorization of the uncategorized classes will be.

Detecting Wrong Categorization. A wrong initial categorization, e.g., if CookBook was categorized as $0'$, can lead or at least hamper the final categorization. One reason for wrong categorization is the evolution of software where classes can change and with them their categories. Another source of error is the manual categorization done initially or after each iteration. To tackle this issue, consistency checks as described, for instance, in [21–23] are suitable. From the dependency matrix in Fig. 5 rules can be derived to check the consistency of the source code and the category graph.

7   Further Dependencies

Up to now, only the technical dependencies of the code are considered for finding generation candidate classes (see Sect. 4). So, for example, if a class A extends a class B, it depends on that class B. But dependencies are not necessarily manifested technically. There can be further dependencies, such as *naming dependencies*. Figure 11 shows an example. The class CookBookWindow does not have any technical dependencies on CookBook, that means, it neither extends CookBook nor does it have any associations to it. It extends AbstractWindow, a T-class, hence, it is probably a T-class, too. However, CookBookWindow contains the name of CookBook as prefix in its class name. Of course, this can be purely coincidental. But, if there are specific conventions dictating that the name of a window for a class is composed of the name of that class and the suffix "Window", the naming dependency in Fig. 11 is very likely no coincidence. Considering this naming dependency, CookBookWindow has both a dependency to the T-class AbstractWindow and the D-class CookBook. Consequently, CookBookWindow is a DT-class and a generation candidate. Please note that from the architecture's point of view a (technical) dependency between CookBookWindow and CookBook might be forbidden. Hence, deriving the dependency rules from the architecture (and not from software category graph) would limit the kinds of possible dependencies.

In Fig. 11 there is a further clue that CookBookWindow refers to the CookBook class: its constructor has the same types as the attributes in CookBook. Hence, the dependencies between classes can be atomic (such as extension) or more complex, matching a specific pattern (for example similarity [24] and design patterns [25]). In sum, what a dependency finally is, depends on the software system and its conventions. This affects the emerging dependency graph of the source code and can also lead to a different candidate list. In any case, the procedure as described in Sects. 5 and 6 remains unchanged.

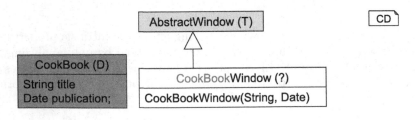

Fig. 11. Naming dependency between classes.

8   Related Work

[26] introduce class-level micro-patterns for common Java programming practices, such as immutability. Each pattern is assigned to a main category and optionally to an additional category. The categories in the approach are similar to our software categories such as they (logically) group together classes based on specific patterns and dependencies, respectively. *TaxTOOL* [27] and *TaxTOOLJ* [28] use a comprehensive taxonomy of OO characteristics (e.g., polymorphism) to classify classes. [29] present an approach to find so called *key classes* of a software project, based on dynamic coupling and webmining. Key classes are identified by their dependencies to other classes, since they "are tightly coupled with other parts of the system".

In [30–32] an approach is presented for finding stereotypes of methods and classes of a software system. Method stereotypes describe characteristics of a method, such as accessor (e.g., getter), mutator (e.g., setter), and creational (e.g., factory). A class stereotype categorizes a class, e.g., `DataClass`. The stereotype of a class depends on the stereotype of its methods. Rules exist for each kind of stereotype. Based on these rules, the concrete stereotypes of methods and classes are determined. Our approach has a lot in common with the one presented in [30–32]. Both approaches conduct static code analysis in order to categorize code (elements). Predefined rules serve as basis. However, the main difference is that in our approach dependencies between (un-)categorized classes are analyzed in order to determine the categorization. Consequently, a higher amount of categorized classes can improve the result. In contrast, method stereotypes, for example, rely on a method's characteristics independent of how it relates to other methods.

Some visualization approaches are presented by [33,34] which enrich classes and methods, respectively, with semantic information in order to improve code understanding.

All approaches have in common that they categorize or classify code using specific rules or patterns. These rules and patterns can be combined with our approach in order to categorize classes.

9   Conclusion

Code generators are crucial to MDD, transforming abstract models to executable source code. The generated source code often depends on handwritten code, e.g., code from the domain framework. When a code generator is developed or evolved, the generator developer manually decides which classes need to be generated and which remain handwritten. This task can be time-consuming, labor-intensive and may generate more code than is necessary, hampering the maintenance of the software.

This paper has introduced an approach that can aid the generator developer in finding candidates for generated code. First, a software category graph is defined. From this graph the allowed dependencies between the corresponding classes (and interfaces) are derived automatically. After an initial categorization of some classes, further classes can be categorized automatically, by analyzing their dependencies. This procedure is conducted iteratively until all classes are categorized or no more categorization is needed. Finally, generation candidates are all classes belonging to the domain categories.

References

1. Mir Seyed Nazari, P., Rumpe, B.: Using software categories for the development of generative software. In: Hammoudi, S., Pires, L.F., Desfray, P., Filipe, J.F. (eds.) Proceedings of the 3rd International Conference on Model-Driven Engineering and Software Development, pp. 498–503. SciTePress, Angers (2015)
2. Kleppe, A.G., Warmer, J., Bast, W.: MDA Explained: the Model Driven Architecture: Practice and Promise. Addison-Wesley Longman Publishing Co., Inc, Boston (2003)
3. Rumpe, B.: Modellierung mit UML, 2te edn. Springer, Berlin (2011)
4. France, R., Rumpe, B.: Model-driven development of complex software: a research roadmap. In: Future of Software Engineering 2007 at ICSE, pp. 37–54 (2007)
5. Kelly, S., Tolvanen, J.P.: Domain-Specific Modeling: Enabling Full Code Generation. Wiley, Hoboken (2008)
6. Schindler, M.: Eine werkzeuginfrastruktur zur agilen entwicklung mit der UML/P. In: Aachener Informatik Berichte, Software Engineering. Shaker Verlag (2012)
7. Krahn, H., Rumpe, B., Völkel, S.: Roles in software development using domain specific modelling languages. In: Gray, J., Tolvanen, J.P., Sprinkle, J., (eds.) Proceedings of the 6th OOPSLA Workshop on Domain-Specific Modeling 2006 (DSM 2006), Volume TR-37 of Technical report., Portland, Oregon, USA, pp. 150–158. Jyväskylä University, Finland (2006)
8. Stahl, T., Voelter, M., Czarnecki, K.: Model-Driven Software Development: Technology, Engineering, Management. Wiley, Chichester (2006)
9. Fowler, M.: Domain Specific Languages. Addison-Wesley Professional, Boston (2010)
10. Rumpe, B.: Agile Modellierung mit UML. Xpert Press, 2nd edn. Springer, Berlin (2012)
11. Greifenberg, T., Hölldobler, K., Kolassa, C., Look, M., Mir Seyed Nazari, P., Müller, K., Navarro Perez, A., Plotnikov, D., Reiss, D., Roth, A., Rumpe, B., Schindler, M., Wortmann, A.: A comparison of mechanisms for integrating handwritten and generated code for object-oriented programming languages. In: Hammoudi, S., Pires, L.F., Desfray, P., Filipe, J.F. (eds.) Proceedings of the 3rd International Conference on Model-Driven Engineering and Software Development, pp. 74–85. SciTePress, Angers (2015)
12. Clements, P., Northrop, L.: Software Product Lines: Practices and Patterns. Addison-Wesley, Reading (2002)
13. Pohl, K., Böckle, G., van der Linden, F.J.: Software Product Line Engineering: Foundations, Principles and Techniques. Springer-Verlag New York, Inc., Secaucus (2005)
14. Siedersleben, J.: Moderne Software-Architektur: Umsichtig Planen, Robust Bauen mit Quasar. Dpunkt.Verlag GmbH, Heidelberg (2004)

15. Grönniger, H., Krahn, H., Rumpe, B., Schindler, M., Völkel, S.: MontiCore: a framework for the development of textual domain specific languages. In: 30th International Conference on Software Engineering (ICSE 2008), Companion Volume, Leipzig, Germany, 10–18 May 2008 (2008)
16. Krahn, H., Rumpe, B., Völkel, S.: Monticore: modular development of textual domain specific languages. In: Paige, R., Meyer, B. (eds.) TOOLS EUROPE 2008. LNBIP 11, vol. 11, pp. 297–315. Springer, Heidelberg (2008)
17. Krahn, H., Rumpe, B., Völkel, S.: MontiCore: a framework for compositional development of domain specific languages. Int. J. Softw. Tools Technol. Transf. (STTT) 12, 353–372 (2010)
18. Völkel, S.: Kompositionale entwicklung domänenspezifischer sprachen. In: Number 9 in Aachener Informatik-Berichte, Software Engineering. Shaker Verlag (2011)
19. Look, M., Navarro Pérez, A., Ringert, J.O., Rumpe, B., Wortmann, A.: Black-box integration of heterogeneous modeling languages for cyber-physical systems. In: Combemale, B., De Antoni, J., France, R.B. (eds.) Proceedings of the 1st Workshop on the Globalization of Modeling Languages (GEMOC). CEUR Workshop Proceedings, vol. 1102, Miami, Florida, USA (2013)
20. Haber, A., Look, M., Mir Seyed Nazari, P., Navarro Perez, A., Rumpe, B., Völkel, S., Wortmann, A.: Integration of heterogeneous modeling languages via extensible and composable language components. In: Hammoudi, S., Pires, L.F., Desfray, P., Filipe, J.F. (eds.) Proceedings of the 3rd International Conference on Model-Driven Engineering and Software Development, pp. 19–31. SciTePress, Angers (2015)
21. Murphy, G.C., Notkin, D., Sullivan, K.J.: Software reflexion models: bridging the gap between design and implementation. IEEE Trans. Softw. Eng. 27, 364–380 (2001)
22. Terra, R., Valente, M.T.: A dependency constraint language to manage object-oriented software architectures. Softw. Pract. Experience 39, 1073–1094 (2009)
23. Passos, L., Terra, R., Valente, M., Diniz, R., Mendon, N.: Static architecture-conformance checking: an illustrative overview. IEEE Softw. 27, 82–89 (2010)
24. Bellon, S., Koschke, R., Antoniol, G., Krinke, J., Merlo, E.: Comparison and evaluation of clone detection tools. IEEE Trans. Softw. Eng. 33, 577–591 (2007)
25. Gamma, E., Helm, R., Johnson, R., Vlissides, J.: Design Patterns: Elements of Reusable Object-Oriented Software. Addison-Wesley Professional, Reading (1995)
26. Gil, J.Y., Maman, I.: Micro patterns in java code. In: Proceedings of the 20th Annual ACM SIGPLAN Conference on Object-oriented Programming, Systems, Languages, and Applications. OOPSLA 2005, pp. 97–116. ACM, New York (2005)
27. Clarke, P., Malloy, B., Gibson, P.: Using a taxonomy tool to identify changes in OO Software. In: Proceedings of Seventh European Conference on Software Maintenance and Reengineering, 2003, pp. 213–222 (2003)
28. Clarke, P.J., Babich, D., King, T.M., Kibria, B.G.: Analyzing clusters of class characteristics in {OO} applications. J. Syst. Soft. 81, 2269–2286 (2008)
29. Zaidman, A., Demeyer, S.: Automatic identification of key classes in a software system using webmining techniques. J. Softw. Maintenance Evol. Res. Pract. 20, 387–417 (2008)
30. Dragan, N., Collard, M.L., Maletic, J.I.: Reverse engineering method stereotypes. In: Proceedings of the 22nd IEEE International Conference on Software Maintenance. ICSM 2006, pp. 24–34. IEEE Computer Society, Washington (2006)
31. Dragan, N., Collard, M.L., Maletic, J.I.: Using method stereotype distribution as a signature descriptor for software systems. In: 2009 IEEE International Conference on Software Maintenance, ICSM 2009, pp. 567–570 (2009)

32. Dragan, N., Collard, M.L., Maletic, J.I.: Automatic identification of class stereo-types. In: Proceedings of the 2010 IEEE International Conference on Software Maintenance, ICSM 2010, pp. 1–10. IEEE Computer Society, Washington (2010)
33. Lanza, M., Ducasse, S.: A categorization of classes based on the visualization of their internal structure: the class blueprint. In: Proceedings of the 16th ACM SIGPLAN Conference on Object-Oriented Programming, Systems, Languages, and Applications, OOPSLA 2001, pp. 300–311. ACM, New York (2001)
34. Robbes, R., Ducasse, S., Lanza, M.: Microprints: a pixelbased semantically rich visualization of methods. In: In Proceedings of ESUG 2005, 13th International Smalltalk Conference, pp. 131–157 (2005)

Applications and Software
Development

Model-in-the-Loop Testing of a Railway Interlocking System

Fabio Scippacercola[1]($\boxtimes$), Roberto Pietrantuono[1], Stefano Russo[1],
and András Zentai[2]

[1] DIETI, Università degli Studi di Napoli Federico II,
Via Claudio 21, 80125 Napoli, Italy
{fabio.scippacercola,roberto.pietrantuono,sterusso}@unina.it
[2] Prolan Process Control Co., Szentendre út 1-3, Budakalász 2011, Hungary
zentai.andras@prolan.hu

Abstract. Model-driven techniques offer new solutions to support
development and verification and validation (V&V) activities of software-
intensive systems. As they can reduce costs, and ease the certification
process as well, they are attractive also in safety-critical domains. We
present an approach for Model-in-the-loop testing within an OMG-based
model-driven process, aimed at supporting system V&V activities. The
approach is based on the definition of a model of the system environment,
named Computation Independent Test (CIT) model. The CIT enables
various forms of system test, allowing early detection of design faults. We
show the benefits of the approach with reference to a pilot project that is
part of a railway interlocking system. The system, required to be CEN-
ELEC SIL-4 compliant, has been provided by the Hungarian company
Prolan Co. in the context of an industrial-academic partnership.

Keywords: Model-Driven Engineering · Safety-critical systems ·
Model-Driven Testing

1 Introduction

The development of systems in safety-critical domains is complex and expensive.
Normative certification standards in such domains require many verification, validation and certification activities to produce evidence that a high level of confidence has been achieved, that take most of resources of the entire development
process. A key role in system V&V activities is played by the environment, whose
correct specification is essential for the generation of proper test sequences.

In critical domains such as railway, automotive, and avionics, Model-Driven
Engineering (MDE) is increasingly adopted with the aim of reducing time and
costs. MDE refers to engineering processes in which models are key artifacts of
the work [1]. Models are defined in (semi-)formal languages, and other artifacts
are derived through defined transformations: model-to-model transformations
(M2M), or model-to-text transformation (M2T) from models to textual documents, source code or testing artifacts (test cases and test scripts).

© Springer International Publishing Switzerland 2015
P. Desfray et al. (Eds.): MODELSWARD 2015, CCIS 580, pp. 375–389, 2015.
DOI: 10.1007/978-3-319-27869-8_22

The current MDE practices emphasize a strong support to system design modeling and automatic generation of artifacts at different level of abstraction: while this is undoubtedly of primary importance, the MDE support to environment modeling, and more generally to system V&V activities, is still underestimated. If we want to fully exploit MDE potentials for critical contexts, the role of correct environment modeling for V&V tasks cannot be disregarded.

In the context of the European project CECRIS[1] – investigating new methods for certification of critical systems – we have defined a model-driven process incorporating concepts of the OMG MDA[2] [2] and MDT[3] [3] techniques, meant to support V&V of safety-critical systems [4]. The process has been experimented in conjunction with Prolan Co., a Hungarian company active in the domain of railway systems, on a pilot project for a new interlocking system.

In this paper, we focus on the topmost part of the process, and we detail how our methodology exploits model-driven techniques to define an environmental model enabling: *(i)* an environment-aware specification supporting the definition of a test plan; *(ii)* the detection of design flaws at early stages of the development lifecycle; *(iii)* the set-up of a framework to run model-, software- and hardware-in-the-loop tests. We experiment the approach on a Prolan's system, named *Prolan Monitor* (PM), which is part of a railway interlocking system required to be certified as SIL-4 (the highest safety level). Results highlight the potential advantages that can be gained when the environment is taken into account from the beginning through modeling support.

In the remainder, we briefly survey the state-of-the-art about model-driven V&V and certification for critical systems (Sect. 2); then, our MD V-model process is described (Sect. 3). Section 4 presents the experience regarding environment modeling for the railway case study. Section 5 discusses the results.

2   Related Work

There are several experiences on the application of MDE in industrial projects; a systematic review of the available literature is in [5]. Although MDE is generally perceived as positive – in terms of productivity, quality improvement, or automation support – not all claimed benefits are fully supported by consolidated empirical evidence. MDE is used mainly for code generation, while few meaningful studies document its use for simulation, test generation, validation and early detection of design flaws. In particular, not many success stories are documented on the adoption of MDA/MDT techniques based on standard (non-proprietary) modeling notations to support evidence of their maturity.

---

[1] CErtification of CRItical Systems, www.cecris-project.eu.

[2] MDA (Model-Driven Architecture) is the specific Model-Driven Development (MDD) approach proposed by the OMG standardization organization.

[3] MDT (Model-Driven Testing) refers to MDE V&V activities. It is not an OMG standard, but it is based on a UML standard profile, the UML Testing Profile (UTP), which adapts UML as a test specification language. In MDT, test infrastructure, test cases, and test scripts are derived from UTP models through transformations.

MDE has found application for safety-critical systems particularly in the railway domain. Authors in [6] report a successful application of Simulink/Stateflow models to the design of an on-board equipment of a Train Protection System. With particular restrictions on models, and using a model-based testing approach called Translation Validation, the authors were able to certify the system according to the CENELEC standards. Another interesting application of MDD for the generation of proper configurations of computer based interlocking systems is presented in [7]: secondary artifacts are automatically generated by model transformations to support CENELEC certification.

Indeed, important MD advantages for certification lie in the support for requirements traceability and for formal V&V. An MDE technique for the assessment of railway control systems is proposed in [8]; it is based on specialized UML profiles enabling translations to specific formalisms, for automated test cases generation and model checking. In the airborne domain, a similar solution for integrating model checking with various synchronous dataflow languages adopted by commercial MDD tools (e.g., MATLAB Simulink or SCADE) is discussed in [9]. SCADE is a DO-178B qualified model-based environment for mission- and safety-critical embedded applications [10]. A study on the use of the SCADE suite for the verification of railway control systems can be found in [11], while a success story of its application is reported in [12]. Techniques to enhance traceability and documentation capabilities of MDE to ease safety inspections and certification processes are proposed in [13,14].

MDE sees a growing adoption for embedded systems development [15], where it enables additional forms of V&V to achieve the required behavior and quality. *Model-in-the-loop* is an iterative testing activity involving the models of the system and of its environment. When the system model is replaced with a concrete software implementation, the testing is named *Software-in-the-loop*, aiming at identifying faults due the translation of the model into code. Finally, *Processor-in-the-loop* and *Hardware-in-the-loop* testing aim at assessing the system in realistic environments, i.e., on the target processor or on the production hardware. Such forms of testing are spread in the automotive industry, where MATLAB Simulink is generally adopted [16,17].

3 The Overall Approach

MDE is often introduced in industrial contexts adapting traditional domain-specific processes. This Section introduces the proposed model-driven process originated from a conventional V-model process (Fig. 1). The activities are grouped in those concerning development (left side) and V&V (right side), where we exploit, respectively, MDA and MDT.

On the left side of the V-model we follow the MDA approach: at each step we focus on one of the three viewpoints of the system (*Computation Independent Viewpoint, Platform Independent Viewpoint* and *Platform Specific Viewpoint*), used to define the *Computation Independent Model* (CIM), the *Platform Independent Model* (PIM), and the *Platform Specific Model* (PSM). The same

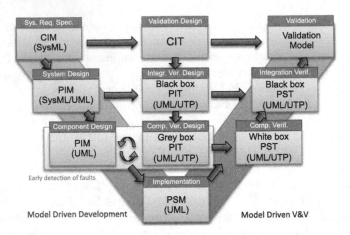

Fig. 1. The proposed model-driven V-Model. Boxes show the activities (e.g., *System Requirements Specification*), the models produced (e.g., CIM), and the formalisms used (e.g., SysML). The arrows indicate that the model at the arrow's origin is exploited by the activity at the arrow's destination (e.g., the *Validation Design* exploits the CIM to derive the CIT model). Note that, in a model-in-the-loop testing, the *Component Design* also exploits the test models to allow early fault detection.

abstractions are adopted in the activities of the center and right side of the 'V', but focusing on defining additional models that support the V&V exploiting the different views of the system.

In *System Requirements Specification*, we define a CIM for modeling the environment and the system requirements. The CIM is defined in SysML; this language is particularly suited for this phase, as it offers requirements diagrams and allows modeling both hardware and software components.

System Design refines the CIM into a PIM, by defining the high-level system architecture and its components. Requirements are assigned to the components. In this phase the PIM describes for each component the allocated requirements, the interfaces, and the expected interactions at components' interfaces. UML *Protocol State Machines* are suited at this stage, because they describe I/O relations without reference to the internal design of components.

Component Design completes the PIM with the internal design of the elements. Considering the software, this model is expressed in UML and should be specific enough to be subject to simulation. Since the *Component Design* focuses on describing the dynamic behavior of the elements, it can exploit UML *Behavioral State Machines*.

In the *Implementation* phase, the PIM is refined into one or more PSMs bound to the target platforms. For instance, a PSM adapts the generic types of the variables with the actual ones provided by a programming language, and binds data and function calls to the interfaces of the middleware and OS that have been chosen for the instantiation. The PSM can be translated into code to provide a partial or a total implementation of the system.

In the *Validation Design* we move to environment modeling. At this stage we exploit the CIM to define a novel model named *Computation Independent Test* model (CIT). The CIT is unaware of computation details, and focuses on the interactions with the actors. It allows expressing such interactions as properties and conditions related to the environment, e.g., "the station (interacting with the interlocking system under development) cannot invert the railway direction if there is a train occupying the block". The CIT allows creating a simulated environment in which engineers are supported in the validation activity of the systems' design models. The CIT is a basic block of the proposed Model-in-the-loop testing approach, as further discussed in the next section.

Integration Verification Design defines a model of the expected behavior of the system's components, independent from their inner design. We refer to it as *Black Box Platform Independent Test* model (BB-PIT). This model provides static and dynamic views of the system's components, and it is mainly used to support functional testing in the unit/integration/system verification. The static description supports the generation of the test infrastructure, including stubs and drivers for unit and integration testing. The dynamic description is composed by: *(i)* behavioral models, such as UML Behavioral State Machines, defined starting from requirements allocation to components in the PIM model; *(ii)* test cases, which are specified by Sequence, Activity and State Machines diagrams using the UTP profile. Behavioral models are useful indeed for automatic generation of test cases. A BB-PIT models the behavior of one component with more state machines, each focusing on a different subset of functionalities, with the possibility of composing test suites by grouping tests derived by several state machines. In addition, a BB-PIT supports the detection of design faults by comparing the behavior it describes with the one defined in the PIM. In fact, the behavior of a component is modeled differently in the PIM and in the BB-PIT, due to their different purposes: a PIM specifies how to build the system, and represents the specification of an actual implementation must comply with; a BB-PIT describes the expected behavior in a way to verify its correspondence between requirements and implementation (e.g., by using the BB-PIT for test case generation, the description represents the specification test cases must comply with). It is worth noting that, since BB-PIT derives from requirements and is barely influenced by design details, it supports validation too.

Component Verification Design refines the BB-PIT defining a *Grey Box PIT* model (GB-PIT), exploiting the PIM at *Component Design*-level that provides a partial internal view of the system. The GB-PIT enables additional verification techniques that can exploit structural features to assess correctness. Following this flow, engineers first focus on a functional V&V modeling in the *Integration Verification Design*, and then move to functional and structural V&V modeling in this phase. Moreover, since an executable PIM is available in this phase, the PIT allows performing a preliminary verification and validation of the design model, in order to detect defects before implementation. In addition, by exploiting the CIT properties on the PIM, model checking techniques can assess the absence of any undesired condition in operation.

The V&V activities of the right side of V-Model refine the CIT and the PITs considering details of the target platform, of implementation, and of the PSM. With these refinements, the BB-PIT and the GB-PIT become the *Black Box* and the *White Box Platform Specific Test* (respectively, BB-PST and WB-PST). For instance, the BB-PST allows to define test cases based on the knowledge of the target platform arithmetic, while the WB-PST can adopt a coverage criterion based on source code. Finally, testing plans, test cases, and artifacts supporting the V&V are derived by the PSTs through (automatic) transformations.

4   Environment Modeling

4.1   The Computation Independent Test Model

We have introduced a new form of environment modeling in the process during the *Validation Design*, through the definition of a Computation Independent Test model. The CIT is an *executable* model of the environment that captures the behavior of the system's context and provides interfaces *complementary* to those of the SUT. Therefore, it can be seen as a *symmetric PIM* and can be linked or put in a feedback loop with the system to enable early V&V.

The CIT is useful to create a simulated environment to reason about the operational aspects of the system in its context: we can validate the system against its expected interactions with the external actors and perform special kinds of system assessment (like performance testing or stress testing) by generating representative operational profiles. Also, whenever model checking techniques are adopted, undesired condition in operation can be detected by analyzing the state space of the SUT combined with the environment.

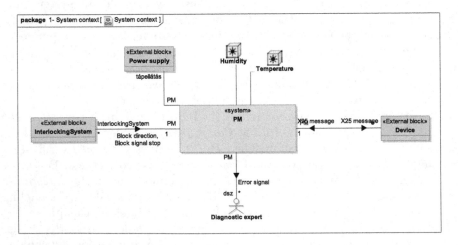

Fig. 2. A SysML Block Definition Diagram of the CIM, showing the PM in its context.

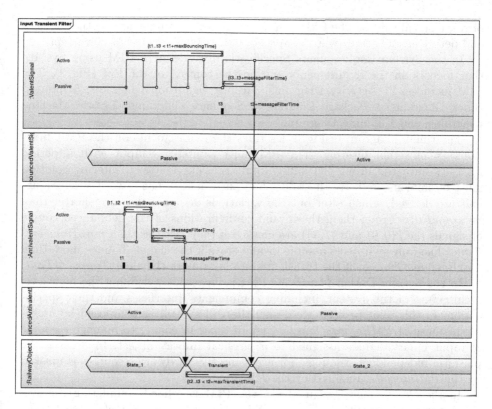

Fig. 3. A UML Timing Diagram included in the CIM, representing the requirements for the functionality of signal debouncing.

4.2 Case Study

In our previous work, we experimented the model-driven process integrated in the V-model in a pilot project of the *Prolan Block* (PB) railway interlocking system, under development by Prolan. Here we focus on the environment modeling, considering the *Prolan Monitor* (PM), another part of the interlocking system, which must be CENELEC EN50126, EN50128 and EN50129 SIL-4 certified. The PB shares with the PM the same hardware and middleware platform (*Prosigma*), which is the basis of the next generation of the company's products: according to the CENELEC terminology, Prosigma is a *generic product*, the PB and the PM are *generic applications*, and their instances are *specific applications*.

The PM is deployed on railway segments, named *blocks*. Each block is equipped with a legacy interlocking system and the PM, whose goal is to receive binary signals from the interlocking system and to transmit the information to newer devices that adopt different protocols, e.g., as datagrams over an IP network. In particular, the PM monitors one or more *railway objects*: these objects send a bit via couples of electric signals coding the information by valent and antivalent physical signal values. The PM must transmit the logical values to other devices and detect invalid states when couples of electric signals are not consistent.

In the System Requirements Specification, we define a CIM using SysML, that focuses on the requirements and on the context of the PM (Fig. 2). The CIM includes: 27 Activity Diagrams, 4 Block Definition Diagrams, 5 Internal Block Diagrams, 1 Package Diagram, 9 Sequence Diagrams, 7 State Machine Diagrams, and 1 Timing Diagram.

The timing diagram in Fig. 3 describes the requirements on the PM's functionality of signal filtering. The PM must sample its input with a period T_{sample}; since the input can suffer from transient states, a filtering solution must be implemented. By the valent and antivalent signals, two *debounced* signals are derived, which filter out the variations of signal that are shorter than *messageFilterTime*; then, the invalid configurations of the debounced couple of signals (i.e., $(0,0)$ and $(1,1)$) are masked if they last less than *maxTransientTime*. The railway objects assume invalid state if the signals bounce more than *maxBouncingTime* or if the transient state lasts more than *maxTransientTime*.

In the System Design phase, the PIM is created, by defining the high level architecture of the system, including components' interfaces and their specification. In this pilot project, we design the PM system as composed by multiple instance of *PMRailwayObjects*, each of those in charge to manage a couple of input binary signals assigned to a physical railway object. In order to be platform-independent, the logic for accessing the hardware resources is masked by the *PMInterface*, required by the *PMSystem*.

In the Component Design phase, the PIM is refined completing the system internal design. The *PMRailwayObject* consists of one *Sampler*, two *PMDebouncers* and one *PMInputFilter* (Fig. 4). The sampler reads from the input channels and notifies the values to the two *PMDebouncers*, filtering the valent and antivalent signal. Finally, the *PMDebouncers* propagate the signals to the *PMInputFilter* that filters out transient states, as specified in Fig. 3.

At this stage, we also define the behavior of the components, by using UML State Machines or Activity Diagrams. The state machine in Fig. 5 models the behavior of the *PMDebouncers* as a two-orthogonal composite state: the state machine in the left monitors if the input is stable and sends *inputStabilizedEvents* to the region in the right. The latter determines if the input is bouncing for a time longer than the maximum allowed.

The PIM is defined using IBM Rhapsody Developer (hereinafter: Rhapsody) [18], following guidelines to let the model be platform-independent.

As the derived model is executable, it can be animated to observe the running program and the system's interactions. This is a feature that we exploited to get an immediate feedback on program behaviour. Moreover, we can easily create prototype of user interface for interacting with the model: by means of the Rhapsody Panel Diagrams, we can set the logical signals and observe the output of the PM (Fig. 9, panel diagram on the left).

In the Implementation phase, we define the PSM. In this project we set several tagged values and tool-dependent parameters to enrich the PIM; then,

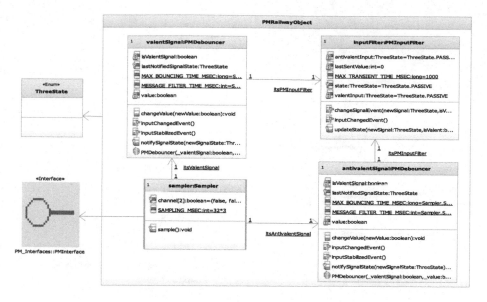

Fig. 4. The UML Internal Structure Diagram of the *PMRailwayObject*, defined in the PIM during Component Design.

the tool uses the additional information for translating the model into code. The automatic translation generated around 4.3 thousands of lines of Java code; the source code is readable, understandable and ready to run.

The Validation Design phase aims at creating an executable model of the environment. For the Prolan Monitor, the architecture of the CIT model is formed by two *CITRailwayObject*s: each *CITRailwayObject* controls the couple of logical signals associated with the binary information that it encapsulates; from the *point of view* of the CIT, the PM is an actor (Fig. 6).

The *CITRailwayObject*s are modeled as composed by one *SignalGenerator* and one *EventGenerator*: the *EventGenerator* determines the next output to be triggered, as specified by a user-defined operational profile. The *EventGenerator* generates the following events:

NoAction: the output is not altered in the next event generation loop;
ChangeStableState: the railway object switches between valid stable states;
CreateSpike: the output moves to an invalid state and then back to the previous stable state in order to simulate a transient in the electric signals;
Fail: the railway object moves to an invalid state and then fails.

According to the events sent by the *EventGenerator*, the *SignalGenerator* properly sets the couple of output signals and manages the duration of the transients. The behavior of the *EventGenerator* is modeled by an activity diagram, while the behavior of the *SignalGenerator* by a state machine (Fig. 7): the *SignalGenerator* can generate sets of valid or invalid signals; when a *changeOutputEvent* is triggered by the *EventGenerator*, it evolves to the next stable

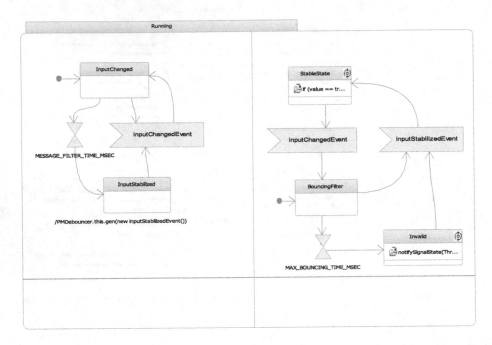

Fig. 5. The UML Behavioral State Machine of the class *PMDebouncer*, defined in the PIM during Component Design.

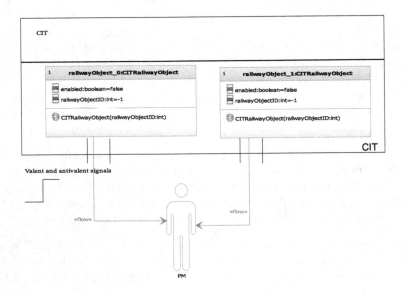

Fig. 6. The architecture of the CIT.

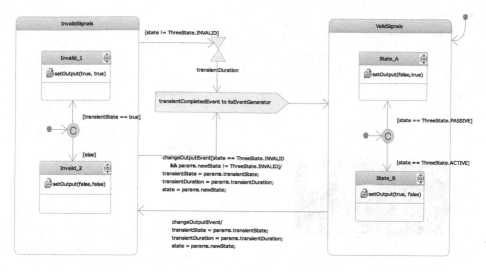

Fig. 7. The UML Behavioral State Machine model of the *SignalGenerator*, defined in the CIT during Validation Design.

state passing through invalid signals (i.e., $(1,1)$ or $(0,0)$) for a time equals to *transientDuration*. Then, if the *CITRailwayObject* is not failed, the *SignalGenerator* notifies the *EventGenerator* that the next stable state has been reached, and it starts to wait for the next event.

A panel diagram allows to interact with the CIT (Fig. 9, on the right): it offers a couple of knobs to set the period of event generation as well as the duration of transient states, and shows the output generated by the railway object.

4.3   Model-in-the-Loop Testing

We integrate the CIT and the PIM in order to perform the Model-in-the-loop testing. Since their interfaces are complementary, we link the two models by an adapter that simulates a physical relay, the *VirtualRelay* (Fig. 8): the CIT sends commands to switch the virtual relays, while the PIM reads their status.

Fig. 8. The software adapter linking the interfaces required by the CIT and the PIM.

Once the CIT and the PIM are linked, we can execute the whole model and examine its evolution by means of the output console and of the panel diagrams of Fig. 9. To use the CIT for Software- and Hardware in-the-loop testing, we just

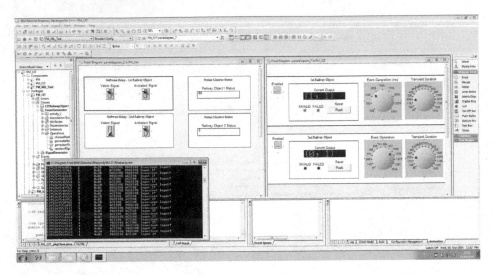

Fig. 9. A screenshot of Rhapsody showing two panel diagrams and an output console: the panel diagram on the left is linked with the PIM, whereas the panel diagram on the right is connected to the CIT. In Model in-the-loop configuration, both are linked through the *VirtualRelay*, and are part of the animation that produces output in the console.

need to change the adapter to forward the events to the actual SUT. Specifically, to run Hardware-in-the-loop tests in our case study, we replace the *VirtualRelay* with a physical relay card connected to Prosigma.

To assess the fulfillment of the requirements for the functionality of signal filtering, we have designed a test plan to assess if the events received by the *External Device* are the expected ones, according to the behavior of the *Interlocking System* and of the input signals (Figs. 2 and 3). We apply category partition testing (CPT) on the CIT's interface (Table 1), deriving six test case obligations: in this type of testing, categories are configurations of the environment (i.e., of the CIT) that lead to the generation of different sequences of effective stimuli to the SUT. The test case specification is summarized in Tables 2 and 3. As test oracle, we implemented a script to analyze the execution traces of the actors and of the PIM in order to detect any undesired behavior.

To execute the tests, the code of the model (in configuration *in-the-loop*) is generated without the instrumentation needed for animating the model in Rhapsody, so as to avoid slowing down the execution. Since the tests TC3 and TC6 require a time granularity of 10 ms, we tuned the *time tick* to 5 ms: this parameter specifies the time resolution to be used to poll the time events of the state machines and of the activities. By analyzing the execution during testing, we assure that the hardware was adequate to meet the timing constraints.

Note that, as the events are sent to a running software system, we are actually performing a form of Software in-the-loop testing. However, tests are not executed on the final software code, but on the instantiation of the PIM generated by Rhapsody that we are adopting for animation and testing purposes.

Table 1. CPT test categories.

Parameter	Categories	Constraints	Test case ID
Input domain	(1.1) Valid values		TC1-4
	(1.2) Valid and invalid values	[ERROR]	TC5
Input frequency	(2.1) Low frequency		TC1-2, TC4-6
	(2.2) High frequency	[SINGLE]	TC3
Duration of transients	(3.1) Undetectable by the SUT	[SINGLE]	TC3, TC6
	(3.2) Detectable by the SUT		TC1-2, TC5
	(3.3) Erroneous for the SUT	[ERROR]	TC4
Signal fluctuations	(4.1) Low probability		TC1, TC3-6
	(4.2) High probability	[SINGLE]	TC2

Table 2. Specification of the test cases. All test cases except TC5 send to the SUT valid input values $((1,0)$ and $(0,1))$ and invalid transient values $((0,0)$ and $(1,1))$.

TC ID	Categories covered	Event generation period	Transient duration	probability of fluctuations
TC1	1.1, 2.1, 3.2, 4.1	2.5 s	100 ms	1 %
TC2	1.1, 2.1, 3.2, 4.2	2.5 s	100 ms	40 %
TC3	1.1, 2.2, 3.2, 4.1	65 ms	10 ms	1 %
TC4	1.1, 2.1, 3.3, 4.1	2.5 s	5,000 ms	1 %
TC5	1.2, 2.1, 3.2, 4.1	2.5 s	100 ms	1 %
TC6	1.1, 2.1, 3.1, 4.1	2.5 s	10 ms	1 %

Table 3. Configuration of the SUT for the experiments.

Parameter	Value
T_{sample}	35 ms
messageFilterTime	$3 * T_{sample} = 105$ ms
maxBouncingTime	$5 * T_{sample} = 175$ ms
maxTransientTime	1,000 ms
Time tick	5 ms
Execution time	300 s

In our experiments, the SUT passed all the tests, behaving correctly. Using this approach, we enabled an early detection of design fault, because we could exercise the design model in its context before a complete implementation was available. Focusing on modeling the environment, we are suggesting a form of separation of concerns to design the test plan, that guides to design test cases considering the conditions of the environment.

5   Discussion and Conclusions

In this study, we presented an approach for Model-in-the-loop testing, embedded in a model-driven process, aimed at supporting the activities of V&V. The approach accounts for the relevant role of the environment, especially in safety-critical system V&V, by introducing modeling activities suited for designing and executing additional forms of verification and validation. The approach is experimented on a pilot project that is part of an interlocking system required to be CENELEC EN50126, EN50128 and EN50129 SIL-4 certified.

By exploiting the newly defined *Computation Independent Test* model (CIT), we guided the generation of tests based on the analysis of the environment, successfully supporting a Model-in-the-loop verification. Such a form of verification can favor the early detection of faults, while taking advantage of the automation offered by MDE tools. By performing testing on the SUT, we were able to verify the design model and show the correctness of the PIM integrated with a model of its environment.

As further remark, it is worth to emphasize that the CIT can be used to assess multiple systems, where the environment is the same: in other words, we are introducing a form of *environment model reuse*. For instance, in our case study, the CIT can be reused with the *Prolan Block*, because the PB is based on the same hardware platform and shares the requirements for input filtering. Additionally, applying a MDA approach for the development of the CIT, we can easily deploy the CIT under different configurations, so as to support verification tasks of a broader range of SUT.

Finally, when the implementation is available, the CIT can be adapted to perform Software-, Processor- and Hardware-in-the-loop testing, offering a ready-to-use environment to execute performance and stress tests.

As future work, we will mainly focus on evaluating the benefits achievable by the proposed process, as well as further improvement margins, under Software- and Hardware-in-the-loop tests.

Acknowledgement. This research has been supported by the EU FP7 Programme 2007-2013 under REA grant agreement n. 324334 CECRIS (CErtification of CRItical Systems, www.cecris-project.eu) within the IAPP (Industry Academia Partnerships and Pathways) Marie Curie Action of the People Programme.

References

1. Brambilla, M., Cabot, J., Wimmer, M.: Model-Driven Software Engineering in Practice, 1st edn. Morgan & Claypool Publishers, USA (2012)
2. OMG: MDA Guide (2003) Version 1.0.1. http://www.omg.org/cgi-bin/doc?omg/03-06-01
3. Baker, P., Dai, Z.R., Grabowski, J., Haugen, Ø., Schieferdecker, I., Williams, C.: Model-Driven Testing: Using the UML Testing Profile, 1st edn. Springer, Heidelberg (2008)

4. Scippacercola, F., Pietrantuono, R., Russo, S., Zentai, A.: Model-driven engineering of a railway interlocking system. In: Proceedings of MODELSWARD 2015, 3rd International Conference on Model-Driven Engineering and Software Development, SCITEPRESS, pp. 509–519 (2015)
5. Mohagheghi, P., Dehlen, V.: Where is the proof? - a review of experiences from applying MDE in industry. In: Schieferdecker, I., Hartman, A. (eds.) ECMDA-FA 2008. LNCS, vol. 5095, pp. 432–443. Springer, Heidelberg (2008)
6. Ferrari, A., Fantechi, A., Magnani, G., Grasso, D., Tempestini, M.: The Metrô Rio case study. Sci. Comput. Program. **78**(7), 828–842 (2013)
7. Svendsen, A., Olsen, G.K., Endresen, J., Moen, T., Carlson, E.J., Alme, K.-J., Haugen, Ø.: The future of train signaling. In: Czarnecki, K., Ober, I., Bruel, J.-M., Uhl, A., Völter, M. (eds.) MODELS 2008. LNCS, vol. 5301, pp. 128–142. Springer, Heidelberg (2008)
8. Marrone, S., Flammini, F., Mazzocca, N., Nardone, R., Vittorini, V.: Towards Model-Driven V&V assessment of railway control systems. Int. J. Softw. Tools Technol. Transf. **16**(6), 669–683 (2014)
9. Miller, S.P., Whalen, M.W., Cofer, D.D.: Software model checking takes off. Commun. ACM **53**(2), 58–64 (2010)
10. Esterel Technologies: SCADE Suite Product Description (2014). http://www.esterel-technologies.com
11. Lawrence, A., Seisenberger, M.: Verification of railway interlockings in SCADE. MRes Thesis, Swansea University (2011)
12. Invensys Rail: Invensys Rail Discovers Agile Development Process with SCADE Suite (2014). http://www.esterel-technologies.com/success-stories/invensys-rail/
13. Nejati, S., Sabetzadeh, M., Falessi, D., Briand, L., Coq, T.: A SysML-based approach to traceability management and design slicing in support of safety certification: framework, tool support, and case studies. Inf. Softw. Technol. **54**(6), 569–590 (2012)
14. Panesar-Walawege, R., Sabetzadeh, M., Briand, L.: A model-driven engineering approach to support the verification of compliance to safety standards. In: Proceedings of ISSRE 2011, IEEE 22nd International Symposium on Software Reliability Engineering, pp. 30–39 (2011)
15. Shokry, H., Hinchey, M.: Model-based verification of embedded software. Computer **42**(4), 53–59 (2009)
16. Amalfitano, D., Fasolino, A.R., Scala, S., Tramontana, P.: Towards automatic model-in-the-loop testing of electronic vehicle information centers. In: Proceedings of WISE '14, International Workshop on Long-term Industrial Collaboration on Software Engineering, pp. 9–12. ACM (2014)
17. Matinnejad, R., Nejati, S., Briand, L., Bruckmann, T., Poull, C.: Automated model-in-the-loop testing of continuous controllers using search. In: Ruhe, G., Zhang, Y. (eds.) SSBSE 2013. LNCS, vol. 8084, pp. 141–157. Springer, Heidelberg (2013)
18. IBM Corp.: Rational Rhapsody Developer (2014). http://www-03.ibm.com/software/products/it/ratirhap

Model Transformation Configuration and Variability Management for User Interface Design

Jean-Sébastien Sottet$^{(\boxtimes)}$, Alain Vagner, and Alfonso García Frey

Luxembourg Institute of Science and Technology,
5 av. des Hauts-Fourneaux, Esch/Alzette, Luxembourg
{jean-sebastien.sottet,alain.vagner,alfonso.garcia}@list.lu

Abstract. User Interfaces (UI) design is a complex and multi-faceted problem, owing to the ever increasing variability of the design options and the interaction context (devices, user profiles, and their environment). Moreover, UI design choices stand on users' needs elicitation, which are difficult to evaluate precisely upfront and require iterative design cycles based on trial and error. All this complex variability should be managed efficiently to ensure moderate design costs. In this article, we propose a variability management approach integrated into a UI rapid prototyping process, which involves the combination of Model-Driven Engineering (MDE) and Software Product Lines. Our approach supports the separation of concerns through multi-step partial configuration of UI features, enabling each stakeholder of the UI design process to define the variability on the assets she manages. We have implemented this approach in our existing MDE UI generation Framework.

Keywords: Software engineering · Software product lines · Variability management · Configuration · Model-driven engineering · Model transformations · Human-computer interaction · Model-based user interfaces · Feature models

1 Introduction

In design and development of User Interfaces (UI) it is often required to produce several versions of the same product, including different look and feel and user tasks for different platforms. As stated by [7] interaction design is a complex and multi-faceted problem. When designing interaction, variability is manifold: variability of devices, users, interaction environments, etc. Moreover, user requirements are difficult to evaluate precisely upfront in UI design processes. Therefore, the main UI design processes, such as User-Centred Design [13], implement an iterative design cycle in which a UI variant is produced, tested on end-users, and their feedback is integrated into design artifacts (e.g., part of the UI, requirements, etc.). Since these processes are mostly based on trial and error, some parts of the UI have to be re-developed many times to fit all the different user

© Springer International Publishing Switzerland 2015
P. Desfray et al. (Eds.): MODELSWARD 2015, CCIS 580, pp. 390–404, 2015.
DOI: 10.1007/978-3-319-27869-8_23

requirements. Moreover these processes involve multiple stakeholders with different roles (software developers, UI/User eXperience designers, business analysts, end-users, etc.) that demand a great amount of time to reach consensus. UI variability has thus a significant impact on the design, development and maintenance costs of the UI.

To overcome variability issues in software engineering, researchers have proposed to rely on the paradigm of Software Product Lines (SPLs) [10]. The SPL paradigm allows to manage variability by producing a family of related product configurations (leading to product variants) for a given domain. Indeed, the SPL paradigm proposes the identification of common and variable sets of features, to foster software reuse in the configuration of new products [22].

Model-Driven Engineering (MDE) has already been used to improve the UI design process [27]. According to [4,11] SPL and MDE are complementary and can be combined in a unified process that aggregates the advantages of both methods.

In this paper, we propose an approach to manage UI variability based on MDE and SPL. Our approach relies on model transformations that support the expression of the variability. This approach enables the separation of concerns of the different stakeholders when expressing the UI variability and their design choices (UI configurations). We considered a Multiple Feature Model approach in which each feature model represents a particular concern allowing, if needed, each stakeholder to work independently. We also support the configuration reconciliation to reach a consensus through constraints and dependencies between UI features. We thus proposed a partial and staged configuration process [12] in which we produce partial UI configurations that can be refined by all stakeholders including the users feedback. Finally, we propose to integrate the configuration inside the transformations, modifying existing UI model transformations and integrate them into our model-driven UI design process [27]. We illustrate these concepts with a concrete example of UI variability.

2   Related Work

2.1   Feature Modelling

Feature models (FM) [22] are popular SPL assets that describe both variability and commonalities of a system. They express, through some defined operators, the decomposition of a product related features. The feature diagram notation used in this article is explained in Fig. 1. The E-Shop FM consists of a mandatory feature "catalogue", two possible payment methods from which one or both could be selected, an exclusive alternative of security levels and an optional search feature. FM constraints can be defined. In this case "credit card" implies a high level of security.

Features composing a FM depict different parts of a system without any clear separation. The absence of feature types makes these models popular as there are no limits for the expression of design artifacts. But at the same time, [8] have

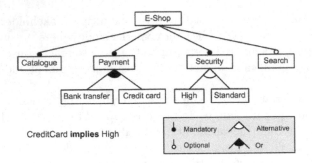

Fig. 1. Feature Model from an E-shop. Source: Wikimedia commons.

demonstrated that depicting information in a single FM leads to feature redundancies due to the tree structure. As a result, separation of variability concerns into multiple FM seems to be crucial for understanding [18] and manipulating [1] the many different faces of variability. Each of these FM focuses on a viewpoint on variability which makes easier to handle variability for each stakeholder.

2.2 SPL Configuration

The configuration process is an important task of SPL management: producing a particular product variant based on a selection of features to fit the customers' needs. In this context, a configuration is a specific combination of FM features such as hierarchical decomposition, operators (Or, optional, etc.) and constraints of FM.

As stated by [29], when designers and developers configure a system according to requirements, the enforcement of FM constraints can limit them in their design choices. Moreover, the separation of the variability in multiple FMs is also a source of complexity due to many dependencies across FMs. The fusion of all FMs into one for configuration purposes seems to solve this issue but results in a large FM that mixes different facets: this may lead to invalid configurations and thus inefficient products. Some solutions exist to overcome these problems. The work by [23] proposes an implementation of a configuration composition system defining a step-by step configuration [12] using partial configurations [5]. Thus, some portion of a FM can be configured independently, without considering all the constraints (coming from other configurations) at configuration time. Then, constraints amongst configurations may be solved by implementing consistency transformations such as in [1].

2.3 Model-Driven User Interfaces Variability

Model-Driven UI calls for specific models and abstraction. These models address the flow of user interfaces, the domain elements manipulated during the interaction, the models of expected UI quality, the layout, the graphical rendering, etc. In addition, each model corresponds to a standard level of abstraction as identified in the CAMELEON Reference Framework (CRF) [9]. The CRF aims at providing a unified view on modelling and adaptation of UIs. In the CRF, each level of abstraction is a potential source of variability. Modifying a model of a specific level of abstraction corresponds to a specific adaptation of the UI.

For instance in the CRF, the most abstract model, the task model, depicts the interaction between the user and the features offered by the software. Adding or removing a task results in modifying the software features. Considering this, we can assume that there is a direct link between classical feature modelling and task modelling such as presented in [21]. In this work, a task model is derived from an initial FM. However the authors did not go any further in describing the variability related to interaction and UI (graphical components, behavior, etc.).

In [14], the authors present an integrated vision of functional and interaction concerns into a single FM. This approach is certainly going a step further by representing variability at the different abstraction levels of the CRF. However, this approach has several drawbacks. On the one hand, this approach derives functional variability only from the task model, limiting the functional variability of the software. On the other hand, all the UI variations are mixed into a single all encompassing FM which blurs the various aspects for comprehension and configuration [18].

Finally, Martinez et al. [19] presented an initial experience on the usage of multiple FMs for web systems. This work showed the feasibility of using multiple FMs and the possibility to define a process around it. It implements FMs for a web system, interaction scenario, a user model (user impairments), and device. However, this approach does not consider the very peculiarity of UI design models and their variability.

A few works in SPL for UI have been published. A large part is dedicated to the main variability depiction (using FMs) but they do not directly address the configuration management. Configuration is a particular issue when considering end-user related requirements which may be fuzzily defined.

3   UI-SPL Approach

Model-driven UI design is a multi-stakeholder process [15,17] where each model – representing a particular subdomain of UI engineering– is manipulated by specific stakeholders. For instance, the choice of graphical widgets to be used (e.g. radio button, drop-down list, etc.) is done by a graphical designer, sometimes in collaboration with the usability expert and/or the client. Our model-driven UI design approach [27] relies on a revised version of the CRF framework (Fig. 2).

It consists of two base metamodels, the Domain metamodel -representing the domain elements manipulated by the application as provided by classical domain analyst- and the Interaction Flow Model (IFM) [20]. From these models we derive the Concrete User Interface model (CUI) which depicts the application "pages" and their content (i.e., widgets) as well as the navigation between pages. The CUI metamodel aims at being independent of the final implementation of any graphical element. Finally, the obtained CUI model is transformed

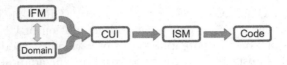

Fig. 2. Model-Driven UI design process.

into an Implementation Specific Model (ISM) that takes into account platform details (here platform refers to UI tool-kits such as HTML/JQuery, Android GUI, etc.). A last model-to-text transformation generates the code according to the ISM. This separation allows for separate evolution of CUI metamodel and implementation specific metamodel and code generation.

We propose a multiple feature models (multi-FM) approach (see Sect. 3.1) to describe the various facets of UI variability (e.g., UI layout, graphical elements, etc.). In a second time, (see Sect. 3.2) we introduce our specific view on configuration on this multi-FM and its implementation in our model-driven UI design approach (see Sect. 4.3).

3.1   Multi-FM Approach

Classical FM approaches combine different functional features [21]. In the specific context of UI design, we propose to rely on a similar approach for managing variability of each UI design concern. UI variability is thus decomposed into FMs (Fig. 3).

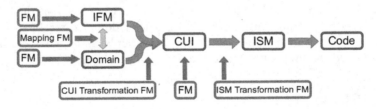

Fig. 3. Variability models (FM) coverage on our UI modeling framework.

Each of these FMs is related either to a model, a metamodel, a mapping or a transformation depending on the nature of the information it conveys.

– Models: Three FMs in Fig. 3 manage variations at the model level (IFM, Domain and CUI). The FM responsible for the Domain configuration can be used to express alternatives of a same concept, e.g., using or not the address, age or photo of a given class "Person". The IFM variability can express for instance the possible navigation alternatives to be activated or not. For instance on a shopping website, shortcuts providing quickly access to a given product can be configured. The CUI FM represents alternative representations of a widget: a panel (i.e., portion of UI displayed on a screen) can become a full window (i.e., displayed has full-screen) on mobile phones.

- Mappings: The variability of the mapping between IFM and Domain can be managed by a mapping FM. Interaction flow elements (UI states) can involve different concepts of the domain model.
- Transformations: Variability can be expressed also at the level of transformations. The variability that a transformation could convey (i.e., multiple output alternatives) can be expressed with FMs. The transformations impacted are (1) between IFM, Domain and CUI, (2) between CUI and ISM. The variability of (1) expresses the possible UI design choices: how an IFM state selection can be represented: a simple list, an indexed list, a tile list, etc. The variability in (2) depends on the target ISM and configures the final representation to be provided to end-users. For instance, a CUI simple list can be represented using, as output of the transformation, the following HTML markup alternatives: "<select>" or "<ul>".

By scoping the FM to a specific concern, our approach allows to focus only on the variations related to the underlying concern. In our approach, the different FM enrich the existing UI design process accompanying, step by step, the design of models and its variability. However, all the concerns are interrelated in the generation process: the IFM, Domain and CUI are in relation together (derivation traceability, explicit mapping, etc.). Thus, the FMs are interrelated as well leading to dependencies and sometimes overlaps between them. As such, the configuration of the transformation IFM-Domain to CUI is overlapping the FM of the CUI. If the UI design stakeholders are following an automated approach, they will rather use the transformation FM. The FM responsible for the CUI transformation configuration (i.e., elements to be displayed) is directly dependent on the mappings between domain elements and IFM. For instance, if the picture (Domain) is not mapped to a selection state (IFM), the generated CUI list would not contain this picture.

3.2   Configuration: The Specific Case of Rapid Prototyping

End-user requirements are crucial in user centred design. They are often not formally defined: most of the time their are expressed as remarks on a portion of produced or prototyped UI. Thus, in order to capture end-user requirements UI designers have to propose various product versions (prototypes) to end-users. A common practice is to use rapid prototyping. Rapid prototyping is a user-centred iterative process where end-users give feedback on each produced prototype. Prototypes are usually mock-ups of UI drawn with dedicated tools (e.g., see balsamiq[1]). In order to show to the users an interaction experience closest to reality we should rely on higher fidelity and on living prototypes (i.e., the user should be able to interact with it). As a result, MDE provides us with semi-automatic generation capabilities. It allows a quick production of prototypes and many assessments in a limited amount of time. End-users will thus elicit the way they prefer interacting with the system, the best widgets and representations for

---

[1] http://balsamiq.com.

their tasks. In fact, through these iterations they elicit the product configuration that best fits their needs.

This user-centred process is composed of many iterations that test only a portion of the UI. If we can test the global interaction experience with the end-users, the designer may also need to focus on one particular UI part/concern in isolation. In previous work [26,27], we have tested the global usability of generated UI prototypes. We will focus here on the configuration of specific UI parts. In order to perform this, we stand on partial configurations [5]. For instance, configuring content of a specific page or a specific interaction state.

The partial configuration does not take into account the external feature[2] constraints which enter in the partial configuration (e.g., requires, implies, excludes, etc.). In other words, if another configuration has a feature which requires/excludes a feature of the partial configuration being set we simply do not consider it. For the features required or excluded by the partial configuration being set, we do not involve the end-users/designer but rather compute the consequences: i.e., provide a configuration for these external features. The constraints that are expressed inside the partial configuration are still to be considered as in traditional approaches.

We designed a generation process of UI prototypes from partial configurations and their evaluation with end-users. We divided this process into 4 steps from the identification of UI parts to be tested to the corresponding prototype generation:

1. **Selection of the Model Parts to be Configured:** in order to target the critical portion(s) of the application to be tested with end-users, the selection should be done on the input design models (e.g., IFM and Domain). Then, we deduce the impacted FMs and provide for each of them the relevant subset.
2. **Combination of the Various FMs Subsets:** the subset of FMs previously selected have to be aggregated (see FMs aggregation [1]) together in order to produce a unified configuration.
3. **Establishment and Use of Configuration UI:** the configuration UI can be derived from the obtained FM. We have developed a FM to CUI transformation that is used to generate the configuration UI.
4. **Executing "Variability Aware" Transformations:** we have finally developed transformation rules that take into account variability rules (that we will call later variability rules) related to the idea of [25]. The variability rules allow for a smarter management of FM in transformations. Secondly, these transformations should also support, with some default heuristics, elements that have no configuration.

In order to illustrate the process above let's introduce a simple application example (Fig. 4). We have realized this application model with our application modeling tool AME [16,17]. The application[3] proposes to search actors that play in a film, whose name is given by the user; then the user is able to select one actor to see more detailed information (birth date, photos, etc.). This simple

---

[2] External features refer to features coming from another partial configuration.
[3] This example is supported by the Neo4J tutorial: Movie DB, www.neo4j.com.

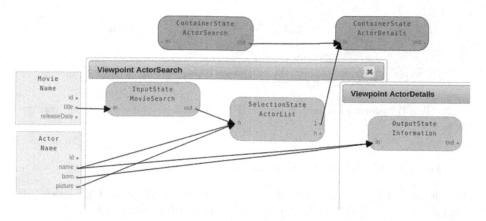

Fig. 4. Model of the application realized with our modeling tool AME [16,17].

application is composed by two interaction flow states: one for searching by film and displaying the list of actors and one for displaying information about the selected actor.

In this example, the UI designer wants to focus on a specific element to test and enhance with end-users: test the most appropriated way to select the actor[4]. Thus, the designer could propose several variations for the actor selection. The actor selection is supported by different types of lists as depicted by the CUI metamodel (tile list, radio-button, etc.) and the information that this list should convey (actors photo, name, etc.).

The rapid prototyping configuration occurs in the transformation between IFM, Domain and CUI Models (Fig. 3). This configuration stands on the combination of two FMs (as described in step 2). Firstly, the "CUI transformation FM" that depicts the variability of the widgets to be generated (see Fig. 5 upper part CUI decomposition). Secondly, the "Mapping FM" (mapping between IFM and domain) which depicts the configuration of the information conveyed by the list of actors (see Fig. 5 right frame Mapping FM). We also added a constraint: to be efficient a tile list requires to show some pictures (Tile List implies picture).

As a summary, the FMs of the Fig. 5 correspond to the UI designer specific viewpoint when he/she starts to configure the actors selection.

4   Implementation

In the following section we will illustrate the process described in Sect. 3.2. As such we introduce the management of design and feature models and the selection of the part of FM from which we will derive (generate) the partial configuration. Finally, we introduce the transformation rules tuned for supporting partial configuration.

---

[4] Here, we focus on a widget but other factors are to be adjusted by the interface designer like style, layout, etc.

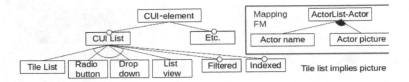

Fig. 5. CUI Transformation and Mapping IFM-Domain FM for excerpt List configuration.

4.1 Feature Models: Selection and Reconciliation

The selection of the part to be configured is done through the design models. On such models the designer is able to select the critical part of the UI. For instance, it can be a crucial part of the application or a problematic situation (e.g., a particularly long interaction with many steps, a page with many information to fill in, etc.). In our simple example, the "ActorList" selection state, related to the concept it manipulates, is central to the application: it is the main entry point for the users.

Once the part of the input design model is selected, the relation with the FM still has to be found. The model transformation gives us a first link to the target metamodel elements. In fact, the transformation is linking elements from the input models (previously selected in the IFM and Domain models) to elements from the target metamodel. Through the transformation scope (e.g., CUI List) we are able to scope the variability of the target metamodel[5]. The IFM states "selection" are transformed into various types of lists. As a result we have selected the portion of CUI transformation FM corresponding to List. We have to do the same for the domain concept mapped to the "selection" state: as shown on Fig. 4 the selection state actor list is mapping to the attributes of concept actor name and picture. The selection can be implemented using the slicing operator defined in Familiar [2].

Once the FM have been selected and rightly scoped (i.e., we obtained FM portions) we have to aggregate them together. We can use the insert operator of Familiar using the following Familiar [2] expression see Listing 1.1.

Listing 1.1. Familiar insertion operator for building complete partial configuration.

```
fml> insert MappingIFMDomain into CUITransformation.CUIList with mand
```

4.2 Generation of the Configuration UI

Once the aggregated FM is produced for the specific point that needs to be configured, it is necessary to build a configuration interface. As the FM are selected and composed on demand, we should significantly improve the production time of it by using UI automatic generation. Indeed, this kind of UI can be

---

[5] We designed the transformation FMs in accordance to the transformations themselves.

automatically generated thanks to simple heuristics, see for instance [6,24]. We implement some of these heuristics in order to produce from a FM a configuration CUI. For instance in Listing 1.2 we generate a label and a check-box (Input of type 'checkox') for each optional feature (using the isInOptionalGroup()). In the same idea, mandatory features are just shown with a label (no user action is required). For the groups (XOR, OR, AND), we generate specific elements: XOR are decomposed into a drop-down list where only one feature can be selected, OR as a checkbox group. Finally, for each level of the FM hierarchy we generate a container (panel or a tab) that would help separating the features.

Listing 1.2. Configuration rule for optional feature.

```
rule FeatureOptionalToCheckBox {
  from
    source : MM!Feature (source.isInOptionalGroup())
  to
    target : MM2!Input (
      id<- 'checkbox_'+source.id,
      type <- 'checkbox',
      content <- source.name ),
    t2: MM2!Label(
      content <- source.name,
      "for" <- target,
      id <- 'checkbox-label_'+source.id )
}
```

As such, we have generated a configuration (see Fig. 6) for the partial aggregated FMs of Fig. 5. We have thus generated a drop-down list for the selection of list type, a group of check-boxes for list options (filtered, indexed) and finally another group of check-boxes for each mapped concept (name and picture).

Fig. 6. Configuration Interface for a given State (here "ActorList").

The configuration UI is filling a configuration model conforms to a configuration metamodel (a generic configuration metamodel dedicated to our UI design process). It sets for the selected interaction state - IFM model - (e.g., ActorList) the value of "WidgetType" to be targeted and the potential options (for a list: filtered, indexed, etc.).

4.3   Transformations

The implementation of our approach relies on an existing system that derives a UI from IFM and domain models using successive model transformations [28].

This initial system was not taking into account the configuration of the variability. We added the possibility of configuring the system using a specific UI dedicated to specific configurations.

In addition, as mentioned in the Sect. 3.2, we should not freeze the UI generation until a complete configuration is provided: we rely on partial configuration. As a result, we have kept our initial tool behavior: it should generate an executable UI even if no explicit configuration is provided for all elements. A default transformation (see Listing 1.3) is executed if it has no configuration (i.getConfiguration.oclIsUndefined()): it will, by default, transform a selection state into a "ListView". The "getConfiguration" helper uses the explicit link between the input models (IFM/Domain) and the configuration model. It is based on a reference of an IFM state previously selected (see Fig. 6 where the reference to the IFM state model is given - State ActorList).

Listing 1.3. Excerpt of the default transformation used if no configuration is defined.

```
rule selectionListViewDefault extends widgetEvents {
  from
    i : SC!SelectionState(i.getConfiguration.oclIsUndefined())
  to
    o : CUI!ListView (
      name <- i.name,
      id <- i.name.regexReplaceAll(' ',''),
      widgets <- i.domainElements->select(e| e.Type = #Image)->collect(e|thisModule.
        ↪image(e))
    )
}
```

We modified our initial tool by adding the configuration as a parameter of the transformation. This has no impact on the other transformations allowing us to reuse the rest of the transformation chain up to the application generation: CUI to ISM and ISM to Code. For each type of widget to be generated a rule is produced (see the Listing 1.4 for a configuration of a tile list). Each particular attribute of the widget (i.e., indexed and filtered) is also dependent on the configuration thus introducing additional conditional expressions (ListFilters and ListDividers conditions in Listing 1.4).

Listing 1.4. Excerpt of Selection to Tile List in CUI transformation including configuration helpers.

```
helper context OclAny def: hasConfig(config:String) : Boolean = if (self.
  ↪getConfiguration.oclIsUndefined())
  then
    false
  else
    self.getConfiguration.WidgetName=config
  endif;
...
rule selectionTileList extends widgetEvents {
  from
    i : SC!SelectionState(i.hasConfig('TileList'))
  using {
    conf:Configuration!Configuration = i.getConfiguration;
  }
  to
    o : CUI!TileList (
      name <- i.name,
      id <- i.name.regexReplaceAll(' ',''),
      icons <- i.domainElements->select(e| e.Type = #Image)->collect(e|thisModule.
        ↪image(e)),
      Listfilters <- if(conf.filtered) then filter else OclUndefined endif,
      listDivider <- if(conf.indexed) then divider else OclUndefined endif
    ),
    filter : CUI!Filter(
```

```
        filterRevealedList <- false),
    divider : CUI!Divider(
        autodivider <- true )
}
```

4.4   Example of Product Configuration

In order to perform a configuration, the designer uses the interface provided in
Fig. 6. He/she first selects the input state model element (e.g., selection state
"ActorList") and the type of widget (e.g., among the type of lists) using the
drop-down menu. In addition he/she can select/de-select the domain elements
manipulated by this state (configuration of the mapping FM), for instance
removing/adding the Actor name and Actor picture that could be displayed
by the list. If the selected type of list is "Tile List", it needed an attribute of
type image (e.g., the actor picture). As a result, the actor picture will be selected
by default and not de-selectable.

Once the designer has finished and saves the configuration (i.e., as a configuration model), he/she can choose to launch the generation process. The
transformation chain will generate the configured UI part within the rest of the
application. End-users are able to evaluate the configured part inside the whole
application interaction process. This task has to be repeated for each identified
configurations. Figure 7 shows the result of two UIs generated from two different
list configurations. A video summarizing the edition of models and the realization of configurations, including the automatic generation of the prototypes, is
available at http://youtu.be/78t11o0jatU.

Fig. 7. At left: List View configuration for actor selection displaying actor names. At
right: Tile List configuration with actor images.

Once a convincing configuration is positively evaluated by the end-users, it
is stored to be used for the final product. The final product configuration should
be done by composing all the relevant configurations, using for instance the
approach by [23].

5   Conclusions and Perspectives

We have considered in this article the issue related to UI variability. UI variability has numerous facets (e.g., graphical design, development, usability, etc.) due to the diversity of stakeholder profiles (including end-users). Moreover, in UI design, one encounters frequently the difficulty to align the products with fuzzily defined user requirements. This complexity can lead to an inefficient UI design process, which has an impact on the UI design costs.

Therefore, we proposed an approach to manage UI variability based on MDE and SPL, integrating SPL management into our current MDE UI design process. Whereas traditional approaches focus on the elicitation of product line from FMs only, we rather claim that FMs are supporting the design of a product line completing the existing design choices (i.e., the one made by expert stakeholders using their design models). In our approach, UI design stakeholders can express the variability on the models, mappings and transformations by defining multiple FMs related to each of these assets.

In order to build a viable product, the stakeholders have to confront their viewpoints when configuring products. The proposed approach is based on iterative-steps and partial configurations that can be refined by all stakeholders including the end-users. As a result, we have worked on the selection and aggregation of FM subsets in order to provide a unified frame for building a partial configuration. Then, in order to support such dynamic definition of partial configuration, we have to automatically derive a configuration UI based on the sliced and aggregated FMs.

Partial configurations are used to parameterize the transformations: it specifies some design choices. Default transformation heuristics are then used to complete the partial configuration. A partial configuration should be independent from other partial configurations (i.e., independent from external constraints) but we should derive all the implications (i.e., required or disabled features) of the current partial configuration in order to generate a proper product.

More particularly, in the context of rapid prototyping, the UI designer can focus on a specific point, using partial configurations and test it with end-users. We implemented this approach in our existing UI model transformations which are parameterized by partial configurations and based on heuristics to generate default UI elements for the features that are not configured.

As future work, we have to further explore the merging of partial configurations in order to produce a final product configuration according (e.g., [23]) to the global product constraints. When trying to solve the global constraints from each individual partial configurations, we can reach a point where the product expected by the end-users enforces some of theses constraints. Thus, we will have to provide some collaborative environment to actually help in reaching consensus and maybe make compromises amongst the partial configurations. As such, we plan to further exploit our collaborative infrastructure [15] for partial configurations reconciliation.

Finally, we discovered that the variability is manifold and multi-dimensional in the design of UIs and that FMs are of several types. We think that building a taxonomy of these different FM could help us in understanding more precisely UI variability and could lead us to a better reuse of variability assets across projects and domains.

Acknowledgements. This work has been supported by the FNR CORE Project MoDEL C12/IS/3977071 and AFR grant agreement 7859308.

References

1. Acher, M., Collet, P., Lahire, P., France, R.B.: Separation of concerns in feature modeling: support and applications. In: Proceedings of the 11th Conference on Aspect-oriented Software Development (2012)
2. Acher, M., Collet, P., Lahire, P., France, R.B.: Familiar: a domain-specific language for large scale management of feature models. Sci. Comput. Program. **78**(6), 657–681 (2013)
3. Acher, M., Lahire, P., Moisan, S., Rigault, J.P.: Tackling high variability in video surveillance systems through a model transformation approach. In: MISE 2009. ICSE Workshop, pp. 44–49. IEEE (2009)
4. Batory, D., Azanza, M., Saraiva, J.: The objects and arrows of computational design. In: Czarnecki, K., Ober, I., Bruel, J.-M., Uhl, A., Völter, M. (eds.) MOD-ELS 2008. LNCS, vol. 5301, pp. 1–20. Springer, Heidelberg (2008)
5. Benavides, D., Segura, S., Ruiz-Cortés, A.: Automated analysis of feature models 20 years later: a literature review. Inf. Syst. **35**(6), 615–636 (2010)
6. Boucher, Q., Perrouin, G., Heymans, P.: Deriving configuration interfaces from feature models: A vision paper. In: Proceedings of the Sixth International Workshop on Variability Modeling of Software-Intensive Systems, pp. 37–44. ACM (2012)
7. Brummermann, H., Keunecke, M., Schmid, K.: Variability issues in the evolution of information system ecosystems. In: Proceedings of the 5th Workshop on Variability Modeling of Software-Intensive Systems (2011)
8. Bühne, S., Lauenroth, K., Pohl, K.: Why is it not sufficient to model requirements variability with feature models. In: Workshop on Automotive Requirements Engineering (AURE04), at RE04, Japan (2004)
9. Calvary, G., Coutaz, J., Thevenin, D., Limbourg, Q., Bouillon, L., Vanderdonckt, J.: A unifying reference framework for multi-target user interfaces. Interact. Comput. **15**(3), 289–308 (2003)
10. Clements, P., Northrop, L.: Software Product Lines. Addison-Wesley Boston, Boston (2002)
11. Czarnecki, K., Antkiewicz, M., Kim, C.H.P., Lau, S., Pietroszek, K.: Model-driven software product lines. In: Companion to the 20th Annual ACM SIGPLAN Conference on Object-Oriented Programming, Systems, Languages, and Applications, pp. 126–127. ACM (2005)
12. Czarnecki, K., Helsen, S., Eisenecker, U.: Staged configuration through specialization and multilevel configuration of feature models. Softw. Process Improv. Pract. **10**(2), 143–169 (2005)
13. DIS, I.: 9241–210: 2010. Ergonomics of human system interaction-part 210: Human-centred design for interactive systems. International Standardization Organization (ISO). Switzerland (2009)
14. Gabillon, Y., Biri, N., Otjacques, B.: Designing multi-context uis by software product line approach. In: ICHCI 2013 (2013)

15. Garcìa Frey, A., Sottet, J.S., Vagner, A.: A multi-viewpoint approach to support collaborative user interface generation. In: 19th IEEE International Conference on Computer Supported Cooperative Work in Design CSCWD (2015)
16. García Frey, A., Sottet, J.S., Vagner, A.: Ame: an adaptive modelling environment as a collaborative modelling tool. In: Proceedings of the 2014 ACM SIGCHI Symposium on Engineering Interactive Computing Systems, pp. 189–192. ACM (2014)
17. García Frey, A., Sottet, J.S., Vagner, A.: Towards a multi-stakehoder engineering approach with adaptive modelling environments. In: Proceedings of the 2014 ACM SIGCHI Symposium on Engineering Interactive Computing Systems, pp. 33–38. ACM (2014)
18. Mannion, M., Savolainen, J., Asikainen, T.: Viewpoint-oriented variability modeling. In: COMPSAC 2009 (2009)
19. Martinez, J., Lopez, C., Ulacia, E., del Hierro, M.: Towards a model-driven product line for web systems. In: 5th Model-Driven Web Engineering Workshop MDWE 2009 (2009)
20. OMG: IFML- interaction flow modeling language, March 2013
21. Pleuss, A., Hauptmann, B., Dhungana, D., Botterweck, G.: User interface engineering for software product lines: the dilemma between automation and usability. In: EICS, pp. 25–34. ACM (2012)
22. Pohl, K., Böckle, G., Van Der Linden, F.: Software Product Line Engineering: Foundations, Principles, and Techniques. Springer, Heidelberg (2005)
23. Rosenmüller, M., Siegmund, N.: Automating the configuration of multi software product lines. In: VaMoS, pp. 123–130 (2010)
24. Schlee, M., Vanderdonckt, J.: Generative programming of graphical user interfaces. In: Proceedings of the Working Conference on Advanced Visual Interfaces, pp. 403–406. ACM (2004)
25. Sijtema, M.: Introducing variability rules in atl for managing variability in mde-based product lines. In: Proceedings of MtATL 2010, pp. 39–49 (2010)
26. Sottet, J.S., Calvary, G., Coutaz, J., Favre, J.M.: A model-driven engineering approach for the usability of plastic user interfaces. In: Gulliksen, Jan, Harning, Morton Borup, van der Veer, Gerrit C., Wesson, Janet (eds.) EIS 2007. LNCS, vol. 4940, pp. 140–157. Springer, Heidelberg (2008)
27. Sottet, J.S., Vagner, A.: Genius: generating usable user interfaces (2013). arXiv preprint arXiv:1310.1758
28. Sottet, J.S., Vagner, A.: Defining domain specific transformations in human-computer interfaces development. In: 2nd International Conference on Model-Driven Engineering and Software Developement (2014)
29. White, J., Dougherty, B., Schmidt, D.C., Benavides, D.: Automated reasoning for multi-step feature model configuration problems. In: Proceedings of the 13th International Software Product Line Conference (2009)

Sustainable Enterprise Interoperability in Dynamic Collaborative Environments: A Knowledge Link Approach

Artur Felic[1,2](✉), Felix Herrmann[1], Christian Hogrefe[1], Michael Klein[1], and Birgitta König-Ries[2]

[1] CAS Software AG, Karlsruhe, Germany
{artur.felic,felix.herrmann,christian.hogrefe,michael.klein}@cas.de
[2] Institut Für Informatik, Friedrich-Schiller-Universität Jena, Jena, Germany
{artur.felic,birgitta.koenig-ries}@uni-jena.de

Abstract. In complex and collaborative ecosystems, different partners need to share their respective expert knowledge in order to be successful. Due to the diversity of business applications and highly customized application suites used by business partners, knowledge exchange and the establishment of interoperability between enterprise applications is extremely difficult. Different meanings of enterprise data lead to incomprehensibility between partners. This paper presents a model-driven approach to support sustainable interoperability for enterprise applications in collaborative environments. Knowledge Links enable dynamic modelling of knowledge transformations between knowledge domains and keep background consistency between the connected domains. Knowledge Links can be created and modified at any time, which enables sustainable interoperability. Business partners may rely on their enterprise applications and sensitive data stays covert due to the nature of modular ontologies. The presented approach is exemplified in the context of the OSMOSE Project and will be evaluated by the proof-of-concept scenarios in this Project.

Keywords: Semantic web · Knowledge links · Semantic interoperability · Sustainable interoperability · Enterprise interoperability

1 Introduction

According to Fowler [13] "Enterprise applications are about the display, manipulation, and storage of large amounts of often complex data and the support or automation of business processes with that data". Enterprises usually compose their highly customized applications suits by applications from different competing vendors, which do not want to reveal sensitive data in order to be integrated.

The paradigm shift from individual businesses to complex and collaborative, globally spread ecosystems also comprising competing business partners has led

© Springer International Publishing Switzerland 2015
P. Desfray et al. (Eds.): MODELSWARD 2015, CCIS 580, pp. 405–420, 2015.
DOI: 10.1007/978-3-319-27869-8_24

to enterprise interoperability problems. Interoperability can be seen as "ability of systems or components to exchange and use information" [18] or the "ability to share and exchange information using common syntax and semantics to meet an application-specific functional relationship through the use of a common interface" (ISO 1610). Enterprise Interoperability concerns data, services, processes and internal business. Emerging Enterprise Interoperability Frameworks like EIF [17], FEI [4], C4IF [32] and AIF [2] aim at enabling Enterprise Interoperability. Sustainable interoperability can be described as "novel strategies, methods and tools to maintain and sustain the interoperability of enterprise systems in networked environments as they evolve with their environments" [19] and takes dynamics in business networks into account. Thus, sustainability and interoperability are two inherently linked and inseparable aspects [7].

The Object Management Group (OMG) [29] proposed Model-Driven Architecture (MDA) [28] as a strategy towards interoperability of heterogeneous systems [36]. MDA can be extended by Semantic Web technologies, i.e. ontologies, to create unambiguous domain vocabularies [41]. Gruber defines ontologies as "an explicit specification of a conceptualization" [15]. Knowledge sharing is fundamental in collaborative ecosystems. Ontologies can be used to structure knowledge and knowledge properties in order to make knowledge understandable for machines and humans. Upper ontologies like SUMO [27] are purposed to structure only very general concepts in order to support semantic interoperability. Modular ontologies [3] divide large monolithic ontologies into smaller domain modules in terms of interchangeability. Domain ontologies are often not comprehensible outside the domain, but the knowledge structured inside is of importance for other domains and need to be linked.

In the OSMOSE Project [31], the aim is to interconnect the real, digital and virtual world for sensing liquid enterprises and to keep background consistency of shadow ambassadors. Applications in each world have to be aware of the meaning of data in order to decide which data has to cross world borders. The three worlds together with the middleware can be seen as an collaborative environment.

This paper is an extended Version of [10], omitting most technical details and going deeper into theoretical background of knowledge links. We propose a model-driven approach using Knowledge Links [11]. Knowledge Links are used to connect the knowledge domains and transform knowledge from one to another. By connecting different knowledge domains in a black box manner, business partners of a collaborative environment can rely on their knowledge structures. We present an event-driven and service oriented architecture approach in which enterprise applications constitute separated knowledge domains. Furthermore, a tool is presented with which knowledge links can be created and maintained at any time during system runtime and thus enable sustainable interoperability.

After this introduction, in Sect. 2, we will explore related work to this paper. In Sect. 3, the modular and hierarchical knowledge base concept is introduced. The proposed Event-Driven Architecture is described in Sect. 4. The two latter sections constitute the foundation of Sect. 5, in which the sustainable interoperability approach is illustrated. In Sect. 7 the paper is concluded and summarized and future research directions are specified.

2   Related Work

[21] identified the lack of scientific foundations of enterprise interoperability and formulated several scientific areas. The main scientific areas the present paper addresses are data, software, knowledge and ecosystems interoperability. While one of the main objectives of semantic web technologies is to induce a common meaning about knowledge for human beings and machines, MDA and EDA are concerned with platform independence and heterogeneity of systems. The following scientific findings and publications give an overview about related work in these scientific areas.

[5] analysed enterprise interoperability architectures from 1985 to 2000 and states that most effort has been put in framework approaches rather architectures of enterprise systems. Furthermore, the authors identified the lack of an enterprise architecture ontology, the absence of scientific methodologies and interoperability between existing architectures as well as weak impact in industry. The authors identified conceptual barriers as one of the main category of interoperability barriers that are "concerned with the syntactic and semantic differences of information to be exchanged", which highly motivates our work. Moreover, they describe the interoperability of data as a category of interoperability concerns that "deals with finding and sharing information from heterogeneous data sources". According to the categorization of interoperability approaches, we present a federated approach, where partners do not impose own models on the enterprise architecture.

The authors of [6] utilize a model driven architecture approach and ontologies to enable knowledge sharing for manufacturing systems interoperability. The Manufacturing Core Ontology constitutes the heart of the Platform Independent Model (PIM), whereas other domains extend the Manufacturing Core Ontology to specify domain specific models. To enable knowledge sharing of the further transformed Platform Specific Model (PSM), knowledge verification mechanisms are specified at PIM level. However, the approach is limited to the specification of constraints on PIM level and does not allow appropriate knowledge propagation with transformations in order to provide partners with new knowledge build from their knowledge base.

Kadar et al. [20] propose a multi-agent system to support sustainable interoperability for networked organizations. Rule based negotiation at business level by agents in a distributed environment enable the re-establishment of interoperability between partners. Although the work of Kadar et al. is inspiring and knowledge negotiation is demanding, the need to transform knowledge between different knowledge domains and the creation of complex knowledge relationships among different partners in terms of sustainable interoperability is not covered. Knowledge Links could therefore complement this work.

[26] present an ontology based approach. Domain ontologies are connected by special collaboration ontologies, which are semi-automatically created. These collaboration ontologies are described by OWL-S [40] in order to "enables automatic service discovery, invocation, composition, interoperation, and execution monitoring". The OWL-S descriptions from these collaboration ontologies are further

transformed to BPEL and WSDL to allow automated execution of ontology mappings. Thus, an business process execution engine is able to react appropriately to requests according to data changes. Although the approach is very closely related to the knowledge link approach, it is strongly dependent on the mechanisms behind the semi-automatic creation process of the collaboration ontologies. Additionally, complex links with operations and transformations cannot be created by hand.

The authors of [1] propose to enhance information systems by traceability functionalities to enable sustainable interoperability. Using model morphisms that allow altering and non-altering model mapping, the relationship of models from different knowledge domains can be formalized. These mappings are translated in executable code in order to exchange mapped or transformed data between business partners. The work of Agostinho et al. is closely related to the Knowledge Links due to the support of morphisms between different knowledge domains. Mappings are created on ontology level, therefore Knowledge Links could complement this work by allowing end users to model the executable connections with given tools for end users. By using Knowledge Links, the presented approach could be enhanced by reusability of mappings. The result of a mapping could further be used to define new mappings.

The approach presented in this paper combines ontology-driven, event-driven and model-driven approaches and is based on three pillars: A modular and hierarchical knowledge base, an event-driven architecture for collaborative environments and a model-driven knowledge link approach with a business process execution engine. In the following sections, we will take a look at these in turn.

3   Knowledge Base Structure

Knowledge links generally link concepts from different ontologies that may have common concepts or may be completely separated. The approach also allows linkage inside the same ontology, thus making it a generic approach for many different purposes. The knowledge base structure for sustainable enterprise interoperability is following the work of [3] about modular ontologies. Major advantages of the modularization approach that are of particular importance are knowledge reuse across application domains, distributed ontology engineering over different knowledge domains and effective management of ontology modules. Modular ontologies allow business partners to rely on their own knowledge structures and maintain their own knowledge base while connecting their knowledge structure to a shared common denominator.

The knowledge base structures for sustainable enterprise interoperability can be categorized in different hierarchy levels. The highest level is constituted by a common ontology structuring necessary knowledge about the business network. At the second hierarchy level the business partners' ontologies are located. Each business partner structures its knowledge separately. The third and lowest hierarchy level comprise the enterprise applications' ontologies. Figure 1 illustrates the hierarchy levels.

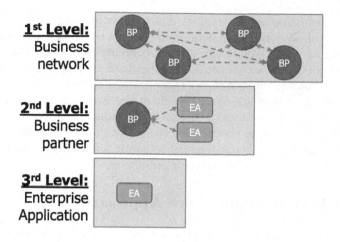

Fig. 1. Knowledge base hierarchy.

Ontologies of lower levels inherit the ontologies of the next higher level and enrich the higher level concepts with new specific concepts or add specific concepts underneath higher level concepts. According to [3], this pattern of imports establishes an unidirectional correspondence between the lower level ontologies and the higher level ontology. More precisely, the highest level ontology constitutes an upper ontology for the underlying ontologies. According to [16], an upper ontology is a high-level, domain independent ontology whose concepts generic and basic and "from which more specific ontologies can be derived". Mid-level ontologies between the lowest and highest level of the ontology hierarchy ease the mapping between these levels, whereas the domain ontologies on the lowest level reuse the concepts from the levels above and extend them with domain specific concepts. Upper ontologies are used to describe generic, platform independent concepts in order to generalise the meaning of domain specific concepts. There are many initiatives that aim to define standard upper ontologies, for instance, the Suggested Upper Merged Ontology [27]. Domain ontologies that are compliant with the upper ontologies are able to interoperate by shared terms and definitions and mapping to these terms. In [30], semantic annotations of various domains are analysed and a unified formal model for semantic annotations is presented. Using such an annotation model allows enterprise application resources to be structured and processable by the event driven knowledge link approach.

In our approach, we use Apache Jena [12] as storage and interface for ontologies. Jena is a semantic web framework consisting of three modules. An OWL [43] and inference API allows interaction with ontologies and reasoning over data. The built-in triple store enables persistence and allows querying over SPARQL [42] and http. An RDF [44] API allows users to create, read and manipulate triples and handles serialization.

The knowledge base structure of the OSMOSE Platform follows the schema described above. Like depicted in Fig. 2, the OSMOSE Upper-Ontology constitutes a common upper ontology for the whole platform at the highest hierarchical level. It contains generic concepts about events, entities, services and processes as well as platform specific concepts like 'OSMOSE World' or 'OSMOSE Process'. This common knowledge base is imported by each of the three worlds allowing the worlds to extend these concepts. The Intra-World Ontologies are ontologies specific for each of the world, acting as a mid-level ontology. Inner world applications use own ontologies by importing the Intra-World Ontology and adding specific concepts. Thus, they define the lowest level of ontologies, the domain ontologies. By semantic annotations, the inner-world applications can map their data to their ontologies.

4   Event-Driven Architecture Approach

An Event-Driven Architecture is a style of Service-Oriented Architecture, where the occurrence of an event can trigger the invocation of services, which in turn can generate new events. [25] Event-driven systems are designed to process events as they occur, allowing the system to observe, react dynamically to and issue personalized data depending on the recipient and situation [9]. Event-driven architectures are deployed in many areas and have proofed as a competitive advantage for a lot of organizations. Thus, they are becoming increasingly popular [14]. Events can be seen as kind of messages that are generated by resources in domains and recognised by information systems. Events can occur and be converted from anywhere in an environment [37], indicating hat an occurrence has been observed in a system [14]. Luckham defines events as objects that are records of activities in a system and can have a relation to other events with a timestamps as properties [22]. According to McGovern, "an event is a change in the state of a resource or request for processing" [24].

Complex events are combinations of multiple events consisting of all the activities that the aggregated events signify [22,35]. Complex Event Processing (CEP) deals with the identification and handling of interdependent events

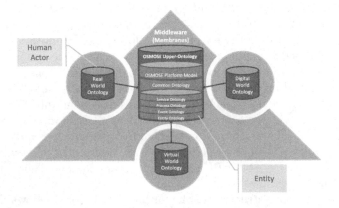

Fig. 2. OSMOSE knowledge base hierarchy.

across organizations, analysing their impact and taking subsequent action in real time into account. It is an emerging technology which allows to find real time relationships between different events using elements such as timing, causality, and membership in a stream of data in order to extract relevant information [33]. Luckham states that "Complex Event Processing (CEP) is a defined as a set of tools and techniques for analysing and controlling the complex series of interrelated events that drive modern distributed information systems" [23].

According to [39], loose coupling among services and applications is the key to building interoperable enterprise systems. Message-Oriented Middleware (MOM) or their extension, the Enterprise Service Bus (ESB), enable loose coupling using message queuing techniques. They implement the Event-Driven Architecture pattern and provide neutral message formats with which applications are able to exchange messages independently and asynchronously using simple transport protocols. Furthermore, it enables communication between different business units with heterogeneous platforms and environments.

Our approach utilizes the WSO2 Enterprise Service Bus [45] together with the RabbitMQ Message Broker [34] and Esper [8] Complex Event Processor in order to take advantage of concepts explained before. Additionally, we've added access to the knowledge base to combine the power of semantic web technologies with complex event processing. Figure 3 illustrates the components of the middleware. Events that are sent have to proceed the middleware, i.e. the event channel. More technical details can be found in [10].

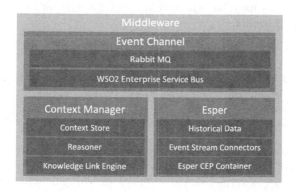

Fig. 3. Middleware components.

WSO2 ESB, RabbitMQ and Esper are used together in the OSMOSE Project in order to allow communication and analysis about events between the real, digital and virtual world. Autonomous components deploy services in a WSO2 ESB. Thereby, they can react to events, call services or negotiate with other autonomous components. The communication is handled by RabbitMQ and analysed by the Esper CEP Engine.

5   Knowledge Links

In the previous two main sections, the foundation of our approach for sustainable interoperability was defined. We have adapted the generic knowledge base concept of knowledge links for business partners with which structuring of different knowledge domains is enabled.

The event driven architecture approach enables business partners to connect their enterprise applications, while all business partners can be connected together to a business network environment. Interoperability can be sustained whenever business partners enter the environment, change enterprise applications or knowledge structures. Knowledge links are connections between knowledge concepts of different knowledge domains in a black box manner. They constitute a morphism of how knowledge in one domain can be constructed by using knowledge from other domains.

5.1   Syntax of Knowledge Links

Knowledge Links can be described by operators and knowledge concepts, i.e. ontology classes, concatenated together. Hereafter, c indicates a knowledge concept from the set of all knowledge concepts C. Operators can be formally described by functions $o(\cdot) \in O$ that transform inputs to an output (1). Like c for Concepts, operators o are generic for the syntax and will be substituted by specific ones. Inputs x_i are ether knowledge concepts c or again operators $o(\cdot)$. Thus, operators may have nested (e.g. $o(o(o(\cdot))))$ and concatenated (e.g. $o(o(\cdot), c, o(\cdot), c, ...))$ inputs.

$$o : (x_1, ..., x_n) \mapsto o(x_1, ..., x_n), \quad o \in O, \quad c \in C, \quad x_i \in O \cup C \qquad (1)$$

The assignment := maps the element on the right side to elements on the left side. A formal representation is given in (2).

$$(c_1, ..., c_m) := (x) \Rightarrow \forall c_i \in (c_1, ..., c_m) : c_i := x, \quad c \in C, \quad x \in C \cup O \qquad (2)$$

(3) to (7) illustrate the structure. Simple assignments from one knowledge concept to one or multiple knowledge concepts are given in (3) and (4). The concepts on the right side are assigned to the concept on the left side indicating direct knowledge propagation from the right to the left side when the knowledge behind the right side knowledge concept changes. General indirect mappings have the form of (5). The result of the operation $o(\cdot)$ with concatenated inputs $x_1, ..., x_m$ is assigned to one or more knowledge concepts c_m. Inside operations, inputs can be again nested operators (6) or concatenations of (nested) operators and concepts (7).

$$(c_1) := (c_2) \qquad (3)$$

$$(c_1, ..., c_n) := (c_m) \qquad (4)$$

$$(c_m) := (o(x_1, ..., x_n)) \qquad (5)$$

$$(c_m) := (o(o(x_1, ..., x_n))) \qquad (6)$$

$$(c_m) := (o(o(x_1, ..., x_n), x_{n+1}, ..., x_o)) \qquad (7)$$

The generic language of knowledge links can be described by the following context-free grammar:

$G_{KL} = (V, \sum, R, S)$
$V = \{$ Assignment, Operation, Concatenation, Concept$\}$
$\sum = \{$ ',', '(', ')', 'o', 'c', ':='$\}$
S as start symbol
with production rules R:
S $\rightarrow$ Assignment(Operation) | Assignment(c)
Operation $\rightarrow$ o(Concept) | o(Concatenation , Concept) | o(Concatenation)
Concatenation $\rightarrow$ Concatenation, Concatenation | Operation
Assignment $\rightarrow$ (Concept):=
Concept $\rightarrow$ c, C | c

The generic terminal symbol 'c' represents knowledge concepts, i.e. classes from ontologies, whereas 'o' represents operators of knowledge links. Let's assume the concepts $c_{SETPOINT}$ and $c_{MEASUREMENT}$ are in one ontology, the concept $c_{DEVIATION}$ in another ontology. To define the deviation as the subtraction result of the set point and measurement, the following knowledge link can be created with the grammar above:

$S \Rightarrow Assignment(Operation) \Rightarrow (Concept) := (Operation) \Rightarrow$
$(Concept) := (o_{SUBTRACTION}(Concept)) \Rightarrow$
$(Concept) := (o_{SUBTRACTION}(c_{SETPOINT}, Concept)) \Rightarrow$
$(Concept) := (o_{SUBTRACTION}(c_{SETPOINT}, c_{MEASUREMENT})) \Rightarrow$
$(c_{DEVIATION}) := (o_{SUBTRACTION}(c_{SETPOINT}, c_{MEASUREMENT}))$

The knowledge link grammar can be formally expressed in Extended Backus-Naur Form (EBNF) (ISO/IEC 14977) for syntax analysis:

$KnowledgeLink = Assignment$ '(' $(Operation|$'c'$)$ ')'
$Operation =$ 'o' '(' $Concatenation$ ')'
$Concatenation = (Operation|Concept) \{$',' $(Operation|Concept)\}$
$Assignment =$ '(' $Concept$ ')' ':='
$Concept =$ 'c' $\{$',' 'c'$\}$

Figure 4 illustrates the resulting syntax diagram of the EBNF grammar.

5.2 Modelling and Execution

In order to model knowledge links, we implemented the Knowledge Link Configurator. This graphical modelling tool allows users to import knowledge structures from different knowledge domains and create knowledge links between them. Creating a new knowledge link or loading an existing one opens a graphical editor that allows dragging and dropping of imported knowledge concepts as well as operators from a palette. Knowledge links are defined by drawing connections

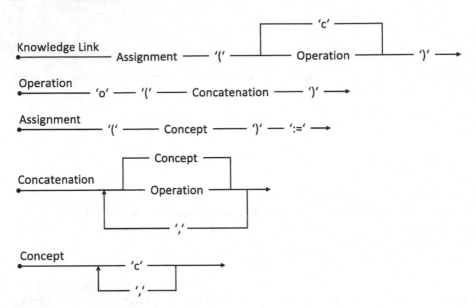

Fig. 4. Knowledge link syntax diagram.

between knowledge concepts and operators dragged and dropped on the editor area. Currently, we have defined a set of numeric (Sum, Subtraction, Average...), textual (Concat...) and boolean (AND, OR, XOR...) operators. After the user finished with modelling, knowledge links can be stored and uploaded to the server. The uploaded knowledge links are further translated and pushed to the Knowledge Link Engine in the Context Store of the middleware.

In Fig. 3, modelling of knowledge links with the Knowledge Link Configurator is illustrated. On the top right corner of the screenshot, the different knowledge base structures are imported. On the lower right side the knowledge link definitions can be found. Creating a new knowledge link definition will create a rule sheet on which the graphical modelling is done (squared area in the middle). The operators can be found on the left side. In the knowledge link on the screenshot, the set point of a machine part is subtracted from it's measurement in order to calculate the deviation of the machine part. The measurement and set point is taken from the real world machine and machine part, more precisely, from the real world ontology. The deviation is a digital world concept and thus described in the digital world ontology. The description of the knowledge link can be interpreted as follows:

1. First two nodes, 'measurement' and 'set point':
   Retrieve 'measurement' and 'set point'.
2. Subtraction node, 'SUB':
   Subtract the set point from the measurement.
3. Equals node, '==':
   Store the result ...
4. Last node, 'deviation':
   ...as 'deviation' in the ontology.

The translation of knowledge links is done in two steps. First, the knowledge concepts of the source domain are identified that participate in the knowledge link. For all of those knowledge concepts, a listener in the CEP Engine is registered that listens to changes of the data behind that knowledge concept. It is assumed that for all changes to data that are relevant for the knowledge base semantic annotations are used and a change of data results in an event that is sent to the middleware having the knowledge concept as subject. Thus, when knowledge concepts of the source domain are recognized in events that represent changes of the data behind, the knowledge link will be executed in order to keep background consistency. After registering the listeners, an event automata is created that handles requests on middleware level. When requesting knowledge that is defined by a knowledge link, events for gathering knowledge from each domain and for calculation need to be executed.

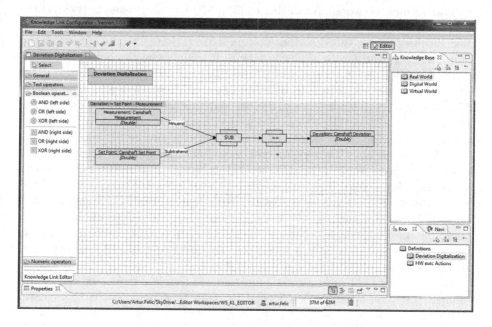

Fig. 5. Knowledge link configurator.

For the latter case, we use business processes to perform actions modelled with palette operators. During the second step of translation, the modelled behaviour is translated into process-files that are associated with the knowledge link. If a listener recognises an event that is relevant for a knowledge link, the data from knowledge bases that refers to the knowledge link is requested by events and passed to the process. The process is built from predefined building blocks that correspond to the palette operators. For instance, the 'Subtraction' palette operator has a predefined building block for business processes. When used, the two values that should be subtracted are loaded by event requests from the appropriate knowledge bases and passed to the business process for calculation. After the business process has finished, the result is passed back to the event automata in order to proceed with another business process or to push the data in the appropriate knowledge base by using events. The translated process file knows about the execution order and the input parameters that are necessary. Because of the flexibility of the predefined building blocks for processes, sequences of them can be reused when similar parts of knowledge links are modelled.

6   Model-Driven Architecture Approach

Knowledge Links follow the Model-Driven Architecture (MDA) [28] approach by separating business and application logic from platform-specific software of dynamic business networks. According to [38], MDA distinguishes between three different MDA Models. The Computation Independent Model (CIM) is also called business model and describes system expectations, i.e. the output of the system, independently from implementation. It bridges the gap between domain experts and information technologists. The Platform Independent Model (PIM) abstracts out technical details by defining appropriate services and exhibiting a sufficient degree of independence to enable mapping to platforms. Contrary, the Platform Specific Model (PSM) combines specifications of the PIM with platform specific details. From their demand to their specification, modelling and translation, knowledge links undergo several model transformations between MDA Models. Figure 6 illustrates the different MDA Models and the transformations that are explained below. Vertical arrows represent CIM to PIM or PIM to PSM transformations respectively. Horizontal arrows represent CIM to CIM or rather PIM to PIM transformations. In some cases, one-to-one transformations may not be suitable. Instead, many-to-one, one-to-many or even many-to-many transformations will be applied. This is illustrated by multiple consecutively arranged boxes as input or output for the arrows in Fig. 6.

Models of the CIM are business requirements that are expressed in natural language. They describe the knowledge demand that business partners have. Further, they can be transformed or consolidated to other, higher-level CIM models to express the knowledge demand inside the business network. These descriptions are computation independent. Knowledge links themselves are models of the PIM. Their description is platform independent and can be graphically modelled with the Knowledge Link Configurator. Furthermore, they are translated into other PIM models, the event automata and business processes (PIM to PIM transformation), after storing them on the platform. The transformation result is independent from enterprise applications that are implemented by business partners. Business processes and event descriptions are also platform independent and could be used by various engines or middleware components in different integrated systems. During knowledge link translation, the PIM models are transformed to PSM models taking semantic annotations into account. Semantic annotations map the knowledge concepts of ontologies to real data like documents in different formats. Thus, knowledge gathering depends on the underlying platform and enterprise application that business partners are using. Additionally, code fragments like event listeners and event triggers are generated in order to control the knowledge and event flow of the knowledge link at the middleware level. Business processes are translated and stored into specific process files that can be executed by the business process execution engine.

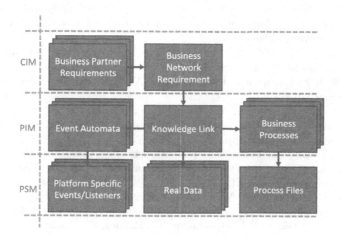

Fig. 6. Model transformations of knowledge links.

7   Summary and Conclusion

We combined semantic web technologies, event-driven and model-driven architecture approaches with knowledge links to propose a solution for sustainable interoperability in collaborative environments. Our approach is based on three pillars: (1) a hierarchical and modular knowledge base concept utilizing upper and modular ontologies, (2) an event-driven and message-message oriented middleware based on enterprise service busses that can be connected and (3) knowledge links, a model-driven approach with which domain ontologies can be linked in order to achieve enterprise interoperability. Sustainable interoperability is enabled due to the possibility to create and maintain knowledge links during runtime allowing to react to changes in collaborative environments by end users that are affected by these changes as they appear. Middleware technologies and a tool to create knowledge links have been presented. Obstacles are reduced due to the ability of business partners to define their own knowledge structures. We exemplified our approach with use cases of the OSMOSE Project and will further evaluate our solution in this Project. The software components of the architecture presented in this paper are currently prototypical and will be evaluated after integration with the proof-of-concept scenarios of the OSMOSE Project.

Acknowledgements. The research leading to these results has received funding from the European Union Seventh Framework Programme (FP7/2007-2013) under grant agreement n°610905, the OSMOSE project.

References

1. Agostinho, C., Sarraipa, J., Goncalves, D., Jardim-Goncalves, R.: Tuple-based semantic and structural mapping for a sustainable interoperability. In: Camarinha-Matos, L.M. (ed.) Technological Innovation for Sustainability. IFIP AICT, vol. 349, pp. 45–56. Springer, Heidelberg (2011)
2. ATHENA Project: Da8.2: Guidelines and best practices for applying the athena interoperability framework to support sme participation in digital ecosystems (2007). http://www.asd-ssg.org/html/ATHENA/Deliverables/Deliverables, 17 November 2014
3. Ben Abbs, S., Scheuermann, A., Meilender, T., D'Aquin, M.: Characterizing modular ontologies. In: 7th International Conference on Formal Ontologies in Information Systems - FOIS 2012, pp. 13–25. Graz, Austria (2012)
4. Chen, D., Daclin, N.: Framework for enterprise interoperability. In: Proceedings of the Workshops and the Doctorial Symposium of the Second IFAC/IFIP I-ESA International Conference: EI2N, WSI, IS-TSPQ 2006, pp. 77–88 (2006)
5. Chen, D., Doumeingts, G., Vernadat, F.: Architectures for enterprise integration and interoperability: past, present and future. Comput. Ind. **59**(7), 647–659 (2008)
6. Chungoora, N., Young, R.I., Gunendran, G., Palmer, C., Usman, Z., Anjum, N.A., Cutting-Decelle, A.F., Harding, J.A., Case, K.: A model-driven ontology approach for manufacturing system interoperability and knowledge sharing. Comput. Ind. **64**(4), 392–401 (2013)
7. Dassisti, M., Jardim-Goncalves, R., Molina, A., Noran, O., Panetto, H., Zdravković, M.M.: Sustainability and interoperability: two facets of the same *gold medal*. In: Demey, Y.T., Panetto, H. (eds.) OTM 2013 Workshops 2013. LNCS, vol. 8186, pp. 250–261. Springer, Heidelberg (2013)
8. EsperTech: Esper - complex event processing (2014). http://esper.codehaus.org/, 30 November 2014
9. Etzion, O., Niblett, P.: Event Processing in Action, 1st edn. Manning Publications Co, Greenwich (2010)
10. Felic, A., Herrmann, F., Hogrefe, C., Klein, M., König-Ries, B.: Enabling sustainable interoperability for enterprise applications with knowledge links. In: Proceedings of the 3rd International Conference on Model-Driven Engineering and Software Development (MODELSWARD) 2015, Special Session on Model-Driven Enterprise Services and Applications for a Sustainable Interoperability (MDE4SI) (in press)
11. Felic, A., König-Ries, B., Klein, M.: Process-oriented semantic knowledge management in product lifecycle management. In: 8th International Conference on Digital Enterprise Technology (DET 2014) Procedia CIRP, vol. 25, pp. 361–368 (2014)
12. Foundation, A.S.: Apache jena - home (2014). https://jena.apache.org/, 30 November 2014
13. Fowler, M.: Patterns of enterprise application architecture. The Addison-Wesley signature series. Addison-Wesley, Boston (2003)
14. Grabs, T., Lu, M.: Measuring performance of complex event processing systems. In: Nambiar, R., Poess, M. (eds.) TPCTC 2011. LNCS, vol. 7144, pp. 83–96. Springer, Heidelberg (2012)

15. Gruber, T.R.: A translation approach to portable ontology specifications. Knowl. Acquisition **5**(2), 199–220 (1993)
16. Healy, M., Poli, R., Kameas, A.: Theory and Applications of Ontology: Computer Applications. Springer, Netherlands (2010)
17. IDABC, Echipa, D.G. Industry: European interoperability framework for pan-european egovernment services: Draft document as basis for eif 2.0. European Communities (2004)
18. IEEE: Ieee standard computer dictionary: a compilation of ieee standard computer glossaries. IEEE Std 610, pp. 1–217, January 1991
19. Jardim-Goncalves, R., Popplewell, K., Grilo, A.: Sustainable interoperability: the future of internet based industrial enterprises. Comput. Ind. **63**(8), 731–738 (2012)
20. Kadar, M., Muntean, M., Cretan, A., Jardim-Goncalves, R.: A multi agent based negotiation system for re-establishing enterprise interoperability in collaborative networked environments. In: 2013 UKSim 15th International Conference on Computer Modelling and Simulation (UKSim), pp. 190–195 (2013)
21. Lampathaki, F., Koussouris, S., Agostinho, C., Jardim-Goncalves, R., Charalabidis, Y., Psarras, J.: Infusing scientific foundations into enterprise interoperability. Comput. Ind. **63**(8), 858–866 (2012)
22. Luckham, D.: The Power of Events, vol. 204. Addison-Wesley Reading, Boston (2002)
23. Luckham, David C.: The power of events: an introduction to complex event processing in distributed enterprise systems. In: Bassiliades, Nick, Governatori, Guido, Paschke, Adrian (eds.) RuleML 2008. LNCS, vol. 5321, pp. 3–3. Springer, Heidelberg (2008)
24. McGovern, J., Sims, O., Jain, A., Little, M.: Event-driven architecture. Enterprise Service Oriented Architectures: Concepts, Challenges, Recommendations, pp. 317–355 (2006)
25. Michelson, B.M.: Event-driven architecture overview. Patricia Seybold Group 2 (2006)
26. Ni, Y., Fan, Y.: Ontology based cross-domain enterprises integration and interoperability. In: IEEE Congress on Services Part II (SERVICES-2), pp. 133–140 (2008)
27. Niles, I., Pease, A.: Towards a standard upper ontology. In: Proceedings of the International Conference on Formal Ontology in Information Systems - vol. 2001, FOIS 2001, pp. 2–9. ACM, New York (2001). http://doi.acm.org/10.1145/505168. 505170
28. Object Management Group: Model driven architecture (mda) (2014). http://www. omg.org/mda, 17 November 2014
29. Object Management Group: Object management group (2014). http://www.omg. org/, 17 November 2014
30. Oren, E., Möller, K.H., Scerri, S., Handschuh, S., Sintek, M.: What are semantic annotations? (2006). http://www.siegfried-handschuh.net/pub/2006/ whatissemannot2006.pdf, 29 November 2014
31. OSMOSE: Osmose project - homepage (2014). http://www.osmose-project.eu/, 29 November 2014
32. Peristeras, V., Tarabanis, K.A.: The connection, communication, consolidation, collaboration interoperability framework (c4if) for information systems interoperability. Ibis **1**(1), 61–72 (2006)
33. Perrochon, L., Kasriel, S., Luckham, D.C.: Managing Event Processing Networks. Stanford University, CA (2001)

34. Pivotal Software, I.: Rabbitmq - messaging that just works (2014). http://www. rabbitmq.com/, 30 November 2014
35. Robins, D.: Complex event processing. In: Second International Workshop on Education Technology and Computer Science, Wuhan (2010)
36. Singh, Y., Sood, M.: Model driven architecture: a perspective. In: 2009 IEEE International Advance Computing Conference (IACC 2009), pp. 1644–1652 (2009)
37. Stojanovic, N., Stojanovic, L., Anicic, D., Ma, J., Sen, S., Stühmer, R.: Foundations for the Web of information and services. Semantic Complex Event Reasoning– beyond Complex Event Processing, pp. 253–279. Springer, Heidelberg (2011)
38. Truyen, F.: The fast guide to model driven architecture. Cephas Consulting Corp (2006)
39. Vernadat, F.B.: Interoperable enterprise systems: principles, concepts, and methods. Annu. Rev. Control 31(1), 137–145 (2007)
40. W3C: Owl-s: Semantic markup for web services (2004). http://www.w3.org/ Submission/OWL-S/, 13 December 2014
41. W3C: Ontology driven architectures and potential uses of the semantic web in systems and software engineering (2006). http://www.w3.org/2001/sw/ BestPractices/SE/ODA/, 17 November 2014
42. W3C: Sparql query language for rdf (2008). http://www.w3.org/TR/ rdf-sparql-query/, 3 December 2014
43. W3C: Owl 2 web ontology language document overview (second edition) (2012). http://www.w3.org/TR/owl2-overview/, 3 December 2014
44. W3C: Rdf - semantic web standards (2014). http://www.w3.org/RDF/, 3 December 2014
45. WSO2: Wso2 enterprise service bus (2014). http://wso2.com/products/ enterprise-service-bus/, 30 November 2014

Services for Business Knowledge Representation and Capture

Carlos Coutinho[1], Ruben Costa[2(✉)], and Ricardo Jardim-Gonçalves[2]

[1] Caixa Mágica Software, Lisbon, Portugal
carlos.coutinho.phd@gmail.com
[2] CTS, Faculdade de Ciências e Tecnologia, Universidade Nova de Lisboa,
UNINOVA, Lisbon, Portugal
{rddc,rg}@uninova.pt

Abstract. The competition inherent to globalisation has led enterprises to gather in nests of specialised business providers with the purpose of building better applications and provide more complete solutions. This, added to the improvements on the Information and Communications Technologies (ICT), led to a paradigm shift from product-centrism to service-centrism and to the need to communicate and interoperate. Traditional segments like banking, insurance and aerospace subcontract a large number of Small and Medium Enterprises (SMEs) that are undergoing this change, and must ensure the criticality and accuracy of their business is not affected or impacted in any way. This also is an excellent motivation for improving the capabilities for capturing the knowledge about businesses, not only their processes and methods but also their surrounding environment. The EU co-founded FP7 TIMBUS project comprises tools and techniques to improve business continuity featuring an intelligent strategy for digital preservation of business assets and environments based on risk-management. This paper proposes the modelling of service-based business information capturing strategies to help in the proper establishment of a knowledge base that permits a seamless interoperability between enterprises. The research addressed here also explores how traditional knowledge representations can be enriched through incorporation of implicit information derived from the complex relationships (semantic associations), modelled by domain ontologies, enhanced by information coming from additional sources of information (e.g. documents).

Keywords: Model-driven development · Servitisation · Ontology modelling · Interoperability

1 Introduction

The service globalisation perpetrated by the Internet has led to a need for change in the traditional businesses. Market terms and conditions dictate a constant need to change and adapt to new environment conditions, new paradigms and solutions, platforms and technology solutions, trends and fashions. Thus, being the best-of-breed no longer means being the most efficient or having the highest performance, it means keeping up with the look & feel trends, being available in many platforms

© Springer International Publishing Switzerland 2015
P. Desfray et al. (Eds.): MODELSWARD 2015, CCIS 580, pp. 421–436, 2015.
DOI: 10.1007/978-3-319-27869-8_25

and heterogeneous environments, i.e., implicates a continuous change. Many manu-facturing enterprises currently have a very clear update and delivery schedule plan, e.g., when deploying a new car model, it is possible to know what the next version(s) of that car will look like and what it shall feature.

This heterogeneity, constant change and subsequent need for interoperability are worrying traditional business areas like finances (banking, insurance), aeronautics and aerospace, which usually tend to be very conservative towards change on account to accuracy and stability. As an example, the aerospace industry is served by a small set of large enterprises that implement projects and missions, and which then subcontract several Small and Medium Enterprises (SMEs) for supporting their development, thus creating a network of dependencies. The need for interoperability with the other players in these networks is as crucial for staying in business, as the ability to do so while maintaining the proprietary business assets protected from the competition.

The evolution of ICT permitted faster, more secure and robust data exchanges, promoting the development of solutions as result of the contributions of the several enterprises working in a network, thus allowing the gathering of multiple competences and expertise into higher-valued products and solutions. Emerging paradigms like the Internet of Things [1, 2] (IoT, which is reshaping the world in the form of categorised discoverable items) and the Internet of Services [3, 4] (IoS), together with the evolving cloud computing's concepts [5] of Infrastructure as a Service (IaaS), Platform as a Service (PaaS) and Software as a Service (SaaS) are gradually transforming the existing reality into a set of available commoditised virtual objects, services, enterprises and networks.

This increase of availability and demand of combined solutions removed all tradi-tional boundaries and allowed the specialisation of enterprises (particularly SMEs) and the building of complex and heterogeneous provider networks. This move from product-concentric to service-dispersed strategies is leading to concerns about reaching and maintaining the interoperability.

To large contractors or even final customers like banks and space agencies, which depend on the performance of this network of SMEs to conduct their business, the improvement coming from the specialisation needs to be balanced with the increase on control of the outcomes that result of multiple sources. The misunderstanding of a concept, a change in a data unit, a mistaken method on a single enterprise in the network can lead to chained mistakes on its counterparts and consequently to errors in the final result that are very difficult to detect and even more difficult to trace and resolve.

It is then essential that more than describing data and interface contracts, the inter-acting enterprises publish their models, ontologies and methods so that their partners can understand and cooperate with them easier. Moreover, it is important that a control-ling entity (e.g., the prime contractor or the customer) is able to control if these models and concepts are aligned with the desired outcome.

Ontologies are the foundation of both content-based information access and semantic interoperability over the web. Various definitions of what constitutes an ontology have been formulated and have evolved over time. A good description of these can be found in [6]. From the authors' perspective, the best definition that captures the essence of an ontology is the one given by Gruber [7]: "an ontology is a formal, explicit specification of a shared conceptualisation". As elaborated in [8], "Conceptualisation" refers to an abstract model of some phenomenon in the world which identifies the relevant concepts of that phenomenon. "Explicit" means that the types of concepts used and the constraints on their use are explicitly defined. "Formal" refers to the fact that the ontology should be machine-processable.

Typically, in human endeavour, shared conceptualisations are defined over a lengthy period of time, based on the shared experience of a group of people, sometimes referred to as a community of practice [9]. They will involve the definition and use of abstractions that are designed to capture the important aspects of some practical context in order to support a particular activity or type of activity. As such, a shared conceptualisation is a socially constructed model or reality that is distinct from reality and is optimised to support the goals and activities of the community of practice in which it was defined. Communities engaged in different activities are likely to form shared conceptualisations that are quite different views of reality, and make up shared "world-views" [10] that provide a basis for highly effective and efficient communications within the respective communities.

This solution is thus essentially targeted to SMEs, so that they are more transparent in their models and interaction. It also helps their prime contractors to monitor whether their requirements are properly addressed.

The EU co-funded FP7 project TIMBUS [11] faces these problems and proposes solutions that include a reasoned Digital Preservation (DP) of business assets, where this reasoning is performed by risk management. The main innovation of the TIMBUS project is therefore its focus on risk assessment based digital preservation of business processes, thus not only bringing together but also advancing traditional digital preservation, risk management and business process management disciplines. Preservation is often considered as a set of activities carried out in isolation within a single domain, without of taking into account the dependencies of third-party services, information and capabilities that will be necessary to validate digital information in the future. Existing DP solutions focus on more simple data objects which are static in nature. The unique aspect of TIMBUS is that it is attempting to advance state of the art by figuring out how more complex digital objects can be preserved and later restored in the same or different environments.

This approach follows the work developed in [12] to define NEGOSEIO as an architecture that handles interoperability negotiations. In this sense, the contribution in this paper comprises the detail of the first step of the NEGOSEIO methodology – The acquisition of business knowledge to develop the MDA and MDI models, establishing a formal model and strategy for capturing the information about businesses, to improve the definition of new solutions for interoperability between enterprises, and also to improve the reasoning behind the risk-management analysis to select business assets for digital preservation. These methods and framework are being evaluated in the scope of the TIMBUS project.

Section 2 presents the background analysis on literature over the proposed solution. Section 3 presents the proposed solutions and how they are being applied to the determined scope. Finally, Sect. 4 presents the conclusions and future work.

2 Literature Review

The proposed methodology is based on the kernel aspect of interoperability, proposing formal models and strategies, supported by a framework which includes several concepts inspired by the work of project Manufacturing SErvice Ecosystem (MSEE), a consortium project of the ICT Work Programme, of the European Community's 7th Framework Programme (FP7) [13], including Model-Driven engineering, SOA, but extending it to Cloud-based solutions.

2.1 SSME and MDSE

The term Services Sciences, Management and Engineering (SSME) was coined by IBM [14] to deal with an holistic approach stating that businesses can be the result of a set of services – the conjunction of people, technology, and organisations to create value, towards becoming very adaptive and flexible, reusable and commoditised. The SSME aims to improve the sustainability of the development processes, monitoring and controlling assets e.g., the quality, productivity and innovation of services and the exchange and widespread of services.

SSME vision states that to define a business, more than dealing only with its tangible assets (hardware, software, and related documentation) – hence Technology, businesses should also be analysed according to their processes, environment, procedures, quality standards, towards achieving the business optimisation that is needed for being competitive.

SSME also notes that an important asset of businesses is the human factor, i.e., the capabilities of its human resources and their interactions determine the agility and flexibility of a business. Issues like motivation, skills, team building and development, leadership, personal involvement and achievements are leading the priorities of enterprises.

All these aspects must be developed in the scope of a business vision and strategy, which itself can be analysed, studied and optimised by statistical methods and Ishikawa (cause-and-effect) diagrams and analysis towards the creation of servitised strategies that can be reused as business development frameworks.

The MSEE project targets to pave the way for service development in Europe, with the creation of virtual manufacturing factories (Factories of the Future), which shall make use of extended servitisation for the shift from product-centrism to product-based services, distributed in virtual organisations and ecosystems.

This project proposed a Model-Driven Service Engineering (MDSE) architecture, largely inspired in the concepts of SSME, which accounts enterprise services to be modelled into three major aspects (views): IT, Machine (and operation) and Human Resources. The MDSE models are developed using various specifications, e.g., the EN/ISO 19440 standard, the GRAI modelling language [15], the POP* language [16] and the Unified Service Description Language (USDL).

2.2 Model-Driven Architectures

The term Model-Driven Architectures (MDA) was coined by the Object Management Group (OMG), and promotes the evolution of solutions through successive transformations of higher-level models into lower-level models, which eventually may result in going down to the level of code generation [17]. This represented a change of the under-going paradigm that professed that system architectures are built by designing and maintaining its code. In this case, the changes are performed in the models, which are then transformed into code.

This means that interoperability may start from the very enterprise foundations, where it is easier to discuss business-related concepts and ideas, and then the progressive steps of transformation into lower-level models may also be synchronised to refine this interoperability, so that the overhead of transforming the concepts into code is performed by automation tools.

The development paradigm of MDA allows the definition of multiple levels of abstraction in the modelling of businesses, using descriptive languages and schemes e.g., UML, OCL, and UEML to define the solution foundations. Applications should be designed right from a high-level abstract Computation Independent Model (CIM) where all business related functionalities, objectives, methods, context, requirements and definitions are specified regardless of any implementation (i.e., pure design).

Then, this model shall be subject to transformations into a more detailed Platform Independent Model (PIM), where the business concepts and rules are converted into activities, tasks, ontologies, structures and algorithms, although still independently of the underlying platform.

Finally, other vertical transformations and conversions shall turn the PIM into a Platform Specific Model (PSM), which provides the foundations for the development of the application, now targeted to a specific platform. Using the proposed framework, changes to any model (CIM, PIM) may trigger alterations in the other parties' models, which then, by transformation towards new PSMs, swiftly change the application towards compliance with the new model.

2.3 Model-Driven Interoperability

The Model-Driven Interoperability (MDI) concept derives from MDA: it comprises the same abstraction layers, but in this case the target to be modelled is the interoperation between the involved parties. The idea behind MDI is to define models for each MDA level that allow the exchange of information. If the MDA can be described as a set of vertical transformations from a conceptual high-level model to a progressively detailed model, then MDI may be seen as a set of horizontal transformations to allow interoperability at each MDA level, e.g., Process, Product and Organisational models with the System Requirements at CIM level and transformations of these models into interoperability models.

Projects like the Advanced Technologies for Interoperability of Heterogeneous Enterprise Networks and their Application (ATHENA) defined a framework that supports interoperability throughout the various abstraction levels and business aspects of enterprise software engineering [18]. Reference [19] provides simplified views over the MDI concept and the ATHENA Interoperability Framework (AIF) concepts and solutions on actions to develop each level of interoperability:

- Interviews, workshops and BPMN choreography diagrams for CIM levels;

- Diagrams, definition of business goals and BPMN collaboration diagrams for PIM levels;
- Service Oriented Architectures (SOA) and BPEL implementations at PSM levels.

Reference [20] defines a roadmap on the possible approaches towards the development of enterprise architectures accounting interoperability.

3   Business Knowledge Capture

The NEGOSEIO (which regards Negotiation for Sustainable Enterprise Interoperability) Framework builds a set of MDA and MDI models that clearly describe the interoperating business assets, processes and interoperability. Hence it assumes the existence of a technology capable of capturing this knowledge and modelling it into their ontologies. This paper covers the issue of capturing business knowledge that is essential to build the models for MDA and MDI, it is essential to first develop a proper container for this information.

Considering its characteristics and the needs that were elicited, ontologies were the natural choice for performing this, because more than storing data, it is essential to also capture the relationships between the business concepts [21]. The ontology classes are capable to define concepts and interrelate them, and the ontology individuals provide the instantiation of the real artefacts of the business.

3.1   Capture Information System

A problem that comes with the ambition to provide a solution that fits all businesses regards their heterogeneity. This fact leads to a lot of difficulties in the TIMBUS intent to perform an automatic capture of the knowledge and assets about the business. This context capture needs to be very flexible and able to address different needs and requirements. It needs to address open-source and proprietary environments, new and legacy applications, and be prepared to handle new platforms and systems, as well as different types of security and secrecy demands. A study analysis performed by project TIMBUS on businesses determines that business knowledge not only spans on different machines, using multiple operating systems and running over multiple platforms, as most times a lot of this information is stored in the people's minds and personal notes, in archives and storage that needs to be also ingested, or in legacy systems that need to be addressed and instantiated, as can be seen in Fig. 1.

To address and resolve these challenges, a Context Model was designed and developed to systematically capture relevant aspects and elements of business processes that are essential for their preservation and verification upon later redeployment [22]. One first difficulty with this matter is that a single ontology would not be able to face the specificities of all businesses. Hence, there was the need to develop a main context model ontology which can be used as-is for all businesses, called a Domain-Independent Ontology (DIO). This ontology was authored in the Web Ontology Language (OWL) with the support of the Enterprise Architecture Modelling Language ArchiMate [23] which developed a framework specifically to address generically the modelling of information of businesses. This is then complemented by a set of other ontologies that are

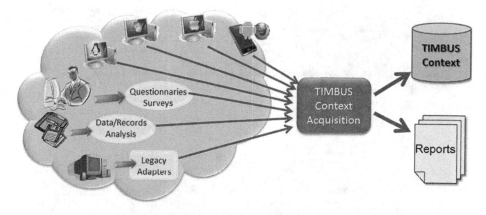

Fig. 1. Heterogeneity in capturing business knowledge.

created for modelling specific use-case scenarios, called Domain-Specific Ontologies (DSOs) [24].

The resulting Context Model is, then, instantiated into process-specific sub-models to provide a fine-grained set of dimensions that surround a particular use-case scenario. These relevant dimensions that surround a business process are called context parameters [25]. The specific scenarios chosen for TIMBUS served as clear illustrations that the Context Model is capable of supporting a vast realm of context parameters. The context model to capture a business' knowledge is then the conjunction of the DIO and the defined DSOs for that particular business [26].

3.2 Knowledge Representation and Enrichment Process

The enrichment process of knowledge representations (KRs) is one of the main contributions of this work, essentially arguing that the domain knowledge represented in a given ontology can be used to semantically enrich representations of knowledge sources [27].

The whole process ranges from the pre-processing stage till the final assessment of results achieved after the enrichment process, in a cyclical way since the assessment will provide inputs to improve the quality of whole process, such as the refinement of the domain ontology.

The overall approach comprises five stages (Fig. 2), namely: (i) pre-processing (preparation of the operational environment and input sources); (ii) ontology evolution (augmenting semantic coverage of the ontology considering the inclusion of new knowledge sources in the KB repository); (iii) semantic enrichment (the enrichment process itself); (iv) classification (application of an unsupervised classification algorithm); and (v) evaluation (measuring accuracy of the overall approach).

The pre-processing stage holds the preparation of both operational environment and input sources. The input sources are the domain ontology and other relevant knowledge sources. These knowledge sources represent the relevant and appropriate elements that will be used to support the semantic enrichment process, as well as to assess the quality

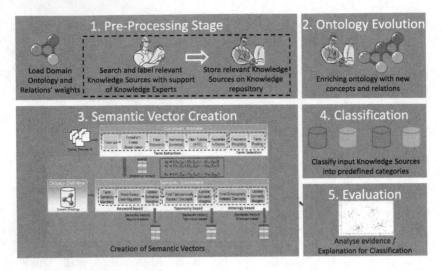

Fig. 2. Knowledge representation enrichment process.

of such enrichment. Logically, experts play a key role to help inspecting and pre-labelling those relevant knowledge sources, in order to provide an initial reference that will be validated against the results produced by the enrichment process. All relevant knowledge sources are selected and stored in a knowledge base repository, to help dealing with the management of all sources to be indexed.

The semantic enrichment is actually the very heart of this process. Indeed, it tackles the enrichment of knowledge representations (here called semantic vectors), extending the classical vector space model approach by including two additional steps in the process: (i) the use of taxonomical relations to improve semantic relevance of neighbours concepts; and (ii) the use of ontological relations with the same purpose of point (i).

The classification stage relies on the application of unsupervised classification algorithm (K-Means clustering [28]) in order to group knowledge sources into various categories, called clusters.

Evaluation, the last stage assesses the overall approach using classical precision and recall metrics to measure performance.

It is worth taking a closer look at the technologies and techniques (both adopted and developed) supporting the whole process, according to each phase, namely:

– *Pre-processing*: Protégé [29] is the ontology editor supporting the ontology creation process, expressed in OWL [30], which is loaded and stored using services provided by the pair JENA/MySQL. Both *Search for relevant KS* and *Label KS into categories* are technical operations performed by domain experts. Liferay [31] is the tool used to manage the knowledge repository, offering the classical functionalities for the purpose. The assignment of weights to ontological relations is performed automatically in the "Ontology Evolution" step, nevertheless the domain expert must analyse such results and update it when he/she considers necessary.
– *Ontology Evolution*: *Generation of Statistical Vectors* (which uses KSs from the knowledge repository), *FP-growth analysis*, and *Association rules learning* are

performed by Rapidminer [32]. It is worth noticing that association rules are automatically discovered based on the semantic liaisons connecting ontological concepts. *Frequent Itemservice Mapping,* implemented as part of this work as a Java-based service, create a map of ontological concepts based on the co-occurrence of equivalent terms.

- *Semantic Vector Creation*: in the Document Analysis step, Rapidminer calculates the *tf-idf* scores for all terms, a stored procedure developed on MySQL [33] reduces the size of the statistical vector according to a certain relevance degree defined by the knowledge expert (*Prune terms below threshold*), and another stored procedure normalise the statistical vector after pruning the terms. Next, the semantic enrichment is performed by three Java services responsible for the generation of the keyword, taxonomy and ontology-based vectors, respectively.
- *KS Classification*: Rapidminer is used to wrap-up the process applying clustering algorithms based on both statistical and semantic vectors, allowing a comparison of results produced. Needless to say that our expectation is to have better results, semantically speaking, in the clusters generated based on the semantic vectors.

It is also worth analysing in detail the following steps within the enrichment process Fig. 3: (i) Document Analysis: extracts terms from knowledge sources, creates the key term set, and produces a term occurrence statistical vector; and (ii) Semantic Enrichment: alters the statistical vector using taxonomical and ontological elements (such as relations, concepts weights) in order to produce a semantically richer KR, called the Semantic Vector.

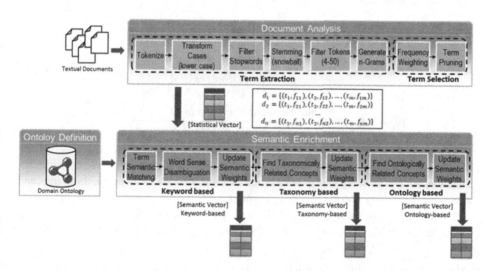

Fig. 3. Semantic vector creation.

Here are two stages in the first module, namely Term Extraction and Term Selection, for reducing the dimensionality of the source document set. Both are described here.

Term Extraction. The whole extraction process is as follows:

1. First of all, each document is broken into sentences. Then, terms in each sentence are extracted as tokens (this process is called tokenisation).
2. All tokens found in the document are transformed to lower case.
3. The terms belonging to a predefined stop word list are removed.
4. Remained terms are converted to their base forms by stemming, using the snowball method [34]. The terms with the same stem are combined for frequency counting. In this paper, a term is regarded as the stem of a single word.
5. Tokens whose length is "< 4" or "> 50" characters are discarded.
6. The n-Grams generation is seen here as a creation of sequences of 1 to N words. For this case we are considering the generation of unigrams, bigrams (e.g., Waste Management) and trigrams (e.g., Electric Power Product).

Term Selection. We understand that terms of low frequencies are supposed as noise and useless, thus we apply the *tf–idf* (term frequency - inverse document frequency) method to choose the key terms for the document set. Equation 1, is used for the measurement of *tfidf$_{ij}$* for the importance of a term t_j within a document d_i. The main limitation of *tf-idf* method is that long documents tend to have higher weights than short ones. It considers only the weighted frequency of the terms in a document, but neglects the length of the document. In Eq. 2, *tf$_{ij}$* is the frequency of t_i in d_j, and the total number of occurrences in d_j is the maximum frequency of all terms in d_j used for normalisation to prevent bias for long documents.

$$tfidf_{ij} = tf_{ij} \times idf_i \qquad (1)$$

$$tf_{ij} = \frac{number\ of\ occurrences\ of\ t_i\ in\ d_j}{total\ number\ of\ occurences\ in\ d_j} \qquad (2)$$

$$idf_i = \log \frac{number\ of\ documents\ in\ D}{number\ of\ documents\ in\ D\ that\ contain\ t_i} \qquad (3)$$

After calculating the weight of each term in each document, those which satisfy the pre-specified minimum *tf–idf* threshold γ are retained. For this work, we consider all terms where its *tf–idf* score was greater or equal than *0.001*. Subsequently, these retained terms form a set of key terms for the document set *D*.

A document, denoted d_i is a logical unit of text, characterised by a set of key terms t_j together with their corresponding frequency f_{ij}, and can be represented by $d_i = \{(t_1, f_{i1}), (t_2, f_{i2}), \dots, (t_j, f_{ij}), \dots, (t_m, f_{im})\}$. Such representation is entitled statistical vector, meaning that, for each document in *D* there is a resultant statistical vector.

3.3 Tools for Business Heterogeneity

Another concern that arises from the need to capture the business knowledge is the establishment of a solution for business context acquisition tool that is capable to be flexible enough to cope with these definitions of the information system (i.e., it is straightforward to develop a solution that works with a single DIO, but handling multiple DSOs that are developed specifically to handle the particular topics of each business is much more complicated). As can be seen in Fig. 1 again, the challenge here is not only coping with the DSOs, but also about developing one solution per business, or one solution per instance of the business, per machine or person, operating system or platform, and so on, or alternatively, to develop a single solution and expect the businesses to adapt to the solution.

Another challenge that relates to this matter regards a different aspect of the information capture which are the changes of information with time. This aspect, which is essential to TIMBUS, is very relevant for any business because the interoperability evolves with time, as business needs change, as also the flows of information between interacting entities. Hence there is the need to maintain a permanent connection to the business to perceive any changes that may conduct to updates in the models that shape the business. However, by being permanently connected to the business this cannot mean that the updates of the business knowledge capturing solution have any impact on the business itself. Therefore, any needs to restart the whole system because of this solution are not acceptable, as so should be avoidable any downtime of the capturing solution. So a big challenge is how to update the capturing solution to cope with the business changes, or with changes in the DSOs without breaking the business itself.

3.4 Proposed Framework

Considering all these issues, the solution architected was to use a framework using the Open Services Gateway Initiative – OSGi [35] philosophy. This solution provides an environment where an application server hosts the context acquisition framework, which consists in a main set of tools (context acquisition) that are able to interact with separate modules called business information extractors. These extractors are tailored pieces of software built as OSGi bundles that interoperate with the framework using a defined interface. OSGi permits these bundles to be installed, removed, started and stopped without the need to affect any of the other components of the system, hence coping with one of the demands of the desired framework.

Figure 4 shows the proposed framework for the acquisition of business information. As can be seen, it comprises a set of static base modules and a variable and flexible set of extractor modules. While the first do the standard operations of information acquisition like the aggregation of the stored information by the multiple extractors, the latter are actually the modules that perform the interconnection to the business premises. These extractors can consist of generic modules that capture standard information (e.g., the information about the hardware installed in a target business machine, or in a whole cluster of multiple machines, or the software packages in a Linux distribution, or the set of Perl modules used for a particular application), and of specific extractors tailored for the specific needs of a business.

These extractors are the instruments for retrieving the business information that is so needed for the development of the MDA and MDI models. Having this set of extractors built as OSGi bundles allows the creation at the same time of a single solution for

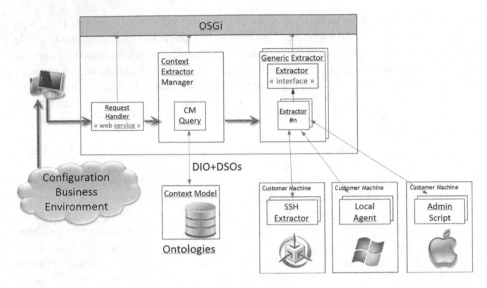

Fig. 4. Business information capturing framework.

all businesses and of a tailored solution for each business context. It allows the evolution of the context acquisition tool to comply with new business requirements or with new DSOs that are defined for storing their information. It finally allows a solution to be fully configurable regarding how to access the information, e.g., a solution may be built that accesses the target machine via SSH and has full access to that machine for retrieving information, another can be built that comprises a local agent installed on the target machine, that performs the extraction of information and publishes it via web-service, or even a solution that consists in a script to be run by a business responsible and then submit the results in the extraction framework. This flexibility permits the development of solutions that are able to be accepted by businesses that have low security demands up to those which have the strictest ones.

Finally, and most important of all, the definition of this philosophy allows the analysis of multiple disciplines for describing the business. Extractors can be built to model the business from the point of view of e.g., infrastructures, software, processes, legalities, organisation, hierarchies, and interoperability. These views can change from site to site of the business, but can also be reused on other businesses. Moreover, extractors may be developed that aggregate other extractors in order to infer information from multiple sources with a specific purpose.

Having this open architecture also allows extractors to be built according to the proper investment performed, i.e., an extractor that is built to describe a particular view of a business can be replaced by another much more thorough and that is able to extract more detailed information if it to be developed e.g., for a defence department or for an aerospace segment. Building more complex and complete extractors may then mean more investment in their development, hence the development of this business context acquisition framework allowed the fostering of another market, which is one of the development of extractors, in a business model similar to the one used in mobile apps.

As can also be seen in Fig. 4, the results of the extractions, coming from multiple disciplines, with multiple sources and degrees of accuracy and time, are then compiled and stored in the context model. All the ontologies in the context model are then merged, thus allowing interesting conclusions to be achieved by reasoning and inferring the properties of the individuals after the consolidation of the various ontologies.

The extractors and reasoners are subsequently applied to the Context Model (or to an instance of it) for extracting, monitoring, and reasoning for digital preservation purposes. The technical dependencies on software and services can be captured and described via CUDF (Common Upgradeability Description Format) defined in the MANCOOSI project [36] for systems which are based on packages. Such an approach enables TIMBUS to capture the complete setup and dependencies of a specific configuration for long-term preservation, which can be re-created, re-executed, and redeployed at a later time on modern hardware and with a different business scenario.

3.5 Use-Case Validation

This research work was being implemented in the scope of the TIMBUS project. This project is now finishing, having validated its results in a set of well-defined real use-cases.

One of these use-cases regards the analysis for business continuity and risk management towards digital preservation of the network of dams in Portugal, performed by the National Civil Engineering Laboratory [37]. The applicability of this paper in this particular use-case was then validated using a set of indicators and validation rules, which include the amount of different terminologies and processes that need to be harmonised throughout the different dams or the different sensor suppliers, the amount, effort and cost of the rework happening due to semantic misalignment before and after the application of the framework, the amount of time spent on harmonising these semantic issues with and without formal negotiation, the advantages in amount of time and cost of having a rich historic record of previous negotiations and negotiation steps and resulting outcomes. While unfortunately most results of TIMBUS have restrictions to their publishing regarding the proprietary rights of each business of the use-cases that were used for the project's assessment, nevertheless several evidences were published documenting the business capturing process success: [38] shows the whole process of capturing information for the sample use-case of preserving an open-source workflow process business, and [39–41] present public assessments and validation of the results of the TIMBUS tools and processes, which include the Business Capturing presented in this document.

4   Conclusions and Future Work

Business complexity is rapidly increasing due to globalisation and, well, evolution. In this fast-pace, there are options and business decisions that need to be taken rapidly as well. The lack of maturity of numerous enterprises leads them to early and poorly designed solutions for enterprise interoperability, leading to some obvious mistakes that can be corrected immediately, and others that are not so obvious or detectable. When these are finally detected, some may require a reinstate of some of the business premises and environment. While the TIMBUS project is aiming to support the development of this by performing risk management and selective digital preservation of assets, it is also based on the traditional risk management empirical analysis. This paper proposed an information model and a framework to support a mature, decision-support analysis of the business continuity, based on the modelling of the various entities and aspects related to enterprise interoperability, supported by a servitised set of supporting activities which are defined to perform the interoperability and to support it. The proposed framework was then validated in the scope of the project TIMBUS's use-cases. As future work, the authors foresee improving the current framework to provide it elements to perform a better decision support with respect to which disciplines to handle, their accuracy, better ways to automate the merging of the ontologies. One possible solution to achieve this is via the use of the negotiation framework NEGOSEIO, thus closing its own loop.

Acknowledgements. The authors wish to acknowledge the support of the European Commission through the funding under the 7th Framework Programme for research and technological development and demonstration activities, through projects TIMBUS (FP7/269940) and FITMAN (FP7/604674).

References

1. CORDIS. Internet of Things - An action plan for Europe, p. 13 (2009)
2. Vermesan, O., Friess, P., Guillemin, P., Gusmeroli, S., Sundmaeker, H., Bassi, A., Jubert, I.S., Mazura, M., Harrison, M., Eisenhauer, M., Doody, P.: Internet of things strategic research roadmap. In: Internet of Things: Global Technological and Societal Trends, River Publishers, pp. 9–52 (2011)
3. Cardoso, J., Voigt, K., Winkler, M.: Service engineering for the internet of services. In: Filipe, J., Cordeiro, J. (eds.) Enterprise Information Systems. LNBIP, vol. 19, pp. 15–27. Springer, Heidelberg (2009)
4. Internet of Services. http://www.internet-of-services.com (2012)
5. Jeffery, K., Neidecker-Lutz, B.: The Future of Cloud Computing: Opportunities for European Cloud Computing Beyond 2010, 1.0 (2010)
6. Corcho, O., Fernández-López, M., Gómez-Pérez, A.: Methodologies, tools and languages for building ontologies. where is their meeting point? Data Knowl. Eng. **46**(1), 41–64 (2003)
7. Gruber, T.R.: Toward Principles for the Design of Ontologies Used for Knowledge Sharing (1993)
8. Studer, R., Benjamins, V.R., Fensel, D.: Knowledge engineering: principles and methods. Data Knowl. Eng. **25**(1–2), 161–197 (1998)
9. Wenger, E.C., Snyder, W.M.: Communities of practice: the organizational frontier. Harv. Bus. Rev. **78**, 139–145 (2000)
10. Checkland, P.: Soft systems methodology: a thirty year retrospective. Syst. Res. Behav. Sci. **17**, 11–58 (2000)
11. TIMBUS. TIMBUS Project page. http://timbusproject.net. Accessed 15 May 2013
12. Jardim-Goncalves, R., Coutinho, C., Cretan, A., da Silva, C.F., Ghodous, P.: Collaborative negotiation for ontology-driven enterprise businesses. Comput. Ind. **65**(9), 1232–1241 (2014)
13. MSEE Project. http://www.msee-ip.eu/project-overview. Accessed 10 Apr 2012

14. Maglio, P.P., Srinivasan, S., Kreulen, J.T., Spohrer, J.: Service systems, service scientists, SSME, and innovation. Commun. ACM Serv. Sci. **49**(7), 81–85 (2006)
15. Doumeingts, G., Vallespir, B., Chen, D.: GRAI GridDecisional modelling. In: Bernus, P., Mertins, K., Schmidt, G. (eds.) Handbook on Architectures of Information Systems, pp. 321–346. Springer, Berlin (2006)
16. Athena Consortium. Athena Interoperability Framework. http://www.modelbased.net/aif. Accessed 20 December 2011
17. OMG. Model Driven Architecture. http://www.omg.org/mda. Accessed 20 December 2011
18. Athena Consortium. ATHENA project: specification of interoperability framework and profiles, guidelines and best practices (2007)
19. Lemrabet, Y., Bigand, M., Clin, D., Benkeltoum, N., Bourey, J.-P.: Model driven interoperability in practice: preliminary evidences and issues from an industrial project. In: First International Workshop on Model-Driven Interoperability (MDI 2010), pp. 3–9 (2010)
20. Chen, D., Doumeingts, G., Vernadat, F.: Architectures for enterprise integration and interoperability: past, present and future. Comput. Ind. **59**(7), 647–659 (2008)
21. Cretan, A., Coutinho, C., Bratu, B., Jardim-Goncalves, R.: NEGOSEIO: a framework for negotiations toward sustainable enterprise interoperability. Annu. Rev. Control **36**(2), 291–299 (2012)
22. Neumann, M.A., Miri, H., Thomson, J., Antunes, G., Mayer, R., Beigl, M.: Towards a decision support architecture for digital preservation of business processes. In: Proceedings of the International Conference on Preservation of Digital Objects (iPRES 2012) (2012)
23. The Open Group. The ArchiMate Modelling Language. http://www.opengroup.org/subjectareas/enterprise/archimate. Accessed 14 December 2012
24. Antunes, G., Bakhshandeh, M., Mayer, R., Borbinha, J., Caetano, A.: Using ontologies for enterprise architecture integration and analysis. Complex Syst. Inform. Model. (1), 1 (2014)
25. Riedel, T.: Federating real world information about business processes into the TIMBUS Context Model (2014)
26. Antunes, G., Caetano, A., Bakhshandeh, M., Mayer, R., Borbinha, J.: Using ontologies to integrate multiple enterprise architecture domains. In: 4th Workshop on Business and IT Alignment (BITA 2013) (2013)
27. Costa, R., Lima, C., Sarraipa, J., Jardim-Gonçalves, R.: Facilitating knowledge sharing and reuse in building and construction domain: an ontology-based approach. J. Intell. Manuf. 1–20 (2013)
28. MacQueen, J.: Some methods for classification and analysis of multivariate observations. In: 5th Berkeley Symposium on Mathematical Statistics and Probability, pp. 281–297 (1967)
29. Protégé-OWL editor. http://protege.stanford.edu/overview/protege-owl.html. Accessed 14 March 2012
30. OWL - Web Ontology Language. http://www.w3.org/2004/OWL. Accessed 14 November 2011
31. LifeRay. LifeRay. http://www.liferay.com/
32. RapidMiner. RapidMiner. https://rapidminer.com/
33. Oracle. MySQL. https://www.mysql.com/
34. Porter, M.F.: An algorithm for suffix stripping. Program **14**(3), 130–137 (1980)
35. Osg. Alliance. Open Services Gateway Initiative. http://www.osgi.org/Specifications/HomePage. Accessed 15 October 2013
36. Mancoosi Consortium. Mancoosi CUDF web page. http://www.mancoosi.org/cudf. Accessed 04 March 2013
37. LNEC. LNEC Portal. http://www.lnec.pt/organizacao/dbb/nmmf/estudos_id. Accessed 10 June 2013

38. TIMBUS. TIMBUS D7.7: Preservation of an open source workflow – Case Description and Analysis (2014)
39. TIMBUS. TIMBUS D7.6: Conceptual/Technical/Business Pilots (2014)
40. TIMBUS. TIMBUS D8.5: Conceptual/Technical/Business Pilots (2014)
41. TIMBUS. TIMBUS D9.5: Conceptual/Technical/Business Pilots (2014)

Author Index

Printed in the United States
By Bookmasters